ALSO BY AMERICA'S TEST KITCHEN

Meat Illustrated

The Complete One Pot

Foolproof Fish

Cooking for One

The Complete Plant-Based Cookbook

How Can It Be Gluten-Free Cookbook Collection

The Complete Summer Cookbook

Bowls

Vegetables Illustrated

The Side Dish Bible

100 Techniques

Easy Everyday Keto

Everything Chocolate

The Perfect Pie

How to Cocktail

Spiced

The Ultimate Burger

The New Essentials Cookbook

Dinner Illustrated

America's Test Kitchen Menu Cookbook

Cook's Illustrated Revolutionary Recipes

Tasting Italy: A Culinary Journey

Cooking at Home with Bridget and Julia

The Complete Diabetes Cookbook

The Complete Slow Cooker

The Complete Make-Ahead Cookbook

The Complete Mediterranean Cookbook

The Complete Vegetarian Cookbook

The Complete Cooking for Two Cookbook

Just Add Sauce

How to Braise Everything

How to Roast Everything

Nutritious Delicious

What Good Cooks Know

Cook's Science

The Science of Good Cooking

The Perfect Cake

The Perfect Cookie

Bread Illustrated

Master of the Grill

Kitchen Smarts

Kitchen Hacks

100 Recipes: The Absolute Best Ways to Make the
  True Essentials

The New Family Cookbook

The America's Test Kitchen Cooking School Cookbook

The Cook's Illustrated Baking Book

The Cook's Illustrated Cookbook

The America's Test Kitchen Family Baking Book

America's Test Kitchen Twentieth Anniversary
  TV Show Cookbook

The Best of America's Test Kitchen (2007–2021 Editions)

The Complete America's Test Kitchen TV Show
  Cookbook 2001–2021

Toaster Oven Perfection

Mediterranean Instant Pot

Cook It in Your Dutch Oven

Vegan for Everybody

Sous Vide for Everybody

Air Fryer Perfection

Multicooker Perfection

Food Processor Perfection

Pressure Cooker Perfection

Instant Pot Ace Blender Cookbook

Naturally Sweet

Foolproof Preserving

Paleo Perfected

The Best Mexican Recipes

Slow Cooker Revolution Volume 2: The Easy-Prep Edition

Slow Cooker Revolution

The America's Test Kitchen D.I.Y. Cookbook

THE COOK'S ILLUSTRATED ALL-TIME BEST SERIES

All-Time Best Brunch

All-Time Best Dinners for Two

All-Time Best Sunday Suppers

All-Time Best Holiday Entertaining

All-Time Best Appetizers

All-Time Best Soups

COOK'S COUNTRY TITLES

Big Flavors from Italian America

One-Pan Wonders

Cook It in Cast Iron

Cook's Country Eats Local

The Complete Cook's Country TV Show Cookbook

FOR A FULL LISTING OF ALL OUR BOOKS

CooksIllustrated.com

AmericasTestKitchen.com

PRAISE FOR AMERICA'S TEST KITCHEN TITLES

"The book's depth, breadth, and practicality makes it a must-have for seafood lovers."

PUBLISHERS WEEKLY (STARRED REVIEW) ON *FOOLPROOF FISH*

"Another flawless entry in the America's Test Kitchen canon, *Bowls* guides readers of all culinary skill levels in composing one-bowl meals from a variety of cuisines."

BUZZFEED BOOKS ON *BOWLS*

Selected as the Cookbook Award Winner of 2019 in the Health and Special Diet Category

INTERNATIONAL ASSOCIATION OF CULINARY PROFESSIONALS (IACP) ON *THE COMPLETE DIABETES COOKBOOK*

"This is a wonderful, useful guide to healthy eating."

PUBLISHERS WEEKLY ON *NUTRITIOUS DELICIOUS*

"*The Perfect Cookie* . . . is, in a word, perfect. This is an important and substantial cookbook. . . . If you love cookies, but have been a tad shy to bake on your own, all your fears will be dissipated. This is one book you can use for years with magnificently happy results."

THE HUFFINGTON POST ON *THE PERFECT COOKIE*

"The book offers an impressive education for curious cake makers, new and experienced alike. A summation of 25 years of cake making at ATK, there are cakes for every taste."

THE WALL STREET JOURNAL ON *THE PERFECT CAKE*

"The sum total of exhaustive experimentation . . . anyone interested in gluten-free cookery simply shouldn't be without it."

NIGELLA LAWSON ON *THE HOW CAN IT BE GLUTEN-FREE COOKBOOK*

"True to its name, this smart and endlessly enlightening cookbook is about as definitive as it's possible to get in the modern vegetarian realm."

MEN'S JOURNAL ON *THE COMPLETE VEGETARIAN COOKBOOK*

"It's all about technique and timing, and the ATK crew delivers their usual clear instructions to ensure success. . . . The thoughtful balance of practicality and imagination will inspire readers of all tastes and skill levels."

PUBLISHERS WEEKLY ON *HOW TO ROAST EVERYTHING*

"Offers a real option for a cook who just wants to learn some new ways to encourage family and friends to explore today's sometimes-daunting vegetable universe. This is one of the most valuable cooking resources for the home chef since Marian Morash's beloved classic *The Victory Garden Cookbook* (1982)."

BOOKLIST (STARRED REVIEW) ON *VEGETABLES ILLUSTRATED*

"A one-volume kitchen seminar, addressing in one smart chapter after another the sometimes surprising whys behind a cook's best practices. . . . You get the myth, the theory, the science, and the proof, all rigorously interrogated as only America's Test Kitchen can do."

NPR ON *THE SCIENCE OF GOOD COOKING*

"The 21st-century *Fannie Farmer Cookbook* or *The Joy of Cooking*. If you had to have one cookbook and that's all you could have, this one would do it."

CBS SAN FRANCISCO ON *THE NEW FAMILY COOKBOOK*

"Some 2,500 photos walk readers through 600 painstakingly tested recipes, leaving little room for error."

ASSOCIATED PRESS ON *THE AMERICA'S TEST KITCHEN COOKING SCHOOL COOKBOOK*

"The go-to gift book for newlyweds, small families, or empty nesters."

ORLANDO SENTINEL ON *THE COMPLETE COOKING FOR TWO COOKBOOK*

"Some books impress by the sheer audacity of their ambition. Backed by the magazine's famed mission to test every recipe relentlessly until it is the best it can be, this nearly 900-page volume lands with an authoritative wallop."

CHICAGO TRIBUNE ON *THE COOK'S ILLUSTRATED COOKBOOK*

"It might become your 'cooking school,' the only book you'll need to make you a proficient cook, recipes included. . . . You can master the 100 techniques with the easy-to-understand instructions, then apply the skill with the recipes that follow."

THE LITCHFIELD COUNTY TIMES ON *100 TECHNIQUES*

THE CHICKEN BIBLE

SAY GOODBYE TO BORING CHICKEN WITH 500 RECIPES FOR
EASY DINNERS, BRAISES, WINGS, STIR-FRIES, AND SO MUCH MORE

AMERICA'S TEST KITCHEN

Library of Congress Cataloging-in-Publication Data

Names: America's Test Kitchen (Firm), author.
Title: The chicken bible : say goodbye to boring chicken with 500 recipes for easy dinners, braises, wings, stir-fries, and so much more / America's Test Kitchen.
Description: Boston, MA : America's Test Kitchen, [2021] | Includes index.
Identifiers: LCCN 2020044422 (print) | LCCN 2020044423 (ebook) | ISBN 9781948703543 (hardcover) | ISBN 9781948703550 (epub)
Subjects: LCSH: Cooking (Chicken) | Quick and easy cooking. | LCGFT: Cookbooks.
Classification: LCC TX714 .A496 2021 (print) | LCC TX714 (ebook) | DDC 641.6/65--dc23
LC record available at https://lccn.loc.gov/2020044422
LC ebook record available at https://lccn.loc. gov/2020044423

AMERICA'S TEST KITCHEN
21 Drydock Avenue, Boston, MA 02210

Manufactured in Canada
10 9 8 7 6 5 4 3 2 1

Distributed by Penguin Random House Publisher Services
Tel: 800.733.3000

Pictured on front cover **Greek Chicken (page 257)**

Pictured on back cover **Two Glazed Grill-Roasted Chickens (page 372), Air-Fryer Spicy Fried-Chicken Sandwich (page 409), Lemon-Braised Chicken Thighs with Chickpeas and Fennel (page 164), Chicken Enchiladas Rojas (page 335), Cashew Chicken (page 209)**

Editorial Director, Books **Adam Kowit**
Executive Food Editor **Dan Zuccarello**
Deputy Food Editor **Stephanie Pixley**
Senior Editors **Sacha Madadian and Sara Mayer**
Executive Managing Editor **Debra Hudak**
Assistant Editors **Brenna Donovan and Kelly Gauthier**
Editorial Assistant **Emily Rahravan**
Contributing Editor **Cheryl Redmond**
Design Director **Lindsey Timko Chandler**
Deputy Art Directors **Katie Barranger, Allison Boales, Courtney Lentz, and Janet Taylor**
Associate Art Director **Kristen Jones**
Graphic Designer **Molly Gillespie**
Photography Director **Julie Bozzo Cote**
Photography Producer **Meredith Mulcahy**
Senior Staff Photographers **Steve Klise and Daniel J. van Ackere**
Staff Photographer **Kevin White**
Additional Photography **Joseph Keller and Carl Tremblay**
Food Styling **Catrine Kelty, Chantal Lambeth, Kendra McKnight, Ashley Moore, Christie Morrison, Marie Piraino, Elle Simone Scott, Kendra Smith, and Sally Staub**
PHOTOSHOOT KITCHEN TEAM
  Photo Team and Special Events Manager **Alli Berkey**
  Lead Test Cook **Eric Haessler**
  Test Cooks **Hannah Fenton and Jacqueline Gochenouer**
  Assistant Test Cooks **Gina McCreadie and Christa West**
Senior Manager, Publishing Operations **Taylor Argenzio**
Imaging Manager **Lauren Robbins**
Production and Imaging Specialists **Tricia Neumyer, Dennis Noble, and Amanda Yong**
Copy Editor **Cheryl Redmond**
Proofreader **Ann-Marie Imbornoni**
Indexer **Elizabeth Parson**

Chief Creative Officer **Jack Bishop**
Executive Editorial Directors **Julia Collin Davison and Bridget Lancaster**

CONTENTS

WELCOME TO AMERICA'S TEST KITCHEN

This book has been tested, written, and edited by the folks at America's Test Kitchen, where curious cooks become confident cooks. Located in Boston's Seaport District in the historic Innovation and Design Building, it features 15,000 square feet of kitchen space including multiple photography and video studios. It is the home of *Cook's Illustrated* magazine and *Cook's Country* magazine and is the workday destination for more than 60 test cooks, editors, and cookware specialists. Our mission is to empower and inspire confidence, community, and creativity in the kitchen.

We start the process of testing a recipe with a complete lack of preconceptions, which means that we accept no claim, no technique, and no recipe at face value. We simply assemble as many variations as possible, test a half-dozen of the most promising, and taste the results blind. We then construct our own recipe and continue to test it, varying ingredients, techniques, and cooking times until we reach a consensus. As we like to say in the test kitchen, "We make the mistakes so you don't have to." The result, we hope, is the best version of a particular recipe, but we realize that only you can be the final judge of our success (or failure). We use the same rigorous approach when we test equipment and taste ingredients.

All of this would not be possible without a belief that good cooking, much like good music, is based on a foundation of objective technique. Some people like spicy foods and others don't, but there is a right way to sauté, there is a best way to cook a pot roast, and there are measurable scientific principles involved in producing perfectly beaten, stable egg whites. Our ultimate goal is to investigate the fundamental principles of cooking to give you the techniques, tools, and ingredients you need to become a better cook. It is as simple as that.

To see what goes on behind the scenes at America's Test Kitchen, check out our social media channels for kitchen snapshots, exclusive content, video tips, and much more. You can watch us work (in our actual test kitchen) by tuning in to *America's Test Kitchen* or *Cook's Country* on public television or on our websites. Download our award-winning podcast *Proof*, which goes beyond recipes to solve food mysteries (AmericasTestKitchen.com/proof), or listen to test kitchen experts on public radio (SplendidTable.org) to hear insights that illuminate the truth about real home cooking. Want to hone your cooking skills or finally learn how to bake—with an America's Test Kitchen test cook? Enroll in one of our online cooking classes. And you can engage the next generation of home cooks with kid-tested recipes from America's Test Kitchen Kids.

Our community of home recipe testers provides valuable feedback on recipes under development by ensuring that they are foolproof. You can help us investigate the how and why behind successful recipes from your home kitchen. (Sign up at AmericasTestKitchen.com/recipe_testing.)

However you choose to visit us, we welcome you into our kitchen, where you can stand by our side as we test our way to the best recipes in America.

facebook.com/AmericasTestKitchen
twitter.com/TestKitchen
youtube.com/AmericasTestKitchen
instagram.com/TestKitchen
pinterest.com/TestKitchen

AmericasTestKitchen.com
CooksIllustrated.com
CooksCountry.com
OnlineCookingSchool.com
AmericasTestKitchen.com/kids

INTRODUCTION

Chicken is always there for you. You most likely have some kind of chicken in your refrigerator or freezer right now, waiting to fill almost any recipe need. If you're wondering just what to do with it this time, you'll find more than 500 answers in _The Chicken Bible_.

We love chicken because it's the ultimate blank culinary canvas. It works with every flavor imaginable and with every technique. We've included dinner options for every night of the week, from a quick dinner such as Pan-Seared Chicken Breasts with Artichokes and Spinach (ready in just 30 minutes) to a whole chicken with One-Hour Broiled Chicken and Pan Sauce (delivers really crisp skin and moist meat) to better-than-store-bought chicken fingers or nuggets for the kids. You can also deploy chicken fajitas or tacos or lettuce wraps for a fun time at the table. Fancy some fried chicken? One of our 20 recipes will keep you happy, from Extra-Crunchy Fried Chicken to Nashville Hot Fried Chicken to Karaage, a supercrispy boneless Japanese version. And if wings are your thing, you can choose from more than a dozen different kinds, starting with classic Buffalo Wings.

Chicken is the basis for all kinds of comfort food we want. Make a pot of Old-Fashioned Chicken Noodle Soup (using a whole chicken to provide both the broth and the meat) or Matzo Ball Soup. Or prepare Classic Chicken Pot Pie or updated Chicken Shepherd's Pie with its rustic topping of boiled chunks of potato. There's plenty of chicken and pasta, too, such as rich Chicken Bolognese with Linguine and the always-popular Chicken, Broccoli, and Ziti Casserole.

Having people over for dinner? You'll find major meal inspiration. Make elegant Chicken Cordon Bleu, Coq au Riesling (a subtler take on coq au vin), or Two Honey Roast Chickens with an easy pan sauce made from the drippings. If you are hosting Thanksgiving, you can take the pressure off with Perfect Roast Turkey and Gravy or try something new with Koji Turkey (both serve 10 to 12).

Taste the world via our recipes that celebrate chicken dishes from various cuisines, such as Chicken B'stilla from Morocco, Murgh Makhani from India, and Chicken Pad See Ew from Thailand, as well as numerous stir-fries and tagines. Or explore regional American favorites like Chicken Riggies (from Utica, New York), Kentucky Burgoo, and Alabama Barbecued Chicken.

So, chicken won't let you down and neither will _The Chicken Bible_. Turn pro with everything chicken you need in one place. And even if you already eat a lot of chicken, you'll be inspired to eat even more—and be very glad of it.

PARTS CHART

When shopping for chicken and turkey, you'll find many options at the supermarket, including a variety of parts, cut-up birds, and whole birds. Here is a listing of the various cuts of chicken and turkey that are in the book and how we used them.

Chicken

TENDERLOIN

The tenderloin (also called a chicken tender) is the flap of meat that's loosely attached to the underside (or rib side) of a boneless, skinless breast. You can buy packages of them or find them as a bonus on boneless, skinless breasts.

Uses Cut up for stir-fries and chicken fingers or shallow-fry for Scampi-Style Chicken (page 194).

CUTLET

A cutlet is a made by cutting a boneless, skinless chicken breast in half either horizontally or crosswise with the thicker piece cut horizontally (see page 8). You can buy cutlets ready to go at the grocery store, but they are often ragged and vary widely in size and thickness. It's better to cut your own from boneless breasts.

Uses Sauté, bread and shallow-fry, or make into sandwiches.

BONELESS, SKINLESS BREAST

A split breast, or breast half, that has had the bones and skin removed. They can weigh between 4 and 8 ounces each but we typically call for 6- to 8-ounce breasts.

Uses This versatile cut does it all: sauté; poach; bake; grill; use in salads, soups, and stews. Cut into cutlets, kebabs, or nuggets or stuff for a company-worthy dinner such as Chicken Kiev (page 279).

SPLIT BREAST

Split chicken breasts have bones and skin, and weigh between 10 and 12 ounces each. Be sure to buy breasts that are the same size so that they will cook at the same rate. To ensure evenly sized pieces, we prefer to buy a whole breast and split it in half ourselves.

Uses Roast (easier than a whole chicken), stuff and bake, make soup or chili, fry, grill, or make an inspired meal in your Instant Pot such as Pressure-Cooker Chicken and Couscous with Chorizo and Saffron (page 397).

WHOLE BREAST

This piece has both bones and skin, and usually weighs about 1½ pounds. Whole breasts can be cooked as is or split in half.

Uses Bake or roast.

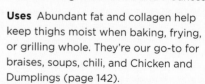

THIGH

The thigh consists of all dark meat and is rich with fat. Thighs that have bones and skin weigh between 5 and 7 ounces.

Uses Abundant fat and collagen help keep thighs moist when baking, frying, or grilling whole. They're our go-to for braises, soups, chili, and Chicken and Dumplings (page 142).

BONELESS, SKINLESS THIGH

A thigh that has had the bone and skin removed.

Uses Include in stews, curries, braises. Holds up well for frying without skin and bones in Karaage (page 283). Stir-fry, broil, cut up for kebabs, or grind for chicken burgers (page 92).

DRUMSTICK

Dark meat with bones and skin weighing between 5 and 6 ounces each. Look for full, round tipped drumsticks that are evenly covered with skin; a poorly butchered drumstick will have the top lopped off with the meat.

Uses Roast, braise, bake, broil, or try grilling Grilled Spice-Rubbed Chicken Drumsticks (page 355).

WHOLE CHICKEN LEG

A whole chicken leg is comprised of a thigh and a drumstick in one piece. It is also known as a thigh-drumstick piece. When a portion of the backbone is attached to it, it is called a chicken leg quarter.

Uses Roast (faster than a whole chicken and still provides drippings for gravy), make rich soup (matzo ball and pho) or a sheet-pan dinner, braise for Chicken Marbella (page 171).

WING

You can cut through the wing joint of a whole chicken wing to create drumettes and flats (see page 10).

Uses Fry, oven-fry, roast, grill, grill-fry, make broth, cook in your pressure cooker or slow cooker.

BACK (AND NECK)

You can purchase chicken backs or save them up in the freezer after butterflying a chicken. Necks usually come in a bag with the giblets.

Uses Make broth.

GROUND CHICKEN

Prepackaged ground chicken is made from either white meat or a mix of white and dark meat. Dark meat has a higher fat content. Do not buy ground breast meat (also labeled 99 percent fat free).

Uses Make burgers, Bolognese, Hearty Chicken and Cabbage Soup (page 113), Phyllo Pie with Chicken (page 339).

CHICKEN SAUSAGE

Raw sausage is made from chicken meat, salt, spices, and water and either prepared skinless or in a pork casing. Also available precooked.

Uses Make skillet dinners and pasta sauce, or make a homey Chicken Sausage Hash for Two (page 474).

WHOLE CHICKEN

Whole chickens can range dramatically in size, from 2½ to 7 pounds. Small, young birds that weigh between 2½ and 4 pounds are called broilers or fryers. Slightly older birds that weigh between 5 and 7 pounds are called roasters. A stewing chicken is an older laying hen and is best used for stews since the meat is tougher and more stringy. A 3½- to 4-pound bird will feed four people.

Uses Roast, skillet-roast, cook en cocotte, vertical roast (in the oven and on the grill), make soup, slow-cook your way to Herbed Chicken with Warm Spring Vegetable Salad (page 442).

SPATCHCOCK CHICKEN

A whole chicken that has been cut, had the backbone removed, and been flattened. Also known as butterflied.

Uses Roast, broil, or grill.

CORNISH HEN

This small hen weighs about 1½ pounds, and one whole bird will serve one person for dinner. Cornish hens feature small breasts and a high ratio of fatty skin to meat.

Uses Roast or grill.

Turkey

BONE-IN TURKEY BREAST

Bone-in turkey breasts can range in size from 5 to 7 pounds and include both the skin and rib bones. They are usually sold fresh, not frozen, and come in two different styles: regular (aka true cut) and hotel (aka country-style). The hotel-cut breast comes with wings attached, as well as a bag containing the neck and giblets for making gravy.

Uses Roast, grill-roast, smoke, cook en cocotte, cook sous vide or in your slow cooker.

BONELESS TURKEY BREAST

Boneless turkey breasts can range in size from 2 to 5 pounds. Often, two boneless breasts are packaged together in netting. The skin is usually left intact, but is often torn or ragged at the edges. For evenly sized breasts with skin that covers the meat, we like to buy a bone-in turkey breast and remove the bone ourselves.

Uses Stuff and roast.

TURKEY CUTLET

Thin slices of meat, usually no more than about ⅜ inch thick, cut from the breast. Inspect packages of cutlets to find the most uniform in shape and thickness.

Uses Sauté.

BONE-IN THIGH

Thighs have bones and skin and consist of all dark meat.

Uses Cook in your slow cooker, grind for burgers, or make superflavorful and tender Sous Vide Turkey Thigh Confit with Citrus-Mustard Sauce (page 416).

LEG QUARTER

A leg quarter consists of the thigh and drumstick in one piece.

Uses Roast as for Koji Turkey (page 245).

GROUND TURKEY

As with ground chicken, ground dark meat has more flavor than white so make sure to buy ground turkey that is a mix of the two. Do not buy ground turkey breast (also labeled 99 percent fat free).

Uses Make burgers, meatballs, meatloaf, tacos, chili.

WHOLE TURKEY

Whole turkeys range in size from 10 to 24 pounds and are sold fresh, frozen, and mail order. A bag containing the neck and giblets can usually be found in the body or neck cavity.

Uses Roast, grill-roast, use the carcass for stock.

HERITAGE TURKEY

Heritage turkeys are often only available via special order or mail order. They have long legs and wings, a more angular breast and high keel bone, almost bluish-purple dark meat (a sign of well-exercised birds), and traces of dark pinfeathers in the skin around the tail. They have an even ratio of white to dark meat and require special cooking instructions.

Uses Roast.

GIBLETS

When you buy a whole chicken or turkey there is usually a small bag in the cavity containing the neck and giblets. The giblets consist of the heart, gizzard, and liver. The heart is the small dark-colored organ. The gizzard is the grinding organ from the bird's digestive tract, recognizable by a butterfly-shaped strip of connective tissue. The liver is the brownish flat organ.

Uses Make gravy.

Our Favorite...

CHICKEN

Boneless, Skinless Breasts

Americans roast plenty of whole chickens, but they cook even more chicken breasts. For that reason, we decided to evaluate this most popular cut. The test kitchen's winner is **Bell & Evans Air Chilled Boneless, Skinless Chicken Breasts**. Thanks to 12 hours of aging before being boned, our favorite chicken breasts were tender and megajuicy, not to mention full of clean, chicken-y flavor.

Whole Chickens

We did an extensive tasting of eight brands of whole chickens and can highly recommend these two brands.

The test kitchen's winning whole chicken is from Mary's, a large, family-owned farm in California. **Mary's Free Range Air Chilled Chicken**, which is air-chilled and has a higher percentage of fat than most brands. Calling its flavor clean and its meat juicy and very chicken-y, our tasters dubbed this brand "really perfect." Our runner up is **Bell & Evans Air Chilled Premium Fresh Chicken**; it had the highest fat percentage of any bird in our lineup. Tasters found its white meat to be perfectly moist, with concentrated chicken flavor, and really fresh and clean-tasting.

TURKEY

We tasted 120 pounds of supermarket turkey to find the best-tasting bird. We avoided those listing anything other than "turkey" on the ingredient list (and you should, too).

Our winner is from the same company that produces our winning chicken and heritage turkey. **Mary's Free Range Non-GMO Verified Turkey** has relatively high fat levels and is fed a vegetarian diet. As a result it has clean, robust turkey flavor and is very tender, with a juicy texture. Our Best Buy, at half the price of our winner, is **Plainville Farms Young Turkey**. Tasters especially liked the texture and rich, meaty flavor of the dark meat, which had the highest fat level in our lineup. It was so good there was no need for gravy.

Our top-pick heritage turkey is also from **Mary's**. It has everything we're looking for in turkey, with rich, full flavor and naturally moist meat. Price is a big factor when considering a heritage turkey. One can cost upwards of $10 per pound; plus, required overnight or two-day shipping can nearly double the price.

SHOPPING FOR CHICKEN (AND TURKEY)

Chicken is endlessly versatile, pretty low in fat, and relatively inexpensive. It's no wonder it is America's favorite type of meat. There is a multitude of chicken choices at the supermarket with potentially confusing labels and a range in cost. Here's what we think is helpful to know when buying chicken and turkey.

Label Language

USDA Organic isn't all hype; it is a tightly regulated term: The poultry must eat organic feed that doesn't contain animal byproducts, must be raised without antibiotics, and must have access to the outdoors (how much access, however, isn't specified). Similar-sounding terms including Raised Without Antibiotics, Natural and All Natural, Hormone-Free (empty reassurance since the U.S. Department of Agriculture, or USDA, does not allow the use of hormones or steroids in poultry production), and Vegetarian Fed and Vegetarian Diet can be misleading and are often unregulated or not strictly enforced.

Buy a Natural Bird

How the chicken was processed makes a big difference in its flavor and texture once cooked. Simply put, buy a natural bird, one that has no artificial ingredients added to the raw meat. We prefer to buy air-chilled rather than water-chilled birds. The latter method (which soaks the bird in a chlorinated bath after slaughtering) causes the bird to absorb water. The water gain must be shown on the product label, so if you see the phrase "contains up to 4% retained water," you know the bird was water-chilled. Besides the fact that you are paying for the water, the water dilutes the chicken flavor and makes it hard to crisp up the skin during cooking. Air-chilled chicken is typically more tender, likely because the slower temperature drop gives enzymes in the meat more time to tenderize muscle tissue.

Avoid chickens that are "enhanced" (injected with broth and flavoring) because they will have a spongy texture. Also avoid "pre-basted" or "self-basting" turkey (injected with a salt-based solution to increase perceived juiciness) because it often tastes weak and washed out, mushy, and waterlogged. Look for an ingredient label—if the turkey has been injected you should see a list of ingredients.

We found the flavor of kosher turkeys to be mild and sometimes spongy. We prefer to salt or brine untreated turkeys because they have a clean flavor and are juicy without being mushy. Also, untreated turkeys are slightly higher in fat than the injected turkeys, which means more flavor.

Kosher Chicken and Turkey

Koshering is a process that is similar to brining; it involves coating the chicken or turkey with salt to draw out any impurities and then rinsing it multiple times during processing. Buying a kosher bird allows you to skip the step of brining. Kosher birds are also all-natural and contain no hormones or antibiotics.

Buying Packaged Parts

The USDA doesn't regulate the weight of chicken parts, so be aware that a package might contain pieces that vary dramatically in weight, which can make it hard to ensure that they cook at the same rate. With prepackaged chicken parts, you can't really tell what you are buying. In packages of split breasts and leg quarters, we found that the largest pieces could weigh twice as much as the smallest. Buying parts individually from the meat counter lets you select similar-size pieces. If you have the time, consider buying a whole chicken and butchering it yourself (see page 12). It is the best way to ensure that parts are the same size.

Looking for a bargain? Buy drumsticks. When we cooked bone-in chicken breasts, thighs, drumsticks, and wings and then stripped the meat from the bones to determine the price per edible ounce, we found that drumsticks were the cheapest and wings were the most expensive.

STORING POULTRY

In the Refrigerator

It's important to refrigerate poultry promptly after bringing it home from the store and to keep it refrigerated until just before cooking. Bacteria thrive at temperatures between 40 and 140 degrees. Keep your chicken and turkey in the coldest part of your refrigerator, generally in the back, where the temperature should be between 32 and 36 degrees. Place chicken packages on a plate or rimmed baking sheet to keep any condensation from dripping down onto other items in the fridge. Raw poultry will keep for two days. Leftover cooked poultry should also be promptly refrigerated and consumed within three days.

In the Freezer and Out Again

We don't recommend freezing chicken in its supermarket packaging (unless it is vacuum-sealed) because most packaging has air gaps that cause freezer burn (and poultry is especially prone to freezer burn). Instead, we wrap each chicken part, including whole birds, tightly in plastic wrap and place the parts in a zipper-lock freezer bag, press out the air, and freeze the parts in a single layer. You can keep poultry frozen for several months, but freezer burn increases with storage time and after two months the flavor and texture will suffer. Never thaw frozen poultry on the counter; this puts it at risk of growing bacteria. Thaw it in its packaging in the refrigerator (on a plate or in a container to catch any juices). Count on 24 hours of defrosting in the refrigerator for every 4 pounds of bird, so a day for a whole chicken and three to four days to defrost a turkey. And don't refreeze poultry: Its texture when cooked becomes significantly tougher.

PREP THIS, MAKE THIS

Learn your way around a chicken with these basic techniques. Practice preparing parts or a whole bird and then make and enjoy all of the recipes that use them.

Chicken Breasts

PREPARING CHICKEN CUTLETS · ▶

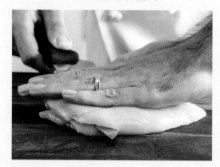

CHICKEN PICCATA, PAGE 192

A. Because a chicken breast is unevenly shaped with a thick and a thin end, it can be tricky to turn it into uniform cutlets. One way is to cut the breast in half horizontally, which yields two cutlets. Gently pound the pieces to desired thickness. The breasts will be easier to slice if you freeze them first for 15 minutes.

B. This cutlet-making method yields three similar-size pieces: Cut breast in half crosswise, and then split the thicker piece in half horizontally. The pieces will require minimal pounding.

POUNDING A CHICKEN BREAST · · · · · · ▶

CURRIED CHICKEN AND RICE, PAGE 39

To create chicken breasts of uniform thickness, simply pound the thicker ends of the breasts until they are all the same thickness. Though some breasts will still be larger in size, at least they will cook at the same rate.

CUTTING A BONE-IN SPLIT CHICKEN BREAST IN HALF CROSSWISE · · · · · · · · · · · · ▶

For more equal parts, we don't cut down the middle.

We halve our chicken breasts so we can cook the thinner tapered ends for less time. To help even out the difference between the tapered end and the thicker broad end, we cut each split breast closer to the broad end, creating pieces of near equal mass, not equal length.

CHICKEN BREASTS WITH KALE AND BUTTERNUT SQUASH, PAGE 26

TRIMMING A BONE-IN, SKIN-ON BREAST · ▶

Besides trimming fat and loose skin, we also trim the rib section so that the breast lies flat in the pan.

1. With breast skin side up, use kitchen shears to trim rib section, following contours of breast.

2. With breast skin side down, use chef's knife to trim any excess fat and skin around edges of breast.

SLOW-COOKER CHICKEN WITH TARRAGON CREAM SAUCE, PAGE 430

SPLITTING A CHICKEN BREAST · ▶

You can buy a package of split chicken breasts, but sometimes it's hard to tell what you're getting. Buying one whole breast and splitting it yourself guarantees evenly sized pieces.

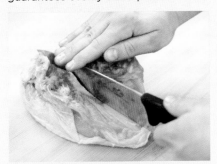

1. With chicken skin side down on cutting board, place knife on breastbone and press firmly to cut through breast plate.

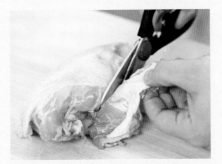

2. Using kitchen shears, trim off rib section of each breast half, following vertical line of fat from tapered end of breast up to socket where wing was attached.

ROASTED BONE-IN CHICKEN BREASTS, PAGE 217

Wings

CUTTING UP WINGS ....▶
Separating wings into two pieces makes them easier to cook.

OVEN-FRIED SOY SAUCE CHICKEN WINGS, PAGE 299

1. Using your fingertip, locate joint between wingtip and midsection. Place blade of chef's knife on joint, between bones, and, using palm of your nonknife hand, press down on blade to cut through skin and tendon.

2. Find joint between midsection and drumette and repeat process to cut through skin and joint. (Save wingtips to use for stock.)

Thighs

TRIMMING A CHICKEN THIGH ....▶

CHICKEN CANZANESE, PAGE 172

With thigh skin side down (or skinned side for boneless, skinless thighs), check long side of thigh for cartilage and short side for fat pocket; trim with chef's knife. Flip thigh and trim any loose skin (or any fat from boneless, skinless thighs).

Drumsticks

TRIMMING A CHICKEN DRUMSTICK ....▶

AIR-FRYER BUFFALO CHICKEN DRUMSTICKS, PAGE 408

When roasting or grilling drumsticks, we like to smooth the skin down over the meat so that it covers as much surface area as possible, which helps the skin render evenly and prevents the meat from overcooking.

Leg Quarters

TRIMMING A LEG QUARTER ·······························

Some leg quarters come with the backbone still attached. Here's an easy way to remove it: Holding leg quarter skin side down, grasp backbone and bend it back to pop thigh bone out of its socket. Place leg on cutting board and cut through joint and any attached skin.

CHICKEN LEG QUARTERS WITH CAULIFLOWER, PAGE 23

Whole Chicken

BUTTERFLYING A CHICKEN ··········

Butterflying or spatchcocking a chicken means cutting out the backbone and pressing the bird flat. We've found the easiest way to do this is with a sturdy pair of kitchen shears.

1. Cut through bones on either side of backbone and trim any excess fat and skin around neck.

2. Flip chicken over and use heel of your hand to flatten breastbone.

ZA'ATAR-RUBBED BUTTERFLIED CHICKEN, PAGE 234

EXTRA-CRUNCHY FRIED CHICKEN, PAGE 285

CUTTING UP A WHOLE CHICKEN

Cutting up a whole chicken is relatively easy and guarantees evenly sized pieces. It's also economical because you use the whole bird.

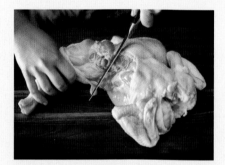

1. Using chef's knife, cut off legs, one at a time, by severing joint between leg and body.

2. Cut each leg into 2 pieces—drumstick and thigh—by slicing through joint that connects them (marked by thin white line of fat).

3. Flip chicken over and remove wings by slicing through each wing joint.

4. Turn chicken on its side and, using kitchen shears, remove back.

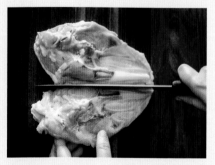

5. Flip breast skin side down and, using chef's knife, cut in half through breast plate (marked by thin white line of cartilage).

6. Flip each breast piece over and cut in half crosswise.

CUTTING A CHICKEN IN HALF ·····················▶

KENTUCKY BOURBON-BRINED GRILLED CHICKEN, PAGE 373

1. Using poultry shears, cut through bones on both sides of backbone; discard backbone.

2. Flip chicken over and use chef's knife to halve chicken through center of breastbone.

Turkey Breast

BONING A TURKEY BREAST ··········▶

Use sharp knife to slice down along both sides of breastbone to remove meat, keeping skin intact.

LEMON-THYME BONELESS TURKEY BREAST WITH GRAVY, PAGE 240

SALTING AND BRINING

Pretreating chicken with salt, whether dry or in brine, helps it cook up juicy and well seasoned.

SALTING

Salting causes juices inside the meat to come to the surface. The salt dissolves in the exuded liquid, forming a brine that is eventually reabsorbed by the meat. The benefits of salting over brining: It's more convenient (no large container needed) and it does not add moisture to the exterior (meaning crispier skin). A con: It takes longer than brining.

Directions

We prefer to use kosher salt for salting because it's easier to distribute the salt evenly. The two leading brands of kosher salt are not the same. We use Diamond Crystal Kosher Salt, which has a more open crystal structure; if using Morton Kosher Salt, reduce the amounts listed by 33 percent (e.g., use ⅔ teaspoon Morton Kosher Salt for 1 teaspoon Diamond Crystal).

Salting chicken under the skin is a very effective way to season it.

CUTS	TIME	KOSHER SALT	METHOD
Whole Chicken	At least 6 hours and up to 24 hours	1 teaspoon per pound	Apply salt evenly inside cavity and under skin of breast and legs and let rest in refrigerator on wire rack set in rimmed baking sheet. (Wrap with plastic wrap if salting for longer than 12 hours.)
Bone-In Chicken Pieces, Boneless or Bone-In Turkey Breast	At least 6 hours and up to 24 hours	¾ teaspoon per pound	If poultry is skin-on, apply salt evenly between skin and meat, leaving skin attached, and let rest in refrigerator on wire rack set in rimmed baking sheet. (Wrap with plastic wrap if salting for longer than 12 hours.)
Whole Turkey	At least 24 hours and up to 2 days	1 teaspoon per pound	Apply salt evenly inside cavity and under skin of breast and legs, wrap tightly with plastic wrap, and let rest in refrigerator.

BRINING

Like other meat, poultry loses moisture when cooked, so brining can be a great way to keep it from drying out. Brining not only seasons the meat but also promotes a change in the structure of its muscle proteins. As the salt is drawn into the meat, the protein structure of the meat changes, creating gaps that increase its ability to hold on to water and stay juicy and tender during cooking. The benefits of brining over salting: It works faster and it makes lean cuts juicier since it adds moisture. The cons: It can inhibit browning on skin or meat exterior and it requires fitting a brining container in the refrigerator.

Directions

Dissolve the salt in the water in a container or bowl large enough to hold the brine and meat, following the amounts in the chart. Submerge the meat completely in the brine. Cover and refrigerate, following the times in the chart (do not brine for longer or the meat will become overly salty). Remove the meat from the brine and pat dry with paper towels.

CUTS	COLD WATER	TABLE SALT	TIME
Chicken			
1 (3- to 8-pound) whole chicken	2 quarts	½ cup	1 hour
2 (3- to 8-pound) whole chickens	3 quarts	¾ cup	1 hour
4 pounds bone-in chicken pieces (whole breasts, split breasts, whole legs, thighs, and/or drumsticks)	2 quarts	½ cup	½ to 1 hour
Boneless, skinless chicken breasts (up to 6 breasts)	1½ quarts	3 tablespoons	½ to 1 hour
Turkey			
1 (12- to 17-pound) whole turkey	2 gallons	1 cup	6 to 12 hours
1 (18- to 24-pound) whole turkey	3 gallons	1½ cups	6 to 12 hours
Bone-in turkey breast	1 gallon	½ cup	3 to 6 hours

Poultry Doneness Temperatures

Do not guess at doneness: Use a thermometer.

Breasts 160 degrees
Thighs and drumsticks 175 degrees

Because breast meat cooks faster than thigh meat, you should take the temperature of both when cooking poultry.

For breast meat
Insert thermometer from neck end, holding thermometer parallel to bird. It should register 160 degrees.

For thigh meat
Insert thermometer at an angle into area between drumstick and breast, taking care not to hit bone. It should register 175 degrees.

LET IT REST

Resting poultry after it is cooked is crucial. It allows the meat to relax and reabsorb its juices, so there's less juice on the cutting board and more inside the meat itself. Small cuts like cutlets need only 5 to 10 minutes of resting time, a whole chicken 10 to 20 minutes. A big turkey, on the other hand, should rest for 30 minutes before being carved. To keep meat warm while it rests, cover it loosely with aluminum foil, unless it has a crisp coating or skin that you don't want to turn soggy. To protect the bottom crust of grilled meat from turning soggy, set the meat on a wire rack as it rests.

MORE SEASONING

There are multiple ways to get flavor into and onto poultry prior to cooking, from rubbing spices on the outside to helping them get directly into the meat.

Applying a Rub
Spice rubs and coatings are one of the simplest ways to add flavor, as they're applied superficially—just coat and cook. And when you make your own rubs (see page 389), you're adding even more flavor.

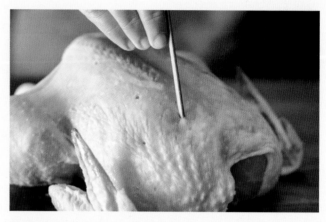

Poking and Seasoning
Use a metal skewer to poke the skin of a whole chicken or thighs (or other part) 10 to 12 times. Pat dry with paper towels, rub skin with oil, and season with salt and pepper.

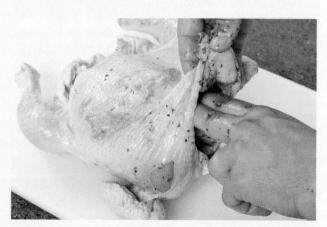

Applying a Paste
The best way to maximize seasoning and flavor is to separate the skin from the meat—to create space for an herb paste or butter. Your best tool is your fingers. Carefully slide them under the skin from the cavity side and sweep them back and forth to loosen the skin. Next, do the same from the neck side. Once the skin is separated from the meat, gently spoon in the paste or butter.

Slashing and Seasoning
Use a boning knife to make several deep cuts through the chicken skin and into the meat—each slash should reach the bone. This exposes more surface area for a marinade and sauce to cling to and helps the chicken cook faster and more evenly.

SERVING

CARVING A WHOLE BIRD

Before you start, make sure that you've let your poultry rest so the juices can redistribute. We've found that a chef's knife works better than a carving knife for this task. The same technique is used for carving a whole roast turkey.

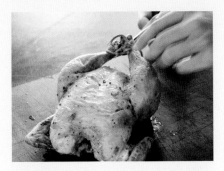

1. Remove any kitchen twine. Start by slicing chicken through skin between leg and breast to expose hip joint.

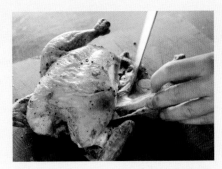

2. Pull leg quarters away from carcass. Separate joint by gently pressing leg out to side and pushing up on joint. Carefully cut through joint.

3. Cut through joint between drumstick and thigh. Slice meat off drumsticks and thighs, leaving some skin attached to each slice.

4. Pull wings away from carcass and carefully cut through joint between wing and breast to remove wings. Cut wings in half for easier eating.

5. Cut down along 1 side following breastbone, pulling meat away from bone as you cut.

6. Cut breast meat crosswise into slices for serving.

CARVING A TURKEY BREAST

Do not skip the resting step or there will be a flood of turkey juices on your carving board.

1. Run chef's or carving knife along 1 side of breastbone. Use your hand (with towel if too hot) to pry entire breast half from bone while cutting, being mindful to keep skin intact if there.

2. Slice breast meat on bias. Repeat process with meat on other side of breastbone.

ESSENTIAL EQUIPMENT FOR PREPPING AND COOKING CHICKEN

CHEF'S KNIFE

A good chef's knife is invaluable in the kitchen for all kinds of poultry tasks, including butchering chicken and carving a roasted one. Our favorite is the **Victorinox Swiss Army Fibrox Pro 8" Chef's Knife** ($31).

PARING KNIFE

A paring knife handles detailed work like poking holes in poultry skin. We prefer 3- to 3½-inch blades, like the one on our favorite paring knife, the **Victorinox Swiss Army Fibrox Pro 3¼" Spear Point Paring Knife** ($7).

BONING KNIFE

A good boning knife should have a narrow, straight, very sharp blade to easily maneuver around joints and bones and trim fat. We like the **Zwilling Pro 5.5" Flexible Boning Knife** ($110).

MEAT CLEAVER

A good meat cleaver is a handy thing to have when chopping chicken and bones for stock. Our favorite is the **Shun Classic Meat Cleaver** ($160); our Best Buy is Lamson Products 7.25" Walnut Handle Meat Cleaver ($56).

KITCHEN SHEARS

A good pair of kitchen shears are life-changing. They're ideal for butterflying a chicken, cutting out the rib portions from bone-in breasts, and much more. Our winning shears are **Kershaw Taskmaster Shears/Shun Multi-Purpose Shears** ($26.30).

MEAT POUNDER

We like to pound chicken cutlets and boneless breasts to a uniform thickness, so our meat pounder gets constant use. We prefer one that weighs at least 1½ pounds and has a vertical handle like our winning **Norpro Grip EZ Meat Pounder** ($19.99).

CUTTING BOARD

Unlike wood cutting boards, plastic ones require no maintenance and can be thrown in the dishwasher, a boon when working with poultry. Our winning large plastic cutting board, **Winco Statik Board Cutting Board** ($45), provides plenty of room to break down a chicken and stays stable when pounding chicken breasts and cleaving chicken parts.

KITCHEN TWINE

For all our chicken and turkey trussing, we prefer a center-fed no-fray cotton or linen twine, such as **Librett Cotton Butcher's Twine** ($7). Make sure your twine is labeled "food-safe" or "kitchen twine."

TRADITIONAL SKILLET

A good stainless-steel skillet is our go-to for searing, sautéing, braising, shallow-frying, pan-roasting, and preparing one-pan dinners. Our favorite is the **All-Clad D3 Stainless 12" Fry Pan with Lid** ($130).

NONSTICK SKILLET

A nonstick skillet is good for cooking thin slices of chicken and turkey including in stir-fries. We like the **OXO Good Grips Non-Stick Pro 12" Open Frypan** ($60).

RIMMED BAKING SHEET

A sturdy rimmed baking sheet is a kitchen workhorse, great for exposing cuts of chicken to the oven's heat and perfect for making a sheet-pan dinner. Our favorite is the **Nordic Ware Baker's Half Sheet** ($20).

WIRE RACK

The combination of a wire rack and a rimmed baking sheet is our top choice for roasting or broiling chicken parts, holding breaded foods before and after frying, and keeping food warm in the oven. We recommend the **Checkered Chef Cooling Rack** ($17).

DUTCH OVEN

Dutch ovens do it all. We use this heavy, deep pot for searing, braising, making stews and chilis, frying, and for sous vide cooking. Our long-time favorite is the **Le Creuset 7¼ Quart Round Dutch Oven** ($380). We also like the Cuisinart Chef's Classic Enameled Cast Iron Covered Casserole ($72).

ROASTING PAN WITH RACK

The large **Calphalon Contemporary Stainless Roasting Pan with Rack** ($140) easily holds a big turkey or two chickens, as does our Best Buy Cuisinart MultiClad Pro Stainless 16" Roasting Pan with Rack ($74).

VERTICAL ROASTER

A vertical roaster cooks a whole roast chicken evenly and crisps the skin all over. Our winner is the **Vertical Roaster with Infuser by Norpro** ($22).

FAT SEPARATOR

A fat separator is a handy tool to have when making gravy or broth. The **Cuisipro Fat Separator** ($27) is versatile and easy to use.

INSTANT-READ THERMOMETER

A good digital instant-read thermometer is essential for testing poultry for doneness. Our favorites are the **Thermoworks Thermapen Mk4** ($99) and Thermoworks ThermoPop ($29).

ELECTRIC PRESSURE COOKER

Our new favorite electric pressure cooker is the **Instant Pot Duo Evo Plus 9-in-1 Electric Pressure Cooker, 8-QT** ($139.95). It makes excellent pressure-cooked and slow-cooked food, and it sears and sautés food evenly.

AIR FRYER

Our winning air fryer is the **Philips Premium Airfryer with Fat Removal Technology** ($279.95). Our Best Buy is the GoWISE USA 3.7-Quart 7-in-1 Air Fryer ($60).

SOUS VIDE MACHINE

Our highly recommended immersion circulator is from **Joule** ($250).

SLOW COOKER

Our winner is the roomy, well-designed **KitchenAid 6-Quart Slow Cooker With Solid Glass Lid** ($74).

GRILLS

The **Weber Performer Deluxe Charcoal Grill** ($439) and **Weber Original Kettle Premium Charcoal Grill, 22-Inch** ($165) are the test kitchen's favorite charcoal grills. The Weber Spirit II E-310 Gas Grill ($499) is our favorite gas grill under $500.

EASY DINNERS

Photos (clockwise from top left): Skillet-Roasted Chicken Breasts with Root Vegetables; Chicken Chow Mein; Roasted Chicken Parts with Potatoes, Carrots, and Brussels Sprouts; Honey-and-Garlic Roasted Chicken with Pearl Couscous Salad

**Pan-Seared Chicken Breasts
with Artichokes and Spinach**

4 (6- to 8-ounce) boneless, skinless
   chicken breasts, trimmed
2 teaspoons minced fresh thyme
1 teaspoon table salt, divided
¾ teaspoon pepper, divided
3 tablespoons unsalted butter, divided
2 cups jarred baby artichoke hearts
   packed in water, patted dry
3 garlic cloves, sliced thin
¼ cup white wine
1 tablespoon grated lemon zest
10 ounces (10 cups) baby spinach
½ cup crème fraîche

1. Pat chicken dry with paper towels and sprinkle with thyme, ½ teaspoon salt, and ½ teaspoon pepper. Melt 2 tablespoons butter in 12-inch nonstick skillet over medium-high heat. Cook until chicken is golden brown on both sides and registers 160 degrees, 12 to 16 minutes. Transfer chicken to plate and tent with aluminum foil.

2. Melt remaining 1 tablespoon butter in now-empty skillet over medium-high heat. Add artichokes and garlic and cook until lightly browned, about 2 minutes. Stir in wine and lemon zest and cook until fragrant, about 30 seconds. Stir in spinach, 1 handful at a time, until wilted, about 3 minutes.

3. Stir in crème fraîche, remaining ½ teaspoon salt, and remaining ¼ teaspoon pepper and cook until sauce is slightly thickened and vegetables are well coated with sauce, about 1 minute. Serve chicken with vegetables.

Pan-Seared Chicken Breasts with Artichokes and Spinach

Serves 4   **Total Time** 30 minutes

Why This Recipe Works Artichokes, creamy spinach, and lemon make a sophisticated flavor combination and a wonderful partner for seared chicken breasts. Our easy one-pan dinner of chicken and these vegetables came together in a flash. We seasoned boneless, skinless chicken breasts with fresh thyme and quickly browned them in butter in less than 15 minutes. While the chicken rested, we sautéed convenient jarred whole baby artichokes (we prefer their flavor and texture) in a little more butter and garlic and then deglazed the pan with white wine and lemon zest. Next we wilted down a pile of baby spinach in the pan. Stirring in crème fraîche added richness and creaminess to our lemony, herby pan sauce. If you can't find crème fraîche, you can substitute sour cream.

Un-Stuffed Chicken Breasts with Ham and Gruyère and Roasted Broccoli

Serves 4   **Total Time** 45 minutes

Why This Recipe Works This inside-out approach to chicken cordon bleu not only bypasses the time-consuming rolling and stuffing process but skips the messy breading and frying as well. We arranged chicken breasts on a sheet pan and topped them with slices of ham and grated Gruyère. Brushing the chicken with mustard added a tangy sharpness and also provided the "glue" to help the ham and cheese stay in place. For the crunchy, golden bread-crumb topping, crumbled Ritz crackers stayed crisp and offered a rich, buttery flavor. We roasted wedges of broccoli alongside the chicken to complete our meal. Swiss cheese can be substituted for the Gruyère.

4 (6- to 8-ounce) boneless, skinless chicken breasts, trimmed
2 tablespoons Dijon mustard
4 ounces deli ham (4 slices), divided
4 ounces Gruyére cheese, shredded (1 cup), divided
15 Ritz crackers, crushed coarse (¾ cup)
1 head broccoli (about 1½ pounds)
2 tablespoons extra-virgin olive oil
½ teaspoon sugar
¼ teaspoon table salt
⅛ teaspoon pepper
Lemon wedges

1. Adjust oven rack to lower-middle position and heat oven to 475 degrees. Grease rimmed baking sheet.

2. Pound chicken breasts to uniform thickness. Pat chicken dry with paper towels. Spread mustard over top of chicken, then top each breast with 1 slice ham and ¼ cup Gruyére. Sprinkle cracker crumbs over cheese and press on crumbs to adhere. Arrange chicken breasts, side by side (and alternating thicker end to thinner end), on 1 side of prepared sheet.

3. Cut broccoli at juncture of florets and stems; remove outer peel from stalk. Cut stalk into ½-inch-thick planks, 2 to 3 inches long. Cut crowns into 4 wedges if 3 to 4 inches in diameter or 6 wedges if 4 to 5 inches in diameter. Toss broccoli with oil, sugar, salt, and pepper. Lay broccoli, cut side down, on opposite side of sheet from chicken. Roast until chicken registers 160 degrees and broccoli is well browned and tender, 20 to 25 minutes, rotating sheet halfway through roasting. Serve with lemon wedges.

Chicken Leg Quarters with Cauliflower and Shallots

Serves 4   **Total Time** 1 hour

Why This Recipe Works A sadly underutilized cut, chicken leg quarters take to roasting like a duck to water, growing tender as they cook while their skin crisps up beautifully. For this sheet-pan dinner, we paired them with cauliflower, which also shines when roasted. Deeply slashing the chicken helped the seasonings (garlic, lemon zest, sage) to penetrate the meat and the fat to render for crispier skin. Arranging the chicken around the pan's edges exposed it to the oven's heat and protected the cauliflower from drying out; the chicken's juices helped soften the cauliflower. Toward the end of cooking, we scattered grape tomatoes over the cauliflower for color and

Chicken Leg Quarters with Cauliflower and Shallots

juicy bursts of acidity and then used the broiler to impart pleasant charring. Some leg quarters are sold with the backbone attached; removing it before cooking makes the chicken easier to serve (see page 11). If you substitute cherry tomatoes for grape tomatoes, halve them before adding them to the pan.

1 head cauliflower (2 pounds), cored and cut into 8 wedges through stem
6 shallots, peeled and halved
¼ cup extra-virgin olive oil, divided
2 tablespoons chopped fresh sage or 2 teaspoons dried, divided
1 teaspoon table salt, divided
1 teaspoon pepper, divided
4 (10-ounce) chicken leg quarters, trimmed
2 garlic cloves, minced
1 teaspoon grated lemon zest, plus lemon wedges for serving
8 ounces grape tomatoes
1 tablespoon chopped fresh parsley

1. Adjust 1 oven rack to lower-middle position and second rack 6 inches from broiler element. Heat oven to 475 degrees. Gently toss cauliflower and shallots with 2 tablespoons oil, 1 tablespoon sage, ½ teaspoon salt, and ½ teaspoon pepper on rimmed baking sheet. Arrange cauliflower pieces cut side down in single layer in center of sheet.

2. Pat chicken dry with paper towels. Make 4 diagonal slashes through skin and meat of each leg quarter with sharp knife (each slash should reach bone). Sprinkle chicken with remaining ½ teaspoon salt and remaining ½ teaspoon pepper. Place each piece of chicken skin side up in 1 corner of sheet; rest chicken directly on sheet, not on vegetables.

3. Whisk garlic, lemon zest, remaining 2 tablespoons oil, and remaining 1 tablespoon sage together in bowl. Brush skin side of chicken with seasoned oil mixture. Transfer sheet to lower rack and roast until chicken registers 175 degrees, cauliflower is browned, and shallots are tender, 25 to 30 minutes, rotating sheet halfway through roasting.

4. Remove sheet from oven and heat broiler. Scatter tomatoes over vegetables. Place sheet on upper rack and broil until chicken skin is browned and crisp and tomatoes have begun to wilt, 3 to 5 minutes.

5. Remove sheet from oven and let rest for 5 minutes. Sprinkle with parsley and serve with lemon wedges.

SEASONING SLASHED CHICKEN

Slashing chicken skin helps fat to render and lets seasoning penetrate meat. Brush skin side of chicken with seasoned oil mixture.

Stir-Fried Chicken Lettuce Wraps

Serves 4   **Total Time** 1¼ hours

Why This Recipe Works Tender morsels of chicken and crunchy vegetables stir-fried in a deeply flavored sauce makes a savory filling for lettuce leaves. We found that Bibb lettuce made the perfect vessel; the tender leaves were soft enough to cradle other ingredients yet sturdy enough to hold together, and their naturally cupped shape begged to be filled with something savory. Boneless chicken thighs brought far more flavor than ground chicken. Freezing them briefly and then pulsing them in a food processor and tossing them in a soy

sauce–rice wine mixture achieved juicy texture. Tasters agreed that including both water chestnuts and celery was ideal. We also added shiitake mushrooms, garlic, and scallions. The stir-fry was as bold and complex as it was light, and it all came together in about an hour. We brought the skillet to the table and let everyone assemble and enjoy their own wraps. Salty-sweet hoisin sauce made the perfect accompaniment.

Chicken
- 1 pound boneless, skinless chicken thighs, trimmed and cut into 1-inch pieces
- 2 teaspoons Shaoxing wine or dry sherry
- 2 teaspoons soy sauce
- 2 teaspoons toasted sesame oil
- 2 teaspoons cornstarch

Sauce
- 3 tablespoons oyster sauce
- 1 tablespoon Shaoxing wine or dry sherry
- 2 teaspoons soy sauce
- 2 teaspoons toasted sesame oil
- ½ teaspoon sugar
- ¼ teaspoon red pepper flakes

Stir-Fry
- 2 tablespoons vegetable oil, divided
- 2 celery ribs, cut into ¼-inch pieces
- 6 ounces shiitake mushrooms, stemmed and sliced thin
- ½ cup water chestnuts, cut into ¼-inch pieces
- 2 scallions, white parts minced, green parts sliced thin
- 2 garlic cloves, minced
- 1 head Bibb lettuce (8 ounces), leaves separated
  Hoisin sauce

1. For the chicken Place chicken on large plate in single layer and freeze until firm and beginning to harden around edges, about 20 minutes.

2. Whisk Shaoxing wine, soy sauce, oil, and cornstarch together in bowl. Pulse half of chicken in food processor until chopped into approximate ¼-inch pieces, about 10 pulses. Transfer to bowl with rice wine mixture and repeat with remaining chicken. Toss chicken to coat and refrigerate for 15 minutes.

3. For the sauce Whisk all ingredients together in bowl; set aside.

4. For the stir-fry Heat 1 tablespoon oil in 12-inch nonstick skillet over high heat until smoking. Add chicken and cook, stirring constantly, until opaque, 3 to 4 minutes. Transfer to clean bowl and wipe out skillet.

5. Heat remaining 1 tablespoon oil in now-empty skillet over high heat until smoking. Add celery and mushrooms and cook, stirring constantly, until mushrooms have reduced in size by half and celery is crisp-tender, 3 to 4 minutes. Add water chestnuts, scallion whites, and garlic and cook, stirring constantly, until fragrant, about 1 minute. Whisk sauce to recombine. Return chicken to skillet and add sauce, tossing to combine. Transfer to serving platter and sprinkle with scallion greens. Serve with lettuce leaves and hoisin sauce.

Chicken Sausage with Braised Red Cabbage and Potatoes

Serves 4 to 6   **Total Time** 1 hour

Why This Recipe Works Chicken sausage is a pleasant change of pace from pork sausage and it pairs well with cabbage for an easy, rustic dinner. Braising cabbage in apple cider with grated apple, bay leaves, and thyme added complexity in 20 minutes and kept the cabbage's texture intact. Simmering the sausage and cabbage together helped unite the dish's sweet, salty, and tart flavors, and a hit of cider vinegar rounded things out. Small red potatoes cooked quickly in the microwave; we then browned and crisped them in the skillet. Chicken sausage is available in a variety of flavors; feel free to substitute any flavor that you think will pair well with this dish. If your potatoes are larger than 2 inches, cut them into 1-inch pieces. You will need a 12-inch skillet with a tight-fitting lid for this recipe. The skillet will be very full once you add the cabbage in step 3 but will become more manageable as the cabbage wilts.

- 1½ pounds small red potatoes, unpeeled, halved
- ¼ cup vegetable oil, divided
- ¾ teaspoon table salt, divided
- ¼ teaspoon pepper
- 1½ pounds raw chicken sausage
- 1 onion, halved and sliced thin
- 1 head red cabbage (2 pounds), cored and shredded
- 1½ cups apple cider
- 1 Granny Smith apple, peeled and grated
- 2 bay leaves
- 1½ teaspoons minced fresh thyme or ½ teaspoon dried
- 2 tablespoons cider vinegar
- 2 tablespoons minced fresh chives

1. Toss potatoes with 1 tablespoon oil, ¼ teaspoon salt, and pepper in bowl. Cover and microwave, stirring occasionally, until potatoes are tender, about 5 minutes; drain well.

Stir-Fried Chicken Lettuce Wraps

Chicken Sausage with Braised Red Cabbage and Potatoes

2. Meanwhile, heat 1 tablespoon oil in 12-inch nonstick skillet over medium heat until shimmering. Brown sausage on all sides, about 5 minutes; transfer to plate.

3. Add onion and remaining ½ teaspoon salt to fat left in skillet and cook over medium heat until onion is softened, about 5 minutes. Stir in cabbage, cider, apple, bay leaves, and thyme. Nestle sausage into vegetables and add any accumulated juices. Cover and cook until cabbage is very tender and sausage is cooked through, 20 to 25 minutes.

4. Uncover and simmer until liquid is almost evaporated, 2 to 3 minutes. Transfer sausage to serving platter and discard bay leaves. Stir vinegar into vegetables and season with salt and pepper to taste. Transfer vegetables to platter with sausage and tent with aluminum foil.

5. Wipe skillet clean with paper towels. Add remaining 2 tablespoons oil to now-empty skillet and heat over medium heat until shimmering. Add potatoes cut side down and cook until browned, 2 to 5 minutes. Transfer to platter with sausage and cabbage, sprinkle with chives, and serve.

Chicken Breasts with Kale and Butternut Squash

Serves 4   Total Time 1 hour

Why This Recipe Works For a hearty but not heavy autumnal dinner of roast chicken and vegetables, we departed from the standard starchy root vegetables by incorporating kale and butternut squash. We hoped to cook the squash, kale, and chicken together in a single sheet pan, but we'd need to get them to cook at the same rate. To start, we chose bone-in split chicken breasts, which cook faster than leg quarters (or a whole chicken) and wouldn't smother the vegetables and cause them to steam or render too much fat. Halving the breasts assisted in even cooking. A simple sage marinade seasoned both the chicken and vegetables. In just 25 minutes, we had crisp-skinned chicken, tender but not mushy squash, and lightly crispy kale. A sprinkling of dried cranberries added color and a sweet-tart chew to the mix. We topped our chicken with a drizzle of light, creamy yogurt sauce accented with orange zest and garlic to bring the dish into harmony. Both curly and Lacinato kale will work in this recipe.

½ cup extra-virgin olive oil
2 tablespoons minced fresh sage
2 teaspoons honey
1 teaspoon table salt
½ teaspoon pepper
¾ cup plain whole-milk yogurt

Chicken Breasts with Kale and Butternut Squash

1 tablespoon water
7 garlic cloves, peeled (6 whole, 1 minced)
1 teaspoon grated orange zest
8 ounces kale, stemmed and cut into 2-inch pieces
2 pounds butternut squash, peeled, seeded, and cut into 1-inch pieces (6 cups)
8 shallots, peeled and halved
½ cup dried cranberries
2 teaspoons paprika
4 (12-ounce) bone-in split chicken breasts, trimmed and halved crosswise

1. Adjust oven rack to upper-middle position and heat oven to 475 degrees. Whisk oil, sage, honey, salt, and pepper in large bowl until well combined. In separate bowl whisk yogurt, water, minced garlic, orange zest, and 1 tablespoon oil mixture together; set yogurt sauce aside for serving.

2. Vigorously squeeze and massage kale with your hands in large bowl until leaves are uniformly darkened and slightly wilted, about 1 minute. Add squash, shallots, cranberries, whole garlic cloves, and ¼ cup oil mixture and toss to combine. Whisk paprika into remaining oil mixture, then add chicken and toss to coat.

3. Spread vegetables in single layer on rimmed baking sheet, then place chicken skin side up on top of vegetables. Roast until chicken registers 160 degrees, 25 to 35 minutes, rotating sheet halfway through roasting.

4. Transfer chicken to serving platter, tent with aluminum foil, and let rest for 5 minutes. Toss vegetables with pan juices, season with salt and pepper to taste, and transfer to platter with chicken. Drizzle ¼ cup yogurt sauce over chicken and serve, passing remaining yogurt sauce separately.

MASSAGING KALE

One way to tenderize kale is to vigorously squeeze and massage it with your hands in a large bowl or on the counter until the leaves are uniformly darkened and slightly wilted, about 1 minute.

Crispy Parmesan Chicken with Warm Fennel, Radicchio, and Arugula Salad

Serves 4   Total Time 1 hour

Why This Recipe Works With its crisp coating and juicy, tender meat, Parmesan chicken is a surefire crowd-pleaser and a guaranteed win for any weeknight dinner. Pasta is a classic pairing, but we were more interested in a fresh, vegetable-heavy side that would brighten up our savory breaded chicken and wouldn't involve another pan. So, after the chicken cutlets had finished cooking through, we took advantage of the preheated skillet to soften thinly sliced fennel and halved cherry tomatoes. We tossed the cooked vegetables in a simple vinaigrette of minced shallot, Dijon mustard, white wine vinegar, and extra-virgin olive oil. Adding raw radicchio and baby arugula to the cooked vegetables added crunch and a light bitterness that paired well with the sweetness of the fennel and contrasted perfectly with rich, juicy chicken. Use the large holes of a box grater to shred the Parmesan. The skillet will be crowded initially but the cutlets will shrink as they cook. For more information about making cutlets, see page 8.

4 (6- to 8-ounce) boneless, skinless chicken breasts, trimmed
2 large eggs
1¼ teaspoons table salt, divided
½ teaspoon pepper
1 cup panko bread crumbs
3 ounces Parmesan cheese, shredded (1 cup)
½ cup vegetable oil for frying, divided
1 tablespoon white wine vinegar
1 small shallot, minced
½ teaspoon Dijon mustard
¼ cup extra-virgin olive oil, divided
1 fennel bulb, stalks discarded, bulb halved, cored, and sliced thin
12 ounces cherry tomatoes, halved
½ head radicchio (5 ounces), cored and sliced thin
2 ounces (2 cups) baby arugula

1. Remove any tenderloins from breasts. Cut each breast horizontally into 2 thin cutlets, then pound to uniform ¼-inch thickness.

2. Beat eggs, 1 teaspoon salt, and pepper together in shallow dish. Combine panko and Parmesan in second shallow dish. Working with 1 cutlet at a time, dredge in egg mixture, allowing excess to drip off, then coat all sides with panko mixture, pressing gently so crumbs adhere. Transfer cutlets to rimmed baking sheet.

3. Adjust oven rack to middle position and heat oven to 200 degrees. Set wire rack in second rimmed baking sheet and line rack with triple layer of paper towels. Heat ¼ cup vegetable oil and small pinch panko mixture in 12-inch nonstick skillet over medium-high heat. When panko has turned golden brown, place 4 cutlets in skillet. Cook, without moving cutlets, until bottoms are deep golden brown, 2 to 3 minutes. Using tongs, carefully flip cutlets and cook on second side until deep golden brown, 2 to 3 minutes.

4. Transfer cutlets to prepared rack, season with salt to taste, and keep warm in oven. Wipe skillet clean with paper towels. Repeat with remaining ¼ cup vegetable oil and remaining 4 cutlets; transfer to rack and keep warm in oven. Wipe skillet clean with paper towels.

5. Whisk vinegar, shallot, mustard, and remaining ¼ teaspoon salt together in large bowl. Whisking constantly, slowly drizzle in 3 tablespoons olive oil until emulsified.

6. Heat remaining 1 tablespoon olive oil in now-empty skillet over medium heat until shimmering. Add fennel and cook until softened and just beginning to brown, 5 to 7 minutes; transfer to bowl with vinaigrette. Add tomatoes, radicchio, and arugula and gently toss to combine. Season with salt and pepper to taste, and serve with chicken.

Mustard-Roasted
Chicken with Warm
Green Bean and
Potato Salad

Teriyaki Chicken Thighs with
Sesame Vegetables

Mustard-Roasted Chicken with Warm Green Bean and Potato Salad

Serves 4   Total Time 1 hour

Why This Recipe Works A simple coating of mustard elevates bone-in chicken parts to flavorful weeknight bistro fare. The cooking is mostly hands-off, leaving ample time to create a simple and delicious side dish. Dressing the potatoes and green beans while still warm helped them absorb the vinaigrette, and adding the fond and juices from the roasted chicken to the salad contributed meaty, mustardy flavor. If the potatoes are larger than 2 inches, cut them into 1-inch pieces.

3 tablespoons plus 1 teaspoon Dijon mustard, divided
¼ cup extra-virgin olive oil, divided
2 teaspoons soy sauce
1 garlic clove, minced
1 teaspoon fresh minced rosemary
¼ teaspoon pepper, divided
3 pounds bone-in chicken pieces (split breasts halved crosswise, drumsticks, and/or thighs), trimmed
½ teaspoon table salt, plus salt for cooking vegetables
1½ pounds small red potatoes, 1 to 2 inches in diameter, halved
8 ounces green beans, trimmed and cut into 1½-inch lengths
2 tablespoons white wine vinegar
1 tablespoon capers, rinsed and minced
2 tablespoons chopped fresh parsley

1. Adjust oven rack to upper-middle position and heat oven to 475 degrees. Combine 3 tablespoons mustard, 1 tablespoon oil, soy sauce, garlic, rosemary, and ⅛ teaspoon pepper in small bowl; set aside.

2. Pat chicken dry with paper towels and sprinkle with ½ teaspoon salt and remaining ⅛ teaspoon pepper. Place chicken skin side up on rimmed baking sheet, arranging breast pieces in center and leg and/or thigh pieces around perimeter. Brush chicken with mustard mixture. Roast until breasts register 160 degrees and drumsticks/thighs register 175 degrees, 25 to 30 minutes, rotating sheet halfway through roasting. Tent with aluminum foil and let rest.

3. Meanwhile, bring 2 quarts water to boil in large saucepan over medium-high heat. Add potatoes and 1½ tablespoons salt to boiling water; return to boil and cook for 10 minutes. Add green beans and cook until both vegetables are tender, about 5 minutes. Drain well, return to pot, and cover to keep warm.

4. Whisk vinegar, remaining 1 teaspoon mustard, and capers together in large bowl. Whisking constantly, slowly drizzle in remaining 3 tablespoons oil until incorporated. Transfer chicken to serving platter. Scrape up any browned bits and pour any accumulated juices from baking sheet into bowl with dressing; whisk to combine. Add warm vegetables, toss gently to combine, and season with salt and pepper to taste. Sprinkle chicken and salad with parsley and serve.

Teriyaki Chicken Thighs with Sesame Vegetables

Serves 4   **Total Time** 1¼ hours

Why This Recipe Works This unique take on teriyaki yields crispy chicken in a sweet-sticky sauce and a vegetable "stir-fry" that cook in the same sheet pan. We first browned bone-in chicken thighs in the oven for 20 minutes, slashing the skin and placing them on a wire rack to render and drain away the fat. We then tossed sliced bell pepper and mushrooms with garlic and ginger and spread them alongside the chicken as it continued to roast. Snap peas went in 10 minutes later so they wouldn't overcook. Briefly broiling everything crisped the thighs' skin further. As for the teriyaki sauce, a few pantry items did the trick; we thickened it in the microwave before brushing it on our chicken. Depending on your wire rack, you may need to place parchment paper underneath the vegetables to prevent them from falling through.

8 (5- to 7-ounce) bone-in chicken thighs, trimmed
2 tablespoons vegetable oil, divided
1 red bell pepper, stemmed, seeded, and cut into ¼-inch-wide strips
8 ounces shiitake mushrooms, stemmed and sliced thin
3 garlic cloves, minced, divided
1 tablespoon grated fresh ginger, divided
8 ounces snap peas, strings removed
5 tablespoons mirin
5 tablespoons soy sauce
¼ cup water
3 tablespoons sugar
2 teaspoons cornstarch
⅛ teaspoon red pepper flakes
1 tablespoon toasted sesame oil
1 tablespoon toasted sesame seeds
½ teaspoon table salt

1. Adjust 1 oven rack to lower-middle position and second rack 8 inches from broiler element. Heat oven to 450 degrees. Set wire rack in rimmed baking sheet lined with aluminum foil. Make 3 diagonal slashes through skin of each thigh with sharp knife (do not cut into meat). Brush chicken with 1 tablespoon vegetable oil. Lay chicken skin side up on half of prepared rack and roast for 20 minutes.

2. Toss bell pepper and mushrooms with remaining 1 tablespoon vegetable oil, half of garlic, and 1½ teaspoons ginger. Spread vegetables over empty side of rack. Rotate rack and continue to roast for 10 minutes. Sprinkle snap peas over vegetables and continue to roast until chicken registers 165 degrees and vegetables start to brown, about 10 minutes.

3. Remove sheet from oven and heat broiler. Place sheet on upper rack and broil until chicken and vegetables are well browned and chicken registers 175 degrees, 3 to 5 minutes. Meanwhile, combine mirin, soy sauce, water, sugar, cornstarch, pepper flakes, remaining garlic, and remaining 1½ teaspoons ginger in bowl and microwave, whisking occasionally, until thickened, 3 to 5 minutes.

4. Remove sheet from oven, brush chicken with 3 tablespoons of sauce, and let rest for 5 minutes. Transfer vegetables to clean bowl; toss with sesame oil, sesame seeds, and salt. Serve vegetables and chicken with remaining sauce.

Skillet-Roasted Chicken Breasts with Root Vegetables

Serves 4   **Total Time** 1¼ hours

Why This Recipe Works Roasted bone-in chicken breasts with moist, tender meat and crispy skin can be the ultimate simple-yet-elegant main course, and this recipe goes the extra mile by incorporating a side of root vegetables for a homey, one-dish meal. To sync the cooking times for chicken and vegetables we first seared our chicken to crisp the skin to golden brown perfection. After the initial sear, we took the chicken out of the skillet and filled the pan with a mix of potatoes, parsnips, carrots, and shallots. We then put the chicken back in the pan on top of the vegetables and moved the whole thing to the oven. Elevating the chicken allowed the meat to gently cook while the vegetables roasted against the hot surface of the pan. Once the chicken was done, we removed it and let it rest while we finished cooking our vegetables. Cutting the vegetables into 1-inch pieces ensured they were done by the time the chicken was rested and ready to serve. A simple sprinkling of chives finished our dish. If your potatoes are larger than 2 inches, cut them into 1-inch pieces. You will need a 12-inch ovensafe skillet for this recipe.

4 (12-ounce) bone-in split chicken breasts, trimmed
1 teaspoon table salt, divided
¾ teaspoon pepper, divided
1 tablespoon vegetable oil
1 pound small red potatoes, unpeeled, quartered
8 ounces parsnips, peeled, halved lengthwise, and cut into 1-inch pieces
4 carrots, peeled, halved lengthwise, and cut into 1-inch pieces
4 shallots, peeled and quartered
1 teaspoon minced fresh rosemary or ¼ teaspoon dried
1 tablespoon minced fresh chives
Lemon wedges

1. Adjust oven rack to middle position and heat oven to 450 degrees. Pat chicken dry with paper towels and sprinkle with ½ teaspoon salt and ½ teaspoon pepper. Heat oil in 12-inch ovensafe skillet over medium-high heat until just smoking. Place chicken skin side down in skillet and cook until well browned on first side, 5 to 7 minutes. Flip chicken and continue to cook until lightly browned on second side, about 3 minutes; transfer to plate.

2. Add potatoes, parsnips, carrots, shallots, rosemary, remaining ½ teaspoon salt, and remaining ¼ teaspoon pepper to fat left in skillet and toss to coat. Place chicken skin side up on top of vegetables, transfer skillet to oven, and roast until chicken registers 160 degrees, 20 to 25 minutes.

3. Using pot holders, remove skillet from oven. Transfer chicken to serving platter, tent with aluminum foil, and let rest while finishing vegetables.

4. Being careful of hot skillet handle, stir vegetables, return skillet to oven, and roast until vegetables are tender, about 15 minutes. Stir in chives and season with salt and pepper to taste. Serve chicken with vegetables and lemon wedges.

VARIATIONS
Skillet-Roasted Chicken Breasts with Red Potatoes, Fennel, and Cauliflower
Omit rosemary. Substitute 1 thinly sliced fennel bulb and ½ head cauliflower, cut into 1-inch florets, for carrots and parsnips. Sprinkle vegetables with 1 tablespoon minced fresh tarragon before serving.

Skillet-Roasted Chicken Breasts with Squash, Carrots, and Brussels Sprouts
Substitute ½ butternut squash, cut into 1-inch pieces (2 cups), and 10 ounces brussels sprouts, trimmed and halved, for potatoes and parsnips. Substitute 1 tablespoon minced fresh thyme for rosemary.

Chicken Bonne Femme

Chicken Bonne Femme
Serves 4 to 6   **Total Time** 1¼ hours

Why This Recipe Works A traditional Creole dish, chicken bonne femme combines browned chicken with bacon, onions, garlic, wine, and potatoes, slow-cooked until rich and savory. Traditional recipes sometimes fry both the chicken and potatoes before combining them with a sauce. We opted to braise; this handily turned our bonne femme into a one-pot meal. We chose bone-in chicken thighs for their rich flavor and ability to stay moist during slow cooking but weren't keen on skin that turned soft during cooking. So after browning the thighs in some of the rendered fat from our bacon (which we'd previously crisped), we discarded the skin. The fond left in the pan during browning combined with the fat rendered from the skin would give our sauce deep flavor, without any soft skin to detract from the dish. We next browned potato halves, then built the sauce, first adding onion to soften, then garlic and thyme, and finally dry white wine, chicken broth, some of the bacon, and a splash of hot sauce. We returned the skinless thighs to braise until they emerged loaded with flavor, ready for a sprinkling of sliced scallions, fresh parsley, and the rest of the bacon. To ensure even cooking and browning, use small red potatoes measuring no more than 1½ inches in diameter for this recipe.

- 3 pounds bone-in chicken thighs, trimmed
- ½ teaspoon table salt
- ¼ teaspoon pepper
- 5 slices bacon, chopped
- 1½ pounds small red potatoes, unpeeled, halved
- 1 onion, chopped fine
- 4 garlic cloves, minced
- 2 teaspoons minced fresh thyme
- ¾ cup dry white wine
- ½ cup chicken broth
- 1 teaspoon hot sauce
- 3 scallions, sliced thin
- 2 tablespoons chopped fresh parsley

1. Pat chicken dry with paper towels and sprinkle with salt and pepper. Cook bacon in Dutch oven over medium heat until rendered and crisp, 5 to 7 minutes. Using slotted spoon, transfer bacon to paper towel–lined plate.

2. Pour off all but 1 tablespoon fat from pot. Heat fat over medium-high heat until just smoking. Cook chicken until browned on both sides, 6 to 8 minutes; transfer to plate. When chicken is cool enough to handle, discard skin.

3. Pour off all but 1½ tablespoons fat from pot. Arrange potatoes cut side down in pot and cook over medium heat until golden brown, about 10 minutes. Stir in onion and cook until softened, about 5 minutes. Stir in garlic and thyme and cook until fragrant, about 30 seconds. Stir in wine, broth, hot sauce, and half of bacon and bring to boil.

4. Return chicken and any accumulated juices to pot. Reduce heat to medium-low, cover, and cook until potatoes are tender and chicken registers 175 degrees, about 25 minutes. Sprinkle with scallions, parsley, and remaining bacon. Season with salt and pepper to taste. Serve.

REMOVING CHICKEN SKIN

Chicken skin is often slippery, making it a challenge to remove by hand, even when chicken has been browned. To simplify the task, use a paper towel to provide extra grip while pulling.

Roasted Chicken Parts with Potatoes, Carrots, and Brussels Sprouts

Serves 4 **Total Time** 1 hour

Why This Recipe Works When we want a dinner of roast chicken with vegetables but prefer not to bother with a whole bird, we often turn to this sheet-pan roast. It accommodates a cut-up chicken or any mix of parts and adds interest by combining root vegetables with sweet-earthy brussels sprouts. But using mixed chicken parts complicated things slightly: By the time the dark meat was cooked through, the delicate white meat was overcooked and dry. We solved this problem by placing the breasts in the center of the pan and putting the thighs and drumsticks around the perimeter where the heat was more intense. A similar treatment for the vegetables—leafy brussels sprouts in the middle, hardier potatoes and carrots on the outside—also proved effective. Use brussels sprouts no bigger than golf balls, as larger ones are often tough and woody.

- 12 ounces red potatoes, unpeeled, cut into 1-inch pieces
- 12 ounces brussels sprouts, trimmed and halved
- 8 shallots, peeled and halved
- 4 carrots, peeled, cut into 2-inch pieces, thick ends halved lengthwise
- ¼ cup vegetable oil, divided
- 6 garlic cloves, peeled
- 4 teaspoons minced fresh thyme or 1½ teaspoons dried, divided
- 2 teaspoons minced fresh rosemary or ½ teaspoon dried, divided
- 3½ pounds bone-in chicken pieces (2 split breasts halved crosswise, 2 drumsticks, and 2 thighs), trimmed
- ¾ teaspoon table salt, divided
- ¼ teaspoon pepper, divided
- 1 teaspoon sugar

1. Adjust oven rack to upper-middle position and heat oven to 475 degrees. Toss potatoes, brussels sprouts, shallots, and carrots with 2 tablespoons oil, garlic, 2 teaspoons thyme, and 1 teaspoon rosemary in bowl.

2. In separate bowl, toss chicken with ¼ teaspoon salt, ⅛ teaspoon pepper, remaining 2 tablespoons oil, remaining 2 teaspoons thyme, and remaining 1 teaspoon rosemary.

3. Spread vegetables in single layer in rimmed baking sheet, discarding any excess liquid and arranging brussels sprouts in center. Season vegetables with sugar, remaining ½ teaspoon salt, and remaining ⅛ teaspoon pepper.

4. Place chicken skin side up on top of vegetables, arranging breast pieces in center and leg and thigh pieces around perimeter of sheet. Roast until breasts register 160 degrees and drumsticks/thighs register 175 degrees, 35 to 40 minutes, rotating sheet halfway through baking.

5. Transfer chicken to serving platter, tent with aluminum foil, and let rest for 5 to 10 minutes. Return vegetables to oven and continue to roast until lightly browned, 5 to 10 minutes. Toss vegetables with any accumulated chicken juices and transfer to platter with chicken. Serve.

Lemon-Thyme Roasted Chicken with Ratatouille

Serves 4　　**Total Time** 1 hour

Why This Recipe Works Roasted chicken and ratatouille offers the flavors of summer in perfect balance. Yet preparations can be onerous, requiring multiple pans for the ratatouille alone. A sheet pan offered an easier method. Its large surface area could accommodate both the chicken and the vegetables, and exposing the food to dry heat would prevent the vegetables from becoming soggy. Bone-in chicken breasts gave us juicy, tender meat without being too fussy or producing too much grease. To get nicely golden skin, we preheated the baking sheet, oiled it to prevent sticking, and placed the chicken, skin side down, on the pan to sear them. We chopped eggplant and zucchini into bite-size pieces and tossed them with canned tomatoes (ideal for year-round cooking), seasoning them with garlic and plenty of thyme to drive home the authentic flavor. We scattered the vegetables opposite the chicken. Halfway through roasting, we flipped the chicken, stirred the vegetables, and added lemon wedges to roast for a flavor boost. Peeking in 5 minutes later, we stirred the vegetables again—they were really beginning to soften—and then once more to ensure that every piece was cooked and all the excess liquid could evaporate. Minutes later, our chicken was ready, the ratatouille was tender and moist but not wet, and we even had juicy roasted lemon wedges to squeeze over everything. All that was missing was some crusty bread.

- 1 (14.5-ounce) can diced tomatoes, drained
- 12 ounces eggplant, cut into ½-inch pieces
- 2 small zucchini (6 ounces each), cut into ½-inch pieces
- 3 tablespoons extra-virgin olive oil, divided
- 1 tablespoon minced fresh thyme or 1 teaspoon dried, divided
- 2 garlic cloves, minced
- 1 teaspoon table salt, divided
- ¾ teaspoon pepper, divided
- 4 (12-ounce) bone-in split chicken breasts, trimmed
- 1 lemon, quartered
- 2 tablespoons minced fresh parsley

1. Adjust oven rack to upper-middle position, place rimmed baking sheet on rack, and heat oven to 450 degrees. Toss tomatoes, eggplant, and zucchini with 2 tablespoons oil, 1 teaspoon thyme, garlic, ½ teaspoon salt, and ¼ teaspoon pepper. Pat chicken dry with paper towels and sprinkle with remaining 2 teaspoons thyme, remaining ½ teaspoon salt, and remaining ½ teaspoon pepper.

2. Brush remaining 1 tablespoon oil evenly over hot sheet. Place chicken skin side down on 1 side of sheet and spread vegetables in single layer on other side. Roast until chicken releases from sheet and vegetables begin to wilt, about 10 minutes.

3. Flip chicken skin side up and stir vegetables. Place lemon quarters cut side down on sheet. Continue to roast, stirring vegetables occasionally, until chicken registers 160 degrees and vegetables are tender, 10 to 15 minutes.

4. Remove sheet from oven, tent with aluminum foil, and let rest for 5 minutes. Transfer chicken to serving platter. Toss vegetables with pan juices, season with salt and pepper to taste, and transfer to platter with chicken. Sprinkle parsley over vegetables and serve with roasted lemon wedges.

Chicken Kebabs with Potatoes and Broccoli

Serves 4　　**Total Time** 1½ hours

Why This Recipe Works Kebabs don't have to be just for grilling. Here, we managed a dinner of chicken, vegetables, and starch on one pan—with a bit of staggered cooking and a bit of help from the kebabs themselves. Briefly marinating the chicken in yogurt and Thai red curry paste seasoned it, kept it juicy, and helped brown the exterior. Beginning the roasting with just a layer of potatoes around the perimeter of the baking sheet (the best place for browning) jump-started their cooking, ensuring that they would finish along with the kebabs. Next, we added broccoli florets to the center of the sheet and broiled them for quick cooking and flavorful browning. Rather than add the chicken directly to the sheet to turn steamy, we used the skewers to prop the chicken pieces on top of the potatoes, closer to the broiler element. A second round under the broiler to cook the chicken and a quick stir-together sauce of more yogurt and a touch more red curry paste finished things off. If your potatoes are larger than 2 inches, cut them into 1-inch pieces. You will need four 12-inch metal skewers for this recipe.

Chicken
- ½ cup plain Greek yogurt
- 2 tablespoons red curry paste
- 1 tablespoon vegetable oil
- 1 teaspoon table salt
- ½ teaspoon pepper
- 2 pounds boneless, skinless chicken breasts, trimmed and cut into 2-inch chunks

Sauce
- ½ cup plain Greek yogurt
- ¼ cup chopped fresh cilantro
- 1 tablespoon lime juice
- 1 tablespoon water
- 1 teaspoon red curry paste
- ¼ teaspoon table salt
- ⅛ teaspoon pepper

Vegetables
- 1½ pounds small red potatoes, unpeeled, halved
- ¼ cup vegetable oil, divided
- ¾ teaspoon table salt, divided
- ½ teaspoon pepper, divided
- 1 pound broccoli florets, cut into 2-inch pieces

1. For the chicken Whisk yogurt, curry paste, oil, salt, and pepper together in medium bowl. Add chicken and toss to combine. Refrigerate for at least 30 minutes or up to 1 hour. Thread chicken onto four 12-inch metal skewers; set aside.

2. For the sauce Whisk all ingredients together in bowl.

3. For the vegetables Adjust oven rack to middle position and heat oven to 475 degrees. Line rimmed baking sheet with aluminum foil. Toss potatoes, 2 tablespoons oil, ½ teaspoon salt, and ¼ teaspoon pepper together on prepared sheet. Arrange potatoes cut side down around outside of sheet. Roast until bottoms begin to brown, about 15 minutes.

4. Remove sheet from oven and heat broiler. Toss broccoli with remaining 2 tablespoons oil, remaining ¼ teaspoon salt, and remaining ¼ teaspoon pepper. Place broccoli in center of sheet. Place kebabs around perimeter of sheet on top of potatoes. Return sheet to oven and broil until chicken is lightly charred on top, about 8 minutes. Flip kebabs and continue to broil until lightly charred on second side and chicken registers 160 degrees, 6 to 8 minutes. Serve kebabs with vegetables and sauce.

Lemon-Thyme Roasted Chicken with Ratatouille

Chicken Kebabs with Potatoes and Broccoli

Chicken Baked in Foil with Fennel, Carrots, and Orange

Chicken Baked in Foil with Zucchini and Tomatoes

Serves 4   Total Time 1 hour (plus 1 hour chilling time)

Why This Recipe Works Despite its reputation for delivering bland, boring food, steaming in a foil packet is actually an excellent way to cook delicate boneless, skinless chicken breasts. The method is fast and convenient, and it keeps food moist. The chicken absorbs the flavors of the other ingredients and everything cooks in the protein's tasty juices. To keep those juices from becoming too watery, we first salted our zucchini to draw out excess moisture. After tossing the vegetables with oil and aromatics, we layered them on the foil, starting with zucchini to insulate the chicken from direct heat, and placing the delicate plum tomatoes on top so they wouldn't break down. Refrigerating the packets for at least an hour enabled the salt to fully season the chicken. The result was moist, perfectly cooked chicken with highly flavorful vegetables. To prevent overcooking, open each packet promptly after baking.

2   zucchini, sliced ¼ inch thick
½   teaspoon table salt, divided
2   tablespoons extra-virgin olive oil
2   garlic cloves, minced
1   teaspoon minced fresh oregano or
    ¼ teaspoon dried
½   teaspoon pepper, divided
⅛   teaspoon red pepper flakes
8   ounces plum tomatoes, cored, seeded,
    and chopped
4   (6- to 8-ounce) boneless, skinless chicken
    breasts, trimmed
¼   cup chopped fresh basil
    Lemon wedges

1. Toss zucchini with ¼ teaspoon salt in colander and let drain for 30 minutes. Spread zucchini out on several layers of paper towels and pat dry; transfer to bowl.

2. Combine oil, garlic, oregano, ¼ teaspoon pepper, and pepper flakes in small bowl. Toss zucchini with half of oil mixture, and toss tomatoes with remaining oil mixture in separate bowl. Spray centers of four 20 by 12-inch sheets of aluminum foil with vegetable oil spray.

3. Pound chicken breasts to uniform thickness. Pat chicken dry with paper towels and sprinkle with remaining ¼ teaspoon salt and remaining ¼ teaspoon pepper. Position 1 piece of prepared foil with long side parallel to edge of counter. In center of foil, arrange one-quarter of zucchini slices in 2 rows perpendicular to edge of counter. Lay 1 chicken breast on top of zucchini slices, then top with one-quarter of tomatoes. Repeat with remaining prepared foil, remaining zucchini slices, remaining chicken, and remaining tomatoes. Drizzle any remaining oil mixture from bowls over chicken.

4. Bring short sides of foil together and crimp to seal tightly. Crimp remaining open ends of packets, leaving as much headroom as possible inside packets. Refrigerate for at least 1 hour or up to 24 hours.

5. Adjust oven rack to lowest position and heat oven to 475 degrees. Place packets on rimmed baking sheet and bake until chicken registers 160 degrees, 18 to 23 minutes. (To check temperature, poke thermometer through foil of 1 packet and into chicken.) Let chicken rest in packets for 3 minutes.

6. Transfer chicken packets to individual serving plates, open carefully (steam will escape), and slide contents onto plates. Sprinkle with basil and serve with lemon wedges.

Chicken Baked in Foil with Fennel, Carrots, and Orange

Total Time 45 minutes (plus 1 hour chilling time)

- 2 tablespoons extra-virgin olive oil
- 1 shallot, sliced thin
- 1 teaspoon minced fresh tarragon
- ½ teaspoon table salt, divided
- ½ teaspoon pepper divided
- 2 oranges, peeled and cut into ¼-inch pieces
- 2 carrots, peeled and cut into matchsticks
- 1 fennel bulb (about 12 ounces), stalks discarded, bulb halved, cored, and sliced thin
- 4 (6- to 8-ounce) boneless, skinless chicken breasts, trimmed
- 2 scallions, sliced thin

1. Combine oil, shallot, tarragon, ¼ teaspoon salt, and ¼ teaspoon pepper in small bowl. Toss oranges with half of oil mixture in separate bowl. Toss carrots and fennel with remaining oil mixture in third bowl. Spray centers of four 20 by 12-inch sheets of aluminum foil with vegetable oil spray.

2. Pound chicken breasts to uniform thickness. Pat chicken dry with paper towels and sprinkle with remaining ¼ teaspoon salt and remaining ¼ teaspoon pepper. Position 1 piece of prepared foil with long side parallel to edge of counter. In center of foil, arrange one-quarter of carrot-fennel mixture. Lay 1 chicken breast on top of carrot-fennel mixture, then top with one-quarter of orange mixture. Repeat with remaining prepared foil, remaining carrot-fennel mixture, remaining chicken, and remaining orange mixture. Drizzle any remaining oil mixture from bowls over chicken.

3. Bring short sides of foil together and crimp to seal tightly. Crimp remaining open ends of packets, leaving as much headroom as possible inside packets. Refrigerate for at least 1 hour or up to 24 hours.

4. Adjust oven rack to lowest position and heat oven to 475 degrees. Place packets on rimmed baking sheet and bake until chicken registers 160 degrees, 18 to 23 minutes. (To check temperature, poke thermometer through foil of 1 packet and into chicken.) Let chicken rest in packets for 3 minutes.

5. Transfer chicken packets to individual serving plates, open carefully (steam will escape), and slide contents onto plates. Sprinkle with scallions and serve.

Apricot-Glazed Chicken with Chickpeas, Chorizo, and Spinach

Apricot-Glazed Chicken with Chickpeas, Chorizo, and Spinach

Serves 4   Total Time 45 minutes

Why This Recipe Works A few potent ingredients give this simple chicken dinner a sophisticated balance of flavors: sweetness from apricot preserves, spice from chorizo sausage, smokiness from smoked paprika, and a hint of fresh bitterness from lemon zest. Bone-in split chicken breasts were easy to cook and still had deep, rich flavor. The addition of canned chickpeas turned this into a full meal. We first browned the chicken to start crisping the skin. We then added our other ingredients to the skillet, placing the chicken on top and brushing it with a seasoned apricot glaze before letting everything cook together in a hot oven. Baby spinach, stirred in at the end, brought freshness to offset the earthy, smoky flavors. If Spanish-style chorizo is not available, Portuguese linguica or Polish kielbasa can be substituted. You will need a 12-inch ovensafe skillet for this recipe.

¼ cup apricot preserves

2 teaspoons grated lemon zest, plus lemon wedges for serving

¾ teaspoon table salt, divided

½ teaspoon pepper, divided

4 (12-ounce) bone-in split chicken breasts, trimmed and halved crosswise

1 tablespoon vegetable oil

1 (15-ounce) can chickpeas

6 ounces Spanish-style chorizo sausage, cut into ½-inch pieces

1 onion, chopped

1½ teaspoons smoked paprika

8 ounces (8 cups) baby spinach

1. Adjust oven rack to middle position and heat oven to 450 degrees. Combine preserves, lemon zest, ⅛ teaspoon salt, and ⅛ teaspoon pepper in bowl; set aside. Pat chicken dry with paper towels and sprinkle with ½ teaspoon salt and ¼ teaspoon pepper.

2. Heat oil in 12-inch ovensafe skillet over medium-high heat until just smoking. Place chicken skin side down in skillet and cook until well browned on first side, 5 to 7 minutes. Flip chicken and continue to cook until lightly browned on second side, about 3 minutes; transfer to plate.

3. Off heat, combine chickpeas, chorizo, onion, paprika, remaining ⅛ teaspoon salt, and remaining ⅛ teaspoon pepper in now-empty skillet. Place chicken skin side up on top of chickpea mixture and brush with apricot mixture. Transfer skillet to oven and roast until chicken registers 160 degrees, 20 to 25 minutes.

4. Using pot holders, remove skillet from oven. Transfer chicken to serving platter, tent with aluminum foil, and let rest while finishing chickpea mixture. Being careful of hot skillet handle, return skillet to medium-high heat. Add spinach, 1 handful at a time, and cook until wilted, about 2 minutes. Season with salt and pepper to taste. Transfer chickpea mixture to platter with chicken. Serve with lemon wedges.

Honey Mustard–Glazed Chicken with Roasted Sweet Potato Salad

Serves 4   Total Time 1 hour

Why This Recipe Works Honey mustard–glazed chicken is appealing because it's so easy to make, but that's no reason to settle for too-sweet store-bought sauce. We made our own balanced and superflavorful glaze, which we microwaved to activate the cornstarch's thickening power. Brushing on the glaze both before and after cooking ensured well-seasoned chicken. To turn our chicken into a full meal, we assembled a salad studded with sweet potatoes, which we roasted right alongside our chicken. When the potatoes were browned and tender, we tossed them with peppery arugula, thinly sliced fennel, and dried cranberries—a simple salad full of fall flavor.

⅓ cup honey

¼ cup soy sauce

¼ cup yellow mustard

2 teaspoons cornstarch

4 (6- to 8-ounce) boneless, skinless chicken breasts, trimmed

1 pound sweet potatoes, peeled and cut into ¾-inch pieces

¼ cup extra-virgin olive oil, divided

½ teaspoon smoked paprika

¾ teaspoon table salt, divided

3 tablespoons cider vinegar

¼ teaspoon pepper

5 ounces (5 cups) baby arugula

½ fennel bulb, stalks discarded, bulb halved, cored, and sliced thin

¼ cup dried cranberries

1. Adjust oven rack to middle position and heat oven to 450 degrees. Line rimmed baking sheet with aluminum foil and spray with vegetable oil spray. Combine honey, soy sauce, mustard, and cornstarch in medium bowl and microwave, whisking occasionally, until slightly thickened, 3 to 5 minutes. Let glaze cool slightly, then reserve half for serving.

2. Pound chicken breasts to uniform thickness. Pat chicken dry with paper towels. Add to bowl with remaining glaze and toss to coat. Arrange chicken breasts, side by side (and alternating thicker end to thinner end), on 1 side of prepared sheet. Drizzle any remaining glaze in bowl over top.

3. Toss sweet potatoes in separate bowl with 2 tablespoons oil, paprika, and ¼ teaspoon salt. Spread potatoes evenly over opposite side of sheet from chicken. Roast until chicken registers 160 degrees and potatoes are well browned and tender, 20 to 25 minutes, rotating sheet halfway through roasting.

4. Whisk vinegar, pepper, remaining 2 tablespoons oil, and remaining ½ teaspoon salt together in large bowl. Transfer potatoes to bowl with dressing and let cool slightly. Tent chicken with aluminum foil and let rest while finishing salad. Add arugula, fennel, and cranberries to cooled potatoes and gently toss to combine. Season with salt and pepper to taste. Brush chicken with reserved glaze and serve with salad.

Garlic-Lime Roasted Chicken Leg Quarters with Swiss Chard and Sweet Potatoes

Serves 4   **Total Time** 1¾ hours (plus 1 hour chilling time)

Why This Recipe Works Peruvian Roast Chicken with Garlic and Lime (page 233) boasts a bronzed exterior seasoned with a robust paste of garlic, spices, lime juice, chile, and mint. While the bird is traditionally roasted whole, we found several advantages to using leg quarters and a roasting pan. The quarters cooked faster than a whole chicken and yielded more surface area to be coated in the tasty paste. And the roasting pan also accommodated a side of sweet potatoes. Smearing the chicken with the paste at least an hour before cooking allowed the flavors to meld and the salt to penetrate the meat. We meanwhile gave the sweet potatoes a head start, browning them before adding the chicken and moving the pan to the oven where the drippings basted the potatoes. We then removed the chicken and potatoes to rest while we cooked 4 pounds of chard in the delicious juices left behind. Some leg quarters are sold with the backbone attached; removing it before cooking makes the chicken easier to serve (see page 11). You can substitute 1 tablespoon of minced serrano chile for the habanero here. Be sure to wear gloves when handling the chile.

- ¼ cup fresh mint leaves
- 10 garlic cloves (5 chopped, 5 sliced)
- ¼ cup extra-virgin olive oil, divided
- 1 tablespoon ground cumin
- 1 tablespoon honey
- 2 teaspoons smoked paprika
- 2 teaspoons dried oregano
- 2 teaspoons grated lime zest plus ¼ cup juice (2 limes), plus lime wedges for serving
- 2 teaspoons pepper
- 1¾ teaspoons table salt, divided
- 1 teaspoon minced habanero chile
- 6 (10-ounce) chicken leg quarters, trimmed
- 3 pounds sweet potatoes, peeled, ends squared off, and sliced into 1-inch-thick rounds
- 4 pounds Swiss chard, stemmed and cut into 1-inch pieces
- 2 tablespoons minced fresh cilantro

1. Adjust oven rack to middle position and heat oven to 425 degrees. Process mint, chopped garlic, 1 tablespoon oil, cumin, honey, paprika, oregano, lime zest and juice, pepper, 1 teaspoon salt, and habanero in blender until smooth, 20 seconds.

Honey Mustard–Glazed Chicken with Roasted Sweet Potato Salad

Garlic-Lime Roasted Chicken Leg Quarters with Swiss Chard and Sweet Potatoes

2. Using your fingers, gently loosen skin covering thighs and drumsticks and spread half of paste directly on meat. Spread remaining half of paste over exterior of chicken. Place chicken in 1-gallon zipper-lock bag and refrigerate for at least 1 hour or up to 24 hours.

3. Toss potatoes with 1 tablespoon oil and ½ teaspoon salt. Heat remaining 2 tablespoons oil in 16 by 12-inch roasting pan over medium-high heat (over 2 burners, if possible) until shimmering. Add potatoes cut side down and cook until well browned on first side, 6 to 8 minutes.

4. Off heat, flip potatoes and lay chicken skin side up on top. Roast until thighs and drumsticks register 175 degrees and potatoes are tender, 40 to 50 minutes, rotating pan halfway through roasting.

5. Remove pan from oven. Transfer potatoes and chicken to serving platter, tent with aluminum foil, and let rest for 5 minutes. Being careful of hot pan handles, pour off all but ¼ cup liquid left in pan. Add sliced garlic and cook over high heat (over 2 burners, if possible) until fragrant, about 30 seconds. Add chard and remaining ¼ teaspoon salt and cook, stirring constantly, until chard is wilted and tender, about 8 minutes; transfer to serving bowl.

6. Sprinkle cilantro over chicken and potatoes and serve with chard and lime wedges.

Chicken and Rice with Peas and Scallions

Serves 4   Total Time 1¼ hours

Why This Recipe Works A good chicken and rice recipe, the kind that becomes a weeknight mainstay, should be simple and dependable but easily adaptable. This master recipe delivers on all fronts. It guarantees juicy, not dry, chicken and tender, not mushy, rice, and takes on different flavors beautifully. To prevent our boneless chicken breasts from drying out, we dredged them in flour before browning, which protected the exterior and created a rich, golden crust. For the rice, we sautéed long-grain rice in butter with onion, garlic, and red pepper flakes before adding liquid; this not only gave the rice deeper flavor but kept the grains distinct and creamy without turning mushy. To ensure the chicken didn't overcook, we cooked it atop the rice just until done and set it aside while the rice finished cooking. Thawed frozen peas (one of our favorite frozen vegetables) needed only 2 minutes to warm through. Lemon juice and scallions, gently folded in at the end, brightened up the flavor. Our variations show off the versatility of the dish and are just as easy to make.

½ cup all-purpose flour
4 (6- to 8-ounce) boneless, skinless chicken breasts, trimmed
1 teaspoon table salt, divided
¼ teaspoon pepper
2 tablespoons vegetable oil
2 tablespoons unsalted butter
1 onion, chopped fine
1½ cups long-grain white rice
3 garlic cloves, minced
Pinch red pepper flakes
4½ cups chicken broth
1 cup frozen peas
5 scallions, sliced thin
2 tablespoons lemon juice

1. Spread flour in shallow dish. Pound chicken breasts to uniform thickness. Pat chicken dry with paper towels and sprinkle with ½ teaspoon salt and pepper. Working with 1 breast at a time, lightly dredge chicken in flour, shaking off excess.

2. Heat oil in 12-inch nonstick skillet over medium-high heat until shimmering. Cook chicken until lightly browned on both sides, 8 to 10 minutes; transfer to plate.

3. Melt butter in now-empty skillet over medium heat. Add onion and remaining ½ teaspoon salt and cook until softened, about 5 minutes. Stir in rice, garlic, and red pepper flakes and cook until fragrant, about 30 seconds.

4. Stir in broth, scraping up any browned bits. Nestle chicken into rice, add any accumulated juices, and bring to simmer. Reduce heat to medium-low, cover, and cook until chicken registers 160 degrees, about 10 minutes.

5. Transfer chicken to clean plate, brushing any rice that sticks to chicken back into skillet, and tent chicken with aluminum foil to keep warm. Cover and continue to cook rice over medium-low heat, stirring occasionally, until liquid has been absorbed and rice is tender, about 10 minutes.

6. Off heat, sprinkle peas over rice, cover, and let sit until heated through, about 2 minutes. Add scallions and lemon juice and gently fold into rice. Season with salt and pepper to taste, and serve with chicken.

VARIATIONS
Chicken and Rice with Broccoli and Cheddar
Serves 4   Total Time 1¼ hours

½ cup all-purpose flour
4 (6- to 8-ounce) boneless, skinless chicken breasts, trimmed
1 teaspoon table salt, divided
¼ teaspoon pepper

3 tablespoons vegetable oil, divided
1 onion, chopped fine
1½ cups long-grain white rice
3 garlic cloves, minced
4½ cups chicken broth
1 (10-ounce) package frozen broccoli florets, thawed
4 ounces cheddar cheese, shredded (1 cup), divided
1 teaspoon hot sauce

1. Spread flour in shallow dish. Pound chicken breasts to uniform thickness. Pat chicken dry with paper towels and sprinkle with ½ teaspoon salt and pepper. Working with 1 breast at a time, lightly dredge chicken in flour, shaking off excess.

2. Heat 2 tablespoons oil in 12-inch nonstick skillet over medium-high heat until shimmering. Cook chicken until lightly browned on both sides, 8 to 10 minutes; transfer to plate.

3. Heat remaining 1 tablespoon oil in now-empty skillet over medium heat until shimmering. Add onion and remaining ½ teaspoon salt and cook until softened, about 5 minutes. Stir in rice and garlic and cook until fragrant, about 30 seconds.

4. Stir in broth, scraping up any browned bits. Nestle chicken into rice, add any accumulated juices, and bring to simmer. Reduce heat to medium-low, cover, and cook until chicken registers 160 degrees, about 10 minutes.

5. Transfer chicken to clean plate, brushing any rice that sticks to chicken back into skillet, and tent chicken with aluminum foil to keep warm. Cover and continue to cook rice over medium-low heat, stirring occasionally, until liquid has been absorbed and rice is tender, about 10 minutes.

6. Off heat, gently fold broccoli, ½ cup of cheddar, and hot sauce into rice and season with salt and pepper to taste. Sprinkle remaining ½ cup cheddar over top, cover, and let sit until cheese melts, about 2 minutes. Serve with chicken.

Curried Chicken and Rice

Serves 4   Total Time 1¼ hours

½ cup all-purpose flour
4 (6- to 8-ounce) boneless, skinless chicken breasts, trimmed
1 teaspoon table salt, divided
¼ teaspoon pepper
3 tablespoons vegetable oil
2 carrots, peeled and cut into ¼-inch pieces
1 onion, chopped fine
1½ cups long-grain white rice
2 garlic cloves, minced
1 tablespoon curry powder
4 cups chicken broth

Curried Chicken and Rice

½ cup canned light coconut milk
1 cup frozen peas
¼ cup minced fresh cilantro
2 tablespoons sliced almonds, toasted

1. Spread flour in shallow dish. Pound chicken breasts to uniform thickness. Pat chicken dry with paper towels and season with ½ teaspoon salt and pepper. Working with 1 breast at a time, lightly dredge chicken in flour, shaking off excess.

2. Heat 2 tablespoons oil in 12-inch nonstick skillet over medium-high heat until shimmering. Cook chicken until lightly browned on both sides, 8 to 10 minutes; transfer to plate.

3. Heat remaining 1 tablespoon oil in now-empty skillet over medium heat until shimmering. Add carrots, onion, and remaining ½ teaspoon salt and cook until softened, about 5 minutes. Stir in rice, garlic, and curry powder and cook until fragrant, about 30 seconds.

4. Stir in broth, scraping up any browned bits. Nestle chicken into skillet along with any accumulated juices. Reduce heat to gentle simmer, cover, and cook until chicken registers 160 degrees, about 8 minutes. Transfer chicken to serving platter, brushing any rice that sticks to chicken back into skillet, and tent loosely with aluminum foil. Let chicken rest while finishing rice.

5. Add coconut milk to skillet, cover, and cook over medium-low heat, stirring occasionally, until liquid has been absorbed and rice is tender, 12 to 15 minutes. Off heat, sprinkle peas over rice, cover, and let sit until heated through, about 2 minutes. Gently fold cilantro and almonds into rice. Season with salt and pepper to taste. Serve chicken with rice.

Chicken and Rice with Coconut Milk and Pistachios

Serves 4   Total Time 1¼ hours
We prefer light coconut milk here; full-fat coconut milk causes the rice to become gummy.

 ½ cup all-purpose flour
 4 (6- to 8-ounce) boneless, skinless chicken breasts, trimmed
 1 teaspoon table salt, divided
 ¼ teaspoon pepper
 3 tablespoons vegetable oil, divided
 1 onion, chopped fine
 1½ cups long-grain white rice
 3 garlic cloves, minced
 1½ teaspoons garam masala
 2¾ cups chicken broth
 1 (14-ounce) can light coconut milk
 1 cup frozen peas
 ½ cup shelled pistachios, toasted and chopped
 ½ cup minced fresh cilantro

1. Spread flour in shallow dish. Pound chicken breasts to uniform thickness. Pat chicken dry with paper towels and sprinkle with ½ teaspoon salt and pepper. Working with 1 breast at a time, lightly dredge chicken in flour, shaking off excess.

2. Heat 2 tablespoons oil in 12-inch nonstick skillet over medium-high heat until shimmering. Cook chicken until lightly browned on both sides, 8 to 10 minutes; transfer to plate.

3. Heat remaining 1 tablespoon oil in now-empty skillet over medium heat until shimmering. Add onion and remaining ½ teaspoon salt and cook until softened, about 5 minutes. Stir in rice, garlic, and garam masala and cook until fragrant, about 30 seconds.

4. Stir in broth and coconut milk, scraping up any browned bits. Nestle chicken into rice, add any accumulated juices, and bring to simmer. Reduce heat to medium-low, cover, and cook until chicken registers 160 degrees, about 10 minutes.

5. Transfer chicken to clean plate, brushing any rice that sticks to chicken back into skillet, and tent chicken with aluminum foil to keep warm. Cover and continue to cook rice over medium-low heat, stirring occasionally, until liquid has been absorbed and rice is tender, about 10 minutes.

6. Off heat, sprinkle peas over rice, cover, and let sit until heated through, about 2 minutes. Add pistachios and cilantro and gently fold into rice. Season with salt and pepper to taste, and serve with chicken.

Chicken and Rice with Chorizo and Saffron

Serves 4   Total Time 1¼ hours
If Spanish-style chorizo is not available, Portuguese linguica or Polish kielbasa can be substituted.

 ½ cup all-purpose flour
 4 (6- to 8-ounce) boneless, skinless chicken breasts, trimmed
 1 teaspoon table salt, divided
 ¼ teaspoon pepper
 3 tablespoons vegetable oil, divided
 8 ounces Spanish-style chorizo sausage, quartered lengthwise and sliced ¼ inch thick
 1 onion, chopped fine
 1 red bell pepper, stemmed, seeded, and chopped fine
 1½ cups long-grain white rice
 3 garlic cloves, minced
 Pinch saffron threads, crumbled
 4½ cups chicken broth
 1 cup frozen peas

1. Spread flour in shallow dish. Pound chicken breasts to uniform thickness. Pat chicken dry with paper towels and sprinkle with ½ teaspoon salt and pepper. Working with 1 breast at a time, lightly dredge chicken in flour, shaking off excess.

2. Heat 2 tablespoons oil in 12-inch nonstick skillet over medium-high heat until shimmering. Cook chicken until lightly browned on both sides, 8 to 10 minutes; transfer to plate.

3. Heat remaining 1 tablespoon oil in now-empty skillet over medium heat until shimmering. Add chorizo, onion, bell pepper, and remaining ½ teaspoon salt and cook until onion is softened, about 5 minutes. Stir in rice, garlic, and saffron and cook until fragrant, about 30 seconds.

4. Stir in broth, scraping up any browned bits. Nestle chicken into rice, add any accumulated juices, and bring to simmer. Reduce heat to medium-low, cover, and cook until chicken registers 160 degrees, about 10 minutes.

5. Transfer chicken to clean plate, brushing any rice that sticks to chicken back into skillet, and tent chicken with aluminum foil to keep warm. Cover and continue to cook rice over medium-low heat, stirring occasionally, until liquid has been absorbed and rice is tender, about 10 minutes.

6. Off heat, sprinkle peas over rice, cover, and let sit until heated through, about 2 minutes. Season with salt and pepper to taste, and serve with chicken.

Turkey Meatballs with Lemony Rice

Serves 4   Total Time 1¼ hours

Why This Recipe Works Savory turkey meatballs cook up tender and juicy in a skillet full of seasoned rice for a satisfying one-pan meal. A bread crumb–egg panade gave the meatballs a light texture, and stirring sliced scallion greens, parsley, and lemon zest into the mix added freshness and character. We rolled and refrigerated the meatballs to set them up and browned them in oil to build their flavor. We then used the meatballs' rendered fat to toast the rice, giving the grains a meaty dimension before adding in aromatics. Chicken broth promised rice with rich flavor, while lemon juice and zest added citrusy brightness. We let the browned meatballs finish cooking directly in the rice, absorbing some of the cooking liquid at the same time. The rice and meat finished up simultaneously, and a sprinkling of nutty Parmesan, scallions, and parsley and a squeeze of lemon made for a perfect finish. Be sure to use ground turkey, not ground turkey breast (also labeled 99 percent fat-free), in this recipe. You will need a 12-inch nonstick skillet with a tight-fitting lid for this recipe.

  2 **slices hearty white sandwich bread, torn into 1-inch pieces**
1¼ **pounds ground turkey**
  1 **large egg**
  6 **scallions, white and green parts separated and sliced thin, divided**
  3 **tablespoons minced fresh parsley, divided**
  1 **tablespoon grated lemon zest, divided, plus 2 tablespoons juice, plus lemon wedges for serving**
  1 **teaspoon table salt, divided**
  ½ **teaspoon pepper**
  2 **tablespoons extra-virgin olive oil**
1½ **cups long-grain white rice**
  3 **garlic cloves, minced**
3¼ **cups chicken broth**
  1 **ounce Parmesan cheese, grated (½ cup)**

Turkey Meatballs with Lemony Rice

1. Pulse bread in food processor to fine crumbs, 10 to 15 pulses; transfer to large bowl. Add turkey, egg, 2 tablespoons scallion greens, 2 tablespoons parsley, 1½ teaspoons lemon zest, ½ teaspoon salt, and pepper and mix with your hands until thoroughly combined. Using your wet hands, pinch off and roll 2 tablespoon–size pieces of mixture into balls and arrange on large plate (you should have about 20 meatballs); refrigerate for 15 minutes.

2. Heat oil in 12-inch nonstick skillet over medium-high heat until shimmering. Brown meatballs on all sides, 5 to 7 minutes; return to plate.

3. Add rice to fat left in skillet and cook over medium-high heat, stirring often, until edges of rice begin to turn translucent, about 1 minute. Stir in scallion whites, garlic, and remaining ½ teaspoon salt and cook until fragrant, about 1 minute. Stir in broth, lemon juice, and remaining 1½ teaspoons lemon zest and bring to boil. Return meatballs to skillet and add any accumulated juices. Cover, reduce heat to low, and cook for 20 minutes.

4. Remove skillet from heat and let sit, covered, for 10 minutes. Sprinkle with Parmesan, remaining scallion greens, and remaining 1 tablespoon parsley. Serve with lemon wedges.

Chicken and Shrimp Jambalaya

Serves 6   Total Time 1½ hours

Why This Recipe Works Done right, jambalaya is a one-pot meal with a standout combination of sweetness, spice, and smoke, but when poorly executed, it's thin-flavored with gummy rice; tough, dry chicken; and overcooked shrimp. To keep the chicken moist, we used chicken thighs, which also let us avoid cutting up a whole chicken as is traditionally done. Classic andouille sausage contributed spice and smoke. Simmering the rice in a combination of chicken broth and clam juice added the requisite brininess of the Cajun classic, and some tomato paste boosted the tomato flavor without overwhelming the other components. Adding the raw shrimp to the pot just 5 minutes before the rice was finished left them perfectly tender. If andouille is not available, Portuguese ca or Polish kielbasa can be substituted. To keep the dish from becoming greasy, remove excess fat from the chicken thighs and trim the skin. Be sure to stir the rice gently when cooking in step 5; aggressive stirring will make the rice gluey.

- 1¼ pounds bone-in chicken thighs, trimmed
- ¼ teaspoon table salt
- ⅛ teaspoon pepper
- 1 tablespoon extra-virgin olive oil
- 8 ounces andouille sausage, halved lengthwise and sliced ¼ inch thick
- 1 onion, chopped fine
- 1 celery rib, chopped fine
- 1 red bell pepper, stemmed, seeded, and chopped fine
- 5 garlic cloves, minced
- 1 teaspoon minced fresh thyme or ¼ teaspoon dried
- ¼ teaspoon cayenne pepper
- 2 teaspoons tomato paste
- 1½ cups chicken broth
- 1 (8-ounce) bottle clam juice
- 1 (14.5-ounce) can diced tomatoes, drained
- 2 cups long-grain white rice
- 1 pound large shrimp (26 to 30 per pound), peeled, deveined, and tails removed
- 3 tablespoons minced fresh parsley

1. Adjust oven rack to middle position and heat oven to 350 degrees. Pat chicken dry with paper towels and sprinkle with salt and pepper.

2. Heat oil in Dutch oven over medium-high heat until just smoking. Brown chicken on both sides, 6 to 8 minutes; transfer to large bowl. Add sausage to fat left in pot and cook until lightly browned, about 5 minutes; transfer to bowl with chicken.

3. Pour off all but 2 tablespoons of fat left in pot. Add onion, celery, and bell pepper and cook until softened, 5 to 7 minutes. Stir in garlic, thyme, and cayenne and cook until fragrant, about 30 seconds. Stir in tomato paste and cook for 1 minute. Stir in broth and clam juice, scraping up any browned bits.

4. Stir in tomatoes, chicken, and sausage with any accumulated juices and bring to simmer. Reduce heat to medium-low, cover, and cook for 20 minutes.

5. Thoroughly stir in rice. Cover, transfer pot to oven, and cook until all of rice is tender and liquid has been absorbed, 20 to 30 minutes, gently stirring rice from bottom of pot to top every 10 minutes.

6. Transfer chicken to carving board. Stir shrimp into rice, cover, and continue to cook in oven until shrimp are opaque throughout, 5 to 7 minutes. Let chicken cool slightly, then shred into large chunks using 2 spoons; discard skin and bones.

7. Gently stir shredded chicken and parsley into rice and season with salt and pepper to taste. Cover and let sit until chicken is heated through, about 5 minutes. Serve.

PEELING AND DEVEINING SHRIMP

 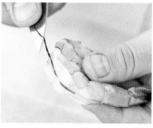

1. Break shell under swimming legs, which will come off as shell is removed. Leave tail intact, if desired, or tug tail to remove shell.

2. Use paring knife to make shallow cut along back of shrimp to expose vein. Use tip of knife to lift out vein. Discard vein by wiping blade against paper towel.

Chicken and Couscous with Fennel and Orange

½ cup all-purpose flour
4 (6- to 8-ounce) boneless, skinless chicken breasts, trimmed
1 teaspoon table salt, divided
¼ teaspoon pepper
½ cup extra-virgin olive oil, divided
1 red onion, sliced thin
1 fennel bulb, stalks discarded, bulb halved, cored, and sliced thin
1 cup couscous
3 garlic cloves, minced
⅛ teaspoon cayenne pepper, divided
1 cup orange juice, divided
¾ cup chicken broth
¼ cup minced fresh cilantro, divided

1. Spread flour in shallow dish. Pound chicken breasts to uniform thickness. Pat chicken dry with paper towels and sprinkle with ½ teaspoon salt and pepper. Working with 1 breast at a time, lightly dredge chicken in flour, shaking off excess.

2. Heat 2 tablespoons oil in 12-inch nonstick skillet over medium-high heat until shimmering. Cook chicken until well browned on both sides and registers 160 degrees, 12 to 16 minutes. Transfer chicken to serving platter, tent with aluminum foil, and let rest while cooking vegetables and couscous.

4. Heat 1 tablespoon oil in now-empty skillet over medium heat until shimmering. Add onion, fennel, and remaining ½ teaspoon salt and cook until vegetables are softened, 5 to 7 minutes. Stir in couscous, garlic, and pinch cayenne and cook until fragrant, about 30 seconds. Stir in ¾ cup orange juice and broth, scraping up any browned bits. Bring to simmer, cover, and let sit off heat until liquid is absorbed, about 5 minutes.

5. Whisk 2 tablespoons cilantro, remaining 5 tablespoons oil, remaining ¼ cup orange juice, and remaining pinch cayenne together in small bowl.

6. Gently fold remaining 2 tablespoons cilantro into couscous with fork and season with salt and pepper to taste. Drizzle oil–orange juice mixture over chicken and couscous before serving.

VARIATION

Chicken and Couscous with Chickpeas and Apricots

Omit fennel. Substitute ground cinnamon for cayenne. Add 1 (15-ounce) can chickpeas, rinsed, and 1 cup coarsely chopped dried apricots to couscous with orange juice.

Chicken and Couscous with Fennel and Orange

Serves 4   Total Time 1 hour

Why This Recipe Works For a change of pace from chicken and rice, couscous offers the perfect option for a quick supper, and this recipe streamlines the process by cooking both elements in one skillet. As with our Chicken and Rice with Peas and Scallions (page 38), we dredged boneless chicken breasts in flour before browning to guard against dryness and give them a nice crust. The fond left in the pan provided a flavor base for our vegetables, aromatic fennel and sharp red onion, which we sautéed to soften slightly before adding our couscous and toasting it briefly to release its nutty flavor and prevent clumping. While couscous is often hydrated in water or chicken broth, for even more flavor we supplemented chicken broth with orange juice. Orange is a marvelous complement to fennel—its acidic sweetness brings out more of the fennel's flavor. Drizzling the final dish with a mix of more orange juice, olive oil, cayenne, and cilantro offered a fragrant flavor boost that elevated everything.

Honey-and-Garlic Roasted Chicken with Pearl Couscous Salad

Serves 4   **Total Time** 1 hour

Why This Recipe Works This savory-sweet recipe shows how employing a few ingredients in multiple ways can pay off when it comes to flavor. Honey, apple cider vinegar, garlic, and paprika formed a sweet and tangy glaze with a gentle kick for this quick and easy roast chicken dish. A warm pearl couscous salad provided a simple pairing. To avoid bland couscous, we whisked up a fragrant dressing using more garlic and cider vinegar plus fresh tarragon, and enhanced that with the pan juices from the roast chicken. Reserving some of the dressing to drizzle over the chicken married all the flavors. Be careful when adding pan juices to the dressing as the pan will be very hot.

¼   cup extra-virgin olive oil, divided
1½   cups pearl couscous
2   cups water
1¼   teaspoons table salt, divided
2   tablespoons plus ½ teaspoon cider vinegar, divided
2   tablespoons honey
¼   teaspoon paprika
3   garlic cloves, minced, divided
3   pounds bone-in chicken pieces (split breasts halved crosswise, drumsticks, and/or thighs), trimmed
½   teaspoon pepper, divided
2   tablespoons minced fresh tarragon
4   ounces (4 cups) baby spinach
2   carrots, peeled and shredded

1. Adjust oven rack to middle position and heat oven to 450 degrees. Heat 1 tablespoon oil and couscous in medium saucepan over medium heat, stirring frequently, until half of grains are golden, about 5 minutes. Stir in water and ¼ teaspoon salt and bring to boil over medium-high heat. Reduce heat to low, cover, and simmer until water is absorbed and couscous is tender, 9 to 12 minutes. Off heat, fluff with fork and cover to keep warm.

2. Whisk ½ teaspoon vinegar, honey, paprika, and two-thirds of garlic together in small bowl. Pat chicken dry with paper towels and sprinkle with ½ teaspoon salt and ¼ teaspoon pepper.

3. Heat 1 tablespoon oil in 12-inch ovensafe skillet over medium-high heat until just smoking. Cook chicken skin side down until well browned, 5 to 7 minutes. Flip chicken and brush with honey mixture. Transfer skillet to oven and roast until breasts register 160 degrees and drumsticks/thighs register 175 degrees, 15 to 20 minutes.

4. Whisk tarragon, remaining 2 tablespoons oil, remaining ½ teaspoon salt, remaining 2 tablespoons vinegar, remaining garlic, and remaining ¼ teaspoon pepper together in large bowl.

5. Using pot holder, remove skillet from oven. Transfer chicken to serving platter, tent with aluminum foil, and let rest, reserving pan juices in skillet. Being careful of hot skillet handle, measure out ¼ cup pan juices from skillet, then add to dressing in bowl and whisk to combine. Measure out ¼ cup dressing and set aside for serving.

6. Add couscous, spinach, and carrots to large bowl with remaining dressing mixture and toss to coat. Drizzle chicken with reserved dressing mixture and serve with couscous salad.

Roasted Chicken with Harissa and Warm Bulgur Salad

Serves 4   **Total Time** 1¼ hours

Why This Recipe Works Blending the pan juices from roasted chicken parts with harissa, the North African paste of ground chiles, garlic, and spices, creates a deeply flavorful, smoky-spicy sauce. We paired the chicken with a robust bulgur salad, incorporating jarred roasted red peppers (which echoed the flavors of the harissa sauce), dill, and cucumber for crunch. For a creamy, cooling foil to the warmly spiced chicken, we seasoned Greek yogurt with salt and pepper to make a simple, delicate sauce. We prefer to use our Harissa (page 125) but you can substitute store-bought harissa, though the spiciness can vary greatly by brand. When shopping, don't confuse bulgur with cracked wheat, which has a much longer cooking time and will not work in this recipe.

2¼   cups chicken broth
1½   cups medium-grind bulgur
1   sprig fresh dill, plus 2 tablespoons minced
1   garlic clove, lightly crushed and peeled
1   teaspoon table salt, divided
3   pounds bone-in chicken pieces (split breasts, drumsticks, and/or thighs), trimmed
½   teaspoon pepper, divided
3   tablespoons extra-virgin olive oil, divided
1   teaspoon grated lemon zest plus 3 tablespoons juice
1   English cucumber, cut into ½-inch pieces
1   cup jarred roasted red peppers, chopped
3   tablespoons harissa
1   cup plain Greek yogurt

1. Adjust oven rack to middle position and heat oven to 450 degrees. Bring broth, bulgur, dill sprig, garlic, and ¼ teaspoon salt to boil in large saucepan over medium-high heat. Reduce heat to low, cover, and simmer gently until bulgur is tender, 16 to 18 minutes. Off heat, let bulgur sit for 10 minutes. Fluff bulgur gently with fork, discard dill and garlic, and cover to keep warm.

2. Pat chicken dry with paper towels and sprinkle with ½ teaspoon salt and ¼ teaspoon pepper. Heat 1 tablespoon oil in 12-inch ovensafe skillet over medium-high heat until just smoking. Cook chicken skin side down until well browned, 5 to 7 minutes. Flip chicken, transfer skillet to oven, and roast until breasts register 160 degrees and drumsticks/thighs register 175 degrees, 15 to 20 minutes.

3. Meanwhile, whisk lemon zest and juice, remaining ¼ teaspoon salt, remaining ¼ teaspoon pepper, and remaining 2 tablespoons oil together in large bowl. Add bulgur, cucumber, red peppers, and minced dill and toss gently to combine. Season with salt and pepper to taste.

4. Transfer chicken to serving platter, reserving pan juices in skillet. In small bowl, whisk harissa together with 2 to 4 tablespoons pan juices, 1 tablespoon at a time, until mixture is loose and spreadable. Brush mixture onto chicken, tent with aluminum foil, and let rest for 5 to 10 minutes. Season yogurt with salt and pepper to taste. Serve chicken with bulgur salad and seasoned yogurt.

Pomegranate-Glazed Bone-In Chicken Breasts with Farro Salad

Serves 4   **Total Time** 1 hour

Why This Recipe Works Pomegranate molasses, a Mediterranean staple, acts as an intensely flavorful glaze for roasted chicken breasts—sweet, sour, and fruity. Our glaze required virtually no prep, just some salt and a bit of cinnamon, which contributed warm spice notes. Brushing on the glaze in two applications during roasting produced richly burnished skin. For a hearty side, a Mediterranean-inspired farro salad perfectly complemented the pomegranate glaze on the chicken. We prefer the flavor and texture of whole farro; pearled farro can be used, but the texture may be softer. Do not use quick-cooking or presteamed farro (read the ingredient list on the package to determine this) in this recipe. The cooking time for farro can vary greatly among different brands, so we recommend beginning to check for doneness after 10 minutes.

Honey-and-Garlic Roasted Chicken with Pearl Couscous Salad

Roasted Chicken with Harissa and Warm Bulgur Salad

Pomegranate-Glazed
Bone-In Chicken Breasts
with Farro Salad

Turkey Cutlets with Barley
and Swiss Chard

1½ cups whole farro
¾ teaspoon table salt, divided, plus salt for cooking farro
4 (12-ounce) bone-in split chicken breasts, trimmed and halved crosswise
¼ teaspoon pepper, divided
¼ cup extra-virgin olive oil, divided
6 tablespoons pomegranate molasses
1 teaspoon ground cinnamon
2 tablespoons plain Greek yogurt
1 shallot, minced
2 tablespoons lemon juice
1 English cucumber, halved lengthwise and cut into ¼-inch pieces
8 ounces cherry tomatoes, halved
¼ cup chopped fresh mint

1. Adjust oven rack to middle position and heat oven to 450 degrees. Set wire rack in aluminum foil–lined rimmed baking sheet. Bring 4 quarts water to boil in Dutch oven. Add farro and 1 tablespoon salt, return to boil, and cook until grains are tender with slight chew, 15 to 30 minutes. Drain farro, spread in second rimmed baking sheet, and let cool completely, about 15 minutes.

2. Pat chicken dry with paper towels and sprinkle with ½ teaspoon salt and ⅛ teaspoon pepper. Heat 1 tablespoon oil in 12-inch skillet over medium-high heat until just smoking. Cook chicken skin side down until well browned, 5 to 7 minutes. Flip chicken and brown lightly on second side, about 3 minutes; transfer skin side up to prepared rack.

3. Meanwhile, combine pomegranate molasses, cinnamon, and ⅛ teaspoon salt in bowl. Brush top of chicken with half of pomegranate glaze. Transfer to oven and roast for 10 minutes. Brush chicken with remaining pomegranate glaze and continue to roast until chicken registers 160 degrees, 5 to 10 minutes. Cover with aluminum foil and let rest.

4. Whisk yogurt, shallot, lemon juice, remaining 3 tablespoons oil, remaining ⅛ teaspoon salt, and remaining ⅛ teaspoon pepper together in large bowl; set aside.

5. Add cooled farro, cucumber, tomatoes, and mint to bowl with vinaigrette and toss gently to combine. Season with salt and pepper to taste. Serve with chicken.

Turkey Cutlets with Barley and Swiss Chard

Serves 4   Total Time 1 hour

Why This Recipe Works For a twist on the traditional chicken-and-rice formula, we paired quick-cooking turkey cutlets with rustic barley and hearty Swiss chard. Since the cutlets cook so quickly, we prepared the barley first, simmering it with aromatics and the chard stems before folding in the chard leaves. To give the turkey bright flavor, we employed a simple trick: We caramelized two lemon halves in the cooking oil, infusing it (and thus the cutlets) with flavor. A hint of lemon zest in the barley complemented the lemony oil. And just a half cup of Parmesan added a salty richness, tying the dish together. Do not substitute hulled, hull-less, quick-cooking, or presteamed barley for the pearl barley in this recipe. You will need a 12-inch nonstick skillet with a tight-fitting lid for this recipe.

- 3 tablespoons extra-virgin olive oil, divided
- 1 cup pearl barley
- ¼ cup onion, chopped fine
- 2 garlic cloves, minced
- 1¾ cups chicken broth
- 12 ounces Swiss chard, stems chopped, leaves cut into 1-inch pieces
- 1 teaspoon grated lemon zest, plus 1 lemon, halved and seeded
- ¾ teaspoon table salt, divided
- 1½ ounces Parmesan cheese, shredded (½ cup), divided
- 6 (4-ounce) turkey cutlets, trimmed
- ⅛ teaspoon pepper

1. Heat 2 tablespoons oil in 12-inch nonstick skillet over medium-high heat until shimmering. Add barley, onion, and garlic and cook until barley is toasted and onion is softened, about 3 minutes. Stir in broth and bring to simmer. Reduce heat to medium-low, cover, and cook until barley is almost tender, about 8 minutes.

2. Add chard stems and cook, covered, until softened, about 3 minutes. Stir in chard leaves, 1 handful at a time, lemon zest, and ½ teaspoon salt. Increase heat to medium-high and cook, uncovered, until barley is tender, about 2 minutes. Stir in ¼ cup Parmesan, transfer to serving platter, and tent with aluminum foil to keep warm. Wipe skillet clean with paper towels.

3. Pat cutlets dry with paper towels and sprinkle with remaining ¼ teaspoon salt and pepper. Heat remaining 1 tablespoon oil in now-empty skillet over medium-high heat until shimmering. Add lemon halves cut side down and cook until browned, about 2 minutes; set aside. Cook cutlets in again-empty skillet until well browned, about 2 minutes per side. Arrange cutlets on top of barley mixture and squeeze lemon halves over cutlets. Sprinkle with remaining ¼ cup Parmesan and serve.

Skillet Chicken Cacciatore with Polenta Topping

Serves 4 to 6   Total Time 35 minutes

Why This Recipe Works For the real-deal chicken cacciatore, see page 176. This shortcut skillet dinner is closer to a pie. It combines precooked chicken with a tomato-mushroom sauce that we top with slices of polenta and a crust of Parmesan. To give our quick sauce deep flavor, we added red wine and potent seasonings—dried porcini mushrooms, garlic, and herbs de Provence. Some flour ensured a thick filling. For an easy topping, we shingled on slices of precooked polenta, sprinkled on a hefty coat of grated Parmesan, and ran everything under the broiler until browned. We like using Perfect Poached Chicken (page 60) here but any cooked chicken would work. You will need a 12-inch ovensafe skillet for this recipe; if your skillet is not ovensafe, transfer the filling to a shallow 2-quart broiler-safe casserole dish before shingling the polenta over the top and broiling.

- 2 tablespoons extra-virgin olive oil
- 8 ounces cremini mushrooms, trimmed and quartered
- 1 onion, chopped fine
- ¼ ounce dried porcini mushrooms, rinsed and minced
- 2 tablespoons all-purpose flour
- 4 garlic cloves, minced
- ¾ teaspoon herbes de Provence
- 1 cup chicken broth
- ¼ cup dry red wine
- 1 (14.5-ounce) can whole peeled tomatoes, drained with juice reserved, chopped
- 3 cups shredded cooked chicken
- 1 (18-ounce) tube precooked polenta, sliced ¼ inch thick
- 2 ounces Parmesan cheese, grated (1 cup)

1. Adjust oven rack 6 inches from broiler element and heat broiler. Heat oil in 12-inch ovensafe skillet over medium-high heat; add cremini mushrooms, onion, and porcini mushrooms and cook, stirring occasionally, until vegetables are softened and lightly browned, 5 to 7 minutes. Stir in flour, garlic, and herbes de Provence and cook until fragrant, about 30 seconds.

2. Gradually whisk in broth and wine, scraping up any browned bits and smoothing out any lumps, and simmer until liquid has reduced to glaze, about 1 minute. Stir in tomatoes and reserved juice and simmer until sauce is thickened, about 5 minutes. Off heat, stir in shredded chicken and season with salt and pepper to taste.

3. Shingle polenta over filling and sprinkle with Parmesan. Transfer skillet to oven and broil until polenta is hot and Parmesan is just beginning to brown, about 5 minutes. Let cool slightly and serve.

Herbes de Provence

Makes about ½ cup   **Total Time** 5 minutes

This delicate, aromatic blend of dried herbs from southern France is easy to make and can freshen up chicken and other kinds of dishes.

2 tablespoons dried thyme
2 tablespoons dried marjoram
2 tablespoons dried rosemary
2 teaspoons fennel seeds, toasted

Combine all ingredients in bowl. (Herbes de Provence can be stored at room temperature in airtight container for up to 1 year.)

Chicken and Orzo with Tomatoes and Parmesan

Serves 4   **Total Time** 1 hour

Why This Recipe Works Our skillet chicken and orzo with tomatoes makes a great one-dish meal after a busy day. Lightly browning the chicken and then finishing it nestled atop the orzo at a gentle simmer resulted in meat that was both flavorful and tender. We liked the subtle nuttiness of orzo and discovered that dry-toasting it before cooking intensified the flavor. A generous amount of aromatics and herbs provided deep flavor without the need for long simmering, and just ¼ cup of Parmesan made the orzo rich and creamy.

1½ cups orzo
½ cup all-purpose flour
4 (6- to 8-ounce) boneless, skinless chicken breasts, trimmed
½ teaspoon table salt
¼ teaspoon pepper
2 tablespoons extra-virgin olive oil, divided
3 garlic cloves, minced
2 teaspoons minced fresh oregano or ½ teaspoon dried
Pinch red pepper flakes
2 cups chicken broth
1 (14.5-ounce) can diced tomatoes
¼ cup grated Parmesan cheese
3 tablespoons chopped fresh basil

1. Toast orzo in 12-inch nonstick skillet over medium-high heat until golden brown, 3 to 5 minutes; transfer to bowl.

2. Spread flour in shallow dish. Pound chicken breasts to uniform thickness. Pat chicken dry with paper towels and sprinkle with salt and pepper. Working with 1 breast at a time, lightly dredge chicken in flour, shaking off excess.

3. Heat 1 tablespoon oil in 12-inch nonstick skillet over medium-high heat until shimmering. Cook chicken until lightly browned on both sides, 8 to 10 minutes; transfer to plate.

4. Cook remaining 1 tablespoon oil, garlic, oregano, and pepper flakes in now-empty skillet over medium heat until fragrant, about 30 seconds. Stir in broth, tomatoes, and toasted orzo.

5. Nestle chicken into orzo, add any accumulated juices, and bring to simmer. Reduce heat to medium-low, cover, and cook until chicken registers 160 degrees, about 10 minutes.

6. Transfer chicken to clean plate, brushing any orzo that sticks to chicken back into skillet, and tent chicken with aluminum foil to keep warm. Cover and continue to cook orzo over medium-low heat, stirring occasionally, until liquid has been absorbed and orzo is tender, about 5 minutes.

7. Off heat, stir in Parmesan and basil and season with salt and pepper to taste. Serve with chicken.

VARIATION
Chicken and Orzo with Spinach and Feta
Omit tomatoes, Parmesan, and basil. Increase chicken broth to 2½ cups. Once orzo is fully cooked in step 6, stir in 10 cups baby spinach, 1 handful at a time, until wilted, about 2 minutes. Off heat, stir in 1 cup crumbled feta cheese and 1 tablespoon lemon juice.

Poached Chicken with Quinoa and Warm Tomato-Ginger Vinaigrette

Serves 4   Total Time 1¼ hours

Why This Recipe Works Poached chicken can be much more than bland health food; ours starts with a flavorful poaching liquid that adds juiciness. Poaching the chicken in a steamer basket ensured gentle even cooking. While the chicken poached, there was time to cook a side of quinoa pilaf. We also made a warm tomato vinaigrette by softening cherry tomatoes in a skillet with ginger, cumin, and fennel. The vinaigrette pulled double duty as a stir-in for the quinoa and a sauce for the chicken. We like the convenience of prewashed quinoa; rinsing removes the quinoa's bitter protective coating (called saponin). If you buy unwashed quinoa, rinse it and then spread it out on a clean dish towel to dry for 15 minutes. You will need a collapsible steamer basket for this recipe.

- 4 (6- to 8-ounce) boneless, skinless chicken breasts
- ½ cup soy sauce for poaching chicken
- 8 garlic cloves (6 smashed, 2 minced)
- ¾ teaspoon table salt, divided, plus salt for poaching chicken
- 3 tablespoons extra-virgin olive oil, divided, plus extra for drizzling
- 1½ cups prewashed white quinoa
- 1 shallot, minced
- 2 teaspoons grated fresh ginger
- ⅛ teaspoon ground cumin
- ⅛ teaspoon ground fennel
- 12 ounces cherry tomatoes, halved
- ¼ cup chopped fresh parsley
- 2 teaspoons red wine vinegar

1. Pound chicken breasts to uniform thickness. Whisk 4 quarts water, soy sauce, smashed garlic cloves, and ¼ cup salt in Dutch oven until salt is dissolved. Arrange breasts skinned side up in steamer basket, making sure not to overlap them. Submerge steamer basket in pot.

2. Heat pot over medium heat, stirring liquid occasionally to even out hot spots, until water registers 175 degrees, 15 to 20 minutes. Turn off heat, cover pot, and let sit until chicken registers 160 degrees, 17 to 22 minutes. Transfer chicken to cutting board, tent with aluminum foil, and let rest.

3. Meanwhile, heat 1 tablespoon oil in large saucepan over medium heat until shimmering. Add quinoa, minced garlic, half of shallot, and ½ teaspoon salt and cook until fragrant, about 3 minutes. Stir in 1¾ cups water and bring to simmer.

Chicken and Orzo with Spinach and Feta

Poached Chicken with Quinoa and Warm Tomato-Ginger Vinaigrette

Reduce heat to low, cover, and simmer until quinoa is tender and water is absorbed, 18 to 22 minutes, stirring once halfway through cooking. Remove pot from heat and let sit, covered, for 10 minutes.

4. Heat 1 tablespoon oil in 10-inch nonstick skillet over medium heat until shimmering. Add ginger, cumin, fennel, and remaining shallot and cook until fragrant, about 30 seconds. Stir in tomatoes and remaining ¼ teaspoon salt and cook, stirring frequently, until tomatoes have softened, 3 to 5 minutes. Off heat, stir in parsley, vinegar, and remaining 1 tablespoon oil and season with salt and pepper to taste.

5. Add half of tomato-ginger vinaigrette to quinoa and stir to combine. Season with salt and pepper and drizzle with extra oil to taste. Slice each chicken breast on bias ¼ inch thick and transfer to platter or individual plates. Serve with remaining warm vinaigrette and quinoa.

Penne with Chicken and Broccoli

Serves 4   **Total Time** 45 minutes

Why This Recipe Works For a chicken and pasta dinner that avoided the need for multiple pot and pans, we browned boneless chicken breasts in a skillet and set them aside while we built the sauce. Chicken broth and water, with minced garlic, red pepper flakes, and white wine, formed the base of the sauce and provided just enough liquid to cook the pasta. Leaving the pan uncovered intensified the flavors as the sauce reduced. For bright-green, tender broccoli, we added it to the pan when the pasta was almost ready. Parmesan added creaminess and rich, savory flavor. Other pasta shapes can be substituted for the penne; however, their cup measurements may vary. To make the chicken easier to slice, freeze it for 15 minutes.

1 pound boneless, skinless chicken breasts, trimmed and sliced thin
¾ teaspoon table salt, divided
⅛ teaspoon pepper
¼ cup extra-virgin olive oil, divided
1 onion, chopped fine
6 garlic cloves, minced
¼ teaspoon red pepper flakes
¼ teaspoon dried oregano
½ cup dry white wine
2½ cups water
2 cups chicken broth
8 ounces (2½ cups) penne
8 ounces broccoli florets, cut into 1-inch pieces
2 ounces Parmesan cheese, grated (1 cup), plus extra for serving

1. Pat chicken dry with paper towels and sprinkle with ¼ teaspoon salt and pepper. Heat 1 tablespoon oil in 12-inch nonstick skillet over medium-high heat until just smoking. Add chicken in single layer and cook without stirring for 1 minute. Stir chicken and continue to cook until nearly cooked through, about 2 minutes; transfer to bowl and cover to keep warm.

2. Add onion, 1 tablespoon oil, and remaining ½ teaspoon salt to now-empty skillet and cook over medium heat until onion is softened, about 5 minutes. Stir in garlic, pepper flakes, and oregano and cook until fragrant, about 30 seconds. Stir in wine, scraping up any browned bits, and simmer until nearly evaporated, 1 to 2 minutes. Stir in water, broth, and pasta. Increase heat to medium-high and cook at vigorous simmer, stirring often, until pasta is nearly tender, about 12 minutes.

3. Stir in broccoli and cook until pasta and broccoli are tender and sauce has thickened, 3 to 5 minutes. Stir in chicken and any accumulated juices and let warm through, about 1 minute. Off heat, stir in remaining 2 tablespoons oil and Parmesan. Season with salt and pepper to taste. Serve with extra Parmesan.

Penne with Chicken Sausage and Spinach

Serves 4   **Total Time** 45 minutes

Why This Recipe Works This supereasy one-pan pasta replaces pork sausage with sweet or hot Italian chicken sausage. To avoid overwhelming the milder-tasting chicken sausage, instead of adding canned tomatoes we incorporated a good amount of baby spinach. Chopped sun-dried tomatoes provided big, bold flavor in quick order. Cooking the pasta and sausage in a measured amount of chicken broth and water ensured that we'd end up with a tasty sauce. Saving the spinach until the end kept this dish bright in both color and flavor. The spinach may seem like a lot at first, but it wilts down substantially. Other pasta shapes can be substituted for the penne; however, their cup measurements may vary.

1 tablespoon extra-virgin olive oil
1 pound sweet or hot Italian chicken sausage, casings removed
3 garlic cloves, minced
2½ cups chicken broth
2 cups water
½ cup oil-packed sun-dried tomatoes, rinsed and chopped fine

½ teaspoon table salt
8 ounces (2½ cups) penne
6 ounces (6 cups) baby spinach
Grated Parmesan cheese

1. Heat oil in 12-inch nonstick skillet over medium-high heat until just smoking. Add sausage and cook, breaking up meat with wooden spoon, until no longer pink, about 4 minutes. Stir in garlic and cook until fragrant, about 30 seconds.

2. Stir in broth, water, tomatoes, salt, and pasta. Increase heat to medium-high and cook at vigorous simmer, stirring often, until pasta is tender and sauce has thickened, 15 to 18 minutes. Stir in spinach, 1 handful at a time, and cook until wilted. Season with salt and pepper to taste, and serve with Parmesan.

Chicken Chow Mein
Serves 4 **Total Time** 50 minutes

Why This Recipe Works This simple take on classic chow mein is packed with stir-fried chicken, vegetables, and noodles. After cooking fresh Chinese noodles, we tossed them in a little oil to prevent them from clumping. We then made a simple sauce and quickly cooked our chicken before adding shiitake mushrooms for earthy flavor and carrots for a dose of sweetness. Scallion greens added crunch and color. Fresh Chinese noodles can be found in the produce section of the supermarket. You can use any thin fresh Chinese egg noodle in this recipe; boil until just tender but still chewy. Or you can substitute 6 ounces angel hair pasta. For more crunch, sprinkle with chopped toasted cashews.

¼ cup oyster sauce
2 tablespoons soy sauce
2 teaspoons sugar
½ teaspoon pepper
12 ounces fresh Chinese noodles
2 tablespoons toasted sesame oil
2 tablespoons vegetable oil, divided
1 pound boneless, skinless chicken breasts, trimmed, halved lengthwise, and sliced thin crosswise, divided
12 ounces shiitake mushrooms, stemmed and sliced thin
2 carrots, peeled and sliced thin on bias
6 scallions, white and green parts separated and sliced thin

Chicken
Chow Mein

1. Whisk ½ cup water, oyster sauce, soy sauce, sugar, and pepper together in bowl; set aside. Bring 4 quarts water to boil in large pot. Add noodles and cook, stirring often, until tender. Drain noodles and rinse thoroughly with cold water, shaking to remove excess water. Toss noodles with sesame oil in bowl and set aside until ready to serve.

2. Heat 1 tablespoon vegetable oil in 12-inch nonstick skillet over medium-high heat until just smoking. Add half of chicken in single layer and cook without stirring for 1 minute. Stir and continue to cook until lightly browned on both sides, about 1 minute; transfer to plate. Repeat with remaining 1 tablespoon vegetable oil and remaining chicken. Return all chicken to skillet. Add mushrooms and carrots to chicken in skillet and cook, stirring frequently, until vegetables are tender and mushrooms begin to brown, about 5 minutes. Stir in scallion whites and cook until fragrant, about 30 seconds. Off heat, stir in sauce.

3. Divide noodles among individual serving bowls, then top with chicken mixture and sprinkle with scallion greens. Serve.

SALADS AND BOWLS

Photos (clockwise from top left): Chicken and Arugula Salad with Figs and Warm Spices; Peanut Soba Noodle Chicken Bowl; Creamy Chicken Salad with Fresh Herbs; Chicken Caesar Salad

Chicken Salad
with Whole-Grain
Mustard Vinaigrette

Grilled Chicken Salad

Chicken Salad with Whole-Grain Mustard Vinaigrette

Serves 4   Total Time 15 minutes

Why This Recipe Works Fresh lemon juice brightens this light and summery version of chicken salad, while sugar snap peas and red grapes add a juicy crunch. Whole-grain mustard helps make a thick, hearty vinaigrette for this salad. The whole seeds also add subtle, tangy mustard flavor and a pleasant pop of texture. You can substitute more delicate Bibb lettuce for the red leaf lettuce if you prefer. We like using Perfect Poached Chicken (page 60) here but any cooked chicken would work.

⅓ cup whole-grain mustard
3 tablespoons lemon juice
¼ teaspoon pepper
⅛ teaspoon table salt
3 tablespoons extra-virgin olive oil
4 cups shredded cooked chicken
1 small head red leaf lettuce (8 ounces), torn into bite-size pieces
8 ounces sugar snap peas, strings removed, halved crosswise on bias
6¾ ounces seedless red grapes, halved (1 cup)
3 tablespoons minced fresh chives

1. Whisk together mustard, lemon juice, pepper, and salt in large bowl. Whisking constantly, slowly drizzle in oil until incorporated.

2. Measure ¼ cup of vinaigrette and toss with chicken until well coated; set aside.

3. Add lettuce, snap peas, grapes, and chives to remaining vinaigrette in bowl and toss until combined. Season with salt and pepper to taste. Divide salad among individual serving dishes and top with chicken. Serve.

Creamy Chicken Salad with Fresh Herbs

Serves 6   Total Time 10 minutes (plus 2 hours chilling time)

Why This Recipe Works The best chicken salads are satisfying yet light, featuring tender chicken, a creamy dressing, and crunchy bites of celery. One of our favorites features cubed chicken bathed in an herby dressing, the classic flavor of mayonnaise brightened with lemon juice. A trio of fresh herbs—chives, tarragon, and dill—shouted springtime.

The salad was so good that we made a more adventurous version featuring dried apricots, curry powder, scallions, and almonds, as well as one inspired by Waldorf salad. This salad can be served over greens or in a sandwich. We like using Perfect Poached Chicken (page 60) here but any cooked chicken would work.

- 4 cups cooked chicken, cut into ½-inch pieces
- ⅔ cup mayonnaise
- ¼ cup finely chopped celery
- 3 tablespoons chopped fresh chives
- 4 teaspoons chopped fresh tarragon
- 1 tablespoon chopped fresh dill
- 1 tablespoon lemon juice
- ½ teaspoon table salt
- ¼ teaspoon pepper

Combine chicken, mayonnaise, celery, chives, tarragon, dill, lemon juice, salt, and pepper in bowl. Cover with plastic and refrigerate for at least 2 hours to allow flavors to meld. Serve. (Salad can be refrigerated for up to 2 days.)

VARIATIONS

Curried Chicken Salad with Dried Apricots
Omit chives, tarragon, and dill. Add ½ cup finely chopped dried apricots, 6 tablespoons toasted slivered almonds, 4 thinly sliced scallions, and 2 teaspoons curry powder to bowl with other ingredients.

Chicken Salad with Grapes and Walnuts
Omit tarragon and dill. Add 1 cup halved seedless red grapes, 6 tablespoons walnuts, toasted and chopped, and 3 tablespoons chopped fresh parsley to bowl with other ingredients. Substitute Dijon mustard for lemon juice.

Grilled Chicken Salad
Serves 4   **Total Time** 1 hour

Why This Recipe Works Just a few perfectly flavorful ingredients and a finishing touch of coarse sea salt elevate this vibrant summer weeknight arugula and grilled chicken salad. We added cherry tomatoes, kalamata olives, and bite-size pieces of fresh mozzarella—all dressed with a sharp red wine vinaigrette—for garden freshness, brininess, and richness, respectively. Then we sprinkled on the coarse sea salt, seasoning the salad as a whole—not just its parts. The crystals offered textural contrast and enhanced the flavors of the soft milky mozzarella, sweet juicy tomatoes, and moist charred chicken. To keep the salt level in check, use a gentle hand when seasoning the chicken before cooking.

- 4 (6- to 8-ounce) boneless, skinless chicken breasts, trimmed
- ¼ teaspoon plus ⅛ teaspoon table salt, divided
- ⅛ teaspoon plus pinch pepper, divided
- 6 tablespoons extra-virgin olive oil
- 2 tablespoons red wine vinegar
- 1 garlic clove, minced
- 8 ounces (8 cups) baby arugula
- 8 ounces fresh whole-milk mozzarella cheese, torn into bite-size pieces (2 cups)
- 8 ounces cherry tomatoes, halved
- ½ cup pitted kalamata olives, chopped

1A. For a charcoal grill Open bottom vent completely. Light large chimney starter filled with charcoal briquettes (6 quarts). When top coals are partially covered with ash, pour evenly over grill. Set cooking grate in place, cover, and open lid vent completely. Heat grill until hot, about 5 minutes.

1B. For a gas grill Turn all burners to high, cover, and heat grill until hot, about 15 minutes. Leave all burners on high.

2. Pat chicken breasts dry with paper towels and sprinkle with ¼ teaspoon salt and ⅛ teaspoon pepper. Clean and oil cooking grate. Place breasts on grill and cook until chicken registers 160 degrees, about 6 minutes per side. Transfer breasts to cutting board, tent with aluminum foil, and let rest for 5 minutes.

3. Slice breasts ½ inch thick. Whisk oil, vinegar, garlic, remaining ⅛ teaspoon salt, and remaining pinch pepper together in large bowl. Add arugula, mozzarella, tomatoes, and olives and toss to combine. Divide salad among individual plates, top with chicken, and sprinkle with coarse sea salt to taste. Serve.

California Chicken Salad with Creamy Avocado Dressing
Serves 4   **Total Time** 15 minutes

Why This Recipe Works You can put avocado on just about any salad and call it "California." We wanted our salad to earn the name with a healthy and hearty chicken salad that paid respect to the Golden State in every bite. Rather than just throw on diced avocado, we prepared a creamy dressing by pureeing ripe avocado with lemon, garlic, and olive oil. To make our salad burst with fresh flavors, we went heavy on the green veggies, while thinly sliced radishes offered a pop of color. To balance all the vegetal flavors, we added a handful of sweet grapes (think Napa Valley). Just when we thought we hit all the points, we realized we were missing something quintessentially Californian: a light, fluffy mound of alfalfa sprouts. We like

California
Chicken Salad
with Creamy
Avocado Dressing

using Seared Chicken Breasts (page 60) here but any cooked chicken would work. For added crunch, sprinkle with chopped Quick Toasted Nuts (page 69) or Orange-Fennel Nuts (page 69).

8 ounces (8 cups) baby spinach
2 scallions, sliced thin
1 recipe Creamy Avocado Dressing (page 69), divided
4 cups cooked chicken, cut into ½-inch pieces
8 ounces seedless grapes, halved (1⅓ cups)
4 ounces sugar snap peas, strings removed, halved
8 radishes, trimmed, halved, and sliced thin
2 ounces (1 cup) alfalfa sprouts

Toss spinach and scallions with half of dressing to coat, then season with salt and pepper to taste. Divide among individual serving bowls, then top with chicken, grapes, snap peas, and radishes. Drizzle with remaining dressing and top with alfalfa sprouts. Serve.

Chicken Caesar Salad
Serves 6   Total Time 35 minutes

Why This Recipes Works A classic Caesar salad is hard to beat, with its combination of crisp romaine, garlicky dressing, and crunchy croutons. Adding chicken makes a great thing better—another vehicle (protein, in this case) for the dressing's intense savoriness. To give our dressing a robust but not aggressive garlic flavor, we grated the garlic into a pulp and steeped it in lemon juice. Cutting the extra-virgin olive oil with vegetable oil made for a less harsh dressing, and using egg yolks instead of a whole egg added richness. We recommend using homemade croutons, but store-bought are fine as well. The eggs in this recipe are not cooked. If you prefer, ¼ cup Egg Beaters may be substituted for the egg yolks. Adjust the amount of anchovies to suit your taste. A rasp-style grater makes quick work of turning the garlic into a paste. We like using Perfect Poached Chicken (page 60) here but any cooked chicken would work.

Dressing
2 tablespoons lemon juice, plus extra for seasoning
1 small garlic clove, minced to paste (¾ teaspoon)
5 tablespoons vegetable oil
5 teaspoons extra-virgin olive oil
6 anchovy fillets, rinsed, patted dry, and minced to paste (1 tablespoon)
2 large egg yolks
½ teaspoon Worcestershire sauce
1 ounce Parmesan cheese, grated fine (½ cup)

Salad
2 heads romaine lettuce (12 ounces each) (large outer leaves discarded), washed, dried, and cut into 1-inch pieces (16 cups)
1 recipe Croutons (page 70)
2 ounces Parmesan cheese, grated (1 cup), divided
4 cups cooked chicken, sliced ¼ inch thick

1. For the dressing Whisk lemon juice and garlic together in medium bowl and let sit for 10 minutes.

2. Transfer vegetable oil and olive oil to small measuring cup so that they are easy to pour. Whisk anchovies, egg yolks, and Worcestershire into lemon mixture. Whisking constantly, slowly drizzle oil mixture into bowl until dressing is emulsified. If pools of oil gather on surface as you whisk, stop addition of oil and whisk mixture well to combine, then resume whisking in oil in slow stream. Dressing should be glossy and lightly thickened, with no surface pools of oil. Whisk in Parmesan and season with pepper and extra lemon juice to taste.

3. For the salad Toss lettuce with croutons, ¾ cup Parmesan, and two-thirds of dressing in large bowl until well combined. Divide dressed lettuce among individual plates. Toss chicken with remaining dressing. Divide chicken equally among plates and season with pepper. Serve immediately, passing remaining ¼ cup Parmesan separately.

VARIATIONS

Southwestern Chicken Caesar Salad

For the dressing: Omit anchovies. Substitute lime juice for lemon juice. Add 2 tablespoons minced canned chipotle chile in adobo sauce to lime mixture with egg yolks.

Asiago-Bacon Chicken Caesar Salad

For the dressing: Line plate with double layer of coffee filters. Spread 2 slices finely chopped bacon in even layer on filters and microwave until crisp, about 4 minutes; let cool slightly. Omit anchovies. Substitute Asiago cheese for Parmesan and add bacon to dressing with Asiago.

Kale Caesar Salad with Chicken

Serves 4   Total Time 25 minutes

Why This Recipe Works Hearty kale is closing in on romaine as the most popular green for a Caesar salad, but its notoriously tough leaves demand special treatment to make them tender enough to enjoy. A 10-minute soak in hot tap water relaxed the leaves just enough to work in a salad. While we love our classic Caesar dressing (page 56), kale's assertive flavor demands something more potent. Instead of eggs, we based our dressing on mayonnaise for a thicker, creamier dressing and increased the Worcestershire to make it super-savory. Adding chicken made the salad into a satisfying meal. We prefer curly kale in this recipe, but you can substitute Lacinato kale. We like using Seared Chicken Breasts (page 60) here but any cooked chicken would work.

Salad
12 ounces curly kale, stemmed and cut into
     1-inch pieces
 1 recipe Croutons (page 70)
 4 cups cooked chicken, sliced ¼ inch thick

Dressing
⅓ cup mayonnaise
 1 ounce Parmesan cheese, grated (½ cup), divided
 1 tablespoon lemon juice
 3 anchovy fillets, rinsed

Kale Caesar Salad
with Chicken

 2 teaspoons white wine vinegar
 2 teaspoons Worcestershire sauce
 2 teaspoons Dijon mustard
 1 garlic clove, minced
¼ teaspoon table salt
¼ teaspoon pepper
 2 tablespoons extra-virgin olive oil

   1. For the salad Place kale in bowl, cover with hot tap water, and let sit for 10 minutes. Swish kale around to remove grit, then drain and spin dry in salad spinner. Pat leaves dry with paper towels if still wet.

   2. For the dressing Process mayonnaise, ¼ cup Parmesan, lemon juice, anchovies, vinegar, Worcestershire, mustard, garlic, salt, and pepper in blender until smooth, about 30 seconds. With blender running, slowly add oil until incorporated.

   3. Add dressing, croutons, and remaining ¼ cup Parmesan to bowl with kale and toss until well coated. Divide salad among individual serving dishes. Arrange chicken over salads. Serve.

Chicken BLT Salad

Green Goodness
Chicken Salad

Chicken BLT Salad

Serves 4   **Total Time** 30 minutes

Why This Recipe Works We love the idea of enjoying a favorite sandwich in salad form. All of the expected ingredients are here—bacon, lettuce, and tomato—along with the addition of chunks of chicken. We cooked the chicken chunks right in the rendered bacon fat, giving the salad even more big bacon flavor. For croutons that had just the right hint of BLT sandwich flavor, we spread thick slices of fresh Italian bread with mayonnaise before toasting and cutting them into cubes. You can substitute grape tomatoes for the cherry tomatoes here.

¾ cup mayonnaise, divided
4 (1-inch-thick) slices Italian bread
1 pound bacon, chopped
1 pound boneless, skinless chicken breasts, trimmed and cut into 1-inch pieces
¼ teaspoon table salt
¼ teaspoon pepper
3 tablespoons red wine vinegar
1½ pounds cherry tomatoes, halved
2 romaine lettuce hearts (12 ounces), torn into bite-size pieces

1. Adjust oven rack to middle position and heat oven to 475 degrees. Spread ¼ cup mayonnaise over both sides of bread, lay on baking sheet, and bake until golden brown, 8 to 10 minutes, flipping bread halfway through cooking. Let cool for 5 minutes, then cut into 1-inch croutons.

2. Meanwhile, cook bacon in 12-inch nonstick skillet over medium-high heat until crisp, 5 to 7 minutes. Transfer bacon to paper towel–lined plate and pour off all but 1 tablespoon fat left in skillet.

3. Pat chicken dry with paper towels and sprinkle with salt and pepper. Heat fat left in skillet over medium-high heat until just smoking. Cook chicken, stirring often, until browned on all sides, 4 to 6 minutes; transfer to plate.

4. Whisk remaining ½ cup mayonnaise and vinegar together in serving bowl. Add tomatoes, lettuce, croutons, bacon, and chicken and toss to combine. Season with salt and pepper to taste, and serve.

Green Goodness Chicken Salad

Serves 4   **Total Time** 30 minutes

Why This Recipe Works A green goddess salad requires just one thing: green goddess dressing, which gets its herbaceous flavor and appealing hue from a wallop of herbs. We took the concept further by creating a green "goodness" chicken salad filled with an abundance of green foods, including baby spinach, edamame, and pistachios. Raw broccoli was dull and harsh but sautéing it gave it some nice char, boosting its flavor and shade of vibrant green. And what would a green goodness salad be without buttery avocado? Since the classic dressing is a bit heavy, we lightened ours by replacing mayonnaise with buttermilk and yogurt. Three herbs (chives, parsley, and dried tarragon) gave the dressing plenty of color, and an anchovy added savory depth. We like using Perfect Poached Chicken (page 60) here but any cooked chicken would work.

1½ tablespoons extra-virgin olive oil, divided
 8 ounces broccoli florets, cut into 1-inch pieces
 ⅛ teaspoon table salt
1½ tablespoons water
 1 garlic clove, minced
 ¼ teaspoon minced fresh thyme or pinch dried
 8 ounces (8 cups) baby spinach
 1 recipe Green Goddess Dressing (page 68), divided
 4 cups shredded cooked chicken
 1 ripe avocado, halved, pitted, and sliced thin
 ½ cup frozen shelled edamame beans, thawed and patted dry
 ¼ cup shelled pistachios, toasted and chopped

1. Heat 1 tablespoon oil in 12-inch skillet over medium high heat until just smoking. Add broccoli and salt and cook, without stirring, until beginning to brown, about 2 minutes. Add water, cover, and cook until broccoli is bright green but still crisp, about 2 minutes. Uncover and continue to cook until water has evaporated and broccoli is crisp-tender, about 2 minutes.

2. Clear center of pan, add remaining 1½ teaspoons oil, garlic, and thyme and cook, mashing garlic into skillet, until fragrant, about 30 seconds. Stir garlic mixture into broccoli. Transfer broccoli to bowl and season with salt and pepper to taste.

3. Toss spinach with half of dressing to coat, then season with salt and pepper to taste. Divide among individual serving bowls, then top with chicken, broccoli, avocado, and edamame. Drizzle with remaining dressing and sprinkle with pistachios. Serve.

Spinach Salad with Chicken, Almonds, and Apricots

Serves 4   **Total Time** 35 minutes

Why This Recipe Works With its combination of fruit, nuts, greens, and chicken, this summery salad makes for a refreshing dinner or lunch. Because fresh apricots can be hard to come by, we turned to the easily found dried variety. Searing the chicken on one side and poaching it on the other in a mixture of water and apricot preserves yielded flavorful and tender meat infused with apricot flavor. While we prefer the earthy flavor of spinach here, more assertively flavored baby arugula would also work.

 2 (6- to 8-ounce) boneless, skinless chicken breasts, trimmed
 ¼ teaspoon table salt
 ¼ teaspoon pepper
 6 tablespoons extra-virgin olive oil, divided
 ½ cup water
 2 tablespoons apricot preserves, divided
 2 tablespoons red wine vinegar
 1 shallot, minced
 2 tablespoons minced fresh tarragon
 6 ounces (6 cups) baby spinach
 ½ cup dried apricots, sliced
 ⅓ cup slivered almonds, toasted

1. Pound chicken breasts to uniform thickness. Pat chicken dry with paper towels and sprinkle with salt and pepper. Heat 1 tablespoon oil in 12-inch nonstick skillet over medium-high heat until just smoking. Cook chicken until browned, about 3 minutes. Flip chicken, then stir in water and 1 tablespoon preserves. Simmer, covered, over medium heat until chicken registers 160 degrees, 5 to 7 minutes. Transfer to cutting board.

2. Combine vinegar, shallot, tarragon, and remaining 1 tablespoon preserves in large bowl. Slowly whisk in remaining 5 tablespoons oil. Season with salt and pepper to taste.

3. Add spinach, apricots, and almonds to bowl with dressing and toss to combine. Transfer salad to individual plates. Slice chicken crosswise and arrange on top of salad. Serve.

CHICKEN FOR SALADS

What kind of cooked chicken works best in a salad? The short answer is whatever you have on hand; most recipes are accommodating to leftovers or a rotisserie bird. That said, there are a few points to consider. Starting from a roast chicken means you get both white and dark meat; the added richness is especially nice in dinner salads built around fresh vegetables and a bright vinaigrette. Poached white-meat chicken, a go-to for creamy chicken salads, offers maximum juiciness and tenderness and no crispy edges to interfere with a smooth texture. Of course, sometimes the golden crust from seared chicken is ideal to stand up to a bold dressing or play off of softer ingredients such as avocado. Choose what suits your tastes.

When cooking chicken for salads, simple methods make sense but there's no reason to settle for bland or rubbery meat. A few tricks guarantee chicken that's juicy and well seasoned. If you use a rotisserie chicken, an average-size chicken will yield 3 to 4 cups of meat.

Perfect Poached Chicken

Makes 4 cups   **Total Time** 1¼ hours

Elevating the chicken in a steamer basket above the pot's hot base ensures even cooking. Bringing the water to 175 degrees and then removing the pot from the burner lets the chicken cook gently in the residual heat, turning supremely juicy and tender. Brining the chicken in the poaching liquid for 30 minutes helps it to absorb extra flavor but you can skip this step. It's important that the chicken breasts are similar in size so that they cook at the same rate. This recipe can easily be halved; do not alter the amount of salt or water.

- ½ cup soy sauce for brining
- ¼ cup table salt for brining
- 4 (6- to 8-ounce) boneless, skinless chicken breasts, trimmed and pounded to even thickness

1. Whisk 4 quarts water, soy sauce, and salt in Dutch oven until salt is dissolved. Arrange chicken skinned side up in steamer basket, submerge in brine, and let sit at room temperature for 30 minutes.

2. Heat pot over medium heat, stirring liquid occasionally to even out hot spots, until water registers 175 degrees, 15 to 20 minutes. Turn off heat, cover pot, remove from burner, and let sit until chicken registers 160 degrees, 17 to 22 minutes.

3. Transfer chicken to cutting board, tent with aluminum foil, and let rest for 5 minutes. Slice, cube, or shred as desired. (Chicken can be refrigerated for up to 2 days.)

Seared Chicken Breasts

Makes 4 cups   **Total Time** 30 minutes

This sear-then-steam method helps the chicken stay moist and tender on the inside and develop flavorful browning on the outside. You will need a 12-inch skillet with a tight-fitting lid for this recipe. To halve the recipe, halve the ingredients and use a 10-inch skillet.

- 4 (6- to 8-ounce) boneless, skinless chicken breasts, trimmed and pounded to even thickness
- ½ teaspoon table salt
- ¼ teaspoon pepper
- 2 teaspoons extra-virgin olive oil or vegetable oil
- ½ cup water

Pat chicken dry with paper towels and sprinkle with salt and pepper. Heat oil in 12-inch skillet over medium-high heat until just smoking. Cook chicken skinned side down until brown, about 6 minutes. Flip chicken, add water, and cover. Reduce heat to medium-low and continue to cook until chicken registers 160 degrees, 5 to 7 minutes. Transfer chicken to cutting board, tent with aluminum foil, and let rest for 5 minutes. Slice, cube, or shred as desired. (Chicken can be refrigerated for up to 2 days.)

OTHER GOOD CHICKEN RECIPES FOR SALADS
- Crispy Pan-Fried Chicken Cutlets (page 268)
- Gluten-Free Crispy Chicken Cutlets (page 274)
- Sous Vide Foolproof Poached Chicken (page 411)
- Grilled Boneless, Skinless Chicken Breasts (page 347)
- Weeknight Roast Chicken (page 224)

Classic Cobb Salad

Serves 6 to 8   **Total Time** 1 hour

Why This Recipe Works Born in the 1920s at the Hollywood hangout the Brown Derby, the Cobb salad is an artfully assembled salad of crunchy greens (both mild and spicy), tender chicken, buttery avocado, juicy tomato, hard-cooked eggs, smoky bacon, and tangy blue cheese. The salad's classic vinaigrette dressing is both the tie that binds the dish together and its biggest problem, with the salad components either drowned in puddles of liquid or sitting high and dry. We found it best to dress each ingredient separately before arranging them. Romaine lettuce gave our salad crunch and watercress added flavor, and we switched from often-tasteless supermarket beefsteak tomatoes to grape tomatoes, which taste sweet year-round. Cooking the chicken in the rendered bacon fat gave the salad even more flavor. You'll need a large platter or a wide, shallow bowl to accommodate this salad. Though watercress is traditional, feel free to substitute an equal amount of arugula, chicory, curly endive, or a mixture of assertive greens. We prefer grape tomatoes here, but cherry tomatoes can also be used.

Vinaigrette

- ½ cup extra-virgin olive oil
- 2 tablespoons red wine vinegar
- 2 teaspoons lemon juice
- 1 teaspoon Worcestershire sauce
- 1 teaspoon Dijon mustard
- 1 garlic clove, minced
- ½ teaspoon table salt
- ¼ teaspoon sugar
- ⅛ teaspoon pepper

Salad

- 8 slices bacon, cut into ¼-inch pieces
- 3 (6- to 8-ounce) boneless, skinless chicken breasts, trimmed
- ¼ teaspoon table salt
- ¼ teaspoon pepper
- 1 large head romaine lettuce (14 ounces), torn into bite-size pieces
- 4 ounces (4 cups) watercress, torn into bite-size pieces
- 10 ounces grape tomatoes, halved
- 2 avocados, halved, pitted, and cut into ½-inch pieces
- 3 Easy-Peel Hard-Cooked Eggs, cut into ½-inch pieces
- 2 ounces blue cheese, crumbled (½ cup)
- 3 tablespoons minced fresh chives

Classic Cobb Salad

Easy-Peel Hard-Cooked Eggs

Makes 1–6 eggs   **Total Time** 45 minutes
Be sure to use large eggs that have no cracks and are cold from the refrigerator.

1–6 large eggs

1. Bring 1 inch water to rolling boil in medium saucepan over high heat. Place eggs in steamer basket. Transfer basket to saucepan. Cover, reduce heat to medium-low, and cook eggs for 13 minutes.

2. When eggs are almost finished cooking, combine 2 cups ice cubes and 2 cups cold water in medium bowl. Using tongs or spoon, transfer eggs to ice bath; let sit for 15 minutes. Peel before using. (Hard-cooked eggs can be refrigerated, peeled or unpeeled, for up to 3 days.)

1. For the vinaigrette Whisk all ingredients in medium bowl until well combined; set aside.

2. For the salad Cook bacon in 12-inch nonstick skillet over medium heat until crispy, 5 to 7 minutes. Using slotted spoon, transfer bacon to paper towel–lined plate and pour off all but 1 tablespoon fat left in skillet.

3. Pound chicken breasts to uniform ¾-inch thickness. Pat chicken dry with paper towels and sprinkle with salt and pepper. Heat fat left in skillet over medium-high heat until just smoking. Cook until chicken is golden brown and registers 160 degrees, about 6 minutes per side. Transfer chicken to plate. When cool enough to handle, cut chicken into ½-inch pieces and set aside.

4. Combine lettuce and watercress with 5 tablespoons vinaigrette in large bowl and toss to coat; arrange on very large, flat serving platter. Add chicken and ¼ cup vinaigrette to now-empty bowl and toss to coat; arrange in row along 1 edge of greens.

5. Add tomatoes and 1 tablespoon vinaigrette to again-empty bowl and toss gently to coat; arrange on opposite edge of greens. Arrange avocados and eggs in separate rows near center of greens and drizzle with remaining vinaigrette. Sprinkle blue cheese, chives, and bacon evenly over salad and serve immediately.

Chicken and Arugula Salad with Figs and Warm Spices

Serves 6   **Total Time** 20 minutes

Why This Recipe Works This salad is light and fresh but still packs a protein punch with chicken, chickpeas, and almonds. Figs have a subtle, seductive flavor that comfortably swings between the sweet and savory sides of the menu, so they're right at home in this sophisticated salad. If you can't find fresh figs, you can substitute dried figs; they have a chewier texture and deeper caramel flavor. To enhance the figs' floral sweetness, we wanted a dressing seasoned with warm spices. We tried a variety of spice combinations in the dressing and finally settled on coriander for its light citrus note, along with smoked paprika and cinnamon for depth. We like using Perfect Poached Chicken (page 60) here but any cooked chicken would work.

6 tablespoons extra-virgin olive oil, divided
1 teaspoon ground coriander
½ teaspoon smoked paprika
¼ teaspoon ground cinnamon
3 tablespoons lemon juice
1 teaspoon honey

½ teaspoon table salt
¼ teaspoon pepper
4 cups shredded cooked chicken
1 (15-ounce) can chickpeas, rinsed
5 ounces (5 cups) baby arugula
½ cup fresh parsley leaves
1 shallot, halved and sliced thin
8 fresh figs, stemmed and quartered
½ cup whole almonds, toasted and chopped coarse

1. Microwave 1 tablespoon oil, coriander, paprika, and cinnamon in large bowl until fragrant, about 30 seconds. Whisk remaining 5 tablespoons oil, lemon juice, honey, salt, and pepper into spice mixture until incorporated.

2. Add shredded chicken, chickpeas, arugula, parsley, and shallot to dressing in bowl and gently toss to combine. Transfer salad to serving dish, arrange figs over top, and sprinkle with almonds. Serve.

Sichuan-Style Chicken Salad

Serves 4 to 6   **Total Time** 40 minutes

Why This Recipe Works Sichuan's famous bangbang ji or bang bang chicken is a dish composed of shredded chicken, julienned cucumber, and a spicy sauce. We liked the idea of turning these components into a main dish salad. Shredding the chicken allowed it to hold plenty of potent dressing. For contrast, we added the dressed chicken to thin-sliced napa cabbage, scallions, celery, loads of cilantro, and toasted sesame seeds for a super-crunchy salad with deep toasty notes. We prefer Sichuan chili powder, but Korean red pepper flakes, called gochugaru, are a good alternative. Vary the amount of Sichuan peppercorns to suit your taste. We like using Perfect Poached Chicken (page 60) here but any cooked chicken would work.

Dressing
¼ cup vegetable oil
1 garlic clove, peeled and smashed
1 (½-inch) piece ginger, peeled and sliced in half
2 tablespoons Sichuan chili powder
2 tablespoons soy sauce
1 tablespoon Chinese black vinegar or sherry vinegar
1 tablespoon toasted sesame oil
1–3 teaspoons Sichuan peppercorns, toasted and ground
2 teaspoons sugar

Salad

- 4 cups shredded cooked chicken
- ½ head napa cabbage, sliced thin (6 cups)
- 1½ cups coarsely chopped fresh cilantro leaves and stems, divided
- 6 scallions, sliced in half lengthwise, then sliced thin on bias, divided
- 1 celery rib, sliced thin on bias
   Pinch table salt
- 2 teaspoons toasted sesame seeds (optional)

1. For the dressing Combine vegetable oil, garlic, and ginger in bowl. Microwave until oil is hot and bubbling, about 2 minutes. Stir in chili powder and let cool for 10 minutes.

2. Strain oil mixture through fine-mesh strainer into large bowl; discard solids. Whisk soy sauce, vinegar, sesame oil, 1 teaspoon peppercorns, and sugar into strained oil. Add up to 1 teaspoon additional peppercorns to taste.

3. For the salad Add chicken to bowl with dressing and toss to coat. Season with salt to taste. Toss cabbage, 1 cup cilantro, two-thirds of scallions, celery, and salt in second large bowl. Arrange cabbage mixture in even layer on large platter. Mound chicken on top of cabbage mixture and sprinkle with remaining ½ cup cilantro, remaining scallions, and sesame seeds, if using. Serve.

Chicken and Arugula
Salad with Figs and Warm Spices

NOTES FROM THE TEST KITCHEN

GIVE COLD CHICKEN THE COLD SHOULDER

If you cook the chicken ahead of time and chill it, be sure to let it come to room temperature before using it in one of our salads. That's because cold meat tastes less juicy and flavorful than meat that's warm or at room temperature. Why? Juiciness and flavor in meat are not just a function of moisture but also of fat and of salivation. When meat is cold, the moisture is gelled and the fat is firm, so neither flows as freely. Less flavor is released, so you also salivate less. In addition, the solidification of the juices means that the muscle fibers don't slide against each other as easily during chewing, which gives the meat a tougher, stringier texture.

Sichuan-Style
Chicken Salad

Chinese Chicken Salad

Serves 6   Total Time 1 hour

Why This Recipe Works This Chinese chicken salad isn't Chinese as all. Wolfgang Puck served a version of chicken salad with Asian flavorings in the early 1980s at his restaurant Chinois and it went on to become a chain-restaurant classic. Given that this salad is so popular, we were inspired to make our own seriously fresh version. The salad bar pile-ons (chow mein noodles, fried wonton strips, water chestnuts, canned oranges) got the ax. Instead, we chose to highlight crisp napa cabbage and romaine lettuce, bell peppers, fresh cilantro, and scallions. We used fresh oranges, cutting out segments to top our salad, and squeezing the remaining juice. We used some of the juice to poach our chicken to flavor it deeply, along with soy sauce, rice vinegar, and ginger. Whisking more of the same ingredients with sesame and vegetable oils made a bold dressing for our salad. The whole shebang was finished with crunchy roasted peanuts and our orange segments.

- 2 oranges
- ¼ cup rice vinegar
- ¼ cup soy sauce
- 3 tablespoons grated fresh ginger
- 3 tablespoons sugar
- 1 tablespoon Asian chili-garlic sauce
- 2 pounds boneless, skinless chicken breasts, trimmed
- 3 tablespoons vegetable oil
- 2 tablespoons toasted sesame oil
- ½ head napa cabbage, cored and sliced thin (5½ cups)
- 2 romaine lettuce hearts (12 ounces), sliced thin
- 2 red bell peppers, stemmed, seeded, and cut into 2-inch-long matchsticks
- 1 cup fresh cilantro leaves
- 1 cup salted dry-roasted peanuts, chopped
- 6 scallions, sliced thin on bias

1. Cut away peel and pith from oranges. Holding fruit over large bowl to catch juice, use paring knife to slice between membranes to release segments; set segments aside for serving. Squeeze juice from membrane into bowl (juice should measure ¼ cup). Whisk in vinegar, soy sauce, ginger, sugar, and chili-garlic sauce. Pound chicken breasts to uniform thickness.

2. Transfer ½ cup orange juice mixture to 12-inch skillet and bring to simmer over medium-high heat; set aside remaining orange juice mixture. Add chicken to skillet, cover, and reduce heat to medium-low. Cook until chicken registers 160 degrees, 10 to 15 minutes, flipping chicken halfway through cooking. Transfer to plate; set aside.

3. Once chicken is cool enough to handle, shred into bite-size pieces using 2 forks.

4. Bring pan juices to boil and cook until reduced to ¼ cup, 1 to 3 minutes. Off heat, stir in chicken and any accumulated juices and let sit for 10 minutes.

5. Slowly whisk vegetable oil and sesame oil into reserved orange juice mixture. Add cabbage, romaine, bell peppers, cilantro, peanuts, and scallions and toss to combine. Transfer to serving platter and top with chicken and reserved orange segments. Serve.

CUTTING CITRUS INTO SEGMENTS

1. Slice off top and bottom of citrus, then cut away peel and pith using paring knife.

2. Holding fruit over bowl, slice between membranes to release individual segments.

Chicken Salad with Thai Basil and Mango

Serves 4 to 6   Total Time 20 minutes

Why This Recipe Works This simple, fragrant salad dresses chicken in a sweet, sour, salty dressing with abundant fresh herbs. Shredding the chicken creates loads of surface area that allows the dressing to soak into the meat, ensuring that every bite is saturated with flavor. We like to serve this salad in leaves of Bibb lettuce to form lettuce cups, but it can also be served on a bed of greens. Toss 6 to 8 cups of greens with 2 teaspoons of lime juice, 1 teaspoon of toasted sesame oil, 1 teaspoon of vegetable oil, and a pinch of salt before spooning the chicken on top. If you can't find Thai basil, you can substitute regular basil. If you can't find Thai chiles, you can substitute two Fresno chiles. We like using Perfect Poached Chicken (page 60) here but any cooked chicken would work.

Chicken Salad with Thai Basil and Mango

Chicken Salad with Spicy Peanut Dressing

Serves 6   **Total Time** 35 minutes

Why This Recipe Works This crunchy chicken salad tossed in a Thai-inspired peanut dressing takes advantage of the emulsifying power of peanut butter, which not only provides stability but also contributes interesting flavor. For further insurance against separation, we used a blender to mix the dressing. Lime juice and brown sugar gave the dressing a sour-sweet balance and red pepper flakes contributed heat. With a bright, creamy dressing at the ready, we just stirred in handfuls of fresh vegetables and herbs along with our chicken and sprinkled everything with toasted peanuts for added flavor and crunch. Don't dress the chicken when it's warm—it will absorb too much of the dressing. This recipe is best served over salad greens. We like using Seared Chicken Breasts (page 60) here but any cooked chicken would work.

½ cup vegetable oil
3 tablespoons smooth peanut butter
½ cup fresh lime juice (4 limes)
2 tablespoons water
¼ teaspoon table salt
3 cloves garlic, minced
2 teaspoons finely grated fresh ginger
2 tablespoons packed light brown sugar
1½ teaspoons red pepper flakes
1 carrot, peeled and grated (about ½ cup)
½ cucumber, peeled, seeded, and cut into 1 inch by ¼-inch matchsticks (about 1 cup)
4 scallions, white and green parts, sliced thin
3 tablespoons minced fresh cilantro leaves
4 cups shredded cooked chicken
½ cup chopped toasted peanuts

1. Puree oil, peanut butter, lime juice, water, salt, garlic, ginger, brown sugar, and red pepper flakes in blender until combined. Transfer to large bowl. (Dressing can be refrigerated overnight. Whisk to recombine before using.)

2. Add carrot, cucumber, scallions, and cilantro to vinaigrette; toss to combine. Add chicken and toss gently to combine; let stand at room temperature 15 minutes. Season with salt to taste, and sprinkle with peanuts. Serve immediately.

Dressing

3 tablespoons lime juice (2 limes)
1 shallot, minced
2 tablespoons fish sauce, plus extra for serving
1 tablespoon packed brown sugar
1 garlic clove, minced
¼ teaspoon red pepper flakes

Salad

4 cups shredded cooked chicken
1 mango, peeled, pitted, and cut into ¼-inch pieces
½ cup chopped fresh mint
½ cup chopped fresh cilantro
½ cup chopped fresh Thai basil
1 head Bibb lettuce (8 ounces), leaves separated
2 Thai chiles, sliced thin

1. For the dressing Whisk all ingredients together in large bowl.

2. For the salad Add chicken to bowl with dressing and toss to coat. Add mango, mint, cilantro, and basil and toss to coat. Season with salt to taste. Serve salad in lettuce cups, passing Thai chiles and extra fish sauce separately.

Chicken Salad with Apricots,
Almonds, and Chickpeas

Turkey Taco Salad

Chicken Salad with Apricots, Almonds, and Chickpeas

Serves 4 to 6   **Total Time** 40 minutes

Why This Recipe Works This creative chicken salad was inspired by some of the flavors of Morocco: apricots, lemon, and warm spices. To give our dressing complex flavor, we reached for garam masala, a blend that often includes coriander, cumin, ginger, cinnamon, and black pepper. We added a little more coriander, honey, and smoked paprika for depth. Blooming the spices in the microwave deepened their flavors for an even bolder dressing. Chickpeas further echoed the Moroccan theme and lent heartiness, and crisp romaine combined with slightly bitter watercress made the perfect bed of greens for our toppings. Reserving a bit of the dressing to drizzle on just before serving made the flavors come alive. We like using Seared Chicken Breasts (page 60) here but any cooked chicken would work.

- ¾ cup extra-virgin olive oil, divided
- 1 teaspoon garam masala
- ½ teaspoon ground coriander
  Pinch smoked paprika
- ¼ cup lemon juice, divided
- 1 tablespoon honey
- ¼ teaspoon table salt
- ¼ teaspoon pepper
- 4 cups cooked chicken, sliced ½ inch thick on bias
- 1 (15-ounce) can chickpeas, rinsed
- ¾ cup dried apricots, chopped coarse
- 1 shallot, sliced thin
- 2 tablespoons minced fresh parsley
- 2 romaine lettuce hearts (12 ounces), cut into 1-inch pieces
- 4 ounces (4 cups) watercress
- ½ cup whole almonds, toasted and chopped coarse

1. Microwave 1 tablespoon oil, garam masala, coriander, and paprika in medium bowl until oil is hot and fragrant, about 30 seconds. Whisk 3 tablespoons lemon juice, honey, salt, and pepper into spice mixture. Whisking constantly, drizzle in remaining oil.

2. In large bowl, combine chicken, chickpeas, apricots, shallot, parsley, and half of dressing and toss to coat. Let mixture sit for 15 to 30 minutes. Whisk remaining 1 tablespoon lemon juice into remaining dressing.

3. Toss romaine, watercress, and almonds together in serving bowl, drizzle remaining dressing over top, and toss to combine. Season with salt and pepper to taste. Top with chicken mixture and serve.

Turkey Taco Salad

Serves 4 **Total Time** 35 minutes

Why This Recipe Works Taco salads are a great way to enjoy the flavors of a taco with no assembly required. We made a quick, well-seasoned ground turkey mixture in a skillet—no seasoning packet required. While the turkey mixture cooked and cooled, we put together the dressing; the trio of lime juice, cilantro, and jalapeño gave the dressing (and salad) tons of zip. Romaine lettuce, chopped tomato, cubed avocado, and shredded cheese rounded out the salad, and crumbled tortilla chips provided a pleasant crunch. Be sure to use ground turkey, not ground turkey breast (labeled 99 percent fat-free), in this recipe. Salsa, sour cream, and minced cilantro also taste great on this salad.

- 1 tablespoon plus ¾ cup extra-virgin olive oil, divided
- 1 onion, chopped fine
- 2 tablespoons chili powder
- 5 garlic cloves, minced, divided
- 1 pound 93 percent lean ground turkey
- 1 (8-ounce) can tomato sauce
- 3 tablespoons lime juice
- 1 jalapeño chile, stemmed, seeded, and chopped
- ½ teaspoon table salt
- ½ cup fresh cilantro leaves
- 1 large head romaine lettuce (14 ounces), torn into bite-size pieces
- 2 tomatoes, cored and chopped
- 1 avocado, halved, pitted, and cut into ½-inch pieces
- 4 ounces shredded cheddar cheese or Mexican cheese blend (1 cup)
- 1 cup crumbled tortilla chips (2 ounces)

1. Heat 1 tablespoon oil in 12-inch nonstick skillet over medium heat until shimmering. Add onion and chili powder and cook until onion is softened, 3 to 5 minutes. Stir in 4 teaspoons garlic and cook until fragrant, about 30 seconds.

2. Stir in turkey and cook, breaking up meat with wooden spoon, until lightly browned, 6 to 8 minutes. Stir in tomato sauce and simmer until slightly thickened, about 2 minutes. Season with salt and pepper to taste.

3. Meanwhile, process lime juice, jalapeño, salt, and remaining garlic in blender until finely chopped, about 15 seconds. With blender running, add cilantro and then remaining ¾ cup oil and continue to process until smooth and emulsified, about 15 seconds.

4. Toss lettuce with ½ cup dressing in bowl. Divide salad among individual plates, top with turkey mixture, and sprinkle with tomatoes, avocado, cheese, and tortilla chips. Drizzle with remaining dressing and serve.

Chopped Salad with Apples, Bacon, and Smoked Turkey

Serves 4 **Total Time** 20 minutes

Why This Recipe Works Chopped salads often are a hodge-podge of leftovers or pantry ingredients, aimlessly tossed together and dressed with whatever dressing is lying around. We wanted a chopped salad that made sense. We paired crispy bacon with sweet apples, rich cheddar cheese, and smoked turkey breast, a collection of ingredients that works well together and is simple to assemble. To finish this light and refreshing salad we tossed these ingredients with romaine lettuce and a simple cider vinegar and Dijon mustard vinaigrette that complemented the other ingredients but did not compete. When buying the turkey for this salad, ask the deli to slice it into a ½-inch-thick slab so that you can easily cut it into ½-inch pieces.

- 8 slices bacon, chopped
- ¼ cup extra-virgin olive oil
- 2 tablespoons cider vinegar
- 1 shallot, minced
- 1 tablespoon Dijon mustard
- ½ teaspoon table salt
- ½ teaspoon pepper
- 2 romaine lettuce hearts (12 ounces), torn into bite-size pieces
- 2 apples, cored, halved, and sliced thin
- 8 ounces deli smoked turkey breast, cut into ½-inch pieces
- 4 ounces cheddar cheese, cut into ½-inch pieces

1. Cook bacon in 12-inch nonstick skillet over medium-high heat until crisp, 5 to 7 minutes; transfer to paper towel–lined plate.

2. Whisk oil, vinegar, shallot, mustard, salt, and pepper together in large bowl. Add bacon, lettuce, apples, turkey, and cheddar and toss to combine. Season with salt and pepper to taste. Divide among individual plates and serve.

VARIATION

Chopped Salad with Apples, Fennel, and Chicken

Omit bacon. Add 1 bulb fennel, sliced ¼ inch thick, and 1 cucumber, halved, seeded, and sliced ½ inch thick. Substitute goat cheese for cheddar. Substitute 2 cups cooked chicken for turkey.

DRESSINGS AND TOPPINGS FOR CHICKEN SALADS

Bright, creamy, and bold dressings all complement chicken salads of one kind or another, but the choice of dressing might influence how you cut up the chicken. Shredded meat has the most surface area and readily soaks up thinner dressings like vinaigrette. Cubed meat loves a clinging creamy coating, while broader slices make a nice foil to the boldest of dressings. Chicken's mildness means that a crispy or tangy topping is a welcome companion in a salad. Toasted (and maybe spiced) nuts or seeds are easy, and much better than store-bought. And if you haven't quick-pickled a grape, a chicken salad is a good reason to do so.

Lemon-Dill Vinaigrette

Makes about ½ cup   **Total Time** 10 minutes

The flavor of fresh herbs and lemon or wine vinegar sings when paired with chicken—in salads or most any other way. A gentle whisking technique keeps the herb's delicate flavor at the fore. Two emulsifiers (mayonnaise and mustard) help to prevent the dressing from breaking.

- 2 tablespoons lemon juice
- 1 teaspoon mayonnaise
- 1 teaspoon Dijon mustard
- ¼ teaspoon table salt
- 6 tablespoons extra-virgin olive oil
- 2 tablespoons minced fresh dill

1. Whisk lemon juice, mayonnaise, mustard, and salt in medium bowl until mixture is milky in appearance and no lumps of mayonnaise remain.

2. Transfer oil to small measuring cup so that it is easy to pour. Whisking constantly, slowly drizzle oil into lemon juice mixture. If pools of oil gather on surface as you whisk, stop addition of oil and whisk mixture well to combine, then resume whisking in oil in slow stream. Vinaigrette should be glossy and lightly thickened, with no surface pools of oil. Whisk in dill and season with salt and pepper to taste. (Vinaigrette can be refrigerated for up to 2 days; whisk to recombine before using.)

VARIATIONS

Tarragon-Caper Vinaigrette

Substitute white wine vinegar for lemon juice, and minced fresh tarragon for dill. Add 2 teaspoons minced shallot and 2 teaspoons chopped capers to vinaigrette with tarragon.

Lime-Cilantro Vinaigrette

Substitute lime juice for lemon juice, and minced fresh cilantro for dill.

Green Goddess Dressing

Makes 1¼ cups   **Total Time** 1 hour

An abundance of herbs gives this boldly flavored dressing its name along with its green color.

- 1 tablespoon lemon juice
- 1 tablespoon water
- 2 teaspoons dried tarragon
- ½ cup buttermilk
- ¼ cup plain yogurt
- ¼ cup sour cream
- ¼ cup minced fresh parsley
- 1 garlic clove, minced
- 1 anchovy fillet, minced (optional)
- ¼ cup minced fresh chives
- ¼ teaspoon table salt
- ⅛ teaspoon pepper

1. Combine lemon juice, water, and tarragon in small bowl and let sit for 15 minutes.

2. Process tarragon mixture; buttermilk; yogurt; sour cream; parsley; garlic; and anchovy, if using, in blender until smooth, scraping down sides of blender jar as needed; transfer dressing to clean bowl. Stir in chives, salt, and pepper. Cover and refrigerate until flavors meld, 30 minutes to 1 hour. Season with salt and pepper to taste. (Dressing can be refrigerated for up to 4 days; whisk to recombine before using.)

Blue Cheese Dressing

Makes 1½ cups **Total Time** 10 minutes

This dressing adds tangy, creamy, funky flavor to salads and bowls. For the hot sauce, Frank's RedHot Original Cayenne Pepper Sauce is the classic choice.

- 1 cup plain yogurt
- 2 ounces blue cheese, crumbled (½ cup)
- 2 tablespoons hot sauce
- 4 teaspoons lemon juice
- 2 garlic cloves, minced
- ½ teaspoon table salt

Whisk all ingredients together in bowl. Season with salt and pepper to taste. (Dressing can be refrigerated for up to 4 days; whisk to recombine before using.)

Creamy Avocado Dressing

Makes 1 cup **Total Time** 10 minutes

Rich avocado makes for a deliciously creamy dressing.

- 1 avocado, halved, pitted, and cut into ½-inch pieces
- 2 tablespoons extra-virgin olive oil
- 1 teaspoon grated lemon zest, plus 3 tablespoons juice
- 1 garlic clove, minced
- ¾ teaspoon table salt
- ¼ teaspoon pepper

Process avocado, oil, lemon zest and juice, garlic, salt, and pepper in food processor until smooth, about 30 seconds, scraping down sides of bowl as needed. Season with salt and pepper to taste. Use immediately.

Quick Toasted Nuts

Makes 2 cups **Total Time** 25 minutes

Nuts are an easy way to add hearty crunch to a salad, and toasting them helps to bring out their flavorful oils.

- 1 tablespoon extra-virgin olive oil or vegetable oil
- 2 cups skin-on raw whole almonds, shelled walnuts, or shelled pistachios
- 1 teaspoon table salt
- ¼ teaspoon pepper

Heat oil in 12-inch nonstick skillet over medium-high heat until just shimmering. Add nuts, salt, and pepper and reduce heat to medium-low. Cook, stirring often, until nuts are fragrant and their color deepens slightly, about 8 minutes. Transfer nuts to paper towel–lined plate and let cool. (Nuts can be stored in airtight container at room temperature for up to 5 days.)

Green Goddess Dressing

VARIATIONS

Rosemary Nuts

Add ½ teaspoon dried rosemary to skillet with nuts.

Orange-Fennel Nuts

Add 1 teaspoon grated orange zest and ½ teaspoon ground fennel seeds to skillet with nuts.

Spiced Nuts

Add 2 teaspoons grated lemon zest, 1 teaspoon ground coriander seeds, and ½ teaspoon hot paprika to skillet with nuts.

Lemon-Garlic Nuts

Add ½ teaspoon grated lemon zest and 1 minced garlic clove to skillet with nuts. Just before serving, toss with another ½ teaspoon grated lemon zest.

Spiced Pepitas or Sunflower Seeds

Makes ½ cup   **Total Time** 10 minutes

Salty, crunchy, spicy seeds make an easy topping that elevates a salad in a snap.

  2 teaspoons extra-virgin olive oil or vegetable oil
  ½ cup pepitas or sunflower seeds
  ½ teaspoon paprika
  ½ teaspoon coriander
  ¼ teaspoon table salt

Heat oil in 12-inch skillet over medium heat until shimmering. Add pepitas, paprika, coriander, and salt. Cook, stirring constantly, until seeds are toasted, about 2 minutes; transfer to bowl and let cool. (Seeds can be stored in airtight container at room temperature for up to 5 days.)

Croutons

Makes 3 cups   **Total Time** 30 minutes

You can make good croutons using nearly any type of bread, from stale pieces of baguette to the end slices of a sandwich loaf.

  3 tablespoons extra-virgin olive oil
  2 garlic cloves, minced
  ¼ teaspoon table salt
  4 cups (½-inch) bread cubes, from baguette or
     hearty white sandwich bread

Adjust oven rack to middle position and heat oven to 350 degrees. Toss all ingredients together in bowl. Bake on rimmed baking sheet until golden and crisp, 20 to 25 minutes. Let croutons cool before serving. (Croutons can be stored at room temperature for up to 1 week.)

VARIATIONS

Parmesan Croutons

Increase oil to 6 tablespoons and toss 1 cup grated Parmesan cheese with other ingredients.

Spiced Croutons

Omit garlic. Toss ½ teaspoon cumin, ½ teaspoon coriander, ¼ teaspoon paprika, and ⅛ teaspoon cayenne pepper with other ingredients.

Herbed Croutons

Toss 2 teaspoons minced fresh rosemary (or ½ teaspoon dried), 2 teaspoons minced fresh thyme, sage, or dill (or ½ teaspoon dried), and ¼ teaspoon pepper with other ingredients.

Quick Pickled Grapes

Quick Pickled Grapes

Makes 1⅓ cups   **Total Time** 50 minutes

Pickling adds vibrantly acidic flavor to grapes, rendering a perfect sweet-tart combination.

  ⅓ cup white wine vinegar
  1 tablespoon sugar
  ½ teaspoon table salt
  8 ounces seedless grapes, halved

Microwave vinegar, sugar, and salt in medium bowl until simmering, 1 to 2 minutes. Stir in grapes and let sit, stirring occasionally, for 45 minutes. Drain. (Drained pickled grapes can be refrigerated for up to 1 week.)

Buffalo Chicken Bowl

Serves 4   **Total Time** 10 minutes

Why This Recipe Works Creamy, tangy, and with plenty of kick, this buffalo bowl translates the appeal of the popular bar snack to a dinner salad suitable for enjoyment any day. Convenient coleslaw mix offered a sturdy base for our salad, but its meager quantity of carrot was barely noticeable, so we shredded an additional carrot. To bring together the iconic pairing of buffalo sauce and blue cheese, we used our Blue Cheese Dressing (page 69), a lighter version of the classic using yogurt mixed with hot sauce, lemon juice, garlic, and pungent blue cheese. And it wouldn't be a buffalo bowl without celery, sliced on the bias into attractive strips. Extra blue cheese on top added even more rich, tangy goodness. We like using Perfect Poached Chicken (page 60) here but any cooked chicken would work.

    4 cups (8 ounces) shredded coleslaw mix
    1 recipe Blue Cheese Dressing (page 69), divided
    4 cups shredded cooked chicken
    1 carrot, peeled and shredded (½ cup)
    1 celery rib, sliced thin on bias, plus ¼ cup celery leaves
    2 tablespoons crumbled blue cheese

Toss coleslaw mix with half of dressing to coat, then season with salt and pepper to taste. Toss chicken and carrot with remaining dressing to coat. Divide dressed coleslaw mix among individual serving bowls, then top with dressed chicken mixture, celery, and blue cheese. Serve.

Turkey Meatball and Barley Bowl

Serves 4   **Total Time** 1 hour

Why This Recipe Works These diminutive turkey meatballs are hard to resist simply popping in your mouth, but save them for topping this hearty grain bowl that's replete with chewy barley, lightly charred cumin-dusted carrots and snow peas. A warmly spiced mix of cumin, paprika, and cilantro gave our meatballs plenty of flavor, while a white bread panade kept them tender. A lemony dressing brightened up the bowl's earthy flavors and a dollop of Greek yogurt offered creamy contrast. Be sure to use ground turkey, not ground turkey breast (also labeled 99 percent fat-free), in this recipe. Top with pickled red onions if desired.

    1 slice hearty white sandwich bread, crust removed, torn into ¼-inch pieces
    2 tablespoons milk
    1 pound ground turkey
    ½ cup chopped fresh cilantro, divided
    2 teaspoons ground cumin, divided
    1½ teaspoons paprika
    ½ teaspoon table salt, divided
    ½ teaspoon pepper
    2 teaspoons plus ¼ cup extra-virgin olive oil, divided
    6 carrots, peeled
    8 ounces snow peas, strings removed, halved lengthwise
    2 teaspoons grated lemon zest plus 2 tablespoons juice
    4 cups cooked barley, warmed
    ½ cup plain Greek yogurt

1. Mash bread and milk into paste in medium bowl using fork. Break turkey into small pieces over bread mixture and add ¼ cup cilantro, 1½ teaspoons cumin, paprika, ¼ teaspoon salt, and pepper. Lightly knead with your hands until well combined. Pinch off and roll mixture into 36 meatballs (about ½ tablespoon each).

2. Heat 2 teaspoons oil in 12-inch nonstick skillet over medium heat until shimmering. Add meatballs and cook until well browned and tender, 5 to 7 minutes. Transfer meatballs to plate, cover with aluminum foil to keep warm, and set aside until ready to serve.

3. Halve carrots crosswise, then halve or quarter lengthwise to create uniformly sized pieces. Heat 2 tablespoons oil in now-empty skillet over medium heat until shimmering. Add carrots, remaining ½ teaspoon cumin, and remaining ¼ teaspoon salt and cook, stirring occasionally, until lightly charred and just tender, 5 to 7 minutes. Stir in snow peas and cook until crisp-tender, 2 to 4 minutes; set aside off heat.

4. Whisk remaining 2 tablespoons oil, remaining ¼ cup cilantro, and lemon zest and juice together in large bowl. Add barley, tossing to coat, then season with salt and pepper to taste. Divide among individual serving bowls, then top with meatballs and carrot mixture. Dollop with yogurt. Serve.

Chimichurri Couscous Chicken Bowl

Serves 4   Total Time 50 minutes

Why This Recipe Works Bold chimichurri sauce highlights the incredible flavor of fresh parsley and comes together in a snap. We used it to add bright flavor and color to a base of hearty pearl couscous. For protein, we crisped cooked chicken with garlic to infuse it with flavor. Hefty portions of parsley on top of the chimichurri added pleasant vegetal flavors, and cucumber added cool crispness. Sun-dried tomatoes rounded out the flavor profile. We like using Seared Chicken Breasts (page 60) here but any cooked chicken would work.

Chimichurri Sauce
- 1 cup fresh parsley leaves
- ¼ cup extra-virgin olive oil
- 1 tablespoon red wine vinegar
- 2 garlic cloves, minced
- ½ teaspoon dried oregano
- ¼ teaspoon red pepper flakes

Bowl
- 1 tablespoon extra-virgin olive oil, divided
- 2 cups pearl couscous
- 2½ cups chicken or vegetable broth
- 2 garlic cloves, minced
- 4 cups shredded cooked chicken
- 1 cup chopped fresh parsley
- 1 English cucumber, chopped fine
- ½ cup oil-packed sun-dried tomatoes, rinsed, patted dry, and chopped fine

1. For the sauce Pulse all ingredients in food processor until coarsely chopped, about 10 pulses, scraping down sides of bowl as needed. Season with salt and pepper to taste. (Sauce can be refrigerated for up to 3 days.)

2. For the bowl Heat 2 teaspoons oil and couscous in medium saucepan over medium heat, stirring frequently, until half of grains are golden brown, about 3 minutes. Stir in broth and bring to boil. Reduce heat to medium-low, cover, and simmer, stirring occasionally, until couscous is tender and broth is absorbed, 9 to 12 minutes.

3. Remove couscous from heat and let sit, covered, for 3 minutes. Transfer to bowl to cool slightly, about 10 minutes.

4. While couscous cools, heat remaining 1 teaspoon oil in 12-inch nonstick skillet over medium-high heat until shimmering. Add garlic and cook, mashing garlic into skillet, until fragrant, about 30 seconds. Stir in chicken, toss to coat, and remove skillet from heat.

5. Stir parsley and ¼ cup chimichurri sauce into cooled couscous in bowl and season with salt and pepper to taste. Divide evenly among individual serving bowls, then top with chicken, cucumber, and sun-dried tomatoes. Drizzle with remaining chimichurri sauce. Serve.

Peanut Soba Noodle Chicken Bowl

Serves 4   Total Time 50 minutes

Why This Recipe Works We love the combination of earthy buckwheat soba noodles and rich peanut sauce as a base for a chicken bowl. The peanut sauce came together easily in a blender and added sweet-salty-spicy flavors. We rinsed the noodles after cooking to cool them down and remove extra starch (which would have overly thickened the sauce) before tossing them in our creamy peanut sauce. For an easy topping that added both texture and color, we turned to vibrant, crunchy shredded red cabbage, although you could easily try out different vegetables with this base. Shredded chicken added a hefty dose of protein. Herbaceous fresh cilantro leaves paired well with the flavors of the sauce. We finished our satisfying bowl with a sprinkle of chopped roasted peanuts and lime wedges for a bit of acidity. You can use store-bought coleslaw mix in place of the red cabbage. We like using Perfect Poached Chicken (page 60) here but any cooked chicken would work.

Sauce
- 3 tablespoons chunky peanut butter
- 3 tablespoons toasted sesame seeds
- 2 tablespoons soy sauce
- 1½ tablespoons rice vinegar
- 1½ tablespoons packed light brown sugar
- 1½ teaspoons grated fresh ginger
- 1 small garlic clove, minced
- ¾ teaspoon hot sauce

Noodles
- 12 ounces soba noodles
- 4 cups shredded cooked chicken
- 1 cup shredded red cabbage
- ¼ cup fresh cilantro leaves
- ¼ cup chopped dry-roasted peanuts
  Lime wedges

1. For the sauce Process all ingredients in blender until smooth and mixture has consistency of heavy cream, about 1 minute (adjust consistency with warm water, 1 tablespoon at a time, as needed). (Sauce can be refrigerated for up to 3 days; add warm water as needed to loosen before using.)

2. For the noodles Bring 4 quarts water to boil in large pot. Add noodles and cook, stirring often, until tender. Drain noodles and rinse thoroughly with cold water, shaking to remove excess water. Toss noodles with sauce, adjust consistency with up to ½ cup hot water as needed, and season with salt and pepper to taste. Divide among individual serving bowls, then top with chicken, cabbage, cilantro, and peanuts. Serve with lime wedges.

Chicken Zoodle Bowl with Ginger and Garam Masala

Serves 4   **Total Time** 45 minutes

Why This Recipe Works Quick-cooking zucchini noodles make a light and refreshing base for this chicken bowl and seasoning them with the Indian spice mixture garam masala gave us exciting flavor. We used more garam masala to season our chicken before cooking it, along with garlic and ginger for balance. A few dollops of cilantro-mint yogurt sauce added cooling freshness and tang, and mango tossed with more cilantro lent a touch of sweetness. Cooking the zoodles in two batches ensured that the delicate vegetable didn't overcook and turn mushy. You will need 2 pounds of zucchini to get 24 ounces of noodles; we prefer to make our own using a spiralizer, but in a pinch you can use store-bought. Cook the zucchini to your desired level of doneness but be careful not to overcook.

- 1 cup plain whole-milk yogurt
- ¼ cup chopped fresh cilantro, divided
- 2 tablespoons minced fresh mint
- 5 garlic cloves, minced, divided
- 1 teaspoon grated lemon zest plus 3 tablespoons juice, divided
- 1 mango, peeled and cut into ¼-inch pieces
- 2 tablespoons plus 2 teaspoons vegetable oil, divided
- 4 teaspoons garam masala, divided
- 2 teaspoons grated fresh ginger
- ½ teaspoon table salt, divided
- ½ teaspoon pepper, divided
- 1 pound boneless, skinless chicken breasts, trimmed and cut into ½-inch pieces
- 24 ounces zucchini noodles, cut into 6-inch lengths, divided

1. Whisk yogurt, 2 tablespoons cilantro, mint, 1 teaspoon garlic, lemon zest, and 2 tablespoons lemon juice together in bowl. Cover and refrigerate until flavors meld, at least 30 minutes. (Sauce can be refrigerated for up to 4 days.)

Chicken Zoodle Bowl with Ginger and Garam Masala

2. Combine mango, remaining 2 tablespoons cilantro, and remaining 1 tablespoon lemon juice in bowl; season with salt and pepper to taste and set aside until ready to serve.

3. Whisk 2 teaspoons oil, 2 teaspoons garam masala, ginger, ¼ teaspoon salt, ¼ teaspoon pepper, and remaining garlic together in medium bowl, then add chicken and toss to coat.

4. Heat 2 teaspoons oil in 12-inch nonstick skillet over medium-high heat until shimmering. Add chicken and cook until browned on all sides, 4 to 6 minutes. Transfer to clean bowl, cover with aluminum foil to keep warm, and set aside until ready to serve.

5. Heat 2 teaspoons oil in now-empty skillet over medium-high heat until shimmering. Add 1 teaspoon garam masala, ⅛ teaspoon salt, ⅛ teaspoon pepper, and half of zucchini noodles and cook, tossing frequently, until crisp-tender, about 1 minute. Transfer to individual serving bowl and repeat with remaining 2 teaspoons oil, remaining 1 teaspoon garam masala, remaining ⅛ teaspoon salt, remaining ⅛ teaspoon pepper, and remaining zucchini noodles. Top zucchini noodles with chicken, mango mixture, and yogurt sauce. Serve.

SANDWICHES, BURGERS, TACOS, AND MORE

Photos (clockwise from top left): Mediterranean Turkey Burger with Shaved Zucchini Salad and Ricotta; Chicken Souvlaki; Red Chile Chicken Tamales; Grilled Chicken Tacos with Salsa Verde

Crispy Chicken Salad Wraps

Serves 4   Total Time 30 minutes

Why This Recipe Works We turned ordinary chicken salad sandwiches into restaurant-style wraps with a crispy, toasted exterior by heating chicken salad–stuffed tortillas in a skillet until crisp. The additions of sharp cheddar and a hit of hot sauce livened up our chicken salad. We like using Perfect Poached Chicken (page 60) here but any cooked chicken would work. To prevent the wraps from unrolling as they cook, be sure to start them seam side down in step 3.

⅓ cup mayonnaise
⅓ cup chopped fresh cilantro
3 scallions, sliced thin
2 celery ribs, minced
2 tablespoons sour cream
2 teaspoons hot sauce
3 cups shredded cooked chicken
4 (10-inch) flour tortillas
8 ounces sharp cheddar cheese, shredded (2 cups)
Vegetable oil spray

1. Whisk mayonnaise, cilantro, scallions, celery, sour cream, and hot sauce together in bowl. Add chicken and toss to combine. Season with salt and pepper to taste.

2. Wrap tortillas in damp dish towel and microwave until warm and pliable, about 1 minute. Lay warm tortillas on counter. Sprinkle ½ cup cheese over center of each tortilla, close to bottom edges, then top with chicken salad. Working with 1 tortilla at a time, fold sides then bottom of tortilla over filling, pulling back on it firmly to tighten it around filling, then continue to roll tightly into wrap; leave seam side down on counter to secure.

3. Spray wraps with vegetable oil spray on all sides. Arrange 2 wraps seam side down in 12-inch nonstick skillet and cook over medium heat until golden brown and crisp, about 1 minute per side. Transfer to plate and repeat with remaining wraps. Serve.

Smoked Turkey Club Panini

Serves 4   Total Time 45 minutes

Why This Recipe Works We love a pressed sandwich—hot, crusty, melty, and dense with tasty fillings—but most of us don't own the ridged press typically used to make panini. To re-create it using more widely available household kitchen equipment, we turned to a cast-iron skillet, which can produce

Smoked Turkey Club Panini

steady, even heat just like that specialized appliance. For our sandwich, we mixed zesty sun-dried tomatoes into mayonnaise for a flavored condiment that would complement smoked turkey. We also brushed some of the oil from the tomatoes onto the bread for a flavor boost and a crispy, golden exterior. Bacon, crisped in the skillet, gave the sandwich more smokiness and crunch, and Swiss cheese added the requisite melted cheese flavorful depth. To weight down our sandwiches as they cooked, we placed a heavy Dutch oven on top; it pressed them perfectly. We like to use rustic artisanal bread for this recipe; do not use a baguette but rather look for a wide loaf that will yield big slices.

8 slices bacon
⅓ cup mayonnaise
⅓ cup oil-packed sun-dried tomatoes, rinsed, patted dry, and minced, plus ¼ cup tomato packing oil
8 (½-inch-thick) slices crusty bread
8 ounces thinly sliced Swiss cheese
8 ounces thinly sliced smoked turkey
2 ounces (2 cups) baby arugula

1. Adjust oven rack to middle position and heat oven to 200 degrees. Set wire rack in rimmed baking sheet. Cook bacon in 12-inch cast-iron skillet over medium heat until crispy, 12 to 15 minutes. Transfer bacon to paper towel–lined plate. Pour off fat from skillet, then wipe skillet clean with paper towels.

2. Combine mayonnaise and tomatoes in bowl. Brush tomato oil on 1 side of bread slices. Flip slices over and spread mayonnaise mixture on second side. Assemble 4 sandwiches by layering ingredients as follows between prepared slices (with mayonnaise mixture inside sandwiches): half of Swiss, turkey, bacon, arugula, and remaining Swiss. Press gently on sandwiches to set.

3. Heat now-empty skillet over medium heat for 3 minutes. Place 2 sandwiches in skillet, reduce heat to medium-low, and set Dutch oven on top. Cook until bread is golden and crispy, 4 to 6 minutes per side, redistributing sandwiches as needed to ensure even browning.

4. Transfer sandwiches to prepared rack and keep warm in oven. Wipe skillet clean with paper towels and repeat with remaining 2 sandwiches. Serve.

MAKING PANINI

Place 2 sandwiches in skillet. Set Dutch oven on top. Cook until bread is crispy, flipping sandwiches and replacing Dutch oven halfway through cooking.

Spicy Chicken Subs

Serves 4   **Total Time** 45 minutes

Why This Recipe Works Topping breaded chicken cutlets with sautéed onion, red bell pepper, and provolone cheese yields a simple but supremely satisfying sandwich, which becomes deliciously melty after a quick stint under the broiler. Giardiniera (a spicy mix of pickled vegetables), mayonnaise, and red pepper flakes combined to make a creamy, tangy relish that gave our subs a kick. Combining the onion and pepper with a little of the giardiniera brine further boosted the flavor of this sandwich.

1   (16-ounce) jar giardiniera, drained, 1 tablespoon brine reserved
1   tablespoon mayonnaise
¼   teaspoon red pepper flakes
4   (3- to 4-ounce) chicken cutlets, ½ inch thick, trimmed
¼   teaspoon table salt
⅛   teaspoon pepper
3   tablespoons olive oil, divided
1   onion, halved and sliced thin
1   red bell pepper, stemmed, seeded, and sliced thin
4   (6-inch) sub rolls, partially split lengthwise
8   slices provolone cheese (8 ounces)

1. Adjust oven rack 8 inches from broiler element and heat broiler. Pulse giardiniera, mayonnaise, and pepper flakes in food processor until finely chopped, about 5 pulses.

2. Pat cutlets dry with paper towels and sprinkle with salt and pepper. Heat 1 tablespoon oil in 12-inch skillet over medium-high heat until just smoking. Cook 2 cutlets until browned, about 2 minutes per side. Transfer to cutting board and tent with aluminum foil. Repeat with 1 tablespoon oil and remaining cutlets.

3. Add onion, bell pepper, and remaining 1 tablespoon oil to now-empty skillet and cook over medium heat until softened, about 5 minutes. Off heat, stir in reserved giardiniera brine and season with salt and pepper to taste.

4. Slice each cutlet on bias into 4 pieces. Place rolls on rimmed baking sheet and layer with giardiniera mixture, chicken, onion mixture, and provolone. Broil until provolone is melted, 1 to 2 minutes. Serve.

OTHER RECIPES TO TRY THAT WILL MAKE GREAT SANDWICHES

- Creamy Chicken Salad with Fresh Herbs (page 54)
- Two Honey Roast Chickens (page 230)
- Crispy Pan-Fried Chicken Cutlets with Tonkatsu Sauce or Garlic-Curry Sauce (page 268)
- Gluten-Free Chicken Parmesan (page 271)
- Grilled Lemon-Parsley Chicken Breasts (page 347)
- Turkey Meatloaf with Ketchup–Brown Sugar Glaze (page 258)
- Italian-Style Turkey Meatballs (page 309)
- Easy Roast Turkey Breast (page 241)
- Smoked Turkey Breast (page 381)

Chicken Parmesan Subs

Serves 4 **Total Time** 45 minutes

Why This Recipe Works Easy enough to pull off for lunch, these chicken subs are crispy, saucy, and satisfying. Using store-bought chicken cutlets meant we didn't have to slice and pound our own. To minimize pans, we used the same skillet to pan-fry the breaded cutlets and then simmer a quick tomato sauce to pour over them. The pan-fried panko coating stayed crisp, even when smothered in sauce and cheese. A brief stint in a hot oven melted the cheese and toasted the rolls. Mangia.

- ½ cup all-purpose flour
- 2 large eggs
- 1½ cups panko bread crumbs
- ½ teaspoon table salt, divided
- ¼ teaspoon pepper, divided
- 4 (3- to 4-ounce) chicken cutlets, ½ inch thick, trimmed
- 5 tablespoons extra-virgin olive oil, divided
- 2 garlic cloves, minced
- 1 (14.5-ounce) can diced tomatoes
- 4 (6-inch) sub rolls, partially split lengthwise
- 4 ounces shredded Italian cheese blend (1 cup)

1. Adjust oven rack to middle position and heat oven to 400 degrees. Spread flour in shallow dish. Beat eggs in second shallow dish. Combine panko, ¼ teaspoon salt, and ⅛ teaspoon pepper in third shallow dish.

2. Pat cutlets dry with paper towels and sprinkle with remaining ¼ teaspoon salt and remaining ⅛ teaspoon pepper. Working with 1 cutlet at a time, dredge in flour, dip in eggs, letting excess drip off, then coat with panko mixture, pressing gently to adhere; transfer to large plate.

3. Heat ¼ cup oil in 12-inch nonstick skillet over medium-high heat until shimmering. Add cutlets, reduce heat to medium, and cook until golden brown and crisp, about 2 minutes per side. Transfer cutlets to paper towel–lined plate.

4. Meanwhile, heat remaining 1 tablespoon oil in medium saucepan over medium-high heat until shimmering. Add garlic and cook until fragrant, about 30 seconds. Stir in tomatoes and their juice and simmer until slightly thickened, about 7 minutes. Mash mixture until only small chunks of tomato remain. Season with salt and pepper to taste.

Chicken Parmesan Subs

5. Place rolls on rimmed baking sheet. Slice each cutlet on bias into 4 pieces (16 pieces total). Lay 4 pieces of cutlet inside each roll. Cover cutlets with tomato sauce, then sprinkle with cheese. Bake until cheese is melted, 3 to 5 minutes. Serve.

VARIATION
Chicken Cordon Bleu Subs

Omit garlic, tomatoes, and Italian cheese blend and skip step 4. Reduce oil to ¼ cup. Combine ¼ cup Dijon mustard and 2 tablespoons mayonnaise in bowl and whisk until smooth. In step 5, after slicing cutlets, spread mustard mixture on cut sides of each roll. Lay 2 slices deli ham on top, then 4 slices chicken, and finish with 2 slices deli Swiss cheese. Add roll tops and press rolls closed. Bake as directed.

Barbecue Chicken Sandwiches with Quick Buttermilk Coleslaw

Serves 4   Total Time 45 minutes

Why This Recipe Works A sandwich filled with smoky chicken smothered in a thick barbecue sauce and coleslaw is an American favorite. This simplified version translates the recipe from the grill to the stovetop. The barbecue sauce acts as a shield for the chicken as it cooks, allowing it to absorb as much sweet and spicy flavor as possible without drying out. Browning the chicken first on one side created fond in the bottom of the pan, which added depth to the pan sauce. Cooking the chicken in butter instead of oil added more richness to the sauce. After the chicken was cooked, we shredded it using two forks. Some vinegar balanced the sweetness of the barbecue sauce with a sharp flavor, and cut through the creamy coleslaw. We prefer our Basic Barbecue Sauce (page 386) in this recipe, but you can use store-bought sauce.

- 4 (6- to 8-ounce) boneless, skinless chicken breasts, trimmed
- ½ teaspoon table salt
- ¼ teaspoon pepper
- 3 tablespoons unsalted butter
- ¾ cup barbecue sauce
- ½ cup plus 1 tablespoon cider vinegar, divided
- 1 tablespoon hot sauce, plus extra for serving
- ½ cup mayonnaise
- ½ cup buttermilk
- 1 (16-ounce) bag shredded coleslaw mix
- 4 hamburger buns, toasted if desired
- ¼ cup bread-and-butter pickle chips

1. Pound chicken breasts to uniform thickness. Pat chicken dry with paper towels and sprinkle with salt and pepper. Melt butter in 12-inch skillet over medium-high heat. Add chicken and cook until lightly browned on first side, about 4 minutes. Flip chicken, stir in barbecue sauce, ½ cup vinegar, and hot sauce, and bring to simmer. Reduce heat to medium-low, cover, and cook until chicken registers 160 degrees, about 10 minutes, flipping chicken halfway through cooking.

2. Transfer chicken to cutting board, let cool slightly, then shred into bite-size pieces using 2 forks. Continue to simmer sauce until thickened, about 3 minutes. Add chicken and toss to combine.

3. Meanwhile, combine mayonnaise, buttermilk, and remaining 1 tablespoon vinegar in large bowl. Stir in coleslaw mix and season with salt and pepper. Serve chicken on buns, topped with coleslaw, pickles, and extra hot sauce.

Texas-Size Barbecue Chicken and Cheddar Sandwiches

Serves 4   Total Time 45 minutes

Why This Recipe Works The combination of bacon, cheddar, chicken, chile, and barbecue sauce ensures that these big, hot, toasty, oven-baked sandwiches also pack Texas-size flavor. We fried bacon until crisp, then browned boneless chicken breasts in some of the rendered fat before finishing them in barbecue sauce mixed with minced chipotle chile in adobo and a splash of water. Once the chicken had cooled, we cut the breasts into pieces and arranged them on rolls. After topping each sandwich with the barbecue sauce mixture, bacon, and shredded cheddar, we baked them open-faced until the cheese melted. With the roll tops back on, the sandwiches were ready to eat. We prefer our Basic Barbecue Sauce (page 386) in this recipe, but you can use store-bought sauce.

- 4 slices bacon, halved crosswise
- 4 (6- to 8-ounce) boneless, skinless chicken breasts, trimmed
- ½ teaspoon table salt
- ¼ teaspoon pepper
- 1 cup barbecue sauce
- 1 teaspoon minced canned chipotle chile in adobo sauce
- ¼ cup water
- 4 deli-style onion rolls, split
- 6 ounces cheddar cheese, shredded (1½ cups)

1. Adjust oven rack to upper-middle position and heat oven to 400 degrees. Cook bacon in 12-inch nonstick skillet over medium-high heat until crispy, about 5 minutes. Using slotted spoon, transfer bacon to paper towel–lined plate. Pour off all but 1 tablespoon fat left in skillet.

2. Pound chicken breasts to uniform thickness. Pat chicken dry with paper towels and sprinkle with salt and pepper. Add chicken to fat left in skillet and cook over medium-high heat until lightly browned on 1 side, about 4 minutes. Flip chicken, stir in barbecue sauce, chipotle, and water, and bring to simmer. Reduce heat to medium-low, cover, and cook until chicken registers 160 degrees and sauce has thickened, about 10 minutes, flipping chicken halfway through cooking.

3. Transfer chicken to cutting board, let cool slightly, then cut crosswise ¼ inch thick.

4. Arrange roll halves cut side up on rimmed baking sheet. Divide chicken among bottom halves of rolls and top with sauce, cheddar, and bacon. Bake open-faced sandwiches in oven until cheese is melted and rolls are lightly toasted, about 4 minutes. Place toasted roll tops on top of sandwiches and serve.

Indoor Pulled Chicken with Sweet and Tangy Barbecue Sauce

Serves 6 to 8   **Total Time** 1 hour

Why This Recipe Works Traditional outdoor barbecued pulled chicken is a beautiful thing, but requires wood, smoke, and time (page 357). For a weeknight sandwich, we turned to this recipe for chicken braised indoors in a smoky barbecue sauce. To keep things as simple as possible, we used boneless chicken thighs, which turn moist and tender during braising, leaving them untrimmed to make use of their rich, flavorful fat. Recreating the smoky flavor of wood chips proved as easy as adding some liquid smoke, which is an all-natural ingredient made from real woodsmoke. We found when simmering our chicken in barbecue sauce that the result lacked concentrated chicken-y flavor and the sauce was thin. So instead of adding our sauce at the start we simmered the chicken in a smaller amount of chicken broth flavored with sugar, salt, molasses for its bittersweet notes, the liquid smoke, and some gelatin to give the sauce body. The sugar and salt seasoned the chicken as it cooked, infusing the meat with the taste of a brined, slowly smoked bird. After shredding the chicken, we reheated it with a little barbecue sauce and some of the braising liquid, and a bit more liquid smoke, before piling it into buns. Do not trim the fat from the chicken thighs; it contributes to the flavor and texture of the pulled chicken. If you don't have 3 tablespoons of fat to add back to the pot in step 4, add melted butter to make up the difference. We like mild molasses in this recipe; do not use blackstrap. Serve on white bread or hamburger buns with pickles and coleslaw.

Barbecue Sauce

1½ cups ketchup
¼ cup molasses
2 tablespoons Worcestershire sauce
1 tablespoon hot sauce
½ teaspoon table salt
½ teaspoon pepper

Chicken

1 cup chicken broth
2 tablespoons molasses
1 tablespoon sugar
1 tablespoon liquid smoke, divided
1 teaspoon unflavored gelatin
1 teaspoon table salt
2 pounds boneless, skinless chicken thighs, halved crosswise
Hot sauce

Indoor Pulled Chicken with Sweet and Tangy Barbecue Sauce

1. For the sauce Whisk all ingredients together in bowl. Set aside.

2. For the chicken Bring broth, molasses, sugar, 2 teaspoons liquid smoke, gelatin, and salt to boil in Dutch oven over high heat, stirring to dissolve sugar. Add chicken and return to simmer. Reduce heat to medium-low, cover, and cook, stirring occasionally, until chicken is easily shredded with fork, about 25 minutes.

3. Transfer chicken to medium bowl and set aside. Strain cooking liquid through fine-mesh strainer set over bowl (do not wash pot). Let liquid settle for 5 minutes; skim fat from surface. Set aside fat and defatted liquid.

4. Using tongs, squeeze chicken until shredded into bite-size pieces. Transfer chicken, 1 cup barbecue sauce, ½ cup reserved defatted liquid, 3 tablespoons reserved fat, and remaining 1 teaspoon liquid smoke to now-empty pot. Cook mixture over medium heat, stirring frequently, until liquid has been absorbed and exterior of meat appears dry, about 5 minutes. Season with salt, pepper, and hot sauce to taste. Serve, passing remaining barbecue sauce separately.

Indoor Pulled Chicken with Lexington Vinegar Barbecue Sauce

Omit sauce ingredients. Whisk together 1 cup cider vinegar, ½ cup ketchup, ½ cup water, 1 tablespoon sugar, ¾ teaspoon table salt, ¾ teaspoon red pepper flakes, and ½ teaspoon pepper in bowl; set aside. Proceed with step 2.

Indoor Pulled Chicken with South Carolina Mustard Barbecue Sauce

Omit sauce ingredients. Whisk together 1 cup yellow mustard, ½ cup distilled white vinegar, ¼ cup packed brown sugar, ¼ cup Worcestershire sauce, 2 tablespoons hot sauce, 1 teaspoon table salt, and 1 teaspoon pepper in bowl; set aside. Proceed with step 2.

NOTES FROM THE TEST KITCHEN

NO BONES ABOUT COOKING WITH GELATIN
When bone-in chicken is braised, the collagen in its skin, bones, and tendons breaks down to form gelatin, giving the liquid a luxurious texture. But when braising boneless chicken how could we avoid a watery sauce? The answer was simply to add powdered gelatin. To be sure the gelatin properly activated, we added it to liquid that was still cool so it hydrated properly (gelatin granules added directly to hot liquid will hydrate too quickly and their interiors will remain undissolved). Then, as we heated the liquid, the protein in the gelatin dissolved. As the liquid eventually cooled, the proteins tangled together, producing the unctuousness that we love in a great sauce.

Sloppy Janes

Serves 4   **Total Time** 45 minutes

Why This Recipe Works This lighter take on the classic sloppy joe trades beef for ground turkey or chicken and brings a more balanced, less sweet flavor. Cooking the ground poultry until just pink—not browned—before adding the sauce ensured that the meat stayed tender. Combining tomato puree and ketchup yielded a sufficiently sweet, rich tomato base. Flavoring the filling with garlic, chili powder, and hot pepper sauce gave the Sloppy Janes some heat to balance their sweetness. Be sure to use ground turkey or chicken, not ground turkey or chicken breast (also labeled 99 percent fat-free),

in this recipe. Be careful not to cook the meat beyond pink in step 1; if you let it brown it will end up dry and crumbly. Serve with your favorite pickles.

- 2 tablespoons vegetable oil
- 1 onion, chopped fine
- ½ teaspoon table salt
- 2 cloves garlic, minced
- ½ teaspoon chili powder
- 1 pound ground turkey or chicken
- 1 cup tomato puree
- ½ cup ketchup
- ¼ cup water
- 1 teaspoon packed brown sugar
- ¼ teaspoon pepper
- ¼ teaspoon hot sauce
- 4 hamburger buns, toasted if desired

1. Heat oil in 12-inch skillet over medium heat until shimmering. Add onion and salt and cook until softened and lightly browned, 5 to 7 minutes. Stir in garlic and chili powder and cook until fragrant, about 30 seconds. Add turkey and cook, breaking up meat with wooden spoon, until just pink, about 3 minutes.

2. Stir in tomato puree, ketchup, water, sugar, pepper, and hot sauce. Bring to simmer and cook, stirring occasionally, until sauce is slightly thicker than ketchup, 8 to 10 minutes. Season with salt and pepper to taste. Spoon meat mixture onto buns and serve.

Fried Chicken Sandwiches

Serves 4   **Total Time** 1¾ hours

Why This Recipe Works This fried chicken sandwich blows the feathers off of fast-food versions. It boasts a craggy coating, properly spiced chicken, and crisp—not limp—toppings on a sturdy mayo-slicked bun. After testing different thicknesses of chicken, we found that breasts that we'd halved crosswise and gently pounded to ½ inch thick cooked through in the time it took our coating to brown properly. A few tablespoons of water in our flour coating created the craggy effect we wanted, and a teaspoon of baking powder made the coating supercrispy. Beaten egg whites helped the coating adhere. Letting the breaded chicken sit for 30 minutes before frying helped the coating set up and enabled the salty spice rub to season the meat throughout. A sturdy potato bun and a few simple toppings took this sandwich to the finish line. Use a Dutch oven that holds 6 quarts or more.

Fried Chicken Sandwiches

Chicken Souvlaki

1 teaspoon paprika
1 teaspoon pepper
1 teaspoon garlic powder
¾ teaspoon table salt
½ teaspoon dried thyme
½ teaspoon dried sage
¼ teaspoon cayenne pepper
2 (6- to 8-ounce) boneless, skinless chicken breasts, trimmed
1½ cups all-purpose flour
1 teaspoon baking powder
3 tablespoons water
2 large egg whites, lightly beaten
2 quarts peanut or vegetable oil for frying
¼ cup mayonnaise
4 hamburger buns, toasted if desired
1 cup shredded iceberg lettuce
½ red onion, sliced thin
¼ cup dill pickle chips

1. Combine paprika, pepper, garlic powder, salt, thyme, sage, and cayenne in bowl. Measure out 1 tablespoon spice mixture and set aside. Cut each breast in half crosswise, then pound each piece to uniform ½-inch thickness. Pat chicken dry with paper towels and sprinkle with remaining 2 teaspoons spice mixture.

2. Whisk flour, baking powder, and reserved spice mixture together in large bowl. Add water to flour mixture and rub together with your fingers until water is evenly incorporated and shaggy pieces form. Place egg whites in shallow dish.

3. Set wire rack in rimmed baking sheet. Working with 1 piece of chicken at a time, dip in egg whites to thoroughly coat, letting excess drip back into dish, then dredge in flour mixture, pressing to adhere. Transfer chicken to prepared rack and refrigerate for at least 30 minutes or up to 1 hour.

4. Line second rimmed baking sheet with triple layer of paper towels. Add oil to large Dutch oven until it measures about 1½ inches deep and heat over medium-high heat to 375 degrees. Add chicken to hot oil and fry, stirring gently to prevent pieces from sticking together, until chicken is golden brown and registers 160 degrees, 4 to 5 minutes, flipping halfway through frying. Adjust burner, if necessary, to maintain oil temperature between 325 and 350 degrees. Transfer chicken to prepared sheet and let cool for 5 minutes.

5. Spread mayonnaise over bun tops. Serve burgers on buns, topped with lettuce, onion, and pickles.

Chicken Souvlaki

Serves 4 to 6   **Total Time** 1½ hours

Why This Recipe Works Souvlaki is a Greek specialty consisting of chunks of marinated meat threaded onto skewers, sometimes with chunks of vegetables such as green pepper and onion, and grilled. Chicken souvlaki is almost always made with boneless, skinless breasts, which have a marked tendency to dry out when grilled. To prevent this, we swapped the traditional overnight soak in an acidic marinade for a quick 30-minute brine while the grill heated. We then tossed the chunks of chicken with a classic and flavorful mixture of lemon, olive oil, herbs, and honey right before grilling. To prevent the end pieces from overcooking, we protected the chicken by threading pepper and onion pieces on the ends of the skewers. Once the chicken was cooked, we tossed it with the reserved marinade to ensure that the exterior was brightly flavored and just as tender and moist as the interior. We finished the sandwich with a traditional Greek yogurt sauce known as tzatziki, which is made from strained yogurt, cucumber, garlic, and herbs. Using Greek yogurt here is key; do not substitute regular plain yogurt or the sauce will be very watery. We like the chicken in a wrap, but you may skip the pita and serve the chicken with vegetables, tzatziki, and rice. If using kosher chicken, do not brine in step 2. You will need four 12-inch metal skewers for this recipe.

Tzatziki
- ½ cucumber, peeled, halved lengthwise, seeded, and shredded
- ¼ teaspoon table salt
- ½ cup whole-milk Greek yogurt
- 1 tablespoon extra-virgin olive oil
- 1 tablespoon minced fresh mint and/or dill
- 1 small garlic clove, minced

Chicken
- 2 tablespoons table salt for brining
- 1½ pounds boneless, skinless chicken breasts, trimmed and cut into 1-inch pieces
- ⅓ cup extra-virgin olive oil
- 2 tablespoons minced fresh parsley
- 1 teaspoon finely grated lemon zest plus ¼ cup juice (2 lemons)
- 1 teaspoon honey
- 1 teaspoon dried oregano
- ½ teaspoon pepper

- 1 green bell pepper, quartered, stemmed, seeded, and each quarter cut into 4 pieces
- 1 small red onion, halved through root end, each half cut into 4 pieces
- 4–6 (8-inch) pita breads

1. For the tzatziki Toss cucumber with salt in colander and let drain for 15 minutes. Whisk yogurt, oil, mint, and garlic together in bowl, then stir in drained cucumber. Season with salt and pepper to taste. Cover and refrigerate until chilled, at least 1 hour or up to 2 days.

2. For the chicken Dissolve salt in 1 quart cold water in large container. Submerge chicken in brine, cover, and refrigerate for 30 minutes. Combine oil, parsley, lemon zest and juice, honey, oregano, and pepper in medium bowl. Reserve ¼ cup oil mixture in large bowl.

3. Remove chicken from brine and pat dry with paper towels. Toss chicken with remaining oil mixture. Thread 4 pieces of bell pepper, concave side up, onto one 12-inch metal skewer. Thread one-quarter of chicken onto skewer. Thread 2 chunks of onion onto skewer and place skewer on plate. Repeat skewering remaining chicken and vegetables on 3 more skewers. Lightly moisten 2 pita breads with water. Sandwich unmoistened pitas between moistened pitas and wrap stack tightly in lightly greased heavy-duty aluminum foil.

4A. For a charcoal grill Open bottom vent completely. Light large chimney starter mounded with charcoal briquettes (7 quarts). When top coals are partially covered with ash, pour evenly over half of grill. Set cooking grate in place, cover, and open lid vent completely. Heat grill until hot, about 5 minutes.

4B. For a gas grill Turn all burners to high, cover, and heat grill until hot, about 15 minutes. Leave primary burner on high and turn off other burner(s).

5. Clean and oil cooking grate. Place skewers on hotter side of grill and cook, turning occasionally, until chicken and vegetables are well browned and chicken registers 160 degrees, 15 to 20 minutes. Using tongs, slide chicken and vegetables off skewers into bowl of reserved oil mixture. Toss gently, breaking up onion chunks. Cover loosely with foil and let sit while heating pitas.

6. Place packet of pitas on cooler side of grill and flip occasionally until heated through, about 5 minutes. Lay each warm pita on 12-inch square of foil. Spread each pita with 2 tablespoons yogurt sauce. Place one-quarter of chicken and vegetables in middle of each pita. Roll into cylindrical shape and serve.

Chicken Spiedies

Classic
Turkey
Burgers

Chicken Spiedies
Serves 6   Total Time 1½ hours

Why This Recipe Works A grilled sandwich popular in upstate New York, the spiedie (pronounced "speedy") gets its named from spiedo, Italian for spit. Cubed chicken (or other meat) sits in an acidic, highly seasoned marinade for up to a week before being skewered and grilled. We wanted to update this custom by creating a marinade that imparted tangy, bright flavor without the wait. Pricking the chicken with a fork before marinating allowed the flavor to penetrate the meat in only 30 minutes. A potent, oil-based marinade kept the chicken moist on the grill, and a drizzle of reserved marinade mixed with lemon juice, vinegar, and mayonnaise reinforced our spiedies' trademark flavors before serving. With these small changes, we had a zesty, full-flavored sandwich ready for dinner in less than 2 hours. You will need six 12-inch metal skewers for this recipe.

½ cup extra-virgin olive oil
2 tablespoons chopped fresh basil
2 garlic cloves, minced
2 teaspoons grated lemon zest plus
    1 tablespoon juice
1 teaspoon table salt
½ teaspoon pepper
½ teaspoon dried oregano
¼ teaspoon red pepper flakes
3 tablespoons mayonnaise
1 tablespoon red wine vinegar
4 (6- to 8-ounce) boneless, skinless
    chicken breasts, trimmed
6 (6-inch) sub rolls, partially split
    lengthwise, or 6 large slices Italian
    bread, toasted if desired

1. Combine oil, basil, garlic, lemon zest, salt, pepper, oregano, and pepper flakes in large bowl. Transfer 2 tablespoons oil mixture to separate bowl and whisk in mayonnaise, vinegar, and lemon juice; refrigerate until ready to serve. (Marinade and sauce can each be refrigerated, covered, for up to 2 days.)

2. Prick breasts all over with fork, cut into 1¼-inch chunks, and transfer to bowl with remaining oil mixture. Refrigerate, covered, for 30 minutes or up to 3 hours.

3. Remove chicken from marinade and thread chunks onto six 12-inch metal skewers.

4A. For a charcoal grill Open bottom vent completely. Light large chimney starter filled with charcoal briquettes (6 quarts). When top coals are partially covered with ash, pour evenly over grill. Set cooking grate in place, cover, and open lid vent completely. Heat grill until hot, about 5 minutes.

4B. For a gas grill Turn all burners to high, cover, and heat grill until hot, about 15 minutes. Leave all burners on high.

5. Clean and oil cooking grate. Place skewers on grill and cook (covered if using gas), turning frequently, until lightly charred and cooked through, 10 to 15 minutes.

6. Transfer chicken to rolls, remove skewers, and drizzle with mayonnaise mixture. Serve.

Classic Turkey Burgers

Serves 4   **Total Time** 45 minutes

Why This Recipe Works A great turkey burger (or chicken burger, for that matter) is light, juicy, savory, and tender. Your average version is more likely to be lean, dry, and poorly seasoned. Ground poultry doesn't cook the same as ground beef. First of all, it's leaner, but also wetter, yet it easily ends up dry since it must be cooked to a higher temperature (160 degrees) than beef. To mitigate dryness, we avoided buying ground breast-only meat in favor of ground turkey or chicken, which contains a mix of white and dark meat. Melted butter added richness and ensured moist, juicy burgers, while a bit of Worcestershire sauce and Dijon mustard added pleasant tang to the mild meat. Burger patties typically bulge as they cook; pressing a slight divot in the patty helped our burgers stay flat. Be sure to use ground turkey or chicken, not ground turkey or chicken breast (also labeled 99 percent fat-free), in this recipe. You can serve these burgers simply with classic condiments, burger sauces (page 94), lettuce, and/or sliced ripe tomatoes.

- 1½ pounds ground turkey or chicken
- 2 tablespoons unsalted butter, melted and cooled
- 2 teaspoons Worcestershire sauce
- 2 teaspoons Dijon mustard
- ½ teaspoon table salt
- ¼ teaspoon pepper
- 2 teaspoons vegetable oil
- 4 slices cheese (4 ounces) (optional)
- 4 hamburger buns, toasted if desired

1. Break ground turkey into small pieces in large bowl. Add melted butter, Worcestershire, and mustard and gently knead with your hands until well combined. Divide turkey mixture into 4 equal portions, then gently shape each portion into ¾-inch-thick patty. Using your fingertips, press center of each patty down until about ½ inch thick, creating slight divot.

2. Sprinkle patties with salt and pepper. Heat oil in 12-inch skillet over medium heat until just smoking. Transfer patties to skillet, divot side up, and cook until well browned on first side, 4 to 6 minutes. Flip patties, top with cheese, if using, and continue to cook until browned on second side and meat registers 160 degrees, 5 to 7 minutes. Transfer burgers to platter and let rest for 5 minutes. Serve burgers on buns.

SHAPING AND COOKING TURKEY AND CHICKEN BURGERS

1. Break ground poultry into small pieces before gently kneading in seasonings.

2. Divide meat mixture into equal portions and gently shape into ¾-inch-thick patties.

3. Using your fingertips, press divots into center of each patty to prevent bulging.

4. Season with salt on outside only to avoid toughening meat and grill or pan-cook, flipping only once.

Turkey Burgers with Sun-Dried Tomatoes, Goat Cheese, and Balsamic Glaze

Serves 4   Total Time 45 minutes

Why This Recipe Works These bright-tasting burgers are infused with deep tomato flavor from sun-dried tomatoes. Adding some of the oil from the jarred tomatoes, along with a little butter, helped keep the turkey moist while the patties cooked. The tomatoes added umami and sweetness to the delicate turkey with the added benefit of providing a pleasing textural contrast to the meat. Minced shallot and some fresh oregano imparted an aromatic depth. At this point, we had the makings of a burger with a delicious Italian flavor profile; with that in mind, we reduced some balsamic vinegar to a concentrated glaze that popped with fruity acidity. The glaze cut through the tang of the creamy goat cheese, which we spread on the burger buns. A final topping of baby arugula added a peppery bite to our elegant-but-easy, full-flavored turkey burgers. Be sure to use ground turkey or chicken, not ground turkey or chicken breast (also labeled 99 percent fat-free), in this recipe.

⅓ cup balsamic vinegar

1¼ pounds ground turkey or chicken

⅓ cup oil-packed sun-dried tomatoes, chopped, plus 1 tablespoon packing oil

1 shallot, minced

2 tablespoons unsalted butter, melted and cooled

1 teaspoon chopped fresh oregano

¼ teaspoon pepper

½ teaspoon table salt

2 teaspoons vegetable oil

2 ounces goat cheese, crumbled (½ cup), room temperature

4 hamburger buns, toasted if desired

1½ ounces (1½ cups) baby arugula

1. Bring vinegar to simmer in small saucepan over medium heat and cook until reduced to 2 tablespoons, 5 to 7 minutes; set aside.

2. Break ground turkey into small pieces in large bowl. Add tomatoes and packing oil, shallot, melted butter, oregano, and pepper and gently knead with your hands until well combined. Divide chicken mixture into 4 equal portions, then gently shape each portion into ¾-inch-thick patty. Using your fingertips, press center of each patty down until about ½ inch thick, creating slight divot.

3. Sprinkle patties with salt. Heat oil in 12-inch nonstick skillet over medium heat until just smoking. Transfer patties to skillet, divot side up, and cook until well browned on first side, 4 to 6 minutes. Flip patties, reduce heat to medium-low, and continue to cook until browned on second side and meat registers 160 degrees, 5 to 7 minutes. Transfer burgers to platter and let rest for 5 minutes. Spread goat cheese over bun tops. Serve burgers on buns, topped with arugula and drizzled with balsamic reduction.

Buffalo Turkey Burgers

Serves 4   Total Time 45 minutes

Why This Recipe Works To translate the flavors of buffalo wings into a great burger, we started off with ground turkey and then added some Worcestershire and shallot for umami; melted butter helped keep the patties moist during cooking. Conventional buffalo sauce is comprised of some combination of butter and hot sauce. For a bold sauce that would be cohesive enough to cling to our patties, we added cornstarch and molasses to the mix. In a nod to the classic buffalo accompaniment, we topped our burgers with thinly sliced celery along with the delicate leaves, which brought pleasing crispness and refreshing contrast. If the delicate leaves attached to the celery stalks are not available, you can omit them. We prefer a mild blue cheese, such as Gorgonzola, in this recipe. Be sure to use ground turkey or chicken, not ground turkey or chicken breast (also labeled 99 percent fat-free) in this recipe.

4 tablespoons unsalted butter, plus 2 tablespoons melted and cooled, divided

6 tablespoons hot sauce

1 tablespoon molasses

½ teaspoon cornstarch

1½ pounds ground turkey or chicken

1 large shallot, minced

2 teaspoons Worcestershire sauce

¼ teaspoon pepper

½ teaspoon table salt

2 teaspoons vegetable oil

4 leaves Bibb or Boston lettuce

4 hamburger buns, toasted if desired

2 ounces mild blue cheese, crumbled (½ cup), room temperature

1 celery rib, sliced thin on bias, plus ¼ cup celery leaves

1. Microwave 4 tablespoons butter, hot sauce, molasses, and cornstarch in bowl, whisking occasionally, until butter is melted and mixture has thickened slightly, 2 to 3 minutes; cover to keep warm and set aside.

2. Break ground turkey into small pieces in large bowl. Add remaining 2 tablespoons melted butter, shallot, Worcestershire, and pepper and gently knead with your hands until well combined. Divide chicken mixture into 4 equal portions, then gently shape each portion into ¾-inch-thick patty. Using your fingertips, press center of each patty down until about ½ inch thick, creating slight divot.

3. Sprinkle patties with salt. Heat oil in 12-inch nonstick skillet over medium heat until just smoking. Transfer patties to skillet, divot side up, and cook until well browned on first side, 4 to 6 minutes. Flip patties, reduce heat to medium-low, and continue to cook until browned on second side and meat registers 160 degrees, 5 to 7 minutes. Transfer burgers to platter, brush with half of buffalo sauce, and let rest for 5 minutes.

4. Arrange lettuce on bun bottoms. Serve burgers on buns, topped with blue cheese, celery, and celery leaves, passing extra buffalo sauce separately.

Crispy California Turkey Burgers

Serves 4   **Total Time** 45 minutes

Why This Recipe Works California has a reputation for embracing the latest health food crazes, and while we don't usually reach for a burger when we're watching our diet, it's hard to deny that avocado and fresh sprouts make fine burger toppings. For a West Coast–style burger, we paired these toppings with turkey burgers. Mixing some Monterey Jack into the lean turkey meat helped the burgers stay moist during cooking, giving us patties with juicy pockets of fat to yield a melting interior texture; the cheese also crisped around the edges of the burger, creating a pleasantly crunchy crust. Adding panko and a little mayonnaise to the turkey mixture kept the burgers from becoming too dense. We loaded the cooked burgers with creamy avocado and tender alfalfa sprouts, and also included some crisp red onion and lettuce for even more freshness. To finish, we slathered some sweet-savory classic burger sauce over simple buns before topping them off. Be sure to use ground turkey or chicken, not ground turkey or chicken breast (also labeled 99 percent fat-free), in this recipe.

Crispy California
Turkey Burgers

Turkey Burgers with Sun-Dried Tomatoes, Goat Cheese, and Balsamic Glaze

1 pound ground turkey or chicken
1 cup panko bread crumbs
2 ounces Monterey Jack cheese, shredded (½ cup)
¼ cup mayonnaise
¼ teaspoon pepper
½ teaspoon table salt
2 teaspoons vegetable oil
½ cup Classic Burger Sauce (page 94), plus extra for serving
4 hamburger buns, toasted if desired
4 leaves Bibb or Boston lettuce
1 tomato, cored and sliced thin
1 ripe avocado, halved, pitted, and sliced ¼ inch thick
¼ cup alfalfa sprouts
½ red onion, sliced thin

1. Break ground turkey into small pieces in large bowl. Add panko, Monterey Jack, mayonnaise, and pepper and gently knead with your hands until well combined. Divide turkey mixture into 4 equal portions, then gently shape each portion into ¾-inch-thick patty. Using your fingertips, press center of each patty down until about ½ inch thick, creating slight divot.

2. Sprinkle patties with salt. Heat oil in 12-inch nonstick skillet over medium heat until just smoking. Transfer patties to skillet, divot side up, and cook until well browned on first side, 4 to 6 minutes. Flip patties, reduce heat to medium-low, and continue to cook until browned on second side and meat registers 160 degrees, 5 to 7 minutes. Transfer burgers to platter and let rest for 5 minutes.

3. Spread burger sauce over bun tops and arrange lettuce on bun bottoms. Serve burgers on buns, topped with tomato, avocado, alfalfa sprouts, and onion, passing extra burger sauce separately.

Spiced Turkey Burgers with Mango Chutney

Serves 4   Total Time 45 minutes

Why This Recipe Works Sweet, spicy, fruity, and jammy, mango chutney is a powerhouse ingredient common in Indian cuisine that can liven up even the most mild-mannered of dishes. To complement the chutney we added some garam masala to the ground turkey, as well as a pinch of cayenne for a little fire. Stirring a little melted butter into the turkey mixture prevented the meat from drying out during cooking, and some Worcestershire added extra meaty flavor. A little mayonnaise generally goes a long way on a burger, but we

Spiced Turkey Burgers with Mango Chutney

opted for creamy Greek yogurt instead, which nicely complemented the other components. We piled on some crunchy red onion for its savory allium flavor and sprigs of cilantro for a final fresh note. Be sure to use ground turkey or chicken, not ground turkey or chicken breast (also labeled 99 percent fat-free), in this recipe.

1½ pounds ground turkey or chicken
2 tablespoons unsalted butter, melted and cooled
2 teaspoons Worcestershire sauce
1 teaspoon garam masala
¼ teaspoon pepper
⅛ teaspoon cayenne pepper
½ teaspoon table salt
2 teaspoons vegetable oil
¼ cup plain Greek yogurt
4 hamburger buns, toasted if desired
4 leaves Bibb or Boston lettuce
¼ cup mango chutney
½ red onion, sliced thin
12 fresh cilantro sprigs, trimmed and cut into 2-inch pieces

1. Break ground turkey into small pieces in large bowl. Add melted butter, Worcestershire, garam masala, pepper, and cayenne and gently knead with your hands until well combined. Divide turkey mixture into 4 equal portions, then gently shape each portion into ¾-inch-thick patty. Using your fingertips, press center of each patty down until about ½ inch thick, creating slight divot.

2. Sprinkle patties with salt. Heat oil in 12-inch nonstick skillet over medium heat until shimmering. Transfer patties to skillet, divot side up, and cook until well browned on first side, 4 to 6 minutes. Flip patties, reduce heat to medium-low, and continue to cook until browned on second side and meat registers 160 degrees, 5 to 7 minutes. Transfer burgers to platter and let rest for 5 minutes.

3. Spread yogurt over bun bottoms and arrange lettuce on top. Serve burgers on buns, topped with chutney, onion, and cilantro.

Brie-Stuffed Turkey Burgers with Red Pepper Relish

Serves 4   **Total Time** 1½ hours

Why This Recipe Works There isn't a more indulgent and comforting bistro starter than baked Brie with a sweet conserve, and we thought this combination of flavors and textures could make for a unique and truly decadent stuffed turkey burger. But we soon learned that there were two challenges to pulling off such a feat: getting the cheese to melt enough, but not too much, and distributing it evenly throughout the burger. We first tried simply packing some brie into our turkey patty and found that it melted very quickly, oozing out of the not-yet-cooked patties and leaving us with an empty cavern of departed cheese. Brie melts at around 130 degrees Fahrenheit, but the turkey patties would need to reach 160 degrees before they were fully cooked through. We next wrapped the cheese in two portions of the burger mixture and refrigerated the patties until the cheese center was fully chilled. This worked perfectly, delaying the cheese's melting long enough for the burgers to cook through. As a perfect foil for the richness of the cheese, we topped the burgers with a spicy-sweet-tangy relish made from a combination of bell and jalapeño pepper, plus a tangle of fresh, crisp frisée lettuce. Be sure to use ground turkey or chicken, not ground turkey or chicken breast (also labeled 99 percent fat-free), in this recipe.

Brie-Stuffed Turkey Burgers with Red Pepper Relish

Relish

- 1 red bell pepper, stemmed, seeded, and cut into 1-inch pieces
- 1 jalapeño chile, stemmed, seeded, and cut into 1-inch pieces
- ⅓ cup chopped onion
- 1 garlic clove, peeled
- ¼ cup distilled white vinegar
- ¼ cup sugar
- ½ teaspoon yellow mustard seeds
- ¼ teaspoon table salt

Burgers

- 4 ounces Brie cheese, rind removed, cut into ½-inch pieces
- 1½ pounds ground turkey or chicken
- 2 tablespoons unsalted butter, melted and cooled
- 2 teaspoons Worcestershire sauce
- ¼ teaspoon pepper
- ½ teaspoon table salt
- 2 teaspoons vegetable oil
- 4 hamburger buns, toasted if desired
- ½ head frisée lettuce (3 ounces), leaves separated

1. For the relish Pulse bell pepper and jalapeño in food processor until coarsely chopped into ¼-inch pieces, 6 to 8 pulses; transfer to bowl. Pulse onion and garlic in now-empty food processor until coarsely chopped into ¼-inch pieces, about 8 pulses; transfer to bowl with bell pepper mixture.

2. Bring vinegar, sugar, mustard seeds, and salt to boil in large saucepan over medium-high heat. Add vegetable mixture, reduce heat to medium, and simmer, stirring occasionally, until mixture has thickened, about 15 minutes. Let relish cool slightly, then transfer to bowl and let cool to room temperature, about 10 minutes. (Relish can be refrigerated for up to 3 months; flavor will deepen over time.)

3. For the burgers Divide Brie into 4 equal portions; using your hands, mash each portion together into rough 2-inch disk. Break ground turkey into small pieces in large bowl. Add melted butter, Worcestershire, and pepper and gently knead with hands until well combined. Divide turkey mixture into 8 equal portions. Encase each disk of cheese with 1 portion of turkey mixture to form mini burger patty. Mold second portion of turkey around each mini patty and seal edges to form ball. Flatten ball to form ¾-inch-thick patty. Cover and refrigerate patties for at least 30 minutes or up to 24 hours.

4. Sprinkle patties with salt. Heat oil in 12-inch nonstick skillet over medium heat until shimmering. Transfer patties to skillet and cook until well browned on first side, 5 to 7 minutes. Flip patties, reduce heat to medium-low, and continue to cook until browned on second side and meat registers 160 degrees, 5 to 7 minutes. Transfer burgers to platter and let rest for 5 minutes. Serve burgers on buns, topped with relish and lettuce.

Turkey-Veggie Burgers with Lemon-Basil Sauce

Serves 4   **Total Time** 45 minutes

Why This Recipe Works Packed with a combo of shredded zucchini and carrot, this great-tasting turkey burger is moist, flavorful, and nutritious. The vegetables didn't require any precooking—adding them raw to the ground turkey gave us the juiciest results. A little grated Parmesan provided a savory balance to the sweetness of the vegetables while an easy, bright sauce made with mayo and yogurt plus lemon and basil added a rich finishing touch. Use the large holes of a box grater to shred the zucchini and carrot. Be sure to use ground turkey or chicken, not ground turkey or chicken breast (also labeled 99 percent fat-free), in this recipe.

Turkey-Veggie Burgers
with Lemon-Basil Sauce

¼ cup mayonnaise

¼ cup plain whole-milk yogurt

2 tablespoons chopped fresh basil

1 tablespoon lemon juice

1 pound ground turkey or chicken

1 small zucchini, shredded (1¼ cups)

1 carrot, peeled and shredded (½ cup)

½ ounce Parmesan cheese, grated (¼ cup)

¼ teaspoon pepper

½ teaspoon table salt

2 teaspoons extra-virgin olive oil

4 hamburger buns, toasted if desired

1. Combine mayonnaise, yogurt, basil, and lemon juice in bowl and season with salt and pepper to taste; cover and refrigerate until ready to serve.

2. Break ground turkey into small pieces in large bowl. Add zucchini, carrot, Parmesan, and pepper and gently knead with your hands until well combined. Divide turkey mixture into 4 equal portions, then gently shape each portion into ¾-inch-thick patty. Using your fingertips, press center of each patty down until about ½ inch thick, creating slight divot.

3. Sprinkle patties with salt. Heat oil in 12-inch nonstick skillet over medium heat until just smoking. Transfer patties to skillet, divot side up, and cook until well browned on first side, 4 to 6 minutes. Flip patties, reduce heat to medium-low, and continue to cook until browned on second side and meat registers 160 degrees, 5 to 7 minutes. Transfer burgers to platter and let rest for 5 minutes. Serve burgers on buns, topped with lemon-basil sauce.

Grilled Turkey Burgers with Spinach and Feta

Serves 4   **Total Time** 1 hour

Why This Recipe Works Turkey burgers on the grill offer a pleasant change from beef; the mild meat benefits from the smoky, flame-kissed flavor. Still, we wanted to start out with patties that had character on their own so we stirred some melted butter and feta cheese into the ground poultry; these simple additions provided plenty of richness and flavor while also preventing the burgers from drying out. For textural interest, we added fresh baby spinach to the meat mixture. Chopped dill lent a hit of freshness, and minced garlic rounded out the flavors. To make sure the patties didn't stick to the grill grates, we cleaned the heated grate with a sturdy grill brush. For further insurance against stuck patties, we grabbed a wad of paper towels with a pair of long-handled tongs and dipped it in a bowl of vegetable oil, then ran it over the cleaned grill grate. Be sure to use ground turkey or chicken, not ground turkey or chicken breast (also labeled 99 percent fat-free), in this recipe.

1¼ pounds ground turkey
  2 ounces (2 cups) baby spinach, chopped
  2 ounces feta cheese, crumbled (½ cup)
  2 tablespoons unsalted butter, melted and cooled
  2 teaspoons minced fresh dill
  1 garlic clove, minced
  ¼ teaspoon pepper
  ½ teaspoon table salt
  4 hamburger buns, toasted if desired

1. Break ground turkey into small pieces in large bowl. Add spinach, feta, melted butter, dill, garlic, and pepper and gently knead with your hands until well combined. Divide turkey mixture into 4 equal portions, then gently shape each portion into ¾-inch-thick patty. Using your fingertips, press center of each patty down until about ½ inch thick, creating slight divot.

2A. For a charcoal grill Open bottom vent completely. Light large chimney starter filled with charcoal briquettes (6 quarts). When top coals are partially covered with ash, pour evenly over grill. Set cooking grate in place, cover, and open lid vent completely. Heat grill until hot, about 5 minutes.

2B. For a gas grill Turn all burners to high, cover, and heat grill until hot, about 15 minutes. Turn all burners to medium.

3. Clean and oil cooking grate. Sprinkle patties with salt. Place patties on grill, divot side up, and cook (covered if using gas) until well browned on first side and meat easily releases from grill, 4 to 6 minutes. Flip patties and continue to cook until browned on second side and meat registers 160 degrees, 5 to 7 minutes. Transfer burgers to platter and let rest for 5 minutes. Serve burgers on buns.

VARIATIONS

Grilled Turkey Burgers with Miso and Ginger
Omit spinach, feta, salt, and pepper. Whisk 2 tablespoons miso paste and 1 tablespoon water in bowl until combined. Add miso mixture to turkey with melted butter. Substitute 1 teaspoon grated fresh ginger for dill and 2 minced scallions for garlic.

Grilled Turkey Burgers with Herbs and Goat Cheese
Omit spinach and garlic. Substitute ¾ cup crumbled goat cheese for feta. Add 1 large minced shallot and 2 tablespoons minced fresh parsley to turkey with melted butter.

Turkey Sliders with Peanut Sauce and Cucumber Salad

Serves 6 (Makes 12 sliders)   **Total Time** 1½ hours

Why This Recipe Works These sliders may be small in size, but with a creamy peanut sauce and a crunchy cucumber topping they're big on flavor. Lean turkey was the perfect base for these mini burgers, and we mixed scallions, cilantro, chili-garlic sauce, and lime right into the patties for a blast of spicy tang. Our simple peanut sauce complements these flavorful burgers with a hint of salt from fish sauce and a touch of sweetness from brown sugar, and using creamy peanut butter makes this traditional sauce easy to replicate at home. For crisp, bright crunch, we created a cucumber salad that makes a perfect topping. Be sure to use ground turkey or chicken, not ground turkey or chicken breast (also labeled 99 percent fat-free), in this recipe.

Turkey Sliders with Peanut Sauce and Cucumber Salad

¼ cup creamy peanut butter
2 tablespoons fish sauce, divided
5 teaspoons packed brown sugar, divided
1 teaspoon grated lime zest plus 5 tablespoons juice (3 limes), divided
½ English cucumber, sliced thin
½ red onion, sliced thin
1½ pounds ground turkey or chicken
4 scallions, chopped fine
¼ cup chopped fresh cilantro
2 tablespoons unsalted butter, melted and cooled
1 tablespoon Asian chili-garlic sauce
12 slider hamburger buns, toasted if desired
½ teaspoon table salt
¼ teaspoon pepper
2 teaspoons vegetable oil, divided

1. Whisk peanut butter, 4 teaspoons fish sauce, 1 tablespoon sugar, and 3 tablespoons lime juice in bowl until smooth; set aside until ready to serve. (Sauce should have consistency of ketchup; if it seems too thick, add water in small increments as needed to adjust consistency.)

2. Combine cucumber, onion, remaining 2 teaspoons fish sauce, remaining 2 teaspoons sugar, and remaining 2 tablespoons lime juice in second bowl; set aside until ready to serve.

3. Break ground turkey into small pieces in large bowl. Add scallions, cilantro, melted butter, chili-garlic sauce, and lime zest and gently knead with your hands until well combined.

4. Cut sides off 1-quart zipper-lock bag, leaving bottom seam intact. Divide turkey mixture into 12 portions (about 2½ ounces each), then roll each portion into balls. Working with 1 ball at a time, enclose in split bag. Using clear pie plate (so you can see size of patty), press ball into even 4-inch patty. Remove patty from bag and transfer to baking sheet. Cover and refrigerate patties until ready to cook.

5. Arrange bun bottoms on platter. Sprinkle patties with salt and pepper. Heat 1 teaspoon oil in 12-inch nonstick skillet over medium heat until just smoking. Using spatula, transfer 6 patties to skillet. Cook patties until well browned, 2 to 3 minutes per side. Transfer sliders to prepared bun bottoms, tent with aluminum foil, and set aside while cooking remaining patties. Wipe skillet clean with paper towels. Repeat with remaining 1 teaspoon oil and 6 patties. Top sliders with peanut sauce, cucumber salad, and bun tops. Serve.

Grind-Your-Own Turkey Burgers

Serves 4   Total Time 1¾ hours

Why This Recipe Works Grinding your own turkey for burgers reaps big rewards when using collagen-rich turkey thighs. Freezing the meat before processing it gave us control over the size of the grind and helped us to produce burgers that were loose-textured and tender. But our burgers were dry. The solution proved to be processing a portion of the meat to a paste along with some salt in the form of soy sauce. This activated the meat's sticky proteins, enabling it to trap copious amounts of moisture and fat. Mixing gelatin into the paste promoted more moisture retention, as did a pinch of baking soda, which tenderized the muscle fibers. Mushrooms, also pulsed in the food processor, broke up the texture of the patty for a more tender burger without muting the flavor; in fact, they improved the burgers' overall meatiness. The result was the juiciest turkey burgers we'd ever tasted. Because these patties are somewhat delicate, if grilling, we partially freeze them to ensure that they will stay together. If you are unable to find boneless, skinless turkey thighs, substitute one 2-pound bone-in thigh, skin and bones removed, trimmed. To double this recipe, spread the turkey over two baking sheets in step 1 and pulse in the food processor in six batches. You can serve these burgers simply with classic condiments, burger sauces (page 94), lettuce, and/or sliced ripe tomatoes.

Turkey Burger Blend

1½ pounds boneless, skinless turkey or chicken thighs, trimmed and cut into ½-inch pieces
1 tablespoon unflavored gelatin
3 tablespoons chicken broth
6 ounces white mushrooms, trimmed
1 tablespoon soy sauce
 Pinch baking soda
2 tablespoons vegetable oil

Burgers

½ teaspoon table salt, divided
¼ teaspoon pepper, divided
2 teaspoons vegetable oil, divided
4 slices cheese (4 ounces) (optional)
4 hamburger buns, toasted if desired

1. For the turkey burger blend Arrange turkey in single layer on rimmed baking sheet and freeze until very firm and starting to harden around edges but still pliable, 35 to 45 minutes.

2. Sprinkle gelatin over broth in small bowl and let sit until gelatin softens, about 5 minutes. Pulse mushrooms in food processor until coarsely chopped, about 7 pulses, stopping and redistributing mushrooms as needed; transfer to bowl.

3. Working in 3 batches, pulse turkey in now-empty processor until ground into ⅛-inch pieces, about 20 pulses, stopping to redistribute meat as needed; transfer to separate large bowl.

4. Return ½ cup (about 3 ounces) ground turkey to again-empty processor along with softened gelatin, soy sauce, and baking soda. Process until smooth, about 2 minutes, scraping down sides of bowl as needed. With processor running, slowly add oil until incorporated, about 10 seconds. Return mushrooms to processor with paste and pulse to combine, 3 to 5 pulses. Transfer mushroom mixture to bowl with turkey and knead with your hands until combined.

5. For the burgers With your lightly greased hands, divide turkey mixture into 4 lightly packed balls, then gently flatten into ¾-inch-thick patties. Using your fingertips, press center of each patty down until about ½ inch thick, creating slight divot. Cover and refrigerate until ready to cook. (Patties can be refrigerated for up to 1 hour or frozen for up to 2 weeks. To freeze, stack patties, separated by parchment paper, wrap in plastic wrap, and place in zipper-lock freezer bag.)

6A. For a skillet Adjust oven rack to middle position and heat oven to 300 degrees. Sprinkle patties with ½ teaspoon salt and ¼ teaspoon pepper. (If previously frozen, thaw at room temperature for 30 minutes before seasoning and increase baking time to 12 to 14 minutes.) Heat 2 teaspoons oil in 12-inch nonstick skillet over high heat until just smoking. Using spatula, transfer patties to skillet, divot side up, and

Grind-Your-Own
Turkey Burgers

cook until well browned on first side, 2 to 4 minutes. Flip patties and cook until well browned on second side, 2 to 4 minutes. Transfer patties to rimmed baking sheet, divot side down, top with cheese, if using, and bake until burgers register 160 degrees, 6 to 10 minutes. Transfer burgers to platter and let rest for 5 minutes. Serve burgers on buns.

6B. For a charcoal grill Freeze patties for 30 minutes. (If previously frozen, do not thaw.) Open bottom vent completely. Light large chimney starter filled with charcoal briquettes (6 quarts). When top coals are partially covered with ash, pour evenly over half of grill. Set cooking grate in place, cover, and open lid vent completely. Heat grill until hot, about 5 minutes. Clean and oil cooking grate. Brush 1 side of patties with 1 teaspoon oil and sprinkle with ¼ teaspoon salt and ⅛ teaspoon pepper. Using spatula, gently flip patties, brush with remaining 1 teaspoon oil, and sprinkle second side with remaining ¼ teaspoon salt and remaining ⅛ teaspoon pepper. Place burgers, divot side up, over hotter part of grill and cook, covered, until well browned and meat easily releases from grill, 5 to 7 minutes. Flip, top with cheese, if using, and cook until well browned on second side and meat registers 160 degrees, 5 to 7 minutes. Transfer burgers to platter and let rest for 5 minutes. Serve burgers on buns.

Classic Burger Sauce

Makes about 1 cup   **Total Time** 5 minutes

½ cup mayonnaise
¼ cup ketchup
2 teaspoons sweet pickle relish
2 teaspoons sugar
2 teaspoons distilled white vinegar
1 teaspoon pepper

Whisk all ingredients together in bowl.

Malt Vinegar–Molasses Burger Sauce

Makes about 1 cup   **Total Time** 5 minutes

¾ cup mayonnaise
4 teaspoons malt vinegar
½ teaspoon molasses
¼ teaspoon Worcestershire sauce
¼ teaspoon table salt
¼ teaspoon pepper

Whisk all ingredients together in bowl.

Chile-Lime Burger Sauce

Makes about 1 cup   **Total Time** 5 minutes

¾ cup mayonnaise
2 teaspoons chile-garlic paste
2 teaspoons lime juice
1 scallion, sliced thin
¼ teaspoon fish sauce
⅛ teaspoon sugar

Whisk all ingredients together in bowl.

6C. For a gas grill Freeze patties for 30 minutes. (If previously frozen, do not thaw.) Turn all burners to high, cover, and heat grill until hot, about 15 minutes. Leave primary burner on high and turn off other burner(s). Clean and oil cooking grate. Brush 1 side of patties with 1 teaspoon oil and sprinkle with ¼ teaspoon salt and ⅛ teaspoon pepper. Using spatula, gently flip patties, brush with remaining 1 teaspoon oil, and sprinkle second side with remaining ¼ teaspoon salt and remaining ⅛ teaspoon pepper. Place burgers, divot side up, over hotter part of grill and cook, covered, until well browned and meat easily releases from grill, 5 to 7 minutes. Flip, top with cheese, if using, and cook until well browned on second side and meat registers 160 degrees, 5 to 7 minutes. Transfer burgers to platter and let rest for 5 minutes. Serve burgers on buns.

Jerk Spice–Rubbed Turkey Burgers with Fried Green Tomatoes

Serves 4   Total Time 1¼ hours

Why This Recipe Works This mouthwatering burger features the sweet, spicy, and bold elements of jerk seasoning to give mild turkey a serious flavor boost. To create an authentic jerk-style spice rub, we started by combining ground allspice berries, black peppercorns, and dried thyme; for heat and depth we added garlic powder, dry mustard, and cayenne. When it came time to top our burgers we chose fried green tomatoes; these cornmeal-crusted tomatoes lent freshness and crunch to each bite. For a creamy element we created a quick aioli and stirred in some habanero for a little extra spice. We prefer our home-made turkey burger blend in this recipe; however, you can substitute 1¾ pounds of ground turkey or chicken tossed with 2 tablespoons melted butter if desired. Avoid ground turkey or chicken breast (also labeled 99 percent fat-free). If a green tomato is unavailable, you can substitute two plum tomatoes. Be sure to wear gloves when mincing the habanero.

1 green tomato, cored and sliced ¼ inch thick
½ cup mayonnaise
1 habanero chile, stemmed, seeds and ribs removed, and minced
½ teaspoon grated lime zest plus 1 tablespoon juice
2½ teaspoons pepper, divided
1¼ teaspoons table salt, divided
½ cup cornmeal
¼ cup all-purpose flour
⅔ cup buttermilk

Jerk Spice-Rubbed Turkey Burgers with Fried Green Tomatoes

1 large egg
2 tablespoons packed brown sugar
2 teaspoons garlic powder
2 teaspoons ground allspice
1½ teaspoons dry mustard
1½ teaspoons dried thyme
1 teaspoon cayenne pepper
1 recipe Grind-Your-Own Turkey Burger Blend (page 92)
2 teaspoons vegetable oil
½ cup vegetable oil for frying
4 hamburger buns, toasted if desired
4 leaves red or green lettuce
2 scallions, sliced thin

1. Place tomato on paper towel–lined plate. Cover with more paper towels and let sit for 20 minutes. Combine mayonnaise, habanero, lime zest and juice, ¼ teaspoon pepper, and ¼ teaspoon salt in bowl; refrigerate until ready to serve.

2. Combine cornmeal, flour, ¼ teaspoon pepper, and ¼ teaspoon salt in shallow dish. Whisk buttermilk and egg together in second shallow dish. Pat tomatoes dry. Working

with 1 tomato slice at a time, dip in buttermilk mixture, letting excess drip off, then dredge in cornmeal mixture, pressing firmly to adhere; transfer to clean baking sheet and set aside.

3. Adjust oven rack to middle position and heat oven to 300 degrees. Whisk sugar, garlic powder, allspice, dry mustard, thyme, cayenne, remaining 2 teaspoons pepper, and remaining ¾ teaspoon salt together in bowl. With your lightly greased hands, divide burger blend into 4 lightly packed balls, then gently flatten into ¾-inch-thick patties. Using your fingertips, press center of each patty down until about ½ inch thick, creating slight divot.

4. Sprinkle patties with brown sugar mixture, pressing gently to adhere. Heat 2 teaspoons oil in 12-inch nonstick skillet over medium heat until shimmering. Using spatula, transfer patties to skillet, divot side up, and cook until well browned on first side, 2 to 4 minutes. Gently flip patties and continue to cook until well browned on second side, 2 to 4 minutes. Transfer patties to rimmed baking sheet, divot side down, and bake until burgers register 160 degrees, 6 to 10 minutes. Transfer burgers to platter and let rest while finishing tomatoes. Wipe skillet clean with paper towels.

5. Heat ½ cup oil in now-empty skillet over medium-high heat until shimmering. Cook tomato slices until golden brown, 2 to 3 minutes per side. Transfer to paper towel–lined plate, let drain briefly, then season with salt and pepper to taste. Spread mayonnaise mixture over bun tops and arrange lettuce on bottoms. Serve burgers on buns, topped with fried tomatoes and scallions.

Mediterranean Turkey Burgers with Shaved Zucchini Salad and Ricotta

Serves 4   Total Time 45 minutes

Why This Recipe Works A great turkey burger deserves some special fixings as much as any other burger. Here we top it with delicate shaved zucchini tossed with a little olive oil, lemon juice, garlic, and red pepper flakes. Not only was this simple zucchini salad delicious, keeping the zucchini raw added a pleasant crunch to our burgers. A sprinkling of basil and toasted pine nuts added further interest. We wanted a creamy element for our burger, and thought ricotta cheese would complement the zucchini. We whisked it until it was light and fluffy and then added a little olive oil and some lemon zest for brightness. Slathered onto each bun, this ricotta spread took our burger to the next level. We prefer our homemade turkey burger blend in this recipe; however, you can substitute

1¾ pounds of ground turkey or chicken tossed with 2 table-spoons melted butter if desired. Avoid ground turkey or chicken breast (also labeled 99 percent fat-free). Look for small zucchini; they will have fewer seeds. Use a vegetable peeler to slice the zucchini into very thin ribbons.

1 recipe Grind-Your-Own Turkey Burger Blend (page 92)
¾ teaspoon table salt, divided
½ teaspoon pepper, divided
2 teaspoons plus 2 tablespoons extra-virgin olive oil, divided
4 ounces (½ cup) whole-milk ricotta cheese
½ teaspoon grated lemon zest plus 1 tablespoon juice
1 pound small zucchini, trimmed and sliced lengthwise into ribbons
¼ cup chopped fresh basil
2 tablespoons pine nuts, toasted
1 small garlic clove, minced
¼ teaspoon red pepper flakes
4 hamburger buns, toasted if desired

1. Adjust oven rack to middle position and heat oven to 300 degrees. With your lightly greased hands, divide burger blend into 4 lightly packed balls, then gently flatten into ¾-inch-thick patties. Using your fingertips, press center of each patty down until about ½ inch thick, creating slight divot.

2. Sprinkle patties with ½ teaspoon salt and ¼ teaspoon pepper. Heat 2 teaspoons oil in 12-inch nonstick skillet over high heat until just smoking. Using spatula, transfer patties to skillet, divot side up, and cook until well browned on first side, 2 to 4 minutes. Gently flip patties and continue to cook until well browned on second side, 2 to 4 minutes. Transfer patties to rimmed baking sheet, divot side down, and bake until burgers register 160 degrees, 6 to 10 minutes. Transfer burgers to platter and let rest while preparing toppings.

3. Whisk ricotta, lemon zest, 1 tablespoon oil, remaining ¼ teaspoon salt, and remaining ¼ teaspoon pepper together in bowl. Toss zucchini with basil, pine nuts, garlic, pepper flakes, remaining 1 tablespoon oil, and lemon juice in separate bowl. Spread ricotta mixture over bun tops. Serve burgers on buns, topped with zucchini salad.

Easy Chipotle Chicken Tacos

Easy Chipotle Chicken Tacos
Serves 4   **Total Time** 45 minutes

Why This Recipe Works Much of the appeal of traditional tacos is their essential simplicity. While we love braised, slow-cooked taco fillings, sometimes we want simple chicken tacos that we can make at home any night of the week. Boneless, skinless breasts were a convenient place to start, and poaching proved to be the easiest way to imbue them with flavor. To build our poaching liquid, we started by sautéing chipotle chile in adobo and garlic for a smoky, savory flavor base. Sautéing our aromatic ingredients in butter instead of oil added richness to the lean breast meat. We then added orange juice for citrusy freshness, cilantro for a pleasant herbal note, and Worcestershire for savory depth. Once the chicken was finished cooking, our poaching liquid pulled double duty: We reduced it to a sauce. A bit of mustard thickened the sauce and provided a sharp counterpoint to the sweet orange juice. Finally, we shredded and sauced the chicken; warm tortillas and a few basic toppings completed our tacos. Serve with shredded cheese, shredded lettuce, chopped tomatoes, diced avocado, and sour cream.

- 3 tablespoons unsalted butter
- 4 garlic cloves, minced
- 2 teaspoons minced canned chipotle chile in adobo sauce
- ¾ cup chopped fresh cilantro, divided
- ½ cup orange juice
- 1 tablespoon Worcestershire sauce
- 1½ pounds boneless, skinless chicken breasts, trimmed
- 1 teaspoon yellow mustard
- 12 (6-inch) corn tortillas, warmed
  Lime wedges

1. Melt butter in 12-inch skillet over medium-high heat. Add garlic and chipotle and cook until fragrant, about 30 seconds. Stir in ½ cup cilantro, orange juice, and Worcestershire and bring to simmer. Nestle chicken into sauce. Reduce heat to medium-low, cover, and cook until chicken registers 160 degrees, 10 to 15 minutes, flipping chicken halfway through cooking.

2. Transfer chicken to cutting board, let cool slightly, then shred into bite-size pieces using 2 forks.

3. Meanwhile, increase heat to medium-high and cook liquid left in skillet until reduced to ¼ cup, about 5 minutes. Off heat, whisk in mustard. Add chicken and remaining ¼ cup cilantro and toss until well combined. Season with salt and pepper to taste. Serve with tortillas and lime wedges.

NOTES FROM THE TEST KITCHEN

THREE WAYS TO WARM TORTILLAS

Warming tortillas not only makes them more pliable but can also add flavorful toasty char, depending on the method. Wrap the tortillas in foil or clean dish towels to keep them warm until serving.

Gas Flame Using tongs, place tortilla directly over medium flame of gas burner until lightly charred, about 30 seconds per side.

Skillet Toast tortilla in dry nonstick skillet over medium-high heat until softened and spotty brown, 20 to 30 seconds per side.

Microwave Wrap up to 6 tortillas in damp, clean dish towel and microwave until warm, 30 to 45 seconds.

Grilled Chicken Tacos with Salsa Verde

Serves 4   Total Time 1¼ hours

Why This Recipe Works Simple grilled chicken, which cooks up quickly with a nice, smoky char, makes a perfect taco filling, especially when accompanied by a piquant green tomatillo salsa known as salsa verde. Since it would be paired with other flavorful elements, we found that our chicken needed only a brief stint in a garlic-lime marinade before being grilled over a hot fire. A bit of salt and sugar in our marinade kept the chicken moist as it cooked and rounded out its flavor. To complement the smoky, charred notes of the chicken, we grilled some of the salsa ingredients as well: sliced onion, a jalapeño chile, and half of the tomatillos. We pulsed our grilled vegetables with additional raw tomatillos, cilantro, lime juice, and garlic for freshness and bite. As a final touch, we grilled our tortillas briefly to warm and lightly char them.

- ¼ cup vegetable oil, divided
- 3 tablespoons lime juice (2 limes), divided
- 2 tablespoons water
- 1 teaspoon plus pinch sugar, divided
- 2¼ teaspoons table salt, divided
- ½ teaspoon pepper
- 5 cloves garlic, minced
- 1½ pounds boneless, skinless chicken breasts, trimmed
- 1 onion, peeled and cut into ½-inch-thick rounds
- 1 jalapeño chile, stemmed, halved, and seeded
- 1 pound tomatillos, husks and stems removed, rinsed well and dried, divided
- 12 (6-inch) corn tortillas
- ½ cup chopped fresh cilantro
- 1 avocado, halved, pitted, and cut into ½-inch pieces
- 4 radishes, trimmed and sliced thin

1. Whisk 3 tablespoons oil, 1 tablespoon lime juice, water, 1 teaspoon sugar, 1½ teaspoons salt, pepper, and half of garlic together in medium bowl. Pound chicken breasts to uniform thickness. Add chicken to marinade, cover, and refrigerate, turning occasionally, for 30 minutes.

2. Brush onion, jalapeño, and half of tomatillos with remaining 1 tablespoon oil and sprinkle with ¼ teaspoon salt. Halve remaining tomatillos; set aside. Remove chicken from marinade, let excess marinade drip off, and transfer to plate.

3A. For a charcoal grill Open bottom vent completely. Light large chimney starter filled with charcoal briquettes (6 quarts). When top coals are partially covered with ash, pour evenly over grill. Set cooking grate in place, cover, and open lid vent completely. Heat grill until hot, about 5 minutes.

Grilled Chicken Fajitas

Chicken Tinga

3B. For a gas grill Turn all burners to high, cover, and heat grill until hot, about 15 minutes. Leave all burners on high.

4. Clean and oil cooking grate. Place chicken and oiled vegetables on grill. Cook (covered if using gas), turning as needed, until chicken is well browned and registers 160 degrees and vegetables are lightly charred and soft, 10 to 15 minutes. Transfer chicken and vegetables to cutting board and tent with aluminum foil.

5. Working in batches, grill tortillas, turning as needed, until warm, about 30 seconds; wrap tightly in foil to keep soft.

6. Chop grilled vegetables coarse, then pulse with cilantro, remaining 2 tablespoons lime juice, remaining pinch sugar, remaining ½ teaspoon salt, remaining garlic, and remaining tomatillos in food processor until slightly chunky, 16 to 18 pulses. Slice chicken thin on bias. Serve with tortillas, tomatillo sauce, avocado, and radishes.

Grilled Chicken Fajitas

Serves 4   Total Time 1¼ hours

Why This Recipe Works We wanted to create a simple fajita recipe with the perfect combination of smoky grilled vegetables and tender chicken. To boost the flavor of the chicken, we made a brightly flavored marinade and added a surprising ingredient—Worcestershire sauce—which lent a subtle but complex savory note. To prepare the vegetables for grilling, we quartered the bell peppers so they'd lie flat on the grill and cut the onion into thick rounds that would hold together during cooking. A two-level fire enabled us to grill the chicken and vegetables at the same time, the latter on the cooler part so they wouldn't burn. We reserved some of the marinade to toss with everything at the end for a bright burst of flavor. Serve with your favorite fajita toppings, including guacamole, salsa, sour cream, shredded cheddar or Monterey Jack cheese, and lime wedges.

  6 tablespoons vegetable oil, divided
  ⅓ cup lime juice (3 limes)
  1 jalapeño chile, stemmed, seeded, and minced
1½ tablespoons minced fresh cilantro
  3 garlic cloves, minced
  1 tablespoon Worcestershire sauce
1½ teaspoons packed brown sugar
2⅛ teaspoons table salt, divided
  ¾ teaspoon plus ⅛ teaspoon pepper, divided
1½ pounds boneless, skinless chicken breasts, trimmed
  2 large red, green, and/or yellow bell peppers, quartered, stemmed, and seeded
  1 large red onion, sliced into ½-inch-thick rounds
12 (6-inch) flour tortillas

1. Whisk ¼ cup oil, lime juice, jalapeño, cilantro, garlic, Worcestershire, sugar, 1 teaspoon salt, and ¾ teaspoon pepper together in large bowl. Measure out ¼ cup marinade and set aside for serving. Whisk 1 teaspoon salt into remaining marinade. Pound chicken breasts to uniform thickness. Add chicken to marinade, cover, and refrigerate, turning occasionally, for 30 minutes.

2. Brush bell peppers and onion with remaining 2 tablespoons oil and sprinkle with remaining ⅛ teaspoon salt and remaining ⅛ teaspoon pepper. Remove chicken from marinade, let excess marinade drip off, and transfer to plate.

3A. For a charcoal grill Open bottom vent completely. Light large chimney starter filled with charcoal briquettes (6 quarts). When top coals are partially covered with ash, pour coals over two-thirds of grill. Set cooking grate in place, cover, and open lid vent completely. Heat grill until hot, about 5 minutes.

3B. For a gas grill Turn all burners to high, cover, and heat grill until hot, about 15 minutes. Leave primary burner on high and turn other burner(s) to medium.

4. Clean and oil cooking grate. Place chicken on hotter side of grill and vegetables on cooler side of grill. Cook (covered if using gas), turning chicken and vegetables as needed, until chicken is well browned and registers 160 degrees and vegetables are tender and slightly charred, 10 to 15 minutes. Transfer chicken and vegetables to cutting board and tent with aluminum foil.

5. Working in batches, grill tortillas, turning as needed, until warm, about 30 seconds; wrap tightly in foil to keep soft.

6. Slice bell peppers into ¼-inch strips, separate onion into rings, and toss together with 2 tablespoons reserved marinade. Slice chicken on bias into ¼-inch-thick slices and toss with remaining 2 tablespoons marinade in separate bowl. Transfer chicken and vegetables to serving platter and serve with tortillas.

Chicken Tinga

Serves 6   Total Time 1½ hours

Why This Recipe Works Tinga de pollo is a traditional taco filling that typically combines shredded chicken breast meat with a flavorful tomato-chipotle sauce. For deeper flavor, we chose boneless thighs and cooked them directly in the sauce. Cooking the chicken until it reached 195 degrees allowed lots of collagen to break down, delivering meat that was supertender and giving the sauce savory depth. Fire-roasted tomatoes increased smokiness, and a little brown sugar and lime juice and zest further created balanced complexity. Simmering the

cooked shredded chicken in the sauce before serving allowed the sauce to thicken and the flavors to meld and penetrate the meat. If you can't find cotija cheese, use farmer's cheese or feta instead.

   2 pounds boneless, skinless chicken thighs, trimmed
   ½ teaspoon table salt
   ¼ teaspoon pepper
   2 tablespoons vegetable oil, divided
   1 onion, halved and sliced thin
   3 garlic cloves, minced
   1 teaspoon ground cumin
   ¼ teaspoon ground cinnamon
   1 (14.5-ounce) can fire-roasted diced tomatoes
   ½ cup chicken broth
   2 tablespoons minced canned chipotle chile in
       adobo sauce plus 2 teaspoons adobo sauce
   ½ teaspoon packed brown sugar
   1 teaspoon grated lime zest plus 2 tablespoons juice
  12 (6-inch) corn tortillas, warmed
   1 avocado, halved, pitted, and cut into ½-inch pieces
   2 ounces cotija cheese, crumbled (½ cup)
   6 scallions, minced
      Fresh cilantro leaves
      Lime wedges

1. Pat chicken dry with paper towels and sprinkle with salt and pepper. Heat 1 tablespoon oil in Dutch oven over medium-high heat until shimmering. Add half of chicken and brown on both sides, 3 to 4 minutes per side. Transfer to large plate and repeat with remaining chicken.

2. Reduce heat to medium, add remaining 1 tablespoon oil to now-empty pot, and heat until shimmering. Add onion and cook, stirring frequently, until softened, about 5 minutes. Add garlic, cumin, and cinnamon and cook until fragrant, about 1 minute. Add tomatoes and their juice, broth, chipotle and adobo sauce, and sugar and bring to boil, scraping up any browned bits.

3. Return chicken and any accumulated juices to pot, reduce heat to medium-low, cover, and simmer until meat registers 195 degrees, 15 to 20 minutes, flipping chicken after 5 minutes. Transfer chicken to cutting board.

4. Transfer cooking liquid to blender and process until smooth, 15 to 30 seconds. Return sauce to pot. When cool enough to handle, shred chicken into bite-size pieces using 2 forks. Return chicken to pot with sauce. Cook over medium heat, stirring frequently, until sauce is thickened and clings to chicken, about 10 minutes. Stir in lime zest and juice and season with salt and pepper to taste. Serve with tortillas, passing avocado, cotija, scallions, cilantro, and lime wedges separately.

Chicken Quesadillas with Roasted Corn and Jack Cheese

Serves 4   Total Time 1¼ hours

Why This Recipe Works The perfect chicken quesadilla is crisp and evenly browned outside with melted cheese and a warm, flavorful filling inside. For quesadillas that were substantial enough for a satisfying meal, we started with 10-inch flour tortillas. We wanted to make four quesadillas, but cooking them one at a time in a skillet was impractical. We turned to the oven to solve this problem. By placing the quesadillas on an oiled baking sheet and then brushing their tops with oil, we were able to achieve perfectly browned, crispy tortillas in only 15 minutes. To ensure that both sides browned evenly, we flipped the quesadillas partway through baking. With our cooking method down, we shifted our attention to creating a flavorful chicken filling. To keep the flavor uncluttered, we seasoned the chicken simply with salt and pepper and sautéed it until golden brown. Sautéed scallion whites, garlic, and cumin added plenty of background flavor. Roasted red peppers and hot sauce were a simple, quick way to give the filling some complex notes of smoke and subtle heat. Fresh cilantro and scallion greens gave the quesadillas a welcome freshness. Just the right amount of Monterey Jack cheese helped hold everything together and became perfectly melty in the oven. We prefer our Quick Tomato Salsa (page 103) in this recipe, but you can use store-bought salsa.

3 tablespoons plus 1 teaspoon vegetable oil, divided
1 pound boneless, skinless chicken breasts, trimmed
¾ teaspoon table salt, divided
⅛ teaspoon pepper
3 scallions, white and green parts separated, sliced thin
2 garlic cloves, minced
1 teaspoon ground cumin
8 ounces Monterey Jack cheese, shredded (2 cups)
½ cup jarred roasted red peppers, patted dry and chopped
¼ cup minced fresh cilantro
1 teaspoon hot sauce
4 (10-inch) flour tortillas
1 cup tomato salsa
¼ cup sour cream

1. Adjust oven rack to middle position and heat oven to 450 degrees. Line rimmed baking sheet with aluminum foil and brush with 1 tablespoon oil.

2. Pound chicken breasts to uniform thickness. Pat chicken dry with paper towels and sprinkle with ¼ teaspoon salt and pepper. Heat 1 tablespoon oil in 12-inch nonstick skillet over medium-high heat until just smoking. Gently lay chicken in skillet and cook, turning as needed, until lightly golden on both sides and registers 160 degrees, about 12 minutes. Transfer chicken to cutting board, let cool slightly, then shred into bite-size pieces using 2 forks.

3. Add 1 teaspoon oil, scallion whites, garlic, cumin, and remaining ½ teaspoon salt to now-empty skillet and cook over medium heat until softened, about 2 minutes; transfer to medium bowl. Add chicken, scallion greens, Monterey Jack, peppers, cilantro, and hot sauce and toss to combine.

4. Lay tortillas on counter. Spread chicken filling over half of each tortilla, leaving ½-inch border around edge. Fold other half of tortilla over top and press firmly to compact. Arrange quesadillas in single layer on prepared sheet with rounded edges facing center of sheet. Brush with remaining 1 tablespoon oil.

5. Bake until quesadillas begin to brown, about 10 minutes. Flip quesadillas over and press gently with spatula to compact. Continue to bake until crisp and golden brown on second side, about 5 minutes. Let quesadillas cool on wire rack for 5 minutes, then slice each into 4 wedges. Serve with salsa and sour cream.

California Chicken Burritos

Serves 4   Total Time 45 minutes

Why This Recipe Works A burrito is a great way to use up cooked chicken, and this version comes together faster than delivery from the local burrito joint: Put some rice on to cook while you prepare the rest. Open a jar of salsa or, better yet, make Quick Tomato Salsa, which takes 10 minutes. To avoid a soggy burrito, we drained the salsa and added the flavorful liquid to canned black beans along with garlic and chipotle in adobo, letting everything cook down a bit before mashing some of the beans against the side of the skillet to thicken the mixture. After stirring in chicken, rice, and shredded cheddar cheese, our burrito was ready to roll up. A sprinkle of additional cheese on top and 10 minutes in the oven delivered burritos with a crispy, bubbly exterior. We like using Perfect Poached Chicken (page 60) and Quick Tomato Salsa (page 103) here but any cooked chicken and store-bought salsa would work. You can use leftover or precooked rice in this recipe.

Chicken Burritos Mojados

3. Meanwhile, microwave rice and chicken in medium covered bowl until hot, stirring occasionally, about 2 minutes. Stir in salsa and 2 cups cheddar.

4. Wrap tortillas in damp dish towel and microwave until warm and pliable, about 1 minute. Lay warm tortillas on counter. Spread one-quarter of bean mixture evenly over center of each tortilla, close to bottom edge. Mound rice mixture on top of beans. Working with 1 tortilla at a time, fold sides then bottom of tortilla over filling, pulling back on it firmly to tighten it around filling, then continue to roll tightly into burrito. (Burritos can be held at room temperature for up to 1 hour before baking.)

5. Arrange burritos on prepared sheet and sprinkle with remaining 1 cup cheese. Bake until cheese is spotty brown and burritos are heated through, about 10 minutes. Serve with extra salsa.

ASSEMBLING CHICKEN BURRITOS

1. After spreading one-quarter of bean mixture on bottom half of each tortilla, leaving 1- to 2-inch border at edge uncovered, mound rice mixture into tidy pile on top.

2. Fold sides of tortilla over filling, tightly roll bottom edge of tortilla up over filling, and continue to roll into burrito.

2 tablespoons vegetable oil

1 (15-ounce) can black beans, rinsed

1 teaspoon minced canned chipotle chile in adobo sauce plus 1 teaspoon adobo sauce

3 garlic cloves, minced

1 cup tomato salsa, drained with juice reserved, plus extra for serving

½ cup water

2 cups cooked rice

1½ cups shredded cooked chicken

12 ounces cheddar cheese, shredded (3 cups), divided

4 (10-inch) flour tortillas

1. Adjust oven rack to middle position and heat oven to 450 degrees. Line rimmed baking sheet with aluminum foil and spray with vegetable oil spray.

2. Heat oil in 12-inch nonstick skillet over medium-high heat until shimmering. Add black beans, chipotle, and garlic and cook until fragrant, about 1 minute. Stir in reserved salsa juice, water, and adobo sauce and cook until liquid has evaporated and beans are soft, about 5 minutes. Off heat, use back of wooden spoon to mash some of beans against side of skillet. Season with salt and pepper to taste.

Chicken Burritos Mojados

Serves 6   Total Time 1½ hours

Why This Recipe Works Festive burritos mojados or "wet burritos" are draped with three distinct sauces—red chile sauce, white Mexican crema, and green tomatillo sauce—representing the colors of the Mexican flag. This is a fork and knife burrito, eaten on a plate. To reduce the hours spent making multiple sauces, we used premade tomatillo salsa and boosted its flavor with fresh cilantro. Cooking the chicken and the red chile sauce together further streamlined the recipe. Any store-bought tomatillo salsa will work here. If the salsa is very thick or chunky, loosen it with several tablespoons of water and puree it quickly in the blender before heating in step 5. If you can't find Mexican crema, you can substitute sour cream.

2¼ cups chicken broth, divided
¾ cup long-grain white rice, rinsed
1 (15-ounce) can pinto beans, rinsed
3½ tablespoons chili powder, divided
1½ teaspoons table salt
2 scallions, sliced thin
2 tablespoons vegetable oil
3 garlic cloves, minced
2 (8-ounce) cans tomato sauce
1½ pounds boneless, skinless chicken breasts, trimmed
6 tablespoons minced fresh cilantro, divided
6 (10-inch) flour tortillas
2 avocados, halved, pitted, and cut into ½-inch pieces
8 ounces Monterey Jack cheese, shredded (2 cups)
1½ cups tomatillo salsa
½ cup Mexican crema

1. Bring 1¼ cups broth, rice, beans, 1½ teaspoons chili powder, and salt to boil in medium saucepan over medium-high heat. Cover, reduce heat to low, and cook until rice is tender and broth is absorbed, about 20 minutes. Remove rice from heat and let sit, covered, for 10 minutes. Add scallions and fluff with fork to incorporate; cover to keep warm.

2. Meanwhile, cook oil, garlic, and remaining 3 tablespoons chili powder in large saucepan over medium-high heat until fragrant, 1 to 2 minutes. Stir in tomato sauce and remaining 1 cup broth and bring to simmer. Nestle chicken into sauce. Reduce heat to medium-low, cover, and cook until chicken registers 160 degrees, 10 to 15 minutes, flipping chicken half-way through cooking.

3. Transfer chicken to cutting board, let cool slightly, then shred into bite-size pieces using 2 forks. Toss chicken with ¼ cup sauce and 2 tablespoons cilantro in bowl. Set remaining sauce aside.

4. Adjust oven rack to middle position and heat oven to 450 degrees. Line baking sheet with aluminum foil. Wrap tortillas in damp dish towel and microwave until warm and pliable, about 1 minute. Lay warm tortillas on counter. Mound rice in center of tortillas, close to bottom edge, then top with chicken, avocado, and Monterey Jack. Working with 1 tortilla at a time, fold sides then bottom of tortilla over filling, pulling back on it firmly to tighten it around filling, then continue to roll tightly into burrito. (Burritos can be held at room temperature for up to 1 hour before baking.) Place burritos seam side down on prepared sheet, cover tightly with foil, and bake until heated through, 20 to 30 minutes.

5. Before serving, whisk salsa and 2 tablespoons cilantro together in bowl, cover, and microwave until hot, about 1 minute. Reheat red sauce in saucepan over medium heat until hot, about 3 minutes, adding water as needed to loosen consistency.

Chicken Chimichangas

6. Arrange burritos on individual plates. Pour tomatillo sauce over half of each burrito and pour red sauce over other half of burrito. Drizzle with crema, sprinkle with remaining 2 tablespoons cilantro, and serve.

Chicken Chimichangas
Serves 4   Total Time 1¾ hours

Why This Recipe Works The chimichanga is a burrito taken to the next level. What gives it the edge is deep frying: The shell becomes crispy and flaky, and the cheese oozes into gooey nirvana. To create great chicken chimichangas, we cooked the chicken right in a flavorful chile sauce, which kept the chicken moist and infused with chile flavor. Some mashed pinto beans thickened the sauce and filling nicely. Cheddar cheese provided a complementary tang. To prevent the folded chimichangas from opening during frying (causing filling to leak into the oil and burn) we mixed a flour and water "glue" and brushed the paste on the edges of the tortillas. We also changed the wrapping method. A standard burrito has folds of dough at either end that would turn oily during frying. To avoid this, we folded each tortilla as though we were wrapping a present, wrapping the top and bottom of the tortilla over the filling before folding in the sides. Use a Dutch oven that holds 6 quarts or more for this recipe. Serve with salsa and sour cream.

1 cup plus 2 tablespoons water, divided
½ cup long-grain white rice, rinsed
¼ teaspoon table salt
2 tablespoons minced fresh cilantro
1 scallion, sliced thin
1 tablespoon vegetable oil
1 onion, chopped fine
2 tablespoons ancho chile powder
1 tablespoon minced canned chipotle chile in adobo sauce
2 garlic cloves, minced
½ teaspoon ground cumin
1 cup chicken broth
1 pound boneless, skinless chicken breasts, trimmed
1 (15-ounce) can pinto beans, rinsed
2 tablespoons all-purpose flour
4 (10-inch) flour tortillas
4 ounces sharp cheddar cheese, shredded (1 cup)
3 cups vegetable oil for frying

1. Bring 1 cup water, rice, and salt to boil in small saucepan over medium-high heat. Reduce heat to low, cover, and cook until rice is tender and water is absorbed, about 20 minutes. Remove rice from heat and let sit, covered, for 10 minutes. Add cilantro and scallion and fluff with fork to incorporate; cover to keep warm.

2. Meanwhile, heat 1 tablespoon oil in 12-inch nonstick skillet over medium heat until shimmering. Add onion and cook until softened, about 5 minutes. Stir in chile powder, chipotle, garlic, and cumin and cook until fragrant, about 1 minute. Stir in broth and bring to simmer. Nestle chicken into sauce. Reduce heat to medium-low, cover, and cook until chicken registers 160 degrees, 10 to 15 minutes, flipping halfway through cooking.

3. Transfer chicken to cutting board, let cool slightly, then cut crosswise into very thin pieces. Continue to simmer sauce until thickened and measures ½ cup, about 10 minutes; remove from heat. Coarsely mash half of beans in bowl using potato masher, then add to sauce with remaining beans and sliced chicken.

4. Whisk flour and remaining 2 tablespoons water together in bowl. Wrap tortillas in damp dish towel and microwave until warm and pliable, about 1 minute. Lay warm tortillas on counter. Mound rice, chicken-bean mixture, and cheddar across center of tortillas. Working with 1 tortilla at a time, brush edges of tortilla with flour paste, then wrap top and bottom of tortilla tightly over filling and press firmly to seal. Brush ends of tortilla thoroughly with paste, fold into center, and press firmly to seal.

5. Adjust oven rack to middle position and heat oven to 200 degrees. Line plate with several layers of paper towels. Set wire rack in rimmed baking sheet. Heat 3 cups oil in large Dutch oven over medium-high heat to 325 degrees. Place 2 chimichangas seam side down in oil and fry, turning as needed, until well browned on both sides, about 4 minutes. Adjust burner, if necessary, to maintain oil temperature between 300 and 325 degrees. Transfer chimichangas to prepared plate, let drain briefly, then transfer to prepared rack and keep warm in oven. Return oil to 325 degrees and repeat with remaining 2 chimichangas. Serve.

FRYING CHIMICHANGAS

Add chimichangas to hot oil, seam side down. Fry, turning as needed, until well browned on all sides, about 4 minutes. Starting chimichangas seam side down ensures a firm seal.

Quick Tomato Salsa
Makes about 3 cups **Total Time** 10 minutes

½ small red onion, quartered
½ cup fresh cilantro leaves
¼ cup drained jarred pickled jalapeños
2 tablespoons lime juice
2 garlic cloves, peeled
½ teaspoon table salt
1 (28-ounce) can diced tomatoes, drained

Pulse onion, cilantro, jalapeños, lime juice, garlic, and salt in food processor until coarsely chopped. Add tomatoes and pulse until combined, about three 1-second pulses. Place salsa in fine-mesh strainer and drain briefly. Transfer to bowl and serve. (Salsa can be refrigerated for up to 2 days.)

Spicy
Chicken
Flautas

Spicy Chicken Flautas

Serves 4 to 6   Total Time 1¾ hours

Why This Recipe Works Take a soft flour tortilla, roll it around a small amount of flavorful filling and fry it until satisfyingly crisp and golden brown, and you have a flauta. Spanish for "flute," these crunchy, fun-to-eat rolls are similar to taquitos, but while taquitos are small and use corn tortillas, flautas are much larger and are made from flour tortillas. To make a rich chicken filling, we built a spicy tomato sauce by sautéing onion, jalapeño, garlic, oregano, chili powder, and cayenne to bloom their flavors. After adding a can of tomato sauce, we simply nestled the chicken in the skillet, covered it, and let the chicken cook through. As the chicken cooked, it absorbed the sauce's spicy flavor; once it was cooked through, we shredded the chicken into bite-size pieces, added it back to the sauce, and stirred in cilantro and lime juice for bright flavor. To make the flautas, we decided to use 8-inch flour tortillas, which were large enough to hold a pleasing amount of filling but small enough to allow us to fry all the flautas in just two batches. But when we rolled the flautas, we found that the tortillas were too long, leaving large flaps of excess tortilla. These flaps

didn't get as crisp when fried and didn't allow the filling to shine. We solved this problem by cutting off one-third of the tortilla before we added the filling. To keep the flautas from opening up during frying, we "glued" the flaps down using a paste made from equal parts flour and water, and then fried them seam side down. Using merely a cup of oil, we were able to turn out flautas with ultracrisp, golden-brown exteriors in just a few minutes. Be sure to use very ripe avocados for the avocado sauce.

Avocado Sauce

- 2 avocados, halved, pitted, and chopped coarse
- ½ cup sour cream
- ¼ cup water
- 3 tablespoons lime juice (2 limes)
- 2 tablespoons minced fresh cilantro

Flautas

- 1 tablespoon vegetable oil
- 1 onion, chopped fine
- 2 jalapeño chiles, stemmed, seeded, and minced
- 1 tablespoon chili powder
- 2 garlic cloves, minced
- ½ teaspoon table salt
- ¼ teaspoon pepper
- ¼ teaspoon dried oregano
- ⅛ teaspoon cayenne pepper
- 1 (8-ounce) can tomato sauce
- 2 pounds boneless, skinless chicken breasts, trimmed
- 2 tablespoons minced fresh cilantro
- 2 tablespoons lime juice
- 2 tablespoons all-purpose flour
- 2 tablespoons water
- 12 (8-inch) flour tortillas
- 1 cup vegetable oil for frying

1. For the sauce Mash all ingredients in bowl with potato masher (or fork) until smooth. Season with salt and pepper to taste; set aside for serving.

2. For the flautas Heat oil in 12-inch nonstick skillet over medium heat until shimmering. Add onion and cook until softened, about 5 minutes. Stir in jalapeños, chili powder, garlic, salt, pepper, oregano, and cayenne and cook until fragrant, about 30 seconds. Stir in tomato sauce and bring to simmer. Nestle chicken into sauce. Reduce heat to medium-low, cover, and cook until chicken registers 160 degrees, 10 to 15 minutes, flipping chicken halfway through cooking.

3. Transfer chicken to cutting board, let cool slightly, then shred into bite-size pieces using 2 forks. Stir chicken, cilantro, and lime juice into sauce.

4. Line rimmed baking sheet with parchment paper. Whisk flour and water together in bowl. Cut off bottom third of each tortilla (discard or reserve for another use). Wrap tortillas in damp dish towel and microwave until warm and pliable, about 1 minute.

5. Lay 6 warm tortillas on clean counter with trimmed edge facing you. Mound half of chicken filling alongside trimmed edges. Roll trimmed edge of 1 tortilla up over filling, then pull back on tortilla to tighten it around filling. Working with 1 tortilla at a time, brush remaining exposed tortilla with flour paste, then roll it up tightly around filling. Press on edges firmly to seal; transfer to prepared baking sheet, seam side down. Repeat with remaining 6 tortillas and remaining filling. (Flautas can be covered with damp towel, wrapped tightly in plastic wrap, and refrigerated for up to 24 hours.)

6. Adjust oven rack to middle position and heat oven to 200 degrees. Line plate with several layers of paper towels. Set wire rack in second rimmed baking sheet. Heat 1 cup oil in clean 12-inch nonstick skillet over medium-high heat to 325 degrees. Place 6 flautas, seam side down, in oil and fry, turning as needed, until golden brown on all sides, 3 to 5 minutes. Adjust burner, if necessary, to maintain oil temperature between 300 and 325 degrees. Transfer flautas to prepared plate, let drain briefly, then transfer to wire rack and keep warm in oven. Return oil to 325 degrees and repeat with remaining flautas. Serve with avocado sauce.

Chicken and Avocado Arepas

Serves 8   Total Time 1¼ hours

Why This Recipe Works Arepas are a type of corn cake popular in Venezuela and Colombia, though iterations exist in other Latin countries. The Venezuelan variety is served as sandwiches that are split open and stuffed with anything from meat and cheese to corn, beans, or even fish. The arepa itself is made using masarepa (precooked corn flour) along with water and salt, but getting the consistency right proved to be a challenge. In the end, we found that using just a half cup more water than masarepa produced a dough that was easy to shape, and a small amount of baking powder lightened the texture just enough. Arepas are traditionally cooked on a griddle or deep-fried, but we found it easiest to brown them in a skillet and finish baking them through in the oven. We made a filling of finely shredded cooked chicken and chopped avocado. Cilantro added freshness, lime juice injected a bit of acidity, and chili powder brought a hint of heat. We like using Perfect Poached Chicken (page 60) here but any cooked chicken would work.

MAKING AREPAS

1. Cook arepas, 4 at a time, in hot, well-oiled skillet until golden on both sides, about 4 minutes per side.

2. Bake arepas on wire rack until they sound hollow when tapped on bottom, about 10 minutes.

3. Using fork, gently split hot arepas open. Stuff each arepa with generous 3 tablespoons filling.

Arepas

- 10 ounces (2 cups) masarepa blanca
- 1 teaspoon table salt
- 1 teaspoon baking powder
- 2½ cups warm tap water
- ¼ cup vegetable oil, divided

Chicken Filling

- 1 cup shredded cooked chicken
- 1 avocado, halved, pitted, and cut into ½-inch pieces
- 2 scallions, sliced thin
- 2 tablespoons minced fresh cilantro
- 1 tablespoon lime juice
- ¼ teaspoon chili powder

1. For the arepas Adjust oven rack to middle position and heat oven to 400 degrees. Whisk masarepa, salt, and baking powder together in large bowl. Gradually add water and stir until combined. Using generous ⅓ cup dough for each, form eight 3-inch rounds, each about ½ inch thick. Set wire rack in rimmed backing sheet.

2. Heat 2 tablespoons oil in 12-inch nonstick skillet over medium-high heat until shimmering. Add 4 arepas and cook until golden on both sides, about 4 minutes per side. Transfer arepas to prepared baking sheet. Wipe out skillet with paper towels and repeat with remaining 2 tablespoons oil and remaining 4 arepas; transfer to baking sheet. (Fried arepas can be refrigerated for up to 3 days or frozen for up to 1 month. Increase baking time as needed in step 3; if frozen, do not thaw before baking.)

3. Bake arepas on wire rack until they sound hollow when tapped on bottom, about 10 minutes.

4. For the filling Using potato masher or fork, mash all ingredients in bowl until well combined. Season with salt and pepper to taste.

5. Using fork, gently split hot, baked arepas open and stuff each with generous 3 tablespoons filling. Serve.

Red Chile Chicken Tamales

Serves 6 to 8   Total Time 3½ hours

Why This Recipe Works Tamales are small, moist corn cakes that can be stuffed with a variety of fillings, wrapped in corn husks, and steamed. Often served during the holidays, tamales are time-consuming to prepare. We wanted to simplify the process while staying true to the tamales' subtle but hearty flavor and light texture. Although masa dough (made from corn kernels that have been cooked with slaked lime, ground to a flour, and mixed with water) is traditional, it can be difficult to find. Instead, we turned to widely available masa harina, but found that when used alone, it was too fine-textured and the corn flavor was bland. Grits, on the other hand, had a granular texture similar to authentic tamales and didn't sacrifice any of the flavor. Most recipes require tying each tamale closed, a process we found we could do without by simply folding the tamales and placing them with the seam sides facing the edges of a steamer basket. For the filling, hearty chicken thighs worked best for the long cooking time. A combination of dried ancho and New Mexican chiles resulted in a sauce with subtle spice and sweetness. Once cooked, the tamales peeled easily away from the moist rich corn cakes. We found it easiest to use large corn husks that measure about 8 inches long by 6 inches wide; if the husks are small, you may need to use two per tamale and shingle them as needed to hold all of the filling. You can substitute butter for the lard if desired, but the tamales will have a distinctive buttery flavor. Be sure to use quick, not instant, grits in this recipe. For an accurate measurement of boiling water, bring a full kettle of water to a boil and then measure out the desired amount.

Tamales
   1 cup plus 2 tablespoons quick grits
   1½ cups boiling water
   1 cup (4 ounces) plus 2 tablespoons masa harina
   20 large dried corn husks
   1½ cups frozen corn, thawed
   6 tablespoons unsalted butter, cut into ½-inch cubes and softened
   6 tablespoons lard, softened
   1 tablespoon sugar
   2¼ teaspoons baking powder
   ¾ teaspoon table salt

Filling
   4 dried ancho chiles, stemmed, seeded, and torn into ½-inch pieces (1 cup)
   4 dried New Mexican chiles, stemmed, seeded, and torn into ½-inch pieces (1 cup)
   3 tablespoons vegetable oil
   1 large onion, chopped
   6 garlic cloves, minced
   ¾ teaspoon ground cumin
   ¾ teaspoon dried oregano
   ¾ teaspoon table salt, divided
   3 cups chicken broth
   1¼ pounds boneless, skinless chicken thighs, trimmed
   1½ tablespoons cider vinegar
   Sugar

1. For the tamales Place grits in medium bowl, whisk in boiling water, and let stand until water is mostly absorbed, about 10 minutes. Stir in masa harina, cover, and let cool to room temperature, about 20 minutes. While mixture cools, place husks in large bowl, cover with hot tap water, and let soak until pliable, about 30 minutes.

2. Process masa dough, corn, butter, lard, sugar, baking powder, and salt in food processor until mixture is light, sticky, and very smooth, about 1 minute, scraping down sides as necessary. Remove husks from water and pat dry with dish towel.

3. For the filling Meanwhile, toast anchos and New Mexican chiles in 12-inch skillet over medium heat, stirring frequently, until fragrant, 2 to 6 minutes; transfer to bowl.

4. Heat oil in now-empty skillet over medium heat until shimmering. Add onion and cook until softened, 5 to 7 minutes. Stir in garlic, cumin, oregano, ½ teaspoon salt, and toasted chiles and cook for 30 seconds. Stir in broth and simmer until slightly reduced, about 10 minutes. Transfer mixture to blender and process until smooth, about 20 seconds; return to skillet.

Red Chile Chicken Tamales

8. Fit large pot or Dutch oven with steamer basket, removing feet from steamer basket if pot is short. Fill pot with water until it just touches bottom of basket and bring to boil. Gently lay tamales in basket with open ends facing up and seam sides facing out. Cover and steam, checking water level often and adding additional water as needed, until tamales easily come free from husks, about 1 hour. Transfer tamales to large platter. Reheat remaining sauce from filling in covered bowl in microwave, about 30 seconds, and serve with tamales.

MAKING TAMALES

1. Lay 1 soaked husk on counter, with long side parallel to edge of counter. Spoon ¼ cup of dough onto bottom right-hand corner. Spread into 4-inch square, flush with bottom edge.

2. Place filling down center of dough, parallel to long side of husk. Roll husk away from you so that dough surrounds filling. Roll tamales tightly so they don't leak while cooking.

3. Fold tapered end of tamale up, leaving top open, and transfer to platter, seam side down.

4. Place tamales in steamer basket with seams facing edge of pot and open ends facing up. Cover and steam for about 1 hour.

5. Season chicken with salt and pepper, nestle into skillet, and bring to simmer over medium heat. Cover, reduce heat to low, and cook until chicken registers 160 degrees, 20 to 25 minutes.

6. Transfer chicken to carving board, let cool slightly, then shred into bite-size pieces using 2 forks. Stir vinegar into sauce and season with salt, pepper, and sugar to taste. Toss shredded chicken with 1 cup sauce. Set filling and remaining sauce aside. (Shredded chicken and remaining sauce can be refrigerated separately for up to 3 days or frozen for up to 1 month; if frozen, thaw completely in refrigerator.)

7. Working with 1 husk at a time, lay on counter, cupped side up, with long side facing you and wide end on right side. Spread ¼ cup tamale dough into 4-inch square over bottom right-hand corner, pushing it flush to bottom edge but leaving ¼-inch border at wide edge. Mound 2 scant tablespoons filling in line across center of dough, parallel to bottom edge. Roll husk away from you and over filling, so that dough surrounds filling and forms cylinder. Fold up tapered end, leaving top open, and transfer seam side down to platter.

SOUPS

Photos (clockwise from top left): Turkey Barley Soup; Tortilla Soup;
Garlic Chicken and Wild Rice Soup; Tom Kha Gai

Old-Fashioned Chicken Noodle Soup

Serves 6 to 8   **Total Time** 2 hours

Why This Recipe Works Chicken noodle soup is one of the all-time great comfort foods and homemade broth is a must. We wanted to make it the old-fashioned way—starting with a whole chicken. We began by cutting the chicken, minus the breast, into small pieces to be browned in batches. Cutting the bones exposed more bone marrow, key for both rich flavor and full body. To develop additional flavor, we sweat the browned pieces in a covered pot with an onion and then simmered them for less than half an hour. Now we had a broth that just needed some salt and bay leaves to round out its flavor. We sautéed the aromatics and carrots for the soup and added in tender chicken breast pieces that had already been poached in our broth. For extra flavor, we cooked the egg noodles right in the soup pot so they could absorb rich, meaty flavor from the broth. With a final sprinkling of chopped parsley, our chicken noodle soup was complete—rich, homemade broth, moist pieces of chicken, tender vegetables, and perfectly cooked noodles. If you use a cleaver you will be able to cut up the chicken parts quickly but a heavy-duty chef's knife or heavy-duty kitchen shears will also work. If desired, substitute chicken fat (skimmed and reserved from making the broth) for the vegetable oil in the soup.

Old-Fashioned Chicken Noodle Soup

Broth
- 1 (3½- to 4-pound) whole chicken
- 1 tablespoon vegetable oil
- 1 onion, chopped
- 8 cups water
- 2 teaspoons table salt
- 2 bay leaves

Soup
- 1 tablespoon vegetable oil
- 1 onion, chopped fine
- 1 carrot, peeled and sliced ¼ inch thick
- 1 celery rib, sliced ¼ inch thick
- 1 teaspoon minced fresh thyme or ¼ teaspoon dried
- 2 cups (3 ounces) wide egg noodles
- 2 tablespoons minced fresh parsley

1. For the broth Cut chicken into 7 pieces (2 split breasts, 2 legs, 2 wings, and backbone). Set split breasts aside, then hack remaining chicken into 2-inch pieces with meat cleaver.

2. Heat oil in large Dutch oven over medium-high heat until just smoking. Add chicken breasts and brown lightly, about 5 minutes. Transfer to plate.

3. Add half of 2-inch chicken pieces and brown lightly, about 5 minutes; transfer pieces to large bowl. Repeat with remaining 2-inch pieces; transfer to bowl.

4. Add onion to fat left in pot and cook until softened, about 3 minutes. Return chicken pieces (not breasts) to pot, along with any accumulated juice, cover, and reduce heat to low. Cook, stirring occasionally, until chicken releases its juice, about 20 minutes.

5. Add reserved chicken breasts, water, salt, and bay leaves and bring to boil. Cover, reduce heat to gentle simmer, and cook, skimming as needed, until chicken breasts register 160 degrees, about 20 minutes.

6. Remove chicken breasts from pot and let cool slightly. Remove and discard skin and bones and shred breast meat into bite-size pieces. Strain broth through fine-mesh strainer, discarding solids, let settle for 10 minutes, then skim off fat. (Broth and chicken can be refrigerated in separate containers for up to 2 days; return broth to simmering before proceeding.)

7. For the soup Heat oil in large Dutch oven over medium heat until shimmering. Add onion, carrot, and celery and cook until softened, 5 to 7 minutes. Stir in thyme and cook until fragrant, about 30 seconds. Stir in broth and bring to boil. Reduce to simmer and cook until vegetables are nearly tender, 6 to 8 minutes.

8. Stir in noodles and simmer until just tender, 10 to 15 minutes. Stir in shredded chicken and let it heat through, about 2 minutes. Off heat, stir in parsley and season with salt and pepper to taste. Serve.

VARIATION

Chicken Noodle Soup with Curried Cauliflower and Cilantro

Serves 6 to 8   **Total Time** 2¼ hours

Broth
- 1 (3½- to 4-pound) whole chicken
- 1 tablespoon vegetable oil
- 1 onion, chopped
- 8 cups water
- 2 teaspoons table salt
- 2 bay leaves

Soup
- 1 tablespoon vegetable oil
- 1 onion, chopped fine
- 1 carrot, peeled and sliced ¼ inch thick
- 1 tablespoon curry powder
- 3 garlic cloves, minced
- 1 teaspoon minced fresh thyme or ¼ teaspoon dried
- 3 ounces (2 cups) wide egg noodles
- ½ head cauliflower, trimmed, cored, and cut into ½-inch pieces (3 cups)
- ½ cup frozen peas
- 2 tablespoons minced fresh cilantro leaves

1. For the broth Cut chicken into 7 pieces (2 split breasts, 2 legs, 2 wings, and backbone). Set split breasts aside, then hack remaining chicken into 2-inch pieces with meat cleaver.

2. Heat oil in large Dutch oven over medium-high heat until just smoking. Add chicken breasts and brown lightly, about 5 minutes. Transfer to plate.

3. Add half of 2-inch chicken pieces and brown lightly, about 5 minutes; transfer pieces to large bowl. Repeat with remaining 2-inch pieces; transfer to bowl.

4. Add onion to fat left in pot and cook until softened, about 3 minutes. Return chicken pieces (not breasts) to pot, along with any accumulated juice, cover, and reduce heat to low. Cook, stirring occasionally, until chicken releases its juice, about 20 minutes.

5. Add reserved chicken breasts, water, salt, and bay leaves and bring to boil. Cover, reduce heat to gentle simmer, and cook, skimming as needed, until chicken breasts register 160 degrees, about 20 minutes.

6. Remove chicken breasts from pot and let cool slightly. Remove and discard skin and bones and shred breast meat into bite-size pieces. Strain broth through fine-mesh strainer, discarding solids, let settle for 10 minutes, then skim off fat. (Broth and chicken can be refrigerated in separate containers for up to 2 days; return broth to simmering before proceeding.)

7. For the soup Heat oil in large Dutch oven over medium heat until shimmering. Add onion and carrot and cook until softened, 5 to 7 minutes. Stir in curry powder, garlic, and thyme and cook until fragrant, about 30 seconds. Stir in broth and bring to boil. Reduce to simmer and cook until vegetables are nearly tender, 6 to 8 minutes.

8. Stir in noodles and cauliflower and simmer until both are tender, 10 to 15 minutes. Stir in shredded chicken and peas and let heat through, about 2 minutes. Off heat, stir in cilantro, season with salt and pepper to taste, and serve.

SKIMMING FAT FROM BROTH

Let broth settle, then use large, flat spoon to skim fat off surface. Be sure to hold spoon parallel to surface of soup; you want to collect as little broth as possible.

Matzo Ball Soup

Serves 6   **Total Time** 3½ hours

Why This Recipe Works Tender dumplings and savory broth make a happy pair in matzo ball soup. This version hits all the marks, delivering substantial but light dumplings and a flavorful broth. For matzo balls that were not too heavy or greasy we settled on a ratio of 1 cup matzo meal to four eggs and 5 tablespoons of water, plus a bit of chopped, cooked onion and minced dill. For the soup, we turned to the classic

Matzo Ball Soup

Hearty Chicken and Cabbage Soup

mirepoix ingredients plus parsnip for its subtle sweetness. To deepen the broth's chicken flavor, we added two whole chicken legs, which we removed after they cooked through. (The meat may be added back in if you like.) Chicken fat, or schmaltz, is available in the refrigerator or freezer section of most supermarkets. Note that the matzo batter needs to be refrigerated for at least 1 hour before shaping.

Matzo Balls
- ¼ cup chicken fat (schmaltz) or vegetable oil
- 1 onion, chopped fine
- 4 large eggs
- 1 teaspoon minced fresh dill
- ¾ teaspoon table salt, plus salt for cooking matzo balls
- ½ teaspoon pepper
- 1 cup (4 ounces) matzo meal

Soup
- 1 tablespoon chicken fat (schmaltz) or vegetable oil
- 1 onion, chopped
- 2 carrots, peeled and cut into ½-inch pieces
- 2 celery ribs, chopped
- 1 parsnip, peeled and cut into ½-inch pieces
- ½ teaspoon table salt
- 8 cups chicken broth
- 1½ pounds chicken leg quarters, trimmed
- 1 teaspoon minced fresh dill

1. For the matzo balls Heat chicken fat in Dutch oven over medium heat until shimmering. Add onion and cook until light golden brown and softened, about 5 minutes. Transfer onion to large bowl and let cool for 10 minutes. (Do not clean pot.)

2. Whisk eggs, 5 tablespoons water, dill, ¾ teaspoon salt, and pepper into cooled onion. Fold in matzo meal until well combined. Cover with plastic wrap and refrigerate for at least 1 hour or up to 2 hours. (Batter will thicken as it sits.)

3. Bring 4 quarts water and 2 tablespoons salt to boil in now-empty Dutch oven. Divide batter into 12 portions (about 1 heaping tablespoon each) and place on greased plate. Roll portions into smooth balls between your wet hands and return to plate. Transfer matzo balls to boiling water, cover, reduce heat to medium-low, and simmer until tender and cooked through, about 30 minutes.

4. Using slotted spoon, transfer matzo balls to colander and drain briefly. Transfer balls to clean plate and let cool to firm up, about 10 minutes. Discard cooking water. (Do not clean pot.)

5. For the soup Meanwhile, heat chicken fat in large saucepan over medium heat until shimmering. Add onion, carrots, celery, parsnip, and salt and cook, covered, until vegetables begin to soften, about 5 minutes. Add broth, chicken, and dill and bring to boil. Cover, reduce heat to low, and cook until chicken is tender, 35 to 45 minutes. Remove from heat and transfer chicken to plate. (Chicken can be used for soup or reserved for another use. If adding to soup, shred with 2 forks into bite-size pieces; discard skin and bones.) Season soup with salt and pepper to taste.

6. Transfer soup to now-empty Dutch oven and bring to simmer over medium heat. Carefully transfer matzo balls to hot soup (along with shredded chicken, if using). Cover and cook until matzo balls are heated through, about 5 minutes. Serve.

VARIATIONS

Herbed Matzo Ball Soup
Add ¼ cup minced fresh dill or parsley to egg mixture in step 2.

Spiced Matzo Ball Soup
Add ½ teaspoon ground nutmeg, ½ teaspoon ground ginger, and ½ teaspoon ground cinnamon to matzo mixture in step 2.

Hearty Chicken and Cabbage Soup

Serves 4   Total Time 1¼ hours

Why This Recipe Works Assertive aromatics and herbs give cabbage an unexpected star quality in this satisfying chicken soup. It makes for a hearty meal thanks to the addition of creamy red potatoes, ground chicken, and bacon, which we crisped and reserved to use as a topping. Caraway seeds brought out the sweetness of the cabbage, and smoked paprika and fresh thyme added depth and complexity. A dollop of yogurt served as a tangy counterpoint to the soup's mild sweetness, and a final sprinkling of fresh dill enhanced the caraway's flavor. Serve with Croutons (page 70), if desired. Be sure to use ground chicken and not ground chicken breast (also labeled 99 percent fat-free) in this recipe.

4 slices bacon, chopped
8 ounces ground chicken
1 large onion, chopped fine
1 teaspoon caraway seeds, toasted
4 garlic cloves, minced
1 teaspoon minced fresh thyme or ¼ teaspoon dried
½ teaspoon hot smoked paprika

½ cup dry white wine
1 small head green cabbage, cored and cut into ¾-inch pieces (6 cups)
5 cups chicken broth
1 pound red potatoes, unpeeled, cut into ¾-inch pieces
½ cup plain Greek yogurt
¼ cup minced fresh dill

1. Cook bacon in Dutch oven over medium-high heat until crisp, about 5 minutes. Using slotted spoon, transfer bacon to paper towel–lined plate; set aside until ready to serve.

2. Pour off all but 2 tablespoons fat from pot. (If necessary, add oil to equal 2 tablespoons.) Add chicken, onion, and caraway seeds to pot and cook over medium heat, breaking up chicken with wooden spoon, until chicken is no longer pink and onion is softened, about 5 minutes.

3. Stir in garlic, thyme, and paprika and cook until fragrant, about 30 seconds. Stir in wine, scraping up any browned bits and smoothing out any lumps, and cook until nearly evaporated, about 30 seconds. Stir in cabbage and broth and bring to simmer. Reduce heat to medium-low, cover, and cook for 15 minutes. Stir in potatoes and cook until vegetables are tender, 15 to 20 minutes. Season soup with salt and pepper to taste.

4. Ladle soup into serving bowls, then top with bacon, yogurt, and dill. Serve.

Hearty Chicken and Vegetable Soup

Serves 8   Total Time 1½ hours

Why This Recipe Works Our ideal bowl of chicken and vegetable soup is rich, satisfying, and complex, with tender chicken and well-cooked vegetables in every bite. For deep vegetable flavor, we started by sautéing meaty cremini mushrooms and boosted their meatiness by adding tomato paste to our aromatics. We knew that root vegetables, with their earthy flavor and hearty texture, would be key, and we really liked the sweet, vegetal flavor of parsnips, celery root, and turnips as well as the more traditional carrots and potatoes. Zucchini provided the perfect fresh counterpoint to the starchy vegetables. A little flour gave our soup some body, and white wine offered nuanced acidity. Thyme and parsley added heady herbal notes. White mushrooms can be substituted for the cremini mushrooms. Our Simple Chicken Broth with Shredded Breast Meat (page 134) delivers the perfect amount of rich broth and cooked chicken for this recipe.

2 tablespoons vegetable oil, divided
8 ounces cremini mushrooms, trimmed and sliced thin
¼ teaspoon table salt
1 onion, chopped fine
3 garlic cloves, minced
1 teaspoon minced fresh thyme or ¼ teaspoon dried
2 tablespoons all-purpose flour
1 tablespoon tomato paste
½ cup dry white wine
8 cups chicken broth
1 pound parsnips, celery root, and/or turnips, peeled and cut into ½-inch pieces
8 ounces red potatoes, unpeeled, cut into ½-inch pieces
2 carrots, peeled and cut into ½-inch pieces
1 zucchini, halved lengthwise, seeded and cut into ½-inch pieces
2 cups shredded cooked chicken
2 tablespoons minced fresh parsley leaves

1. Heat 1 tablespoon oil in large Dutch oven over medium heat until shimmering. Add mushrooms and salt, cover, and cook until mushrooms have released their liquid, about 5 minutes. Uncover and continue to cook until mushrooms are dry and browned, 5 to 10 minutes.

2. Stir in remaining 1 tablespoon oil and onion and cook until softened, 5 to 7 minutes. Stir in garlic and thyme and cook until fragrant, about 30 seconds. Stir in flour and tomato paste and cook for 1 minute. Stir in wine, scraping up any browned bits and smoothing out any lumps, and cook until almost completely evaporated, about 1 minute.

3. Gradually whisk in broth, smoothing out any lumps. Stir in parsnips, potatoes, and carrots and bring to boil. Partially cover, reduce to gentle simmer, and cook until vegetables are just tender, 20 to 25 minutes.

4. Stir in zucchini and continue to simmer gently until just tender, 5 to 10 minutes. Stir in shredded chicken and let heat through, about 2 minutes. Off heat, stir in parsley, season with salt and pepper to taste, and serve.

Lemony Chicken and Rice Soup
Serves 4 to 6 **Total Time** 45 minutes

Why This Recipe Works Our easy lemony chicken and rice soup is based loosely on the Greek classic soup Avgolemono (page 121). It has rich flavor and can be ready in under an hour. Egg yolks gave our soup a velvety texture and fennel, thyme, and lemon zest and juice supplied fresh flavor. Adding pre-cooked rice at the end of cooking provided tender grains in a flash. Feel free to use leftover or precooked rice here. Be careful not to overcook the chicken in step 3 or it will taste dry. To avoid scrambling the eggs, add the hot broth to the egg yolks slowly in step 5. Also, be sure to heat the soup very gently after adding the egg yolks in step 5 or they may curdle.

2 tablespoons vegetable oil, divided
1 pound boneless, skinless chicken breasts, trimmed
¼ teaspoon table salt
¼ teaspoon pepper
3 carrots, peeled and sliced ¼ inch thick
1 fennel bulb, stalks discarded, bulb halved, cored, and sliced ¼ inch thick
1 onion, chopped fine
1 teaspoon minced fresh thyme or ¼ teaspoon dried
6 cups chicken broth
6 (3-inch) strips lemon zest plus 2 tablespoons juice
2 cups cooked rice
4 large egg yolks
2 tablespoons minced fresh parsley or tarragon

1. Heat 1 tablespoon oil in Dutch oven over medium-high heat until just smoking. Pat chicken dry with paper towels and sprinkle with salt and pepper. Cook chicken until lightly browned on both sides, about 5 minutes; transfer to plate.

2. Add remaining 1 tablespoon oil, carrots, fennel, and onion to fat left in pot and cook over medium heat until vegetables are softened, about 5 minutes. Stir in thyme and cook until fragrant, about 30 seconds. Stir in broth and lemon zest, scraping up any browned bits.

3. Add browned chicken, cover, and simmer gently until it registers 160 degrees, about 10 minutes. Transfer chicken to cutting board and shred into bite-size pieces.

4. Meanwhile, remove lemon zest and return soup to simmer. Stir in shredded chicken and rice and cook until heated through, about 1 minute. Turn heat to low.

5. Whisk egg yolks and lemon juice together in medium bowl. Stir 3 tablespoons hot broth into yolk mixture to temper, then whisk yolk mixture into soup. Continue to cook soup gently, whisking constantly, until it thickens slightly, about 1 minute. Promptly remove from heat. Stir in parsley and season with salt and pepper to taste. Serve.

Chicken and Rice Soup with Ginger and Scallions

Chicken and Rice Soup with Ginger and Scallions

Serves 4   Total Time 45 minutes

Why This Recipe Works This very simple chicken and rice soup is perfumed with ginger and the sweet allium flavor of scallions. The base of the soup started with onion and earthy shiitake mushrooms, whose flavor we punched up with grated fresh ginger. Simmering a half-cup of uncooked rice directly in the broth allowed it to soak up chicken flavor while the starch it released helped to thicken the soup. Scallions and cilantro contributed a final layer of green herbal freshness. We like using Simple Chicken Broth with Shredded Breast Meat (page 134) here.

2 tablespoons vegetable oil
1 onion, chopped fine
4 ounces shiitake mushrooms, stemmed and sliced thin
2 tablespoons grated fresh ginger
½ teaspoon table salt
½ teaspoon pepper
8 cups chicken broth
½ cup long-grain white rice
2 cups shredded cooked chicken
2 scallions, white parts sliced thin, green parts cut into 1-inch pieces
½ cup fresh cilantro leaves

1. Heat oil in large saucepan over medium-high heat until shimmering. Add onion, mushrooms, ginger, salt, and pepper and cook until just beginning to brown, about 4 minutes.

2. Add broth and rice, scraping up any browned bits, and bring to boil. Reduce heat to medium-low and simmer until rice is tender, about 12 minutes. Stir in chicken and scallions and continue to cook until heated through, about 2 minutes longer. Season with salt and pepper to taste. Ladle soup into serving bowls, sprinkle with cilantro, and serve.

Garlic Chicken and Wild Rice Soup

Serves 6   Total Time 1½ hours

Why This Recipe Works There's nothing like a bowl of steaming chicken soup, especially when you're feeling under the weather. We supercharged one of our homemade chicken broths (pages 134–137) with a health-boosting megadose of garlic before adding tender morsels of chicken. To our surprise, tasters rallied behind a whopping ½ cup of minced garlic, praising its bright yet balanced presence in our soup. To build flavor, we added aromatic vegetables, thyme, bay leaves, and tomato paste along with the broth. We opted for nutritious wild rice, cooking it directly in the soup to infuse it with garlicky flavor. To keep our chicken tender, we simmered it during the last few minutes of cooking. Finally, baby spinach and chopped fresh parsley gave our soup a vegetal boost.

3 tablespoons extra-virgin olive oil
½ cup minced garlic (about 25 cloves)
2 carrots, peeled and sliced ¼ inch thick
1 onion, chopped fine
1 celery rib, minced
¼ teaspoon table salt
2 teaspoons minced fresh thyme or ½ teaspoon dried
1 teaspoon tomato paste
6 cups chicken broth
2 bay leaves
⅔ cup wild rice, rinsed
8 ounces boneless, skinless chicken breasts, trimmed and cut into ¾-inch pieces
3 ounces (3 cups) baby spinach
¼ cup chopped fresh parsley

1. Heat oil and garlic in Dutch oven over medium-low heat, stirring occasionally, until garlic is light golden, 3 to 5 minutes. Add carrots, onion, celery, and salt, increase heat to medium, and cook, stirring occasionally, until vegetables are just beginning to brown, 10 to 12 minutes.

2. Stir in thyme and tomato paste and cook until fragrant, about 30 seconds. Stir in broth and bay leaves, scraping up any browned bits, and bring to simmer. Stir in rice, return to simmer, cover, and cook over medium-low heat until rice is tender, 40 to 50 minutes.

3. Discard bay leaves. Stir in chicken and spinach and cook over low heat, stirring occasionally, until chicken is cooked through and spinach is wilted, 3 to 5 minutes. Off heat, stir in parsley and season with salt and pepper to taste. Serve.

Hearty Chicken Soup with Orzo and Spring Vegetables

Serves 6 to 8   **Total Time** 45 minutes

Why This Recipe Works This fresh-tasting vegetable soup comes together easily. We started the base with the mildly sweet flavor of leek, which we sautéed along with carrot and celery. Earthy grassy asparagus contributed the taste of springtime while green peas added more springy flavor and verdant color. Quick-cooking orzo added the right amount of substance to our soup and cooked right in the broth. The distinct anise flavor of tarragon added a final burst of herbal freshness. We like using Simple Chicken Broth with Shredded Breast Meat (page 134) here.

- 8 cups chicken broth
- 1 carrot, peeled and sliced ¼ inch thick
- 1 celery rib, sliced ¼ inch thick
- 1 leek, quartered lengthwise, sliced thin crosswise, and washed thoroughly
- ¼ teaspoon dried thyme
- 2 cups shredded cooked chicken
- ½ cup orzo
- ¼ pound asparagus, trimmed and cut into 1-inch lengths
- ¼ cup green peas (fresh or frozen)
- 2 tablespoons minced fresh tarragon

Bring broth to simmer over medium-high heat. Add carrot, celery, and leek and cook until softened, about 5 minutes. Add thyme and chicken and simmer until vegetables are tender and flavors meld, 10 to 15 minutes. Add orzo, asparagus, and peas and cook until just tender, about 5 minutes. Stir in tarragon, season with salt and pepper to taste, and serve.

Easy Alphabet Soup with Chicken

Serves 4 to 6   **Total Time** 45 minutes

Why This Recipe Works There's nothing more inviting than a bowl of chicken noodle soup that you can find your name in. We knew this soup would appeal to kids, but we wanted the flavor to appeal to adults as well. We started by browning boneless, skinless chicken breasts, which we then poached in broth. We added depth to the broth with a small amount of tomato paste and a couple of garlic cloves, and we limited the vegetables to classic carrots and celery. The result: a flavorful, comforting soup that is on the table in less than an hour. Ditalini or orzo can be substituted for the alphabet pasta if necessary. Be careful not to overcook the chicken in step 3 or it will taste dry.

- 1 tablespoon vegetable oil
- 1 pound boneless, skinless chicken breasts, trimmed
- ¼ teaspoon table salt
- ¼ teaspoon pepper
- 2 carrots, peeled and cut into ¼-inch pieces
- 1 celery rib, cut into ¼-inch pieces
- 1 tablespoon tomato paste
- 2 garlic cloves, minced
- 1 teaspoon minced fresh thyme or ¼ teaspoon dried
- 6 cups chicken broth
- 3 ounces alphabet pasta

1. Heat oil in Dutch oven over medium-high heat until just smoking. Pound chicken breasts to uniform thickness, then pat dry with paper towels and sprinkle with salt and pepper. Cook chicken until lightly browned on both sides, about 5 minutes; transfer to plate.

2. Add carrots and celery to fat left in pot and cook over medium heat until softened, about 5 minutes. Stir in tomato paste, garlic, and thyme and cook until fragrant, about 1 minute. Stir in broth, scraping up any browned bits.

3. Add browned chicken and any accumulated juices, cover, and simmer gently until it registers 160 degrees, about 10 minutes. Transfer chicken to cutting board and, using 2 forks, shred into bite-size pieces.

4. Meanwhile, return soup to simmer and stir in pasta and cook until tender, 7 to 9 minutes. Stir in shredded chicken and season with salt and pepper to taste. Serve.

Chicken and Spinach Tortellini Soup

Serves 4 to 6   **Total Time** 25 minutes

Why This Recipe Works We developed an easy but impressive last-minute chicken and tortellini soup by using pantry staples and a simple procedure. Browning the aromatics in rendered bacon fat created a rich base on which to build the soup and provided a crisp bacon garnish. Once we added the broth, we poached boneless chicken breasts in it, which gave both the broth and the chicken deeper flavor. Frozen spinach and packaged tortellini were convenient and quick-cooking hearty additions.

- 3 slices bacon, cut into ½-inch pieces
- ½ onion, chopped fine
- 1 clove garlic, minced
- ½ teaspoon red pepper flakes
- 1½ quarts chicken broth
- 12 ounces boneless, skinless chicken breasts, trimmed
- 5 ounces frozen spinach, thawed, squeezed dry, and chopped
- 1 package fresh spinach tortellini (18 ounces) Grated Parmesan cheese

1. Cook bacon in large Dutch oven over medium heat until crispy, 5 to 7 minutes. With slotted spoon, transfer bacon to paper towel–lined plate.

2. Stir onion into fat in pot and cook until browned, about 6 minutes. Stir in garlic and red pepper flakes and cook until fragrant, about 30 seconds.

3. Add broth and chicken, bring to boil, reduce heat, and simmer until chicken registers 160 degrees, about 20 minutes. Off heat, remove chicken with slotted spoon. Let cool slightly and shred into bite-size pieces.

4. Return soup to simmer. Add spinach and tortellini and simmer until tortellini are tender, about 3 minutes. Add shredded chicken and season with salt and pepper to taste. Ladle soup into serving bowls and garnish with bacon and Parmesan. Serve, passing more Parmesan separately.

Hearty Chicken Soup with Orzo and Spring Vegetables

Easy Alphabet Soup with Chicken

Italian Chicken Soup with Parmesan Dumplings

Serves 4 to 6 **Total Time** 2 hours

Why This Recipe Works This rustic Northern Italian specialty features tender, plump dumplings deeply flavored with Parmesan and served in a light chicken broth. We modernized the classic recipe, making it more hearty and a bit easier by adding flavor to the broth using browned chicken thighs. We used a little of the rendered chicken fat along with extra cheese to boost the savory flavor of the dumplings while egg whites kept them light. Fennel, carrots, and escarole complemented the shredded chicken and the flavorful dumplings. To ensure that the dumplings remain intact during cooking, hand-roll them until their surfaces are smooth and no cracks remain.

Italian Chicken Soup with
Parmesan Dumplings

- 1½ pounds bone-in chicken thighs, trimmed
- ¾ teaspoon table salt, divided
- ¼ teaspoon pepper, divided
- 1 teaspoon vegetable oil
- 1 fennel bulb, 1 tablespoon fronds minced, stalks discarded, bulb halved, cored, and cut into ½-inch pieces
- 1 onion, chopped fine
- 2 carrots, peeled and cut into ¾-inch pieces
- ½ cup dry white wine
- 8 cups chicken broth
- 1 Parmesan cheese rind, plus 3 ounces Parmesan, shredded (1 cup)
- 2 slices hearty white sandwich bread, torn into 1-inch pieces
- 2 large egg whites
- ¼ teaspoon grated lemon zest
   Pinch ground nutmeg
- ½ small head escarole (6 ounces), trimmed and cut into ½-inch pieces

1. Pat chicken dry with paper towels and sprinkle with ¼ teaspoon salt and ⅛ teaspoon pepper. Heat oil in Dutch oven over medium-high heat until just smoking. Add chicken, skin side down, and cook until well browned, 6 to 8 minutes. Transfer chicken to plate and remove skin.

2. Pour off all but 1 teaspoon fat from pot and set aside 1 tablespoon fat for dumplings. Add fennel bulb, onion, carrots, and remaining ½ teaspoon salt and cook over medium heat, stirring occasionally, until vegetables soften and begin to brown, 5 to 7 minutes. Stir in wine and cook, scraping up any browned bits, until nearly dry, about 2 minutes. Return

chicken to pot; add broth and Parmesan rind and bring to boil. Reduce heat to low, cover, and simmer until chicken is tender and registers 175 degrees, about 30 minutes. Transfer chicken to clean plate. Discard Parmesan rind. Cover broth and remove from heat. When cool enough to handle, use 2 forks to shred chicken into bite-size pieces; discard bones.

3. While broth is simmering, adjust oven rack to middle position and heat oven to 350 degrees. Pulse bread in food processor until finely ground, 10 to 15 pulses. Measure out 1 cup bread crumbs and transfer to parchment paper–lined rimmed baking sheet (set aside remainder for another use). Bake until lightly browned, about 5 minutes. Transfer to large bowl and set aside to cool completely.

4. Pulse shredded Parmesan in now-empty food processor until finely ground, 10 to 15 pulses. Transfer Parmesan to bowl with cooled bread crumbs and add reserved 1 tablespoon fat, egg whites, lemon zest, nutmeg, and remaining ⅛ teaspoon pepper. Mix until thoroughly combined, then refrigerate for 15 minutes.

5. Working with 1 teaspoon dough at a time, roll into balls and place on parchment-lined sheet (you should have about 28 dumplings).

6. Return broth to simmer over medium-high heat. Add escarole and chicken and return to simmer. Add dumplings and cook, adjusting heat to maintain gentle simmer, until dumplings float to surface and are cooked through, 3 to 5 minutes. Stir in fennel fronds, season with salt and pepper to taste, and serve. (Soup, shredded chicken, and dumplings, prepared through step 5, can be refrigerated separately for up to 24 hours. To reheat, bring soup, covered, to gentle simmer, stirring often, and continue with step 6.)

Pennsylvania Dutch Chicken, Corn, and Rivel Soup

Serves 6 to 8   **Total Time** 1¼ hours

Why This Recipe Works Since this hearty soup is meant to highlight sweet corn, we maximized corn flavor in three ways: steeping the shorn cobs in the broth while the chicken poached; grating half the kernels to release more juice, flavor, and body-building starch; and cooking the kernels just long enough to enhance their sweetness without losing their crisp-tender bite. Rivels—tiny doughballs that most closely resemble German spaetzle—completed our soup, adding texture and a slight thickness as they simmer. Do not substitute frozen corn for the fresh corn here; fresh corn is crucial to the flavor of this soup. The rivel dough is quite soft and sticky; dip your fingers in cool water as needed to prevent it from sticking to your hands when shaping. We like using Simple Chicken Broth with Shredded Breast Meat (page 134) here.

- 1 tablespoon unsalted butter
- 1 onion, chopped fine
- 3 garlic cloves, minced
- 1 teaspoon minced fresh thyme or ¼ teaspoon dried
- 8 cups chicken broth
- 2 cups plus 3 tablespoons water, divided
- 3 ears corn, husks and silk removed, kernels and cob pulp removed and reserved separately
- 1½ cups all-purpose flour
- 2 large eggs, lightly beaten
- ¼ teaspoon table salt
- 2 cups shredded cooked chicken
- 2 tablespoons minced fresh parsley

1. Melt butter in large Dutch oven over medium heat. Add onion and cook until softened, 5 to 7 minutes. Stir in garlic and thyme and cook until fragrant, about 30 seconds. Stir in broth, 2 cups water, and corn cob pulp and bring to simmer.

Pennsylvania Dutch Chicken, Corn, and Rivel Soup

2. Meanwhile, combine flour, eggs, and salt in large bowl with rubber spatula until sticky dough forms. If dough does not come together easily, add remaining 3 tablespoons water, 1 tablespoon at a time, until it forms sticky, cohesive mass.

3. Using your moistened fingers, pinch dough into ½-inch rivels and drop them into the simmering soup. Cover and simmer gently, stirring occasionally, until the rivels are tender, about 30 minutes.

4. Stir in corn kernels and simmer gently until tender, 5 to 7 minutes. Stir in shredded chicken and let heat through, about 2 minutes. Off heat, stir in parsley, season with salt and pepper to taste, and serve.

Mulligatawny with Chicken

Serves 6   **Total Time** 2 hours

Why This Recipe Works Mulligatawny is a classic Anglo-Indian soup that features a potently spiced and pureed base enriched with lentils and tender shredded chicken. Its flavor profile comes from curry powder and coconut, which adds a touch of sweetness. We decided to make our own curry spice

Mulligatawny with Chicken

Avgolemono

blend, as most Indian home cooks do, using garam masala, cumin, coriander, and turmeric. To give the soup the right amount of body, we made a roux with our aromatics, added chicken broth, and gently poached bone-in chicken breasts that we had previously browned. Setting aside the chicken to cool, we pureed our soup to a smooth consistency then added the lentils. While the lentils cooked through, we shredded the chicken. A dollop of yogurt and a sprinkling of cilantro were the crowning touches on our richly spiced, velvety mulligatawny. French green lentils (lentilles du Puy) will also work well here; the cooking time will remain the same.

1½ pounds bone-in split chicken breasts, trimmed
¼ teaspoon table salt
¼ teaspoon pepper
1 tablespoon vegetable oil
2 tablespoons unsalted butter
2½ teaspoons garam masala
1½ teaspoons ground cumin
1½ teaspoons ground coriander
1 teaspoon ground turmeric
2 onions, chopped fine
2 carrots, peeled and chopped
1 celery rib, chopped
½ cup sweetened shredded or flaked coconut
4 garlic cloves, minced
4 teaspoons grated fresh ginger
¼ cup all-purpose flour
1 teaspoon tomato paste
7 cups chicken broth
½ cup dried brown lentils, picked over and rinsed
2 tablespoons minced fresh cilantro
1 cup plain yogurt, for serving

1. Pat chicken dry with paper towels and sprinkle with salt and pepper. Heat oil in Dutch oven over medium-high heat until just smoking. Cook chicken until lightly browned on both sides, about 5 minutes, then transfer to plate.

2. Melt butter in now-empty Dutch oven over medium heat. Stir in garam masala, cumin, coriander, and turmeric and cook until fragrant, about 30 seconds. Stir in onions, carrots, celery, and coconut and cook until softened, 5 to 7 minutes. Stir in garlic and ginger and cook until fragrant, about 30 seconds. Stir in flour and tomato paste and cook for 1 minute. Gradually whisk in broth, scraping up any browned bits and smoothing out any lumps, and bring to boil.

3. Add browned chicken, cover, and simmer gently until chicken registers 160 degrees, 15 to 20 minutes. Remove chicken from pot, let cool slightly, then shred meat into bite-size pieces, discarding skin and bones.

4. Working in batches, puree soup in blender until smooth, return to clean pot, and simmer. Stir in lentils, cover, and simmer gently until lentils are tender, 35 to 45 minutes.

5. Stir in shredded chicken and let heat through, about 2 minutes. Off heat, stir in cilantro and season with salt and pepper to taste. Ladle soup into serving bowls, dollop with yogurt, and serve.

New Orleans Chicken and Sausage Soup

Serves 8 to 10   **Total Time** 1¼ hours

Why This Recipe Works We're fans of both spicy jambalaya and chicken soup, so we created a New Orleans–inspired recipe that combined the two. This soup uses easy-to-prep boneless, skinless chicken breasts and andouille sausage for complex meaty flavor. The rendered fat from browning the sausage added smoky flavor to the Cajun trio of onions, bell pepper, and celery, which formed the aromatic base of the soup. The rice is efficiently cooked right in the broth. We like using authentic spicy andouille sausage but kielbasa can be substituted. We found that this soup is especially good the day after it's cooked, when the flavors have had time to mingle.

- 1 tablespoon vegetable oil
- 1 pound smoked sausage, such as andouille, cut into ¼-inch pieces
- 2 onions, chopped fine
- 1 red bell pepper, stemmed, seeded, and chopped fine
- 1 celery rib, chopped fine
- 6 garlic cloves, minced
- 1 teaspoon dried thyme
- ½ teaspoon cayenne pepper
- ¼ cup all-purpose flour
- 8 cups chicken broth
- 2 cups water
- 1½ pounds boneless, skinless chicken breasts, cut into ½-inch pieces
- 1 cup long-grain rice

1. Heat oil in large Dutch oven over medium-high heat. Add sausage and cook until lightly browned, about 8 minutes. With slotted spoon, transfer sausage to paper towel–lined plate.

2. Add onions, bell pepper, and celery to fat in pot and cook over medium heat, stirring frequently, until softened, about 8 minutes. Stir in garlic, thyme, and cayenne and cook until fragrant, about 30 seconds. Add flour and stir constantly with wooden spoon until mixture is golden brown, about 10 minutes.

3. Whisk in chicken broth and water and bring to boil. Add chicken and rice and simmer until rice is tender and chicken is cooked through, about 10 minutes. Add reserved sausage and simmer until soup is slightly thickened, about 5 minutes. Season with salt and pepper to taste. Serve. (Soup can be refrigerated in airtight container for up to 3 days.)

Avgolemono

Serves 6 to 8   **Total Time** 1¼ hours

Why This Recipe Works Avgolemono, or Greek chicken and rice soup, gets its name from the egg-lemon mixture that thickens and flavors it. Our version contains tender shreds of chicken that are poached to perfection by sitting off the heat in hot broth. We flavored the broth with citrusy coriander and lemon zest, which gave it savory depth and enhanced the soup's lemon flavor. Processing eggs, yolks, and a portion of the cooked rice in a blender and then stirring this puree into the hot broth gave our avgolemono a velvety consistency. Make sure to zest the lemons before juicing them. The longer the final soup cooks after the eggs have been added, the thicker it becomes. Serve the soup immediately; it thickens to a gravy-like consistency when reheated.

- 1½ pounds boneless, skinless chicken breasts, trimmed
- 1¾ teaspoons table salt
- 12 (3-inch) strips lemon zest plus 6 tablespoons juice, plus extra juice for seasoning (3 lemons)
- 2 sprigs fresh dill, plus 2 teaspoons chopped
- 2 teaspoons coriander seeds
- 1 teaspoon black peppercorns
- 1 garlic clove, peeled and smashed
- 8 cups chicken broth
- 1 cup long-grain rice
- 2 large eggs plus 2 large yolks, room temperature

1. Cut each chicken breast in half lengthwise. Toss with salt and let stand at room temperature for at least 15 minutes or up to 30 minutes. Cut 8-inch square of triple-thickness cheesecloth. Place lemon zest, dill sprigs, coriander seeds, peppercorns, and garlic in center of cheesecloth and tie into bundle with kitchen twine.

2. Bring broth, rice, and spice bundle to boil in large saucepan over high heat. Reduce heat to low, cover, and cook for 5 minutes. Turn off heat, add chicken, cover, and let stand for 15 minutes.

3. Transfer chicken to large plate and discard spice bundle. Using 2 forks, shred chicken into bite-size pieces. Using ladle, transfer 1 cup cooked rice to blender (leave any liquid in pot). Add lemon juice and eggs and yolks to blender and process until smooth, about 1 minute.

4. Return chicken and any accumulated juices to pot. Return soup to simmer over high heat. Remove pot from heat and stir in egg mixture until fully incorporated. Stir in chopped dill and season with salt, pepper, and extra lemon juice to taste. Serve.

Cock-a-Leekie

Serves 6 to 8   **Total Time** 45 minutes

Why This Recipe Works Rumored to be a favorite of Mary, Queen of Scots, the first recorded version of cock-a-leekie (chicken and leek soup) dates back to the late 1500s. Our modernized recipe makes an authentic-tasting yet streamlined soup. Many recipes disagree on what role the leeks should play. We wanted full, rich leek flavor and for the leeks to contribute some texture too, so we sautéed them until soft to start and then stirred some sliced leeks in after adding the broth. A pinch of cloves and some minced garlic provided just the right amount of warm spice flavor while prunes, a traditional ingredient, made our soup more balanced and complex with a mellow sweetness. Look for leeks with large white and light green parts. If your leeks are small, you may need a few extra for this recipe. We like using Simple Chicken Broth with Shredded Breast Meat (page 134) here.

 2 tablespoons unsalted butter
 6 leeks, white and light green parts only,
      halved lengthwise, sliced ¼ inch thick,
      and rinsed thoroughly, divided
 ¼ teaspoon table salt
 2 garlic cloves, minced
      Pinch ground cloves
 8 cups chicken broth
 2 cups shredded cooked chicken
 10 pitted prunes, cut into ½-inch pieces
 2 tablespoons minced fresh parsley

1. Melt butter in large Dutch oven over medium heat. Add half of leeks and salt and cook until very soft, 8 to 10 minutes. Stir in garlic and cloves and cook until fragrant, about 30 seconds. Stir in broth, scraping up any browned bits, and bring to boil.

2. Stir in remaining leeks, reduce to gentle simmer, and cook until leeks are just tender, 5 to 7 minutes. Stir in shredded chicken and prunes and let them heat through, about 2 minutes. Off heat, stir in parsley, season with salt and pepper to taste, and serve.

Turkey Meatball Soup with Saffron

Serves 6 to 8   **Total Time** 2 hours

Why This Recipe Works Spanish-style meatball soup boasts a deeply flavorful sunset-colored broth and tender meatballs. For extra flavor and texture, we added grated Manchego, a sharp Spanish sheep's-milk cheese, shallot, parsley, and olive oil to lean ground turkey along with a bread and milk paste to keep them moist. We rolled 2-inch balls and placed them in the refrigerator to firm up. For a full-flavored broth, we started with a traditional Spanish sofrito of onion, bell pepper, and garlic, then added saffron threads for a potent impact. Paprika contributed some sweetness to the broth while a bit of red pepper flakes delivered just enough heat. We deglazed the pot with white wine for brightness, poured in chicken broth, and then carefully dropped in the chilled meatballs. Finally, we added body to the soup with a traditional picada, a simple mixture of ground almonds, bread crumbs, and olive oil. A sprinkling of minced parsley made for a bright, fresh finish. Parmesan or Asiago cheese can be substituted for the Manchego. Be sure to use ground turkey, not ground turkey breast (also labeled 99 percent fat-free), in this recipe.

Meatballs
 2 slices high-quality white sandwich bread,
      torn into quarters
 ⅓ cup whole milk
 1 pound ground turkey or chicken
 1 ounce Manchego cheese, grated (½ cup)
 3 tablespoons minced fresh parsley
 1 shallot, minced
 2 tablespoons extra-virgin olive oil
 ½ teaspoon table salt
 ½ teaspoon pepper

Turkey Meatball Soup with Saffron

1. For the meatballs Using fork, mash bread and milk into paste in large bowl. Stir in ground turkey, Manchego, parsley, shallot, oil, salt, and pepper until combined. Pinch off and roll 2-teaspoon-size pieces of mixture into balls and arrange in rimmed baking sheet (you should have 30 to 35 meatballs). Cover with plastic wrap and refrigerate until firm, at least 30 minutes.

2. For the picada Adjust oven rack to middle position and heat oven to 375 degrees. Pulse almonds in food processor to fine crumbs, about 20 pulses. Add bread, oil, salt, and pepper and pulse bread to coarse crumbs, about 10 pulses. Spread mixture evenly in rimmed baking sheet and bake, stirring often, until golden brown, about 10 minutes. Set aside to cool. (Picada can be stored in airtight container for up to 2 days.)

3. For the soup Heat oil in large Dutch oven over medium-high heat until shimmering. Add onion and bell pepper and cook until softened and lightly browned, 8 to 10 minutes. Stir in garlic, paprika, saffron, and pepper flakes and cook until fragrant, about 30 seconds. Stir in wine, scraping up any browned bits, and cook until almost completely evaporated, about 1 minute.

4. Stir in broth and bring to simmer. Gently add meatballs and simmer until cooked through, 10 to 12 minutes. Off heat, stir in picada and parsley and season with salt and pepper to taste. Serve.

VARIATION

Turkey Meatball Soup with Saffron and Kale
Add 8 ounces kale, stemmed and chopped, to soup with meatballs.

Harira
Serves 8   Total Time 1¾ hours

Why This Recipe Works Harira is an intensely flavored Moroccan soup of lentils, tomatoes, chickpeas, and often chicken or lamb. We chose to use split chicken breasts, and after browning them, bloomed our aromatics in the rendered fat. We began with chopped onion, next adding a fragrant combination of fresh ginger, cumin, paprika, cinnamon, cayenne, saffron, and black pepper, which produced a sweet, smoky, deeply flavorful base with just a touch of heat. Cooking the chicken through in the broth boosted the base's meaty flavor, and brown lentils both held their shape and took on a tender texture when added with the browned chicken. Once the chicken was cooked, we removed it and then shredded it and stirred it back into the pot. Canned chickpeas added heft while plum tomatoes added just the right amount of tomato

Picada
¼ cup slivered almonds
2 slices hearty white sandwich bread, torn into quarters
2 tablespoons extra-virgin olive oil
⅛ teaspoon table salt
    Pinch pepper

Soup
1 tablespoon extra-virgin olive oil
1 onion, chopped fine
1 red bell pepper, stemmed, seeded, and cut into ¾-inch pieces
2 garlic cloves, minced
1 teaspoon paprika
¼ teaspoon saffron threads, crumbled
⅛ teaspoon red pepper flakes
1 cup dry white wine
8 cups chicken broth
2 tablespoons minced fresh parsley

Harira

Tortilla Soup

flavor and acidity. Harissa, a superspicy paste of hot chiles, spices, garlic, and olive oil, is a critical finishing touch to every harira recipe; for the best and most potent flavor, we made our own. We stirred plenty of this potent paste into the pot along with bright, fresh cilantro. Large green or brown lentils work well in this recipe; do not use French green lentils (lentilles du Puy). We prefer to use our homemade Harissa (page 125), but you can substitute store-bought harissa if you wish, though spiciness can vary greatly by brand.

1½ pounds bone-in split chicken breasts, trimmed
½ teaspoon pepper, divided
¼ teaspoon table salt
1 tablespoon extra-virgin olive oil
1 onion, chopped fine
1 teaspoon grated fresh ginger
1 teaspoon ground cumin
½ teaspoon paprika
¼ teaspoon ground cinnamon
¼ teaspoon cayenne pepper
Pinch saffron threads, crumbled
1 tablespoon all-purpose flour
10 cups chicken broth
¾ cup green or brown lentils, picked over and rinsed
1 (15-ounce) can chickpeas, rinsed
4 plum tomatoes, cored and cut into ¾-inch pieces
⅓ cup minced fresh cilantro
¼ cup harissa, plus extra for serving

1. Pat chicken dry with paper towels and sprinkle with ¼ teaspoon pepper and salt. Heat oil in Dutch oven over medium-high heat until just smoking. Cook chicken until lightly browned on both sides, about 6 minutes; transfer to plate.

2. Add onion to fat left in pot and cook over medium heat until softened, about 5 minutes. Stir in ginger, cumin, paprika, cinnamon, cayenne, saffron, and remaining ¼ teaspoon pepper and cook until fragrant, about 30 seconds. Stir in flour and cook for 1 minute. Slowly whisk in broth, scraping up any browned bits and smoothing out any lumps, and bring to boil.

3. Stir in lentils and chickpeas, then nestle chicken into pot and bring to simmer. Cover, reduce heat to low, and simmer gently until chicken registers 160 degrees, 15 to 20 minutes.

4. Transfer chicken to cutting board, let cool slightly, then shred into bite-size pieces using 2 forks; discarding skin and bones. Meanwhile, continue to simmer lentils, covered, for 25 to 30 minutes.

5. Stir in shredded chicken and cook until heated through, about 2 minutes. Stir in tomatoes, cilantro, and harissa and season with salt and pepper to taste. Serve, passing extra harissa separately.

Tortilla Soup

Serves 8   **Total Time** 45 minutes

Why This Recipe Works Packed with layers of ingredients, tortilla soup is a classic Mexican meal in a bowl full of authentic flavor yet very easy to prepare. The classic recipe has three main components—the flavor base, the chicken stock, and the garnishes. To simplify the vegetables for the flavor base, we made a puree from smoky chipotles, plus tomatoes, onion, garlic, and jalapeño, and fried the puree in oil over high heat. We poached chicken in broth infused with onion, garlic, cilantro, and oregano, which gave our base plenty of flavor. We oven-toasted tortilla strips instead of frying them. For mild spiciness, trim the ribs and seeds from the jalapeño (or omit it altogether) and use 1 teaspoon chipotle chile pureed with the tomatoes in step 3. For a spicier soup, add up to 1 tablespoon adobo sauce in step 5 before you add the chicken. Although the chicken and broth can be prepared ahead of time, the tortilla strips and garnishes are best prepared the day of serving.

- 8 (6-inch) corn tortillas, cut into ½-inch-wide strips
- 2 tablespoons vegetable oil, divided
- 1½ pounds bone-in split chicken breasts, trimmed
- 8 cups chicken broth
- 1 white onion, quartered, divided
- 4 garlic cloves, peeled, divided
- 8–10 sprigs fresh cilantro, plus leaves for serving
- 1 sprig fresh oregano
- ½ teaspoon plus ⅛ teaspoon table salt, divided
- 2 tomatoes, cored and quartered
- ½ jalapeño chile
- 1 tablespoon minced canned chipotle chile in adobo sauce
- 1 avocado, halved, pitted, and diced
- 8 ounces cotija cheese, crumbled (2 cups)
  Lime wedges

1. Adjust oven rack to middle position and heat oven to 425 degrees. Toss tortilla strips with 1 tablespoon oil and bake on rimmed baking sheet until crisp and deep golden, about 14 minutes, stirring occasionally. Season with salt to taste, and let cool on paper towel–lined plate.

2. Meanwhile, bring chicken, broth, 2 onion quarters, 2 garlic cloves, cilantro sprigs, oregano sprig, and ½ teaspoon salt to boil over medium-high heat in Dutch oven. Reduce heat to low, cover, and simmer gently until chicken registers 160 degrees, about 20 minutes. Transfer chicken to cutting board, let cool slightly, and shred into bite-size pieces; discarding skin and bones. Strain broth through fine-mesh strainer.

3. Puree tomatoes, jalapeño, chipotle, remaining 2 onion quarters, and remaining 2 garlic cloves in food processor until smooth. Heat remaining 1 tablespoon oil in now-empty Dutch oven over high heat until shimmering. Add tomato-onion puree and remaining ⅛ teaspoon salt and cook, stirring frequently, until mixture has darkened in color, about 10 minutes.

4. Stir in strained broth and bring to boil, then reduce heat to low and simmer gently until flavors meld, 15 to 20 minutes.

5. Stir in shredded chicken and let heat through, about 2 minutes. Place portions of tortilla strips in serving bowls, ladle soup over top, and serve with avocado, cotija, lime wedges, and cilantro leaves.

Mexican-Style Chicken and Chickpea Soup

Serves 6 to 8   **Total Time** 1½ hours

Why This Recipe Works Caldo tlalpeño is a spicy chicken soup from the south of Mexico. It is laden with tender pieces of chicken, meaty chickpeas, and savory bites of avocado in a broth filled with the smoky flavor of chipotle chiles. Other vegetables vary by cook. We built our soup base by browning bone-in, skin-on chicken breasts (a traditional cut for this soup), developing flavorful fond in the pan. After removing the browned breasts, we softened our aromatic ingredients in

Mexican-Style Chicken and Chickpea Soup

1 (15-ounce) can chickpeas, rinsed
3 tablespoons minced fresh cilantro
1 teaspoon minced fresh oregano

1. Pat chicken dry with paper towels and sprinkle with salt and pepper. Heat oil in Dutch oven over medium-high heat until just smoking. Cook chicken until lightly browned on both sides, 4 to 6 minutes; transfer to plate.

2. Add onions and carrots to fat left in pot and cook over medium heat until softened and lightly browned, 8 to 10 minutes. Stir in garlic, chipotle, and thyme and cook until fragrant, about 30 seconds. Stir in flour and cook for 1 minute. Slowly whisk in broth, scraping up any browned bits and smoothing out any lumps, and bring to simmer.

3. Return browned chicken and any accumulated juices to pot, reduce heat to low, cover, and simmer gently until chicken registers 160 degrees, 15 to 20 minutes.

4. Transfer chicken to cutting board and let cool slightly. Using 2 forks, shred chicken into bite-size pieces; discard skin and bones. Meanwhile, stir zucchini and chickpeas into soup and simmer until zucchini is just tender, 5 to 10 minutes.

5. Stir shredded chicken into soup and simmer until heated through, about 2 minutes. Off heat, stir in cilantro and oregano and season with salt and pepper to taste. Serve.

the rendered fat before stirring in a bit of flour, which produced a rich broth with great substance. Zucchini, added along with the chickpeas, provided a fresh if nontraditional counterpoint to our soup. We shredded the chicken and added it back to the soup just a few minutes before serving to ensure that the delicate meat wouldn't overcook and turn tough. Stirring in the herbs last provided a burst of freshness for the finished soup. Serve with lime wedges, diced avocado, and/or sliced radishes.

1½   pounds bone-in split chicken breasts, trimmed
¼   teaspoon table salt
¼   teaspoon pepper
 1   tablespoon vegetable oil
 2   onions, chopped fine
 2   carrots, peeled and sliced ½ inch thick
 5   garlic cloves, minced
 2   teaspoons minced canned chipotle chile in adobo sauce
1½   teaspoons minced fresh thyme or ½ teaspoon dried
 2   tablespoons all-purpose flour
 8   cups chicken broth
 2   zucchini, cut into ½-inch pieces

Chicken Pho

Serves 6 to 8   Total Time 3¼ hours

Why This Recipe Works Pho is a Vietnamese noodle soup that is usually judged by the quality of its most important element, the broth. To extract the most flavor from collagen-rich bone-in chicken parts for our broth, we hacked the parts into pieces before browning them to create fond. We then set the chicken aside while we cooked an aromatic mixture of onion, ginger, a cinnamon stick, star anise, cloves, and black peppercorns in the flavorful fond. We returned the chicken to the pot, added water and a bit of fish sauce, and cooked the broth on the stovetop until it was rich and flavorful. Cooking boneless chicken thighs in the broth added even more chicken flavor and provided meat for the soup; while it simmered, we prepared our rice noodles. We topped our pho with Crispy Shallots (optional but recommended) and served it with fresh cilantro, crunchy bean sprouts, lime wedges, sriracha, hoisin, and extra fish sauce. Use a Dutch oven that holds 6 quarts or more for this recipe. The finished broth in step 4 should taste overseasoned; the addition of noodles before serving will temper the flavor of the broth. If you use a cleaver you will be able to cut up the chicken parts quickly, but a heavy-duty chef's knife or heavy-duty kitchen shears will also work.

Broth

- 4 pounds whole chicken legs, backs, and/or wings
- 2 tablespoons vegetable oil, divided
- 1 onion, quartered
- 1 (4-inch) piece ginger, sliced into thin rounds
- 1 cinnamon stick
- 6 star anise pods
- 6 whole cloves
- 1 teaspoon black peppercorns
- 3½ quarts water, plus extra as needed
- 2 tablespoons fish sauce, plus extra for serving
- 2 tablespoons sugar
- 1 tablespoon table salt

Soup

- 1½ pounds boneless, skinless chicken thighs, trimmed
- 16 ounces (¼-inch-wide) flat rice noodles
- 1 recipe Crispy Shallots (optional)
  Bean sprouts
  Fresh cilantro sprigs, Thai or Italian basil sprigs, and/or mint sprigs
  Lime wedges
  Sriracha
  Hoisin sauce

1. For the broth Hack chicken into 2-inch pieces using meat cleaver and pat chicken dry with paper towels. Heat 1 tablespoon oil in large Dutch oven over medium-high heat until just smoking. Brown half of chicken on all sides, 5 to 7 minutes; transfer to large bowl. Repeat with remaining 1 tablespoon oil and remaining chicken; transfer to bowl.

2. Add onion, ginger, cinnamon stick, star anise, cloves, and peppercorns to fat left in pot and cook over medium heat until fragrant, about 1 minute. Return chicken and any accumulated juices to pot. Partially cover, reduce heat to medium-low, and cook until chicken releases additional juices, 15 to 20 minutes, scraping bottom of pot occasionally to release fond.

3. Add water, fish sauce, sugar, and salt and bring to boil. Reduce heat to low, cover, and simmer, skimming away foam as needed, until broth is flavorful, about 1 hour.

4. Set fine-mesh strainer over large bowl or container and line with triple layer of cheesecloth. Discard chicken. Strain broth through prepared strainer and let settle for 5 minutes; discard solids. Using wide, shallow spoon, skim excess fat from surface of broth. Season with salt to taste. (You should have 12 cups broth; add extra water as needed to equal 12 cups. Broth can be refrigerated for up to 4 days or frozen for up to 1 month; thaw frozen broth completely before proceeding with recipe.)

Crispy Shallots

Makes about 1½ cups fried shallots and 1¾ cups shallot oil   **Total Time** 1 hour

We love crispy shallots as a topping for soups like Chicken Pho (page 126) because they add texture and oniony flavor. The golden oil infused with rich shallot flavor that this recipe yields is also great over soups and stews. The shallots should be sliced to a consistent thickness to cook and brown evenly; a mandoline works perfectly. It is crucial to strain the shallots from the oil while they are deep golden—not brown—to prevent them from turning bitter. This recipe can be halved and cooked in a small saucepan.

- 1 pound shallots
- 2 cups vegetable oil for frying
- ½ teaspoon kosher salt

1. Adjust oven rack to middle position and heat oven to 200 degrees. Using mandoline or V-slicer, slice shallots 1/16 inch thick. Set fine-mesh strainer over heatproof bowl. Line baking sheet with double layer of paper towels.

2. Combine shallots and oil in medium saucepan and heat over high heat, stirring frequently, until shallots wilt and lose bright pink color and oil is bubbling vigorously over entire surface of pot, about 4 minutes. Continue to cook over high heat, stirring frequently, until few shallots turn golden, 8 to 11 minutes.

3. Reduce heat to medium-low so that oil is bubbling gently, and continue to cook, stirring frequently, until shallots are deep golden, 2 to 4 minutes.

4. Immediately strain oil into prepared bowl. Quickly spread shallots onto prepared sheet and sprinkle evenly with salt; stir shallots to incorporate salt and allow paper towels to blot up oil. Slide shallots off paper towels directly onto sheet; discard paper towels. Bake until shallots are dry and firm to touch, 15 to 25 minutes. Let shallots and oil cool completely and store separately in airtight containers. (Shallots can be stored at room temperature for up to 1 month; shallot oil can be stored in refrigerator for up to 1 month.)

5. For the soup Return broth to now-empty pot and bring to simmer over medium heat. Add chicken and cook until tender, about 20 minutes. Transfer chicken to cutting board, let cool slightly, then slice thin.

6. Meanwhile, bring 4 quarts water to boil in large pot. Remove from heat, add noodles, and let sit, stirring occasionally, until noodles are soft and pliable but not fully tender. Drain noodles and distribute evenly among serving bowls.

7. Bring broth to rolling boil over high heat. Shingle chicken evenly over noodles, then ladle hot broth into each bowl and top with shallots, if using. Serve immediately, passing bean sprouts, cilantro sprigs, lime wedges, sriracha, hoisin, and extra fish sauce separately.

Tom Kha Gai

Serves 6   **Total Time** 1 hour

Why This Recipe Works With this recipe in your arsenal, you can enjoy the heady flavors of Thai-style chicken soup anytime. For an authentic-tasting soup, we began by making a rich base with chicken broth and coconut milk. Store-bought Thai red curry paste was a good substitution for the assortment of ingredients like makrut lime leaves, galangal, and bird chiles used in from-scratch recipes. Pungent fish sauce and tart lime juice contributed the salty and sour flavors. Although we prefer the deeper, richer flavor of regular coconut milk, light coconut milk can be substituted for one or both cans. The fresh lemongrass can be omitted, but the soup will lack some complexity; don't be tempted to use jarred or dried lemongrass, as both have characterless flavor. If you want a spicier soup, add more red curry paste to taste. To make the chicken easier to slice, freeze it for 15 minutes.

1 teaspoon vegetable oil
3 stalks lemongrass, trimmed to bottom 6 inches and minced
3 shallots, chopped coarse
8 sprigs fresh cilantro, chopped, plus whole leaves for serving
3 tablespoons fish sauce, divided
4 cups chicken broth
2 (14-ounce) cans coconut milk, divided
1 tablespoon sugar
8 ounces white mushrooms, trimmed and sliced thin
1 pound boneless, skinless chicken breasts, trimmed, halved lengthwise, and sliced ¼ inch thick
3 tablespoons lime juice (2 limes), plus wedges for serving
2 teaspoons Thai red curry paste
2 fresh Thai, serrano, or jalapeño chiles, stemmed, seeded, and sliced thin
2 scallions, sliced thin on bias

1. Heat oil in large saucepan over medium heat until shimmering. Add lemongrass, shallots, chopped cilantro sprigs, and 1 tablespoon fish sauce and cook, stirring often, until just softened but not browned, 2 to 5 minutes.

2. Stir in broth and 1 can coconut milk and bring to simmer. Cover, reduce heat to gentle simmer, and cook until flavors meld, about 10 minutes. Strain broth through fine-mesh strainer. (Broth can be refrigerated for up to 1 day.)

3. Return strained broth to clean saucepan, stir in sugar and remaining can coconut milk, and bring to simmer. Stir in mushrooms and cook until just tender, 2 to 3 minutes. Stir in chicken and cook until no longer pink, 1 to 3 minutes.

4. Off heat, whisk lime juice, curry paste, and remaining 2 tablespoons fish sauce together in bowl to dissolve curry, then stir mixture into soup. Ladle soup into bowls and sprinkle with cilantro leaves, chiles, and scallions. Serve with lime wedges.

Hearty Cream of Chicken Soup

Serves 6   **Total Time** 1¾ hours

Why This Recipe Works Cream of chicken soup is usually a distillation of chicken captured in cream. It is rich and silky-smooth, enlivened with herbs and punctuated with tiny bits of tender chicken. To make our cream of chicken soup more substantial, we added potatoes and carrots, along with leeks for sweetness. We used chicken skin to build flavor in two ways: by browning the skin to create fond, which we then used to make a roux, our preferred thickener for silky soup, and by leaving the browned skin in the simmering soup to extract even more flavor from it. We made a roux of butter and flour, and settled on 2 quarts of broth and ½ cup of heavy cream for the liquid. Whisking in the broth gradually helped prevent the formation of lumps. Finally, sherry, fresh herbs, and a bay leaf added deep, complex flavor. This soup can be made with whole milk, half-and-half, or heavy cream, depending on the desired richness.

2 (12-ounce) bone-in split chicken breasts, skin removed and reserved, trimmed
¼ teaspoon table salt
⅛ teaspoon pepper
1 tablespoon water
1 pound leeks, white and light green parts only, halved lengthwise, sliced ¼ inch thick, and washed thoroughly (2½ cups)
2 tablespoons unsalted butter
½ cup all-purpose flour
⅓ cup dry sherry
8 cups chicken broth
12 ounces Yukon gold potatoes, peeled and cut into ¾-inch pieces
3 carrots, peeled and cut into ½-inch pieces
3 sprigs fresh thyme
1 bay leaf
½ cup heavy cream
3 tablespoons minced fresh chives

1. Sprinkle chicken with salt and pepper. Place water and chicken skin in Dutch oven and cook over medium-low heat with lid slightly ajar until enough fat has rendered from skin to coat bottom of pot, about 7 minutes.

2. Uncover pot, increase heat to medium, and continue to cook until skin has browned, about 3 minutes, flipping skin halfway through cooking. Add leeks and butter and cook until leeks are just softened, about 3 minutes. Stir in flour and cook for 1 minute. Stir in sherry and cook until evaporated, about 1 minute.

3. Slowly whisk in broth until incorporated. Add potatoes, carrots, thyme sprigs, bay leaf, and chicken and bring to boil. Reduce heat to medium-low and simmer, uncovered, until chicken registers 160 degrees, 20 to 25 minutes.

4. Transfer chicken to plate and let cool for 20 minutes. While chicken cools, continue to simmer soup for 20 minutes. Using shallow spoon, skim grease and foam from surface of soup. Discard chicken bones and shred meat into 1-inch pieces. Discard chicken skin, thyme sprigs, and bay leaf. Off heat, stir in cream and chicken. Season with salt and pepper to taste. Sprinkle individual portions with chives and serve.

Tom Kha Gai

Hearty Cream of Chicken Soup

Farmhouse Chicken Chowder with
Corn, Poblano Chile, and Cilantro

Turkey Barley Soup

Farmhouse Chicken Chowder

Serves 8 **Total Time** 1¼ hours

Why This Recipe Works This hearty, rustic chicken chowder hails from landlocked rural America. To create the ultimate chowder, we first made a rich chicken broth, which also provided white meat for the soup. We built flavor by rendering bacon and cooking the aromatics in the fat and added flour as a thickener. Then the broth was added along with potatoes and a few other vegetables. Once everything was tender we stirred in heavy cream to add richness and added the chicken. We like using Simple Chicken Broth with Shredded Breast Meat (page 134) here.

- 4 slices bacon, chopped
- 1 onion, chopped fine
- 3 garlic cloves, minced
- 1 teaspoon minced fresh thyme or ¼ teaspoon dried
- ⅓ cup all-purpose flour
- 8 cups chicken broth
- 2 pounds Yukon Gold potatoes, peeled and cut into ½-inch pieces
- 1 carrot, peeled and sliced ¼ inch thick
- 1 red bell pepper, stemmed, seeded, and cut into ½-inch pieces
- 1 cup heavy cream
- 2 cups shredded cooked chicken
- 2 tablespoons minced fresh parsley

1. Cook bacon in Dutch oven over medium heat until crispy, 5 to 7 minutes; transfer half of bacon to paper towel–lined plate. Add onion to bacon left in pot and cook until softened, 5 to 7 minutes. Stir in garlic and thyme and cook until fragrant, about 30 seconds. Stir in flour and cook for 1 minute.

2. Gradually whisk in broth, scraping up any browned bits and smoothing out any lumps. Stir in potatoes and carrot and bring to boil. Reduce to gentle simmer and cook until vegetables are nearly tender, about 10 minutes. Stir in bell pepper and simmer until all vegetables are tender, 10 to 15 minutes.

3. Stir in cream and bring to simmer. Stir in shredded chicken and let heat through, about 2 minutes. Off heat, stir in parsley and season with salt and pepper to taste. Ladle chowder into serving bowls, sprinkle with reserved bacon, and serve.

VARIATION

Farmhouse Chicken Chowder with Corn, Poblano Chile, and Cilantro

Substitute 1 stemmed, seeded, and chopped poblano chile for bell pepper. Add 1 ear corn, husk and silk removed, kernels cut from cob, or 1 cup thawed frozen corn, and chile with carrot in step 2. Substitute minced fresh cilantro for parsley.

STORING AND REHEATING SOUPS, STEWS, AND CHILIS

As tempting as it might seem, do not transfer hot foods straight to the refrigerator. This can increase the fridge's internal temperature to unsafe levels, which is dangerous for all the other food stored there. Letting the pot cool on the countertop for an hour helps its temperature drop to about 75 degrees, at which point you can transfer it safely to the fridge.

To reheat soups, stews, and chilis, we prefer to simmer them gently on the stovetop in a heavy-bottomed pot, but a spin in the microwave works, too. Just be sure to cover the dish to prevent a mess. And note that while most soups, stews, and chilis freeze just fine, those that contain dairy or pasta do not—the dairy curdles as it freezes, and the pasta turns bloated and mushy. Instead, make and freeze the dish without including the dairy or pasta. After thawing the soup, stew, or chili, and heating it through, stir in the uncooked pasta and simmer until just tender, or stir in the dairy and continue to heat gently until hot (do not boil).

Simple Turkey Stock

Makes 8 cups   **Total Time** 2¾ hours (plus 1½ hours cooling time)

Why This Recipe Works We took a simple approach to stock making that delivered pure turkey flavor with very little effort: Our stock is made with just bones and water. Using the roasted carcass as is, without further browning the bones in the oven, saved time and allowed the turkey flavor to come to the fore. Gently simmering the bones in water for just 2 hours extracted enough gelatin to give this stock rich homemade flavor and body. Omitting mirepoix (carrot, celery, and onion) from the recipe allowed the essence of the poultry to shine through and eliminated the effort involved in peeling and dicing vegetables. Pick off most of the meat clinging to the carcass and reserve it. However, don't pick the carcass clean: The stock will have a fuller flavor if there is some meat and skin still attached. If you have the bones from the drumsticks and thighs, add them to the pot.

1 carcass from 12- to 14-pound turkey
10 cups water

1. Remove wings from carcass and separate each wing at joints into 3 pieces. Cut through ribs to separate breastbone from backbone, then cut backbone into 3 to 4 pieces. Using kitchen shears or heavy knife, remove ribs from both sides of breastbone. (You should have roughly 4 pounds of bones broken into 10 to 12 pieces.)

2. Arrange bones in stockpot or large Dutch oven in compact layer. Add water and bring to boil over medium-high heat. Reduce heat to low, cover, and cook for 2 hours, using shallow spoon to skim foam and impurities from surface as needed.

3. Strain stock through fine-mesh strainer into large container; discard solids. Let stock cool slightly, about 20 minutes. Skim any fat from surface (reserve fat for making soup). Let stock cool for 1½ hours before refrigerating. (Stock can be refrigerated for up to 2 days or frozen for up to 4 months.)

Turkey Barley Soup

Serves 6   Total Time 1½ hours

Why This Recipe Works We wanted a turkey soup that would highlight the flavor of our homemade stock. Along with leftover turkey meat, we included starchy barley and simple celery and carrots for vegetables. Limiting the seasonings to thyme, bay leaf, garlic, and a pinch of red pepper flakes along with a squeeze of lemon juice allowed the pure flavor of the turkey stock to shine through. If you don't have turkey fat, you can substitute unsalted butter. This soup is made using the leftovers from a roast turkey; you will use the turkey carcass to make the broth and will need 2 cups of leftover meat for the soup.

2 tablespoons turkey fat
1 onion, chopped fine
½ teaspoon dried thyme
   Pinch red pepper flakes
2 garlic cloves, minced
1 recipe Simple Turkey Stock
¾ cup pearl barley
1 bay leaf
2 celery ribs, cut into ¼-inch pieces
2 carrots, peeled and cut into ¼-inch pieces
2 cups shredded cooked turkey
1 tablespoon lemon juice

1. Heat fat in Dutch oven over medium heat until shimmering. Add onion, thyme, and pepper flakes and cook, stirring occasionally, until onion is softened and translucent, about 5 minutes. Add garlic and cook until fragrant, about 1 minute.

Add stock, barley, and bay leaf, increase heat to high and bring to simmer. Reduce heat to medium-low and simmer, partially covered, for 15 minutes.

2. Add celery and carrots and simmer, partially covered, until vegetables start to soften, about 15 minutes.

3. Add turkey and cook until barley and vegetables are tender, about 10 minutes. Off heat, stir in lemon juice and season with salt and pepper to taste. Serve.

VARIATIONS

Turkey Orzo Soup with Kale and Chickpeas

Serves 6   **Total Time** 1 hour

If you don't have turkey fat, you can substitute extra-virgin olive oil. Our favorite canned chickpeas are from Pastene.

    2 tablespoons turkey fat
    1 onion, chopped fine
      Pinch red pepper flakes
    3 garlic cloves, minced
    ¼ teaspoon ground cumin
    ¼ teaspoon ground coriander
    1 recipe Simple Turkey Stock (page 131)
    3 ounces curly kale, stemmed and cut into
      ½-inch pieces (6 cups)
    1 (15-ounce) can chickpeas, rinsed
    ½ cup orzo
    2 cups shredded cooked turkey
    2 tablespoons lemon juice

1. Heat fat in Dutch oven over medium heat until shimmering. Add onion and pepper flakes and cook, stirring occasionally, until onion is softened and translucent, about 5 minutes. Add garlic, cumin, and coriander and cook until fragrant, about 1 minute. Add stock; increase heat to high and bring to simmer. Stir in kale, chickpeas, and orzo; reduce heat to medium-low and simmer, partially covered, for 10 minutes.

2. Add turkey and cook until orzo and kale are tender, about 2 minutes. Off heat, stir in lemon juice and season with salt and pepper to taste. Serve.

Turkey Rice Soup with Mushrooms and Swiss Chard

Serves 6   **Total Time** 1¼ hours

If you don't have turkey fat, you can substitute extra-virgin olive oil.

    2 tablespoons turkey fat
    1 onion, chopped fine
    ½ teaspoon dried sage
      Pinch red pepper flakes
    3 garlic cloves, minced

    1 recipe Simple Turkey Stock (page 131)
    ¾ cup long-grain white rice
    4 ounces cremini mushrooms, trimmed and sliced thin
    3 ounces Swiss chard, stems chopped fine, leaves
      sliced into ½-inch-wide strips (5 cups)
    2 cups shredded cooked turkey
    2 tablespoons lemon juice

1. Heat fat in Dutch oven over medium heat until shimmering. Add onion, sage, and pepper flakes and cook, stirring occasionally, until onion is softened and translucent, about 5 minutes. Add garlic and cook until fragrant, about 1 minute. Add stock; increase heat to high and bring to simmer. Stir in rice, reduce heat to medium-low, and simmer, partially covered, for 10 minutes.

2. Add mushrooms and chard stems and simmer, partially covered, until vegetables start to soften, about 5 minutes.

3. Add chard leaves and turkey and cook until rice is cooked and chard leaves are wilted, about 2 minutes. Off heat, stir in lemon juice and season with salt and pepper to taste. Serve.

Creamy Turkey and Wild Rice Soup

Serves 6 to 8   **Total Time** 2¼ hours

Why This Recipe Works Turkey and rice soup is a great way to make use of leftover Thanksgiving turkey. We wanted a full-flavored soup with a rich broth studded with perfectly cooked rice and tender turkey. Our turkey soup delivered carrots, wild rice, and a thick creamy texture. To speed up the cooking of the rice, we added a small amount of baking soda to the soup—this helped break down the tough fibers in the rice and reduced our cooking time by about 15 minutes. This soup is made using the leftovers from a roast turkey; you will use the turkey carcass to make the broth (page 131) and will need 3 cups of leftover meat for the soup.

    1 cup wild rice
    1 recipe Simple Turkey Stock (page 131)
    2 carrots, peeled and chopped
    ½ teaspoon dried thyme
    ¼ teaspoon baking soda
    1 cup heavy cream
    ¼ cup all-purpose flour
    3 cups chopped cooked turkey

1. Toast rice over medium heat in Dutch oven until rice begins to pop, 5 to 7 minutes. Stir in turkey stock, carrots, thyme, and baking soda and bring to boil. Reduce heat to low and simmer, covered, until rice is tender, about 1 hour.

2. Whisk cream and flour in bowl until smooth. Slowly whisk flour mixture into soup. Add turkey and simmer until soup is slightly thickened, about 10 minutes. Season with salt and pepper to taste. Serve.

Italian Wedding Soup with Kale and Farro

Serves 6   Total Time 2¼ hours

Why This Recipe Works Italian wedding soup is so named because of the harmonious marriage of meatballs, greens, and pasta in a savory, fortified broth. For a complex broth, we simmered chicken broth with aromatic fennel, onion, garlic, and dried porcini mushrooms, adding white wine for sharpness and Worcestershire for meaty depth. In place of traditional beef and pork, we prepared turkey meatballs, boosting their flavor with parsley, Parmesan, and minced fronds from our fennel bulb. After gently poaching them in the broth, we were pleasantly surprised to find that they turned out delicate and tender. Chopped kale lent its assertive texture. Finally, we replaced ditalini pasta with hearty whole-grain farro. A rasp-style grater makes quick work of turning the garlic into a paste. Be sure to use ground turkey, not ground turkey breast (also labeled 99 percent fat-free), or the meatballs will be tough.

- 1 tablespoon extra-virgin olive oil
- 1 fennel bulb, fronds minced to make ¼ cup, stalks discarded, bulb halved, cored, and sliced thin
- 1 onion, sliced thin
- 5 garlic cloves, peeled (4 smashed, 1 minced to paste)
- ¼ ounce dried porcini mushrooms, rinsed and minced
- ½ cup dry white wine
- 1 tablespoon Worcestershire sauce
- 4 cups chicken broth
- 4 cups water
- 1 slice hearty sandwich bread, torn into 1-inch pieces
- 5 tablespoons milk
- 12 ounces ground turkey
- ¼ cup grated Parmesan cheese
- ¼ cup minced fresh parsley
- 1 teaspoon table salt, divided
- ⅛ teaspoon pepper
- 1 cup whole farro, rinsed
- 8 ounces kale, stemmed and cut into ½-inch pieces

1. Heat oil in Dutch oven over medium-high heat until just shimmering. Stir in sliced fennel, onion, smashed garlic, and

Italian Wedding Soup with Kale and Farro

porcini and cook, stirring frequently, until just softened and lightly browned, 5 to 7 minutes. Stir in wine and Worcestershire and cook for 1 minute. Stir in broth and water and bring to simmer. Reduce heat to low, cover, and simmer for 30 minutes.

2. Meanwhile, combine bread and milk in large bowl and, using fork, mash mixture to uniform paste. Add turkey, Parmesan, parsley, minced fennel fronds, minced garlic, ½ teaspoon salt, and pepper to bowl with bread mixture and knead gently with your hands until evenly combined. Using your wet hands, roll heaping 1 teaspoons of meat mixture into meatballs and transfer to rimmed baking sheet. (You should have 35 to 40 meatballs.) Cover with greased plastic wrap and refrigerate for 30 minutes.

3. Strain broth through fine-mesh strainer set over large bowl, pressing on solids to extract as much broth as possible; discard solids. Wipe pot clean with paper towels and return strained broth to pot.

4. Bring broth to boil over medium-high heat. Add farro and remaining ½ teaspoon salt, reduce heat to medium-low, cover, and simmer until farro is just tender, about 15 minutes. Uncover, stir in meatballs and kale and cook, stirring occasionally, until meatballs are cooked through and farro is tender, 5 to 7 minutes. Season with salt and pepper to taste, and serve.

MAKING CHICKEN BROTH

Making chicken broth from scratch is a simple process of gently cooking bones and aromatics in water, and great homemade broth is like liquid gold. It is a building block of flavor that can improve everything you cook—not only soups but also stews, sauces, bean dishes, and more. Here we have collected the best ways to make broth, whether you want to make it on the stovetop in a stockpot or Dutch oven or use your electric pressure cooker, slow cooker, or sous vide circulator. For our simple turkey stock recipe, see page 131.

Classic Chicken Broth

Makes 8 cups   **Total Time** 5½ hours

This classic approach to making chicken broth calls for gently simmering a mix of chicken backs and wings in water for several hours and requires almost no hands-on work. The long, slow simmer helps the bones and meat release both deep flavor and gelatin and results in a full-bodied all-purpose broth. If you have a large pot (at least 12 quarts), you can easily double this recipe to make 1 gallon.

- 4 pounds chicken backs and wings
- 3½ quarts water
- 1 onion, chopped
- 2 bay leaves
- 2 teaspoons table salt

1. Heat chicken and water in large stockpot or Dutch oven over medium-high heat until boiling, skimming off any scum that comes to surface. Reduce heat to low and simmer gently for 3 hours.

2. Add onion, bay leaves, and salt and continue to simmer for 2 hours.

3. Strain broth through fine-mesh strainer into large pot or container, pressing on solids to extract as much liquid as possible. Let broth settle for about 5 minutes, then skim off fat. (Broth can be refrigerated for up to 4 days or frozen for up to 2 months.)

Simple Chicken Broth with Shredded Breast Meat

Makes about 8 cups broth with 2 cups cooked, shredded meat   **Total Time** 2 hours

This broth is quicker to make than our classic version and delivers a rich, golden broth and edible meat from water, an onion, and one chicken. Choose this broth when you want to have some cooked breast meat for your soup. If you use a cleaver you will be able to cut up the chicken parts quickly, but a heavy-duty chef's knife or heavy-duty kitchen shears will also work. See page 12 for how to cut up a whole chicken.

- 1 (3½- to 4-pound) whole chicken
- 1 tablespoon vegetable oil
- 1 onion, chopped
- 8 cups water
- 2 teaspoons table salt
- 2 bay leaves

1. Cut chicken into 7 pieces (1 breast split into 2 pieces, 2 legs, 2 wings, and backbone). Set breast halves aside and hack remaining parts into 2-inch pieces with meat cleaver.

2. Heat oil in large Dutch oven over medium-high heat until just smoking. Add chicken breasts and brown lightly, about 5 minutes. Transfer to plate.

3. Add half of 2-inch chicken pieces and brown lightly, about 5 minutes; transfer pieces to large bowl. Repeat with remaining 2-inch chicken pieces; transfer to bowl.

4. Add onion to fat left in pot and cook until softened, about 3 minutes. Return chicken pieces (not breasts) to pot, along with any accumulated juices; cover and reduce heat to low. Cook, stirring occasionally, until chicken releases its juice, about 20 minutes.

5. Add reserved chicken breasts, water, salt, and bay leaves and bring to boil. Cover, reduce to gentle simmer, and cook, skimming as needed, until chicken breasts register 160 degrees, about 20 minutes.

6. Remove chicken breasts from pot and let cool slightly. Remove and discard skin and bones and shred breast meat into bite-size pieces. Strain broth through fine-mesh strainer, discarding solids. Let settle for 10 minutes, then skim off fat. (Broth and chicken can be refrigerated separately in airtight containers; broth can be refrigerated for up to 4 days or frozen for up to 2 months, and chicken can be refrigerated for up to 2 days.)

Pressure-Cooker Chicken Broth

Makes 3 quarts   **Total Time** 2¼ hours

To maximize the chicken flavor in our pressure-cooker broth, we tested many combinations of chicken parts and found chicken wings to be the best option. The electric pressure cooker eked out every last bit of chicken-y goodness and gelatin from the bones, resulting in a broth that was remarkably clear and that had a great silky texture. Browning the chicken wings was an easy way to deepen their flavor; we also browned some onion and garlic. A few bay leaves were the only other seasoning we needed to complement the broth.

- 3 **pounds chicken wings**
- 1 **tablespoon vegetable oil**
- 1 **onion, chopped**
- 3 **garlic cloves, lightly crushed and peeled**
- 12 **cups water, divided**
- ½ **teaspoon table salt**
- 3 **bay leaves**

1. Pat chicken wings dry with paper towels. Using highest sauté or browning function, heat oil in electric pressure cooker for 5 minutes (or until just smoking). Brown half of chicken wings on all sides, about 10 minutes; transfer to bowl. Repeat with remaining chicken wings; transfer to bowl.

Classic
Chicken
Broth

2. Add onion to fat left in pressure cooker and cook until softened and well browned, 8 to 10 minutes. Stir in garlic and cook until fragrant, about 30 seconds. Stir in 1 cup water, scraping up any browned bits. Stir in remaining 11 cups water, salt, bay leaves, and chicken along with any accumulated juices.

3. Lock lid in place and close pressure release valve. Select high pressure cook function and cook for 1 hour. Turn off pressure cooker and let pressure release naturally for 15 minutes. Quick-release any remaining pressure, then carefully remove lid, allowing steam to escape away from you.

4. Strain broth through fine-mesh strainer into large container, pressing on solids to extract as much liquid as possible; discard solids. Using wide, shallow spoon, skim excess fat from surface of broth. (Broth can be refrigerated for up to 4 days or frozen for up to 2 months.)

Slow-Cooker Chicken Broth

Makes 3 quarts   **Cook Time** 6 to 8 hours on low or
4 to 6 hours on high
Slow Cooker Size 4 to 7 quarts

Making a tasty chicken broth in a slow cooker is a breeze.
We tested many combinations of chicken parts, finding a
whole cut-up chicken too fussy, and chicken backs, legs,
and necks too liver-y. Using just chicken wings produced
a clear and refined broth, and the long simmering time
pulled every last bit of flavor from the chicken bones.
Roasting the chicken wings was an easy way to incorporate dark color and pleasantly deep caramelized flavor.
Additionally, we found that an onion, a little garlic, and
some salt were all we needed to complement, and not
distract from, the chicken.

  3 **pounds chicken wings**
  1 **onion, chopped**
 12 **cups water**
  3 **garlic cloves, peeled and smashed**
 ½ **teaspoon salt**

   1. Adjust oven rack to lower-middle position and heat
oven to 450 degrees. Line rimmed baking sheet with
aluminum foil and lightly spray with vegetable oil spray.
Distribute chicken and onion evenly on prepared sheet
and roast until golden, about 40 minutes; transfer to
slow cooker.
   2. Stir water, garlic, and salt into slow cooker, cover,
and cook until broth is deeply flavored and rich, 6 to
8 hours on low or 4 to 6 hours on high.
   3. Strain broth through fine-mesh strainer into large
container, pressing on solids to extract as much liquid as
possible. Using large spoon, skim fat from surface of
broth. (Broth can be refrigerated for up to 4 days or
frozen for up to 2 months.)

Slow-Cooker Chicken Broth

Sous Vide Chicken Broth

Makes about 2 quarts   **Cook Time** 4 to 5 hours

With the sous vide method of making broth, a precise, temperature-controlled environment ensures flavor extraction from the chicken bones without evaporation. We found that chicken wings worked best to produce a clear broth with unadulterated chicken flavor. The simple additions of onion, bay leaves, and a little salt complemented the chicken flavor without overpowering it. If you want more roasted chicken flavor, try our Sous Vide Rich Brown Chicken Broth variation. To fit all of the ingredients in one bag, this recipe calls for 2-gallon zipper-lock freezer bags. If you do not have 2-gallon bags, simply divide the ingredients between two 1-gallon bags. Be sure to double-bag the mixture to protect against seam failure. Note that this recipe requires a 12-quart container.

2½ pounds chicken wings, cut into 2-inch pieces
 1 large onion, chopped
 8 cups water
 3 bay leaves
 1 teaspoon table salt

1. Using sous vide circulator, bring water to 185 degrees in 12-quart container.

2. Place all ingredients in 2-gallon zipper-lock freezer bag and seal bag, pressing out as much air as possible. Place bag in second 2-gallon zipper-lock freezer bag and seal. Gently lower bag into prepared water bath until chicken is fully submerged, and then clip top corner of bag to side of water bath container, allowing remaining air bubbles to rise to top of bag. Reopen 1 corner of zipper, release remaining air bubbles, and reseal bag. Cover and cook for at least 4 hours or up to 5 hours.

3. Strain broth through fine-mesh strainer into large container; discard solids. Let broth settle for 5 to 10 minutes, then skim excess fat from surface using wide, shallow spoon. Let cool, then transfer to airtight container and refrigerate or freeze until ready to use. (Broth can be refrigerated for up to 4 days or frozen for up to 2 months.)

VARIATION

Sous Vide Rich Brown Chicken Broth

Note that this variation takes about 20 minutes longer to make than the master recipe.

Heat 1 tablespoon vegetable oil in Dutch oven over medium-high heat until just smoking. Pat chicken dry with paper towels. Brown half of chicken, about 5 minutes; transfer to bowl. Repeat with remaining chicken; transfer to bowl. Add onion to fat left in pot and cook over medium heat until softened, about 5 minutes. Stir in 1 cup water, scraping up any browned bits; transfer to bowl with chicken. Proceed with step 2 as directed.

NOTES FROM THE TEST KITCHEN

FREEZING BROTH

To save extra broth, we either store it in an airtight container in the refrigerator for up to four days or freeze it for up to two months using one of these methods.

Ice Cube Tray After cubes have frozen, transfer them to zipper-lock bag.

Muffin Tin Once frozen, transfer 1-cup portions to zipper-lock bag.

Zipper-Lock Bag Line 4-cup measuring cup with zipper-lock bag; pour in cooled stock. Lay bag flat to freeze.

STEWS, CHILIS, AND CURRIES

Photos (clockwise from top left): Chicken and Dumplings; Chicken Maque Choux; White Chicken Chili; Vindaloo-Style Chicken

Classic Chicken Stew

Serves 6 to 8   **Total Time** 2 hours

Why This Recipe Works We love a good chicken stew: moist chunks of meat and hearty vegetables enveloped in a glossy, thick sauce. That kind of supper can easily take all day to prepare; this one comes together more quickly than many but is deeply flavorful. Rather than fussing with browning and simmering a cut-up chicken, navigating bones and skin, we looked to boneless thighs. More than just convenient, they stayed tender and juicy during slow cooking, giving up enough flavor and collagen to make a rich sauce while retaining plenty of flavor and juiciness (no bland, dried-out meat here). Cooking the stew in a low oven, rather than on the stovetop, ensured consistent, gentle heat transfer. About an hour in the oven allowed time for the thighs' connective tissue to break down, providing gelatin to thicken the sauce and rendering the meat exceedingly tender. Some white wine added an acidic note to cut through the hearty flavors, and thyme added depth. Our stew formula works so well that it easily accommodates other flavor variations. Serve with Easiest-Ever Drop Biscuits (page 141), if desired.

Classic Chicken Stew

3 pounds boneless, skinless chicken thighs, trimmed and cut into 1-inch pieces
1 teaspoon table salt, divided
½ teaspoon pepper
3 tablespoons vegetable oil, divided
2 onions, chopped fine
4 garlic cloves, minced
1 teaspoon minced fresh thyme or ¼ teaspoon dried
¼ cup all-purpose flour
½ cup dry white wine
3½ cups chicken broth
1½ pounds red potatoes, unpeeled, cut into ¾-inch pieces
1 pound carrots, peeled and sliced ½ inch thick
2 bay leaves
1 cup frozen peas
¼ cup minced fresh parsley

1. Adjust oven rack to lower-middle position and heat oven to 300 degrees. Pat chicken dry with paper towels and sprinkle with ¾ teaspoon salt and pepper. Heat 1 tablespoon oil in Dutch oven over medium-high heat until just smoking. Brown half of chicken, 6 to 8 minutes; transfer to bowl. Repeat with 1 tablespoon oil and remaining chicken; transfer to bowl.

2. Heat remaining 1 tablespoon oil in now-empty pot over medium heat until shimmering. Add onions and remaining ¼ teaspoon salt and cook until softened, about 5 minutes. Stir in garlic and thyme and cook until fragrant, about 30 seconds. Stir in flour and cook for 1 minute. Stir in wine, scraping up any browned bits.

3. Slowly whisk in broth, smoothing out any lumps. Stir in potatoes, carrots, bay leaves, and chicken with any accumulated juices and bring to simmer. Cover, transfer pot to oven, and cook until chicken is very tender, 50 minutes to 1 hour.

4. Remove pot from the oven and discard bay leaves. Stir in peas, cover, and let sit until heated through, about 5 minutes. Stir in parsley and season with salt and pepper to taste. Serve.

VARIATIONS

Classic Chicken Stew with Winter Root Vegetables

Turnips, rutabagas, or parsley root can be substituted for the carrots, celery root, or parsnips, if desired. Omit peas. Reduce amount of potatoes and carrots to 8 ounces each. Add 1 pound celery root, peeled and cut into ¾-inch pieces, and 8 ounces parsnips, peeled and sliced ½ inch thick to pot with potatoes.

Classic Chicken Stew with Leeks and Saffron

Substitute 4 leeks, white and light green parts only, halved lengthwise, and sliced ½ inch thick, for onions. Add ¼ teaspoon saffron threads, crumbled, to pot with garlic.

Classic Chicken Stew with Chipotle and Hominy

For a spicier stew, include the jalapeño seeds and ribs when mincing. Omit potatoes. Add 2 jalapeño chiles, stemmed, seeded, and minced, and 1 tablespoon minced canned chipotle chile in adobo sauce to pot with garlic. Substitute 2 (15-ounce) cans white or yellow hominy, rinsed, for peas and ¼ cup minced fresh cilantro for parsley.

Classic Chicken Stew with Red Peppers, White Beans, and Spinach

Omit potatoes and peas. Reduce amount of carrots to 8 ounces. Add 2 red bell peppers, stemmed, seeded, and cut into 1-inch pieces, to pot with carrots. After discarding bay leaves in step 4, mash 1 (15-ounce) can cannellini beans, rinsed, with ⅓ cup of stew liquid in bowl until smooth. Stir mashed bean mixture, additional 1 (15-ounce) can cannellini beans, rinsed, and 4 ounces baby spinach into stew and let sit until spinach is wilted, about 5 minutes, before adding parsley.

Quick Provençal-Style Chicken Stew with Mushrooms and Olives

Serves 4   Total Time 45 minutes

Why This Recipe Works Cooking sliced chicken breasts in a deeply flavored base (essentially poaching them) offers a quick route to a bold chicken stew. To build complexity without long simmering, we first browned mushrooms and onions with herbes de Provence, and then introduced a host of flavor boosters: a healthy dose of tomato paste, six garlic cloves, some red pepper flakes, plus a full cup of kalamata olives, stirred in right at the end for a rich and balanced brininess. Slicing the chicken meant it needed a mere 3 minutes of simmering to cook through while staying perfectly tender. To make the chicken easier to slice, freeze it for 15 minutes. Be sure to crumble any large pieces of rosemary in the herbes de Provence before adding it to the pot.

- 1 pound white mushrooms, trimmed and quartered
- 2 onions, chopped fine
- 2 tablespoons extra-virgin olive oil
- 1 teaspoon herbes de Provence
- ¼ teaspoon table salt
- ¼ cup all-purpose flour

Easiest-Ever Drop Biscuits

Serves 10   Total Time 40 minutes

- 3 cups (15 ounces) all-purpose flour
- 4 teaspoons sugar
- 1 tablespoon baking powder
- ¼ teaspoon baking soda
- 1¼ teaspoons table salt
- 2 cups heavy cream
- 2 tablespoons unsalted butter, melted (optional)

1. Adjust oven rack to upper-middle position and heat oven to 450 degrees. Line rimmed baking sheet with parchment paper. In medium bowl, whisk together flour, sugar, baking powder, baking soda, and salt. Microwave cream until just warmed to body temperature (95 to 100 degrees), 60 to 90 seconds, stirring halfway through microwaving. Stir cream into flour mixture until soft, uniform dough forms.

2. Spray ⅓-cup dry measuring cup with vegetable oil spray. Drop level scoops of batter 2 inches apart on prepared sheet (biscuits should measure about 2½ inches wide and 1¼ inches tall). Respray measuring cup after every 3 or 4 scoops. If portions are misshapen, use your fingertips to gently reshape dough into level cylinders. Bake until tops are light golden brown, 10 to 12 minutes, rotating sheet halfway through baking. Brush hot biscuits with melted butter, if using. Serve warm. (Biscuits can be stored in zipper-lock bag at room temperature for up to 24 hours. Reheat biscuits in 300-degree oven for 10 minutes.)

- 6 garlic cloves, minced
- 2 tablespoons tomato paste
- ⅛ teaspoon red pepper flakes
- 3 cups chicken broth
- 1 (14.5-ounce) can diced tomatoes
- 1 pound boneless, skinless chicken breasts, trimmed, halved lengthwise, and sliced ½ inch thick
- 1 cup pitted kalamata olives, halved
- ¼ cup minced fresh parsley

1. Combine mushrooms, onions, oil, herbes de Provence, and salt in Dutch oven. Cover and cook over medium heat, stirring occasionally, until vegetables are softened, about 5 minutes. Uncover, increase heat to medium-high, and cook until vegetables are lightly browned, about 8 minutes.

2. Stir in flour, garlic, tomato paste, and pepper flakes and cook until fragrant, about 1 minute. Slowly whisk in broth, scraping up any browned bits and smoothing out any lumps. Stir in tomatoes and simmer until thickened and flavors meld, about 10 minutes.

3. Stir in chicken and cook until no longer pink, about 3 minutes. Stir in olives and parsley and season with salt and pepper to taste. Serve.

Chicken and Dumplings

Serves 6 to 8   **Total Time** 3¾ hours

Why This Recipe Works There's no disguising a leaden dumpling. Our goal was dumplings that were light yet substantial, and tender yet durable, cozily nestled in a chicken and vegetable stew bound in a rich sauce. After sampling dumplings that ranged from tough and chewy to fragile and disintegrated, we landed on a method for light and fluffy dumplings that held up beautifully. The secret was adding warm liquid rather than cold to the flour and fat. The reason? The heat expands and sets the flour so that the dumplings don't absorb liquid in the stew. The best-tasting dumplings also contain some chicken fat left from browning the chicken. We cooked bone-in, skin-on chicken thighs skin side down to render some of the requisite fat for our dumplings (and to build fond in the pan) before discarding the skin. Using dry sherry instead of wine gave our sauce bright, fruity flavor, and adding extra liquid gave us plenty of sauce for our dumplings. If you prefer not to use chicken fat in the dumplings, 3 tablespoons melted unsalted butter can be substituted. For tender dumplings, the dough should be gently mixed right before the dumplings are dropped onto the stew.

Stew

    5 pounds bone-in chicken thighs, trimmed
1¼ teaspoons table salt, divided
 ½ teaspoon pepper
    2 teaspoons vegetable oil, plus extra as needed
    4 tablespoons unsalted butter
    4 carrots, peeled and sliced ¼ inch thick
    2 celery ribs, sliced ¼ inch thick
    1 onion, chopped fine
    6 tablespoons all-purpose flour
    1 teaspoon minced fresh thyme or ¼ teaspoon dried
 ¼ cup dry sherry
4½ cups chicken broth
 ¼ cup whole milk
    2 bay leaves
    1 cup frozen green peas
    3 tablespoons minced fresh parsley, divided

Dumplings

    2 cups all-purpose flour
    1 tablespoon baking powder
    1 teaspoon table salt
    1 cup whole milk
    3 tablespoons reserved chicken fat

1. For the stew Adjust oven rack to lower-middle position and heat oven to 300 degrees. Pat chicken dry with paper towels and sprinkle with 1 teaspoon salt and pepper. Heat oil in Dutch oven over medium-high heat until just smoking. Brown half of chicken on both sides, 8 to 10 minutes; transfer to plate. Repeat with remaining chicken; transfer to plate. When chicken is cool enough to handle; remove skin. Pour off and reserve 3 tablespoons chicken fat (if necessary, add extra oil to equal 3 tablespoons).

2. Melt butter in now-empty Dutch oven over medium heat. Add carrots, celery, onion, and remaining ¼ teaspoon salt and cook until softened, 5 to 7 minutes. Stir in flour and thyme and cook for 1 minute. Stir in sherry, scraping up any browned bits. Slowly whisk in broth, milk, and bay leaves, smoothing out any lumps. Nestle chicken into pot. Add any accumulated chicken juices and bring to simmer. Cover, transfer pot to oven, and cook until chicken is tender and registers at least 175 degrees, about 1 hour.

3. Remove pot from oven. Transfer chicken to cutting board, let cool slightly, then shred into bite-size pieces using 2 forks; discard bones. Discard bay leaves. Stir in chicken, peas, and 2 tablespoons parsley. Season with salt and pepper to taste.

ADDING DUMPLINGS TO STEW

1. Gather golf ball–size portion of dumpling batter onto soupspoon. Push dumpling onto stew using second spoon, leaving about ¼ inch between each.

2. Cover stew. When fully cooked, dumplings will have doubled in size.

4. For the dumplings Whisk flour, baking powder, and salt together in large bowl. Microwave milk and reserved chicken fat in separate bowl until just warm, about 1 minute. Stir milk mixture into flour mixture with wooden spoon until incorporated (dough will be very thick and shaggy).

5. Bring stew to simmer over medium heat. Using 2 large soupspoons, drop golf ball–size dumplings onto stew about ¼ inch apart (you should have 16 to 18 dumplings). Reduce heat to low, cover, and cook until dumplings have doubled in size, 15 to 18 minutes. Sprinkle with remaining 1 tablespoon parsley and serve.

VARIATION
Chicken and Herbed Dumplings
Mix ¼ cup minced fresh parsley, chives, dill, and tarragon in with flour in step 4.

Gluten-Free Chicken and Dumplings

Serves 6 to 8   **Total Time** 1¾ hours

Why This Recipe Works For a gluten-free version of this comfort food classic, we first swapped in our Gluten-Free Flour Blend in the usual mixture of flour, milk, melted butter, and a hefty dose of baking powder, but these dumplings simply melted into the stew. We tried adding a little xanthan gum for binding, and while these dumplings retained their shape better, they sank into the stew and had a texture that was more akin to gnocchi than to biscuits. Switching from whole milk to low-fat lightened up the batter and got us closer, but our stew still could not support the starchier dumplings. For a thicker stew, we cut back the broth to 3 cups and added more chopped carrots and celery so the dumplings could rest on a raft of chicken and vegetables while they simmered. They cooked through properly, yielding moist, tender dumplings that soaked up the sauce perfectly. Using boneless, skinless chicken thighs kept the stew simple. We prefer to use our ATK All-Purpose Gluten-Free Flour Blend (page 328); however, an equal amount by weight of your favorite store-bought gluten-free flour blend can be substituted.

Stew
- 2 pounds boneless, skinless chicken thighs, trimmed
- ½ teaspoon table salt
- ¼ teaspoon pepper
- 3 tablespoons vegetable oil, divided

Chicken and Dumplings

Gluten-Free Chicken and Dumplings

4 carrots, peeled and cut into ¾-inch pieces
2 celery ribs, chopped fine
1 onion, chopped fine
1 teaspoon minced fresh thyme
2 tablespoons ATK All-Purpose Gluten-Free Flour Blend (page 328)
¼ cup dry sherry
3 cups chicken broth
½ cup frozen peas
¼ cup minced fresh parsley

Dumplings

9 ounces (2 cups) ATK All-Purpose Gluten-Free Flour Blend (page 328)
1 tablespoon baking powder
½ teaspoon table salt
⅛ teaspoon xanthan gum
½ cup plus 1 tablespoon 2 percent low-fat milk
½ cup plus 1 tablespoon water
3 tablespoons unsalted butter, melted

1. For the stew Pat chicken dry with paper towels and sprinkle with salt and pepper. Heat 2 tablespoons oil in Dutch oven over medium-high heat until shimmering. Brown chicken on both sides, 8 to 10 minutes; transfer to plate.

2. Add remaining 1 tablespoon oil, carrots, celery, onion, and thyme to fat left in pot and cook over medium heat, stirring often, until vegetables are softened and well browned, 6 to 8 minutes. Stir in flour blend and cook for 1 minute. Stir in sherry, scraping up any browned bits. Slowly whisk in broth, smoothing out any lumps. Stir in chicken and any accumulated juices and bring to simmer. Reduce heat to medium-low, cover, and simmer until chicken is tender and registers at least 175 degrees, about 15 minutes.

3. Remove pot from heat. Transfer chicken to cutting board, let cool slightly, then shred into bite-size pieces using 2 forks. Stir in chicken, peas, and parsley. Season with salt and pepper to taste.

4. For the dumplings Whisk flour blend, baking powder, salt, and xanthan gum together in large bowl. Microwave milk, water, and butter in separate bowl until just warm, about 1 minute. Using rubber spatula, stir warmed milk mixture into flour mixture until incorporated and no flour pockets remain; mixture will begin to bubble immediately.

5. Return stew to vigorous simmer over medium heat. Using greased tablespoon measure, spoon portions of dumpling batter evenly over top of stew; you should have about 24 dumplings. Cover, reduce heat to medium-low, and cook until dumplings have doubled in size and toothpick inserted into center comes out clean, about 15 minutes. Serve.

Southern-Style Stewed Chicken and Rice

Serves 6 to 8   **Total Time** 1½ hours

Why This Recipe Works This supremely satisfying dish boasts the clear, unambiguous flavor of chicken and little else. White rice is softened and plumped with chicken stock and tossed with tender pieces of stewed chicken. With so few ingredients to rely on, we had to treat them just right: Gently simmering bone-in, skin-on chicken thighs in broth coaxed out gorgeous flavor and made an ultrasavory base in which to cook our rice. After stewing and shredding our chicken, we returned it to the pot along with the rice, leaving the pot uncovered, and let everything simmer. The rice emerged soft and creamy—just right for this comforting meal. Butter and a chopped onion proved to be the only worthwhile additions, lending savory richness.

4 tablespoons unsalted butter, divided
1 onion, chopped fine
1½ teaspoons table salt, divided
2 pounds bone-in chicken thighs, trimmed
4 cups chicken broth
3 cups water
1 teaspoon pepper
2 cups long-grain white rice, rinsed

1. Melt 2 tablespoons butter in Dutch oven over medium-high heat. Add onion and ½ teaspoon salt and cook until onion is softened, about 5 minutes. Add chicken, broth, water, pepper, and remaining 1 teaspoon salt and bring to boil. Reduce heat to low, cover, and simmer until chicken is tender and registers at least 175 degrees, about 30 minutes.

2. Remove pot from heat. Transfer chicken to cutting board, let cool slightly, then shred into bite-size pieces using 2 forks; discard skin and bones.

3. Return broth to boil over high heat and stir in rice, chicken, and remaining 2 tablespoons butter. Reduce to simmer and cook, uncovered, stirring occasionally, until rice is tender and liquid level drops just below surface of rice, 17 to 20 minutes. Season with salt and pepper to taste. Serve.

Chicken Maque Choux

Serves 4 to 6   **Total Time** 2 hours

Why This Recipe Works Just about every Cajun family has its own version of maque choux, a simple but bold and spicy dish featuring fresh corn. We added chicken and sausage to create a chunky, satisfying stew. To ensure fresh corn flavor, we not only stripped the kernels from six cobs but scraped off the sweet, milky pulp as well. For aromatics, we looked to the Cajun trinity of onions, celery, and bell peppers (red in this case, as we liked their sweetness and color), plus garlic, thyme, and cayenne for pungent warmth. Boneless chicken thighs stayed tender over the slow simmer. Though spicy andouille sausage is traditional, kielbasa offered a milder but still smoky flavor that didn't overpower the corn. We browned and softened the ingredients in stages before adding our corn and broth and transferring the pot to the oven. A final sprinkling of fresh cilantro and a few dashes of hot sauce countered the dish's richness. This stew tastes best with fresh sweet corn; do not substitute frozen corn.

- 6 ears corn, husks and silk removed
- 2 pounds boneless, skinless chicken thighs, trimmed and cut into 1-inch pieces
- ¾ teaspoon table salt, divided
- ¼ teaspoon pepper
- 3 tablespoons vegetable oil, divided
- 1 pound kielbasa sausage, sliced ¼ inch thick
- 2 onions, chopped fine
- 2 red bell peppers, stemmed, seeded, and cut into ½-inch pieces
- 2 celery ribs, minced
- 4 garlic cloves, minced
- 1 teaspoon minced fresh thyme or ¼ teaspoon dried
- ¼ teaspoon cayenne pepper
- 2 tablespoons all-purpose flour
- 2½ cups chicken broth
- 2 bay leaves
- ¼ cup minced fresh cilantro
  Hot sauce

1. Adjust oven rack to lower-middle position and heat oven to 300 degrees. Working with 1 ear of corn at a time, stand ears on end inside large bowl and cut kernels from cob using a paring knife. Using back of butter knife, scrape remaining pulp from all cobs into bowl with corn.

2. Pat chicken dry with paper towels and sprinkle with ½ teaspoon salt and pepper. Heat 1 tablespoon oil in Dutch oven over medium-high heat until just smoking. Brown half of chicken, 6 to 8 minutes; transfer to bowl with corn. Repeat with 1 tablespoon oil and remaining chicken; transfer to bowl.

Southern-Style Stewed Chicken and Rice

Chicken Maque Choux

3. Heat remaining 1 tablespoon oil in now-empty pot over medium heat until shimmering. Brown kielbasa, about 2 minutes. Stir in onions, bell peppers, celery, and remaining ¼ teaspoon salt and cook until vegetables are softened, 8 to 10 minutes. Stir in garlic, thyme, and cayenne and cook until fragrant, about 30 seconds. Stir in flour and cook for 1 minute.

4. Slowly whisk in broth, scraping up any browned bits and smoothing out any lumps. Stir in corn, chicken, and bay leaves and bring to simmer. Cover, transfer pot to oven, and cook until chicken is very tender, 50 minutes to 1 hour.

5. Remove pot from oven and discard bay leaves. Stir in cilantro and season with salt and pepper to taste. Serve with hot sauce.

PREPARING FRESH CORN FOR STEW

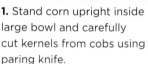

1. Stand corn upright inside large bowl and carefully cut kernels from cobs using paring knife.

2. Before discarding cobs, scrape remaining pulp from each using back of butter knife.

Chicken Pepper Pot

Serves 6 to 8   **Total Time** 1¾ hours

Why This Recipe Works A Caribbean pepper pot is a classic island stew traditionally made with beef, mutton, or pork and aggressively flavored with hot peppers. Okra and cassava are typical vegetable additions. We used boneless, skinless chicken thighs for a lighter dinner option, and the combination of okra, collards, and sweet potatoes (in place of cassava) made this a flavorful and colorful one-pot meal. One Scotch bonnet pepper was all it took to give this dish its characteristic heat, while allspice and thyme were traditional seasonings. Salting the okra drew out some of its viscous liquid to minimize sliminess. While we prefer the flavor and texture of fresh okra in this recipe, you can substitute frozen cut okra, thawed and thoroughly patted dry, for fresh. Skip step 1 if using frozen okra. To make this dish spicier, mince all or a portion of the ribs and seeds from the Scotch bonnet and add them in. Be sure to wear gloves when working with the chile.

1   pound okra, stemmed
¼   teaspoon table salt, plus 1 teaspoon for salting okra
1½   pounds boneless, skinless chicken thighs, trimmed and cut into 1-inch pieces
⅛   teaspoon pepper
2   tablespoons vegetable oil, divided
1   onion, chopped fine
6   garlic cloves, minced
2   tablespoons tomato paste
1   teaspoon dried thyme
½   teaspoon ground allspice
4   cups chicken broth
1   Scotch bonnet or habanero chile, stemmed, seeded, and minced
2¼   pounds sweet potatoes, peeled and cut into 1-inch pieces
1   pound collard greens, stemmed and chopped
    Lime wedges

1. Toss okra with 1 teaspoon salt in colander and let sit for 1 hour, tossing again halfway through. Rinse well, cut into 1-inch pieces, and set aside.

2. Pat chicken dry with paper towels and sprinkle with salt and pepper. Heat 1 tablespoon oil in Dutch oven over medium-high heat until just smoking. Brown half of chicken, 6 to 8 minutes; transfer to bowl. Repeat with remaining 1 tablespoon oil and remaining chicken; transfer to bowl.

3. Reduce heat to medium-low, add onion to fat left in pot, and cook until softened, about 5 minutes. Stir in garlic, tomato paste, thyme, and allspice and cook until fragrant, about 30 seconds. Stir in chicken broth, scraping up any browned bits. Stir in Scotch bonnet chile, sweet potatoes, collard greens, and chicken with any accumulated juices. Bring to simmer and cook until chicken and sweet potatoes are almost tender, 15 to 20 minutes. Stir in okra and cook until chicken and potatoes are completely tender, about 5 minutes. Season with salt and pepper to taste, and serve with lime wedges.

Brunswick Stew

Serves 4   **Total Time** 1½ hours

Why This Recipe Works At many Southern barbecues it's common to find a pot of rich, tomato-based stew full of assorted meats and vegetables simmering near the smoking pits. Recipes can vary by cook and by region, and often the stew becomes bogged down by too many additions. We sampled versions from Georgia, Virginia, and the Appalachians before settling on a North Carolina style made with barbecue sauce, which added complexity to the tomato base, as well as potatoes, which thickened it up. For meat, collagen-rich boneless, skinless chicken thighs were tender and forgiving, and kielbasa provided smoky, porky flavor. Since barbecue sauces vary widely in style, we built our own right in the skillet by browning ketchup before stirring in mustard, cider vinegar, Worcestershire sauce, and red pepper flakes. Staggering the addition of potatoes, crushed tomatoes, and frozen lima beans and corn ensured that all the vegetables finished cooking at the same time. Just before serving, we added final doses of cider vinegar and Worcestershire for a Brunswick stew any North Carolinan would be proud of.

Chicken Pepper Pot

- 1 tablespoon vegetable oil
- 1 onion, chopped fine
- ¾ cup ketchup
- 4 cups water, divided
- 2 pounds boneless, skinless chicken thighs, trimmed
- 1 pound russet potatoes, peeled and cut into ½-inch pieces
- 8 ounces kielbasa sausage, sliced ¼ inch thick
- 6–8 tablespoons cider vinegar
- 2 tablespoons Worcestershire sauce, divided
- 1 tablespoon yellow mustard
- 1 teaspoon garlic powder
- 1 teaspoon table salt
- 1 teaspoon pepper
- ¼ teaspoon red pepper flakes
- 1 cup canned crushed tomatoes
- ½ cup frozen lima beans
- ½ cup frozen corn

Brunswick Stew

1. Heat oil in Dutch oven over medium heat until shimmering. Add onion and cook until softened, about 5 minutes. Add ketchup and ¼ cup water and cook, stirring frequently, until fond begins to form on bottom of pot and mixture has thickened, about 6 minutes.

2. Stir in chicken, potatoes, kielbasa, 6 tablespoons vinegar, 1½ tablespoons Worcestershire, mustard, garlic powder, salt, pepper, pepper flakes, and remaining 3¾ cups water and bring to simmer. Reduce heat to low, cover, and simmer gently until potatoes are tender, 30 to 35 minutes, stirring frequently.

3. Transfer chicken to cutting board, let cool slightly, then shred into bite-size pieces using 2 forks.

4. Meanwhile, stir tomatoes, lima beans, and corn into stew and simmer, uncovered, for 15 minutes. Stir in chicken and remaining 1½ teaspoons Worcestershire and cook until heated through, about 2 minutes. Season with salt, pepper, and remaining vinegar (up to 2 tablespoons) to taste. Serve.

Kentucky Burgoo

Serves 4 to 6   **Total Time** 3 hours

Why This Recipe Works A Kentucky favorite, burgoo is a hunter's style stew, the kind that originally made use of whatever meat was caught and vegetables were harvested, and boasts a warming, slow heat and compelling tangy quality. The stew achieves its rich meatiness from incorporating multiple meats—here, chicken and lamb, an update on the traditional mutton—but it's Worcestershire sauce that's responsible for the unusual tang and savory depth, while a healthy dose of black pepper bestows the spicy warmth. For our meats, bone-in chicken thighs were flavorful enough to stand up to lamb shoulder chops, a favorite cut for stew since they become fall-apart tender and the bones add body to the liquid. To round out the stew we chose traditional vegetables: tomatoes, potatoes, corn, and lima beans, opting for frozen corn and beans to reduce the amount of prep work. A splash of lemon juice at the end brightened up our meaty stew. If you can't find lamb shoulder chops, you can substitute 1½ pounds of boneless leg of lamb or boneless beef chuck-eye roast, cut into 1½ inch pieces.

Kentucky Burgoo

2 pounds bone-in chicken thighs, trimmed
3 pounds lamb shoulder chops (blade or round bone), ½ inch thick, trimmed
1¼ teaspoons pepper, divided
1 teaspoon table salt
1 tablespoon vegetable oil, plus extra as needed
2 onions, chopped
2 tablespoons all-purpose flour
2 garlic cloves, minced
6 cups chicken broth
1 (14.5-ounce) can diced tomatoes
¼ cup Worcestershire sauce
1½ pounds Yukon Gold potatoes, peeled and cut into ½-inch pieces
1½ cups frozen corn
1½ cups frozen baby lima beans
¼ cup lemon juice (2 lemons)

1. Adjust oven rack to lower-middle position and heat oven to 300 degrees. Pat chicken and lamb dry with paper towels and sprinkle with ½ teaspoon pepper and 1 teaspoon salt. Heat oil in Dutch oven over medium-high heat until just smoking. Cook chicken until browned on both sides, 8 to 10 minutes; transfer to large plate. Pour off all but 1 tablespoon fat from pot and reserve (you should have 2 tablespoons; if necessary, supplement with extra oil). Heat fat left in pot until just smoking.

Brown half of chops on both sides, 8 to 10 minutes; transfer to plate. Repeat with 1 tablespoon reserved fat and remaining chops; transfer to plate.

2. Heat remaining 1 tablespoon reserved fat in now-empty pot, add onions, and cook until softened, about 5 minutes. Stir in flour and garlic and cook for 1 minute. Slowly whisk in broth, scraping up any browned bits and smoothing out any lumps. Stir in tomatoes and their juice and Worcestershire and bring to simmer. Nestle chicken and lamb into pot and add any accumulated juices. Cover, transfer pot to oven, and cook until chicken and lamb are very tender and chicken registers at least 195 degrees, about 1½ hours.

3. Transfer chicken and lamb to cutting board, let cool slightly, then shred into bite-size pieces using 2 forks; discard skin and bones.

4. Meanwhile, add potatoes to stew and simmer over medium heat until tender, about 15 minutes. Stir in corn, lima beans, chicken, and lamb and simmer until heated through, about 5 minutes. Stir in lemon juice and remaining ¾ teaspoon pepper and season with salt to taste. Serve.

Gumbo

Serves 4 to 6   **Total Time** 1¼ hours

Why This Recipe Works One of the trademark dishes of Cajun cooking, gumbo is a thick, hearty stew featuring a host of meats—some combination of seafood, poultry, small game, and sausages—and vegetables. But its defining ingredient is a dark roux, a slow-cooked combination of fat and flour that adds flavor and thickens the dish. To avoid having to stand over a pot and carefully stir for upwards of an hour, we found a neat workaround: We toasted the flour by itself on the stovetop for just 5 minutes until it began to brown and then added the oil and let the roux finish unattended in the gentle heat of the oven. When selecting meats, for simplicity, we chose bone-in chicken thighs, andouille sausage, and shrimp. Store-bought chicken broth fortified with fish sauce was an easy substitute for traditional homemade shrimp stock. Fish sauce is important to the flavor of this stew; do not omit it. If andouille is not available, Portuguese linguica or Polish kielbasa can be substituted. The roux cooking time in step 2 may be longer depending on the type of pot you use; the color of the finished roux should be that of a dark copper penny.

¾ cup plus 1 tablespoon all-purpose flour, divided
½ cup vegetable oil
1 onion, chopped fine
1 green bell pepper, stemmed, seeded, and cut into ¾-inch pieces
1 celery rib, minced
5 garlic cloves, minced
1 teaspoon minced fresh thyme or ¼ teaspoon dried
¼ teaspoon cayenne pepper
1 (14.5-ounce) can diced tomatoes, drained
3¾ cups chicken broth
¼ cup fish sauce
2 pounds bone-in chicken thighs, skin removed and trimmed
½ teaspoon table salt
¼ teaspoon pepper
8 ounces andouille sausage, halved lengthwise and sliced ¼ inch thick
2 cups frozen okra, thawed (optional)
2 pounds extra-large shrimp (21 to 25 per pound), peeled, deveined, and tails removed

1. Adjust oven rack to lowest position and heat oven to 300 degrees. Toast ¾ cup flour in Dutch oven over medium heat, stirring constantly, until it just begins to brown, about 5 minutes.

Gumbo

2. Off heat, whisk in oil until smooth. Cover pot, transfer to oven, and cook until mixture is deep brown and fragrant, about 45 minutes. Remove pot from oven and whisk roux to combine.

3. Stir onion, bell pepper, and celery into hot roux and cook over medium heat, stirring often, until vegetables are softened, about 10 minutes. Stir in remaining 1 tablespoon flour, garlic, thyme, and cayenne and cook until fragrant, about 1 minute. Stir in tomatoes and cook until they look dry, about 1 minute. Slowly whisk in broth and fish sauce, scraping up any browned bits and smoothing out any lumps.

4. Sprinkle chicken with salt and pepper and nestle into pot. Bring to simmer, cover, and transfer pot to oven. Cook until chicken is tender and registers at least 175 degrees, about 1 hour.

5. Remove pot from oven. Transfer chicken to cutting board, let cool slightly, then shred into bite-size pieces using 2 forks; discard bones.

6. Stir chicken; sausage; and okra, if using, into stew. Bring to simmer over medium heat and cook until heated through, about 5 minutes. Stir in shrimp and simmer until opaque throughout, about 5 minutes. Season with salt and pepper to taste. Serve.

Chicken
Posole
Verde

Chicken Posole Verde

Serves 6 to 8   Total Time 2 hours

Why This Recipe Works Posole is the Mexican name for both hominy (dried field corn kernels treated with lime and boiled until tender but still chewy) and the full-flavored stew made with hominy and meat. We decided to create a green chicken posole—a style with a trademark tanginess that comes from a puree of tomatillos, jalapeños, and cilantro. Using whole bone-in chicken thighs resulted in easy-to-shred meat, giving our stew a pleasant rustic texture. We quickly browned the chicken, then sautéed our aromatics after we removed the chicken from the pot, allowing us to incorporate the flavorful browned bits into our broth. After discarding the skin, we returned our partially cooked chicken to the pot and moved the cooking to the oven where the stew could cook more gently. Adding the tomatillo puree late in the cooking process allowed the flavors to meld without dulling the puree's bright freshness. Serve with lime wedges, diced avocado, and/or sliced radishes.

- 4 pounds bone-in chicken thighs, trimmed
- 1 teaspoon table salt, divided
- ¼ teaspoon pepper
- 2 teaspoons vegetable oil
- 1 onion, chopped fine
- 3 garlic cloves, minced
- 1 tablespoon chopped fresh oregano or 1 teaspoon dried
- 4½ cups chicken broth, divided
- 12 ounces tomatillos, husks and stems removed, rinsed well, dried, and quartered
- 2 jalapeños, stemmed, halved, and seeded
- 2½ cups fresh cilantro leaves and stems, trimmed (2 bunches)
- 2 (15-ounce) cans white or yellow hominy, rinsed

1. Adjust oven rack to lower-middle position and heat oven to 300 degrees. Pat chicken dry with paper towels and sprinkle with ¾ teaspoon salt and pepper. Heat oil in Dutch oven over medium-high heat until just smoking. Brown half of chicken on both sides, 8 to 10 minutes; transfer to plate. Repeat with remaining chicken; transfer to plate. When chicken is cool enough to handle, remove skin.

2. Pour off all but 1 tablespoon fat from pot. Add onion and remaining ¼ teaspoon salt and cook over medium heat until softened, about 5 minutes. Stir in garlic and oregano and cook until fragrant, about 30 seconds. Stir in 4 cups broth, scraping up any browned bits, and bring to simmer. Nestle chicken into pot and add any accumulated juices. Cover, transfer pot to oven, and cook until chicken is tender and registers at least 175 degrees, about 1 hour.

3. Remove pot from oven. Transfer chicken to cutting board, let cool slightly, then shred into bite-size pieces using 2 forks; discard bones.

4. Meanwhile, process tomatillos, jalapeños, cilantro, and remaining ½ cup broth in blender until smooth, about 30 seconds. Stir tomatillo mixture and hominy into stew, bring to simmer over medium heat, and cook until flavors meld, 10 to 15 minutes. Stir in chicken and cook until heated through, about 2 minutes. Season with salt and pepper to taste. Serve.

Chicken Stew with Sweet Potato, Pineapple, and Plantains

Serves 6 to 8   **Total Time** 2 hours

Why This Recipe Works Rooted in the flavor profile of the Oaxacan dish called manchamanteles (literally, "tablecloth stainer"), this spicy, sweet, and savory stew is as flavorful as it is complex. Traditional manchamanteles consists of a vibrant red sauce made from chiles, nuts, and seeds, served over tender pieces of braised chicken, pineapple, plantains, sweet potatoes, and pinto beans. We set out to create a stew that incorporated each of these elements and brought all of the flavors into focus. To re-create the chile paste for the base of the stew, we ground toasted dried ancho chiles, a portion of our pineapple, onion, peanuts and sesame seeds, garlic, and jalapeño until we had a smooth, rich puree. Sautéing this mixture before adding the broth gave us a heady medium for braising the chicken, sweet potatoes, and beans. We found that using the oven was the ideal hands-off method for simmering our stew. Stirring ripe plantains and pieces of pineapple into the finished stew ensured that the tender fruit didn't turn to mush during cooking. A small amount of red wine vinegar helped to round out the deep chile flavor. If plantains are not available, ripe but firm bananas may be substituted; however, the flavor will be somewhat sweeter.

1½ ounces (about 3) dried ancho chiles, stemmed, seeded, and torn into ½-inch pieces (¾ cup)
4½ cups chicken broth, divided
2 cups ½-inch pineapple pieces, divided
1 onion, quartered
¼ cup unsalted dry-roasted peanuts
3 tablespoons sesame seeds, toasted, plus extra for serving
3 garlic cloves, peeled
1 jalapeño chile, stemmed
3 tablespoons vegetable oil
1¾ teaspoons table salt, divided
1 pound sweet potatoes, peeled and cut into ½-inch pieces
1 (15-ounce) can pinto beans, rinsed
4 pounds bone-in chicken thighs, skin removed, trimmed
½ teaspoon pepper
2 ripe plantains, peeled, quartered lengthwise and sliced 1 inch thick
1 tablespoon red wine vinegar
4 scallions, sliced thin

1. Adjust oven rack to lower-middle position and heat oven to 300 degrees. Toast anchos in Dutch oven over medium-high heat, stirring frequently, until fragrant, 2 to 6 minutes, reducing heat if anchos begin to smoke; transfer to blender. Add ½ cup broth, 1 cup pineapple, onion, peanuts, sesame seeds, garlic, and jalapeño and process until smooth, about 60 seconds.

2. Heat oil in now-empty pot over medium-high heat until shimmering. Add ancho mixture and 1 teaspoon salt and cook, stirring frequently, until mixture has darkened in color and liquid has evaporated, about 10 minutes. Stir in remaining 4 cups broth, scraping up any browned bits. Stir in sweet potatoes and beans and bring to simmer. Sprinkle chicken with pepper and remaining ¾ teaspoon salt and nestle into pot. Cover, transfer pot to oven, and cook until chicken is tender and registers at least 175 degrees, about 1 hour.

3. Remove pot from oven. Transfer chicken to cutting board, let cool slightly, then shred into bite-size pieces using 2 forks; discard bones. Stir shredded chicken, plantains, and remaining 1 cup pineapple into stew and bring to simmer over medium heat. Stir in vinegar and season with salt and pepper to taste. Sprinkle individual portions with scallions and extra sesame seeds before serving.

White Chicken Chili

Serves 6 to 8   **Total Time** 1½ hours

Why This Recipe Works The bold flavors of Mexican green chiles take the forefront in this alternative featuring moist chicken breasts and tender beans. For complex flavor, we used a combination of chiles: spicy jalapeños, mild Anaheims, and sweet-vegetal poblanos. The food processor made quick work of chopping them. To avoid a watery sauce, we pureed some of the chili base with a portion of beans and some broth, which thickened the chili without compromising its flavor. To ensure that the chicken breasts stayed moist, we browned them and then poached them in the chili. A minced raw jalapeño stirred in before serving provided a shot of heat and color. If you can't find Anaheim chiles, add an additional poblano and jalapeño to the chili. Serve with lime wedges, sour cream, and tortilla chips.

White Chicken Chili

Quick Green
Chicken Chili

3 poblano chiles, stemmed, seeded, and cut into
  1-inch pieces, divided
3 Anaheim chiles, stemmed, seeded, and cut into
  1-inch pieces, divided
1 pound onions, cut into 1-inch pieces, divided
3 pounds bone-in split chicken breasts, trimmed
¾ teaspoon table salt, divided
¼ teaspoon pepper
2 tablespoons vegetable oil, divided
3 jalapeño chiles, stemmed, seeded, and minced,
  divided
6 garlic cloves, minced
1 tablespoon ground cumin
1½ teaspoons ground coriander
2 (15-ounce) cans cannellini beans, rinsed, divided
3 cups chicken broth, divided
3 tablespoons lime juice (2 limes)
¼ cup minced fresh cilantro
4 scallions, sliced thin

1. Pulse half of poblanos, half of Anaheims, and half of onions in food processor until consistency of chunky salsa, 10 to 12 pulses, scraping down sides of bowl as needed; transfer to medium bowl. Repeat with remaining poblanos, Anaheims, and onions; transfer to bowl (do not clean food processor).

2. Pat chicken dry with paper towels and sprinkle with ½ teaspoon salt and pepper. Heat 1 tablespoon oil in Dutch oven over medium-high heat until just smoking. Brown half of chicken on both sides, 8 to 10 minutes; transfer to plate. Repeat with remaining 1 tablespoon oil and remaining chicken. When chicken is cool enough to handle; remove skin.

3. Pour off all but 2 tablespoons fat from pot and reduce heat to medium. Add chile mixture, two-thirds of jalapeños, garlic, cumin, coriander, and remaining ¼ teaspoon salt. Cover and cook, stirring occasionally, until vegetables are softened, about 10 minutes. Remove pot from heat.

4. Transfer 1 cup cooked vegetable mixture to now-empty food processor. Add 1 cup beans and 1 cup broth and process until smooth, about 20 seconds. Add vegetable-bean mixture and remaining 2 cups broth to pot and bring to simmer over medium-high heat. Nestle chicken into pot along with any accumulated juices. Reduce heat to low, cover, and simmer gently until chicken registers 160 degrees, 15 to 20 minutes.

5. Transfer chicken to cutting board, let cool slightly, then shred into bite-size pieces using 2 forks; discard bones.

6. Meanwhile, stir remaining beans into chili and simmer, uncovered, until beans are heated through and chili has thickened slightly, about 10 minutes. Stir in chicken and remaining jalapeño into chili and cook until heated through, about 2 minutes. Off heat, stir in lime juice, cilantro, and scallions. Season with salt and pepper to taste. Serve.

Quick Green Chicken Chili

Serves 4   Total Time 35 minutes

Why This Recipe Works Jarred green salsa makes this bold green chili simple to make. To ensure that our chili had plenty of flavor, we used chicken broth as our cooking liquid and added a few potent seasonings—cumin, garlic, and fresh cilantro. Mashing some of the white beans against the side of the pot helped to thicken our chili without the need for any starchy thickener. We like using Perfect Poached Chicken (page 60) here but any cooked chicken would work. Serve with lime wedges, sour cream, and tortilla chips.

- 1 tablespoon vegetable oil
- 1 onion, chopped fine
- ¾ teaspoon pepper
- ½ teaspoon table salt
- 3 garlic cloves, minced
- 2 teaspoons ground cumin
- 4 cups chicken broth
- 2 (15-ounce) cans cannellini beans, rinsed
- 1 cup jarred tomatillo salsa
- 3 cups shredded cooked chicken
- ½ cup chopped fresh cilantro

1. Heat oil in Dutch oven over medium heat until shimmering. Add onion, pepper, and salt and cook until softened, about 5 minutes. Stir in garlic and cumin and cook until fragrant, about 1 minute. Stir in broth, beans, and salsa, bring to simmer, and cook until flavors meld, about 10 minutes.

2. Using back of wooden spoon, mash some beans against side of pot until chili is slightly thickened. Stir in chicken and cilantro and cook until heated through, about 2 minutes. Serve.

Mole Chicken Chili

Serves 6 to 8   Total Time 2½ hours

Why This Recipe Works Inspired by the moles of the Puebla region of Mexico, this chili boasts a rich, bittersweet flavor and deep, dark brown coloring derived from a blend of chiles (dried anchos and canned chipotles), almond butter, sesame seeds, raisins, and chocolate. Moles are typically made by cooking each ingredient individually before pureeing and cooking the mixture until the flavors meld. We realized that cooking some ingredients in stages was critical to layering flavor, but it could be done in a single pot. After browning and removing bone-in chicken thighs, we sautéed dried ancho chiles in the rendered fat until dark red and toasted, then added sesame seeds to toast, then the onion, and finally the chocolate, raisins, and

almond butter. After the mixture cooked down, we added chicken broth and diced tomatoes, pureed the mixture, and returned it to the pot with the chicken to gently simmer in the oven before shredding the meat. After a sprinkling of sesame seeds and scallions, our mole-style chili was complete—glossy, dark, and rich. Serve with warmed corn tortillas.

- ¼ cup raisins
- ¼ cup almond butter
- 1 ounce bittersweet, semisweet, or Mexican chocolate, broken into pieces
- 2 garlic cloves, minced
- 1 teaspoon minced canned chipotle chile in adobo sauce
- ½ teaspoon ground cinnamon
- ⅛ teaspoon ground cloves
- 4 pounds bone-in chicken thighs, trimmed
- ¾ teaspoon table salt
- ¼ teaspoon pepper
- 2 teaspoons vegetable oil
- 1 ounce (about 2) dried ancho chiles, stemmed, seeded, and torn into ½-inch pieces (½ cup)
- 2 tablespoons sesame seeds, plus extra for serving
- 1 onion, chopped fine
- 2 cups chicken broth
- 1 (14.5-ounce) can diced tomatoes
- 1 teaspoon packed dark brown sugar, plus extra for seasoning
- 2 scallions, sliced thin

1. Adjust oven rack to lower-middle position and heat oven to 300 degrees. Combine raisins, almond butter, chocolate, garlic, chipotle, cinnamon, and cloves in small bowl and set aside. Pat chicken dry with paper towels and sprinkle with salt and pepper.

2. Heat oil in Dutch oven over medium-high heat until just smoking. Brown half of chicken on both sides, 8 to 10 minutes; transfer to plate. Repeat with remaining chicken; transfer to plate. When chicken is cool enough to handle; remove skin.

3. Pour off all but 2 tablespoons fat from pot. Add anchos, and cook over medium heat, stirring constantly, until dark red and toasted, about 5 minutes. Stir in sesame seeds and cook until golden, about 1 minute. Stir in onion and cook until just softened, about 2 minutes.

4. Stir in raisin-chocolate mixture and cook, stirring constantly, until chocolate is melted and bubbly, 1 to 2 minutes (do not let chocolate burn). Stir in broth, scraping up any browned bits.

5. Stir in tomatoes and their juice and sugar and bring to simmer. Process sauce in blender until smooth, 1 to 2 minutes, then return it to clean pot and season with salt, pepper, and extra sugar to taste.

6. Nestle chicken into pot and add any accumulated juices. Spoon sauce over chicken and bring to simmer. Cover pot, transfer to oven, and cook until chicken is tender and registers at least 175 degrees, about 1 hour.

7. Remove pot from oven. Transfer chicken to cutting board, let cool slightly, then shred into bite-size pieces using 2 forks; discard bones. Whisk sauce to re-emulsify, then stir in chicken and reheat gently over low heat, 1 to 2 minutes. Sprinkle individual portions with scallions and extra sesame seeds before serving.

Classic Turkey Chili

Serves 6 to 8   **Total Time** 1½ hours

Why This Recipe Works Turkey chili is a great alternative to classic ground beef chili, providing a leaner but no less flavorful meal. To keep the ground turkey moist and tender while slow cooking, we treated it with salt and baking soda. Both helped the meat hold on to moisture, so it didn't shed liquid during cooking. To buttress the mild turkey with plenty of flavor, we weren't shy with seasonings, incorporating a full ¼ cup of chili powder, six cloves of garlic, and plenty of other spices, blooming them in fat to release their full flavor before adding our tomatoes. Because turkey works so well as a blank canvas for other flavors, we were inspired to create two lively variations, one using the bright, tangy flavors of tequila and lime, and another that packs a hot and spicy punch with habaneros and chipotle chiles. Be sure to use ground turkey, not ground turkey breast (also labeled 99 percent fat-free), in this recipe. Serve with your favorite chili toppings and cornbread, if desired.

    2 pounds ground turkey
    1 tablespoon water, plus extra as needed
    1 teaspoon table salt, divided
    ¼ teaspoon baking soda
    ¼ cup chili powder
    6 garlic cloves, minced
    1 tablespoon ground cumin
    2 teaspoons ground coriander
    1 teaspoon red pepper flakes
    1 teaspoon dried oregano
    ½ teaspoon cayenne pepper
    2 tablespoons vegetable oil
    2 onions, chopped fine
    2 red bell peppers, stemmed, seeded,
       and cut into ½-inch pieces
    1 (28-ounce) can diced tomatoes
    1 (28-ounce) can tomato puree
    2 (15-ounce) cans dark red kidney beans,
       drained and rinsed

Southern-Style Cornbread

Makes 1 loaf   **Total Time** 1 hour

    2¼ cups (11¼ ounces) stone-ground cornmeal
    1½ cups sour cream
    ½   cup whole milk
    ¼   cup vegetable oil
    5   tablespoons unsalted butter
    2   tablespoons sugar
    1   teaspoon baking powder
    1   teaspoon baking soda
    ¾   teaspoon salt
    2   large eggs

1. Adjust oven rack to middle position and heat oven to 450 degrees. Toast cornmeal in 10-inch cast-iron skillet over medium heat, stirring frequently, until fragrant, about 3 minutes. Transfer cornmeal to large bowl, whisk in sour cream and milk, and set aside.

2. Wipe skillet clean with paper towels. Add oil to now-empty skillet, place skillet in oven, and heat until oil is shimmering, about 10 minutes. Using pot holders, remove skillet from oven, carefully add butter, and gently swirl to incorporate. Being careful of hot skillet handle, pour all but 1 tablespoon oil-butter mixture into cornmeal mixture and whisk to incorporate. Whisk sugar, baking powder, baking soda, and salt into cornmeal mixture until combined, then whisk in eggs.

3. Quickly transfer batter to skillet with remaining fat and smooth top. Transfer skillet to oven and bake until top begins to crack and sides are golden brown, 12 to 15 minutes, rotating skillet halfway through baking. Using pot holders, transfer skillet to wire rack and let cornbread cool for at least 15 minutes before serving.

1. Toss turkey, 1 tablespoon water, ½ teaspoon salt, and baking soda in bowl until thoroughly combined; set aside for 20 minutes. Combine chili powder, garlic, cumin, coriander, pepper flakes, oregano, and cayenne in bowl.

2. Heat oil in Dutch oven over medium heat until shimmering. Add onions, bell peppers, and remaining ½ teaspoon salt and cook until softened, 8 to 10 minutes. Increase heat to medium-high, add turkey, and cook, breaking up meat with wooden spoon, until no longer pink, 4 to 6 minutes. Stir in spice and garlic mixture and cook until fragrant, about 30 seconds.

Stir in tomatoes and their juice and tomato puree and bring to simmer. Reduce heat to low, cover, and simmer gently, stirring occasionally, for 1 hour.

3. Stir in beans, cover, and continue to cook until slightly thickened, about 45 minutes. (If chili begins to stick to bottom of pot or looks too thick, stir in extra water as needed.) Season with salt and pepper to taste. Serve.

VARIATIONS

Tequila-Lime Turkey Chili with Pinto Beans
Substitute 2 (15-ounce) cans pinto beans for kidney beans. Add ¼ cup tequila and 1 tablespoon honey to chili with turkey in step 2. Stir additional 2 tablespoons tequila, 1 teaspoon grated lime zest, and 2 tablespoons lime juice into chili before serving.

Firecracker Turkey Chili
To make this chili spicier, mince all or a portion of the ribs and seeds from the habanero and add them in. Be sure to wear gloves when working with the chile.

Omit red pepper flakes and cayenne. Add 2 habanero chiles, stemmed, seeded, and minced, and 2 tablespoons minced canned chipotle chile in adobo sauce to spice mixture in step 1. Add 1 tablespoon brown sugar to chili with beans in step 3.

Pumpkin
Turkey Chili

Pumpkin Turkey Chili
Serves 6 to 8   **Total Time** 1½ hours

Why This Recipe Works Folding pumpkin puree into healthy, hearty turkey chili gives it a silky texture and subtle squashy flavor that marvelously complements the chili's smokier notes. To safeguard against rubbery turkey, we followed the lead of our previous chili and treated the ground poultry with salt and baking soda, which helped it hold on to moisture. To give our dish an aromatic backbone, we made our own chili powder by grinding toasted ancho chiles, cumin, coriander, paprika, and oregano. For even more substance and texture, we loaded up the chili with sweet red bell peppers and black beans. The result is a chili with rich flavor that belies its virtuous ingredient makeup. Be sure to use ground turkey, not ground turkey breast (also labeled 99 percent fat-free), in this recipe. Serve with your favorite chili toppings and cornbread, if desired.

- 2 **pounds ground turkey**
- 2 **cups plus 1 tablespoon chicken broth, divided, plus extra as needed**
- 1 **teaspoon table salt, divided**
- ¼ **teaspoon baking soda**
- 2 **ounces (4 to 6) dried ancho chiles, stemmed, seeded, and torn into ½-inch pieces (1 cup)**
- 1½ **tablespoons ground cumin**
- 1½ **teaspoons ground coriander**
- 1½ **teaspoons dried oregano**
- 1½ **teaspoons paprika**
- 1 **teaspoon pepper**
- 1 **(28-ounce) can whole peeled tomatoes**
- 2 **tablespoons extra-virgin olive oil**
- 2 **onions, chopped fine**
- 2 **red bell peppers, stemmed, seeded, and cut into ½-inch pieces**
- 6 **garlic cloves, minced**
- 1 **cup canned unsweetened pumpkin puree**
- 2 **(15-ounce) cans black beans, rinsed**

1. Toss turkey, 1 tablespoon broth, ½ teaspoon salt, and baking soda in bowl until thoroughly combined; set aside for 20 minutes.

2. Toast anchos in Dutch oven over medium-high heat, stirring frequently, until fragrant, 2 to 6 minutes, reducing heat if anchos begin to smoke. Transfer to food processor and let cool about 5 minutes.

3. Add cumin, coriander, oregano, paprika, and pepper to food processor with anchos and process until finely ground, about 2 minutes; transfer mixture to bowl. Process tomatoes and their juice in now-empty food processor until smooth, about 30 seconds.

4. Heat oil in now-empty pot over medium heat until shimmering. Add onions, bell peppers, and remaining ½ teaspoon salt and cook until softened, 8 to 10 minutes. Increase heat to medium-high, add turkey, and cook, breaking up meat with wooden spoon, until no longer pink, 4 to 6 minutes. Stir in spice mixture and garlic and cook until fragrant, about 30 seconds. Stir in pureed tomatoes, pumpkin, and remaining 2 cups broth and bring to simmer. Reduce heat to low, cover, and simmer gently, stirring occasionally, for 1 hour.

5. Stir in beans, cover, and continue to cook until slightly thickened, about 45 minutes. (If chili begins to stick to bottom of pot or looks too thick, stir in extra broth as needed.) Season with salt to taste. Serve.

Chicken Curry
Serves 4 to 6   **Total Time** 2 hours

Why This Recipe Works We set out to create a bold-tasting chicken curry using supermarket staples. Working with bone-in, skin-on chicken pieces meant we would have flavorful rendered fat to enrich the sauce. After browning the chicken, we softened chopped onion and bloomed curry powder and garam masala in the juices for a fragrant, richly spiced base. Garlic, jalapeño, fresh ginger, and tomato paste brought in more flavor. Coconut milk and butter added richness and body while plum tomatoes and frozen peas contributed color and freshness. The sauce was plenty thick, so we cooked it just enough to warm the vegetables through. For more heat, include the jalapeño seeds and ribs when mincing. If you are using both chicken breasts and thighs/drumsticks, we recommend cutting the breast pieces in half so that each serving can include both white and dark meat. The breasts and thighs/drumsticks do not cook in the same amount of time; if using both, note that the breast pieces are added partway through the cooking time. We prefer the richer flavor of regular coconut milk here; however, light coconut milk can be substituted. Serve with rice.

- 4 pounds bone-in, skin-on chicken pieces (split breasts cut in half, drumsticks, and/or thighs), trimmed
- 1 teaspoon table salt, divided
- ½ teaspoon pepper
- 2 tablespoons vegetable oil, divided, plus extra as needed

- 2 tablespoons curry powder
- 1 teaspoon garam masala
- 2 onions, chopped fine
- 6 garlic cloves, minced
- 1 jalapeño chile, stemmed, seeded, and minced
- 1 tablespoon grated fresh ginger
- 1 tablespoon tomato paste
- 1 cup water
- 2 plum tomatoes, cored, seeded, and chopped fine
- ½ cup frozen peas
- ½ cup coconut milk
- 2 tablespoons unsalted butter
- ¼ cup minced fresh cilantro

1. Pat chicken dry with paper towels and sprinkle with ¾ teaspoon salt and pepper. Heat 1 tablespoon oil in large Dutch oven over medium-high heat until just smoking. Add half of chicken and cook until browned on both sides, 7 to 10 minutes. Transfer chicken to large plate. Repeat with remaining 1 tablespoon oil and remaining chicken; transfer to plate. (If using thighs and/or drumsticks; discard skin.)

2. Pour off all but 2 tablespoons of fat left in pot (or add more oil if necessary). Add curry powder and garam masala and cook over medium heat until fragrant, about 10 seconds. Stir in onions and remaining ¼ teaspoon salt and cook until softened, 5 to 7 minutes. Stir in garlic, chile, ginger, and tomato paste and cook until fragrant, about 30 seconds.

3. Gradually stir in water, scraping up any browned bits. Nestle browned chicken along with any accumulated juices into pot and bring to simmer.

4. Cover, reduce to gentle simmer, and cook until chicken is fully cooked, about 1 hour for thighs and drumsticks (175 degrees) or 20 minutes for breasts (160 degrees), flipping pieces halfway through cooking. (If using both types of chicken, simmer thighs and drumsticks for 40 minutes before adding breasts.)

5. Transfer chicken to serving dish, tent with foil, and let rest while finishing sauce. Using large spoon, skim excess fat from surface of sauce.

6. Stir in tomatoes, peas, coconut milk, and butter and simmer gently until butter is melted and vegetables are heated through, 1 to 2 minutes. Off heat, stir in cilantro and season with salt and pepper to taste. Spoon sauce over chicken and serve.

VARIATIONS
Chicken Curry with Red Potatoes and Green Beans
Omit tomatoes and peas. Add 12 ounces unpeeled red potatoes, cut into ½-inch pieces, to pot during last 20 minutes of cooking in step 4 (with breast pieces, if using). Stir 8 ounces

green beans, trimmed and cut into 1-inch lengths, into pot with coconut milk and butter in step 6; cover and simmer until beans are tender, 10 to 12 minutes.

Chicken Curry with Sweet Potatoes and Cauliflower

Omit tomatoes and peas. Add 12 ounces sweet potato, peeled and cut into 1-inch pieces, to pot during last 20 minutes of cooking in step 4 (with breast pieces, if using). Stir ½ head cauliflower, trimmed, cored, and cut into 1-inch florets (3 cups), into pot with coconut milk and butter in step 6; cover and simmer until cauliflower is tender, 10 to 12 minutes.

Chicken Curry

Vindaloo-Style Chicken

Serves 6   Total Time 2 hours

Why This Recipe Works Vindaloo is a complex dish that has both Indian and Portuguese influences. The hallmark is its interplay of sweet and sour flavors in a thick, reddish-orange sauce. Traditional vindaloos are made with pork, but chicken, lamb, and sometimes potatoes have found their way into this dynamic stew. Cumin, cardamom, cloves, and paprika give our version its distinct flavor. Tomatoes, mustard seeds, and chicken broth, along with some aromatic onion and garlic, provided a good base. Red wine vinegar contributed the classic tanginess, and some chopped fresh cilantro provided a burst of color and a distinct herbal note. Do not substitute chicken breasts in this recipe. Serve with rice.

- 3 pounds boneless, skinless chicken thighs, trimmed and cut into 1½-inch pieces
- 1¼ teaspoons table salt, divided
- ¼ teaspoon pepper
- 3 tablespoons vegetable oil, divided
- 3 onions, chopped fine
- 8 garlic cloves, minced
- 1 tablespoon paprika
- ¾ teaspoon ground cumin
- ½ teaspoon ground cardamom
- ¼ teaspoon cayenne pepper
- ¼ teaspoon ground cloves
- 3 tablespoons all-purpose flour
- 1½ cups chicken broth
- 1 (14.5-ounce) can diced tomatoes
- 2 tablespoons red wine vinegar
- 1 tablespoon mustard seeds
- 2 bay leaves
- 1 teaspoon sugar
- ¼ cup minced fresh cilantro

Vindaloo-Style Chicken

1. Adjust oven rack to lower-middle position and heat oven to 325 degrees. Pat chicken dry with paper towels and sprinkle with 1 teaspoon salt and pepper. Heat 1 tablespoon oil in Dutch oven over medium-high heat until just smoking. Add half of chicken and brown well, about 8 minutes; transfer to bowl. Repeat with 1 tablespoon oil and remaining chicken.

2. Add remaining 1 tablespoon oil to now-empty pot and place over medium heat until shimmering. Add onions and remaining ¼ teaspoon salt and cook until softened, 5 to 7 minutes. Stir in garlic, paprika, cumin, cardamom, cayenne, and cloves and cook until fragrant, about 30 seconds. Stir in flour and cook for 1 minute.

3. Gradually whisk in broth, scraping up any browned bits and smoothing out any lumps. Stir in tomatoes with their juice, vinegar, mustard seeds, bay leaves, sugar, and browned chicken along with any accumulated juices. Bring to simmer. Cover pot, place in oven, and cook until chicken is tender, about 1 hour.

4. Remove stew from oven and discard bay leaves. Stir in cilantro, season with salt and pepper to taste, and serve.

Thai Green Curry with Chicken, Bell Peppers, and Mushrooms

Serves 4   **Total Time** 1 hour

Why This Recipe Works Thai green curry starts with an aromatic flavor paste. The paste is simmered with coconut milk, which carries the flavors and forms the base of the sauce. Though store-bought spice pastes are available, we made our own by processing Thai green chiles with shallots, lemongrass, cilantro stems, garlic, galangal, makrut lime leaves, coriander, and cumin in a blender. We bloomed the paste in oil to release its flavors, then simmered it with coconut milk and a little fish sauce to make the silky, intensely rich sauce before adding slices of boneless chicken, shiitake mushrooms, and red bell peppers to cook until tender. Do not substitute light coconut milk here. Shake the coconut milk to combine before using. If you can't find makrut lime leaves (sometimes sold as kaffir lime leaves), substitute one 3-inch strip each of lemon zest and lime zest, adding them to the pot with the coconut milk in step 3; remove the zest before serving. For a spicier dish, include all or a portion of the chile seeds when blending the paste. If fresh Thai chiles are unavailable, substitute 4 serranos or 2 jalapeños. Serve with jasmine rice.

Green Curry Paste
- ⅓ cup water, plus extra as needed
- 12 Thai green chiles, stemmed, seeded, and chopped
- 3 shallots, quartered
- 8 garlic cloves, peeled
- 2 lemongrass stalks, trimmed to bottom 6 inches and chopped
- 2 tablespoons chopped fresh cilantro stems
- 2 tablespoons vegetable oil
- 1 tablespoon grated fresh galangal or ginger
- 2 makrut lime leaves, torn if large
- 2 teaspoons ground coriander
- 1 teaspoon ground cumin
- 1 teaspoon table salt

Curry
- 2 tablespoons vegetable oil
- 2 (14-ounce) cans coconut milk
- 2 tablespoons fish sauce
- 1 tablespoon packed brown sugar
- 1½ pounds boneless, skinless chicken breasts, trimmed and sliced ¼ inch thick
- 8 ounces shiitake mushrooms, stemmed and quartered
- 2 red bell peppers, stemmed, seeded, and sliced thin
- ½ cup fresh Thai or Italian basil leaves
- ½ cup fresh mint leaves
- 1 tablespoon lime juice

1. For the green curry paste Process all ingredients in blender until smooth paste forms, about 4 minutes, scraping down sides of blender jar as needed; transfer to bowl. (If paste does not come together after 1 minute, add up to 3 tablespoons extra water, 1 tablespoon at a time, until it does. Curry paste can be refrigerated for up to 1 week or frozen for up to 2 months; if frozen, let thaw completely before using.)

2. For the curry Heat oil in Dutch oven over medium heat until shimmering. Add curry paste and cook, stirring frequently, until paste is fragrant and darkens in color, 5 to 8 minutes.

3. Stir in coconut milk, fish sauce, and sugar, scraping up any browned bits. Bring to simmer and cook until sauce thickens, about 5 minutes.

4. Stir in chicken and mushrooms and cook until chicken is tender, 5 to 10 minutes. Stir in bell peppers and cook until crisp-tender, 2 to 5 minutes. Off heat, stir in basil, mint, and lime juice. Serve.

Massaman Curry with Potatoes and Peanuts

Serves 4 to 6   **Total Time** 1½ hours

Why This Recipe Works Savory-sweet massaman curry is a Thai dish that's spiced but not spicy. Traditionally, massaman has a warm, faintly sweet, spiced profile from a mix of warm spices (including cinnamon, cloves, cardamom, and cumin), roasted dried chiles, and fresh aromatics. Shrimp paste or fish sauce and tangy tamarind or lime juice are usually added to balance the rich sauce, which is typically paired with chicken (or beef), potato chunks, and roasted peanuts. For chiles, we used dried New Mexican chiles for their relatively moderate heat, and five-spice powder offered a useful stand-in for the traditional massaman lineup of spices. Broiling the chiles, shallots, and garlic yielded more-robust flavors and made the ingredients easier to process into a smooth paste. We sautéed the paste to intensify the flavors before stirring in coconut milk and chicken broth. Then it was just a matter of simmering the potatoes, onion, chicken, and peanuts until they were tender. A final garnish of lime zest and cilantro added both color and brightness. Serve with jasmine rice.

Curry Paste

- 6 dried New Mexican chiles
- 4 shallots, unpeeled
- 7 garlic cloves, unpeeled
- ½ cup chopped fresh ginger
- ¼ cup water
- 1½ tablespoons lime juice
- 1½ tablespoons vegetable oil
- 1 tablespoon fish sauce
- 1 teaspoon five-spice powder
- ½ teaspoon ground cumin
- ½ teaspoon pepper

Curry

- 1 teaspoon vegetable oil
- 1 (14-ounce) can coconut milk
- 1¼ cups chicken broth
- 1 pound Yukon Gold potatoes, unpeeled, cut into ¾-inch pieces
- 1 onion, cut into ¾-inch pieces
- ⅓ cup dry-roasted peanuts
- ¾ teaspoon table salt
- 1 pound boneless, skinless chicken thighs, trimmed and cut into 1-inch pieces
- 2 teaspoons grated lime zest
- ¼ cup chopped fresh cilantro

1. For the curry paste Adjust oven rack to middle position and heat oven to 350 degrees. Line rimmed baking sheet with aluminum foil. Arrange New Mexican chiles on prepared sheet and toast until puffed and fragrant, 4 to 6 minutes. Transfer chiles to large plate. Heat broiler.

2. Place shallots and garlic on now-empty sheet and broil until softened and skins are charred, 6 to 9 minutes.

3. When cool enough to handle, stem and seed chiles and tear into 1½-inch pieces. Process chiles in blender until finely ground, about 1 minute. Peel shallots and garlic. Add shallots, garlic, ginger, water, lime juice, oil, fish sauce, five-spice powder, cumin, and pepper to blender. Process to smooth paste, 2 to 3 minutes, scraping down sides of blender jar as needed. (You should have 1 cup paste. Paste can be refrigerated for up to 1 week or frozen for up to 2 months; if frozen, let thaw completely before using.)

4. For the curry Heat oil in large saucepan over medium heat until shimmering. Add curry paste and cook, stirring constantly, until paste begins to brown, 2½ to 3 minutes. Stir in coconut milk, broth, potatoes, onion, peanuts, and salt, scraping up any browned bits. Bring to simmer and cook until potatoes are just tender, 12 to 14 minutes.

5. Stir in chicken; continue to simmer until chicken is cooked through, 10 to 12 minutes. Off heat, stir in lime zest. Sprinkle with cilantro and serve.

Massaman Curry with Potatoes and Peanuts

CLASSIC BRAISES

Photos (clockwise from top left): Chicken Bouillabaisse; Chicken in Adobo; Chicken Provençal; Country Captain

Chicken with
40 Cloves of Garlic

Chicken with 40 Cloves of Garlic

Serves 4   **Total Time** 1¼ hours

Why This Recipe Works When the iconic James Beard first published his recipe for chicken with 40 cloves of garlic in the 1970s, he reassured home cooks about the "wonderful, buttery paste perfumed with garlic" that would result from this recipe. Luckily for us today, they believed him. This rustic but fancy-sounding dish is very easy to make and yields huge flavor dividends. We gave the garlic a head start on cooking in the microwave to soften and begin to mellow it. The small amount of sugar added also helped it brown more quickly when it went into the skillet. Chicken broth, heavy cream, dry sherry, and fresh thyme combined to make the luscious sauce, and mashing half of the garlic cloves into the sauce ensured sweet garlic flavor in every bite. You will need three or four heads of garlic to yield 40 cloves. You can substitute four bone-in, skin-on chicken breasts (halved crosswise) for the thighs, but reduce the cooking time in step 3 to 15 to 20 minutes. Serve this dish with plenty of crusty bread to scoop up the rich, garlicky sauce.

40 garlic cloves, peeled
2 teaspoons vegetable oil, divided
½ teaspoon sugar
8 (5- to 7-ounce) bone-in chicken thighs, trimmed
½ teaspoon table salt
¼ teaspoon pepper
½ cup dry sherry
¾ cup chicken broth
½ cup heavy cream
2 teaspoons cornstarch dissolved in 1 tablespoon water
2 sprigs fresh thyme
1 bay leaf

1. Adjust oven rack to upper-middle position and heat oven to 450 degrees. Toss garlic in bowl with 1 teaspoon oil and sugar. Microwave garlic until slightly softened, with light brown spotting, about 4 minutes, stirring halfway through microwaving.

2. Pat chicken dry with paper towels and sprinkle with salt and pepper. Heat remaining 1 teaspoon oil in 12-inch ovensafe skillet over medium-high heat until just smoking. Cook chicken skin side down until browned, 7 to 10 minutes. Transfer to plate, skin side up. Pour off all but 1 tablespoon fat from skillet. Reduce heat to medium-low, add garlic, and cook until evenly browned, about 1 minute.

3. Off heat, add sherry to skillet. Return skillet to medium heat and bring sherry to simmer, scraping up any browned bits. Cook until sherry coats garlic and pan is nearly dry, about 4 minutes. Stir in broth, cream, cornstarch mixture, thyme sprigs, and bay leaf and simmer until slightly thickened, about 3 minutes. Return chicken skin side up to skillet along with any accumulated juices. Transfer skillet to oven and roast until chicken registers 175 degrees, 18 to 22 minutes.

4. Using pot holder (skillet handle will be hot), remove skillet from oven. Transfer chicken and half of garlic to serving platter. Discard thyme sprig and bay leaf. Using potato masher, mash remaining garlic into sauce and season with salt and pepper to taste. Pour half of sauce around chicken. Serve, passing remaining sauce separately.

PEELING A LOT OF GARLIC

Break heads of garlic into cloves and place in zipper-lock bag. Squeeze out air, seal bag, and gently pound garlic with rolling pin. Remove peeled cloves from bag, zip bag up with skins inside, and discard.

Braised Chicken with Mustard and Herbs

Braised Chicken with Mustard and Herbs

Serves 4 to 6   **Total Time** 1½ hours

Why This Recipe Works Chicken is great for braising. Its skin renders fat and collagen, which add flavor and body to the sauce, and the meat turns tender and gives up savory juices. For well-seasoned, juicy chicken pieces, we brined bone-in halved breasts, thighs, and drumsticks. We then browned the chicken (except for the tapered breast ends) to create a flavorful fond, to which we added aromatics and just enough flour to emulsify the fat and make the sauce silky. Deglazing the pot with white wine and water created the perfect braising liquid. Staggering the cooking of the dark and white meat ensured that the tough collagen in the dark meat broke down before the white meat dried out. Adding the broad breast pieces first gave them a jump start before the thinner tapered pieces went into the pot. Finally, we transferred the pot to the oven and let the chicken pieces simmer gently until tender. We created a classic sauce with mustard, fresh parsley, and lemon juice. Chicken breasts are broader at

one end than the other, so cut more than halfway up each breast to create two pieces of equal mass. There's no need to take the temperature of the dark meat; it will be properly cooked by the time the white meat reaches its target temperature. If you prefer not to serve the skin, wait until step 6 to remove it; browning the skin produces flavorful compounds that add complexity to the sauce, and braising it releases gelatin, which gives the sauce a rich texture.

½ cup table salt for brining
3½ pounds bone-in chicken pieces (2 split breasts halved crosswise, 2 drumsticks, and 2 thighs), trimmed
1 tablespoon vegetable oil
1 onion, chopped fine
3 garlic cloves, minced
1 tablespoon minced fresh thyme
1 teaspoon pepper
1 tablespoon all-purpose flour
⅓ cup dry white wine
3 tablespoons minced fresh parsley
1½ tablespoons whole-grain mustard
2 teaspoons lemon juice

1. Dissolve salt in 2 quarts cold water in large container. Submerge chicken in brine, cover, and refrigerate for 30 minutes to 1 hour. Remove chicken from brine and thoroughly pat dry with paper towels. Set aside tapered breast pieces.

2. Adjust oven rack to middle position and heat oven to 300 degrees. Heat oil in Dutch oven over medium-high heat until just smoking. Cook all chicken except reserved tapered breast pieces skin side down until browned, 5 to 8 minutes. Transfer to plate. Pour off all but 2 tablespoons fat from pot, then reduce heat to medium.

3. Add onion and cook, stirring occasionally, until softened, 5 to 7 minutes. Stir in garlic, thyme, and pepper and cook until fragrant, about 30 seconds. Stir in flour and cook, stirring constantly, for 1 minute. Stir in wine and 1¼ cups water, scraping up any browned bits.

4. Place thighs and drumsticks skin side up in pot and bring to simmer over medium heat. Cover and cook for 8 minutes. (Sauce will have consistency of thick gravy but will thin as chicken cooks.) Add broad breast pieces, skin side down, along with any accumulated juices. Cover and cook until broad breast pieces register 105 to 115 degrees, 3 to 5 minutes. Remove pot from heat.

5. Flip broad breast pieces skin side up. Add tapered breast pieces, skin side up, to pot and cover. Transfer pot to oven and cook until breast pieces register 160 degrees, 15 to 30 minutes.

6. Transfer chicken to serving dish. Discard skin from tapered breast pieces (or all skin, if desired). Sauce should thinly coat back of spoon; if necessary, simmer until slightly thickened, 1 to 2 minutes. Stir parsley, mustard, and lemon juice into sauce. Season with salt and pepper to taste. Pour sauce over chicken and serve.

VARIATION
Braised Chicken with Herbes de Provence and Lemon

Substitute 2 teaspoons herbes de Provence for thyme. Omit mustard. Increase lemon juice to 1 tablespoon and add ¾ teaspoon lemon zest with juice.

PATTING CHICKEN DRY

Excess moisture on the skin will cause it to stick to the pot and tear away from the meat, so be sure to pat the chicken dry before cooking. Doing so will also remove excess salt from brining.

Lemon-Braised Chicken Thighs with Chickpeas and Fennel

Lemon-Braised Chicken Thighs with Chickpeas and Fennel

Serves 4   **Total Time** 1½ hours

Why This Recipe Works This skillet meal-in-one builds ample flavor in little time. We first browned meaty bone-in chicken thighs to create a savory base. Next, we layered in aromatics like sweet fennel, garlic, lemon zest, and citrusy coriander for brightness and complexity. Canned whole chickpeas added heft to the dish, while mashed chickpeas helped thicken the sauce. To keep the chicken skin crispy, we nestled the browned chicken thighs on top of the aromatics and braised the mixture uncovered in the oven. Keeping the skillet uncovered allowed the sauce to reduce as the chicken braised, and placing the skillet on the upper rack took advantage of reflected, top-down heat, ensuring crispy skin. Cooking the chicken to an internal temperature of 185 degrees rendered the fat and melted the tough connective tissue into rich gelatin. Note that only the skin side of the chicken is seared in step 2. Leave the core in the fennel so the wedges don't fall apart. We prefer briny green olives like Manzanilla, Picholine, or Cerignola in this recipe; look for them in your grocery store's salad bar section or in the pickle aisle.

2 (15-ounce) cans chickpeas, rinsed, divided
6 (5- to 7-ounce) bone-in chicken thighs, trimmed
¾ teaspoon table salt, divided
¼ teaspoon pepper
1 tablespoon extra-virgin olive oil
1 large fennel bulb, stalks discarded, bulb halved and cut into ½-inch-thick wedges through core
4 garlic cloves, minced
2 teaspoons grated lemon zest plus 1½ tablespoons juice
1 teaspoon ground coriander
½ teaspoon red pepper flakes
½ cup dry white wine
1 cup pitted large brine-cured green olives, halved
¾ cup chicken broth
1 tablespoon honey
2 tablespoons chopped fresh parsley
1 baguette, sliced

1. Adjust oven rack to upper-middle position and heat oven to 350 degrees. Place ½ cup chickpeas in bowl and mash to coarse puree with potato masher; set aside. Pat chicken dry with paper towels and sprinkle with ½ teaspoon salt and pepper.

2. Heat oil in ovensafe 12-inch skillet over medium-high heat until just smoking. Cook chicken skin side down until browned, 8 to 10 minutes. Transfer chicken to plate, skin side up.

3. Pour off all but 2 tablespoons fat from skillet, then heat fat left in skillet over medium heat until shimmering. Add fennel, cut side down, and sprinkle with remaining ¼ teaspoon salt. Cook, covered, until lightly browned, 3 to 5 minutes per side. Add garlic, lemon zest, coriander, and pepper flakes and cook, uncovered, until fragrant, about 30 seconds. Stir in wine, scraping up any browned bits, and cook until almost evaporated, about 2 minutes.

4. Stir in olives, broth, honey, lemon juice, mashed chickpeas, and remaining whole chickpeas and bring to simmer. Nestle chicken into liquid, keeping skin above surface. Transfer skillet to oven and bake, uncovered, until fennel is tender and chicken registers 185 degrees, 35 to 40 minutes. Sprinkle with parsley and serve with baguette slices.

NOTES FROM THE TEST KITCHEN

"OVERCOOKING" CHICKEN
Braising unlocks the delicious flavor already inherent in the food you're cooking. When you braise fattier, meaty chicken thighs, collagen—the main protein that makes up the chewy connective tissue that surrounds meat's muscle fibers—doesn't even start to break down until the chicken reaches 140 degrees. But cook this collagen-rich cut past this point and the collagen melts into gooey gelatin, which lubricates the fibers, making the meat tender—even more tender than before the moisture was pushed out. At 175 degrees, the dark meat chicken is tender but clings to the bone. A thigh slowly cooked to 195 degrees is something else: meltingly tender and exceptionally succulent, with rich poultry flavor. Take the thighs too far, to 210 degrees, and the meat slumps off the bone, can look gray, and tastes bland, losing its flavor to the surrounding liquid.

175 degrees

195 degrees

210 degrees

Braised Chicken with Leeks and Saffron

Serves 4 to 6   **Total Time** 1¼ hours

Why This Recipe Works Saffron gives this braise a yellow-orange hue as well as a rich, earthy flavor that's supported by gently aromatic leeks. Leeks take especially well to braising; to make the most of their oniony sweetness, we cooked them until soft before adding our braising liquid. Cooking the saffron along with the leeks and a couple of garlic cloves allowed its flavor to bloom. We nestled the chicken into the pot and cooked it until tender; we then removed the chicken pieces and simmered the liquid to make a sauce. A splash of lemon juice and a handful of chopped parsley added a bright finish. If you are using both chicken breasts and thighs/drumsticks, we recommend cutting the breast pieces in half so that each serving includes both white and dark meat. Using thighs or drumsticks will increase the total cooking time by 40 minutes. For the best flavor, buy saffron threads (not powder) and crumble them yourself. Serve with Classic Mashed Potatoes (page 169).

4 pounds bone-in chicken pieces (split breasts halved crosswise, drumsticks, and/or thighs), trimmed
1 teaspoon table salt, divided
½ teaspoon pepper
2 tablespoons vegetable oil, plus more as needed
2 large leeks, white and light green parts only, halved lengthwise, sliced thin, and washed thoroughly
¼ teaspoon saffron threads
2 garlic cloves, minced
1 tablespoon all-purpose flour
1½ cups chicken broth
½ cup dry white wine
1½ teaspoons minced fresh thyme or ½ teaspoon dried
2 bay leaves
2 teaspoons lemon juice
¼ cup minced fresh parsley

1. Pat chicken dry with paper towels and sprinkle with ¾ teaspoon salt and pepper. Heat oil in Dutch oven over medium-high heat until just smoking. Cook half of chicken skin side down until browned, 5 to 8 minutes. Flip chicken and brown on second side, about 5 minutes; transfer to plate. Repeat with remaining chicken; transfer to plate.

2. Pour off all but 1 tablespoon fat from pot. (Add additional oil to equal 1 tablespoon, if needed.) Add leeks, saffron, and remaining ¼ teaspoon salt to pot and cook over medium heat, stirring occasionally, until leeks are softened, 5 to 7 minutes.

Stir in garlic and cook until fragrant, about 30 seconds. Stir in flour and cook for 1 minute. Whisk in broth, wine, thyme, and bay leaves, scraping up any browned bits.

3. Nestle chicken, along with any accumulated juice, into pot and bring to simmer. Cover, turn heat to medium-low, and simmer until chicken is fully cooked, about 20 minutes for breasts to register 160 degrees and 1 hour for drumsticks/thighs to register 175 degrees. (If using both types of chicken, simmer thighs and drumsticks for 40 minutes before adding breasts.)

4. Transfer chicken to serving dish, tent with foil, and let rest while finishing sauce. Remove bay leaves. Skim as much fat as possible off surface of sauce and return to simmer until sauce has thickened slightly, 4 to 6 minutes. Off heat, stir in lemon juice and season with salt and pepper to taste. Pour sauce over chicken, sprinkle with parsley, and serve.

Braised Lemon Chicken Breasts
Serves 4   **Total Time** 1 hour

Why This Recipe Works Chicken and lemon are a classic pairing, but infusing the meat with bold lemon flavor can be a challenge. We took a two-step approach: After browning bone-in chicken breasts, we braised them in broth with lemon juice so they would pick up lemon flavor as they cooked. Once the breasts were done, we added a few lemon slices to the braising liquid and reduced it to make a sauce. The slices provided a fresh lemon flavor that brightened the whole dish. A tablespoon of honey complemented the flavor of the lemon, and a generous dollop of sour cream, whisked in at the end, underscored the tangy flavor of this chicken dish. Adding the sour cream to the sauce off the heat will prevent the sauce from curdling. Shallots are used as a vegetable here, but if you prefer you can add one medium red onion, minced, with the whole garlic cloves instead.

- 4 (12-ounce) bone-in split chicken breasts, trimmed
- 1 teaspoon table salt, divided
- ¼ teaspoon pepper
- 2 tablespoons extra-virgin olive oil
- 12 shallots, peeled and halved lengthwise if large
- 16 garlic cloves, peeled (12 whole, 4 minced)
- 1 tablespoon chopped fresh thyme
- 1½ cups chicken broth
- 3 tablespoons lemon juice plus 4 thin lemon slices (2 lemons)
- 1 tablespoon honey
- ¼ cup sour cream
- 1 tablespoon chopped fresh parsley

1. Pat chicken dry with paper towels and sprinkle with ½ teaspoon salt and pepper. Heat oil in 12-inch skillet over medium-high heat until just smoking. Cook chicken skin side down until browned, 4 to 6 minutes. Transfer to plate.

2. Reduce heat to medium and add shallots, whole garlic cloves, and remaining ½ teaspoon salt to now-empty pan. Cook until vegetables begin to soften and turn spotty brown, about 5 minutes. Add minced garlic and thyme and cook until fragrant, about 30 seconds. Stir in broth, lemon juice, and honey. Return chicken, skin side up, and accumulated juices to skillet. Bring to boil, cover, and reduce heat to medium-low. Simmer until thickest part of chicken registers 160 degrees, 20 to 25 minutes.

3. Transfer chicken to serving platter and tent with foil. Add lemon slices to pan, increase heat to high, and boil until sauce is slightly thickened, about 7 minutes. Off heat, whisk in sour cream and parsley and season with salt and pepper to taste. Pour sauce over chicken. Serve.

Southern-Style Smothered Chicken
Serves 4   **Total Time** 1¼ hours

Why This Recipe Works For our take on smothered chicken, we had two goals: big chicken flavor and weeknight ease. For perfectly tender, evenly cooked Southern-style smothered chicken, we started with chicken parts rather than a whole bird. We browned the pieces and then shallow-braised them in a savory gravy built from pantry ingredients: chicken broth, flour, sautéed onions, celery, garlic, and dried sage. We found that we needed just 2 tablespoons of flour to thicken the gravy to a rich—but not stodgy—consistency. A splash of cider vinegar brightened the sauce and helped the chicken's flavor shine. This dish is best served with rice, but it's also good with potatoes. You may substitute ground sage for the dried sage leaves, but decrease the amount to ¼ teaspoon.

- 3 pounds bone-in chicken pieces (split breasts halved crosswise, drumsticks, and/or thighs), trimmed
- 1½ teaspoons table salt, divided
- ¾ teaspoon pepper, divided
- ½ cup plus 2 tablespoons all-purpose flour, divided
- ¼ cup vegetable oil
- 2 onions, chopped fine
- 2 celery ribs, chopped fine
- 3 garlic cloves, minced
- 1 teaspoon dried sage leaves
- 2 cups chicken broth
- 1 tablespoon cider vinegar
- 2 tablespoons minced fresh parsley

1. Pat chicken dry with paper towels and sprinkle with ½ teaspoon salt and ¼ teaspoon pepper. Spread ½ cup flour in shallow dish. Working with 1 piece at a time, dredge chicken in flour, shaking off excess, and transfer to plate.

2. Heat oil in Dutch oven over medium-high heat. Cook half of chicken skin side down until browned, 5 to 8 minutes. Flip chicken and brown on second side, about 5 minutes; transfer to plate. Repeat with remaining chicken; transfer to plate.

3. Pour off all but 2 tablespoons fat and return pot to medium heat. Add onions, celery, remaining 1 teaspoon salt, and remaining ½ teaspoon pepper and cook until softened, 6 to 8 minutes. Stir in garlic, sage, and remaining 2 tablespoons flour and cook until vegetables are well coated with flour and garlic is fragrant, about 1 minute. Whisk in broth, scraping up any browned bits.

4. Nestle chicken into sauce, add any accumulated juices from plate, and bring to boil. Reduce heat to low, cover, and simmer until breasts register 160 degrees and drumsticks/thighs register 175 degrees, 30 to 40 minutes.

5. Transfer chicken to serving dish. Stir vinegar into sauce and season with salt and pepper to taste. Pour sauce over chicken, sprinkle with parsley, and serve.

Braised Chicken Thighs with Chard and Mustard

Serves 4   Total Time 2¼ hours

Why This Recipe Works Rich-tasting chicken thighs and slightly bitter Swiss chard make a good combination for a simple, satisfying one-pot dinner. Braised bone-in thighs become juicy and tender as they simmer and flavor the surrounding sauce. Browning brings rich flavor, but we weren't excited about eating flabby skin—inevitable after a long simmer. So, after browning skin-on thighs to develop lots of flavorful fond, we discarded the skin. Then we built our braise with bold ingredients: sturdy chard; garlic, thyme, and an umami-packed anchovy fillet for flavor; lemon zest for brightness; and bay leaves for depth. Cooking the chicken thighs for a full hour allowed the collagen to melt into rich gelatin, adding body and depth to the sauce. A dollop of mustard added sharp contrast to the sauce's richness. We like to use green or white Swiss chard here; if using red chard, note that the sauce will take on a reddish hue. Serve with rice or egg noodles.

Southern-Style Smothered Chicken

Braised Chicken Thighs with Chard and Mustard

8 (5- to 7-ounce) bone-in chicken thighs, trimmed
¾ teaspoon table salt
¼ teaspoon pepper
1 tablespoon extra-virgin olive oil
1 pound Swiss chard, stems chopped fine, leaves
   sliced thin
1 onion, chopped fine
6 garlic cloves, minced
1 tablespoon minced fresh thyme or
   2 teaspoons dried
1 anchovy fillet, rinsed and minced
2 tablespoons all-purpose flour
1½ cups chicken broth
½ cup dry white wine
2 bay leaves
1 teaspoon grated lemon zest
1 tablespoon whole-grain mustard

1. Adjust oven rack to lower-middle position and heat oven to 300 degrees. Pat chicken dry with paper towels and sprinkle with salt and pepper. Heat oil in Dutch oven over medium-high heat until just smoking. Add half of chicken and brown on both sides, 7 to 10 minutes; transfer to plate and remove skin. Repeat with remaining chicken.

2. Pour off all but 2 tablespoons fat left in pot and heat over medium-high heat until shimmering. Add chard stems and onion and cook until softened and lightly browned, 5 to 7 minutes. Stir in garlic, thyme, and anchovy and cook until fragrant, about 30 seconds. Stir in flour and cook for 30 seconds. Whisk in broth and wine, scraping up any browned bits and smoothing out any lumps.

3. Add bay leaves and browned chicken with any accumulated juices. Bring to simmer, cover, and transfer pot to oven. Cook until chicken is very tender and almost falling off bone, about 1 hour.

4. Remove pot from oven. Transfer chicken to platter, tent with aluminum foil, and let rest while finishing sauce. Let liquid in pot settle for 5 minutes, then skim any fat from surface using large spoon. Stir in chard leaves and lemon zest, bring to simmer, and cook until sauce is thickened, about 10 minutes.

5. Off heat, discard bay leaves, stir in mustard, and season with salt and pepper to taste. Pour sauce over chicken and serve. (Chicken and sauce can be refrigerated for up to 2 days; add additional broth as needed to loosen sauce when reheating.)

VARIATION
Braised Chicken Thighs with Spinach and Garlic
Omit chard and mustard. Add 10 ounces chopped curly-leaf spinach and 2 additional minced garlic cloves to pot with lemon zest.

Quick Chicken Fricassee

Quick Chicken Fricassee
Serves 4 to 6   Total Time 50 minutes

Why This Recipe Works Fricassee of chicken is a French dish of cut-up chicken that's braised and then served with its sauce. It has a lot going for it but we found the classic recipes to be a bit bland and too time-consuming. Using boneless, skinless chicken breasts and thighs considerably cut down our fricassee's cooking time. To add back richness, we browned the meat in a combination of butter and oil, and then browned vegetables until they developed their own fond to serve as the base of the sauce. We used a generous pound of glutamate-rich mushrooms to boost the fricassee's meaty flavor. As a final step, we finished our chicken's sauce with sour cream, which added body and pleasant tang. Whisking an egg yolk into the sour cream thickened the sauce and made it incredibly silky. Two tablespoons of chopped fresh parsley can be substituted for the tarragon in this recipe.

2 pounds boneless, skinless chicken
   breasts and thighs, trimmed
1 teaspoon table salt
½ teaspoon pepper

1 tablespoon unsalted butter
1 tablespoon extra-virgin olive oil
1 pound cremini mushrooms, trimmed and sliced ¼ inch thick
1 onion, chopped fine
¼ cup dry white wine
1 tablespoon all-purpose flour
1 garlic clove, minced
1½ cups chicken broth
⅓ cup sour cream
1 large egg yolk
2 teaspoons lemon juice
2 teaspoons minced fresh tarragon
½ teaspoon ground nutmeg

1. Pat chicken dry with paper towels and sprinkle with salt and pepper. Heat butter and oil in 12-inch skillet over medium-high heat until butter is melted. Cook chicken until browned on both sides, 8 to 10 minutes; transfer to plate.

2. Add mushrooms, onion, and wine to now-empty skillet and cook, stirring occasionally, until liquid has evaporated and mushrooms are browned, 8 to 10 minutes. Add flour and garlic and cook, stirring constantly, for about 1 minute. Add broth and bring mixture to boil, scraping up any browned bits. Add chicken and any accumulated juices to skillet. Reduce heat to medium-low, cover, and simmer until breasts register 160 degrees and thighs register 175 degrees, 5 to 10 minutes.

3. Transfer chicken to platter and tent with aluminum foil. Whisk sour cream and egg yolk together in medium bowl. Whisking constantly, slowly stir ½ cup heated sauce into sour cream mixture to temper. Stirring constantly, slowly pour sour cream mixture into simmering sauce. Stir in lemon juice, tarragon, and nutmeg; return to simmer. Season sauce with salt and pepper to taste, pour over chicken, and serve.

Chicken California

Serves 4 to 6   Total Time 1¼ hours

Why This Recipe Works This century-old recipe surrounds braised chicken with several iconic California ingredients, including red wine, almonds, and olives. To make the most of each element, we added them at various stages in cooking. While the original recipe calls for thickening at the end with a cornmeal slurry, tasters preferred toasting the cornmeal early and allowing it to braise with the chicken. This also helped the sauce stay smooth rather than gritty. Be sure to wait until the last minute for the final toss of cilantro, so it maintains its fresh flavor. Serve with Classic Mashed Potatoes or rice.

Classic Mashed Potatoes

Serves 4 to 6   Total Time 50 minutes
Russet potatoes make fluffier mashed potatoes, but Yukon Golds have an appealing buttery flavor and can be used. Mashed potatoes are a good match for just about any braise.

2 pounds russet potatoes, unpeeled
8 tablespoons unsalted butter, melted
1 cup half-and-half, warmed

1. Place potatoes in large saucepan and cover with cold water by 1 inch. Bring to boil over high heat, reduce heat to simmer, and cook until potatoes are just tender (paring knife can be slipped in and out of potatoes with little resistance), 30 to 45 minutes. Drain.

2. Using pot holder or folded dish towel to hold potatoes, peel skins from potatoes with paring knife. For slightly chunky texture, return peeled potatoes to now-empty pot and mash smooth using potato masher. For creamy texture, set ricer or food mill over now-empty pot; cut peeled potatoes into large chunks and press or mill into saucepan in batches. Stir in melted butter until incorporated. Gently whisk in half-and-half and season with salt and pepper to taste. Serve.

VARIATIONS
Garlic Mashed Potatoes

Toasting the garlic is essential for mellowing it. Avoid using unusually large garlic cloves, as they will not soften.

Toast 20 unpeeled garlic cloves in covered 8-inch skillet over lowest heat possible until spotty dark brown and slightly softened, about 22 minutes. Off heat, let sit, covered, until fully softened, 15 to 20 minutes. Peel and mince garlic, then stir into mashed potatoes with half-and-half. (If using ricer or food mill, softened garlic cloves can be processed along with potatoes.)

Mashed Potatoes with Scallions and Horseradish

Stir ¼ cup prepared horseradish and 3 minced scallions, green parts only, into warm half-and-half before adding to mashed potatoes.

3 pounds bone-in chicken pieces (split breasts halved crosswise, drumsticks, and/or thighs), trimmed
1 teaspoon table salt, divided
¾ teaspoon pepper, divided
½ cup plus 2 tablespoons cornmeal, divided
5 tablespoons extra-virgin olive oil, divided
1 onion, chopped fine
3 garlic cloves, minced
1 tablespoon chili powder
1 cup dry red wine
1¼ cups chicken broth
1 tablespoon packed brown sugar
⅓ cup sliced almonds, toasted
⅓ cup pitted green olives, chopped coarse
⅓ cup chopped fresh cilantro

1. Pat chicken dry with paper towels and sprinkle with ½ teaspoon salt and ¼ teaspoon pepper. Place ½ cup cornmeal in shallow dish. Dredge chicken in cornmeal, shaking off excess; transfer to plate. Heat 2 tablespoons oil in Dutch oven over medium heat until shimmering. Cook half of chicken skin side down until browned, about 3 minutes. Flip chicken and brown on second side, about 3 minutes; transfer to plate. Wipe out pot with paper towels and repeat with 2 tablespoons oil and remaining chicken; transfer to plate. Wipe out pot.

2. Return now-empty pot to medium heat, add remaining 1 tablespoon oil and onion, and cook until soft, about 3 minutes. Add garlic, chili powder, and remaining 2 tablespoons cornmeal and cook until fragrant, about 30 seconds. Stir in wine and cook until reduced by half, about 3 minutes.

3. Add broth, sugar, remaining ½ teaspoon salt, remaining ½ teaspoon pepper, and chicken and bring to boil. Cover, reduce heat to low, and simmer for 10 minutes. Flip chicken and continue to simmer, covered, until breasts register 160 degrees and thighs/drumsticks register 175 degrees, 8 to 10 minutes longer.

4. Off heat, transfer chicken to shallow casserole dish. Season sauce with salt and pepper to taste. Pour sauce over chicken and sprinkle with almonds, olives, and cilantro. Serve.

Country Captain
Serves 6   Total Time 1¼ hours

Why This Recipe Works Mildly curried braised country captain chicken originated in India, was adopted by the British, and was transformed again after reaching U.S. shores in the early 1800s. We wanted to freshen up this dish so it boasted the perfect balance of heat and sweet. After browning the chicken, we used the rendered fat to cook onions and green bell pepper.

We upped our spices' impact by cooking a generous amount of curry powder and garlic with tomato paste, flour, and brown sugar. Raisins and chopped sweet-tart apple contributed subtle sweetness and brightness when stirred in with canned diced tomatoes. Before cooking the chicken in this flavorful sauce, we discarded its skin, which would have turned flabby and made the sauce greasy. Lime juice added before serving provided a final citrusy kick. If you can't find petite diced tomatoes, pulse one 28-ounce can of diced tomatoes in a food processor until coarsely ground. This dish is traditionally served with rice and a host of garnishes that include crumbled bacon, sliced scallions, toasted coconut, toasted almonds, chopped banana, toasted peanuts, and chopped pineapple; use as few or as many as you like.

4 pounds bone-in chicken pieces (2 split breasts halved crosswise, 2 drumsticks, and 2 thighs), trimmed
¾ teaspoon table salt
½ teaspoon pepper
1 tablespoon vegetable oil
2 onions, chopped fine
1 green bell pepper, stemmed, seeded, and chopped fine
2 tablespoons tomato paste
2 tablespoons curry powder
2 tablespoons all-purpose flour
2 garlic cloves, minced
1 teaspoon packed brown sugar
1 (28-ounce) can petite diced tomatoes
1 Granny Smith apple, cored, halved, and chopped fine
½ cup raisins or dried currants
2 teaspoons lime juice

1. Pat chicken dry with paper towels and sprinkle with salt and pepper. Heat oil in Dutch oven over medium-high heat until just smoking. Brown half of chicken on both sides, 8 to 10 minutes; transfer to plate. Repeat with remaining chicken; transfer to plate. When chicken is cool enough to handle, discard skin.

2. Pour off all but 2 tablespoons fat from pot. Add onions and bell pepper and cook, covered, until softened, about 8 minutes. Stir in tomato paste, curry powder, flour, garlic, and sugar and cook until fragrant and color deepens, about 2 minutes. Stir in tomatoes and their juice, apple, and raisins and bring to boil.

3. Return chicken and any accumulated juices to pot. Reduce heat to low and simmer, covered, until breasts register 160 degrees and drumsticks/thighs register 175 degrees, 20 to 25 minutes. Stir in lime juice, season with salt and pepper to taste, and serve.

Chicken Marbella

Serves 4 to 6   Total Time 1¼ hours

Why This Recipe Works More than 35 years ago, Chicken Marbella put *The Silver Palate Cookbook* on the map with its unusual (for the time) combination of ingredients: prunes, olives, and wine. To save time, we skipped the original marinade and instead made a potent paste including prunes, olives, capers, garlic, and anchovies and caramelized a portion of it to bloom its complex flavors. After deglazing the skillet with wine and pouring the sauce around the chicken, we transferred the pan to the oven. Using a skillet resulted in a concentrated sauce. Once the skin was well rendered and browned, we added the remainder of the paste to the chicken. Last-minute additions of butter, vinegar, and parsley pulled everything together. Serve with Simple Couscous (page 189).

Paste

- ⅓ cup pitted green olives, rinsed
- ⅓ cup pitted prunes
- 3 tablespoons extra-virgin olive oil
- 2 tablespoons capers, rinsed
- 4 garlic cloves, peeled
- 3 anchovy fillets, rinsed
- ½ teaspoon dried oregano
- ½ teaspoon pepper
- ¼ teaspoon kosher salt
- Pinch red pepper flakes

Chicken

- 2½–3 pounds bone-in, skin-on split chicken breasts and/or leg quarters, trimmed
- 1½ teaspoons table salt
- ¼ teaspoon pepper
- 2 teaspoons extra-virgin olive oil
- ¾ cup chicken broth
- ⅓ cup white wine
- ⅓ cup pitted green olives, rinsed and halved
- 1 tablespoon capers, rinsed
- 2 bay leaves
- ⅓ cup pitted prunes, chopped coarse
- 1 tablespoon unsalted butter
- 1 teaspoon red wine vinegar
- 2 tablespoons minced fresh parsley, divided

1. Adjust oven rack to middle position and heat oven to 400 degrees.

2. For the paste Pulse all ingredients in food processor until finely chopped, about 10 pulses. Scrape down bowl and continue to process until mostly smooth, 1 to 2 minutes. Transfer to bowl. (Paste can be refrigerated for up to 24 hours.)

Country Captain

Chicken Marbella

3. For the chicken Pat chicken dry with paper towels and sprinkle with salt and pepper. Heat oil in 12-inch ovensafe skillet over medium-high heat until just smoking. Cook chicken skin side down until browned, 5 to 8 minutes. Transfer chicken to plate. Drain off all but 1 teaspoon fat from skillet and return to medium-low heat.

4. Add ⅓ cup paste to skillet and cook, stirring constantly, until fragrant and fond forms on pan bottom, 1 to 2 minutes. Stir in broth, wine, olives, capers, and bay leaves, scraping up any browned bits. Return chicken to pan, skin side up (skin should be above surface of liquid), and roast, uncovered, for 15 minutes.

5. Remove skillet from oven and use back of spoon to spread remaining paste over chicken pieces; sprinkle prunes around chicken. Continue to roast until paste begins to brown, breasts register 160 degrees, and leg quarters register 175 degrees, 7 to 12 minutes longer.

6. Transfer chicken to serving platter and tent with aluminum foil. Remove bay leaves from sauce and whisk in butter, vinegar, and 1 tablespoon parsley; season with salt and pepper to taste. Pour sauce around chicken, sprinkle with remaining 1 tablespoon parsley, and serve.

Chicken Marengo

Serves 4   Total Time 1½ hours

Why This Recipe Works Chicken Marengo is a robust French dish that reportedly dates back to Napoleon. By the time the recipe appeared in *The Joy of Cooking*, the focus was on the big flavors of tomato, brandy, and olive. We wanted our version to focus on those bold flavors without extra effort. To do this, we used bone-in chicken breasts: The bones added depth to the braise, and the skin browned and contributed even more flavor. Crushed tomatoes didn't add enough flavor, so we switched to fresher-tasting canned diced tomatoes, which we chopped a bit to make the sauce more cohesive. A half-cup of brandy added a strong hit of flavor in the sauce. We liked kalamata olives in this recipe—adding them at the outset allowed their briny taste to permeate the sauce. To prevent the chicken skin from becoming chewy during stewing, we made sure to have only enough sauce in the pot to come halfway up the chicken breasts as they cooked skin side up. You can roughly chop the tomatoes by hand or pulse them three or four times in a food processor.

4 (12-ounce) bone-in split chicken breasts, trimmed
¾ teaspoon table salt, divided
¼ teaspoon pepper
1 tablespoon extra-virgin olive oil
1 onion, chopped fine

4 garlic cloves, minced
10 ounces cremini or white mushrooms, sliced thin
2 teaspoons minced fresh thyme
2 tablespoons tomato paste
1 (28-ounce) can diced tomatoes, drained and chopped coarse
¾ cup chicken broth
½ cup brandy
¼ cup pitted kalamata olives, chopped fine
¼ teaspoon red pepper flakes
3 tablespoons unsalted butter

1. Adjust oven rack to middle position and heat oven to 450 degrees. Pat chicken dry with paper towels and sprinkle with ½ teaspoon salt and pepper. Heat oil in Dutch oven over medium-high heat until just smoking. Cook chicken skin side down until brown, about 5 minutes. Flip chicken and brown on second side, about 2 minutes. Transfer to plate.

2. Reduce heat to medium. Add onion to fat in pan and cook until softened, about 5 minutes. Stir in garlic and cook until fragrant, about 30 seconds. Add mushrooms, thyme, and remaining ¼ teaspoon salt. Cover and cook, stirring occasionally, until mushrooms have released their juices, about 10 minutes. Stir in tomato paste and cook until thickened, about 2 minutes.

3. Stir in tomatoes, broth, brandy, olives, and pepper flakes and bring to boil. Add chicken pieces, skin side up, along with any accumulated juices. Transfer pot to oven and cook, uncovered, until chicken registers 160 degrees, about 30 minutes. Transfer chicken to serving platter. Stir butter into sauce and season with salt and pepper to taste. Pour sauce around chicken. Serve.

Chicken Canzanese

Serves 4 to 6   Total Time 2 hours

Why This Recipe Works Chicken Canzanese is a heady Italian braised chicken dish flavored with prosciutto, rosemary, sage, garlic, red pepper flakes, and cloves. For chicken that would be fork-tender and juicy, we opted for bone-in chicken thighs, which contain more connective tissue than breasts. We made a rich flavor base with prosciutto and garlic and then added white wine and chicken broth, which we simmered in a skillet. We then returned the chicken to the pan and cooked it in the oven uncovered, which allowed the sauce to reduce and also preserved the chicken's crispy skin. When seasoning the dish at the end, be mindful that the prosciutto adds a fair amount of salt. It is important to use a piece of thickly sliced prosciutto in this recipe; thin strips will become tough and stringy.

Chicken Canzanese

1. Adjust oven rack to lower-middle position and heat oven to 325 degrees. Heat 1 teaspoon oil in 12-inch ovensafe skillet over medium heat until shimmering. Add prosciutto and cook, stirring frequently, until just starting to brown, about 3 minutes. Add garlic and cook, stirring frequently, until garlic is golden brown, about 1½ minutes. Using slotted spoon, transfer prosciutto and garlic to small bowl and set aside.

2. Increase heat to medium-high; add remaining 2 teaspoons oil to skillet and heat until just smoking. Pat chicken dry with paper towels and sprinkle with pepper. Cook chicken skin side down until browned, 5 to 8 minutes. Flip chicken and brown on second side, about 5 minutes longer. Transfer chicken to plate.

3. Pour off all but 2 tablespoons fat from skillet. Sprinkle flour over fat and cook, stirring constantly, for 1 minute. Slowly add wine and broth; bring to simmer, scraping up any browned bits. Cook until liquid is slightly reduced, 3 minutes. Stir in cloves, rosemary stem, sage leaves, bay leaves, pepper flakes, and prosciutto-garlic mixture. Nestle chicken into liquid, skin side up (skin should be above surface of liquid), and bake, uncovered, until meat offers no resistance when poked with fork but is not falling off bones, about 1¼ hours. (Check chicken after 15 minutes; broth should be barely bubbling. If bubbling vigorously, reduce oven temperature to 300 degrees.)

4. Using tongs, transfer chicken to serving platter; tent with aluminum foil. Discard cloves, rosemary stem, sage leaves, and bay leaves. Place skillet over high heat and bring sauce to boil. Cook until sauce is reduced to 1¼ cups, 2 to 5 minutes. Off heat, stir in butter, lemon juice, and minced rosemary. Season with salt and pepper to taste. Pour sauce around chicken and serve.

An equal amount of thickly sliced pancetta or bacon can be used in place of the prosciutto. For a spicier dish, use the larger amount of red pepper flakes. Serve the chicken with boiled potatoes, noodles, or polenta to absorb extra sauce.

- 1 tablespoon extra-virgin olive oil, divided
- 2 ounces prosciutto (¼ inch thick), cut into ¼-inch cubes
- 4 garlic cloves, sliced thin lengthwise
- 8 (5- to 7-ounce) bone-in chicken thighs, trimmed
- ¼ teaspoon pepper
- 2 teaspoons all-purpose flour
- 2 cups dry white wine
- 1 cup chicken broth
- 4 whole cloves
- 1 (4-inch) sprig fresh rosemary, leaves removed and minced fine (½ teaspoon), stem reserved
- 12 fresh sage leaves
- 2 bay leaves
- ¼–½ teaspoon red pepper flakes
- 2 tablespoons unsalted butter
- 1 tablespoon lemon juice

Spicy Braised Chicken Abruzzo
Serves 4   Total Time 40 minutes

Why This Recipe Works The Abruzzo region in Italy, well known for its spicy cuisine and liberal use of hot peppers, is the inspiration for this lively chicken dish, which gets its flavor from two different kinds of peppers: Pickled hot cherry peppers provide a complex heat and tang, while fresh red bell peppers add sweetness and a slight crunch. To reinforce the hot pepper flavor, we added some of the vinegary brine to the sauce. A few cloves of garlic offered warm complexity and contributed even more heat. We quickly braised boneless, skinless chicken breasts right in the spicy sauce, which simultaneously kept the chicken moist and ensured that it took on big flavor. This dish is not for the faint of heart (or palate); its sweet-hot pepper combo packs a wallop.

2 tablespoons extra-virgin olive oil, divided
4 (6- to 8-ounce) boneless, skinless chicken breasts, trimmed
½ teaspoon table salt
¼ teaspoon pepper
2 red bell peppers, stemmed, seeded, and cut into 2-inch strips
¼ cup jarred sliced hot cherry peppers, plus 2 teaspoons brine
3 garlic cloves, minced
¾ cup chicken broth

1. Heat 1 tablespoon oil in 12-inch skillet over medium-high heat until just smoking. Pat chicken dry with paper towels and sprinkle with salt and pepper. Cook chicken until lightly browned on both sides, about 5 minutes; transfer to plate.

2. Heat remaining 1 tablespoon oil in now-empty skillet over medium-high heat until shimmering. Stir in bell peppers and cherry peppers and cook until bell peppers begin to soften, about 5 minutes. Add garlic and cook until fragrant, about 30 seconds.

3. Stir in broth and cherry pepper brine. Nestle chicken and any accumulated juices into skillet. Cover and simmer gently until chicken registers 160 degrees, 10 to 15 minutes.

4. Transfer chicken to platter and cover to keep warm. Return sauce to simmer and cook until slightly reduced, 2 to 4 minutes. Season with salt and pepper to taste. Pour over chicken and serve.

Chicken Scarpariello
Serves 4 to 6   **Total Time** 1¼ hours

Why This Recipe Works Chicken scarpariello is an Italian American creation of browned chicken and sausage bathed in a spicy, garlicky sauce chock-full of onions, bell peppers, and pickled hot cherry peppers. Its exact origins are murky, but it first became popular stateside in the early 1900s among New York City's burgeoning Italian population. We wanted our version to be bright and flavorful, not too briny and not too spicy. We started by tempering the heat of the cherry peppers by removing their seeds. We wanted some extra flavor, so we added just a couple of tablespoons of the vinegary cherry pepper brine. After browning the sausage and chicken, we sautéed the vegetables and then nestled in the chicken and sausage to finish cooking in the oven, which kept the chicken skin crispy. A tablespoon of flour and ¾ cup of chicken broth resulted in a sauce with the perfect consistency—thick enough to coat the chicken and sausage without being gloppy. We used sweet Italian sausage to balance the spiciness of the cherry peppers. Feel free to substitute hot Italian sausage if you prefer a spicier dish.

3 pounds bone-in chicken pieces (2 split breasts halved crosswise, 2 drumsticks, and 2 thighs), trimmed
1 teaspoon table salt
½ teaspoon pepper
1 tablespoon vegetable oil
8 ounces sweet Italian sausage, casings removed
1 onion, halved and sliced thin
1 red bell pepper, stemmed, seeded, and sliced thin
5 jarred hot cherry peppers, seeded, rinsed, and sliced thin (½ cup), plus 2 tablespoons brine
5 garlic cloves, minced
1 teaspoon dried oregano
1 tablespoon all-purpose flour
¾ cup chicken broth
2 tablespoons chopped fresh parsley

1. Adjust oven rack to middle position and heat oven to 350 degrees. Pat chicken dry with paper towels and season with salt and pepper. Heat oil in 12-inch ovensafe skillet over medium-high heat until just smoking. Add chicken to skillet, skin side down, and cook without moving until well browned, about 5 minutes. Flip chicken and continue to cook until browned on second side, about 3 minutes. Transfer chicken to plate.

2. Add sausage to fat left in skillet and cook, breaking up with spoon, until browned, about 3 minutes. Transfer sausage to paper towel–lined plate.

3. Pour off all but 1 tablespoon fat from skillet and return to medium-high heat. Add onion and bell pepper and cook until vegetables are softened and lightly browned, about 5 minutes. Add cherry peppers, garlic, and oregano and cook until fragrant, about 1 minute. Stir in flour and cook for 30 seconds. Add broth and cherry pepper brine and bring to simmer, scraping up any browned bits.

4. Remove skillet from heat and stir in sausage. Arrange chicken pieces, skin side up, in single layer in skillet and add any accumulated juices. Transfer skillet to oven and bake until breasts register 160 degrees and drumsticks/thighs register 175 degrees, 20 to 25 minutes.

KEEPING SKIN CRISP

Arrange chicken pieces skin side up on top of other ingredients so that they are above surface of liquid.

5. Being careful of hot skillet handle, carefully remove skillet from oven. Transfer chicken to serving platter. Season onion mixture with salt and pepper to taste, then spoon over chicken. Sprinkle with parsley. Serve.

Chicken Arrabbiata

Serves 4   Total Time 1¼ hours

Why This Recipe Works "Angry" chicken (arrabbiata means "angry" in Italian) gets its complex and bold bite from not just one spicy ingredient but three. We bloomed fiery red pepper flakes, bright and briny pepperoncini, and lots of garlic in a heavy dose of extra-virgin olive oil to build the base for an intense tomato sauce. Browning chicken leg quarters first allowed us to cook the aromatics in the flavorful rendered fat and added complex chicken flavor to the sweet crushed tomatoes. Once we built the sauce, the chicken was returned to the pot to braise until cooked through and tender. You can substitute eight 5- to 7-ounce bone-in chicken thighs for the leg quarters, if desired. Good-quality olive oil makes a difference here. The anchovies add a background of savory richness without tasting like fish; we encourage even nonfans to give them a try here. Be sure to remove the stems from the pepperoncini before mincing them. You can substitute Parmesan for the Pecorino Romano, if desired. Some leg quarters are sold with the backbone attached; removing it before cooking makes the chicken easier to serve (see page 11). We recommend serving this dish over polenta.

- 4 (10- to 12-ounce) chicken leg quarters, trimmed
- 1 teaspoon table salt, divided
- ½ teaspoon pepper
- ¼ cup extra-virgin olive oil
- 1 small onion, chopped fine
- 2 tablespoons minced pepperoncini
- 2 anchovy fillets, rinsed and minced
- 2 tablespoons tomato paste
- 4 garlic cloves, minced
- 1½ teaspoons red pepper flakes
- 1 (28-ounce) can crushed tomatoes
- ¼ cup grated Pecorino Romano cheese, plus extra for serving

1. Adjust oven rack to middle position and heat oven to 350 degrees. Pat chicken dry with paper towels and sprinkle with ½ teaspoon salt and pepper. Heat oil in Dutch oven over medium heat until just smoking. Cook chicken skin side down until browned, about 9 minutes. Transfer to plate; set aside.

Chicken Scarpariello

Chicken Arrabbiata

2. Add onion, pepperoncini, and anchovies to now-empty pot. Cook until onion is just softened, about 3 minutes. Add tomato paste, garlic, and pepper flakes and cook until fragrant, about 1 minute. Stir in tomatoes, Pecorino, and remaining ½ teaspoon salt, scraping up any browned bits.

3. Nestle chicken into sauce, skin side up, and bring to boil. Transfer pot to oven and cook, uncovered, until chicken registers 200 degrees, 35 to 40 minutes. Transfer chicken to serving platter. Stir sauce to recombine and spoon over chicken. Serve.

Chicken Pomodoro
Serves 4 **Total Time** 45 minutes

Why This Recipe Works Not every Italian braised dish requires lengthy simmering. For chicken pomodoro in a deeply flavored creamy tomato sauce, we started with a hefty dose of sautéed onion, garlic, and oregano, as well as a few red pepper flakes for spice. Heavy cream added a pleasant richness to the sauce, and fresh basil brought out the bright flavor of the tomatoes. Gently simmering boneless chicken breasts in the tomato sauce enriched the flavor of both the sauce and the chicken. While certain dried herbs like oregano work just as well as fresh, delicate herbs like basil are best used fresh. Be careful not to overcook the chicken in step 3 or it will taste dry. Serve over pasta, egg noodles, or rice.

 4 (6- to 8-ounce) boneless, skinless chicken
   breasts, trimmed
 ¾ teaspoon table salt, divided
 ¼ teaspoon pepper
 2 tablespoons extra-virgin olive oil, divided
 1 onion, chopped fine
 4 garlic cloves, minced
 1 tablespoon minced fresh oregano or
   1 teaspoon dried
 ¼ teaspoon red pepper flakes
 1 (14.5-ounce) can diced tomatoes
 ⅓ cup heavy cream
 ¼ cup chopped fresh basil

1. Pound chicken breasts to uniform thickness, then pat dry with paper towels and sprinkle with ½ teaspoon salt and pepper. Heat 1 tablespoon oil in 12-inch skillet over medium-high heat until just smoking. Brown chicken lightly on both sides, about 5 minutes; transfer to plate.

2. Add remaining 1 tablespoon oil and onion to now-empty skillet and cook over medium heat until softened, about 5 minutes. Stir in garlic, oregano, and pepper flakes and cook until

fragrant, about 30 seconds. Stir in tomatoes and their juice, cream, and remaining ¼ teaspoon salt.

3. Add browned chicken and any accumulated juices, cover, and simmer gently until chicken registers 160 degrees, about 10 minutes. Transfer chicken to platter and tent with aluminum foil.

4. Continue to simmer sauce until slightly thickened, about 5 minutes. Stir in basil and season with salt and pepper to taste. Pour sauce over chicken and serve.

Chicken Cacciatore with Portobellos and Sage
Serves 4 **Total Time** 1½ hours

Why This Recipe Works Cacciatore, which means "hunter-style" in Italian, refers to a rustic dish of freshly caught game, foraged mushrooms, and rosemary that's traditionally long-simmered and served after a hunt. For our version, bone-in chicken thighs supplied hearty flavor. Removing the skin after a quick rendering solved the problems of soggy skin and greasy sauce in our chicken cacciatore. Cooking the chicken in a combination of red wine and chicken broth, adding earthy mushrooms and a Parmesan cheese rind, and finishing with fresh sage gave us the lavish, substantial cacciatore we desired. If your Dutch oven is large enough to hold all the chicken pieces in a single layer without crowding, brown all the pieces at once instead of in batches. The Parmesan cheese rind is optional, but we highly recommend it for the rich, savory flavor it adds to the dish. An equal amount of minced fresh rosemary can be substituted for the sage.

 8 (5- to 7-ounce) bone-in chicken thighs, trimmed
 1½ teaspoons table salt, divided
 ¼ teaspoon pepper
 1 teaspoon extra-virgin olive oil
 1 onion, chopped
 3 portobello mushroom caps, cut into ¾-inch cubes
 4 garlic cloves, minced
 1½ tablespoons all-purpose flour
 1½ cups dry red wine
 1 (14.5-ounce) can diced tomatoes, drained
 ½ cup chicken broth
 1 Parmesan cheese rind (optional)
 2 teaspoons minced fresh thyme
 2 teaspoons minced fresh sage

Chicken Cacciatore with Portobellos and Sage

1. Pat chicken dry with paper towels and sprinkle with ½ teaspoon salt and pepper. Heat oil in Dutch oven over medium-high heat until shimmering. Brown half of chicken on both sides, 8 to 10 minutes; transfer to plate. Repeat with remaining chicken, transfer to plate, and set aside.

2. Pour off all but 1 tablespoon fat from pot. Add onion, mushrooms, and ½ teaspoon salt and cook over medium-high heat, stirring occasionally, until vegetables are beginning to brown, 6 to 8 minutes.

3. When chicken is cool enough to handle, discard skin. Once vegetables have browned, add garlic to pot and cook until fragrant, about 30 seconds. Stir in flour and cook, stirring constantly, for about 1 minute. Add wine, scraping up any browned bits. Stir in tomatoes; broth; Parmesan rind, if using; thyme; and remaining ½ teaspoon salt (omit salt if using Parmesan rind) and season with pepper to taste. Submerge chicken pieces in liquid and bring to boil; cover, reduce heat to low, and simmer until chicken is tender and registers 175 degrees, about 45 minutes, turning chicken pieces halfway through cooking. Discard Parmesan rind, stir in sage, season with salt and pepper to taste, and serve.

VARIATION

Chicken Cacciatore with White Wine and Tarragon

This variation is based on chicken chasseur, the French version of Italian cacciatore.

Substitute 3 large shallots, minced, for onion; 10 ounces white mushrooms, trimmed and quartered if large, halved if medium, for portobellos; dry white wine for red wine; and tarragon for sage.

Chicken Provençal

Serves 4 to 6   **Total Time** 1 hour

Why This Recipe Works This southern France–inspired chicken dinner with a bright, savory sauce is ready in about an hour. Dredging the chicken in a bit of flour helped create a crispy exterior. We reserved a bit of the flour dredge to thicken the drippings in the pan and create a luscious sauce. After we seared the chicken, we sautéed a potent mix of shallots, garlic, thyme, and supersavory anchovies in the rendered fat to give our sauce a flavorful base. From there, we stirred in bright, sweet-savory cherry tomatoes; briny kalamata olives; and a splash of complex, mildly acidic vermouth to create a sauce with compelling character. You can substitute four 10- to 12-ounce bone-in split chicken breasts for the thighs, if desired. Simply extend the cooking time in step 4 to 30 minutes or until the chicken registers 160 degrees. You can substitute any dry white wine for the vermouth, if desired.

8 (5- to 7-ounce) bone-in chicken thighs, trimmed
½ teaspoon table salt, divided
½ teaspoon pepper, divided
½ cup all-purpose flour
3 tablespoons extra-virgin olive oil
2 shallots, halved and sliced thin
3 garlic cloves, minced
3 sprigs fresh thyme
2 anchovy fillets, rinsed and minced
¼ teaspoon red pepper flakes
12 ounces cherry tomatoes, halved
½ cup pitted kalamata olives, halved
½ cup dry vermouth
½ cup fresh parsley leaves

1. Adjust oven rack to middle position and heat oven to 400 degrees. Pat chicken dry with paper towels and sprinkle chicken with ¼ teaspoon salt and ¼ teaspoon pepper.

Place flour in shallow dish. Dredge chicken in flour, 1 piece at a time, turning to coat all sides. Shake to remove any excess flour, then transfer chicken to large plate. Reserve 1 teaspoon flour; discard remaining flour.

2. Heat oil in 12-inch ovensafe skillet over medium-high heat until just smoking. Add chicken and cook until golden brown on both sides, about 3 minutes per side. Return chicken to plate, skin side up. Carefully pour off all but 2 tablespoons fat from skillet.

3. Return skillet to medium heat. Add shallots to fat left in skillet and cook until softened, about 2 minutes. Stir in garlic, thyme sprigs, anchovies, pepper flakes, and reserved flour and cook until fragrant, about 30 seconds. Stir in tomatoes, olives, vermouth, remaining ¼ teaspoon salt, and remaining ¼ teaspoon pepper, scraping up any browned bits.

4. Return chicken to skillet, skin side up, and bring sauce to boil. Transfer skillet to oven and cook until chicken registers 175 degrees, about 25 minutes. Sprinkle with parsley and serve.

Chicken in Adobo

Serves 4   Total Time 1¾ hours

Why This Recipe Works Adobo is a potent, pleasantly bitter sauce made from dried chiles that is found in the cuisines of Mexico and the American Southwest. It isn't fiery, but it will add spark to your weeknight chicken routine. The intense depth of flavor in this adobo comes from a balanced mixture of dried chiles. We combined guajillo and fruity ancho chiles to create a complex and vibrant red sauce to coat tender pieces of chicken. Lightly toasting the chiles removed their bitterness; we then soaked the chiles in water until they softened and blended them with vinegar and a bit of orange juice to enhance their sweetness. Once we brought the adobo to a simmer and stirred in browned chicken pieces, we transferred the pot to the oven to braise. We finished the dish with a splash of lime to brighten things up. One ounce of guajillo chiles is about eight chiles; ½ ounce of ancho chiles is approximately one chile. Remove the strips of orange zest with a vegetable peeler. You can use all white-meat or all dark-meat chicken pieces, if desired. Serve with warm flour tortillas or rice.

- 1   ounce dried guajillo chiles, stemmed and seeded
- ½   ounce dried ancho chiles, stemmed and seeded
- 1½ cups chicken broth
- ¼   cup cider vinegar
- 2   (3-inch) strips orange zest plus 2 tablespoons juice
- 1   tablespoon packed brown sugar
- 1¾ teaspoons table salt, divided
- 1   teaspoon pepper, divided

Chicken in Adobo

- 3   pounds bone-in chicken pieces (2 split breasts halved crosswise, 2 drumsticks, and 2 thighs), trimmed
- 2   tablespoons vegetable oil
- 1   onion, chopped fine
- 5   garlic cloves, minced
- 1   tablespoon tomato paste
- 2   teaspoons dried oregano
- 1   teaspoon ground cumin
- ½   teaspoon ground cinnamon
- 3   tablespoons chopped fresh cilantro
    Lime wedges

1. Adjust oven rack to lower-middle position and heat oven to 300 degrees. Place guajillos and anchos on rimmed baking sheet. Bake until fragrant and guajillos are deep red and have curled edges, about 7 minutes. Immediately transfer chiles to bowl and cover with hot water. Let stand until pliable, about 5 minutes.

2. Drain chiles and transfer to blender. Add broth, vinegar, orange juice, sugar, 1¼ teaspoons salt, and ½ teaspoon pepper and process until smooth, 1 to 2 minutes, scraping down sides of blender jar as needed. Set aside adobo.

3. Pat chicken dry with paper towels and sprinkle with remaining ½ teaspoon salt and remaining ½ teaspoon pepper. Heat oil in Dutch oven over medium-high heat until shimmering. Add chicken and cook until well browned on both sides, about 8 minutes. Transfer to plate.

4. Add onion to now-empty pot and reduce heat to medium. Cook until softened, about 4 minutes. Stir in garlic, tomato paste, oregano, cumin, cinnamon, and orange zest and cook until fragrant, about 30 seconds. Whisk in adobo until combined. Return chicken, skin side up, to pot along with any accumulated juices; bring to simmer. Transfer pot to oven and bake, uncovered, until chicken is tender and breasts register 160 degrees and drumsticks/thighs register 175 degrees, 35 to 40 minutes.

5. Transfer chicken to platter. Stir sauce to combine and season with salt and pepper to taste. Pour sauce over chicken and sprinkle with cilantro. Serve with lime wedges.

Coq au Vin

Serves 4   **Total Time** 1½ hours

Why This Recipe Works Although conventional recipes for coq au vin take upwards of 3 hours to prepare, we felt that this rustic dish shouldn't be so time-consuming. After all, it's basically a chicken fricassee. We wanted a dish with tender, juicy chicken infused with the flavors of red wine, onions, mushrooms, and bacon in under 2 hours. We decided to use chicken parts; this way, we could pick the parts we liked best. If using a mix of dark and white meat, we found it was essential to start the dark before the white, so that all the meat finished cooking at the same time. To thicken the stewing liquid, we sprinkled flour over the sautéed vegetables and whisked in butter toward the end of cooking; the butter also provided a nice richness in the sauce. Chicken broth added a savory note to the sauce and gave it some body; an entire bottle of red wine provided a great base of flavor. Tomato paste was a fuss-free way to add extra depth and body to the sauce, while a sprinkling of crisp, salty bacon rounded out the acidity of the wine. Use any $10 bottle of fruity, medium-bodied red wine, such as Pinot Noir, Côtes du Rhône, or Zinfandel. If you are using both chicken breasts and thighs/drumsticks, we recommend cutting the breast pieces in half so that each serving includes both white meat and dark meat. Note that using thighs or drumsticks will increase the total cooking time by 40 minutes. Serve with egg noodles.

6 ounces thick-cut bacon (about 5 slices), chopped
4 pounds bone-in, skin-on chicken pieces
(split breasts halved crosswise, drumsticks, and/or thighs), trimmed
Vegetable oil, as needed

Coq au Vin

¾ teaspoon table salt
½ teaspoon pepper
2 cups frozen pearl onions
10 ounces white mushrooms, trimmed and quartered
1 tablespoon tomato paste
2 garlic cloves, minced
3 tablespoons all-purpose flour
1 (750-ml) bottle red wine
2½ cups chicken broth
1 teaspoon minced fresh thyme or
¼ teaspoon dried
2 bay leaves
2 tablespoons unsalted butter, cut into
2 pieces and chilled
2 tablespoons minced fresh parsley

1. Cook bacon in Dutch oven over medium heat until crispy, 5 to 7 minutes. Using slotted spoon, transfer bacon to paper towel–lined plate; set aside.

2. Pat chicken dry with paper towels and sprinkle with salt and pepper. If necessary, add vegetable oil to fat left in pot to equal about 2 tablespoons. Heat over medium-high heat until shimmering. Cook half of chicken skin side down until

Coq au Riesling

Chicken
Bouillabaisse

browned, 5 to 8 minutes. Flip chicken and brown on second side, about 5 minutes; transfer chicken to plate. Repeat with remaining chicken; transfer chicken to plate.

3. Pour off all but 1 tablespoon of fat in pot (or add vegetable oil if needed to make this amount). Add onions and mushrooms and cook over medium heat, stirring occasionally, until lightly browned, about 10 minutes. Stir in tomato paste and garlic and cook until fragrant, about 30 seconds. Stir in flour and cook for 1 minute. Stir in wine, broth, thyme, and bay leaves, scraping up any browned bits.

4. Nestle chicken, along with any accumulated juices, into pot and bring to simmer. Cover, turn heat to medium-low, and simmer until breasts register 160 degrees, about 20 minutes, and thighs/drumsticks register 175 degrees, about 1 hour. (If using both types of chicken, simmer thighs and drumsticks for 40 minutes before adding breasts.)

5. Transfer chicken to serving dish and tent with foil. Skim as much fat as possible from surface of sauce and return to simmer until thickened and measures about 2 cups, about 20 minutes. Off heat, discard bay leaves, whisk in butter, and season with salt and pepper to taste. Pour sauce over chicken, sprinkle with reserved bacon and parsley, and serve.

Coq au Riesling
Serves 4 to 6   **Total Time** 1½ hours

Why This Recipe Works This subtler take on coq au vin swaps red wine for dry white. We began by cutting a whole chicken to get even-size pieces and so that we could use the back and wings to give our braise a good boost of meaty flavor. To establish a base, we cooked chopped bacon and used the rendered fat to brown the chicken wings and back. We also browned the skin from the breasts, drumsticks, and thighs to extract flavor before discarding it. These elements, though not part of the finished dish, contributed richness and more flavor. A mirepoix of shallots, carrots, celery, and garlic, added with flour, solidified the complex flavor profile. Stirring in 2½ cups of dry Riesling created a crisp, balanced finish. We then added water, herbs, and the chicken pieces. When the chicken was cooked, we removed it and then strained the liquid to finish off the sauce. While the liquid settled, we used the empty pot to sauté white mushrooms with some of the reserved fat. We returned the liquid to the pot, simmered to thicken it, and added tangy crème fraîche for an elegantly creamy sauce. A dry Riesling is the best wine for this recipe, but a Sauvignon Blanc or Chablis will also work. Avoid a heavily oaked wine such as Chardonnay. Serve this dish with egg noodles or Classic Mashed Potatoes (page 169).

1 (4- to 5-pound) whole chicken, cut into
    8 pieces (4 breast pieces halved crosswise,
    2 drumsticks, 2 thighs), giblets discarded,
    wings and back reserved
1½ teaspoons table salt, divided
½ teaspoon pepper
2 slices bacon, chopped
3 shallots, chopped
2 carrots, peeled and chopped coarse
2 celery ribs, chopped coarse
4 garlic cloves, lightly crushed and peeled
3 tablespoons all-purpose flour
2½ cups dry Riesling
1 cup water
2 bay leaves
6 sprigs fresh parsley, plus 2 teaspoons minced
6 sprigs fresh thyme
1 pound white mushrooms, trimmed and
    halved if small or quartered if large
¼ cup crème fraîche

1. Remove skin from chicken breast pieces, drumsticks, and thighs and set aside. Sprinkle chicken pieces with 1¼ teaspoons salt and pepper; set aside. Cook bacon in large Dutch oven over medium-low heat, stirring occasionally, until beginning to render fat, 2 to 4 minutes. Add chicken skin, back, and wings to pot; increase heat to medium; and cook, stirring frequently, until bacon is browned, skin is rendered, and chicken back and wings are browned on all sides, 10 to 12 minutes. Remove pot from heat; carefully transfer 2 tablespoons fat to small bowl and set aside.

2. Return pot to medium heat. Add shallots, carrots, celery, and garlic and cook, stirring occasionally, until vegetables are softened, 4 to 6 minutes. Add flour and cook, stirring constantly, until no dry flour remains, about 30 seconds. Slowly add wine, scraping up any browned bits. Increase heat to high and simmer until mixture is slightly thickened, about 2 minutes. Stir in water, bay leaves, parsley sprigs, and thyme springs and bring to simmer. Place chicken pieces in even layer in pot, reduce heat to low, cover, and cook until breasts register 160 degrees and thighs/drumsticks register 175 degrees, 25 to 30 minutes, stirring halfway through cooking. Transfer chicken pieces to plate as they come up to temperature.

3. Discard back and wings. Strain cooking liquid through fine-mesh strainer set over large bowl, pressing on solids to extract as much liquid as possible; discard solids. Let cooking liquid settle for 10 minutes. Using wide shallow spoon, skim fat from surface and discard.

4. While liquid settles, return pot to medium heat and add reserved fat, mushrooms, and remaining ¼ teaspoon salt; cook, stirring occasionally, until lightly browned, 8 to 10 minutes.

5. Return liquid to pot and bring to boil. Simmer briskly, stirring occasionally, until sauce is thickened to consistency of heavy cream, 4 to 6 minutes. Reduce heat to medium-low and stir in crème fraîche and minced parsley. Return chicken to pot along with any accumulated juices, cover, and cook until just heated through, 5 to 8 minutes. Season with salt and pepper to taste, and serve.

Chicken Bouillabaisse
Serves 6   Total Time 1¼ hours

Why This Recipe Works Bouillabaisse is a traditional French stew bursting with fish and shellfish and the flavors of Provence. We thought its potent flavors would work well with chicken. Adapting the recipe involved several steps: We substituted chicken broth for fish stock and added flour and tomato paste to the saffron and cayenne to give the sauce extra body. White wine and orange zest brought complexity, and adding the pastis, an anise-flavored liqueur, early on gave the alcohol time to cook off and leave behind a hint of sweetness. To help the chicken skin stay crisp after browning, we switched from stovetop to oven cooking. We rested the chicken on the potatoes as the bouillabaisse cooked in the oven so that the skin stayed out of the liquid and remained crisp. A finishing blast from the broiler before serving further enhanced the crispness. Serve with Rouille (page 182) and Garlic Toasts (page 182), if desired.

3 pounds bone-in chicken pieces (split breasts halved
    crosswise, drumsticks, and/or thighs), trimmed
½ teaspoon table salt
¼ teaspoon pepper
2 tablespoons extra-virgin olive oil
1 large leek, white and light green parts only, halved
    lengthwise, sliced thin, and washed thoroughly
1 small fennel bulb, stalks discarded, bulb halved,
    cored, and sliced thin
4 garlic cloves, minced
1 tablespoon tomato paste
1 tablespoon all-purpose flour
¼ teaspoon saffron threads, crumbled
¼ teaspoon cayenne pepper
3 cups chicken broth
1 (14.5-ounce) can diced tomatoes, drained
12 ounces Yukon Gold potatoes, unpeeled,
    cut into ¾-inch pieces
½ cup dry white wine
¼ cup pastis or Pernod
1 (3-inch) strip orange zest
1 tablespoon chopped fresh tarragon or parsley

Rouille

Makes 1 cup   **Total Time** 25 minutes
Leftover rouille will keep refrigerated for up to one week and can be used as a sauce for vegetables and fish.

    3 tablespoons boiling water
    ¼ teaspoon saffron threads, crumbled
    1 (3-inch) piece baguette, crusts removed, torn into 1-inch pieces (1 cup)
    4 teaspoons lemon juice
    1 large egg yolk
    2 teaspoons Dijon mustard
    2 small garlic cloves, minced
    ¼ teaspoon cayenne pepper
    ½ cup vegetable oil
    ½ cup extra-virgin olive oil

Combine boiling water and saffron in medium bowl and let steep for 5 minutes. Stir bread pieces and lemon juice into saffron-infused water and let soak for 5 minutes. Using whisk, mash soaked bread mixture until uniform paste forms, 1 to 2 minutes. Whisk in egg yolk, mustard, garlic, and cayenne until smooth, about 15 seconds. Whisking constantly, slowly drizzle in vegetable oil until smooth mayonnaise-like consistency is reached, scraping down bowl as necessary. Slowly whisk in olive oil in steady stream until smooth. Season with salt and pepper to taste.

Garlic Toasts

Makes 8 slices   **Total Time** 10 minutes
Be sure to use a high-quality crusty bread, such as a baguette; do not use sliced sandwich bread.

    8 (1-inch-thick) slices rustic bread
    1 large garlic clove, peeled
    3 tablespoons extra-virgin olive oil

Adjust oven rack 6 inches from broiler element and heat broiler. Spread bread evenly in rimmed baking sheet and broil, flipping as needed, until well toasted on both sides, about 4 minutes. Briefly rub 1 side of each toast with garlic, drizzle with oil, and season with salt and pepper to taste. Serve.

1. Adjust oven racks to upper-middle and lowest positions and heat oven to 375 degrees. Pat chicken dry with paper towels and sprinkle with salt and pepper. Heat oil in Dutch oven over medium-high heat until just smoking. Cook chicken skin side down until browned, 5 to 8 minutes. Flip chicken and brown on second side, about 5 minutes; transfer to plate.

2. Add leek and fennel to fat left in pot and cook, stirring often, until beginning to soften and turn translucent, about 4 minutes. Stir in garlic, tomato paste, flour, saffron, and cayenne and cook until fragrant, about 30 seconds. Slowly whisk in broth, scraping up any browned bits and smoothing out any lumps. Stir in tomatoes, potatoes, wine, pastis, and orange zest. Bring to simmer and cook for 10 minutes.

3. Nestle chicken thighs and drumsticks into pot with skin above surface of liquid. Cook, uncovered, for 5 minutes. Nestle breast pieces into pot, adjusting pieces as necessary to ensure that skin stays above surface of liquid. Transfer pot to upper rack and cook, uncovered, until breasts register 145 degrees and thighs/drumsticks register 160 degrees, 10 to 20 minutes.

4. Remove pot from oven and heat broiler. Return pot to oven and broil until chicken skin is crisp and breasts register 160 degrees and drumsticks/thighs register 175 degrees, 5 to 10 minutes (smaller pieces may cook faster than larger pieces; remove individual pieces as they reach correct temperature and return to pot before serving).

5. Using large spoon, skim excess fat from surface of stew. Stir in tarragon and season with salt and pepper to taste. Serve in wide, shallow bowls.

Pollo en Pepitoria

Serves 4   **Total Time** 1½ hours

Why This Recipe Works Pollo en pepitoria is a classic dish from Spain's saffron-producing Castilla–La Mancha region. It consists of chicken in a luxurious sherry-based sauce thickened with ground almonds and egg yolks. We brightened and balanced the lush sauce with canned tomatoes (more consistent year-round than fresh tomatoes) and a little lemon juice. We added some of the braising liquid to the nut mixture when blending it to make the sauce; this helped it puree thoroughly but still retain a pleasantly coarse consistency. Chicken thighs are fully cooked when they reach 175 degrees, but we purposely overcooked them—and did it slowly—which allowed collagen in the meat to break down into gelatin, making the meat more tender. Chopped egg whites are the traditional garnish. We were happy to find that we could also make this rich braise well in advance and keep it in the freezer. Any dry sherry, such as fino or Manzanilla, will work in this dish.

Pollo en Pepitoria

1. Adjust oven rack to middle position and heat oven to 300 degrees. Pat chicken dry with paper towels and sprinkle with ½ teaspoon salt and pepper. Heat oil in 12-inch ovensafe skillet over high heat until just smoking. Cook chicken until browned on both sides, 8 to 10 minutes; transfer to plate. When chicken is cool enough to handle, discard skin. Pour off all but 2 teaspoons fat from skillet.

2. Return skillet to medium heat, add onion and remaining ¼ teaspoon salt and cook, stirring frequently, until just softened, about 3 minutes. Add 2 teaspoons garlic, bay leaf, and cinnamon and cook until fragrant, about 1 minute. Add sherry and cook, scraping up any browned bits, until beginning to thicken, about 2 minutes. Stir in tomatoes and broth and bring to simmer. Return thighs to skillet, cover, transfer to oven, and cook until chicken registers 195 degrees, 45 to 50 minutes. Transfer thighs to serving platter and tent with aluminum foil to keep warm.

3. Discard bay leaf. Transfer ¾ cup chicken cooking liquid, egg yolks, almonds, saffron, and remaining garlic to blender. Process until smooth, about 2 minutes, scraping down blender jar as needed. Return almond mixture to skillet. Add 1 tablespoon parsley and lemon juice and bring to simmer over medium heat. Cook, whisking frequently, until thickened, 3 to 5 minutes. Season with salt and pepper to taste.

4. Pour sauce over chicken, sprinkle with remaining 1tablespoon parsley and egg whites, and serve.

  8 (5- to 7-ounce) bone-in chicken thighs, trimmed
  ¾ teaspoon table salt, divided
  ¼ teaspoon pepper
  1 tablespoon extra-virgin olive oil
  1 onion, chopped fine
  3 garlic cloves, minced
  1 bay leaf
  ¼ teaspoon ground cinnamon
  ⅔ cup dry sherry
  1 (14.5-ounce) can whole peeled tomatoes, drained and chopped fine
  1 cup chicken broth
  2 Easy-Peel Hard-Cooked Eggs (page 61), peeled, yolks and whites separated, whites minced
  ½ cup slivered blanched almonds, toasted
    Pinch saffron threads, crumbled
  2 tablespoons chopped fresh parsley, divided
  1½ teaspoons lemon juice

Chicken with Pumpkin Seed Sauce
Serves 4   Total Time 1¼ hours

Why This Recipe Works Pipian verde, or pumpkin seed sauce, is a traditional Pueblan sauce made with tangy fresh tomatillos and nutty toasted pumpkin seeds. Our first move was to toast sesame seeds and pumpkin seeds (we chose pepitas over unhulled pumpkin seeds for a smoother sauce) in a skillet, which we then used to build our sauce. Onion, garlic, and thyme gave the sauce an aromatic base while fresh jalapeño lent it lively spice. We chopped the tomatillos so they would soften nicely. Poaching our chicken right in the sauce kept our recipe streamlined and ensured moist, flavorful chicken. Once the chicken was done, we pureed the sauce in the blender; lime juice, cilantro, and a pinch of sugar added at this point gave the sauce just the right brightness and rounded out the flavors. Serve with rice.

⅓ cup pepitas

¼ cup sesame seeds

2 tablespoons vegetable oil

1 onion, chopped fine

1 teaspoon table salt, divided

1 jalapeño chile, stemmed, seeded, and chopped

3 garlic cloves, minced

1 teaspoon minced fresh thyme or ¼ teaspoon dried

6 ounces tomatillos, husks and stems removed, rinsed well, dried, and chopped

1½ cups chicken broth

4 (6- to 8-ounce) boneless, skinless chicken breasts, trimmed

¼ teaspoon pepper

1 cup fresh cilantro leaves

1 tablespoon lime juice

Pinch sugar

1. Toast pepitas and sesame seeds in 12-inch nonstick skillet over medium heat until seeds are golden and fragrant, about 15 minutes; transfer to bowl. Set aside 1 tablespoon seeds for garnish.

2. Add oil, onion, and ½ teaspoon salt to now-empty skillet and cook over medium-high heat until softened, 5 to 7 minutes. Stir in jalapeño, garlic, and thyme and cook until fragrant, about 30 seconds. Stir in tomatillos, broth, and toasted seeds; cover; and cook until tomatillos begin to soften, about 10 minutes.

3. Sprinkle chicken with pepper and remaining ½ teaspoon salt, then nestle into mixture in skillet. Cover, reduce heat to medium-low, and cook until chicken registers 160 degrees, 10 to 15 minutes, flipping halfway through cooking. Transfer chicken to platter, tent with aluminum foil, and let rest for 5 to 10 minutes.

4. Carefully transfer mixture left in skillet to blender. Add cilantro, lime juice, and sugar to blender and process until mostly smooth, about 1 minute. Season with salt and pepper to taste. Spoon some of sauce over chicken and sprinkle chicken with reserved seeds. Serve with remaining sauce.

TOASTING SEEDS

Toast pepitas and sesame seeds in dry 12-inch nonstick skillet over medium heat until seeds are golden and fragrant, about 15 minutes.

Pollo Encacahuatado

Serves 4   Total Time 1 hour

Why This Recipe Works A specialty of the Puebla region, pollo encacahuatado is a chicken dish with a thick, hearty sauce made with tomatoes, ground peanuts, and chiles. A variation of a classic mole, the rich red sauce boasts deep chile flavor that is beautifully complemented by the sweetness of the tomatoes and the savory, nutty, peanut flavor. For our version, we settled on traditional ancho chiles; their naturally smoky, fruity, complex flavor and mild heat made them an excellent option. We also added a bit of chipotle chile in adobo for an even deeper, smokier flavor. As for the peanuts, we chose dry-roasted peanuts to save ourselves the time of roasting them ourselves. Toasted sesame seeds gave the sauce an even more complex nutty flavor. We blended the chiles, peanuts, and sesame seeds with tomatoes, warm spices, and aromatics to create a thick paste. We then fried the paste in oil to deepen its flavor; this also created a rich and flavorful fond. To this base, we added some savory chicken broth, which tasted better than plain water. The gentle, even heat of poaching left the chicken juicy and infused it with the complex chile-nut flavor. For textural contrast, we dressed the finished dish with more chopped peanuts as well as some cilantro for freshness. Serve with rice.

3 dried ancho chiles, stemmed, seeded, and torn into ½-inch pieces (¾ cup)

1 onion, chopped fine

2 tomatoes, cored and chopped coarse

1 cup whole unsalted dry-roasted peanuts, plus ¼ cup chopped

1½ cups chicken broth, divided

2 tablespoons sesame seeds, toasted

2 garlic cloves, minced

2 teaspoons cider vinegar

1 teaspoon sugar, plus extra as needed

1 teaspoon minced canned chipotle chile in adobo sauce

1 teaspoon table salt, divided

½ teaspoon ground cinnamon

⅛ teaspoon ground cloves

3 tablespoons vegetable oil

4 (6- to 8-ounce) boneless, skinless chicken breasts, trimmed

¼ teaspoon pepper

2 tablespoons chopped fresh cilantro

1. Toast anchos in 12-inch skillet over medium heat, stirring frequently, until fragrant, 2 to 6 minutes; transfer to blender. Add onion, tomatoes, whole peanuts, ¼ cup broth, sesame seeds, garlic, vinegar, sugar, chipotle, ½ teaspoon salt, cinnamon, and cloves to blender and process until smooth, about 1 minute.

2. Heat oil in now-empty skillet over medium-high heat until shimmering. Add pureed chile mixture and cook, stirring often, until mixture has thickened and darkened in color, about 8 minutes.

3. Stir in remaining 1 ¼ cups broth, scraping up any browned bits, and bring to simmer. Sprinkle chicken with pepper and remaining ½ teaspoon salt and nestle into sauce. Cover, reduce heat to medium-low, and cook until chicken registers 160 degrees, 10 to 15 minutes, flipping halfway through cooking.

4. Transfer chicken to platter, tent with aluminum foil, and let rest for 5 to 10 minutes. Season sauce with sugar, salt, and pepper to taste, and spoon over chicken. Sprinkle with cilantro and chopped peanuts and serve.

Chicken Paprikash

Serves 4 to 6   **Total Time** 1¼ hours

Why This Recipe Works To allow vibrant paprika to shine in this comforting Hungarian braised chicken dish, we added it with the chicken broth (blooming it in hot oil burned it and turned it bitter almost instantly). We removed the skin from bone-in chicken thighs for tender meat without the grease and added sweetness to the stew with softened bell pepper and onion. A bit of cayenne added warmth and enhanced the paprika's earthy flavor. Finishing the dish with a mixture of sour cream and flour thickened and enriched the rust-hued stew. Rather than discarding the chicken skin, try crisping it in a skillet in a little oil set over medium-high heat and setting it aside for a snack. Be sure to use sweet Hungarian paprika here, not hot or smoked, and make sure it's fresh (once opened, paprika loses its flavor quickly). Serve with buttered egg noodles.

- ¼ cup extra-virgin olive oil
- 1 large onion, halved and sliced thin
- 1 red bell pepper, stemmed, seeded, and sliced thin
- 1 (14.5-ounce) can diced tomatoes, drained
- 5 garlic cloves, chopped fine
- 2 teaspoons table salt, divided
- 8 (5- to 7-ounce) bone-in chicken thighs, skin removed, trimmed
- ¾ teaspoon pepper
- 2½ cups chicken broth
- 2 tablespoons paprika, plus extra for serving
- ¼ teaspoon cayenne pepper

Chicken Paprikash

- ⅓ cup sour cream, plus extra for serving
- 3 tablespoons all-purpose flour
- 2 tablespoons chopped fresh parsley

1. Heat oil in Dutch oven over medium-high heat until shimmering. Add onion, bell pepper, tomatoes, garlic, and 1 teaspoon salt and cook, stirring often, until vegetables are softened and fond begins to develop on bottom of pot, about 10 minutes.

2. Sprinkle chicken with pepper and remaining 1 teaspoon salt. Stir broth, paprika, and cayenne into pot, scraping up any browned bits. Submerge chicken in broth mixture and bring to simmer. Reduce heat to medium-low, cover, and simmer until chicken is very tender and registers at least 195 degrees, about 30 minutes, stirring and flipping chicken halfway through simmering.

3. Whisk sour cream and flour together in bowl. Slowly whisk ½ cup cooking liquid into sour cream mixture. Stir sour cream mixture into pot until fully incorporated. Continue to simmer, uncovered, until thickened, about 5 minutes longer. Off heat, season with salt and pepper to taste. Let stand for 5 minutes. Sprinkle with chopped parsley and serve with extra paprika and extra sour cream.

Filipino
Chicken
Adobo

Chicken Tagine with
Olives and Lemon

Filipino Chicken Adobo

Serves 4   Total Time 1½ hours

Why This Recipe Works Adobo is the national dish of the Philippines, and chicken adobo is among the most popular of its countless variations. Its supercharged, pantry-ready ingredient list is short as is the prep time. The dish consists of chicken simmered in a mixture of vinegar, soy sauce, garlic, bay leaves, and black pepper. Some recipes cut the braising liquid with water, which dulls the flavor. We preferred to use coconut milk, traditional in some regional adobos, since it paired well with the tart and salty elements of the dish. The coconut milk's richness tempered the bracing acidity of the vinegar and complemented the briny soy sauce, bringing the sauce into balance. To render the gummy fat layer in the chicken skin and crisp its surface, we started the meat in a room-temperature nonstick skillet and then turned up the heat. As the pan heated, the fat had time to melt before the exterior burned. Light coconut milk can be substituted for the coconut milk, if desired. Serve over white rice.

8 (5- to 7-ounce) bone-in chicken thighs, trimmed
⅓ cup soy sauce
1 (14-ounce) can coconut milk
¾ cup cider vinegar
8 garlic cloves, peeled
4 bay leaves
2 teaspoons pepper
1 scallion, sliced thin

1. Add chicken and soy sauce to large bowl and toss until chicken is thoroughly coated. Refrigerate for at least 30 minutes or up to 1 hour.

2. Place chicken skin side down in 12-inch nonstick skillet; set aside bowl with soy sauce. Place skillet over medium-high heat and cook until fat is rendered and skin is browned, 7 to 10 minutes.

3. Meanwhile, add coconut milk, vinegar, garlic, bay leaves, and pepper to bowl with soy sauce and whisk to combine.

4. Transfer chicken to plate and pour off all fat from skillet. Return chicken, skin side down, to skillet, add coconut milk mixture, and bring to boil. Reduce heat to medium-low and simmer, uncovered, for 20 minutes. Using tongs, flip chicken skin side up and continue to cook, uncovered, until chicken registers 175 degrees, about 15 minutes longer. Transfer chicken to platter and tent with aluminum foil.

5. Discard bay leaves and skim any fat from surface of sauce. Return skillet to medium-high heat and cook until sauce is thickened, 5 to 7 minutes. Pour sauce over chicken, sprinkle with scallion, and serve.

Red-Cooked Chicken

Serves 4 to 6   **Total Time** 1¼ hours

Why This Recipe Works Red-cooked chicken is braised in a soy sauce–based liquid. Dark soy sauce gives this dish its characteristic red color and deep, fruity flavor. Dark soy sauce is slightly thicker and is aged longer than standard soy sauce and is sweetened with molasses to give it its distinctive appearance and slightly bittersweet flavor. It's intense stuff and our first versions of this recipe came on too strong. We scaled back the amount in subsequent tests, making up for the decreased volume with chicken broth, Chinese rice cooking wine (or dry sherry), and a few tablespoons of sesame oil. Light brown sugar added enough richness to balance the flavor, and adding just three pieces of star anise and 1 teaspoon of peppercorns invested our broth with an inviting warmth and aroma. You can substitute regular soy sauce for the dark soy sauce, but the color will not be very dark and the flavor will be blander. If you are using both chicken breasts and thighs/drumsticks, we recommend cutting the breast pieces in half so that each serving includes both white and dark meat. Note that using thighs or drumsticks will increase the total cooking time by 40 minutes. Serve with white rice.

- 4 pounds bone-in, skin-on chicken pieces (split breasts halved crosswise, drumsticks, and/or thighs), trimmed
- 2 tablespoons vegetable oil, plus more as needed
- 6 garlic cloves, minced
- 2 tablespoons grated fresh ginger
- 1 teaspoon Sichuan peppercorns
- 3 star anise pods
- ½ cup dark soy sauce
- ⅓ cup chicken broth
- ¼ cup Shaoxing wine or dry sherry
- 3 tablespoons toasted sesame oil
- 3 tablespoons packed light brown sugar
- 4 Easy-Peel Hard-Cooked Eggs, peeled (page 61)

1. Pat chicken dry with paper towels. Heat oil in large Dutch oven over medium-high heat until just smoking. Cook half of chicken skin side down until browned, 5 to 8 minutes. Flip chicken and brown on second side, about 5 minutes; transfer to plate. Repeat with remaining chicken; transfer chicken to plate.

2. Pour off all but 1 tablespoon fat from pot. (Add additional oil to equal 1 tablespoon, if needed.) Add garlic, ginger, Sichuan peppercorns, and star anise and cook over medium heat until

fragrant, about 30 seconds. Stir in soy sauce, chicken broth, rice wine, sesame oil, and brown sugar, scraping up any browned bits.

3. Nestle hard-cooked eggs and chicken, along with any accumulated juices, into pot and bring to simmer. Cover, turn heat to medium-low, and simmer until breasts register 160 degrees, about 20 minutes, and thighs/drumsticks register 175 degrees, about 1 hour, turning over chicken and eggs halfway through cooking to ensure even coloring from sauce. (If using both types of chicken, simmer thighs and drumsticks for 40 minutes before adding breasts.)

4. Transfer chicken and eggs to serving dish, tent with foil, and let rest while finishing sauce. Discard star anise. Skim as much fat as possible off surface of sauce. Pour sauce over chicken and eggs and serve.

Chicken Tagine with Olives and Lemon

Serves 4   **Total Time** 1¼ hours

Why This Recipe Works A tagine is a warmly spiced, assertively-flavored North African stew, traditionally slow-cooked in an earthenware vessel of the same name. For our chicken tagine, spices, olives, and lemon gave the dish its character. Cumin, ginger, and cinnamon added depth and warmth, cayenne offered a little heat, coriander echoed the lemon's citrusy notes, and paprika brought a smokiness and deep color. Browning the chicken skin-on gave our braising liquid deep flavor but then we pulled off and discarded the skin since it had turned rubbery. Placing the thighs and drumsticks on the bottom of the pot gave them a head start. Arranging the breast pieces on top of the carrots raised the white meat above the simmering liquid and allowed it to cook gently. Greek green olives had the assertiveness we were looking for and adding them before serving retained their flavor and texture. Traditionally, preserved lemons are used to flavor tagines, but we found that cooking broad lemon zest strips with the onion and spices gave our tagine a rich citrus back note, and stirring in grated lemon zest and lemon juice at the end brought a welcome brightness. Use a vegetable peeler to remove wide strips of zest from the lemon before juicing it; be sure to trim away the bitter-tasting white pith from the zest before using. If your olives are particularly salty, rinse and dry them first. Serve with Simple Couscous (page 189).

1¼ teaspoons paprika
½ teaspoon ground cumin
½ teaspoon ground ginger
¼ teaspoon cayenne pepper
¼ teaspoon ground coriander
¼ teaspoon ground cinnamon
3 (2-inch) strips lemon zest, divided, plus
  3 tablespoons juice
5 garlic cloves, minced, divided
4 pounds bone-in chicken pieces (2 split
  breasts halved crosswise, 2 drumsticks,
  and 2 thighs), trimmed
¾ teaspoon table salt
¾ teaspoon pepper
1 tablespoon extra-virgin olive oil
1 large onion, halved and sliced ¼ inch thick
1¾ cups chicken broth
1 tablespoon honey
2 carrots, peeled and cut crosswise into
  ½-inch-thick rounds, very large pieces
  cut into half-moons
1 cup pitted cracked green olives, halved
2 tablespoons chopped fresh cilantro

1. Combine paprika, cumin, ginger, cayenne, coriander, and cinnamon in small bowl and set aside. Mince 1 strip lemon zest, add 1 teaspoon minced garlic, and mince together until reduced to fine paste; set aside.

2. Sprinkle chicken pieces with salt and pepper. Heat oil in Dutch oven over medium-high heat until just beginning to smoke. Add chicken, skin side down, and cook without moving until skin is deep golden, about 5 minutes. Using tongs, flip chicken and brown on second side, about 4 minutes. Transfer chicken to large plate; when cool enough to handle, remove and discard skin. Pour off and discard all but 1 tablespoon fat from pot.

3. Add onion and remaining 2 lemon zest strips to pot and cook, stirring occasionally, until onion slices have browned at edges but still retain their shape, 5 to 7 minutes (add 1 tablespoon water if pot gets too dark). Add remaining garlic and cook until fragrant, about 30 seconds. Add spice mixture and cook, stirring constantly, until darkened and very fragrant, 45 to 60 seconds. Stir in broth and honey, scraping up any browned bits. Add thighs and drumsticks, reduce heat to medium, and simmer for 5 minutes.

4. Add carrots and breast pieces with any accumulated juices to pot, arranging breast pieces in single layer on top of carrots. Cover, reduce heat to medium-low, and simmer until breast pieces register 160 degrees, 10 to 15 minutes.

5. Transfer chicken to plate and tent with aluminum foil. Add olives to pot; increase heat to medium-high and simmer until liquid has thickened slightly and carrots are tender, 4 to 6 minutes. Return chicken to pot and stir in garlic mixture, lemon juice, and cilantro; season with salt and pepper to taste. Serve immediately.

Chicken Tagine with Fennel, Chickpeas, and Apricots

Serves 4 to 6   **Total Time** 1½ hours

Why This Recipe Works For this simple skillet tagine, we found that just a few spices were necessary to create a blend that was short on ingredients but long on flavor. We used skin-on chicken thighs and browned the meat; we then browned fennel in the rendered fat and bloomed a blend of spicy, earthy, and warm ground spices and a whole cinnamon stick, which cooked with the dish and infused the whole thing with flavor. We added a few broad ribbons of lemon zest as well to give the tagine its citrus back note. Brine-cured olives provided meatiness and piquant flavor, and some dried apricots, which plumped among the chickpeas in broth, created well-rounded sweetness for this well-spiced dish. Chopped parsley, stirred in right before serving, was the perfect finishing touch to freshen the flavors.

  2 tablespoons extra-virgin olive oil, divided,
    plus extra as needed
  5 garlic cloves, minced
1½ teaspoons paprika
  ½ teaspoon ground turmeric
  ½ teaspoon ground cumin
  ¼ teaspoon ground ginger
  ¼ teaspoon cayenne pepper
  2 (15-ounce) cans chickpeas, rinsed, divided
  8 (5- to 7-ounce) bone-in chicken thighs, trimmed
  ¾ teaspoon table salt, divided
  ¼ teaspoon pepper

Chicken Tagine with Fennel, Chickpeas, and Apricots

2. Pat chicken dry with paper towels and sprinkle with salt and pepper. Heat remaining 1 tablespoon oil in 12-inch oven-safe skillet over medium-high heat until just smoking. Cook chicken skin side down until skin is crisped and well browned, 8 to 10 minutes; transfer chicken skin side up to plate.

3. Pour off all but 2 tablespoons fat from skillet (or, if necessary, add extra oil to equal 2 tablespoons). Heat fat left in skillet over medium heat until shimmering. Arrange fennel cut side down in skillet and sprinkle with remaining ¼ teaspoon salt. Cover and cook until lightly browned, 3 to 5 minutes per side. Push fennel to sides of skillet. Add spice mixture, lemon zest, and cinnamon stick to center and cook, mashing spice mixture into skillet, until fragrant, about 30 seconds. Stir spice mixture into fennel. Stir in wine, scraping up any browned bits, and cook until almost evaporated, about 2 minutes.

4. Stir in broth, olives, apricots, mashed chickpeas, and whole chickpeas and bring to simmer. Nestle chicken skin side up into skillet, keeping skin above liquid. Roast until fennel is tender and chicken registers 185 degrees, 35 to 40 minutes. Using pot holders, carefully remove skillet from oven. Discard lemon zest and cinnamon stick. Season with salt and pepper to taste. Sprinkle with parsley and serve with lemon wedges.

1 large fennel bulb, stalks discarded, bulb halved and cut into ½-inch-thick wedges through core
3 (2-inch) strips lemon zest, plus lemon wedges for serving
1 cinnamon stick
½ cup dry white wine
1 cup chicken broth
1 cup pitted large brine-cured green or black olives, halved
½ cup dried apricots, halved
2 tablespoons chopped fresh parsley

1. Adjust oven rack to upper-middle position and heat oven to 350 degrees. Combine 1 tablespoon oil, garlic, paprika, turmeric, cumin, ginger, and cayenne in bowl; set aside. Place ½ cup chickpeas in second bowl and mash to coarse paste with potato masher.

Simple Couscous

Serves 6   Total Time 15 minutes
Couscous is an easy side dish to prepare and nice to serve with a braise or stew to soak up its flavorful sauce.

2 tablespoons extra-virgin olive oil
2 cups couscous
1 cup water
1 cup chicken or vegetable broth
1 teaspoon table salt

Heat oil in medium saucepan over medium-high heat until shimmering. Add couscous and cook, stirring frequently, until grains are just beginning to brown, 3 to 5 minutes. Stir in water, broth, and salt. Cover, remove saucepan from heat, and let sit until couscous is tender, about 7 minutes. Gently fluff couscous with fork and season with pepper to taste. Serve.

SIMPLE SAUTÉS AND STIR-FRIES

Photos (clockwise from top left): Chicken Piccata; Chicken Florentine; Three Cup Chicken; Cashew Chicken

Sautéed Chicken Breasts with Vermouth and Tarragon Sauce

Serves 4 **Total Time** 45 minutes

Why This Recipe Works For an easy and flavorful dinner, few choices can compete with boneless chicken breasts dressed up with a savory pan sauce. This formula is a go-to, so we wanted to get it right. To cook chicken breasts that were well browned yet moist and tender, we found that the key was to use plenty of heat (cooking over low or moderate heat draws the meat's moisture to the surface, preventing browning). We cooked the chicken in a traditional, not nonstick, 12-inch skillet so that it had room to brown and would leave behind tasty bits of fond to flavor our sauce. After transferring the chicken to a warm oven, we built a simple sauce in the skillet using a shallot, vermouth, and broth. Whisking in a few tablespoons of chilled butter thickened the sauce and turned it glossy, and fresh tarragon lent an anise note. For a cream sauce, replace the butter with ¼ cup of heavy cream and simmer it until thickened. Parsley, basil, thyme, or dill can be substituted for the tarragon. You can also substitute any of the pan sauces on pages 196–197 to accompany the chicken.

Chicken
- ½ cup all-purpose flour
- 4 (6- to 8-ounce) boneless, skinless chicken breasts, trimmed
- ½ teaspoon table salt
- ¼ teaspoon pepper
- 2 tablespoons vegetable oil

Vermouth and Tarragon Sauce
- 1 tablespoon vegetable oil
- 1 shallot, minced
- ¼ teaspoon table salt
- ¾ cup chicken broth
- ½ cup dry vermouth or white wine
- 3 tablespoons unsalted butter, cut into 3 pieces and chilled
- 2 teaspoons minced fresh tarragon

1. For the chicken Adjust oven rack to lower-middle position and heat oven to 200 degrees. Spread flour in shallow dish. Pound chicken breasts to uniform thickness. Pat dry with paper towels and sprinkle with salt and pepper. Dredge in flour to coat, shaking off any excess.

2. Heat oil in 12-inch skillet over medium-high heat until just smoking. Cook chicken until browned on both sides and registers 160 degrees, about 10 minutes. Transfer to platter and keep warm in oven.

3. For the sauce Add oil to now-empty skillet and heat over medium-high heat until shimmering. Add shallot and salt and cook until softened, about 2 minutes. Stir in broth and vermouth, scraping up any browned bits, and simmer until reduced and slightly syrupy, about 8 minutes.

4. Stir in any accumulated chicken juices. Reduce heat to low and whisk in butter, 1 piece at a time. Off heat, stir in tarragon and season with salt and pepper to taste. Spoon sauce over chicken and serve.

Chicken Piccata

Serves 4 to 6 **Total Time** 1 hour

Why This Recipe Works The best chicken piccata consists of tender chicken cutlets in a complex, lemony sauce that clings to every inch of chicken. To fashion even cutlets for our recipe, we cut each breast in half crosswise. Then, we halved the thicker portion horizontally to make three pieces that required only minimal pounding to become cutlets. We salted the thin cutlets briefly to boost their ability to retain moisture and then lightly coated them in flour, which helped with browning. We seared the cutlets quickly on both sides and set them aside to build the sauce. For complexity and textural appeal, we included both lemon juice and lemon slices—peel and all. We then returned the cutlets to the pan to cook through in the sauce; any excess starch from the chicken washed into the sauce, thickening it and eliminating a gummy coating. Briny capers and a few tablespoons of butter finished our bright-tasting sauce, while a sprinkling of parsley added freshness. For more information about making cutlets, see page 8.

- 4 (6- to 8-ounce) boneless, skinless chicken breasts, trimmed
- 2 teaspoons kosher salt
- ½ teaspoon pepper
- 2 large lemons
- ¾ cup all-purpose flour
- ¼ cup plus 1 teaspoon vegetable oil, divided
- 1 shallot, minced
- 1 garlic clove, minced
- 1 cup chicken broth
- 3 tablespoons unsalted butter, cut into 6 pieces
- 2 tablespoons capers, drained
- 1 tablespoon minced fresh parsley

1. Cut each chicken breast in half crosswise, then cut thick half in half horizontally, creating 3 cutlets of similar thickness. Pound cutlets to uniform ½-inch thickness. Place cutlets in bowl and toss with salt and pepper. Set aside for 15 minutes.

2. Halve 1 lemon lengthwise. Trim ends from 1 half, halve lengthwise again, then cut crosswise into ¼-inch-thick slices; set aside. Juice remaining half and whole lemon and set aside 3 tablespoons juice.

3. Spread flour in shallow dish. Working with 1 cutlet at a time, dredge cutlets in flour, shaking gently to remove excess. Place on wire rack set in rimmed baking sheet. Heat 2 tablespoons oil in 12-inch skillet over medium-high heat until just smoking. Place 6 cutlets in skillet, reduce heat to medium, and cook until golden brown on both sides, 4 to 6 minutes. Return cutlets to wire rack. Repeat with 2 tablespoons oil and remaining 6 cutlets; return to wire rack.

4. Add remaining 1 teaspoon oil and shallot to skillet and cook until softened, 1 minute. Add garlic and cook until fragrant, 30 seconds. Add broth, reserved lemon juice, and reserved lemon slices and bring to simmer, scraping up any browned bits.

5. Add cutlets to sauce and simmer for 4 minutes, flipping halfway through simmering. Transfer cutlets to platter. Sauce should be thickened to consistency of heavy cream; if not, simmer 1 minute longer. Off heat, whisk in butter, 1 piece at a time. Stir in capers and parsley. Season with salt and pepper to taste. Spoon sauce over chicken and serve.

VARIATIONS

Chicken Piccata with Black Olives

Add ¼ cup pitted and chopped black olives to sauce with capers.

Chicken Piccata with Prosciutto

Add 2 ounces thinly sliced prosciutto, cut into 1 by ¼-inch strips, to skillet with shallot and cook until prosciutto is lightly crisped, about 45 seconds.

Chicken Marsala

Serves 4 to 6   **Total Time** 1½ hours

Why This Recipe Works Chicken Marsala is beloved for its winey mushroom sauce. White mushrooms are often used, but we opted for woodsy cremini, along with even more intensely flavored dried porcini, for the deepest mushroom flavor. We used reduced dry Marsala balanced with chicken broth for rich flavor in our sauce, saving some of the Marsala to add at the end along with lemon juice for a hit of booze and brightness. A little powdered gelatin added to the initial dose of Marsala created a silky, full-bodied texture, as if we'd cooked with bone-in chicken. Cooking pancetta after browning the chicken gave the dish a rich savor that tied the components together. Use a good-quality dry Marsala for this recipe. For more information about making cutlets, see page 8.

Chicken Piccata

Chicken Marsala

2¼ cups dry Marsala, divided

4 teaspoons unflavored gelatin

1 ounce dried porcini mushrooms, rinsed

4 (6- to 8-ounce) boneless, skinless chicken breasts, trimmed

1 teaspoon table salt

½ teaspoon pepper

2 cups chicken broth

¾ cup all-purpose flour

¼ cup plus 1 teaspoon vegetable oil, divided

3 ounces pancetta, cut into ½-inch pieces

1 pound cremini mushrooms, trimmed and sliced thin

1 shallot, minced

1 tablespoon tomato paste

1 garlic clove, minced

2 teaspoons lemon juice

1 teaspoon minced fresh oregano

3 tablespoons unsalted butter, cut into 6 pieces

2 teaspoons minced fresh parsley

1. Bring 2 cups Marsala, gelatin, and porcini mushrooms to boil in medium saucepan, then reduce heat to medium-high and simmer vigorously until reduced by half, 6 to 8 minutes.

2. Meanwhile, cut each chicken breast in half crosswise, then cut thick half in half horizontally, creating 3 cutlets of similar thickness. Pound cutlets to uniform ½-inch thickness. Place cutlets in bowl and toss with salt and pepper. Set aside for 15 minutes.

3. Strain Marsala reduction through fine-mesh strainer, pressing on solids to extract as much liquid as possible; discard solids. Return Marsala reduction to saucepan, add broth, and return to boil. Reduce heat to medium-high and simmer until reduced to 1½ cups, 10 to 12 minutes; set aside.

4. Spread flour in shallow dish. Working with 1 cutlet at a time, dredge cutlets in flour, shaking gently to remove excess. Place on wire rack set in rimmed baking sheet. Heat 2 tablespoons oil in 12-inch skillet over medium-high heat until just smoking. Place 6 cutlets in skillet, reduce heat to medium, and cook until golden brown on both sides, 4 to 6 minutes. Return cutlets to wire rack. Repeat with 2 tablespoons oil and remaining 6 cutlets; return to wire rack.

5. Cook pancetta in now-empty skillet over medium-low heat, scraping up any browned bits, until brown and crisp, about 4 minutes. Stir in cremini mushrooms, increase heat to medium-high, and cook until mushrooms begin to brown, about 8 minutes. Using slotted spoon, transfer cremini mushrooms and pancetta to bowl. Add remaining 1 teaspoon oil and shallot to fat left in pan and cook until softened, 1 minute. Add tomato paste and garlic and cook until fragrant, 30 seconds. Stir in lemon juice, oregano, reduced Marsala mixture, and remaining ¼ cup Marsala and bring to simmer.

6. Nestle cutlets into sauce and simmer for 3 minutes, flipping halfway through simmering. Transfer cutlets to platter. Off heat, whisk butter into sauce in skillet. Stir in parsley and cremini mushroom mixture and season with salt and pepper to taste. Spoon sauce over chicken and serve.

Scampi-Style Chicken

Serves 4 to 6   **Total Time** 1 hour

Why This Recipe Works Shrimp isn't the only scampi; we wanted to re-create the chicken version, an Italian restaurant favorite, at home. We took a cue from restaurants and very-shallow-fried chicken tenderloins in a 12-inch skillet with just 2 tablespoons of oil and paired them with a garlicky sauce that we embellished with sweet strips of tender red bell pepper. Just before tossing all the components together, we finished the sauce with butter to give it the proper consistency—ideal for swiping up with crusty bread or pouring over pasta. If you can't find chicken tenderloins, slice boneless, skinless chicken breasts lengthwise into ¾-inch-thick strips. You can substitute torn basil for the parsley, if desired. Serve with lemon wedges.

2 large eggs

1 teaspoon table salt, divided

¾ cup plus 1 tablespoon all-purpose flour, divided

2 pounds chicken tenderloins, trimmed

6 tablespoons extra-virgin olive oil, divided

1 red bell pepper, stemmed, seeded, and sliced thin

8 garlic cloves, sliced thin

1¼ cups chicken broth

¾ cup dry white wine

4 tablespoons unsalted butter, cut into 4 pieces

2 tablespoons chopped fresh parsley

1. Lightly beat eggs and ½ teaspoon salt together in shallow dish. Spread ¾ cup flour in second shallow dish. Pat chicken dry with paper towels and season with salt and pepper. Working with 1 piece of chicken at a time, dip in eggs, allowing excess to drip off, then dredge in flour, shaking off any excess. Transfer to large plate.

2. Heat 2 tablespoons oil in 12-inch nonstick skillet over medium-high heat until just smoking. Cook half of chicken until golden brown on both sides and registers 160 degrees, about 6 minutes. Transfer chicken to clean plate and tent with aluminum foil. Wipe skillet clean with paper towels and repeat with 2 tablespoons oil and remaining chicken; transfer to plate.

3. Wipe skillet clean with paper towels. Heat remaining 2 tablespoons oil in now-empty skillet over medium-high heat until just smoking. Add bell pepper and remaining ½ teaspoon salt and cook until softened and well browned, 5 to 7 minutes. Add garlic and cook until fragrant and golden brown, about 1 minute. Stir in remaining 1 tablespoon flour and cook for 1 minute.

4. Stir in broth and wine and bring to boil, scraping up any browned bits. Cook until mixture is reduced to about 1½ cups, 5 to 7 minutes. Reduce heat to low and stir in butter until melted. Return chicken to skillet and cook, turning to coat with sauce, until heated through, about 2 minutes. Season with salt and pepper to taste. Transfer to platter and sprinkle with parsley. Serve.

Chicken Scaloppini with Mushrooms and Pepper

Serves 4 **Total Time** 1 hour

Why This Recipe Works "Scaloppini" refers to thinly sliced cuts of meat, traditionally veal but also chicken and turkey. The classic recipe calls for dredging the "scallops" (aka cutlets) in flour, cooking them in a hot pan, and serving them in a pan sauce with vegetables. In most recipes, you brown the chicken before building the sauce, but we found that the thin cutlets became dry as they sat while the sauce simmered. So we made the sauce first and then browned the chicken. Mushrooms, red bell pepper, and capers came together for a flavorful sauce. For more information about making cutlets, see page 8.

3 (6- to 8-ounce) boneless, skinless chicken breasts, trimmed
½ teaspoon table salt, divided
⅛ teaspoon pepper
6 tablespoons vegetable oil, divided
8 ounces white mushrooms, trimmed and quartered
1 red bell pepper, stemmed, seeded, and cut into thin matchsticks
1 shallot, sliced thin
¼ cup capers, rinsed
2 garlic cloves, minced
1¼ cups chicken broth
¾ cup white wine
¼ cup all-purpose flour
3 tablespoons unsalted butter, cut into 3 pieces
1 tablespoon chopped fresh parsley

1. Starting on thick side, cut each chicken breast in half horizontally. Pound cutlets to uniform ½-inch thickness. Pat cutlets dry with paper towels and sprinkle with ¼ teaspoon salt and pepper; set aside.

Scampi-Style Chicken

2. Heat 2 tablespoons oil in 12-inch nonstick skillet over medium-high heat until just smoking. Add mushrooms, bell pepper, shallot, and remaining ¼ teaspoon salt and cook until liquid has evaporated and vegetables begin to brown, 8 to 10 minutes. Add capers and garlic and cook until fragrant, about 1 minute. Add broth and wine and bring to boil, scraping up any browned bits. Cook until slightly thickened and mixture is reduced to 2 cups (measured with vegetables), about 8 minutes. Set aside in measuring cup. Wipe out skillet with paper towels.

3. Spread flour in shallow dish. Working with 1 cutlet at a time, dredge cutlets in flour, shaking off excess, and transfer to plate. Heat 2 tablespoons oil in now-empty skillet over medium-high heat until just smoking. Cook 3 cutlets until golden on both sides and cooked through, about 4 minutes. Transfer to platter and tent with aluminum foil. Repeat with remaining 2 tablespoons oil and remaining 3 cutlets; transfer to platter.

4. Discard any oil remaining in skillet. Return sauce to now-empty skillet and bring to boil. Once boiling, remove skillet from heat and whisk in butter, 1 piece at a time. Stir in any accumulated chicken juices. Season with salt and pepper to taste. Spoon sauce and vegetables over chicken and sprinkle with parsley. Serve.

PAN SAUCES FOR CHICKEN

A pan sauce is a quick way to dress up chicken. Sauté the chicken (you can reference Sautéed Chicken Breasts with Vermouth and Tarragon Sauce on page 192) before making a sauce.

Cream Sauce with Mushrooms
Serves 4   **Total Time** 30 minutes

    1 tablespoon vegetable oil
    2 shallots, minced
    ¼ teaspoon table salt
    8 ounces white mushrooms, trimmed and sliced thin
    ⅓ cup dry sherry or white wine
    1 cup heavy cream
    ½ cup chicken broth
    2 tablespoons minced fresh parsley
      Pinch nutmeg or mace

After sautéing chicken, heat oil in now-empty skillet over medium-high heat until shimmering. Add shallots and salt and cook until softened, about 2 minutes. Add mushrooms and cook until brown, about 8 minutes. Add sherry, scraping up any browned bits, and cook until pan is dry, about 1 minute. Stir in cream and broth and simmer until thickened, about 8 minutes. Stir in any accumulated chicken juices. Off heat, stir in parsley and nutmeg. Season with salt and pepper to taste.

Mustard and Cider Sauce
Serves 4   **Total Time** 25 minutes

    1 tablespoon vegetable oil
    1 shallot, minced
    ¼ teaspoon table salt
    1¼ cups apple cider
    2 tablespoons cider vinegar
    3 tablespoons unsalted butter, cut into
      3 pieces and chilled
    2 tablespoons minced fresh parsley
    2 teaspoons whole-grain mustard

After sautéing chicken, heat oil in now-empty skillet over medium-high heat until shimmering. Add shallot and salt and cook until softened, about 2 minutes. Stir in cider and vinegar, scraping up any browned bits, and simmer until reduced and slightly syrupy, about 8 minutes. Stir in any accumulated chicken juices. Reduce heat to low and whisk in butter, 1 piece at a time. Off heat, stir in parsley and mustard. Season with salt and pepper to taste.

Sherry-Rosemary Sauce
Serves 4   **Total Time** 20 minutes

    1 tablespoon vegetable oil
    1 shallot, minced
    ¼ teaspoon table salt
    ¾ cup chicken broth
    ½ cup dry sherry
    2 sprigs fresh rosemary
    3 tablespoons unsalted butter,
      cut into 3 pieces and chilled

After sautéing chicken, heat oil in now-empty skillet over medium-high heat until shimmering. Add shallot and salt and cook until softened, about 2 minutes. Stir in broth, sherry, and rosemary sprigs, scraping up any browned bits. Bring to simmer and cook until thickened and measures ⅔ cup, about 6 minutes. Stir in any accumulated chicken juices. Reduce heat to low and whisk in butter, 1 piece at a time. Off heat, discard rosemary sprigs. Season with salt and pepper to taste.

Tomato, Basil, and Caper Sauce
Serves 4   **Total Time** 20 minutes

    1 tablespoon vegetable oil
    1 shallot, minced
    ¼ teaspoon table salt
    2 tomatoes (12 ounces), cored,
      seeded, and chopped (2 cups)
    4 garlic cloves, minced
    ¼ cup dry white wine
    2 tablespoons capers, rinsed
    2 tablespoons minced fresh basil

After sautéing chicken, heat oil in now-empty skillet over medium-high heat until shimmering. Add shallot and salt and cook until softened, about 2 minutes. Stir in tomatoes and garlic. Cook until tomatoes have broken down into lumpy puree, about 2 minutes. Stir in wine and capers, scraping up any browned bits, and simmer until thickened, about 2 minutes. Stir in any accumulated chicken juices. Off heat, stir in basil and season with salt and pepper to taste.

Hearty Brown Ale Sauce

Serves 4   Total Time 25 minutes

- 1 tablespoon vegetable oil
- ½ onion, sliced thin
- ¼ teaspoon table salt
- ¾ cup chicken broth
- ½ cup brown ale
- 2 teaspoons minced fresh thyme or 1 teaspoon dried
- 1 teaspoon packed brown sugar
- 1 bay leaf
- 3 tablespoons unsalted butter, cut into 3 pieces and chilled
- ½ teaspoon cider vinegar

After sautéing chicken, heat oil in now-empty skillet over medium-high heat until shimmering. Add onion and salt and cook until softened, about 5 minutes. Stir in broth, ale, thyme, brown sugar, and bay leaf, scraping up any browned bits. Simmer until thickened, about 8 minutes. Stir in any accumulated chicken juices. Reduce heat to low and whisk in butter, 1 piece at a time. Off heat, remove bay leaf. Stir in vinegar. Season with salt and pepper to taste.

Apricot-Orange Sauce

Serves 4   Total Time 20 minutes

- 1 tablespoon unsalted butter
- 1 shallot, minced
- 2 garlic cloves, minced
- 1 cup orange juice (2 oranges), plus 1 orange, peeled and chopped coarse
- 1 cup dried apricots, chopped medium
- 2 tablespoons minced fresh parsley

After sautéing chicken, melt butter in now-empty skillet over medium-high heat. Add shallot and cook until softened, about 2 minutes. Stir in garlic and cook until fragrant, about 15 seconds. Stir in orange juice, chopped orange, and apricots. Simmer until thickened, about 4 minutes. Stir in any accumulated chicken juices. Stir in parsley and season with salt and pepper to taste.

Mustard and Cider Sauce

MAKING A PAN SAUCE

1. Add small amount of minced shallot or onion to pan and cook until softened, then add liquid, such as broth and/or wine. Liquid loosens fond and browned bits dissolve and enrich sauce with flavor.

2. Many pan sauces involve whisking in chilled unsalted butter, 1 small piece at a time. Chilled butter pulls sauce together and makes it thick and glossy. Add fresh herbs or potent ingredients (they don't need any cooking time) and season with salt and pepper.

Chicken Saltimbocca

Chicken Florentine

Chicken Saltimbocca

Serves 4 Total Time 45 minutes

Why This Recipe Works It looks and sounds fancy, but chicken saltimbocca is really a pretty package of simple staples: chicken, ham (prosciutto), and sage. Our challenge was neatly assembling the packages and making the sage sing. We cut four boneless, skinless chicken breasts in half horizontally to form eight evenly sized cutlets. The natural tackiness of raw chicken helped the thinly sliced prosciutto adhere without our having to resort to toothpicks or other tricks. We cooked the cutlets first, in two batches, and then set them aside while we stirred together a lemon-and-butter pan sauce. Fried sage leaves looked and tasted impressive and, as they were done in just 20 seconds, they made a perfect garnish. Make sure to buy prosciutto that is thinly sliced, not shaved; also avoid slices that are too thick, as they won't stick to the chicken. The prosciutto slices should be large enough to fully cover one side of each cutlet. To make the chicken easier to slice, freeze it for 15 minutes. Although whole sage leaves make a beautiful presentation, they are optional and can be omitted from step 3. For more information about making cutlets, see page 8.

4 (6- to 8-ounce) boneless, skinless chicken breasts, tenderloins removed, trimmed
½ cup all-purpose flour
1 teaspoon pepper
1 tablespoon minced fresh sage, plus 8 large leaves (optional)
8 thin slices prosciutto (4 ounces)
¼ cup extra-virgin olive oil, divided
1¼ cups dry vermouth or dry white wine
2 teaspoons lemon juice
4 tablespoons unsalted butter, cut into 4 pieces and chilled
1 tablespoon minced fresh parsley

1. Starting on thick side, cut each chicken breast in half horizontally. Pound cutlets to uniform ¼-inch thickness. Combine flour and pepper in shallow dish.

2. Pat cutlets dry with paper towels. Working with 1 cutlet at a time, dredge cutlets in flour mixture, shaking off excess, and transfer to large platter. Sprinkle cutlets evenly with minced sage. Place 1 prosciutto slice on top of each cutlet, covering sage, and press lightly to adhere.

3. Heat 2 tablespoons oil in 12-inch skillet over medium-high heat until shimmering. Add sage leaves, if using, and cook until leaves begin to change color and are fragrant, 15 to 20 seconds. Using slotted spoon, transfer leaves to paper towel–lined plate; set aside.

4. Place 4 cutlets in skillet, prosciutto side down, and cook over medium-high heat until golden brown on first side, about 3 minutes. Using tongs, flip cutlets, reduce heat to medium, and continue to cook until no longer pink and lightly browned on second side, about 2 minutes longer; transfer cutlets to second large platter. Wipe out skillet with paper towels. Repeat with remaining 2 tablespoons oil and remaining 4 cutlets. Tent with aluminum foil and set aside while preparing sauce.

5. Pour off fat from skillet. Add vermouth, scraping up any browned bits. Bring to simmer and cook until reduced to ⅓ cup, 5 to 7 minutes. Stir in lemon juice. Reduce heat to low and whisk in butter, 1 piece at a time. Off heat, stir in parsley and season with salt and pepper to taste. Pour sauce over cutlets; place sage leaf, if using, on top of each cutlet; and serve immediately.

Chicken Florentine

Serves 4   **Total Time** 1 hour

Why This Recipe Works Legend has it that spinach was the favorite vegetable of Catherine de' Medici of Florence, and that the dishes featuring spinach that her cooks created for her in France were the origins of the culinary term "Florentine." To restore chicken Florentine to its elegant roots, we started with fresh spinach. To prevent the water from the spinach from washing out the other flavors in the dish, we drained excess liquid from the cooked spinach by pressing the leaves with the back of a spoon in a colander. For flavorful browning, we seared the chicken breasts first and then poached them in the sauce before broiling. We used cream to make the sauce silky and built volume with equal amounts of chicken broth and water. We also added a squeeze of lemon juice and a hit of zest to brighten the sauce, along with Parmesan cheese for its nutty, savory punch. You will need a broiler-safe dish for this recipe.

  2 **tablespoons vegetable oil, divided**
12 **ounces (12 cups) baby spinach**
  4 **(6- to 8-ounce) boneless, skinless chicken breasts, trimmed**
  ½ **teaspoon table salt**
  ¼ **teaspoon pepper**
  1 **shallot, minced**
  2 **garlic cloves, minced**
1¼ **cups chicken broth**
1¼ **cups water**
  1 **cup heavy cream**
  6 **tablespoons grated Parmesan cheese, divided**
  1 **teaspoon grated lemon zest plus 1 teaspoon juice**

1. Adjust oven rack to upper-middle position and heat broiler. Heat 1 tablespoon oil in 12-inch skillet over medium-high heat until shimmering. Add spinach and cook, stirring occasionally, until wilted, 1 to 2 minutes. Transfer spinach to colander to drain and let cool slightly. Once cool enough to handle, transfer spinach to clean dish towel, wrap towel tightly around spinach to form ball, and wring until dry; set aside.

2. Pat chicken dry with paper towels and sprinkle with salt and pepper. Wipe skillet dry with paper towels. Heat remaining 1 tablespoon oil in now-empty skillet over medium-high heat until just smoking. Lightly brown chicken on both sides, 4 to 6 minutes. Add shallot and garlic to skillet and cook until fragrant, about 30 seconds. Stir in broth, water, and cream and bring to boil.

3. Reduce heat to medium-low and simmer until chicken registers 160 degrees, about 10 minutes. Transfer chicken to plate and tent with aluminum foil. Continue to simmer sauce until reduced to 1 cup, about 10 minutes. Off heat, stir in ¼ cup Parmesan and lemon zest and juice.

4. Slice chicken crosswise ½ inch thick and arrange in broiler-safe dish. Scatter spinach over chicken and pour sauce over spinach. Sprinkle with remaining 2 tablespoons Parmesan and broil until golden brown, 3 to 5 minutes. Serve.

Chicken and Artichokes with Honey and Herbes de Provence

Serves 4   **Total Time** 40 minutes

Why This Recipe Works We wanted a dish with juicy chicken breasts, golden brown skin, and a flavorful pan sauce accented with the floral, woodsy flavor of the French dried herb mixture, herbes de Provence—and we wanted it to come together quickly. We chose bone-in chicken breasts; after browning the skin, we covered the pan to speed up the process of cooking the breasts through. To add substance to our sauce, we sautéed convenient frozen artichoke hearts. A generous amount of honey gave the sauce remarkable character, underscoring the floral nature of the dried herbs, and a splash of white wine vinegar balanced the sauce. Herbes de Provence is a mixture of dried herbs representative of those used most frequently in the south of France, usually a combination of basil, fennel seed, lavender, marjoram, rosemary, sage, summer savory, and thyme. It can be found in the jarred herb section of the supermarket. This sauce is brightened with white wine vinegar, but you may substitute cider or white vinegar if desired.

4 (12-ounce) bone-in split chicken breasts,
    halved crosswise
½ teaspoon table salt
¼ teaspoon pepper
1 tablespoon vegetable oil
1 (9-ounce) box frozen artichoke hearts, thawed
½ cup chicken broth
2 tablespoons honey
2 teaspoons herbes de Provence
4 tablespoons unsalted butter, cut into 4 pieces
2 teaspoons white wine vinegar

1. Pat chicken dry with paper towels and sprinkle with salt and pepper. Heat oil in large skillet over medium-high heat until just smoking. Cook chicken skin-side down until browned, 5 to 8 minutes. Reduce heat to medium, cover, and cook until chicken registers 160 degrees, about 15 minutes. Transfer chicken to platter and tent with foil.

2. Pour off all but 1 tablespoon fat from skillet. Add artichokes and cook until lightly browned, about 3 minutes; transfer to platter with chicken. Add broth, honey, herbs, and any accumulated chicken juices to skillet and simmer, scraping up any browned bits, until reduced to ¼ cup, about 3 minutes. Off heat, whisk in butter, 1 piece at a time, and vinegar. Pour sauce over chicken and artichokes. Serve.

Chicken
Véronique

Chicken Véronique

Serves 4   Total Time 40 minutes

Why This Recipe Works Like its more well-known sibling, sole Véronique, this French classic combines wine, cream sauce, tarragon, and a garnish of bright grapes, which invigorate the mild meat and rich sauce. The name is elegant, but the dish is simple. We started by pounding chicken breasts to an even thinness and sautéing them in butter to develop richly browned fond. Then we built a simple, delicately flavored sauce with shallot, cream, and wine and thickened it to a silky consistency with a cornstarch slurry. We added halved green grapes, fresh tarragon, and lemon juice right at the end for a complex, elegant, yet no-fuss dish that was as delicious as we imagined.

4 (6-ounce) boneless, skinless chicken breasts,
    trimmed
¼ teaspoon table salt
⅛ teaspoon pepper
1 tablespoon plus ¾ cup chicken broth, divided
1 teaspoon cornstarch
2 tablespoons unsalted butter
1 shallot, minced

¾ cup dry white wine
⅓ cup heavy cream
4½ ounces seedless green grapes,
    halved lengthwise (¾ cup)
1 tablespoon chopped fresh tarragon
½ teaspoon lemon juice

1. Pound chicken breasts to uniform ½-inch thickness. Sprinkle with salt and pepper. Whisk 1 tablespoon broth and cornstarch together in small bowl to make slurry; set aside. Melt butter in 12-inch nonstick skillet over medium heat. Lightly brown chicken on both sides, about 4 minutes; transfer to plate.

2. Add shallot to now-empty skillet and cook until softened, about 1 minute. Add wine and cook until reduced to ½ cup, about 3 minutes. Add remaining ¾ cup broth, chicken, and any accumulated juices; reduce heat to medium-low; cover; and simmer until chicken registers 160 degrees, 5 to 7 minutes.

3. Transfer chicken to platter and tent with aluminum foil. Increase heat to medium-high, add cream and cornstarch slurry to skillet, and cook until reduced to ¾ cup, 5 to 7 minutes. Stir grapes, tarragon, lemon juice, and any accumulated juices from chicken into sauce until heated through, about 1 minute. Season with salt and pepper to taste. Pour sauce over chicken. Serve.

Chicken Francese

Serves 4 **Total Time** 1 hour

Why This Recipe Works Chicken Francese is neither French nor Italian in origin but was a 1970s invention from Rochester, New York. This popular dish features pan-fried cutlets with a light but eggy coating dressed in a silky, tangy lemon-butter sauce that nestles into all the nooks of the soft coating. Dredging the cutlets in cornstarch before dipping them in the egg mixture ensured optimal adherence of sauce to coating to chicken. We made sure that the quick-cooking cutlets spent as little time as possible in the pan so that the coating didn't burn or scramble. The coating adhered tightly to the cutlets, soaking up the tangy, buttery sauce without sloughing off. To make the chicken easier to slice, freeze it for 15 minutes. To help keep the fragile egg coating in place, use a fork to flip the cutlets. For more information about making cutlets, see page 8.

- ½ cup plus 1 teaspoon cornstarch, divided
- 2 large eggs
- 2 tablespoons milk
- 1 cup chicken broth
- ½ cup dry white wine
- ¾ teaspoon table salt, divided
- 4 (6- to 8-ounce) boneless, skinless chicken breasts, trimmed
- ¼ teaspoon pepper
- 6 tablespoons unsalted butter, cut into 6 pieces, divided
- 2 tablespoons capers, rinsed
- 1 garlic clove, minced
- 2 tablespoons lemon juice
- 1 tablespoon chopped fresh parsley

1. Adjust oven rack to middle position and heat oven to 200 degrees. Set wire rack in rimmed baking sheet.

2. Meanwhile, place ½ cup cornstarch in shallow dish. Whisk eggs and milk together in second shallow dish. Whisk broth, wine, ¼ teaspoon salt, and remaining 1 teaspoon cornstarch together in bowl.

3. Starting on thick side, cut each chicken breast in half horizontally. Pound cutlets to uniform ¼-inch thickness. Pat cutlets dry with paper towels and sprinkle with remaining ½ teaspoon salt and ¼ teaspoon pepper. Working with 1 cutlet at a time, dredge cutlets in cornstarch, shaking off excess; dip in egg mixture to coat, letting excess drip off; then place on large plate in single layer.

4. Melt 2 tablespoons butter in 12-inch nonstick skillet over medium-high heat. Cook 4 cutlets until golden brown on both sides and cooked through, 4 to 6 minutes, using fork to flip.

Chicken Francese

Transfer to prepared rack and place in oven to keep warm. Repeat with 2 tablespoons butter and remaining 4 cutlets; transfer to rack.

5. Add capers and garlic to now-empty skillet and cook until fragrant, about 30 seconds. Add broth mixture to skillet and bring to boil. Cook until reduced by half, about 5 minutes. Off heat, stir in lemon juice and remaining 2 tablespoons butter.

6. Transfer chicken to platter. Spoon sauce over chicken and sprinkle with parsley. Serve.

GETTING THE PAN HOT

Don't rush preheating; the temperature of the cooking surface drops when food is added. If sautéing in butter, wait until butter has melted and foaming subsides. If using oil, wait until it lets off wisps of smoke.

Circassian Chicken

Blackened Chicken with Pineapple-Cucumber Salsa

Circassian Chicken

Serves 4   **Total Time** 1 hour

Why This Recipe Works Circassian chicken is tender poached chicken served at room temperature in a creamy Turkish walnut sauce and drizzled with chile or olive oil, often as part of a meze spread. In developing our own version of this rich, nutty pita accompaniment, we cooked boneless, skinless chicken breasts with a hybrid method. We browned them on one side only, turned them, poured in chicken broth, and gently simmered them until they were done and we could shred them. The broth that remained not only facilitated pureeing the sauce but also added depth to it. Toasting the walnuts for the sauce increased their nutty flavor. The simple combination of sautéed onion and garlic, spiced with paprika for complexity and cayenne for a little heat, perfectly complemented the nuts. To give the sauce the right thickness, we turned to the traditional Turkish technique of pureeing bread with the other ingredients. A sprinkle of parsley and a bit of extra oil were the perfect simple garnish. This dish is commonly served at room temperature. To serve hot, transfer the sauce and chicken mixture to a large skillet and reheat over medium heat. Serve with fresh warm pitas.

4   (4- to 6-ounce) boneless, skinless chicken breasts, trimmed
¾   teaspoon table salt, divided
⅛   teaspoon pepper
3   tablespoons extra-virgin olive oil, divided, plus extra for serving
3   cups chicken broth
1   onion, chopped fine
4   teaspoons paprika
3   garlic cloves, minced
½   teaspoon cayenne pepper
2   slices hearty white sandwich bread, crusts removed, torn into 1-inch pieces
2   cups walnuts, toasted
2   tablespoons minced fresh parsley

1. Pound chicken breasts to uniform thickness. Pat chicken dry with paper towels and sprinkle with ¼ teaspoon salt and pepper. Heat 1 tablespoon oil in 12-inch skillet over medium-high heat until just smoking. Brown chicken on 1 side, about 4 minutes. Flip chicken, add broth, and bring to simmer. Reduce heat to medium-low, cover, and cook until chicken registers 160 degrees, about 8 minutes.

2. Transfer chicken to cutting board, let cool slightly, then shred into bite-size pieces using 2 forks. Transfer chicken to large bowl and set aside. Strain and reserve broth, discarding white foam.

3. Wipe skillet clean with paper towels. Heat remaining 2 tablespoons oil in now-empty skillet over medium heat until shimmering. Add onion and remaining ½ teaspoon salt and cook until softened, about 5 minutes. Stir in paprika, garlic, and cayenne and cook until fragrant, about 30 seconds.

4. Process onion mixture, bread, walnuts, and 2½ cups reserved broth in food processor until smooth, about 20 seconds, scraping down sides of bowl as needed. Adjust sauce consistency with remaining reserved broth as needed. (Sauce should be slightly thicker than heavy cream.) Add sauce to chicken and toss to coat. Season with salt and pepper to taste. Transfer chicken to serving platter, sprinkle with parsley, and drizzle with extra oil. Serve.

Blackened Chicken with Pineapple-Cucumber Salsa

Serves 4   Total Time 45 minutes

Why This Recipe Works The appeal of blackened chicken lies in the crisp spice crust that envelops juicy meat. However, most of the time this dish ends up with a burnt-tasting exterior and chalk-dry meat. The key to cooking blackened boneless chicken breasts successfully is managing the heat level: too low and the chicken will exude moisture that prevents browning; too high and the spice rub will burn before the meat has a chance to cook through. To keep the spices from burning, we first pounded the thicker ends of the breasts to make them even so that they would cook through faster, ensuring that the spice rub spent less time exposed to intense heat. We used a high-low cooking method: We got a great initial sear over medium-high heat in a cast-iron skillet that we preheated in a hot 500-degree oven. Then we finished the chicken at a lower, gentler temperature. For the rub, we chose a robust combination of ingredients: coriander, ground ginger, garlic powder, allspice, and cayenne, plus a tablespoon of brown sugar—enough to sweeten and caramelize without burning. Tangy pineapple and cooling cucumber created a fruity salsa that balanced the rub's sharp, bold flavors, perfectly complementing our spicy chicken.

- 2 cups ½-inch pineapple pieces
- ½ cucumber, peeled, halved lengthwise, seeded, and cut into ½-inch pieces
- 1 small shallot, minced
- 1 serrano chile, stemmed, seeded, and minced
- 2 tablespoons chopped fresh mint
- 1 tablespoon lime juice
- 1½ teaspoons table salt, divided
- 1 tablespoon packed brown sugar
- 2 teaspoons ground coriander
- 1½ teaspoons ground ginger
- 1½ teaspoons garlic powder
- ¾ teaspoon ground allspice
- ¾ teaspoon pepper
- ½ teaspoon cayenne pepper
- 4 (6- to 8-ounce) boneless, skinless chicken breasts, trimmed
- 2 tablespoons vegetable oil

1. Adjust oven rack to middle position, place 12-inch cast-iron skillet on rack, and heat oven to 500 degrees. Meanwhile, combine pineapple, cucumber, shallot, serrano, mint, lime juice, and ½ teaspoon salt in bowl; set aside salsa.

2. Combine sugar, coriander, ginger, garlic powder, allspice, pepper, cayenne, and remaining 1 teaspoon salt in bowl, breaking up any clumps. Pound chicken breasts to uniform thickness. Pat chicken dry with paper towels and rub evenly with spice mixture.

3. When oven reaches 500 degrees, remove skillet from oven using pot holders and place over medium-high heat; turn off oven. Being careful of hot skillet handle, add oil and heat until just smoking. Lightly brown chicken on both sides, about 4 minutes.

4. Flip chicken, reduce heat to medium, and cook until very dark brown and chicken registers 160 degrees, 4 to 7 minutes, flipping chicken halfway through cooking. Serve with salsa.

Stir-Fried Sesame Chicken with Broccoli and Red Pepper

Serves 4   Total Time 30 minutes

Why This Recipe Works Making a chicken stir-fry presents a challenge: The lean meat can become dry and stringy when cooked over high heat. We wanted juicy, bite-size pieces of chicken paired with vegetables in a complex sesame sauce. For tender, supple chicken we turned to the Chinese technique known as velveting: We coated the pieces with a mixture of cornstarch and oil to protect them from the high heat of the pan, ensuring that they remained tender. As an added benefit, the cornstarch helped create a rough surface on the chicken that prevented the sauce from sliding off. For our vegetables, we chose colorful broccoli and red pepper. We peeled the broccoli stalks and sliced them thin so they would cook at the same rate as the tender florets. We flavored our sauce with potent sesame oil and stirred in fresh ginger at the end to add a final punch of flavor to this stir-fry. You will need a 12-inch nonstick skillet or 14-inch flat-bottomed wok, each with a tight-fitting lid, for this recipe.

Stir-Fried Sesame Chicken with Broccoli and Red Pepper

just smoking. Add chicken, increase heat to high, and cook, tossing slowly but constantly, until no longer pink, 2 to 6 minutes. Transfer to plate and tent with aluminum foil.

3. Add broccoli and remaining ¼ cup broth to now-empty pan and cook, covered, until broccoli begins to soften, about 2 minutes. Uncover and cook, tossing constantly, until liquid evaporates, about 1 minute. Stir in remaining 1 tablespoon vegetable oil and bell pepper and cook until spotty brown, 3 to 4 minutes. Reduce heat to medium.

4. Push vegetables to sides of pan. Add ginger to clearing and cook, mashing ginger into pan, until fragrant, about 30 seconds. Stir ginger into vegetables.

5. Whisk sauce to recombine, then add to pan along with chicken and any accumulated juices. Increase heat to high and cook until sauce is thickened, about 1 minute. Sprinkle with sesame seeds and serve immediately.

VELVETING CHICKEN

The Chinese technique of velveting keeps chicken in stir-fries from overcooking and turning out chewy and dry. A cornstarch and oil mixture forms a barrier around meat and keeps moisture inside.

¾ cup chicken broth, divided
¼ cup soy sauce, divided
3½ teaspoons cornstarch, divided
2 teaspoons toasted sesame oil
3 tablespoons vegetable oil, divided
12 ounces boneless, skinless chicken breasts, trimmed and cut into 1-inch pieces
1 pound broccoli, florets cut into 1-inch pieces, stalks peeled and sliced ¼ inch thick
1 red bell pepper, stemmed, seeded, and cut into 2-inch-long matchsticks
1 tablespoon grated fresh ginger
1 tablespoon sesame seeds, toasted

1. Whisk ½ cup broth, 3 tablespoons soy sauce, 1 tablespoon cornstarch, and sesame oil together in medium bowl. Whisk 1 tablespoon vegetable oil, remaining 1 tablespoon soy sauce, and remaining ½ teaspoon cornstarch together in large bowl. Add chicken and toss to coat.

2. Heat 1 tablespoon vegetable oil in 12-inch nonstick skillet or 14-inch flat-bottomed wok over medium-high heat until

Stir-Fried Chicken with Bok Choy and Crispy Noodle Cake

Serves 4   Total Time 1¼ hours

Why This Recipe Works White rice is a versatile stir-fry accompaniment, but a pan-fried noodle cake, with its crispy-crunchy contrasting exterior and tender-chewy interior, can be a nice change of pace. We had the most success with fresh Chinese egg noodles, which made for a cohesive cake. A non-stick skillet was crucial, as it kept the cake from sticking and falling apart and allowed us to use less oil so the cake wasn't greasy. After cooking the noodle cake, we put together a colorful stir-fry of chicken, bok choy, and red bell pepper. A quick soak in a salty soy marinade flavored our chicken and helped it retain moisture, and a savory stir-fry sauce with soy sauce and oyster sauce tied everything together. Fresh Chinese noodles are often found in the produce section of larger supermarkets. To make the chicken easier to slice, freeze it for 15 minutes.

Sauce

- ¼ cup chicken broth
- 2 tablespoons soy sauce
- 1 tablespoon Shaoxing wine or dry sherry
- 1 tablespoon oyster sauce
- 1 teaspoon sugar
- 1 teaspoon cornstarch
- ¼ teaspoon red pepper flakes

Noodle Cake

- 1 (9-ounce) package fresh Chinese noodles
  Table salt for cooking noodles
- 2 scallions, sliced thin
- ¼ cup vegetable oil, divided

Stir-Fry

- 1 tablespoon soy sauce
- 1 tablespoon Shaoxing wine or dry sherry
- 2 tablespoons toasted sesame oil
- ½ teaspoon cornstarch
- 1 pound boneless, skinless chicken breasts, trimmed and sliced thin
- 2 tablespoons plus 2 teaspoons vegetable oil, divided
- 1 tablespoon grated fresh ginger
- 1 garlic clove, minced
- 1 pound bok choy, stalks sliced ¼ inch thick on bias, greens sliced ½ inch thick
- 1 small red bell pepper, stemmed, seeded, and cut into ¼-inch-wide strips

1. For the sauce Whisk all ingredients together in small bowl; set aside.

2. For the noodle cake Bring 6 quarts water to boil in large pot. Add noodles and 1 teaspoon salt and cook, stirring often, until almost tender, 2 to 3 minutes. Drain noodles, then toss with scallions.

3. Heat 2 tablespoons oil in 12-inch nonstick skillet over medium heat until shimmering. Spread noodles evenly across bottom of pan and press with spatula to flatten. Cook until bottom of cake is crispy and golden brown, 5 to 8 minutes.

4. Slide noodle cake onto large plate. Add remaining 2 tablespoons oil to pan and swirl to coat. Invert noodle cake onto second plate and slide, browned side up, back into pan. Cook until golden brown on second side, 5 to 8 minutes.

5. Slide noodle cake onto cutting board and let sit for at least 5 minutes before slicing into wedges. (Noodle cake can be transferred to wire rack set in rimmed baking sheet and kept warm in 200-degree oven for up to 20 minutes.) Wipe pan clean with paper towels.

Stir-Fried Chicken
with Bok Choy and
Crispy Noodle Cake

NOTES FROM THE TEST KITCHEN

TIPS FOR SUCCESSFUL STIR-FRYING

No matter what ingredient you're stir-frying, follow these guidelines to ensure success:

- Be ready for quick cooking: Prep ingredients in advance.
- For even browning, use a nonstick skillet or flat-bottomed wok.
- Cook large amounts of meat in batches so the meat doesn't steam.
- Toss ingredients slowly but constantly, making sure all pieces get some time at the hottest part of the pan.
- In most cases, add aromatics toward the end of cooking to avoid scorching, mashing them into the base of the pan to release their flavor.
- If cooking vegetables, first remove any protein from the pan. Stir-fry delicate vegetables briefly; for hardy vegetables like broccoli, cover the wok briefly to allow the vegetable to cook through.
- If cooking a sauce, do so once the other ingredients are cooked.

6. For the stir-fry While water for noodles comes to boil, whisk soy sauce, Shaoxing wine, sesame oil, and cornstarch together in large bowl. Add chicken and toss to coat. Combine 1 teaspoon vegetable oil, ginger, and garlic in small bowl; set aside.

7. Heat 2 teaspoons vegetable oil in now-empty pan over medium-high heat until just smoking. Add half of chicken and increase heat to high. Cook, tossing slowly but constantly, until no longer pink, 2 to 6 minutes. Transfer chicken to clean, dry large bowl and cover with aluminum foil. Repeat with 2 teaspoons vegetable oil and remaining chicken; transfer to bowl.

8. Heat remaining 1 tablespoon vegetable oil in again-empty pan over high heat until just smoking. Add bok choy stalks and bell pepper and cook, tossing constantly, until lightly browned, 2 to 3 minutes.

9. Push vegetables to sides of pan and reduce heat to medium. Add ginger mixture to clearing and cook, mashing mixture into pan, until fragrant, about 30 seconds. Stir mixture into vegetables. Add bok choy greens and cook until beginning to wilt, about 30 seconds.

10. Add chicken and any accumulated juices to pan. Whisk sauce to recombine, then add to pan. Increase heat to high and cook, tossing constantly, until sauce is thickened, about 30 seconds. Serve immediately with noodle cake.

Gingery Stir-Fried
Chicken and Bok Choy

Gingery Stir-Fried Chicken and Bok Choy

Serves 4   Total Time 55 minutes

Why This Recipe Works For a stir-fry that merited "ginger" in its name, we included grated fresh ginger in the oil mixture that we stir-fried in so it gave the whole dish foundational fragrance, as well as in the velvety sauce that coated every bite. For vegetables to complement this gingery profile, we balanced more savory, vegetal bok choy with pleasantly sweet red bell pepper. After removing the chicken from the pan, we stir-fried the vegetables in batches. This dish takes only 5 minutes once you turn on the stove. To make the chicken easier to slice, freeze it for 15 minutes. You will need a 12-inch nonstick skillet or 14-inch flat-bottomed wok for this recipe.

Sauce
- ¼ cup chicken broth
- 2 tablespoons Shaoxing wine or dry sherry
- 1 tablespoon soy sauce
- 1 tablespoon oyster sauce
- 2 teaspoons grated fresh ginger
- ½ teaspoon toasted sesame oil
- 1 teaspoon cornstarch
- 1 teaspoon sugar
- ¼ teaspoon red pepper flakes

Stir-Fry
- 2 tablespoons plus 2 teaspoons vegetable oil, divided
- 2 teaspoons grated fresh ginger
- 1 garlic clove, minced
- 1 tablespoon soy sauce
- 1 tablespoon Shaoxing wine or dry sherry
- 2 tablespoons toasted sesame oil
- ½ teaspoon cornstarch
- 1 pound boneless, skinless chicken breasts, trimmed and sliced thin
- 1 pound bok choy, stalks sliced ¼ inch thick on bias and greens cut into ½-inch strips
- 1 small red bell pepper, stemmed, seeded, and cut into ¼-inch-wide strips

1. For the sauce Whisk all ingredients together in small bowl; set aside.

2. For the stir-fry Combine 1 teaspoon vegetable oil, ginger, and garlic in small bowl; set aside. Whisk soy sauce, Shaoxing wine, sesame oil, and cornstarch together in large bowl. Add chicken and toss to coat.

3. Heat 2 teaspoons vegetable oil in 12-inch skillet or 14-inch flat-bottomed wok over medium-high heat until just smoking. Add half of chicken, increase heat to high, and cook, tossing slowly but constantly, until no longer pink, 2 to 6 minutes. Transfer chicken to clean, dry large bowl and cover with aluminum foil. Repeat with 2 teaspoons vegetable oil and remaining chicken; transfer to bowl.

4. Heat remaining 1 tablespoon vegetable oil in now-empty pan over high heat until just smoking. Add bok choy stalks and bell pepper and cook, tossing constantly, until lightly browned, 2 to 3 minutes.

5. Push vegetables to sides of pan and reduce heat to medium. Add ginger mixture to clearing and cook, mashing mixture into pan, until fragrant, about 30 seconds. Stir mixture into vegetables. Add bok choy greens and cook until beginning to wilt, about 30 seconds.

6. Add chicken and any accumulated juices to pan. Whisk sauce to recombine, then add to pan. Increase heat to high and cook until sauce is thickened, about 30 seconds. Serve immediately.

Stir-Fried Chicken and Chestnuts

Serves 4   Total Time 40 minutes

Why This Recipe Works Silky chicken pairs with a number of vegetables in stir-fries, but here we match it with chestnuts. No, not water chestnuts, one of the common stir-fry vegetables, but the delicate, sweet, roasty-toasty nut. A yellow bell pepper supplied further sweetness (and looked attractive), while scallions, sliced into 2-inch pieces for visible presence, added contrast with their allium bite. We tossed the chicken (thighs for welcome savory flavor) with honey before cooking—a surprising addition that amped up the flavor of the chestnuts but also browned the chicken deeply. Brought together with a simple soy–oyster sauce the stir-fry cooked easily, with components gradually added to the pan. Chestnuts are sold jarred or vacuum-packed in many supermarkets.

1½   pounds boneless, skinless chicken thighs, trimmed and cut into 1-inch pieces
2   tablespoons honey

2   tablespoons vegetable oil
6   scallions, white parts sliced thin, green parts cut into 2-inch pieces
3   garlic cloves, minced
2   teaspoons grated fresh ginger
1   yellow bell pepper, stemmed, seeded, and cut into ½-inch-wide strips
5   ounces peeled, cooked chestnuts, cut into ½-inch pieces
3   tablespoons soy sauce
1   tablespoon oyster sauce

1. Pat chicken dry with paper towels and toss with honey in bowl until coated. Heat oil in 12-inch nonstick skillet over medium-high heat until just smoking. Add chicken and cook, stirring frequently, until well browned, about 6 minutes.

2. Add scallion whites, garlic, and ginger and cook until fragrant, about 30 seconds. Add bell pepper and cook until crisp-tender, about 7 minutes. Stir in chestnuts, soy sauce, oyster sauce, and scallion greens and cook until sauce is slightly thickened, about 1 minute. Serve.

Sticky Rice

Serves 4 to 6   Total Time 25 minutes

For rice grains that are sticky, not distinct, we rinsed the rice in cold water and then drained it; this rid the rice of certain starches and allowed others to be released, making the rice tacky. Do not stir the rice as it cooks. The finished rice can stand off the heat, covered, for up to 15 minutes. Medium-grain or jasmine rice can also be used. If serving with a dish that's on the saltier side, such as Three Cup Chicken (page 210), you can omit the salt in step 2.

2   cups long-grain white rice
3   cups water
½   teaspoon table salt

1. Place rice in fine-mesh strainer set over bowl. Rinse under running water, swishing with your hands, until water runs clear. Drain rice thoroughly.

2. Bring rice, water, and salt to boil in medium saucepan over medium-high heat. Cook, uncovered, until water level drops below surface of rice and small holes form, about 5 minutes. Reduce heat to low, cover, and cook until rice is tender and water is fully absorbed, about 15 minutes. Serve.

Sweet and Savory Chicken with Pineapple and Broccoli

Cashew Chicken

Spicy Stir-Fried Sesame Chicken with Green Beans and Shiitake Mushrooms

Serves 4   Total Time 45 minutes

Why This Recipe Works Stir-fried sesame chicken should feature moist, tender, perfectly cooked pieces of flavorful chicken coated with a sweet-spicy-nutty sauce; it shouldn't be a dry and tasteless vehicle for sauce. We employed our go-to solution for combating dry chicken in stir-fries, tossing the chicken in a combination of oil, cornstarch, and soy sauce to keep it moist during the high-heat cooking. We used sesame oil for the mixture and tossed in some toasted sesame seeds as well, for a base layer of sesame flavor. Our sauce also contained sesame oil and sesame seeds, along with sriracha for heat. The result was a stir-fry with plump, tasty slices of chicken and tender-crisp vegetables in a spicy sauce. As a final touch, a drizzle of sesame oil and a sprinkle of toasted seeds over the finished stir-fry really drove home the sesame flavor. To make the chicken easier to slice, freeze it for 15 minutes. For a less spicy stir-fry, reduce the amount of sriracha to 2 teaspoons. You will need a 12-inch nonstick skillet or 14-inch flat-bottomed wok for this recipe.

Sauce
- ½ cup plus 2 tablespoons chicken broth
- 2 tablespoons Shaoxing wine or dry sherry
- 5 teaspoons sugar
- 4 teaspoons sriracha
- 1 tablespoon soy sauce
- 2 teaspoons sesame seeds, toasted
- 2 teaspoons toasted sesame oil
- 1 teaspoon cornstarch
- 1 garlic clove, minced

Stir-Fry
- 2 tablespoons plus 1 teaspoon toasted sesame oil, divided
- 4 teaspoons sesame seeds, toasted, divided
- 2 teaspoons soy sauce
- ½ teaspoon cornstarch
- 1 pound boneless, skinless chicken breasts, trimmed, halved lengthwise, and sliced ¼ inch thick
- 2 tablespoons plus 2 teaspoons vegetable oil, divided
- 2 garlic cloves, minced
- 1 teaspoon grated fresh ginger
- 1 pound green beans, trimmed and cut on bias into 1-inch pieces
- 8 ounces shiitake mushrooms, stemmed and sliced ⅛ inch thick

1. For the sauce Whisk all ingredients together in bowl; set aside.

2. For the stir-fry Whisk 2 tablespoons sesame oil, 1 tablespoon sesame seeds, soy sauce, and cornstarch together in large bowl. Add chicken and toss to coat. Combine 1 teaspoon vegetable oil, garlic, and ginger in separate bowl.

3. Heat 2 teaspoons vegetable oil in 12-inch nonstick skillet or 14-inch flat-bottomed wok over medium-high heat until just smoking. Add half of chicken, increase heat to high, and cook, tossing slowly but constantly, until no longer pink, 2 to 6 minutes. Transfer chicken to clean, dry large bowl and cover with aluminum foil. Repeat with 2 teaspoons vegetable oil and remaining chicken; transfer to bowl.

4. Heat remaining 1 tablespoon vegetable oil in now-empty pan over high heat until just smoking. Add green beans and cook for 1 minute. Stir in mushrooms and cook, tossing constantly, until mushrooms are lightly browned and beans are crisp-tender, 3 to 4 minutes.

5. Push vegetables to sides of pan and reduce heat to medium. Add garlic mixture, and cook, mashing mixture into pan, until fragrant, about 30 seconds. Stir garlic mixture into vegetables.

6. Add chicken and any accumulated juices to pan. Whisk sauce to recombine, then add to pan. Increase heat to high and cook until sauce is thickened, about 30 seconds. Transfer to platter, drizzle with remaining 1 teaspoon sesame oil and sprinkle with remaining 1 teaspoon sesame seeds. Serve.

Sweet and Savory Chicken with Pineapple and Broccoli

Serves 4 **Total Time** 40 minutes

Why This Recipe Works This stir-fry gets its sweet-and-sour profile from pineapple juice, soy sauce, and Asian sweet chili sauce. Letting the chicken marinate in a portion of the sauce not only added flavor but also helped encourage browning. We rounded out our stir-fry with sturdy-yet-tender broccoli and juicy pineapple chunks. We covered the skillet briefly to trap steam so the broccoli would cook quickly. We like to serve this over vermicelli rice noodles. You will need a 12-inch nonstick skillet with a tight-fitting lid for this recipe.

1 cup pineapple juice
3 tablespoons soy sauce
3 tablespoons Asian sweet chili sauce
2 tablespoons cornstarch
3 garlic cloves, minced

1½ pounds boneless, skinless chicken breasts, trimmed and sliced crosswise ½ inch thick
1 tablespoon vegetable oil
12 ounces broccoli florets, cut into 1½-inch pieces
1 cup 1-inch pineapple chunks
¼ teaspoon table salt
¼ cup water
¼ cup fresh cilantro leaves

1. Whisk pineapple juice, soy sauce, chili sauce, cornstarch, and garlic in bowl until smooth. Combine chicken and 3 tablespoons pineapple juice mixture in second bowl and let sit for 15 minutes.

2. Heat oil in 12-inch nonstick skillet over medium-high heat until just smoking. Add chicken and increase heat to high. Cook, stirring frequently, until no longer pink, 2 to 6 minutes; transfer to bowl.

3. Add broccoli, pineapple, and salt to now-empty pan. Cover and cook over high heat, shaking pan occasionally, until broccoli is tender, about 3 minutes. Add chicken and any accumulated juices to pan. Add water and remaining pineapple juice mixture and cook until slightly thickened, about 1 minute. Sprinkle with cilantro leaves and serve immediately.

Cashew Chicken

Serves 4 **Total Time** 35 minutes

Why This Recipe Works Our version of cashew chicken features crunchy, golden-brown, buttery cashews and tender morsels of juicy stir-fried chicken in a salty-sweet sauce—yes, the cashews are as important as the chicken. As with most of our stir-fries, we coated the lean chicken in a cornstarch mixture that served as a protectant, but it also thickened the sauce and gave it a glossy sheen. We wanted our cashews to be much more than a garnish, so we deeply toasted them in the same oil we later used for the stir-fry; this let their flavor permeate the whole dish. Once we toasted them we set them aside to recombine with the stir-fry at the end. You will need a 12-inch nonstick skillet or 14-inch flat-bottomed wok for this recipe.

5 tablespoons soy sauce, divided
1 tablespoon Shaoxing wine or dry sherry
1 teaspoon toasted sesame oil
1 teaspoon cornstarch
1½ pounds boneless, skinless chicken breasts, trimmed and cut into ¾-inch pieces
⅓ cup hoisin sauce

⅓ cup water

1 tablespoon Chinese black vinegar or balsamic vinegar

3 tablespoons vegetable oil

1 cup raw cashews

2 celery ribs, sliced ¼ inch thick on bias

6 scallions, white parts sliced thin, green parts cut into 1-inch pieces

2 garlic cloves, minced

1 teaspoon grated fresh ginger

½ teaspoon red pepper flakes

1. Whisk 2 tablespoons soy sauce, Shaoxing wine, sesame oil, and cornstarch together in large bowl. Add chicken and toss to coat. Whisk hoisin, water, vinegar, and remaining 3 tablespoons soy sauce together in separate bowl.

2. Heat vegetable oil in 12-inch nonstick skillet or 14-inch flat-bottomed wok over medium heat until shimmering. Add cashews and cook, tossing slowly but constantly, until golden brown, 4 to 6 minutes, reducing heat if cashews begin to darken too quickly. Using slotted spoon, transfer cashews to small bowl.

3. Heat oil left in pan over medium-high heat until just smoking. Add chicken and increase heat to high. Cook, tossing slowly but constantly, until no longer pink, 2 to 6 minutes. Add celery, scallion whites, garlic, ginger, and pepper flakes and cook, tossing constantly, until celery is just beginning to soften, about 2 minutes.

4. Add hoisin mixture, bring to boil, and cook until chicken is cooked through and sauce is thickened, 1 to 3 minutes. Off heat, stir in scallion greens and cashews. Serve.

Gai Pad Krapow

Serves 4 **Total Time** 35 minutes

Why This Recipe Works This Thai street food stars stir-fried bite-size pieces of chicken and the bright flavor of basil. The dish traditionally uses holy basil, which can handle prolonged cooking. Since we were using Thai or Italian basil, we needed to keep its flavor intact and ultimately added it in three ways: processed with garlic and Thai chiles for the base, added to our finishing sauce, and stirred into the dish before serving. Pulsing boneless chicken breast in the food processor mimicked the hand-chopping employed by Thai cooks. This dish is normally very spicy; we halved the amount of chiles. If fresh Thai chiles are unavailable, use two serranos or one medium jalapeño. Pass red pepper flakes and sugar at the table, along with extra fish sauce and white vinegar, so that the dish can be adjusted to suit individual tastes. You will need a 12-inch nonstick skillet or 14-inch flat-bottomed wok for this recipe.

2 cups fresh basil leaves, divided

6 green or red Thai chiles, stemmed

3 garlic cloves, peeled

2 tablespoons fish sauce, divided, plus extra for serving

1 tablespoon oyster sauce

1 tablespoon sugar, plus extra for serving

1 teaspoon distilled white vinegar, plus extra for serving

1 pound boneless, skinless chicken breasts, trimmed and cut into 2-inch pieces

3 shallots, sliced thin

2 tablespoons vegetable oil
Red pepper flakes

1. Pulse 1 cup basil, Thai chiles, and garlic in food processor until finely chopped, 6 to 10 pulses, scraping down sides of bowl as needed. Transfer 1 tablespoon basil mixture to small bowl and stir in 1 tablespoon fish sauce, oyster sauce, sugar, and vinegar; set aside. Transfer remaining basil mixture to 12-inch nonstick skillet or 14-inch flat bottomed wok.

2. Pulse chicken and remaining 1 tablespoon fish sauce in now-empty food processor until meat is chopped into approximately ½-inch pieces, 6 to 8 pulses. Transfer to bowl and refrigerate for 15 minutes.

3. Stir shallots and oil into basil mixture in pan. Heat over medium-low heat (mixture should start to sizzle after about 1½ minutes; if it doesn't, adjust heat accordingly), tossing slowly but constantly, until garlic and shallots are golden brown, 5 to 8 minutes.

4. Add chicken, increase heat to medium, and cook, tossing slowly but constantly, breaking up chicken with rubber spatula, until only traces of pink remain, 2 to 4 minutes. Add reserved basil–fish sauce mixture and continue to cook, tossing constantly, until chicken is no longer pink, about 1 minute. Stir in remaining 1 cup basil and cook, stirring constantly, until basil is wilted, 30 seconds to 1 minute. Serve immediately, passing extra fish sauce, sugar, vinegar, and pepper flakes separately.

Three Cup Chicken

Serves 4 **Total Time** 50 minutes

Why This Recipe Works A national dish of sorts in Taiwan, san bei ji, or three cup chicken, gets its name from the three liquids—sesame oil, soy sauce, and rice wine—used in equal amounts to keep the chicken moist and give it flavor. Chiles are included for heat, along with generous amounts of ginger, garlic, scallions, and Thai basil. We scaled down the amount

Three Cup Chicken

3 tablespoons vegetable oil
1 (2-inch) piece ginger, peeled, halved lengthwise, and sliced into thin half-moons
12 garlic cloves, peeled and halved lengthwise
½–¾ teaspoon red pepper flakes
6 scallions, white and green parts separated and sliced thin on bias
1 tablespoon water
1 teaspoon cornstarch
1 cup fresh Thai basil leaves, large leaves halved lengthwise
1 tablespoon toasted sesame oil

1. Whisk soy sauce, Shaoxing wine, and sugar together in large bowl. Add chicken and toss to coat; set aside.

2. Add vegetable oil, ginger, garlic, and pepper flakes to 12-inch nonstick skillet or 14-inch flat-bottomed wok over medium-low heat. Cook, tossing slowly but constantly until garlic is golden brown and beginning to soften, 8 to 10 minutes.

3. Add chicken and marinade to pan, increase heat to medium-high, and bring to simmer. Reduce heat to medium-low and simmer for 10 minutes, tossing constantly. Stir in scallion whites and continue to cook until chicken registers about 200 degrees, 8 to 10 minutes longer.

4. Whisk water and cornstarch together in small bowl, then stir into sauce; simmer until sauce is slightly thickened, about 1 minute. Off heat, stir in basil, sesame oil, and scallion greens. Serve immediately.

Spicy Orange Chicken
Serves 4   Total Time 35 minutes

Why This Recipe Works Featuring tender pieces of meat in a spicy orange sauce, orange chicken too often features overcooked chicken or a sauce that is all spice and no citrus. We found that the combination of orange zest and orange juice created a rich orange flavor, while hoisin sauce offered a mix of sweet, tangy, and salty. Just ½ teaspoon of red pepper flakes contributed the perfect amount of heat. We added red bell pepper and scallions to provide flavor and textural contrast to the tender chicken breasts. Since an intensely flavored sauce is key here, we simmered it for several minutes longer than the sauces in most of our stir-fries to concentrate the flavors. We also waited to add the chicken until after the sauce reduced so it wouldn't overcook. To make the chicken easier to slice, freeze it for 15 minutes. You will need a 12-inch nonstick skillet or 14-inch flat-bottomed wok for this recipe.

of liquid to reduce the cook time. Untoasted sesame oil is the typical cooking oil, but we got similar flavor from using vegetable oil to cook the chicken and finishing with a little toasted sesame oil, which has more potent flavor than untoasted oil. To avoid cutting a whole chicken into pieces with a cleaver, we used boneless chicken thighs; their rich flavor stood up to the sauce. When it came to the aromatics, we left them in larger pieces; the original recipe calls for minced aromatics, but we appreciated the spicy pop that halved garlic cloves and half-moons of ginger provided. Slicing the scallions thin on the bias delivered a pleasant texture. For deep flavor, we marinated the chicken in the soy sauce and rice wine along with a touch of brown sugar. We prefer the flavor of Thai basil in this recipe, but you can substitute sweet Italian basil, if desired. For a spicier dish, use the larger amount of red pepper flakes. You will need a 12-inch nonstick skillet or 14-inch flat-bottomed wok for this recipe.

⅓ cup soy sauce
⅓ cup Shaoxing wine or dry sherry
1 tablespoon packed brown sugar
1½ pounds boneless, skinless chicken thighs, trimmed and cut into 2-inch pieces

1 tablespoon soy sauce
1 tablespoon Shaoxing wine or dry sherry
2 teaspoons toasted sesame oil
½ teaspoon cornstarch
1½ pounds boneless, skinless chicken breasts, trimmed and sliced ¼ inch thick
3 tablespoons hoisin sauce
2 teaspoons grated orange zest plus ¾ cup juice (2 oranges)
3 tablespoons vegetable oil, divided
3 garlic cloves, minced
2 teaspoons grated fresh ginger
½ teaspoon red pepper flakes
1 red bell pepper, stemmed, seeded, and cut into ⅛-inch-wide strips
2 scallions, sliced thin

1. Whisk soy sauce, Shaoxing wine, sesame oil, and cornstarch together in large bowl. Add chicken and toss to coat. Whisk hoisin and orange zest and juice together in second bowl; set aside. Combine 2 teaspoons vegetable oil, garlic, ginger, and red pepper flakes in small bowl; set aside.

2. Heat 2 teaspoons vegetable oil in 12-inch nonstick skillet or 14-inch flat-bottomed wok over medium-high heat until just smoking. Add half of chicken, increase heat to high, and cook, tossing slowly but constantly, until no longer pink, 2 to 6 minutes. Transfer chicken to clean, dry large bowl and cover with aluminum foil. Repeat with 2 teaspoons vegetable oil and remaining chicken; transfer to bowl.

3. Heat remaining 1 tablespoon oil in now-empty pan until just smoking. Add bell pepper and cook, tossing constantly, until bell pepper is just softened, about 3 minutes. Push bell pepper to sides of pan and reduce heat to medium. Add garlic mixture and cook, mashing mixture into pan, until fragrant, about 30 seconds. Stir garlic mixture into bell pepper.

4. Add chicken and any accumulated juices to pan. Whisk sauce to recombine, then add to pan. Increase heat to high and cook until sauce is thickened, about 30 seconds. Sprinkle with scallions and serve.

Kung Pao Chicken
Serves 4 to 6   Total Time 35 minutes

Why This Recipe Works Kung pao chicken is a spicy, savory mix of chicken, peanuts, and chiles. It also includes Sichuan peppercorns, which contribute an intriguing tingling sensation that complements the chiles' heat. (The interplay between the two ingredients is so foundational to Sichuan cuisine that it has a name, ma la, "numbing heat.") Toasting peanuts in a skillet or wok maximized their crunch. Next, we toasted crushed Sichuan peppercorns and arbol chiles that we'd halved to release their heat. We stirred in garlic and ginger and then added marinated diced chicken thighs. Covering the skillet facilitated quick and even cooking. When the chicken was almost done, we added crisp celery then a concentrated sauce that cooked down to a glaze. Stirring in scallions and toasted peanuts last ensured that they retained their crunch. Kung pao chicken should be quite spicy. To adjust the heat level, use more or fewer chiles, depending on the size (we used 2-inch-long chiles) and your taste. Do not eat the chiles. Use a spice grinder or mortar and pestle to coarsely grind the Sichuan peppercorns. You will need a 12-inch nonstick skillet or 14-inch flat-bottomed wok, each with a tight-fitting lid, for this recipe.

Chicken and Sauce
1½ pounds boneless, skinless chicken thighs, trimmed and cut into ½-inch pieces
¼ cup soy sauce, divided
1 tablespoon cornstarch
1 tablespoon Shaoxing wine or dry sherry
½ teaspoon white pepper
1 tablespoon Chinese black vinegar or sherry vinegar
1 tablespoon packed dark brown sugar
2 teaspoons toasted sesame oil

SLICING CHICKEN FOR STIR-FRIES

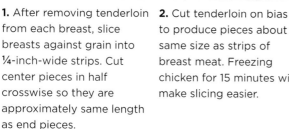

1. After removing tenderloin from each breast, slice breasts against grain into ¼-inch-wide strips. Cut center pieces in half crosswise so they are approximately same length as end pieces.

2. Cut tenderloin on bias to produce pieces about same size as strips of breast meat. Freezing chicken for 15 minutes will make slicing easier.

Stir-Fry

> 2 tablespoons plus 1 teaspoon vegetable oil, divided
> 1 tablespoon minced garlic
> 2 teaspoons grated fresh ginger
> ½ cup dry-roasted peanuts
> 10–15 dried arbol chiles, halved lengthwise and seeded
> 1 teaspoon Sichuan peppercorns, ground coarse
> 2 celery ribs, cut into ½-inch pieces
> 5 scallions, white and light green parts only, cut into ½-inch pieces

1. For the chicken and sauce Combine chicken, 2 tablespoons soy sauce, cornstarch, Shaoxing wine, and white pepper in large bowl and toss to coat; set aside. Stir vinegar, sugar, oil, and remaining 2 tablespoons soy sauce together in small bowl; set aside.

2. For the stir-fry Stir 1 tablespoon oil, garlic, and ginger together in second small bowl. Combine peanuts and 1 teaspoon oil in 12-inch nonstick skillet or 14-inch flat-bottomed wok over medium-low heat. Cook, tossing slowly but constantly, until peanuts just begin to darken, 3 to 5 minutes. Transfer peanuts to plate and spread into even layer to cool. Return now-empty pan to medium-low heat. Add remaining 1 tablespoon oil, arbols, and peppercorns and cook, tossing constantly, until arbols begin to darken, 1 to 2 minutes. Add garlic mixture and cook, tossing constantly, until all clumps are broken up and mixture is fragrant, about 30 seconds.

3. Add chicken and spread into even layer. Cover pan, increase heat to medium-high, and cook, without stirring, for 1 minute. Stir chicken and spread into even layer. Cover and cook, without stirring, for 1 minute. Add celery and cook uncovered, tossing constantly, until chicken is cooked through, 2 to 3 minutes. Add soy sauce mixture and cook, tossing constantly, until sauce is thickened and shiny and coats chicken, 3 to 5 minutes. Stir in scallions and peanuts and serve.

NOTES FROM THE TEST KITCHEN

LUBRICATE YOUR AROMATICS
The small bits of garlic and ginger in a typical stir-fry can clump up when you add them to the pan, preventing some bits from blooming in the oil and their flavors from distributing evenly throughout the dish. The easy work-around? Combine the aromatics with a tablespoon of oil and add this mixture to the pan. The oil helps the garlic and ginger distribute evenly.

Spicy Orange Chicken

Kung Pao Chicken

ROASTED

Photos (clockwise from top left): Skillet-Roasted Chicken in Lemon Sauce; Spice-Rubbed Turkey Breast with Sour Orange Sauce; Roasted Chicken Thighs with Pistachio and Currant Sauce; Classic Roast Chicken

Pan-Roasted Chicken Breasts with Sage-Vermouth Sauce

Serves 4   Total Time 1¼ hours

Why This Recipe Works Our master recipe for roasted bone-in chicken breasts (or parts, see the variation) napped in a luscious sauce utilizes pan roasting, a technique in which food is browned in a skillet on the stovetop and then finished in the oven. A short brine seasoned the chicken and guarded against it drying out in the 450-degree oven, which helped to crisp the skin. The combination of searing and high-heat roasting left plenty of caramelized drippings, or fond, in the skillet to use as the base for a number of quick and flavorful pan sauces.

Chicken
- ½ cup table salt for brining
- 4 (10- to 12-ounce) bone-in split chicken breasts, trimmed
- ¼ teaspoon pepper
- 1 teaspoon vegetable oil

Sage-Vermouth Sauce
- 1 large shallot, minced
- ¾ cup chicken broth
- ½ cup dry vermouth
- 4 fresh sage leaves, each leaf torn in half
- 3 tablespoons unsalted butter, cut into 3 pieces, chilled

1. For the chicken Dissolve salt in 2 quarts cold water in large container. Submerge chicken in brine, cover, and refrigerate for 30 minutes. Remove chicken from brine and pat dry with paper towels. Sprinkle with pepper.

2. Adjust oven rack to lowest position and heat oven to 450 degrees.

3. Heat oil in 12-inch ovenproof skillet over medium-high heat until beginning to smoke; swirl skillet to coat with oil. Brown chicken skin side down until deep golden, about 5 minutes; turn chicken pieces and brown until golden on second side, about 3 minutes longer. Turn chicken skin side down and place skillet in oven. Roast until breast registers 160 degrees, 15 to 18 minutes. Transfer chicken to platter and let rest while making sauce. (If not making sauce, let chicken rest 5 minutes before serving.)

4. For the sage-vermouth sauce Using pot holder to protect your hands from hot skillet handle, pour off most of fat from skillet; add shallot, then set skillet over medium-high heat and cook, stirring frequently, until shallot is softened, about 1½ minutes. Add chicken broth, vermouth, and sage;

increase heat to high and simmer rapidly, scraping skillet bottom with wooden spoon to loosen browned bits, until slightly thickened and reduced to about ¾ cup, about 5 minutes. Pour accumulated chicken juices into skillet, reduce heat to medium, and whisk in butter 1 piece at a time; season with salt and pepper to taste and discard sage. Spoon sauce around chicken breasts and serve immediately.

VARIATIONS

Pan-Roasted Chicken Breasts with Garlic-Sherry Sauce
Substitute 7 thinly sliced garlic cloves for shallot, dry sherry for vermouth, and 2 sprigs fresh thyme for sage. After whisking in butter, discard thyme sprigs and stir ½ teaspoon lemon juice into sauce.

Pan-Roasted Chicken Breasts with Onion and Ale Sauce
Newcastle Brown Ale and Samuel Smith Nut Brown Ale are good choices.

Omit sage. Substitute ½ onion, thinly sliced, for shallot; cook until softened, about 3 minutes. Substitute brown ale for vermouth. Add 1 sprig fresh thyme, 1 bay leaf, and 1 teaspoon packed brown sugar with broth and ale. After whisking in butter, discard thyme sprig and bay leaf and stir ½ teaspoon cider vinegar into sauce.

Pan-Roasted Chicken Breasts with Sweet-Tart Red Wine Sauce
This sauce is a variation on the Italian combination agrodolce.

Substitute ¼ cup red wine and ¼ cup red wine vinegar for vermouth and 1 bay leaf for sage. Add 1 tablespoon sugar and ¼ teaspoon pepper before simmering sauce. After whisking in butter, discard bay leaf.

Pan-Roasted Chicken Breasts with Cognac-Mustard Sauce
Substitute ¼ cup cognac or brandy and ¼ cup white wine for vermouth. Substitute 2 sprigs fresh thyme for sage. Simmer until reduced to ⅔ cup, about 6 minutes. After whisking in butter, discard thyme and add 1 tablespoon Dijon mustard.

Pan-Roasted Chicken Parts
This recipe works with the pan sauces found in the Pan-Roasted Chicken Breasts variations above.

Substitute 1 (4-pound) whole chicken, cut into 8 pieces (2 split breasts halved crosswise, 2 drumsticks, and 2 thighs), trimmed, wings and giblets discarded, for chicken breasts. Roast until breasts register 160 degrees and drumsticks and thighs register 175 degrees, 10 to 15 minutes.

Roasted Bone-In Chicken Breasts

1. Adjust oven rack to lower-middle position and heat oven to 325 degrees. Line rimmed baking sheet with aluminum foil. Working with 1 breast at a time, use your fingers to carefully separate chicken skin from meat. Peel skin back, leaving it attached at top and bottom of breast and at ribs. Sprinkle salt evenly over all chicken, then lay skin back in place. Using metal skewer or tip of paring knife, poke 6 to 8 holes in fat deposits in skin. Arrange breasts skin side up on prepared sheet. Roast until chicken registers 160 degrees, 35 to 45 minutes.

2. Heat 12-inch skillet over low heat for 5 minutes. Add oil and swirl to coat surface. Add chicken breasts, skin side down, and increase heat to medium-high. Cook chicken without moving it until skin is well browned and crispy, 3 to 5 minutes. Using tongs, flip chicken and prop against side of skillet so thick side of breast is facing down; continue to cook until browned, 1 to 2 minutes longer. Transfer to platter and let rest for 5 minutes before serving.

Roasted Bone-In Chicken Thighs

Serves 4   Total Time 50 minutes

Why This Recipe Works Chicken thighs are more flavorful and less prone to overcooking than lean breasts. The only problem is that the layer of fat underneath the skin that helps keep them moist during cooking often leads to flabby skin. To combat this, we cooked the thighs, skin side down, on a preheated baking sheet until the skin was browned and the fat had been rendered. Poking the skin with a skewer before cooking helped the fat to render. We then flipped the thighs over and put them under the broiler briefly to dry and crisp the skin. The result was chicken thighs with succulent and juicy meat under a sheer layer of crackly crisp, deeply browned skin. For the best results, trim all visible fat from the thighs. Use a heavy-duty baking sheet and fully preheat the oven and baking sheet before adding the chicken.

8 (6- to 8-ounce) bone-in chicken thighs, trimmed
1¼ teaspoons table salt
½ teaspoon pepper
Vegetable oil spray

1. Adjust oven racks to middle and lowest positions, place rimmed baking sheet on lower rack, and heat oven to 450 degrees.

2. Using metal skewer, poke skin side of chicken thighs 10 to 12 times. Sprinkle both sides of thighs with salt and pepper; spray skin lightly with vegetable oil spray. Place thighs skin side down on preheated baking sheet. Return baking sheet to lower rack.

Roasted Bone-In Chicken Breasts

Serves 4   Total Time 1¼ hours

Why This Recipe Works If you are looking for supremely crisp skin and tender meat, the extra steps in this method really deliver. Here we employed a reverse-searing method, using the oven first and finishing on the stovetop. We started by applying salt under the skin to season the meat deeply without the need to brine and help retain moisture. Then we poked small holes in the skin to help drain excess fat. Gently baking the breasts at 325 degrees minimized moisture loss and resulted in even cooking from the breasts' thick to their thin ends. It also helped the surface of the skin to dry out so that a quick sear in a hot skillet was all that was required for a crackly, burnished finish. Thanks to this largely hands-off cooking method, there's time to make a separate sauce to serve alongside, if desired (page 403). Be sure to remove excess fatty skin from the thick ends of the breasts when trimming.

4 (10- to 12-ounce) bone-in split chicken breasts, trimmed
¾ teaspoon table salt
1 tablespoon vegetable oil

3. Roast chicken until skin side is beginning to brown and meat registers 160 degrees, 20 to 25 minutes, rotating pan after 10 minutes. Remove chicken from oven and heat broiler.

4. While broiler heats, flip chicken skin side up. Broil chicken on upper rack until skin is crisp and well browned and meat registers 175 degrees, about 5 minutes, rotating pan as needed for even browning. Transfer chicken to platter and let rest for 5 minutes before serving.

ROASTING CHICKEN THIGHS

 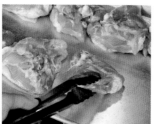

1. Using metal skewer, poke skin side of thighs 10 to 12 times. Pat thighs dry, season, and spray with oil spray.

2. Place thighs skin side down on preheated sheet and roast until skin begins to brown. Flip chicken and broil until skin is crisp and well browned.

Roasted Chicken Thighs with Pistachio and Currant Sauce

Serves 4   Total Time 1 hour

Why This Recipe Works Moroccan b'stilla (see page 340) is a sweet and savory tart filled with tender game or chicken and flavored nuts and warm spices. We loved the idea of capturing it in simpler form. To mimic the shattering crispness of the pastry covering juicy meat, we turned to chicken thighs, cooking them using a two-step roasting method, skin side down on a preheated baking sheet and then under the broiler. To pull together a savory sauce, we caramelized shallots in a foil packet in the oven with the chicken. While the chicken rested, we pulsed the shallots with parsley, pistachios, and lime juice. Cinnamon and orange blossom water recalled Moroccan versions. For the best results, trim all visible fat from the thighs. Use a heavy-duty rimmed baking sheet and fully preheat the oven and baking sheet before adding the chicken.

  3 shallots, sliced thin (½ cup)
  5 tablespoons extra-virgin olive oil, divided
  8 (5- to 7-ounce) bone-in chicken thighs, trimmed

  ½ teaspoon table salt, divided
  ¼ teaspoon pepper
  ½ cup fresh parsley leaves
  6 tablespoons water
  ¼ cup dried currants
  ¼ cup shelled pistachios, toasted
  1 tablespoon lime juice
  ½ teaspoon ground cinnamon
  ¼ teaspoon orange blossom water

1. Adjust oven racks to middle and lowest positions, place rimmed baking sheet on lower rack, and heat oven to 450 degrees.

2. Toss shallots with 1 tablespoon oil in bowl. Cover and microwave until shallots are softened, about 3 minutes, stirring once halfway through microwaving. Place shallots in center of 12-inch square of aluminum foil. Cover with second 12-inch square of foil and fold edges together to create packet about 7 inches square; set aside.

3. Using metal skewer, poke skin side of each chicken thigh 10 to 12 times. Pat thighs dry with paper towels, rub skin with 1 tablespoon oil, and sprinkle with ¼ teaspoon salt and pepper. Place thighs skin side down on hot sheet and place foil packet on upper rack. Roast chicken until skin side is beginning to brown and chicken registers 160 degrees, 17 to 22 minutes, rotating sheet and removing foil packet after 10 minutes. Remove chicken from oven and heat broiler.

4. Flip chicken skin side up and broil on upper rack until skin is crisp and well browned and chicken registers 175 degrees, about 5 minutes, rotating sheet as needed for even browning. Transfer chicken to serving platter and let rest while preparing sauce.

5. Pulse shallots, parsley, water, currants, pistachios, lime juice, cinnamon, orange blossom water, and remaining ¼ teaspoon salt in food processor until finely chopped, about 10 pulses. With processor running, slowly drizzle in remaining 3 tablespoons oil and process until incorporated, scraping down sides of bowl as needed. Season with salt and pepper to taste. Serve chicken with sauce.

VARIATION
Roasted Chicken Thighs with Fennel, Olive, and Orange Sauce
Increase parsley to ¾ cup and decrease water to ¼ cup. Omit currants, pistachios, lime juice, cinnamon, and orange blossom water. Add ¼ cup chopped pitted oil-cured black olives, 2 teaspoons red wine vinegar, 1 rinsed anchovy fillet, 1 teaspoon grated orange zest, ½ teaspoon ground fennel seeds, and ¼ teaspoon red pepper flakes to processor along with shallots, parsley, water, and salt.

Mahogany Chicken Thighs

Serves 4 to 6   **Total Time** 1½ hours

Why This Recipe Works Part braising, part roasting, this hybrid method delivers the best of both: well-rendered, deeply seasoned meat that comes from slow cooking in a flavorful liquid, plus the crispy skin that requires a blast of high heat. Gently simmering bone-in chicken thighs in a potent mix of soy sauce, sherry, ginger, and garlic to an internal temperature of 195 degrees rendered fat and melted the tough connective tissues into rich gelatin. A brief flash under the broiler crisped the skin and gave it a rich mahogany color. For the best results, trim all visible fat and skin from the underside of the thighs. Serve with steamed rice.

1½ cups water, divided
1 cup soy sauce
¼ cup dry sherry
2 tablespoons sugar
2 tablespoons molasses
1 tablespoon distilled white vinegar
8 (5- to 7-ounce) bone-in chicken thighs, trimmed
1 (2-inch) piece ginger, peeled, halved, and smashed
6 garlic cloves, peeled and smashed
1 tablespoon cornstarch

1. Adjust oven rack to middle position and heat oven to 300 degrees. Whisk 1 cup water, soy sauce, sherry, sugar, molasses, and vinegar in ovensafe 12-inch skillet until sugar is dissolved. Arrange chicken, skin side down, in soy sauce mixture and nestle ginger and garlic between pieces of chicken.

2. Bring soy sauce mixture to simmer over medium heat and simmer for 5 minutes. Transfer skillet to oven and cook, uncovered, for 30 minutes.

3. Flip chicken skin side up and continue to cook, uncovered, until chicken registers 195 degrees, 20 to 30 minutes longer. Being careful of hot skillet handle, transfer chicken to platter, taking care not to tear skin. Pour cooking liquid through fine-mesh strainer into fat separator and let settle for 5 minutes. Turn oven to broil.

4. Whisk cornstarch and remaining ½ cup water together in bowl. Pour 1 cup defatted cooking liquid into now-empty skillet and bring to simmer over medium heat. Whisk cornstarch mixture into cooking liquid and simmer until thickened, about 1 minute. Pour sauce into bowl and set aside.

5. Return chicken skin side up to now-empty skillet and broil until well browned, about 4 minutes. Return chicken to platter and let rest for 5 minutes. Serve, passing reserved sauce separately.

Roasted Chicken Thighs with Pistachio and Currant Sauce

Mahogany Chicken Thighs

Skillet-Roasted
Chicken Leg Quarters
and Potatoes

Cast Iron Roast
Chicken Parts

Skillet-Roasted Chicken Leg Quarters and Potatoes

Serves 4   Total Time 1¼ hours

Why This Recipe Works This recipe delivers a chicken and potatoes dinner in just one skillet in just over an hour. Chicken leg quarters, which are underused (and therefore often priced less than other cuts), are substantial enough for one serving and offer plenty of crispy skin. They also rendered enough juices to flavor the potatoes. After browning the leg quarters, we browned potato slices along with some halved shallots; Yukon Golds were starchy enough to soak up the chicken juices, but not so starchy that they'd fall apart. Placing the chicken directly on top of the potatoes allowed the drippings to season the potatoes beneath, bumping up their creamy texture and their flavor. You can substitute four 10- to 12-ounce bone-in split chicken breasts for the leg quarters, if desired. Be sure to cook the breasts to 160 degrees in step 4, about 35 minutes.

  4 (10- to 12-ounce) chicken leg quarters, trimmed
  2 teaspoons minced fresh thyme
1½ teaspoons plus pinch table salt, divided
  1 teaspoon pepper, divided
  2 pounds Yukon Gold potatoes, peeled and
      sliced into ½-inch-thick rounds
  4 shallots, halved through root end
  ¼ cup extra-virgin olive oil, divided
  2 tablespoons chopped fresh parsley
  1 teaspoon grated lemon zest, plus lemon wedges
      for serving
  1 garlic clove, minced

1. Adjust oven rack to middle position and heat oven to 400 degrees. Pat chicken dry with paper towels and sprinkle with thyme, 1 teaspoon salt, and ½ teaspoon pepper. Toss potatoes, shallots, 2 tablespoons oil, ½ teaspoon salt, and remaining ½ teaspoon pepper together in bowl. Combine parsley, lemon zest, garlic, and remaining pinch salt in small bowl; set aside.

2. Heat remaining 2 tablespoons oil in 12-inch ovensafe nonstick skillet over medium heat until shimmering. Add chicken, skin side down, and cook until well browned, about 5 minutes. Transfer chicken to plate, skin side up.

3. Place potatoes and shallots in single layer in now-empty skillet. Cook over medium heat, without moving vegetables, until bottoms of potatoes are golden brown, about 5 minutes.

4. Place chicken, skin side up, on top of vegetables and transfer skillet to oven. Roast until chicken registers 175 degrees and potatoes are tender, about 30 minutes. Sprinkle with parsley mixture. Serve, passing lemon wedges separately.

Cast Iron Roast Chicken Parts

Serves 4   **Total Time** 1 hour

Why This Recipe Works This utterly simple approach requires no stovetop searing pre- or post-roasting; instead it relies on the heat-retaining powers of a cast-iron skillet. We initially tried roasting chicken parts in a traditional skillet, but the skin wasn't nearly as evenly rendered or crispy as we wanted. Using cast iron, preheated thoroughly in the oven, made all the difference. Once the oven and skillet were hot, we carefully added our chicken parts skin side down. They immediately began to sizzle. Halfway through roasting, we flipped the pieces, and 15 minutes later the skin had taken on a beautiful color and crunched faintly against the juicy meat. A spice rub of onion powder, granulated garlic, salt, and pepper further aided in getting a burnished crust. For a finishing touch, we added six sprigs of thyme and a couple of tablespoons of butter to the skillet, which combined with the chicken juices to create a lovely sauce. Note that the skillet should be preheated along with the oven. You will not achieve the same browning with a conventional skillet. A 4-pound chicken will yield the 3 pounds of parts called for in the recipe.

2 teaspoons paprika
2 teaspoons table salt
1 teaspoon pepper
½ teaspoon onion powder
½ teaspoon granulated garlic
3 pounds bone-in chicken pieces (2 split breasts, 2 drumsticks, 2 thighs, and 2 wings with wingtips discarded), trimmed
2 tablespoons unsalted butter
6 sprigs fresh thyme

1. Adjust oven rack to middle position, place 12-inch cast-iron skillet on rack, and heat oven to 450 degrees. Combine paprika, salt, pepper, onion powder, and granulated garlic in bowl. Pat chicken dry with paper towels and sprinkle all over with spice mixture.

2. When oven is heated, carefully remove hot skillet. Add butter, let it melt, and add thyme sprigs. Place chicken in skillet skin side down, pushing thyme sprigs aside as needed. Transfer skillet to oven and bake for 15 minutes.

3. Remove skillet from oven and flip chicken. Return skillet to oven and bake until breasts register 160 degrees and drumsticks/thighs register at least 175 degrees, about 15 minutes longer.

4. Let chicken rest in skillet for 10 minutes. Transfer chicken to platter and spoon pan juices over top. Serve.

Spice-Rubbed Roast Chicken Parts

Serves 4   **Total Time** 1 hour

Why This Recipe Works Need a fresh idea to liven up weeknight roasted chicken? A spice rub is the solution when you don't have a plan, and this spicy, citrusy paste offers potent flavor. We started with a generous handful of mint and offset its coolness with the bite of garlic and the fruity heat of habanero chile. Lime zest and juice brightened up the mixture and smoked paprika added depth. The paste came together quickly in the blender. We shaved off cooking time by using chicken parts instead of a whole chicken, which also created more surface area for our spice paste. Applying it was easy; we simply added the chicken parts and paste to a large zipper-lock bag and tossed it until the parts were well coated. After roasting for less than half an hour, the chicken was done to perfection and sported a lip-smacking spicy crust. For milder heat, substitute jalapeño for the habanero.

½ cup fresh mint leaves
⅓ cup extra-virgin olive oil
6 garlic cloves, peeled
1 tablespoon table salt
1 tablespoon pepper
1 tablespoon ground cumin
1 tablespoon smoked paprika
1 tablespoon dried oregano
2 teaspoons grated lime zest plus ¼ cup juice (2 limes), plus lime wedges for serving
1 teaspoon minced habanero chile
3 pounds bone-in chicken pieces (split breasts halved crosswise, drumsticks, and/or thighs), trimmed

1. Adjust oven rack to lowest position and heat oven to 450 degrees. Line rimmed baking sheet with aluminum foil. Process mint, oil, garlic, salt, pepper, cumin, paprika, oregano, lime zest and juice, and habanero in blender to smooth paste, about 30 seconds. Transfer spice paste to 1-gallon zipper-lock bag. Add chicken to bag, seal, and gently toss to coat chicken evenly with paste.

2. Arrange chicken skin side up on prepared sheet. Roast until well browned and breasts register 160 degrees and drumsticks/thighs register 175 degrees, about 25 minutes. Transfer to platter and let rest for 5 minutes. Serve with lime wedges.

Pan-Roasted Chicken Parts with Vinegar-Tarragon Sauce

Serves 4   Total Time 50 minutes

Why This Recipe Works The success of this dish, inspired by the French classic poulet au vinaigre, rests on avoiding soggy skin and taming the astringent bite of the vinegar. After browning chicken parts in a skillet, we removed them to build our sauce. We then returned the chicken to the pan, keeping the browned skin above the liquid and moving the pan to the oven so that the meat could finish cooking gently in the simmering liquid while the exposed skin crisped. For the sauce, we found cider vinegar to be softer and sweeter than wine vinegar, and perfect balance came when we added a touch of honey. Garlic and shallot added dimension, and just a teaspoon of cornstarch gave the sauce enough body that we only needed to whisk in a tablespoon of butter at the end to create a silky texture. Fresh tarragon brought the requisite French flair.

1 teaspoon cornstarch
1 cup chicken broth, divided
½ cup cider vinegar
2 teaspoons honey
3 pounds bone-in chicken pieces (split breasts halved crosswise, drumsticks, and/or thighs), trimmed
1 teaspoon table salt
½ teaspoon pepper
2 teaspoons vegetable oil
1 shallot, minced
4 garlic cloves, lightly crushed and peeled
1 tablespoon unsalted butter, chilled
1 tablespoon chopped fresh tarragon

1. Adjust oven rack to upper-middle position and heat oven to 450 degrees. Dissolve cornstarch in 2 tablespoons broth in 2-cup liquid measuring cup. Whisk in vinegar, honey, and remaining broth; set aside.

2. Pat chicken dry with paper towels and sprinkle with salt and pepper. Heat oil in 12-inch ovensafe skillet over medium-high heat until just smoking. Cook chicken, skin side down, until well browned, 6 to 8 minutes. Transfer to plate, skin side up.

3. Pour off all but 1 tablespoon fat from skillet and return to medium-high heat. Add shallot and garlic and cook until fragrant, about 30 seconds. Whisk broth mixture to redistribute cornstarch and add to skillet, scraping up any browned bits. Bring to boil and return chicken to skillet, skin side up, along with any accumulated juices. Move skillet to oven and cook until breasts register 160 degrees and drumsticks/thighs register 175 degrees, 10 to 15 minutes.

4. Transfer chicken to serving platter, tent with aluminum foil, and let rest while preparing sauce. Return skillet to medium-high heat (skillet handle will be hot), bring to boil, and cook until sauce is slightly thickened, 5 to 7 minutes. Off heat, whisk butter, tarragon, and any accumulated juices from platter into sauce. Season with salt and pepper to taste. Spoon sauce over chicken and serve.

Skillet-Roasted Chicken in Lemon Sauce

Serves 4   Total Time 1¼ hours

Why This Recipe Works Even if you've never landed a table at Rao's, the legendary tiny East Harlem restaurant, you may have heard of its famous pollo al limone in which two small chickens are split and cooked under a salamander, a powerful restaurant broiler. The bronzed birds are cut into pieces and bathed in a sauce of lemon juice (a cup per bird), olive oil, red wine vinegar, garlic, and oregano before being briefly broiled again and served with crusty bread. We substituted chicken parts, which don't require butchering. Because home broilers are not as powerful as restaurant broilers, we browned the skin in a skillet and then braised the chicken pieces in the pan with a lemon-juice-and-chicken-broth-based sauce; the skin was above the liquid, so it continued to brown and crisp in the oven. We browned the dark-meat pieces on both sides so that they would finish cooking at the same time as the breasts. A mere ¼ cup of lemon juice gave the sauce just the right brightness, and lemon zest gave us more lemon flavor without acidity. We like to serve this chicken with crusty bread, but it can also be served with rice, potatoes, or egg noodles. To ensure crisp skin, dry the chicken well after brining and pour the sauce around, not on, the chicken right before serving.

½ cup table salt for brining
3 pounds bone-in chicken pieces (2 split breasts halved crosswise, 2 drumsticks, and 2 thighs), trimmed
1 teaspoon vegetable oil
2 tablespoons unsalted butter
1 large shallot, minced
1 garlic clove, minced
4 teaspoons all-purpose flour
1 cup chicken broth
4 teaspoons grated lemon zest, divided, plus ¼ cup juice (2 lemons)
1 tablespoon fresh parsley leaves
1 teaspoon fresh oregano leaves

1. Dissolve salt in 2 quarts cold water in large container. Submerge chicken in brine, cover, and refrigerate for 30 minutes to 1 hour. Remove chicken from brine and pat dry with paper towels.

2. Adjust oven rack to lower-middle position and heat oven to 475 degrees. Heat oil in ovensafe 12-inch skillet over medium-high heat until just smoking. Place chicken skin side down in skillet and cook until skin is well browned and crisp, 8 to 10 minutes. Transfer breasts to large plate. Flip thighs and legs and continue to cook until browned on second side, 3 to 5 minutes longer. Transfer thighs and legs to plate with breasts.

3. Pour off and discard fat in skillet. Return skillet to medium heat; add butter, shallot, and garlic and cook until fragrant, 30 seconds. Sprinkle flour evenly over shallot-garlic mixture and cook, stirring constantly, until flour is lightly browned, about 1 minute. Slowly stir in broth and lemon juice, scraping up any browned bits, and bring to simmer. Cook until sauce is slightly reduced and thickened, 2 to 3 minutes. Stir in 1 tablespoon zest and remove skillet from heat. Return chicken, skin side up (skin should be above surface of liquid), and any accumulated juices to skillet and transfer to oven. Cook, uncovered, until breasts register 160 degrees and thighs and legs register 175 degrees, 10 to 12 minutes.

4. While chicken cooks, chop parsley, oregano, and remaining 1 teaspoon zest until finely minced and well combined. Remove skillet from oven and let chicken stand for 5 minutes.

5. Transfer chicken to serving platter. Whisk sauce, incorporating any browned bits from sides of pan, until smooth and homogeneous, about 30 seconds. Whisk half of herb-zest mixture into sauce and sprinkle remaining half over chicken. Pour some sauce around chicken. Serve, passing remaining sauce separately.

Slow-Roasted Chicken Parts with Shallot-Garlic Pan Sauce

Serves 8   Total Time 2¼ hours

Why This Recipe Works Slow roasting allows chicken to retain far more natural juices than high-heat roasting does, but offers little in the way of crispy skin. The solution is to sear the chicken, which is more easily done with parts. We left the skin wet before searing in order to promote fond development, which we later used for a robust jus. After searing, we moved the chicken to a 250-degree oven to slowly roast, but the skin had turned soft and yielding. A final spin under the broiler turned the rendered skin shatteringly crisp and golden brown. To serve four people, halve the ingredient amounts.

Pan-Roasted Chicken Parts with Vinegar-Tarragon Sauce

Skillet-Roasted Chicken in Lemon Sauce

5 pounds bone-in chicken pieces (4 split breasts and 4 leg quarters), trimmed
1 teaspoon table salt
½ teaspoon pepper
¼ teaspoon vegetable oil
1 tablespoon unflavored gelatin
2¼ cups chicken broth
2 tablespoons water
2 teaspoons cornstarch
4 tablespoons unsalted butter, cut into 4 pieces
4 shallots, sliced thin
6 garlic cloves, sliced thin
1 teaspoon ground coriander
1 tablespoon minced fresh parsley
1½ teaspoons lemon juice

1. Adjust 1 oven rack to lowest position and second rack 8 inches from broiler element. Heat oven to 250 degrees. Line baking sheet with aluminum foil and place wire rack on top. Sprinkle chicken pieces with salt and pepper (do not pat chicken dry).

2. Heat oil in 12-inch skillet over medium-high heat until shimmering. Place leg quarters skin side down in skillet; cook, turning once, until golden brown on both sides, 5 to 7 minutes total. Transfer to prepared sheet, arranging legs along 1 long side of sheet. Pour off fat from skillet. Place breasts skin side down in skillet; cook, turning once, until golden brown on both sides, 4 to 6 minutes total. Transfer to sheet with legs. Discard fat; do not clean skillet. Place sheet on lower rack, orienting so legs are at back of oven. Roast until breasts register 160 degrees and legs register 175 degrees, 1 hour 25 minutes to 1¾ hours. Let chicken rest on sheet for 10 minutes.

3. While chicken roasts, sprinkle gelatin over broth in bowl and let sit until gelatin softens, about 5 minutes. Whisk water and cornstarch together in small bowl; set aside.

4. Melt butter in now-empty skillet over medium-low heat. Add shallots and garlic; cook until golden brown and crispy, 6 to 9 minutes. Stir in coriander and cook for 30 seconds. Stir in gelatin mixture, scraping up browned bits. Bring to simmer over high heat and cook until reduced to 1½ cups, 5 to 7 minutes. Whisk cornstarch mixture to recombine. Whisk into sauce and simmer until thickened, about 1 minute. Off heat, stir in parsley and lemon juice; season with salt and pepper to taste. Cover to keep warm.

5. Heat broiler. Transfer sheet to upper rack and broil chicken until skin is well browned and crisp, 3 to 6 minutes. Serve, passing sauce separately.

Weeknight Roast Chicken

Weeknight Roast Chicken
Serves 4   Total Time 1½ hours

Why This Recipe Works When you want a hands-off, absolutely foolproof way to roast a chicken, this is the recipe to use. In fact, we think everyone should memorize it—it's that good. Rather than fussing with a V-rack or flipping the chicken, we simply preheated a skillet in the oven. Direct contact with the superhot pan jump-started the thighs' cooking. Roasting the chicken in a 450-degree oven and then turning the oven off allowed the more delicate white meat to remain moist and tender as the bird finished cooking in the oven's residual heat. We prefer to use a 3½- to 4-pound chicken for this recipe. If roasting a larger bird, increase the time when the oven is on in step 2 to 35 to 40 minutes. Cooking the chicken in a preheated skillet will ensure that the breast and thigh meat finish cooking at the same time.

1½ teaspoons table salt
½ teaspoon pepper
1 (3½- to 4-pound) whole chicken, giblets discarded
1 tablespoon extra-virgin olive oil

1. Adjust oven rack to middle position, place 12-inch oven-safe skillet on rack, and heat oven to 450 degrees. Combine salt and pepper in bowl. Pat chicken dry with paper towels. Rub entire surface with oil. Sprinkle evenly all over with salt mixture and rub in mixture with your hands to coat evenly. Tie legs together with twine and tuck wing tips behind back.

2. Transfer chicken, breast side up, to preheated skillet in oven. Roast chicken until breast registers 120 degrees and thighs register 135 degrees, 25 to 35 minutes. Turn off oven and leave chicken in oven until breast registers 160 degrees and thighs register 175 degrees, 25 to 35 minutes.

3. Transfer chicken to carving board and let rest, uncovered, for 20 minutes. Carve chicken and serve with pan sauce, if using.

NOTES FROM THE TEST KITCHEN

COOKING WITH RESIDUAL HEAT
In our Weeknight Roast Chicken, turning off the oven partway through roasting is the secret to supremely moist meat. How? In meat with a lot of surface area, most of the moisture loss during cooking is through surface evaporation. Shutting off the oven cools the chicken's exterior relatively rapidly, slowing the evaporation of juices. Heat already inside the chicken will continue to be conducted deeper into the interior, eventually bringing it to the desired safe temperature (the same carryover cooking that occurs when meat is resting). The net result is a juicier chicken with virtually no chance of overcooking.

Classic Roast Chicken

Serves 4 **Total Time** 1½ hours (plus 1 hour brining time)

Why This Recipe Works Roasting chicken should be a simple affair but getting the white and dark meat to cook at the same rate while also developing crisp, golden skin is often a challenge. After testing almost every variable we could think of—oven temperature, turning the bird halfway through cooking, basting, and trussing—we found that roasting a chicken is actually quite easy as long as you use the proper technique. Roasting the chicken at 400 degrees for the duration of cooking (rather than adjusting the temperature partway) worked best. Continuous basting didn't improve our roast chicken; we found that applying butter under the skin and rubbing the bird with olive oil before it went into the oven gave it great color

and a crisp texture. Trussing also proved unnecessary; the dark meat cooked more quickly when left untrussed. The only extra step we found truly important was turning the bird twice for evenly cooked meat and crisp, browned skin. If using kosher chicken, do not brine in step 1, and season with salt as well as pepper in step 3. We recommend using a V-rack to roast the chicken. If you don't have a V-rack, set the bird on a regular roasting rack and use balls of aluminum foil to keep the chicken propped up on its side.

- ½ cup table salt for brining
- 1 (3½- to 4-pound) whole chicken, giblets discarded
- 2 tablespoons unsalted butter, softened
- 1 tablespoon extra-virgin olive oil
- ½ teaspoon pepper

1. Dissolve salt in 2 quarts cold water in large container. Submerge chicken in brine, cover, and refrigerate for 1 hour. Remove chicken from brine and pat dry with paper towels.

2. Adjust oven rack to lower-middle position, place roasting pan on rack, and heat oven to 400 degrees. Coat V-rack with vegetable oil spray and set aside.

3. Using your fingers, gently loosen center portion of skin covering each side of breast; place butter under skin, directly on meat in center of each breast. Gently press on skin to distribute butter over meat. Tuck wings behind back. Rub skin with oil, sprinkle with pepper, and place chicken, wing side up, on prepared V-rack. Place V-rack in preheated roasting pan and roast for 15 minutes.

4. Remove roasting pan from oven and, using 2 large wads of paper towels, rotate chicken so that opposite wing side is facing up. Return roasting pan to oven and roast for another 15 minutes.

5. Using 2 large wads of paper towels, rotate chicken again so that breast side is facing up and continue to roast until breast registers 160 degrees and thighs register 175 degrees, 20 to 25 minutes longer. Transfer chicken to carving board and let rest, uncovered, for 20 minutes. Carve and serve.

POSITIONING A CHICKEN IN A V-RACK

For even cooking, roast chicken with 1 wing facing up. Flip chicken and roast with opposite wing facing up. Finish bird breast side up.

Two Roast Chickens

Herbed Roast Chicken

Two Roast Chickens

Serves 8 **Total Time** 1¾ hours (plus 1 hour brining time)

Why This Recipe Works Cooking two whole chickens at once is simple, and leftover roast chicken offers lots of options for second meals. To guarantee juicy, well-seasoned chicken we turned to a brine. Adding sugar along with the salt encouraged browning. Arranging the chickens in opposite directions on a V-rack ensured even airflow between the birds so they cooked and browned evenly. Cooking the chickens at 450 degrees kept the delicate breast meat from drying out; we then turned up the oven to crisp and brown the skin. Brushing the skin with melted butter gave it beautiful color. If using kosher birds, skip the brining. You will need a large V-rack and roasting pan to fit both chickens. If you are reserving some of the chicken for leftovers, pull the meat from the bone and keep in an airtight container for up to two days.

1 cup table salt for brining
1 cup sugar for brining
2 (3½- to 4-pound) whole chickens, giblets discarded
4 tablespoons unsalted butter, softened
2 tablespoons extra-virgin olive oil
1 teaspoon pepper

1. Dissolve salt and sugar in 1 gallon cold water in large container. Submerge chickens in brine, cover, and refrigerate for 1 hour.

2. Adjust oven rack to lower-middle position, place roasting pan on rack, and heat oven to 450 degrees. Coat V-rack with nonstick cooking spray and set aside. Remove chickens from brine, rinse well, and pat dry with paper towels.

3. Using your fingers, gently loosen center portion of skin covering each side of breast. Place 1 tablespoon butter under skin, directly on meat in center of each side of breast on each chicken. Gently press on skin to distribute butter over the meat. Tuck wings behind backs. Rub skin of each chicken with 1 tablespoon oil and season with pepper. Place chickens wing side up, facing in opposite directions, on prepared V-rack. Place V-rack in preheated roasting pan and roast for 25 minutes.

4. Remove roasting pan from oven and, using 2 large wads of paper towels, rotate chickens so that opposite wing sides are facing up. Return roasting pan to oven and roast for another 25 minutes.

5. Using 2 large wads of paper towels, rotate chickens again so that breast sides are facing up. Add ½ cup water to bottom of pan to prevent drippings from burning and continue to roast until breasts register 160 degrees and thighs register 175 degrees, 25 to 30 minutes. Transfer chickens to carving board and let rest, uncovered, for 20 minutes. Carve chickens and serve, reserving some as desired for leftovers.

Herbed Roast Chicken

Serves 4 to 6   Total Time 1½ hours (plus 1 hour brining time)

Why This Recipe Works One of our favorite ways to roast a chicken is to pack it with fresh herb flavor, but the heat of the oven tends to destroy the flavor of fresh herbs. The most common approach is to spread herb butter under the skin of the breast. After much testing with herb pastes (and lots of torn chicken skin), we decided to butterfly the chicken. This made it easier both to spread the paste and to get crisp skin. After brining, we made shallow cuts in the dark meat, which not only helped the skin render its fat but also created pockets to trap the herbs. We rubbed part of our herb paste under the skin on the breast and then browned the chicken in a skillet before moving it to the oven. Halfway through cooking, we slathered on more of the herb paste. Just to make sure that every bite of chicken was bursting with herby flavor, we made a quick pan sauce using the drippings, finishing it off with extra herb butter and lemon juice. You can substitute an equal amount of basil for the tarragon and replace the thyme with rosemary, oregano, or sage. If using a kosher chicken, do not brine in step 1. The chicken may slightly overhang the skillet at first, but once browned it will fit.

Chicken

- 1 (5-pound) whole chicken, giblets discarded
- ½ cup table salt for brining
- 6 tablespoons unsalted butter, softened
- 6 scallions, green parts only, minced
- ¼ cup minced fresh tarragon
- 1 tablespoon minced fresh thyme
- 1 garlic clove, minced
- ¼ teaspoon table salt
- ¼ teaspoon pepper
- 1 tablespoon vegetable oil

Sauce

- 1–1½ cups chicken broth
- 2 teaspoons all-purpose flour
- 1 teaspoon lemon juice

1. For the chicken With chicken breast side down, use kitchen shears to cut through bones on either side of backbone and discard backbone. Flip chicken over and press on breastbone to flatten. Using sharp knife, cut 2 slashes, ⅛ inch deep, into skin of thighs and legs, about ¾ inch apart. Dissolve ½ cup salt in 2 quarts cold water in large container. Submerge chicken in brine, cover, and refrigerate for 1 hour.

2. Meanwhile, adjust oven rack to middle position and heat oven to 450 degrees. Combine softened butter, scallions, tarragon, thyme, garlic, salt, and pepper in bowl. Transfer 2 tablespoons herb butter to small bowl and refrigerate; set remaining herb butter aside.

3. Remove chicken from brine and pat dry with paper towels. Using your fingers, carefully loosen center portion of skin covering each side of breast. Place 1 tablespoon room-temperature herb butter underneath skin over center of each side of breast. Gently press on skin to distribute butter over meat. Season chicken with pepper.

4. Heat oil in 12-inch ovensafe skillet over medium-high heat until just smoking. Add chicken skin side down and reduce heat to medium. Cook until lightly browned, 8 to 10 minutes. Transfer skillet to oven and roast chicken for 25 minutes.

5. Using pot holder, remove chicken from oven. Using 2 large wads of paper towels, flip chicken skin side up. Using spoon or spatula, evenly coat chicken skin with remaining room-temperature herb butter and return to oven. Roast chicken until skin is golden brown, breast registers 160 degrees, and thighs register 175 degrees, 15 to 20 minutes. Transfer chicken to carving board and let rest, uncovered, for 20 minutes.

6. For the sauce While chicken rests, pour pan juices into fat separator. Let liquid settle for 5 minutes, then pour juices into 2-cup liquid measuring cup. Add enough broth to measure 1½ cups. Heat 2 teaspoons fat from fat separator in now-empty skillet over medium heat until shimmering. Add flour and cook, stirring constantly, until golden, about 1 minute. Slowly whisk in broth mixture, scraping up any browned bits. Bring to rapid simmer and cook until reduced to 1 cup, 5 to 7 minutes. Stir in any accumulated chicken juices, return to simmer, and cook for 30 seconds. Off heat, whisk in lemon juice and reserved cold herb butter. Season with salt and pepper to taste. Carve chicken and serve, passing sauce separately.

Roast Lemon Chicken

Serves 4   Total Time 1½ hours

Why This Recipe Works To infuse a whole roast chicken with bright lemon flavor, we first used a pair of kitchen shears to butterfly the bird; this made it easier to flavor the meat as well as speeding up the roasting time. We rubbed a mixture of lemon zest, sugar, and salt into the chicken under the skin. For even more lemon flavor, we roasted the chicken in a sauce of fresh lemon juice mixed with water, more lemon zest, and chicken broth. The butterflied chicken lay flat in the roasting pan so that all of the meat rested in the liquid and the skin remained safely above the juice to let it get crisp. Roasting the bird at a higher temperature—475 degrees—for the entire time also ensured crisp skin. While the chicken rested, we skimmed the fat from the lemony sauce, reduced it to concentrate its flavor, and then thickened it with butter and cornstarch for body and richness. Avoid using nonstick or aluminum roasting pans in this recipe. The former can cause the chicken to brown too quickly, while the latter may react with the lemon juice, producing off-flavors.

- 1 (3½- to 4-pound) whole chicken, giblets discarded
- 3 tablespoons grated lemon zest plus ⅓ cup juice (3 lemons)
- 1 teaspoon sugar
- 1 teaspoon table salt
- ½ teaspoon pepper
- 2 cups chicken broth
- 1 cup plus 1 tablespoon water, divided
- 1 teaspoon cornstarch
- 3 tablespoons unsalted butter, cut into 3 pieces and chilled
- 1 tablespoon finely chopped fresh parsley

1. Adjust oven rack to middle position and heat oven to 475 degrees. With chicken breast side down, use kitchen shears to cut through bones on either side of backbone and discard backbone. Flip chicken over and press on breastbone to flatten. Pat chicken dry with paper towels.

2. Combine lemon zest, sugar, and salt in small bowl. Using your fingers, carefully loosen center portion of skin covering each side of breast. Rub 2 tablespoons zest mixture under skin of chicken. Sprinkle chicken with pepper and transfer to roasting pan. (Seasoned chicken can be refrigerated for 2 hours.)

3. Whisk broth, 1 cup water, lemon juice, and remaining zest mixture in 4-cup liquid measuring cup, then pour into roasting pan. (Liquid should just reach skin of thighs. If it does not, add enough water to reach skin of thighs.) Roast until skin is golden brown and thighs register 175 degrees, 40 to 45 minutes. Transfer chicken to carving board and let rest, uncovered, for 20 minutes.

4. Pour liquid from pan, along with any accumulated chicken juices, into saucepan (you should have about 1½ cups). Skim fat, then cook over medium-high until reduced to 1 cup, about 5 minutes. Whisk cornstarch with remaining 1 tablespoon water in small bowl until no lumps remain, then whisk into saucepan. Simmer until sauce is slightly thickened, about 2 minutes. Off heat, whisk in butter and parsley and season with salt and pepper. Carve chicken and serve, passing sauce at table.

Garlic-Rosemary Roast Chicken with Jus

Serves 4   Total Time 1¾ hours (plus 1 hour brining time)

Why This Recipe Works Simply applying loads of garlic and rosemary under a chicken's skin before roasting does not work (the results are harsh and unpleasant). Instead, we used a restrained amount and added the flavors in other ways, using garlic and rosemary to infuse the brine, rubbing some into the cavity (which seasoned the drippings), and roasting additional cloves in the pan, which we mashed and incorporated into the final jus (flavored with an additional sprig of rosemary). If the roasting pan is considerably larger than the chicken, keep an eye on the pan drippings; the greater surface area may mean more rapid evaporation and a risk of burnt drippings. Add water to the pan as necessary if the liquid evaporates.

Chicken
- ½ cup table salt for brining
- 10 garlic cloves, unpeeled
- 3 sprigs fresh rosemary
- 1 (3½- to 4-pound) whole chicken, giblets discarded

Garlic-Rosemary Paste
- 1 tablespoon plus 2 teaspoons extra-virgin olive oil, divided
- 2 teaspoons minced fresh rosemary
- 2 garlic cloves, minced
- ¼ teaspoon pepper
- ⅛ teaspoon table salt

Jus
- 10 garlic cloves, unpeeled
- 1½ teaspoons extra-virgin olive oil, divided
- 1¾ cups chicken broth, divided
- ½ cup water, plus extra as needed
- ¼ cup dry white wine or vermouth
- 1 sprig fresh rosemary

1. For the chicken Combine salt, garlic, and rosemary in zipper-lock bag; seal, pressing out air. Pound with meat pounder or rolling pin until garlic cloves are crushed. Transfer mixture to large container or stockpot and stir in 2 cups hot tap water; let stand 10 minutes to release flavors. Add 1½ quarts cold tap water and stir until salt is dissolved. Submerge chicken in brine and refrigerate for 1 hour.

2. Remove chicken from brine and pat dry with paper towels. Adjust oven rack to lower-middle position and heat oven to 450 degrees. Set V-rack in roasting pan and lightly spray rack with nonstick cooking spray.

3. **For the paste** Stir together 1 tablespoon oil, rosemary, garlic, pepper, and salt in small bowl. Rub about 1½ teaspoons of paste in cavity of chicken. Using your fingers, carefully loosen center portion of skin covering each side of breast and both thighs. Slip half of remaining paste under skin on each side of breast, then, using your fingers, distribute paste over breast and thigh by rubbing surface of skin. Tie ends of drumsticks together with kitchen twine and tuck wings behind back. Rub all sides of chicken with remaining 2 teaspoons oil and season with pepper. Set chicken breast side down on prepared V-rack and roast for 15 minutes.

4. **For the jus** While chicken is roasting, toss garlic cloves with ½ teaspoon oil; after chicken has roasted for 15 minutes, scatter cloves in pan and roast for 15 minutes longer.

5. Remove roasting pan from oven; decrease oven temperature to 375 degrees. Using tongs or wads of paper towels, rotate chicken breast side up; brush breast with remaining 1 teaspoon oil. Add 1 cup broth and ½ cup water to pan and continue to roast until chicken is medium golden brown, breast registers 160 degrees, and thighs register 175 degrees, about 20 minutes, adding more water to roasting pan if liquid evaporates. Tip V-rack to allow juices in cavity to run into roasting pan. Transfer chicken to large plate.

6. Transfer garlic cloves to cutting board. Using wooden spoon, scrape up browned bits in roasting pan and pour liquid into 2-cup liquid measuring cup. Allow liquid to settle; meanwhile, peel garlic and mash to paste with fork. Using soupspoon, skim fat off surface of liquid (you should have about ⅔ cup skimmed liquid; if not, supplement with water). Transfer liquid to small saucepan, then add wine, rosemary sprig, remaining ¾ cup broth, and garlic paste; simmer over medium-high heat, until reduced to about 1 cup, about 8 minutes. Add accumulated juices from chicken and discard rosemary sprig; season with salt and pepper to taste. Carve chicken and serve with jus.

Glazed Roast Chicken
Serves 6 to 8   Total Time 3 hours

Why This Recipe Works To achieve roast chicken coated in a sweet, tangy glaze without sacrificing crackling skin, we dehydrated the skin with a salt and baking powder rub and poked holes in the fat deposits, which facilitated rendering. Roasting the bird vertically on a beer can achieved allover crispness and made it easier to apply the glaze. We roasted the chicken at two temperatures, gently cooking the meat before blasting it with heat for a burnished finish. Brushing glaze on at the end gave it just enough time to caramelize; a second coat added a luminous sheen. If using table salt, reduce the

Glazed Roast Chicken

amount to 2½ teaspoons. For best results, use a 16-ounce can of beer. A larger can will work, but a 12-ounce can will not support the chicken. A vertical roaster can be used; you will need a model that can be placed in a roasting pan (see page 19). If your marmalade is overly sweet, reduce the maple syrup by 2 tablespoons.

Chicken
- 1 (6- to 7-pound) whole chicken, giblets discarded
- 5 teaspoons kosher salt
- 1 teaspoon baking powder
- 1 teaspoon pepper
- 1 (16-ounce) can beer

Glaze
- 1 teaspoon cornstarch
- 1 tablespoon water
- ½ cup maple syrup
- ½ cup orange marmalade
- ¼ cup cider vinegar
- 2 tablespoons unsalted butter
- 2 tablespoons Dijon mustard
- 1 teaspoon pepper

1. For the chicken Place chicken breast side down on work surface. Use tip of sharp knife to make 1-inch incisions below each thigh and breast along back of chicken (4 incisions total). Using your fingers, carefully loosen center portion of skin covering each side of breast and both thighs. Using metal skewer, poke 15 to 20 holes in fat deposits on top of breasts and thighs. Tuck wingtips underneath chicken.

2. Combine salt, baking powder, and pepper in small bowl. Pat chicken dry with paper towels and sprinkle evenly all over with salt mixture. Rub in mixture with your hands, coating entire surface evenly. Set chicken, breast side up, on rimmed baking sheet and refrigerate, uncovered, for 30 minutes to 1 hour. Meanwhile, adjust oven rack to lowest position and heat oven to 325 degrees.

3. Open beer can and pour out (or drink) about half of liquid. Spray can lightly with nonstick cooking spray and place in middle of roasting pan. Slide chicken over can so drumsticks reach down to bottom of can, chicken stands upright, and breast is perpendicular to bottom of pan. Roast until skin starts to turn golden and breast registers 140 degrees, 1¼ hours to 1½ hours. Carefully remove chicken and pan from oven and increase oven temperature to 500 degrees.

4. For the glaze While chicken cooks, stir cornstarch and water in small bowl until no lumps remain; set aside. Bring maple syrup, marmalade, vinegar, butter, mustard, and pepper to simmer in medium saucepan over medium-high heat. Cook, stirring occasionally, until reduced to ¾ cup, 6 to 8 minutes. Slowly whisk cornstarch mixture into glaze. Return to simmer and cook 1 minute. Remove pan from heat.

5. When oven is heated to 500 degrees, pour 1½ cups water into roasting pan and return to oven. Roast until entire chicken skin is browned and crisp, breast registers 160 degrees, and thighs register 175 degrees, 24 to 30 minutes. Check chicken halfway through roasting; if top is becoming too dark, place 7-inch square piece of foil over neck and wingtips of chicken and continue to roast (if pan begins to smoke and sizzle, add additional ½ cup water to roasting pan).

6. Brush chicken with ¼ cup glaze and continue to roast until browned and sticky, about 5 minutes. (If glaze has become stiff, return to low heat to soften.) Carefully remove chicken from oven; transfer chicken, still on can, to carving board; and brush with another ¼ cup glaze. Let rest for 20 minutes.

7. While chicken rests, strain juices from pan through fine-mesh strainer into fat separator; allow liquid to settle for 5 minutes. Whisk ½ cup juices into remaining ¼ cup glaze in saucepan and set over low heat. Using dish towel, carefully lift chicken off can and onto carving board. Carve chicken, adding any accumulated juices to sauce. Serve, passing sauce separately.

Two Honey Roast Chickens

Serves 8   Total Time 2¼ hours

Why This Recipe Works The only thing better than a honey roast chicken is two honey roast chickens, so we developed our recipe to feed a small crowd. We first rubbed the skin and meat of both chickens with a mixture of salt, pepper, and paprika so they would be nicely seasoned throughout and then set them on a V-rack in a roasting pan to cook. We waited until the chickens were almost done before coating them with a honey–cider vinegar glaze, which kept the skin crisp and didn't give the glaze enough time to burn—at least the glaze that stayed on the chicken. Inevitably, some of the glaze dripped onto the roasting pan, where it sizzled and burned. Our solution was to add water and chicken broth to the pan, which had the added benefit of serving as the base for a flavorful sauce.

1 tablespoon table salt
2 teaspoons pepper
1 teaspoon paprika
2 (3½- to 4-pound) whole chickens, giblets discarded
1 cup plus 1 tablespoon water, divided
1 teaspoon cornstarch
½ cup honey
5 tablespoons cider vinegar, divided
1 cup chicken broth
1 teaspoon minced fresh thyme
2 tablespoons unsalted butter, cut into 2 pieces and chilled

1. Adjust oven rack to middle position and heat oven to 375 degrees. Combine salt, pepper, and paprika in small bowl. Pat chickens dry with paper towels. Working with 1 chicken at a time, using your fingers, carefully loosen center portion of skin covering each side of breast and both thighs. Rub mixture under skin and over outside of each chicken. Tuck wings behind back, and tie legs together with kitchen twine.

2. Stir 1 tablespoon water and cornstarch in bowl until no lumps remain; set aside. Bring honey and ¼ cup vinegar to simmer in saucepan over medium-high heat. Cook, stirring occasionally, until reduced to ½ cup, 3 to 5 minutes. Slowly whisk cornstarch mixture into glaze. Return to simmer and cook for 1 minute.

3. Arrange chickens, breast side down and facing opposite directions, on V-rack set inside roasting pan. Roast until just golden, about 35 minutes. Remove chickens from oven and, using wad of paper towels, flip breast side up. Raise oven temperature to 450 degrees. Pour remaining 1 cup water and broth into roasting pan. Return chickens to oven and roast until thighs register 165 to 170 degrees, 30 to 40 minutes. Brush chickens evenly with thick layer of glaze, and continue to roast until glaze is golden brown, about 10 minutes. Transfer chickens to carving board, brush with remaining glaze, and let rest, uncovered, for 20 minutes.

4. Meanwhile, pour pan juices and any accumulated chicken juices into saucepan; skim fat. Stir in thyme, bring to simmer, and cook until sauce is slightly thickened and reduced to 1 cup, about 10 minutes. Off heat, whisk in butter and remaining 1 tablespoon vinegar. Season with salt and pepper to taste. Carve chickens and serve, passing sauce at table.

Spice-Roasted Chicken with Chili and Oregano

Serves 4   Total Time 1¾ hours

Why This Recipe Works One of the simplest—and best— ways to flavor a roast chicken is with a spice rub, and here we offer several options paired with a walkaway skillet-roasted chicken that's nearly as easy to make as buying a rotisserie bird. We rubbed the chicken with oil (which helped the spices stick) and sprinkled on a combination of chili powder, granulated garlic, and dried oregano. The chicken emerged from the oven browned (not burnt) and superflavorful. Roasting at a moderately high temperature helped ensure rendered fat and slightly crispy skin. The skillet captured the seasoned drippings, which (after a quick skim to remove excess fat) became an easy pan sauce for the carved bird. We used a stainless-steel skillet when developing this recipe, but you can also use a 12-inch cast-iron skillet. If using table salt, reduce the amount to 1 teaspoon.

- 1 tablespoon chili powder
- 1 tablespoon dried oregano
- 2 teaspoons kosher salt
- 1 teaspoon granulated garlic
- 1 teaspoon pepper
- 1 (3½- to 4-pound) whole chicken, giblets discarded
- 2 tablespoons extra-virgin olive oil, divided
- 1 teaspoon cornstarch
- ½ cup water
- 2 teaspoons lemon juice

1. Adjust oven rack to middle position and heat oven to 400 degrees. Combine chili powder, oregano, salt, granulated garlic, and pepper in bowl. Pat chicken dry with paper towels. Transfer chicken, breast side down, to 12-inch ovensafe skillet and rub exposed side with 1 tablespoon oil. Sprinkle with half of spice mixture. Flip chicken breast side up and rub exposed side with remaining 1 tablespoon oil and sprinkle with remaining spice mixture.

Two Honey Roast Chickens

Spice-Roasted Chicken with Chili and Oregano

2. Transfer skillet to oven and roast until breast registers 160 degrees and thighs register 175 degrees, about 1 hour. Transfer chicken to carving board and let rest, uncovered, for 20 minutes. Reserve drippings in skillet.

3. While chicken rests, dissolve cornstarch in water. Carefully skim as much fat as possible from drippings and discard. Add cornstarch mixture to drippings and place over medium-high heat, whisking to scrape up any browned bits. Cook until mixture is boiling and slightly thickened, about 2 minutes. Off heat, whisk in lemon juice. Carve chicken and serve, passing sauce separately.

VARIATIONS

Spice-Roasted Chicken with Dill and Garlic
Substitute 1 tablespoon dried dill weed for chili powder and oregano.

Spice-Roasted Chicken with Fennel, Coriander, and Lemon
Substitute 1 tablespoon fennel seeds, 1 tablespoon ground coriander, and 1 tablespoon lemon zest for chili powder and oregano.

Chile-Rubbed Roast Chicken
Serves 4   Total Time 1¾ hours

Why This Recipe Works For a juicy, tender roast chicken infused with Mexican flavors we needed the right mix of spices; a technique that ensured the spices flavored the chicken throughout; and a simple, foolproof cooking method. A combination of New Mexican and dried chipotle chiles gave us deep, smoky, earthy flavors. To round out our chile rub, we used nutty cumin and citrusy coriander; toasting and grinding whole seeds gave the rub deeper flavor and texture. Onion powder and garlic powder added aromatic depth, warm cinnamon and cloves gave a hint of sweetness, and cayenne and black pepper provided some extra piquant flavor. To keep the cooking method simple, we roasted the chicken in a preheated skillet. This jump-started the cooking of the thighs, which normally take longer than the breasts. Halfway through the cooking time, we shut off the oven, which allowed the chicken to cook through gently in the residual heat, resulting in moist, tender meat. Feel free to substitute ½ teaspoon ground chipotle chile powder for the dried chipotle chile and add it to the spice grinder with the other spices. If using table salt, reduce the amount of salt in the spice rub to 1½ teaspoons.

Chile-Rubbed
Roast Chicken

4 dried New Mexican chiles, stemmed, seeded, and torn into ½-inch pieces (1 cup)
1 dried chipotle chile, stemmed, seeded, and torn into ½-inch pieces (1½ tablespoons)
1 tablespoon cumin seeds
1 tablespoon coriander seeds
½ teaspoon pepper
½ teaspoon onion powder
½ teaspoon garlic powder
¼ teaspoon ground cloves
¼ teaspoon ground cinnamon
⅛ teaspoon cayenne pepper
¼ cup vegetable oil
1 tablespoon kosher salt
2 teaspoons sugar
1 (3½- to 4-pound) whole chicken, giblets discarded
   Lime wedges

1. Toast New Mexican and chipotle chiles, cumin seeds, and coriander seeds in 12-inch ovensafe skillet over medium heat, stirring frequently, until fragrant, 2 to 6 minutes.

Transfer mixture to spice grinder and let cool slightly. Add pepper, onion powder, garlic powder, cloves, cinnamon, and cayenne to grinder and process until coarsely ground, 5 to 10 seconds. Transfer spice mixture to bowl and stir in oil, salt, and sugar.

2. Wipe out now-empty skillet, place on middle rack of oven, and heat oven to 450 degrees. Pat chicken dry with paper towels. Using your fingers, gently loosen skin covering breast and thighs. Rub 3 tablespoons spice paste underneath skin over breast, thighs, and legs. Rub remaining spice paste over top and sides of chicken (do not rub bottom of chicken). Tuck wings behind back and tie legs together loosely with kitchen twine.

3. Transfer chicken, breast side up, to preheated skillet in oven. Roast chicken until breast registers 120 degrees and thighs register 135 degrees, 25 to 35 minutes. Turn off oven and leave chicken in oven until breast registers 160 degrees and thighs register 175 degrees, 25 to 35 minutes.

4. Transfer chicken to carving board and let rest, uncovered, for 20 minutes. Carve and serve with lime wedges.

Peruvian Roast Chicken with Garlic and Lime

Serves 4   **Total Time** 2 hours (plus 6 hours marinating time)

Why This Recipe Works The Peruvian dish pollo a la brasa is deeply bronzed from its slow rotation in a wood-fired oven and impressively seasoned with garlic, spices, lime juice, chiles, and a paste made with huacatay, or black mint. To replicate this dish for the home kitchen we used standard spearmint along with a bit of dried oregano as a substitute for the huacatay, and smoked paprika added a bit of rotisserie flavor. We first tried salting the bird and rubbing the paste over it, but the flavor didn't penetrate much beyond the surface. So instead, we combined the salt with the paste, rubbed it under the skin as well as on top, and refrigerated the chicken for at least 6 hours; this gave the meat deep flavor. A vertical roaster and two-pronged cooking process filled in for the rotisserie, allowing for plenty of hot air circulation around the chicken, which led to perfectly cooked meat and crisp skin. This recipe calls for a vertical poultry roaster. If you don't have one, substitute a 12-ounce can of beer. Open the beer and pour out (or drink) about half of the liquid. Spray the can lightly with nonstick cooking spray and proceed with the recipe. If the top of the chicken is becoming too dark during roasting in step 3, place a 7-inch square piece of foil over the neck and wingtips.

You can substitute 1 tablespoon of minced serrano chile for the habanero here. Wear gloves when working with hot chiles. Spicy Mayonnaise (page 234) takes this dish over the top.

3 tablespoons extra-virgin olive oil
¼ cup lightly packed fresh mint leaves
2 tablespoons kosher salt
6 garlic cloves, chopped coarse
1 tablespoon ground black pepper
1 tablespoon ground cumin
1 tablespoon sugar
2 teaspoons smoked paprika
2 teaspoons dried oregano
2 teaspoons grated lime zest plus ¼ cup juice (2 limes)
1 teaspoon minced habanero chile
1 (3½- to 4-pound) whole chicken, giblets discarded

1. Process oil, mint, salt, garlic, pepper, cumin, sugar, paprika, oregano, lime zest and juice, and habanero in blender until smooth paste forms, 10 to 20 seconds. Using your fingers or handle of wooden spoon, carefully loosen skin over thighs and breast and remove any excess fat. Rub half of paste beneath skin of chicken. Spread entire exterior surface of chicken with remaining paste. Tuck wingtips underneath chicken. Place chicken in gallon-size zipper-lock bag and refrigerate for at least 6 hours or up to 24 hours.

2. Adjust oven rack to lowest position and heat oven to 325 degrees. Place vertical roaster on rimmed baking sheet. Slide chicken onto vertical roaster so chicken stands upright and breast is perpendicular to bottom of pan. Roast until skin just begins to turn golden and breast registers 140 degrees, 45 to 55 minutes. Carefully remove chicken and pan from oven and increase oven temperature to 500 degrees.

FLAVORING PERUVIAN ROAST CHICKEN

1. Use your fingers to gently loosen chicken skin from over thighs and breast and rub half of paste directly over meat.

2. Spread remaining paste over skin of entire chicken.

3. When oven is heated to 500 degrees, place 1 cup water in bottom of pan and return pan to oven. Roast until entire skin is browned and crisp, breast registers 160 degrees, and thighs register 175 degrees, about 20 minutes (replenish water as necessary to keep pan from smoking), rotating bird 180 degrees halfway through cooking.

4. Carefully remove chicken from oven and let rest, still on vertical roaster, 20 minutes. Using dish towel, carefully lift chicken off vertical roaster and onto carving board. Carve chicken and serve.

Spicy Mayonnaise

Makes about 1 cup   **Total Time** 15 minutes

If you have concerns about consuming raw eggs, use ¼ cup egg substitute in place of the egg.

  1 large egg
  2 tablespoons water
  1 tablespoon minced onion
  1 tablespoon lime juice
  1 tablespoon finely chopped fresh cilantro
  1 tablespoon minced jarred jalapeños
  1 garlic clove, minced
  1 teaspoon yellow mustard
  ¼ teaspoon table salt
  1 cup vegetable oil

Process egg, water, onion, lime juice, cilantro, jalapeños, garlic, mustard, and salt in food processor until combined, about 5 seconds. With machine running, slowly drizzle in oil in steady stream until mayonnaise-like consistency is reached, scraping down bowl as necessary.

Za'atar-Rubbed Butterflied Chicken

Serves 4   **Total Time** 1¼ hours

Why This Recipe Works For an easy but impressive weeknight dinner, we turned to a simple dish of roast chicken rubbed with za'atar, an irresistible spice mixture of thyme, sumac, and sesame. To quickly render the fat so that the skin would become crisp, we borrowed the Italian technique of cooking under a brick: We butterflied the chicken, seasoned it, and cooked it on the stove skin side down under a heavy pot to maximize its

contact with the hot skillet. Next, we combined the za'atar with oil to make a paste, flipped the chicken skin side up and brushed the paste over the surface; as the chicken finished cooking in the oven, the paste turned into a crust. While the chicken cooked, we created a zesty vinaigrette that brightened up the finished dish. We prefer to use our homemade Za'atar (page 235), but you can substitute store-bought za'atar, though flavor can vary by brand. If you can't find preserved lemons, you can microwave four 2-inch strips of lemon zest, minced; 1 teaspoon of lemon juice; ½ teaspoon of water; ¼ teaspoon of sugar; and ¼ teaspoon of salt at 50 percent power until the liquid evaporates, about 1½ minutes, stirring and mashing the lemon with the back of a spoon every 30 seconds.

  2 tablespoons za'atar
  5 tablespoons plus 1 teaspoon extra-virgin olive oil, divided
  1 (3½- to 4-pound) whole chicken, giblets discarded
  1 teaspoon plus ⅛ teaspoon table salt, divided
  ½ teaspoon plus ⅛ teaspoon pepper, divided
  1 tablespoon minced fresh mint
  ¼ preserved lemon, pulp and white pith removed, rind rinsed and minced (1 tablespoon)
  2 teaspoons white wine vinegar
  ½ teaspoon Dijon mustard

1. Adjust oven rack to lowest position and heat oven to 450 degrees. Combine za'atar and 2 tablespoons oil in small bowl. With chicken breast side down, use kitchen shears to cut through bones on either side of backbone. Discard backbone and trim away excess fat and skin around neck. Flip chicken and tuck wingtips behind back. Press firmly on breastbone to flatten, then pound breast to be same thickness as legs and thighs. Pat chicken dry with paper towels and season with 1 teaspoon salt and ½ teaspoon pepper.

2. Heat 1 teaspoon oil in 12-inch ovensafe skillet over medium-high heat until just smoking. Place chicken skin side down in skillet, reduce heat to medium, and place heavy pot on chicken to press it flat. Cook chicken until skin is crisp and browned, about 25 minutes. (If chicken is not crisp after 20 minutes, increase heat to medium-high.)

3. Off heat, remove pot and carefully flip chicken. Brush skin with za'atar mixture, transfer skillet to oven, and roast until breast registers 160 degrees and thighs register 175 degrees, 10 to 20 minutes.

4. Transfer chicken to carving board and let rest, uncovered, for 10 minutes. Meanwhile, whisk mint, preserved lemon, vinegar, mustard, remaining ⅛ teaspoon salt, and remaining ⅛ teaspoon pepper in bowl until combined. Whisking constantly, slowly drizzle in remaining 3 tablespoons oil until emulsified. Carve chicken and serve with dressing.

**Za'atar-Rubbed
Butterflied Chicken**

Za'atar

Makes about ½ cup   **Total Time** 5 minutes

Za'atar is an aromatic eastern Mediterranean spice blend that is used as both a seasoning and a condiment.

- ½ **cup dried thyme, ground**
- 2 **tablespoons sesame seeds, toasted**
- 1½ **tablespoons ground sumac**

Combine all ingredients in bowl. (Za'atar can be stored at room temperature in airtight container for up to 1 year.)

Crisp-Skin High-Roast Butterflied Chicken with Potatoes

Serves 4   **Total Time** 1½ hours (plus 1 hour brining time)

Why This Recipe Works "High roasting" chicken simply means cooking it at a very high temperature—above 450 degrees—in order to achieve crispy bronzed skin. Sounded good to us, but we weren't willing to sacrifice moist meat and we didn't want a kitchen full of smoke. We started by butterflying the chicken, which allowed for more even and faster roasting. A sugar-and-salt brine protected the meat against the drying heat of the oven. Rubbing the bird under the skin with a flavored butter added moisture and flavor without burning, as herbs rubbed on the surface of the skin would likely do. To keep the juices from burning and smoking in the pan, we placed a layer of potatoes under the chicken; the potatoes absorbed the juices before they could hit the hot pan beneath and burn. The resulting potatoes were extremely tasty. If you prefer not to brine, use a kosher chicken; it is salted and has a taste and texture similar to a brined bird. For extra-crisp skin, after applying the flavored butter, let the chicken dry uncovered in the refrigerator 8 to 24 hours. Russet potatoes have the best potato flavor, but Yukon Golds have beautiful color and better retain their shape after cooking. Either works well in this recipe. A food processor makes quick and easy work of slicing the potatoes.

- 1 **(3½- to 4-pound) whole chicken, giblets discarded**
- ½ **cup table salt for brining**
- ½ **cup granulated sugar for brining**
- 2½ **pounds russet potatoes (4 to 5 medium), or Yukon Gold potatoes, peeled and sliced ⅛ to ¼ inch thick**

- 2 **tablespoons extra-virgin olive oil, divided**
- ½ **teaspoon table salt**
- ¼ **teaspoon pepper**
- 3 **tablespoons unsalted butter or flavored butter (recipes follow), softened**

1. With chicken breast side down, using kitchen shears, cut through bones on either side of backbone; discard backbone. Trim any excess fat or skin. Flip chicken over and press on breastbone to flatten. Dissolve ½ cup salt and sugar in 2 quarts cold water in large container. Submerge chicken in brine, cover, and refrigerate for 1 hour.

2. Adjust oven rack to lower-middle position and heat oven to 500 degrees. Line broiler pan bottom with heavy-duty aluminum foil. Toss potatoes with 1 tablespoon oil, salt, and pepper in bowl. Spread potatoes in even layer on prepared pan bottom and cover with broiler pan top.

3. Remove chicken from brine, rinse thoroughly, and pat dry with paper towels. Using your fingers, carefully loosen center portion of skin covering each side of breast and both thighs. Place butter under skin, directly on meat in center of each side of breast and on thighs. Gently press on skin to distribute butter evenly over meat. Rub skin with remaining 1 tablespoon oil and season with pepper. Transfer chicken to pan top and push each leg up to rest between thigh and breast.

4. Roast chicken until skin is crispy and deep brown, breast registers 160 degrees, and thighs register 175 degrees, 40 to 45 minutes, rotating pan halfway through roasting. Transfer chicken to carving board and let rest, uncovered, for 10 minutes.

5. While chicken rests, remove broiler pan top and soak up excess grease from potatoes with paper towels. Invert pan bottom with potatoes onto cutting board. Carefully peel back foil, using metal spatula to help scrape potatoes off foil as needed. Soak up any remaining grease with additional paper towels. Transfer potatoes to platter. Carve chicken, transfer to platter with potatoes, and serve.

Mustard-Garlic Butter with Thyme
Makes about 3 tablespoons
Total Time 5 minutes

  2 tablespoons unsalted butter, softened
  1 garlic clove, minced
  1 tablespoon Dijon mustard
  1 teaspoon minced fresh thyme leaves

Mash together all ingredients in small bowl and season with pepper to taste.

Chipotle Butter with Lime and Honey
Makes about 3 tablespoons
Total Time 5 minutes

  2 tablespoons unsalted butter, softened
  1 garlic clove, minced
  1 teaspoon honey
  1 teaspoon grated lime zest
  1 minced canned chipotle chile in adobo sauce
  1 teaspoon adobo sauce

Mash together all ingredients in small bowl.

Roast Chicken with Warm Bread Salad

Serves 4 **Total Time** 1½ hours (plus 24 hours chilling time)

Why This Recipe Works San Francisco's famed Zuni Café serves a perfect roast chicken over a chewy-crisp, warm bread-and-greens salad that has a cult-like following. We pay homage with this simplified take which still hits all the right notes: salty, savory, sweet, and bright. To preserve the soft texture of the arugula and highlight the way its pepperiness offsets the moist chicken and unctuous bread, we served the salad on the side. Salting and refrigerating the chicken drew moisture from the flesh, forming a brine that was reabsorbed, seasoning the meat and keeping it juicy. The salt also made the skin crisp up better when roasted. This recipe was developed using Diamond Crystal Kosher Salt. If you have Morton Kosher Salt, which is denser, use only ½ teaspoon in the chicken cavity. For the bread, we prefer a round rustic loaf with a chewy, open crumb and a sturdy crust.

  1 (3½- to 4-pound) whole chicken, giblets discarded
3½ teaspoons kosher salt, divided
  4 (1-inch-thick) slices crusty bread (8 ounces), bottom crust removed, cut into ¾- to 1-inch pieces (5 cups)
  ¼ cup chicken broth
  6 tablespoons plus 2 teaspoons extra-virgin olive oil, divided
  ½ teaspoon pepper, divided
  2 tablespoons champagne vinegar
  1 teaspoon Dijon mustard
  3 scallions, sliced thin
  2 tablespoons dried currants
  5 ounces (5 cups) baby arugula

1. With chicken breast side down, use kitchen shears to cut through bones on either side of backbone and discard backbone. Do not trim any excess fat or skin. Flip chicken over and press on breastbone to flatten.

2. Using your fingers, carefully loosen center portion of skin covering each side of breast and both thighs. Rub ½ teaspoon salt under skin of each side of breast, ½ teaspoon salt under skin of each leg, and 1 teaspoon salt into bird's cavity. Tuck wingtips behind back and turn legs so drumsticks face inward toward breasts. Place chicken on large plate and refrigerate, uncovered, for 24 hours.

3. Adjust oven rack to middle position and heat oven to 475 degrees. Spray 12-inch skillet with vegetable oil spray. Toss bread with broth and 2 tablespoons oil until pieces are evenly moistened. Arrange bread in skillet in single layer, with majority of crusted pieces near center, crust side up.

4. Pat chicken dry with paper towels and place, skin side up, on top of bread, centered over crusted pieces. Brush 2 teaspoons oil over chicken skin and sprinkle with ¼ teaspoon salt and ¼ teaspoon pepper. Roast chicken until skin is deep golden brown, breast registers 160 degrees, and thighs register 175 degrees, 45 to 50 minutes, rotating skillet halfway through roasting. (Bread should be mix of softened, golden-brown, and crunchy pieces.)

5. While chicken roasts, whisk vinegar, mustard, remaining ¼ teaspoon salt, and remaining ¼ teaspoon pepper together in large bowl. While whisking constantly, slowly drizzle in remaining ¼ cup oil until combined. Stir in scallions and currants and set aside.

6. Transfer chicken to carving board and let rest, uncovered, for 10 minutes. Carve chicken and whisk any accumulated juices into vinaigrette. Add bread and arugula to vinaigrette and toss to coat. Transfer salad to serving platter and serve with chicken.

Skillet-Roasted Chicken and Stuffing

Serves 4   **Total Time** 2 hours

Why This Recipe Works To translate this holiday classic into a one-pan meal, we took the stuffing out of the chicken. Sautéed aromatics are the base of the dish, and we roasted the chicken—brushed with a flavorful herb butter—right on top of them in the skillet. Scattering the bread cubes around the bird before it went into the oven simultaneously toasted them and allowed them to soak up the flavorful juices as the chicken roasted. While the chicken rested on a carving board, we gave the stuffing a quick stir and a splash of broth to moisten it, and a few minutes later we had dinner on the table. You can find Italian bread in the bakery section of your grocery store. Take care when stirring the contents of the skillet in steps 4 and 5, as the skillet handle will be very hot.

- 1 (3½- to 4-pound) whole chicken, giblets discarded
- 6 tablespoons unsalted butter, divided
- 2 tablespoons minced fresh sage, divided
- 2 tablespoons minced fresh thyme, divided
- 1½ teaspoons table salt, divided
- 1 teaspoon pepper, divided
- 2 onions, chopped fine
- 2 celery ribs, minced
- 7 ounces Italian bread, cut into ½-inch cubes (6 cups)
- ⅓ cup chicken broth

Roast Chicken with Warm Bread Salad

Skillet-Roasted Chicken and Stuffing

1. Adjust oven rack to lower-middle position and heat oven to 375 degrees. Pat chicken dry with paper towels. Melt 4 tablespoons butter in small bowl in microwave, about 45 seconds. Stir in 1 tablespoon sage, 1 tablespoon thyme, 1 teaspoon salt, and ½ teaspoon pepper. Brush chicken with herb butter.

2. Melt remaining 2 tablespoons butter in 12-inch ovensafe skillet over medium heat. Add onions, celery, remaining ½ teaspoon salt, and remaining ½ teaspoon pepper and cook until softened, about 5 minutes. Add remaining 1 tablespoon sage and remaining 1 tablespoon thyme and cook until fragrant, about 1 minute. Off heat, place chicken, breast side up, on top of vegetables. Arrange bread cubes around chicken in bottom of skillet.

3. Transfer skillet to oven and roast until breast registers 160 degrees and thighs register 175 degrees, about 1 hour, rotating skillet halfway through roasting.

4. Carefully transfer chicken to plate and tent with aluminum foil. Holding skillet handle with pot holder (handle will be hot), stir bread and vegetables to combine, cover, and let sit for 10 minutes.

5. Add broth and any accumulated chicken juice from plate and cavity to skillet and stir to combine. Warm stuffing, uncovered, over low heat until heated through, about 3 minutes. Remove from heat, cover, and let sit while carving chicken. Transfer chicken to carving board, carve, and serve with stuffing.

Chicken en Cocotte with Thyme and Lemon

Serves 4 to 6   **Total Time** 2½ hours

Why This Recipe Works If you're ready to put your love of crisp chicken skin aside in favor of truly succulent meat, it's time to try chicken en cocotte (chicken in a pot). Cooking chicken in a covered Dutch oven without even a splash of liquid concentrates the chicken's flavor and preserves its supermoist texture. Yet in our tests, we found it challenging to prevent the humidity in the pot from washing the flavor from the meat as it cooked. We discovered that the few vegetables we had been adding for their aromatic flavors were making the pot too steamy. When we omitted them and cooked the chicken by itself, tightly sealing the pot with foil before adding the lid, we got the tender, flavorful chicken we were looking for. After developing the basic technique, we revisited the possibility of including vegetables, finding that we could add a small amount of potently flavored, aromatic vegetables if they were lightly browned with the chicken first to remove most of their moisture.

1 (4½- to 5-pound) whole chicken, giblets discarded
¾ teaspoon table salt
½ teaspoon pepper
2 tablespoons extra-virgin olive oil
1 small onion, halved and sliced thin
6 garlic cloves, peeled and crushed
1 bay leaf
2 sprigs fresh thyme
½–1 teaspoon lemon juice

1. Adjust oven rack to lowest position and heat oven to 250 degrees. Pat chicken dry with paper towels, tuck wings behind back, and sprinkle with salt and pepper.

2. Heat oil in large Dutch oven over medium-high heat until just smoking. Add chicken, breast side down, and scatter onion, garlic, bay leaf, and thyme around chicken. Cook until chicken breast is lightly browned, about 5 minutes. Flip chicken breast side up and continue to cook until back of chicken and vegetables are well browned, 6 to 8 minutes, reducing heat if pot begins to scorch.

3. Off heat, place large sheet of aluminum foil over pot and press to seal, then cover tightly with lid. Transfer pot to oven and cook until breast registers 160 degrees and thighs register 175 degrees, 1 hour 20 minutes to 1 hour 50 minutes.

4. Remove pot from oven. Transfer chicken to carving board, tent with foil, and let rest for 20 minutes. Strain juices from pot into fat separator, reserving strained vegetables. Let juices settle for about 5 minutes.

5. Add defatted juices back to pot, add strained vegetables and any accumulated juices from chicken, and cook over low heat until hot. Discard bay leaf and thyme and season with lemon juice, salt, and pepper to taste. Carve chicken and serve, passing sauce separately.

VARIATIONS

Chicken en Cocotte with Garlic and Rosemary
Increase amount of garlic to 12 cloves. Substitute 2 sprigs fresh rosemary for thyme. Before returning strained vegetables to pot in step 5, mash cooked garlic with back of spoon to create paste, then whisk into sauce.

Chicken en Cocotte with Chorizo, Onion, and Saffron
Substitute pinch of saffron for thyme and 1 to 2 teaspoons sherry vinegar for lemon juice. Before browning chicken in step 2, brown 4 ounces chorizo, cut into ¼-inch pieces, in hot oil until golden, about 5 minutes; transfer chorizo to small bowl, leaving fat in pot. Continue with recipe as directed, returning browned chorizo to pot before covering with foil in step 3.

Chicken en Cocotte with Ginger and Shiitake Mushrooms

Substitute 1 to 1½ teaspoons rice wine vinegar for lemon juice. Add 4 ounces shiitake mushrooms, stemmed, wiped clean, and chopped fine, and 1 tablespoon minced or grated fresh ginger to pot with onion in step 2. Continue with recipe as directed, adding 1 more teaspoon minced or grated fresh ginger and 1 tablespoon soy sauce to sauce in step 5.

Turkey Breast en Cocotte with Pan Gravy

Serves 8 to 10   Total Time 2¾ hours

Why This Recipe Works Roasting an entire turkey can be tedious. But we didn't want to relegate roast turkey to holiday-only status. So that we could enjoy our turkey year-round, we opted for a bone-in breast, which was easier to maneuver and required no fancy carving, and we set out to cook it en cocotte (in a covered pot over low heat for an extended period of time) so the meat would be moist and tender. We started by browning the turkey in our Dutch oven to build flavor. After setting the cooked turkey aside for a brief rest, we used the drippings left behind in the pot to build a rich gravy. Use a Dutch oven that holds 7 quarts or more. Don't buy a turkey breast larger than 7 pounds; it won't fit in the pot. For a smaller turkey breast, reduce the cooking time as necessary.

- 1 (6- to 7-pound) bone-in whole turkey breast, trimmed
- ¾ teaspoon table salt
- ½ teaspoon pepper
- 2 tablespoons extra-virgin olive oil
- 1 onion, chopped
- 1 carrot, peeled and chopped
- 1 celery rib, chopped
- 6 garlic cloves, peeled and crushed
- 2 sprigs fresh thyme
- 1 bay leaf
- 2 tablespoons all-purpose flour
- 2 cups chicken broth

1. Adjust oven rack to lowest position and heat oven to 250 degrees. Pat turkey breast dry with paper towels and sprinkle with salt and pepper.

Turkey Breast en Cocotte with Pan Gravy

2. Heat oil in large Dutch oven over medium-high heat until just smoking. Add turkey, skin side down, and scatter onion, carrot, celery, garlic, thyme, and bay leaf around turkey. Cook, turning breast on its sides and stirring vegetables as needed, until turkey and vegetables are well browned, 12 to 16 minutes, reducing heat if pot begins to scorch.

3. Off heat, place large sheet of aluminum foil over pot and press to seal, then cover tightly with lid. Transfer pot to oven and cook until breast registers 160 degrees, 1½ to 1¾ hours.

4. Remove pot from oven. Transfer turkey to carving board, tent with foil, and let rest while making gravy.

5. Place pot with juices and vegetables over medium-high heat and simmer until almost all liquid has evaporated, 15 to 20 minutes. Stir in flour and cook, stirring constantly, until browned, 2 to 5 minutes. Slowly whisk in chicken broth, bring to simmer and cook, stirring often, until gravy is thickened and measures about 2½ cups, 10 to 15 minutes.

6. Strain gravy through fine-mesh strainer and season with salt and pepper to taste. Discard solids. Carve turkey and serve, passing gravy separately.

Lemon-Thyme Boneless Turkey Breast with Gravy

Serves 8 to 10 **Total Time** 4½ hours (plus 2 hours chilling time)

Why This Recipe Works This rolled and tied roast offers a new look for the Thanksgiving table (or any night) that is just as impressive as the whole bird; plus, it's a breeze to carve. We started at the meat counter, selecting a bone-in, skin-on turkey breast instead of deboned turkey breasts, which vary greatly in size, even when packaged together. Deboning a full breast at home ensured consistency in the size of the two halves—and gave us a breastbone that we could roast and use as the base for a flavorful gravy. Since white-meat turkey is prone to drying out, we seasoned the meat with salt, lemon zest, and thyme and roasted the breasts in a low 275-degree oven. Tying the two halves together ensured even cooking and made for a roast fit for a celebration. A quick sear in a skillet before the turkey went into the oven jump-started the exterior's photo-worthy bronzed hue. Plan ahead: The salted turkey needs to be refrigerated for at least 2 hours before cooking. We prefer a natural (unbrined) turkey breast here, but both self-basting and kosher also work well. Omit the salt in step 1 if you buy a self-basting or kosher turkey breast. You can make soup with the excess turkey stock, if desired.

Turkey

- 1 (6- to 7-pound) bone-in whole turkey breast, trimmed
- 1 tablespoon kosher salt
- 2 teaspoons minced fresh thyme
- 2 teaspoons grated lemon zest
- ½ teaspoon pepper
- 1 tablespoon vegetable oil

Turkey Stock

- 1 onion, chopped
- 1 carrot, peeled and chopped
- 1 celery rib, chopped
- 6 sprigs fresh thyme
- 1 bay leaf

Gravy

- 4 tablespoons unsalted butter
- ¼ cup all-purpose flour
- ⅓ cup dry white wine
- ¾ teaspoon table salt
- ½ teaspoon pepper

1. For the turkey Position turkey breast skin side up on cutting board. Using sharp knife, remove each breast half from bone by cutting through skin on top of breast on either side of center bone. Continue to work knife along bone until each breast half is removed. Reserve breastbone for stock. Combine salt, thyme, lemon zest, and pepper in bowl. Sprinkle breast halves all over with salt mixture.

2. Lay two 24-inch pieces of kitchen twine crosswise in middle of 8½ by 4½-inch loaf pan, about 1 inch apart. Arrange 1 breast half skin side down in pan on top of twine. Position remaining breast half over first, skin side up, with thick end over tapered end. Tuck turkey into edges of pan to fit if necessary. Tie twine tightly to secure. Remove turkey from pan and continue to tie at 1-inch intervals. Wrap in plastic wrap and refrigerate for at least 2 hours or up to 24 hours.

3. For the turkey stock Meanwhile, adjust oven rack to middle position and heat oven to 450 degrees. Line rimmed baking sheet with aluminum foil. Place reserved breastbone on prepared sheet and roast until well browned, about 1 hour. Let sit until cool enough to handle, about 15 minutes.

4. Place breastbone in large saucepan (if necessary, use kitchen shears to break down bone to fit). Add onion, carrot, celery, thyme sprigs, and bay leaf. Add water to cover by 1 inch and bring to boil over high heat. Reduce heat to medium-low and simmer for 1 hour. (Bone should remain covered with water throughout simmer.)

5. Discard breastbone. Strain turkey stock through fine-mesh strainer set over large bowl. Using spoon, press on solids to extract liquid; discard solids. Reserve turkey stock to make gravy when ready.

6. Three hours before serving, adjust oven rack to middle position and heat oven to 275 degrees. Set wire rack in rimmed baking sheet. Heat oil in 12-inch nonstick skillet over medium-high heat until just smoking. Add turkey and cook until well browned on all sides, about 10 minutes. Transfer turkey to

---

BONING AND TYING A WHOLE TURKEY BREAST

1. Use sharp knife to slice down along both sides of breastbone to remove meat, keeping skin intact.

2. Use loaf pan to keep both breast halves in compact, manageable shape to tie them together.

prepared wire rack. Roast until turkey registers 160 degrees, 2¼ to 2¾ hours. Transfer turkey to carving board and let rest, uncovered, for 15 minutes.

7. For the gravy Meanwhile, melt butter in large saucepan over medium heat. Whisk in flour until smooth. Cook, whisking frequently, until peanut butter–colored, about 5 minutes. Slowly whisk in 3 cups turkey stock until no lumps remain. (Remaining stock can be refrigerated for up to 2 days or frozen for up to 2 months.) Whisk in wine, salt, and pepper and bring to boil. Reduce heat to medium-low and simmer until slightly thickened and reduced to about 2½ cups, 8 to 10 minutes. Off heat, season with salt and pepper to taste. Cover and keep warm.

8. Slice turkey ½ inch thick, removing twine as you slice. Serve, passing gravy separately.

Easy Roast Turkey Breast

Serves 8 to 10   **Total Time** 2¼ hours

Why This Recipe Works To produce a foolproof roast turkey breast, we used a two-part roasting technique: a high temperature to crisp the skin and a low temperature for moist meat. The optimal combination was to start the turkey breast in a 425-degree oven for the first half-hour and then reduce the heat to 325 degrees for the remaining hour. This recipe works equally well with any type of turkey breast. We recommend brining a natural turkey breast; if brining (see page 14), omit the salt from the recipe. Using a kosher or self-basting breast eliminates the need for brining. If the breast has a pop-up timer, do not remove it; ignore it (they pop too late) and follow the times and temperatures in the recipe. A turkey breast doesn't yield much in the way of drippings, so a classic pan gravy recipe is not an option. Instead, try our All-Purpose Gravy (page 242). You will need at least a 7-quart Dutch oven for this recipe. Don't buy a turkey breast larger than 7 pounds; it won't fit in the pot.

- 4 **tablespoons unsalted butter, softened**
- ¾ **teaspoon table salt**
- ¼ **teaspoon pepper**
- 1 **(6- to 7-pound) bone-in whole turkey breast, trimmed**
- 1 **cup water**

1. Adjust oven rack to middle position and heat oven to 425 degrees. Mix butter, salt, and pepper in medium bowl with rubber spatula until thoroughly combined. Using your fingers, carefully separate turkey skin from meat.

Lemon-Thyme
Boneless
Turkey Breast
with Gravy

Easy Roast Turkey Breast

2. Work butter mixture under skin on both sides of breast and rub skin of turkey to evenly distribute butter over breast. Spray V-rack with nonstick cooking spray and set inside large roasting pan. Place turkey in rack with skin side facing up; pour water into roasting pan.

3. Roast turkey for 30 minutes. Reduce oven temperature to 325 degrees. Continue to roast until breast registers 160 degrees, about 1 hour longer. Transfer turkey to carving board and let rest, uncovered, for 20 minutes. Carve and serve.

All-Purpose Gravy

Makes about 2 cups **Total Time** 1 hour

If you happen to have drippings from your chicken or turkey, you can use them to replace some or all of the oil.

    3 tablespoons vegetable oil
    1 small onion, chopped
    1 small carrot, peeled and chopped
    1 small celery rib, chopped
    ½ teaspoon pepper
    ¼ cup all-purpose flour
    4 cups chicken broth
    ¼ cup dry white wine
    2 sprigs fresh thyme
    1 bay leaf

1. Heat oil in large saucepan over medium heat until shimmering. Add onion, carrot, celery, and pepper and cook over medium heat until vegetables are softened and well browned, about 8 minutes. Stir in flour and cook for 1 minute. Slowly whisk in broth and wine, scraping up any browned bits and smoothing out any lumps. Stir in thyme sprigs and bay leaf, bring to simmer, and cook until gravy is thickened and reduced to 3 cups, about 15 minutes.

2. Strain gravy through fine-mesh strainer into bowl, pressing on solids to extract as much liquid as possible; discard solids. Season with salt and pepper to taste. (Gravy can be frozen for up to 1 month. To thaw, place the gravy and 1 tablespoon water in a saucepan over low heat and bring slowly to a simmer. The gravy may appear broken or curdled as it thaws, but a vigorous whisking will recombine it.)

VARIATIONS

Easy Roast Turkey Breast with Lemon and Thyme

Add 2 tablespoons minced fresh thyme, 3 minced garlic cloves, and 1 teaspoon grated lemon zest to butter mixture.

Easy Roast Turkey Breast with Southwestern Flavors

Add 3 minced garlic cloves, 1 tablespoon minced fresh oregano, 2 teaspoons ground cumin, 2 teaspoons chili powder, ¾ teaspoon cocoa powder, and ½ teaspoon cayenne pepper to butter mixture.

Easy Roast Turkey Breast with Orange and Rosemary

Add 3 minced garlic cloves, 1 tablespoon minced fresh rosemary, 1 teaspoon grated orange zest, and ¼ teaspoon red pepper flakes to butter mixture.

Spice-Rubbed Turkey Breast with Sour Orange Sauce

Serves 8 to 10 **Total Time** 2½ hours (plus 6 hours chilling time)

Why This Recipe Works As far as roasts go, a bone-in turkey breast is a relatively inexpensive, versatile cut. For a fresh change of pace from standard gravy and potatoes, here we rubbed our turkey with a potent spice paste that provided mellow heat and deep flavor. To crisp the skin without drying out the meat, we browned the turkey in a Dutch oven before transferring it to roast in a low oven. Instead of building a sauce from drippings, we simmered a bright, sweet-sour sauce using fruit juice, vinegar, and tarragon. We prefer either a natural (unbrined) or kosher turkey breast for this recipe. If using a kosher turkey breast (rubbed with salt and rinsed during processing) or self-basting turkey breast (injected with salt and water), do not salt it in step 1.

Turkey
    2 tablespoons vegetable oil, divided
    2 teaspoons five-spice powder
    1½ teaspoons ground cumin
    1½ teaspoons table salt
    1 teaspoon pepper
    1 teaspoon garlic powder
    ¼ teaspoon cayenne pepper
    ¼ teaspoon ground cardamom
    1 (6- to 7-pound) bone-in whole turkey breast, trimmed

Sour Orange Sauce
- 1 tablespoon vegetable oil
- 1 shallot, minced
- 1 garlic clove, minced
- 2 cups chicken broth
- 2 cups orange juice (4 oranges)
- 2 tablespoons white wine vinegar, plus extra for seasoning
- 1 tablespoon cornstarch
- 1 tablespoon water
- 2 teaspoons chopped fresh tarragon

1. For the turkey Combine 1 tablespoon oil, five-spice powder, cumin, salt, pepper, garlic powder, cayenne, and cardamom in bowl. Using your fingers, carefully separate turkey skin from meat. Rub paste evenly under skin. Place turkey breast on large plate, cover with plastic wrap, and refrigerate for at least 6 hours or up to 24 hours.

2. Adjust oven rack to middle position and heat oven to 325 degrees. Heat remaining 1 tablespoon oil in Dutch oven over medium heat until just smoking. Place turkey, skin side down, in Dutch oven and cook, turning breast on its sides as needed, until lightly browned, 8 to 10 minutes.

3. Rotate turkey skin side up and transfer pot to oven. Roast until turkey registers 160 degrees, about 1½ hours. Transfer turkey to carving board, tent with aluminum foil, and let rest, uncovered, for 20 minutes.

4. For the sour orange sauce Meanwhile, heat oil in large saucepan over medium heat until shimmering. Add shallot and cook until softened, about 3 minutes. Add garlic and cook until fragrant, about 30 seconds. Stir in broth, orange juice, and vinegar, increase heat to high, and bring to boil. Cook, stirring occasionally, until sauce is reduced to 1¼ cups, about 20 minutes.

5. Whisk cornstarch and water together in small bowl, then whisk mixture into sauce and cook until thickened, about 1 minute; remove from heat and cover to keep warm.

6. Stir 1 tablespoon turkey pan drippings and tarragon into orange sauce. Season with salt, pepper, and additional vinegar to taste. Remove skin if desired, carve turkey, and serve with sauce.

Maple Roast Turkey Breast
Serves 8 to 10   **Total Time** 2¼ hours

Why This Recipe Works Sometimes, the simplest approach is the best. For our Maple Roast Turkey Breast recipe, we used just two ingredients in the glaze: maple syrup and Dijon mustard. Brushing the glaze onto the bird at the end of the roasting time kept it from burning. Before roasting, we rubbed butter under

Spice-Rubbed Turkey Breast with Sour Orange Sauce

Maple Roast Turkey Breast

Stuffed Roast Turkey Breast

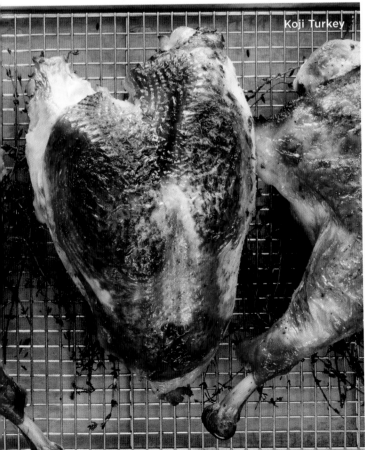

Koji Turkey

the skin to add moisture and flavor to the delicate white meat. This recipe works equally well with any type of turkey breast. We recommend brining a natural turkey breast; if brining (see page 14), omit the salt from the recipe. Using a kosher turkey breast or self-basting turkey breast eliminates the need for brining. After the turkey has been rubbed with butter, it can be covered and refrigerated for up to 24 hours prior to roasting.

- 4 tablespoons unsalted butter, softened
- ¾ teaspoon table salt
- ¼ teaspoon pepper
- ¼ cup maple syrup
- 1 tablespoon Dijon mustard
- 1 (6- to 7-pound) bone-in whole turkey breast, trimmed

1. Adjust oven rack to lower-middle position and heat oven to 425 degrees. Mix butter, salt, and pepper in small bowl. Combine maple syrup and mustard in second small bowl.

2. Using your fingers, carefully separate turkey skin from meat. Rub butter mixture under skin. (After rubbed with butter, turkey can be covered and refrigerated for up to 24 hours.) Arrange turkey breast skin side up on greased V-rack set inside large roasting pan. Pour 2 cups water into bottom of pan and roast until turkey is golden, about 30 minutes.

3. Decrease oven temperature to 325 degrees. Roast until turkey is deep golden brown, about 1 hour. Begin basting turkey with maple mixture every 15 minutes until skin is glossy and meat registers 160 degrees, 15 to 30 minutes. Transfer turkey to carving board and let rest, uncovered, for 20 minutes. Carve and serve.

Stuffed Roast Turkey Breast
Serves 6 to 8   **Total Time** 2¾ hours

Why This Recipe Works Stuffed, rolled, and roasted, this turkey breast makes a stunning presentation and tastes as good as it looks. A simple rub and rich stuffing provided plenty of flavor. After butterflying and pounding the breast, we spread the turkey with an assertive vegetable and cheese stuffing and rolled it into a tight cylinder. Applying a sugar rub to the breast and roasting it in a moderate oven added both color and flavor and kept the turkey moist. Some stores sell only boneless turkey breasts with the skin still attached; the skin can be removed with a paring knife. This recipe calls for one turkey breast half; an entire breast with two lobes of meat is too large for this recipe. Before stuffing the turkey, make sure that the stuffing is completely chilled.

1 (3- to 4-pound) boneless, skinless turkey breast, trimmed
1 recipe stuffing (see box)
2 tablespoons vegetable oil
1 tablespoon sugar
2 teaspoons pepper
1 teaspoon table salt

1. Adjust oven rack to middle position and heat oven to 325 degrees. With turkey smooth side down, slice into thickest part, keeping knife ½ inch above cutting board and stopping ½ inch from edge of breast. Lay butterflied meat flat on cutting board, cover with plastic wrap, and pound lightly with meat mallet until about ½ inch thick. Spread stuffing in even layer over turkey. Starting with short side nearest you, roll up turkey and tie with kitchen twine at 1½-inch intervals.

2. Rub roast with oil and sprinkle evenly with sugar, pepper, and salt. Place on wire rack set in rimmed baking sheet and roast, turning every 30 minutes, until turkey registers 160 degrees, about 2 hours. Transfer turkey to carving board and let rest, uncovered, for 20 minutes. Remove twine and slice ½ inch thick. Serve.

Koji Turkey

Serves 10 to 12   **Total Time** 2½ hours (plus 12 hours brining time)

Why This Recipe Works After learning about the great tenderizing and radical flavor-enhancing properties of the Japanese seasoning shio koji while making Koji Fried Chicken (page 291), we wanted to put them to use again. The enzymes present in shio koji tenderize meats and enhance their flavor, adding intense savory depth. We decided to blend the shio koji with water and additional salt to make a brine for turkey, which added water and seasoning along with koji's meat-enhancing properties. We even lacquered the skin at the end of cooking with a coat of shio koji–spiked butter to give a burnished appearance and add even more savory-sweet flavor. We included some vegetables to roast underneath the turkey, where they could catch all the amazing koji-fied drippings. Shio koji takes at least a week to make, so start it well in advance of when you plan to make this recipe. We prefer the flavor of our homemade shio koji, but if time is short you can purchase ready-made shio koji. We call for one whole bone-in turkey breast, also known as a turkey crown, and two turkey leg quarters (thigh and drumstick attached), but you can also buy a 12- to 14-pound whole turkey and butcher it yourself into these same parts.

Mushroom Marsala Stuffing

Makes about 2 cups   **Total Time** 45 minutes
To avoid flare-ups, remove the pan from the heat before adding the Marsala.

2 tablespoons unsalted butter
1 onion, chopped fine
1 pound white mushrooms, trimmed and chopped fine
2 garlic cloves, minced
2 teaspoons minced fresh thyme
¼ cup sweet Marsala
2 ounces Parmesan cheese, grated (1 cup)
2 tablespoons minced fresh parsley

1. Melt butter in 12-inch skillet over medium-high heat. Add onion and cook until softened, about 5 minutes. Reduce heat to medium, add mushrooms, and cook until liquid has evaporated, 10 to 15 minutes. Add garlic and thyme and cook until fragrant, 30 seconds. Off heat, stir in Marsala.

2. Return to heat and cook until mushrooms are dry and golden brown, about 5 minutes. Remove from heat and let cool for 10 minutes. Stir in Parmesan, parsley, and salt and pepper to taste. Stuffing can be refrigerated for up to 3 days.

Lemon, Spinach, and Fontina Stuffing

Makes about 2 cups   **Total Time** 30 minutes
Soggy spinach can make for a watery filling, so wring out moisture in cheesecloth or a dish towel.

2 tablespoons extra-virgin olive oil
1 onion, chopped fine
8 ounces frozen spinach, thawed, squeezed dry, and chopped
3 garlic cloves, minced
¼ teaspoon grated lemon zest
8 ounces fontina cheese, shredded (2 cups)

1. Heat oil in 12-inch skillet over medium-high heat until shimmering. Add onion and cook until softened, about 5 minutes. Stir in spinach, garlic, and lemon zest and cook until fragrant, 30 seconds. Remove from heat and let cool for 10 minutes.

2. Stir in fontina and season with salt and pepper to taste. Stuffing can be refrigerated for up to 3 days.

2 cups Shio Koji (page 291)

4 quarts water

1½ cups sugar for brining

1½ cups kosher salt for brining

1 (6- to 7-pound) bone-in whole turkey breast, trimmed

2 (1½- to 1¾-pound) turkey leg quarters

2 pounds small red potatoes, quartered

1 pound carrots, peeled and sliced on bias 2 inches thick

10 shallots, peeled and halved

3 tablespoons vegetable oil, divided

1 teaspoon kosher salt

¾ teaspoon pepper, divided

1 bunch thyme sprigs

3 tablespoons unsalted butter, melted

1. Process shio koji in blender until smooth, about 30 seconds. Reserve 3 tablespoons blended shio koji in airtight container in refrigerator. Transfer remaining blended shio koji to large stockpot or large plastic container and whisk in water, sugar, and 1½ cups salt until dissolved. Add turkey parts to brine, cover, and refrigerate for at least 12 hours or up to 16 hours.

2. Remove turkey parts from brine and pat dry with paper towels; set aside at room temperature. Adjust oven rack to lower-middle position and heat oven to 400 degrees. Line rimmed baking sheet with aluminum foil.

3. Toss potatoes, carrots, shallots, 2 tablespoons oil, salt, and 2 tablespoons reserved shio koji in large bowl to combine. Sprinkle with ¼ teaspoon pepper. Arrange vegetables on prepared sheet and top with wire rack (rack will rest on vegetables). Arrange thyme sprigs in single layer on rack. Whisk melted butter and remaining 1 tablespoon shio koji until combined; set aside.

4. Place turkey parts on prepared rack, skin side up, and brush skin with remaining 1 tablespoon oil. Sprinkle with remaining ½ teaspoon pepper and cover loosely with foil. Roast for 30 minutes. Remove foil and continue to roast for 25 minutes. Rotate sheet, brush skin with shio koji–butter mixture (if butter mixture has solidified, reheat in microwave for 10 to 20 seconds), and roast until breast registers 155 degrees and thighs register 170 degrees, 25 to 45 minutes, removing pieces as they come to temperature. (If any portions of the turkey skin are browning too rapidly, re-cover them with foil.) Increase oven temperature to 450 degrees.

5. Transfer turkey to carving board, tent with foil, and let rest for 30 minutes. Remove rack and continue to roast vegetables until vegetables are tender and potatoes are spotty brown, about 30 minutes, stirring halfway through. Transfer vegetables to serving bowl. Carve turkey and transfer to serving platter. Serve.

Perfect Roast Turkey and Gravy

Serves 10 to 12   Total Time 3½ hours (plus 24 hours chilling time)

Why This Recipe Works To produce a fuss-free classic roast turkey and a fast, richly flavored gravy, we borrowed a tool from pizza making. To prep the turkey, we first rubbed it with a salt and sugar blend and refrigerated it for 24 hours. Over time, the salt mixed with the moisture from the meat to form a concentrated brine; this both seasoned the turkey and helped to keep it juicy and also dried out the skin. To roast the turkey, we preheated a roasting pan on a baking stone to create an extra-hot oven. Roasting the bird directly in the preheated pan (with no V-rack) helped the dark meat finish cooking at the same time as the white meat. Adding an aluminum foil shield over the breast protected it during the initial roasting; removing the foil and finishing the turkey in a cooler oven ensured a browned exterior and moist meat. The juices reduced in the pan, laying the foundation for a rich gravy. Note that this recipe requires refrigerating the salted turkey for at least 24 hours or up to 2 days before cooking (a longer chilling time is preferable). If using a self-basting turkey (such as a frozen Butterball) or a kosher turkey, omit salt from rub in step 1.

¼ cup kosher salt

4 teaspoons sugar

1 (12- to 14-pound) turkey, neck and giblets removed and reserved for gravy

2½ tablespoons vegetable oil, divided

1 teaspoon baking powder

1 small onion, chopped fine

1 carrot, sliced thin

5 sprigs fresh parsley

2 bay leaves

5 tablespoons all-purpose flour

3¼ cups water

¼ cup dry white wine

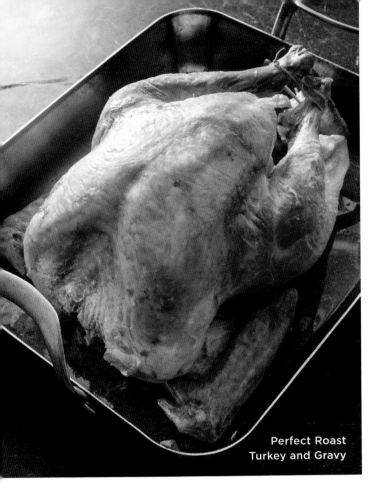

Perfect Roast Turkey and Gravy

4. Remove foil, reduce oven temperature to 325 degrees, and continue to roast until breast registers 160 degrees and thighs register 175 degrees, 1 to 1½ hours longer.

5. Using spatula, loosen turkey from pan; transfer to carving board and let rest, uncovered, for 45 minutes. While turkey rests, scrape up any browned bits from bottom of pan. Strain mixture through fine-mesh strainer set over bowl. Transfer drippings to fat separator and let rest for 10 minutes. Reserve 3 tablespoons fat and defatted liquid (you should have 1 cup of liquid; add water as needed to equal 1 cup). Discard remaining fat.

6. Heat reserved fat in large saucepan over medium-high heat until shimmering. Add reserved neck and giblets and cook until well browned, 10 to 12 minutes. Transfer neck and giblets to large plate. Reduce heat to medium; add onion, carrot, parsley sprigs, and bay leaves; and cook, stirring frequently, until vegetables are softened, 5 to 7 minutes. Add flour and cook, stirring constantly, until flour is well coated with fat, about 1 minute. Slowly whisk in reserved defatted liquid and cook until thickened, about 1 minute. Whisk in water and wine, return neck and giblets to saucepan, and bring to simmer. Simmer for 10 minutes, then season with salt and pepper to taste. Discard neck. Strain gravy through fine-mesh strainer, discarding solids, and transfer to serving bowl. Carve turkey and serve, passing gravy separately.

1. Combine salt and sugar in bowl. Place turkey, breast side up, on counter. Using your fingers or handle of spoon, gently loosen skin covering breast, thighs, and drumsticks. Rub 4 teaspoons salt mixture under skin of each side of breast, 2 teaspoons under skin of each leg, and remaining salt mixture inside cavity. Tie legs together with kitchen twine and tuck wings behind back. Place turkey on wire rack set in rimmed baking sheet and refrigerate, uncovered, for at least 24 hours or up to 2 days.

2. At least 30 minutes before roasting turkey, adjust oven rack to lowest position, set baking stone on rack, set roasting pan on baking stone, and heat oven to 500 degrees. Combine 1½ teaspoons oil and baking powder in small bowl. Pat turkey dry with paper towels. Rub oil mixture evenly over turkey. Cover turkey breast with double layer of aluminum foil.

3. Remove pan from oven and drizzle remaining 2 tablespoons oil into pan. Place turkey, breast side up, in pan and return pan to oven. Reduce oven temperature to 425 degrees and roast for 45 minutes.

TUCKING TURKEY WINGS AND SECURING LEGS

1. Tuck wings under bird to prevent them from burning. Using your hands, twist wing back behind bird—it should stay in place by itself.

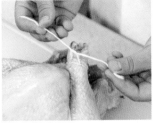

2. Remove and discard any plastic trussing. Using kitchen twine, tie legs together at ankles.

BAKED AND BROILED

Photos (clockwise from top left): Chicken Mole Poblano; Baked Ricotta Chicken;
Murgh Makhani; One-Hour Broiled Chicken and Pan Sauce

Simple Baked Chicken Parts

Serves 4 to 6   **Total Time** 50 minutes

Why This Recipe Works Here's a weeknight chicken dish that you can walk away from after putting it in the oven. For a baked chicken recipe that was light on prep work but delivered on flavor, we used bone-in, skin on chicken parts and seasoned them simply with melted butter, salt, and pepper. The heat of the oven did the rest, producing chicken with crisp skin and moist, savory meat. Baking the chicken on a wire rack allowed the fat to drain away and helped to prevent greasiness, and lining the baking sheet with aluminum foil made cleanup as easy as prep. To ensure that this recipe provides maximum rotation in your cooking schedule, we came up with four flavorful variations. Because different cuts of chicken cook at different rates, we recommend one of the following options: Use only one cut of chicken (such as all breasts or all thighs) or be prepared to remove the various different cuts from the oven as soon as they reach their appropriate temperature for doneness. Note that using dark meat will increase the cooking time by about 20 minutes.

    4   pounds bone-in chicken pieces (split breasts,
        whole legs, thighs, and/or drumsticks), trimmed
    2   tablespoons unsalted butter, melted
    ¼   teaspoon table salt
    ¼   teaspoon pepper

1. Adjust oven rack to upper-middle position and heat oven to 450 degrees. Set wire rack in aluminum foil–lined rimmed baking sheet.

2. Pat chicken dry with paper towels and arrange skin side up on wire rack. Brush chicken with melted butter and sprinkle with salt and pepper.

3. Roast until breasts register 160 degrees and legs, thighs, or drumsticks register 175 degrees, 30 to 50 minutes. Transfer chicken to cutting board and let rest for 5 minutes before serving.

VARIATIONS

Simple Baked Chicken Parts with Honey and Mustard

Mix ¼ cup Dijon mustard, 2 tablespoons honey, and 1 teaspoon brown sugar together. Brush over chicken several times during last 5 minutes of cooking.

Simple Baked Chicken Parts with Lemon and Herbs

Any strong-flavored fresh herb, such as rosemary, tarragon, or sage, can be substituted for thyme.

Mix 3 tablespoons softened unsalted butter with 1 tablespoon minced fresh thyme, 1 teaspoon grated lemon zest, ¼ teaspoon salt, and ¼ teaspoon pepper. Rub butter mixture underneath skin of chicken. Proceed to brush skin with melted butter and sprinkle with salt and pepper before cooking.

Simple Baked Chicken Parts with Five-Spice Powder and Ginger

Omit butter, salt, and pepper. Mix 3 tablespoons softened unsalted butter with 1 tablespoon grated ginger, 1 teaspoon five-spice powder, ¼ teaspoon salt, and ¼ teaspoon pepper. Rub butter mixture underneath skin of chicken before cooking.

Simple Honey-Baked Chicken Parts with Ginger and Soy

Omit butter, salt, and pepper. Mix 3 tablespoons softened unsalted butter with 1 tablespoon soy sauce, 1 tablespoon grated ginger, 1 minced garlic clove, and ¼ teaspoon pepper. Rub butter underneath skin of chicken before cooking. During last 10 minutes of cooking, brush chicken with 2 tablespoons honey, then sprinkle with 1 tablespoon sesame seeds.

Baked Chicken Imperial

Serves 4   **Total Time** 1¾ hours

Why This Recipe Works Chicken Imperial may sound fancy but it's actually an easy weeknight dish of chicken baked under a thick blanket of buttery seasoned bread crumbs. We favored boneless, skinless breasts for our recipe; the mild flavor of the white meat was the best partner for the buttery crumbs, and the meat proved to be a stronger anchor for the crumbs than skin was. We salted the chicken for deep seasoning. Pureeing fresh bread crumbs with softened butter allowed us to press them against the breast into a cohesive mass that stayed put during cooking. Cooking the chicken right in the sauce allowed for maximum flavor transfer between the two, and using a skillet instead of a baking dish enabled us to reduce the sauce to the proper consistency after the chicken had baked. The shallow depth of the sauce kept the crumb coating dry and crisp in the oven. Do not salt the chicken for longer than the recommended hour or it will become too salty. Don't worry if some of the crumb topping falls into the skillet in step 3. It will disappear into the sauce.

4 (6- to 8-ounce) boneless, skinless
chicken breasts, trimmed
1½ teaspoons table salt
4 ounces French baguette, cut or torn into
1-inch pieces (4 cups)
⅓ cup grated Parmesan cheese
3 tablespoons unsalted butter, softened,
plus 2 tablespoons melted and cooled
3 tablespoons minced fresh parsley, divided
2 garlic cloves, minced
2 teaspoons minced fresh thyme
½ teaspoon pepper
1 cup heavy cream
¾ cup chicken broth
⅓ cup dry white wine
1 shallot, minced
2 teaspoons Dijon mustard

1. Sprinkle chicken all over with salt, cover with plastic wrap, and refrigerate for 30 minutes to 1 hour. Adjust oven rack to middle position and heat oven to 425 degrees.

2. Meanwhile, process bread in food processor until coarsely ground, about 20 seconds. Add Parmesan, softened butter, 2 tablespoons parsley, garlic, thyme, and pepper and process to combine, about 15 seconds, scraping down bowl as needed.

3. Pat chicken dry with paper towels and season with pepper. Arrange chicken, skinned side up, in 12-inch ovensafe skillet with narrow ends pointing toward center of skillet. Brush chicken with melted butter. Top each breast with equal amount (generous ½ cup) crumb mixture, pressing firmly to adhere.

4. Whisk cream, broth, wine, shallot, and mustard together in 4-cup liquid measuring cup. Carefully pour 1½ cups around chicken breasts, taking care not to wet crumbs on top of chicken. Transfer skillet to oven and bake until crumbs are deep golden brown and chicken registers 160 degrees, 30 to 35 minutes.

5. Using spatula, carefully transfer chicken to platter and tent with aluminum foil. Pour remaining ½ cup sauce mixture into skillet and bring to boil over medium-high heat. Cook until thickened and reduced to 1 cup, about 5 minutes. Stir in remaining 1 tablespoon parsley. Season with salt and pepper to taste. Serve, passing sauce with chicken.

Simple Baked
Chicken Parts with
Lemon and Herbs

Baked Chicken Imperial

Chicken Mole Poblano

Chicken Mole Poblano

Serves 4 to 6   Total Time 1½ hours

Why This Recipe Works From the Puebla region of Mexico, mole poblano is a rich deep-red sauce made from chiles, nuts, spices, fruit, and chocolate. Traditional mole poblano relies on as many as six types of chiles, but we found that we could get good depth of flavor and rich color by using just two: ancho, which lent a full chile flavor base, and chipotle, which amped up the intensity of the chile flavor and provided a hint of heat and smokiness. Breaking the chiles into small pieces and rehydrating them right in the sauce (rather than in plain water) ensured that our sauce was fully infused with chile flavor. As for the nuts and seeds, we liked the rich, creamy flavors of toasted almonds and sesame seeds. Using almond butter instead of ground almonds was a simple shortcut that lent a luxurious, velvety texture to the sauce. For the chocolate, just 1 ounce added richness and depth but didn't make the sauce taste chocolaty. To round out the flavor of the mole, we added warmth and a touch of sweetness with cinnamon, cloves, and raisins. Bone-in chicken pieces worked perfectly with our mole, although removing the skin was essential since it turned inedibly soggy when covered in sauce. Feel free to substitute ½ teaspoon ground chipotle chile powder or ½ teaspoon minced canned chipotles in adobo sauce for the chipotle chile (we noted little difference in flavor) and add with the cinnamon in step 2. Serve with warm tortillas or rice.

2   dried ancho chiles, stemmed, seeded, and torn into ½-inch pieces (½ cup)
½   dried chipotle chile, stemmed, seeded, and torn into ½-inch pieces (scant tablespoon)
3   tablespoons vegetable oil
1   onion, chopped fine
½   teaspoon ground cinnamon
⅛   teaspoon ground cloves
1   ounce bittersweet, semisweet, or Mexican chocolate, chopped coarse
2   garlic cloves, minced
2   cups chicken broth
1   (14.5-ounce) can diced tomatoes, drained
¼   cup raisins
¼   cup almond butter
2   tablespoons sesame seeds, plus extra for garnish, toasted
     Sugar
3½ pounds bone-in chicken pieces (split breasts halved crosswise, legs, and/or thighs), skin removed, trimmed
¼   teaspoon table salt
¼   teaspoon pepper

Chicken Baked in Foil with Potatoes and Carrots

1. Toast anchos and chipotle in 12-inch skillet over medium heat, stirring frequently, until fragrant, 2 to 6 minutes; transfer to plate. Add oil and onion to now-empty skillet and cook over medium-high heat until softened, 5 to 7 minutes.

2. Stir in cinnamon, cloves, chocolate, and toasted chiles and cook until chocolate is melted and bubbly, about 2 minutes. Stir in garlic and cook until fragrant, about 30 seconds. Stir in broth, tomatoes, raisins, almond butter, and sesame seeds and bring to simmer. Reduce heat to medium and simmer gently, stirring occasionally, until slightly thickened and measures about 3½ cups, about 7 minutes.

3. Transfer mixture to blender and process until smooth, about 20 seconds. Season with salt, pepper, and sugar to taste. (Sauce can be refrigerated for up to 3 days; loosen with water as needed before continuing.)

4. Adjust oven rack to middle position and heat oven to 400 degrees. Pat chicken dry with paper towels and sprinkle with salt and pepper. Arrange chicken in single layer in shallow baking dish and cover with mole sauce, turning to coat chicken evenly. Bake, uncovered, until breasts register 160 degrees, and thighs/drumsticks register 175 degrees, 35 to 45 minutes.

5. Remove chicken from oven, tent with aluminum foil, and let rest for 5 to 10 minutes. Sprinkle with sesame seeds and serve.

Chicken Baked in Foil with Potatoes and Carrots

Serves 4   **Total Time** 1¾ hours

Why This Recipe Works Baking chicken and vegetables together in foil packets makes for an easy dinner and one that can be made ahead. Filling the packets with fragrant vegetables and juicy chicken sounded promising, but when we first tried it, the results were bland and mushy. To ensure full-flavored vegetables, we tossed garlic with olive oil, thyme, and red pepper flakes and browned it in the microwave. We then tossed our potatoes, carrots, and onion with this potent mixture. To protect the quick-cooking but lean boneless chicken breasts we had chosen for this meal from the pan's direct heat, we layered the potatoes under the chicken in the packets, leaving space for steam to circulate. We then nested the other vegetables around the chicken. This method ensured that all the components cooked to perfection. Make sure to buy chicken breasts that are roughly the same size to ensure even cooking. Note that this recipe calls for kosher salt; if using table salt, cut all salt amounts by half. The packets need to be refrigerated for at least 1 hour before cooking but can be assembled the day before.

5 tablespoons extra-virgin olive oil
6 garlic cloves, sliced thin
1 teaspoon minced fresh thyme or ¼ teaspoon dried
¼ teaspoon red pepper flakes
12 ounces Yukon Gold potatoes, unpeeled, sliced ¼ inch thick
2 carrots, peeled, quartered lengthwise, and cut into 2-inch lengths
½ large red onion, sliced ½ inch thick, layers separated
2 teaspoons kosher salt, divided
½ teaspoon pepper
4 (6- to 8-ounce) boneless, skinless chicken breasts, trimmed
2 tablespoons lemon juice
2 tablespoons minced fresh chives

1. Spray centers of four 20 by 12-inch sheets of heavy-duty aluminum foil with vegetable oil spray. Combine oil, garlic, thyme, and pepper flakes in large bowl and microwave until garlic begins to brown, 1 to 1½ minutes. Add potatoes, carrots, onion, and 1 teaspoon salt to garlic oil and toss to coat.

2. Pat chicken dry with paper towels. Sprinkle ⅛ teaspoon salt evenly on each side of each chicken breast, then sprinkle with pepper. Position 1 piece of prepared foil with long side parallel to edge of counter.

COOKING CHICKEN IN FOIL

1. Layer potato slices on sheet of foil to insulate chicken. Place remaining vegetables next to chicken.

2. Seal packets tightly, but allow plenty of headroom so that steam can circulate.

3. To determine doneness, poke thermometer through foil.

3. In center of foil, arrange one-quarter of potatoes in 2 rows perpendicular to edge of counter. Lay 1 chicken breast on top of potatoes. Place carrots and onion around chicken. Repeat with remaining foil, chicken, and vegetables. Drizzle any remaining garlic oil left in bowl over chicken.

4. Bring short sides of foil together and crimp to seal tightly. Crimp remaining open ends of packets, leaving as much headroom as possible inside packets. Place packets on large plate and refrigerate for at least 1 hour or up to 24 hours.

5. Adjust oven rack to lowest position and heat oven to 475 degrees. Place packets on rimmed baking sheet and bake until chicken registers 160 degrees, 18 to 23 minutes. (To check temperature, poke thermometer through foil of 1 packet and into chicken.) Remove sheet from oven and let chicken rest in packets for 3 minutes.

6. Transfer packets to plates, open carefully (steam will escape), and slide contents onto plates. Drizzle lemon juice over chicken and vegetables, sprinkle with chives, and serve.

VARIATIONS

Chicken Baked in Foil with Sweet Potatoes and Radishes

Substitute 1 tablespoon grated fresh ginger for thyme; 12 ounces peeled sweet potato, sliced ¼ inch thick, for Yukon Gold potatoes; 2 celery ribs, quartered lengthwise and cut into 2-inch lengths, for carrots; rice vinegar for lemon juice; and minced fresh cilantro for chives. Add 4 radishes, trimmed and quartered, to vegetables in step 1.

Chicken Baked in Foil with Fennel and Sun-Dried Tomatoes

Substitute 1 fennel bulb, stalks discarded, bulb halved, cored, and cut into ½-inch-thick wedges, layers separated, for carrots; balsamic vinegar for lemon juice; and basil for chives. Add ¼ cup oil-packed sun-dried tomatoes, rinsed, patted dry, and chopped fine, and ¼ cup pitted kalamata olives, chopped fine, to vegetables in step 1.

Un-Stuffed Chicken Breasts with Prosciutto, Sage, and Porcini

Serves 4   **Total Time** 45 minutes

Why This Recipe Works Chicken cordon bleu consists of a thin piece of chicken breast wrapped around ham and cheese. We decided to take the dish in an Italian direction. Bypassing the fussier preparation, we went the deconstructed route, putting the ham and cheese stuffing outside the chicken. First, we browned boneless, skinless breasts in a skillet before flipping

them and topping the meat with prosciutto and a mound of shredded provolone (sliced cheese slid off). To bring textural contrast we added crunchy Ritz crumbs, and we baked our unstuffed chicken in a quick cream sauce flavored with porcini and sage, using the skillet in which they were browned. If the sauce becomes too thick, thin it to the desired consistency with hot chicken broth or hot water before serving.

    4 (6- to 8-ounce) boneless, skinless chicken
       breasts, trimmed
    ¼ teaspoon table salt
    ¼ teaspoon pepper
    2 teaspoons vegetable oil
    4 slices prosciutto
    4 ounces provolone cheese, shredded (1 cup)
   15 Ritz crackers, crushed coarse (¾ cup)
    1 cup heavy cream
    ½ cup dry white wine
    ¼ ounce dried porcini mushrooms, rinsed and minced
    1 tablespoon minced fresh sage

1. Adjust oven rack to upper-middle position and heat oven to 475 degrees. Pat chicken dry with paper towels and pound to uniform thickness. Sprinkle with salt and pepper. Heat oil in 12-inch nonstick skillet over medium-high heat until just smoking. Brown chicken lightly on 1 side, about 3 minutes.

2. Off heat, turn chicken over and lay 1 slice prosciutto on top of each breast. Mound ¼ cup of provolone over prosciutto. Sprinkle cracker crumbs over cheese and press on crumbs to adhere.

3. Whisk cream, wine, mushrooms, and sage together in 2-cup liquid measuring cup and pour into skillet around chicken, without disturbing crumbs. Return skillet to medium-high heat and bring to simmer. Immediately transfer to oven. Bake until chicken registers 160 degrees, 12 to 15 minutes.

4. Transfer chicken to individual plates. Spoon sauce over chicken and serve.

Simple Stuffed Bone-In Chicken Breasts with Boursin

Serves 4   **Total Time** 50 minutes

Why This Recipe Works This simplified approach to stuffed bone-in chicken breasts utilizes the simplest of fillings—creamy Boursin cheese. Instead of cutting pockets in the chicken to hold the filling, which can be a fussy process, we used the skin on the chicken as a natural pocket. We loosened the skin and fit about 1½ tablespoons of the cheese underneath. The skin held the filling in place, and when the chicken emerged from the oven it was moist and tender, with a creamy, sauce-like filling. It is important to buy chicken breasts with the skin still attached and intact; otherwise, the stuffing will leak out. Try to buy chicken breasts of similar size so that they will cook at the same rate.

4 (10- to 12-ounce) bone-in split chicken breasts, trimmed
¼ teaspoon table salt
¼ teaspoon pepper
1 (5.2-ounce) package Boursin Garlic and Fine Herbs cheese, softened
1 tablespoon unsalted butter, melted

1. Adjust oven rack to middle position and heat oven to 450 degrees. Line rimmed baking sheet with aluminum foil.

2. Pat chicken dry with paper towels and sprinkle with salt and pepper. Use your fingers to gently loosen center portion of skin covering each breast. Spoon Boursin equally underneath skin of each breast. Gently press on skin to spread out cheese.

3. Arrange chicken, skin side up, on prepared baking sheet. Brush chicken with melted butter and bake until chicken registers 160 degrees, about 30 minutes, rotating sheet halfway through baking. Let chicken cool for 5 minutes. Serve.

VARIATION

Simple Stuffed Bone-In Chicken Breasts with Gorgonzola and Walnuts
Substitute 4 ounces softened Gorgonzola, mixed with ¼ cup walnuts, toasted and chopped, for Boursin.

Baked Ricotta Chicken
Serves 4   Total Time 50 minutes

Why This Recipe Works Part of the appeal of stuffed chicken breasts is the contrast in textures: tender meat, creamy filling, crunchy topping. Here we aimed for the same effect by taking an uncomplicated layered approach using milky ricotta cheese, zesty pasta sauce, and toasted panko. Ricotta has a tendency to break and dry out when baked, so we processed it with some oil to both add richness and smooth out its texture, and we punched up the flavor with Parmesan and oregano. We jump-started the chicken by browning it before shingling the pieces in a pasta sauce–lined baking dish (store-bought sauce kept things simple). Then we layered on more sauce, added our ricotta mixture, and crowned the chicken with a bread-crumb topping that crisped up in the oven. We like a thicker and richer ricotta so it stays in place when the chicken is baked. Serve the chicken with pasta or bread.

Baked Ricotta Chicken

Bread Crumbs
½ cup panko bread crumbs
1 tablespoon extra-virgin olive oil
⅛ teaspoon salt
⅛ teaspoon pepper

Chicken
8 ounces (1 cup) whole-milk ricotta cheese
1½ ounces Parmesan cheese, grated (¾ cup)
1 teaspoon dried oregano
½ teaspoon table salt, divided
½ teaspoon pepper, divided
¼ cup extra-virgin olive oil, divided
4 (6- to 8-ounce) boneless, skinless chicken breasts, trimmed
1½ cups jarred pasta sauce, divided
2 tablespoons coarsely chopped fresh basil

1. For the bread crumbs Combine all ingredients in bowl. Microwave until panko is light golden brown, 1 to 2 minutes, stirring occasionally; set aside.

2. For the chicken Adjust oven rack to upper-middle position and heat oven to 425 degrees. Process ricotta, Parmesan, oregano, ¼ teaspoon salt, and ¼ teaspoon pepper in food processor until smooth, about 10 seconds. With processor running, slowly add 3 tablespoons oil until incorporated; transfer ricotta mixture to bowl and set aside.

3. Pat chicken dry with paper towels and pound to uniform thickness. Season with remaining ¼ teaspoon salt and remaining ¼ teaspoon pepper. Heat remaining 1 tablespoon oil in 12-inch skillet over medium heat until shimmering. Cook chicken until browned on both sides, about 6 minutes.

4. Evenly spread ¾ cup sauce in bottom of 13 by 9-inch baking dish. Transfer chicken to dish, shingling breasts in center of dish on top of sauce. Pour remaining ¾ cup sauce over chicken, then top each piece with ⅓ cup ricotta mixture. Sprinkle chicken evenly with panko mixture. Bake until chicken registers 160 degrees, about 15 minutes. Sprinkle with basil and serve.

Chicken Vesuvio

Serves 4 to 6   **Total Time** 1 hour

Why This Recipe Works Chicken Vesuvio is a favorite Chicago restaurant dish of crisp-skinned chicken and deeply browned potatoes in a potent garlic and white wine sauce. To bring chicken Vesuvio into our kitchen, we traded a big skillet for a large roasting pan, which gave us room for four servings. We heated oil in the roasting pan on top of the stove, browned bone-in chicken thighs and halved Yukon Gold potatoes, and added dried herbs and plenty of garlic. We poured wine into the pan and moved it to the oven to finish cooking unattended. After transferring the cooked chicken and potatoes to a platter, we returned the pan to the stovetop to reduce the sauce further. Mashing the cooked garlic cloves brought the oil and wine together in a rich emulsion, and some fresh minced garlic, tempered with lemon juice, delivered robust flavor. For this recipe you'll need a roasting pan that measures at least 16 by 12 inches. Trim all the skin from the underside of the chicken thighs but leave the skin on top intact. To ensure that all the potatoes fit in the pan, halve them crosswise to minimize their surface area. For the most efficient browning, heat the roasting pan over two burners. Combining the garlic with lemon juice in step 1 makes the garlic taste less harsh, but only if the lemon juice is added immediately after the garlic is minced.

 8 (5- to 7-ounce) bone-in chicken thighs, trimmed
1¼ teaspoons table salt, divided
 ½ teaspoon pepper
1½ pounds Yukon Gold potatoes, 2 to 3 inches in diameter, halved crosswise

Chicken Vesuvio

 2 tablespoons vegetable oil, divided
14 garlic cloves, peeled (2 whole, 12 halved lengthwise)
 1 tablespoon lemon juice
1½ teaspoons dried oregano
 ½ teaspoon dried thyme
1½ cups dry white wine
 2 tablespoons minced fresh parsley, divided

1. Adjust oven rack to upper-middle position and heat oven to 450 degrees. Pat chicken dry with paper towels and sprinkle on both sides with ¾ teaspoon salt and pepper. Toss potatoes with 1 tablespoon oil and remaining ½ teaspoon salt. Mince 2 whole garlic cloves and immediately combine with lemon juice in small bowl; set aside.

2. Heat remaining 1 tablespoon oil in large roasting pan over medium-high heat until shimmering. Place chicken, skin side down, in single layer in pan and cook, without moving it, until chicken has rendered about 2 tablespoons of fat, 2 to 3 minutes. Place potatoes cut side down in chicken fat, arranging so that cut sides are in complete contact with surface of pan. Sprinkle chicken and potatoes with oregano and thyme. Continue to cook until chicken and potatoes are deeply browned and crisp, 8 to 12 minutes longer, moving chicken and potatoes to ensure even browning and flipping pieces when fully browned. When all pieces have been flipped, tuck halved garlic cloves among chicken and potatoes. Remove pan from heat and pour wine into pan (do not pour over chicken or potatoes). Transfer pan to oven and roast until potatoes are tender when pierced with tip of paring knife and chicken registers 185 to 190 degrees, 15 to 20 minutes.

3. Transfer chicken and potatoes to deep platter, browned sides up. Place pan over medium heat (handles will be hot) and stir to incorporate any browned bits. Using slotted spoon, transfer garlic cloves to cutting board. Chop coarse, then mash to smooth paste with side of knife. Whisk garlic paste into sauce. Continue to cook until sauce coats back of spoon, 3 to 5 minutes longer. Remove from heat and whisk in reserved lemon juice mixture and 1 tablespoon parsley. Pour sauce around chicken and potatoes. Sprinkle with remaining 1 tablespoon parsley and serve.

Greek Chicken

Serves 4   Total Time 1¾ hours

Why This Recipe Works We found inspiration for this superflavorful Greek chicken at Johnny's Restaurant in Homewood, Alabama, where the menu reflects the chef's Greek heritage and Alabama upbringing. The chicken there is tender and juicy, marinated and roasted to perfection and flavored with tons of herbs and lemon. To re-create this dish, we first tested our way to the perfect marinade: a blend of olive oil, fresh and dried herbs and spices, and lemon. To make sure the marinade penetrated past the surface of the chicken, we cut ½-inch-deep slashes in each piece. To achieve lovely browning, we roasted our chicken at a relatively hot 425 degrees and gave it a blast of heat from the broiler at the end of cooking. Use a vegetable peeler to remove six strips of zest from the lemon. If you prefer to zest the lemon, you will need about 1 tablespoon of zest. Make sure to use kosher salt here; we developed this recipe using Diamond Crystal Kosher Salt.

¼ cup extra-virgin olive oil
2 tablespoons chopped fresh rosemary
2 tablespoons chopped fresh thyme
5 garlic cloves, chopped
6 (3-inch) strips lemon zest, chopped, plus 1 tablespoon juice
1 tablespoon kosher salt
1½ teaspoons dried oregano
1 teaspoon ground coriander
½ teaspoon red pepper flakes
½ teaspoon pepper

Greek Chicken

3 pounds bone-in chicken pieces (2 split breasts, 2 drumsticks, 2 thighs, and 2 wings, wingtips discarded)

1. Combine oil, rosemary, thyme, garlic, lemon zest, salt, oregano, coriander, pepper flakes, and pepper in large bowl. Cut three ½-inch-deep slits in skin side of each chicken breast, two ½-inch-deep slits in skin side of each thigh, and two ½-inch-deep slits in each drumstick; leave wings whole. Transfer chicken to bowl with marinade and turn to thoroughly coat, making sure marinade gets into slits. Cover and refrigerate for at least 30 minutes or up to 2 hours.

2. Adjust oven rack 6 inches from broiler element and heat oven to 425 degrees. Place chicken, skin side up, in 12-inch oven-safe skillet. Using rubber spatula, scrape any remaining marinade from bowl over chicken. Roast until breasts register 160 degrees and drumsticks/thighs register 175 degrees, 30 to 35 minutes.

3. Remove skillet from oven and spoon pan juices over top of chicken to wet skin. Heat broiler. Broil chicken until skin is lightly browned, about 3 minutes, rotating skillet as necessary for even browning. Let chicken rest in skillet for 10 minutes. Transfer chicken to shallow platter. Stir lemon juice into pan juices, then spoon over chicken. Serve.

Turkey Meatloaf with Ketchup–Brown Sugar Glaze

Serves 4 to 6   **Total Time** 2¼ hours

Why This Recipe Works Meatloaf made with turkey instead of beef promises comfort food with a lighter touch. When we simply swapped store-bought ground turkey into a traditional meatloaf recipe, however, we wound up with a dense, mushy loaf, thanks to the turkey's fine, pasty texture. We dropped the usual panade from our recipe since it only exacerbated the mushiness. Instead, we stirred in quick oats, which added just the right amount of chew and helped open up the texture of the densely packed turkey. Cornstarch, along with grated Parmesan cheese and butter, gave the turkey's thin juices richer flavor and fuller body, and we used egg yolks in our mix instead of whole eggs. To complement the mild flavor of the meat, we stirred in a modest amount of onion, as well as garlic, Worcestershire, fresh thyme, and Dijon mustard. We finished off our loaf with a flavor-packed glaze and ensured that it stuck by applying a first coat and letting it cook until it was tacky. We then added a second coat of glaze, which stuck to the base coat. To help the loaf cook evenly, we baked it on a foil-lined wire rack set in a rimmed baking sheet. Do not use 99 percent lean ground turkey in this recipe; it will make a dry meatloaf. Three tablespoons of rolled oats, chopped fine, can be substituted for the quick oats; do not use steel-cut oats.

Meatloaf

- 3 tablespoons unsalted butter
  Pinch baking soda
- ½ onion, chopped fine
- 1 teaspoon table salt, divided
- 1 garlic clove, minced
- 1 teaspoon minced fresh thyme
- 2 tablespoons Worcestershire sauce
- 3 tablespoons quick oats
- 2 teaspoons cornstarch
- ½ teaspoon pepper
- 2 large egg yolks
- 2 tablespoons Dijon mustard
- 2 pounds 85 or 93 percent lean ground turkey
- 1 ounce Parmesan cheese, grated (½ cup)
- ⅓ cup chopped fresh parsley

Glaze

- 1 cup ketchup
- ¼ cup packed brown sugar
- 2½ teaspoons cider vinegar
- ½ teaspoon hot sauce

Turkey Meatloaf with Ketchup–Brown Sugar Glaze

1. For the meatloaf Adjust oven rack to upper-middle position and heat oven to 350 degrees. Line wire rack with aluminum foil and set in rimmed baking sheet. Melt butter in 10-inch skillet over low heat. Stir baking soda into melted butter. Add onion and ¼ teaspoon salt, increase heat to medium, and cook, stirring frequently, until onion is softened and beginning to brown, 3 to 4 minutes. Add garlic and thyme and cook until fragrant, about 1 minute. Stir in Worcestershire and continue to cook until slightly reduced, about 1 minute. Transfer onion mixture to large bowl and set aside. Combine oats, cornstarch, pepper, and remaining ¾ teaspoon salt in second bowl.

2. For the glaze Whisk all ingredients in saucepan until sugar dissolves. Bring mixture to simmer over medium heat and cook until slightly thickened, about 5 minutes; set aside.

3. Stir egg yolks and mustard into cooled onion mixture until well combined. Add turkey, Parmesan, parsley, and oat mixture; using your hands, mix until well combined. Transfer turkey mixture to center of prepared rack. Using your wet hands, shape into 9 by 5-inch loaf. Using pastry brush, spread half of glaze evenly over top and sides of meatloaf. Bake meatloaf for 40 minutes.

4. Brush remaining glaze onto top and sides of meatloaf and continue to bake until meatloaf registers 160 degrees, 35 to 40 minutes longer. Let meatloaf cool for 20 minutes before slicing and serving.

Simple Broiled Bone-In Chicken with Garlic, Lemon, and Rosemary

VARIATION
Turkey Meatloaf with Apricot-Mustard Glaze
Microwave ¼ cup apricot preserves until hot and fluid, about 30 seconds. Strain preserves through fine-mesh strainer into bowl; discard solids. Stir in 2 tablespoons Dijon mustard, 2 tablespoons ketchup, and pinch salt. Substitute apricot mixture for glaze.

Simple Broiled Bone-In Chicken Parts

Serves 4 **Total Time** 1¼ hours

Why This Recipe Works Broiling chicken parts makes for a quick and easy dinner. When done right, the result is moist meat encased in crisp skin. Broiling uses direct heat to cook the chicken quickly and give it a browned crust. We found it best to use bone-in parts. Brining the chicken was a must for moist, well-seasoned meat, and adding sugar to the brine ensured caramelized skin. We broiled the chicken on the lowest rack to prevent the skin from charring, but moved it up closer to the heating element for the last minute of cooking for better browning. Finally, slashing the skin and starting the chicken skin side down ensured that plenty of fat rendered from the skin, resulting in a crisp exterior. This chicken tastes great as is, but to dress it up a little we created two flavorful—but still simple—variations. If using kosher chicken, do not brine in step 1, and season with salt as well as pepper. For more information on brining, see page 15.

½ cup table salt for brining
½ cup sugar for brining
 3 pounds bone-in chicken pieces (split breasts halved crosswise, drumsticks, and/or thighs), trimmed
¼ teaspoon pepper

1. Dissolve salt and sugar in 2 quarts cold water in large container. Submerge chicken in brine, cover, and refrigerate for 30 minutes to 1 hour. Remove chicken from brine and pat dry with paper towels. Using sharp knife, make 2 or 3 short slashes into skin of each piece of chicken, taking care not to cut into meat; sprinkle with pepper.

2. Meanwhile, adjust 1 oven rack to lowest position and second rack 5 inches from broiler element; heat broiler.

Set wire rack in aluminum foil–lined rimmed baking sheet. Place chicken pieces skin side down on prepared wire rack.

3. Broil chicken on lower rack until just beginning to brown, 12 to 16 minutes. Flip chicken pieces skin side up and continue to broil on lower rack until skin is slightly crisp and breasts register 160 degrees, about 10 minutes longer (if some chicken parts are browning too quickly, cover only those pieces with small pieces of foil). Transfer breast pieces to large plate and tent with foil. Continue to broil thighs and drumsticks on lower rack until they register 175 degrees, 5 to 10 minutes longer.

4. Return breast pieces skin side up to wire rack and broil on upper rack until chicken is spotty brown and skin is thin and crisp, about 1 minute. Serve immediately.

VARIATIONS
Simple Broiled Bone-In Chicken Breasts
Substitute four 12-ounce bone-in split chicken breasts, trimmed of rib sections, for chicken parts. Broil chicken on lower rack until just beginning to brown, 12 to 16 minutes. Flip chicken skin side up and continue to broil on lower rack until skin is slightly crisp and breasts register 160 degrees, about 10 minutes longer, before broiling on upper rack.

Simple Broiled Bone-In Chicken Thighs

Substitute eight 6-ounce bone-in chicken thighs for chicken parts. Broil chicken on bottom rack until just beginning to brown, 12 to 16 minutes. Flip chicken skin side up and continue to broil on lower rack until thighs register 175 degrees, 15 to 20 minutes longer, before broiling on upper rack.

Simple Broiled Bone-In Chicken with Garlic, Lemon, and Rosemary

While chicken is brining, combine 5 minced garlic cloves, 1 tablespoon minced fresh rosemary, 2 teaspoons grated lemon zest, and ¼ teaspoon pepper in small bowl; set aside. Combine ¼ cup lemon juice (2 lemons) and 3 tablespoons extra-virgin olive oil in second small bowl; set aside. After drying chicken with paper towels, use your fingers to gently loosen skin covering chicken pieces and spread garlic mixture under skin. Slash chicken skin as directed. In step 4, brush chicken pieces with lemon juice mixture before broiling to crisp skin.

Simple Broiled Bone-In Chicken with Spicy Jerk Dipping Sauce

While chicken is brining, toast 1 unpeeled garlic clove and 1 habanero chile in 8-inch skillet over medium heat, shaking pan occasionally, until softened and spotty brown, about 8 minutes. When cool enough to handle, peel and mince garlic and stem, seed, and mince habanero. Whisk ¼ cup lime juice (2 limes) and ¼ cup packed brown sugar in bowl until sugar is completely dissolved. Combine ½ cup finely chopped onion, 2 minced scallions, 1½ tablespoons minced ginger, ½ teaspoon dried thyme, pinch ground allspice, minced garlic, and minced habanero in second small bowl. Stir in 2 tablespoons lime juice mixture and set aside as dipping sauce for cooked chicken. In step 4, brush chicken pieces with lime juice mixture before broiling to crisp skin. Serve with dipping sauce.

CREATING CRISPIER SKIN

Make 2 or 3 diagonal slashes in skin of each chicken piece to help render fat.

Broiled Paprika Chicken

Serves 4   Total Time 40 minutes

Why This Recipe Works For a quicker broiled version of the Hungarian dish Chicken Paprikash (page 185), we started with bone-in, skin-on split chicken breasts. Smearing a mixture of butter, garlic, and paprika beneath the chicken skin ensured that the spread wouldn't slide off the meat. Coating the exposed surface of the breasts with additional paprika, salt, and pepper gave the chicken a deeply flavored brick-red exterior. We broiled the chicken breasts skin side down and then finished them skin side up, which made for crisp, bronzed skin. Broilers vary in heat output, so cooking times can vary dramatically. When you are broiling chicken, it is best to use an instant-read thermometer or cut into the thickest part of the breast to check for doneness.

2 tablespoons unsalted butter, softened
3 cloves garlic, minced
1 tablespoon paprika, divided
¾ teaspoon table salt, divided
½ teaspoon pepper, divided
4 (10- to 12-ounce) bone-in split chicken breasts, trimmed

1. Adjust 1 oven rack to lowest position (rack should be 13 inches away from broiler element) and second oven rack to highest position (about 5 inches away from broiler element) and heat broiler. Set wire rack in aluminum foil–lined rimmed baking sheet.

2. Mash butter, garlic, 2 teaspoons paprika, ¼ teaspoon salt, and ¼ teaspoon pepper in small bowl to form paste. Using your fingers, carefully loosen skin from meat. Spoon about 2 teaspoons of butter mixture under skin of each breast, then work butter evenly under skin. Rub both sides of chicken breasts with remaining 1 teaspoon paprika, remaining ½ teaspoon salt, and remaining ¼ teaspoon pepper. Place chicken skin side down on wire rack.

3. Broil on lower rack until just beginning to brown, 12 to 16 minutes. Turn chicken skin side up and continue to broil on lower rack until skin is slightly crisp and thickest part of meat registers 160 degrees, 10 to 16 minutes. Move pan to upper rack and broil until skin is spotty brown and crisp, about 1 minute. Serve.

Chipotle Chicken Kebabs with Creamy Cilantro Dipping Sauce

Serves 4   **Total Time** 30 minutes

Why This Recipe Works Tasty chicken kebabs can be made indoors in a flash with the help of the broiler and the right spices. For these kebabs, chipotle chile in adobo sauce provided a smoky, slightly spicy flavor, which was rounded out nicely by brown sugar and fresh cilantro. We were looking for a flavorful cooling sauce to accompany our kebabs, and a sour cream–mayonnaise combination with lime juice did the trick. It was light and tangy and was the perfect balance for our chipotle chicken. These kebabs are fairly spicy; to make them more mild, reduce the amount of chipotle. You will need four 12-inch metal skewers for this recipe.

   2 pounds boneless, skinless chicken breasts, trimmed and cut into 1½-inch chunks
   ¼ cup packed light brown sugar
   ¼ cup minced fresh cilantro, divided
   2 tablespoons minced canned chipotle chile in adobo sauce
   1½ teaspoons table salt
   ½ teaspoon garlic powder, divided
   ¼ teaspoon pepper
   ½ cup sour cream
   2 tablespoons mayonnaise
   3 tablespoons lime juice (2 limes)
   2 scallions, minced

   1. Adjust oven rack 6 inches from broiler element and heat broiler. Set wire rack in aluminum foil–lined rimmed baking sheet.

   2. Toss chicken with sugar, 2 tablespoons cilantro, chipotle, salt, ¼ teaspoon garlic powder, and pepper in bowl. Thread chicken onto four 12-inch skewers.

   3. Arrange skewers on prepared wire rack. Broil skewers, turning occasionally, until chicken is charred around edges and registers 160 degrees, about 10 minutes.

   4. Meanwhile, combine sour cream, mayonnaise, lime juice, scallions, remaining 2 tablespoons cilantro, and remaining ¼ teaspoon garlic powder in bowl, and season with salt and pepper to taste. Serve skewers with sauce.

Chicken Tandoori

Chicken Tandoori

Serves 4   **Total Time** 1½ hours

Why This Recipe Works The lightly charred pieces of juicy Indian tandoori chicken are infused with smoke, garlic, ginger, and spices. We thought it would provide a flavorful addition to our chicken routine. Traditional tandoori chicken is marinated in yogurt and spices and roasted in a superhot tandoor oven to produce tender, flavorful meat and a beautiful char. To make it at home, we built a fragrant paste, blooming ginger and garlic in oil before adding garam masala, cumin, and chili powder. We used this paste twice, applying some directly to the meat (which we slashed so the flavors penetrated) and stirring the rest into yogurt for our marinade. Arranged on a wire rack set in a baking sheet, our chicken roasted gently and evenly in a moderate oven; a few minutes under the broiler delivered char. A quick raita cooled things down. We prefer to make this dish with whole-milk yogurt, but you can substitute low-fat yogurt.

If you are using large chicken breasts (about 1 pound each), cut each breast into three pieces. To serve eight, double all the ingredients, adjust the oven racks to the upper-middle and lower-middle positions, arrange the chicken on two baking sheets in step 3, and broil each sheet of chicken individually in step 4. Serve with Raita and basmati rice, if desired. We prefer to use our Garam Masala (page 263) in this recipe, but you can use store-bought.

- 2 tablespoons vegetable oil
- 6 garlic cloves, minced
- 2 tablespoons grated fresh ginger
- 1 tablespoon garam masala
- 2 teaspoons ground cumin
- 2 teaspoons chili powder
- 1 cup plain whole-milk yogurt
- ¼ cup lime juice (2 limes), divided, plus lime wedges for serving
- 2 teaspoons table salt
- 3 pounds bone-in chicken pieces (split breasts cut in half, drumsticks, and/or thighs), skin removed, trimmed

1. Heat oil in 10-inch skillet over medium heat until shimmering. Add garlic and ginger and cook until fragrant, about 30 seconds. Stir in garam masala, cumin, and chili powder and continue to cook until fragrant, 30 seconds longer. Transfer half of garlic mixture to medium bowl, stir in yogurt and 2 tablespoons lime juice, and set aside. In large bowl, combine remaining garlic mixture, remaining 2 tablespoons lime juice, and salt.

2. Using sharp knife, make 2 or 3 short slashes in each piece of chicken. Transfer chicken to large bowl and gently rub with lime juice mixture until all pieces are evenly coated. Let sit at room temperature for 30 minutes.

3. Adjust oven rack to upper-middle position and heat oven to 325 degrees. Set wire rack in aluminum foil–lined rimmed baking sheet. Pour yogurt mixture over chicken and toss until chicken is evenly and thickly coated. Arrange chicken pieces, scored side down, on prepared wire rack. Discard excess yogurt mixture. Roast chicken until breast pieces register 125 degrees and drumsticks/thighs register 130 degrees, 15 to 25 minutes. (Smaller pieces may cook faster than larger pieces. Remove pieces from oven as they reach correct temperature.)

4. Adjust oven rack 6 inches from broiler element and heat broiler. Return chicken to wire rack, scored side up, and broil until chicken is lightly charred in spots and breast pieces register 160 degrees and drumsticks/thighs register 175 degrees, 8 to 15 minutes. Transfer chicken to plate, tent with foil, and let rest for 5 minutes. Serve with lime wedges.

Raita

Makes about 1 cup   **Total Time** 5 minutes

We prefer to use whole-milk yogurt for this recipe, but you can substitute low-fat yogurt. Do not substitute nonfat yogurt here; the sauce will be too thin and will taste bland. The test kitchen's favorite whole-milk yogurt is Brown Cow Cream Top Plain Yogurt. This recipe can easily be doubled if you like more sauce with your Chicken Tandoori (page 261) or if you want extra sauce for another use. Refrigerate the sauce until you are ready to serve it.

- 1 cup plain whole-milk yogurt
- 2 tablespoons minced fresh cilantro
- 1 garlic clove, minced
  Cayenne pepper

Mix yogurt, cilantro, and garlic together in medium bowl. Season with salt and cayenne to taste. (Raita can be refrigerated for up to 24 hours.)

Chicken Tikka Masala

Serves 4 to 6   **Total Time** 1¼ hours

Why This Recipe Works It is said that chicken tikka masala, tender pieces of chicken napped with a lightly spiced tomato-cream sauce, was created in a London curry house in the 1970s. It became, and has stayed, a very popular dish. To create a foolproof method for producing moist chunks of chicken in a rich tomato sauce, we began by coating boneless chicken breasts in a spice mixture and refrigerating it for half an hour, during which time we made a creamy tomato-masala sauce. To cook the chicken we first dipped it in a protective coating of yogurt and oil. Using the broiler was quick and imitated the high heat of a traditional tandoor. The basic combination of garam masala, fresh ginger, and fresh cilantro gave our masala sauce an authentic taste. The dish is best when prepared with whole-milk yogurt, but low-fat yogurt can be substituted. For a spicier dish, add the minced ribs and seeds from the serrano chile as desired. We prefer to use our Garam Masala (page 263) but you can substitute store-bought. Serve with rice.

Chicken

- 1 teaspoon table salt
- ½ teaspoon ground cumin
- ½ teaspoon ground coriander
- ¼ teaspoon cayenne pepper
- 2 pounds boneless, skinless chicken breasts, trimmed
- 1 cup plain whole-milk yogurt
- 2 tablespoons vegetable oil
- 1 tablespoon grated fresh ginger
- 2 garlic cloves, minced

Sauce

- 3 tablespoons vegetable oil
- 1 onion, chopped fine
- 1 serrano chile, stemmed, seeded, and minced
- 1 tablespoon tomato paste
- 1 tablespoon garam masala
- 2 garlic cloves, minced
- 2 teaspoons grated fresh ginger
- 1 (28-ounce) can crushed tomatoes
- 2 teaspoons sugar
- ½ teaspoon table salt
- ⅔ cup heavy cream
- ¼ cup chopped fresh cilantro

1. For the chicken Combine salt, cumin, coriander, and cayenne in small bowl. Place chicken on plate and sprinkle both sides with spice mixture, pressing gently to adhere. Cover chicken with plastic wrap and refrigerate for 30 minutes to 1 hour. Meanwhile, whisk yogurt, oil, ginger, and garlic together in large bowl and set aside.

2. For the sauce Heat oil in Dutch oven over medium heat until shimmering. Add onion and cook, stirring frequently, until light golden, 8 to 10 minutes. Add serrano, tomato paste, garam masala, garlic, and ginger and cook, stirring frequently, until fragrant, about 3 minutes. Add tomatoes, sugar, and salt and bring to boil. Reduce heat to medium-low, cover, and simmer for 15 minutes, stirring occasionally. Stir in cream and return to simmer. Remove pot from heat and cover to keep warm.

3. While sauce simmers, adjust oven rack 6 inches from broiler element and heat broiler. Set wire rack in aluminum foil–lined rimmed baking sheet. Dip chicken in yogurt mixture to coat with thick layer and transfer to prepared wire rack; discard excess yogurt mixture. Broil until chicken registers 160 degrees and is lightly charred in spots, 10 to 18 minutes, flipping chicken halfway through broiling.

4. Let chicken rest for 5 minutes, then cut into 1-inch chunks and stir into warm sauce (do not simmer chicken in sauce). Stir in cilantro, season with salt to taste, and serve.

Chicken Tikka Masala

Garam Masala

Makes about ½ cup   **Total Time** 5 minutes

The warm, floral, and earthy flavor profile of garam masala ("warm spice blend") makes it a welcome addition to most curries. The garam masala can be stored in an airtight container for up to one month.

- 3 tablespoons black peppercorns
- 8 teaspoons coriander seeds
- 4 teaspoons cardamom pods
- 2½ teaspoons cumin seeds
- 1½ (3-inch) cinnamon sticks

Process all ingredients in spice grinder until finely ground, about 30 seconds.

One-Hour Broiled Chicken and Pan Sauce

Murgh Makhani

Serves 4 to 6   Total Time 1¼ hours

Why This Recipe Works Murgh makhani, also known as Indian butter chicken, is a dish in which charred chicken is bathed in a rich tomato-based gravy enriched with butter (and often cream). It should taste rich and creamy but also vibrant and complex. We started by softening lots of onion, garlic, ginger, and chile in butter followed by aromatic spices such as garam masala, coriander, cumin, and black pepper. Instead of chopped or crushed tomatoes, we opted for a hefty portion of tomato paste and water, which lent the sauce bright acidity, punch, and deep color without making it too liquid-y. A full cup of heavy cream gave the sauce lush, velvety body, and we finished it by whisking in a couple more tablespoons of solid butter for extra richness. To imitate the deep charring produced by a tandoor oven, we broiled chicken thighs coated in yogurt (its milk proteins and lactose brown quickly and deeply) before cutting them into chunks and stirring them into the sauce. Traditionally, butter chicken is mildly spiced. If you prefer a spicier dish, reserve, mince, and add the ribs and seeds from the chile. We prefer to use our Garam Masala (page 263) but you can substitute store-bought. Serve with basmati rice and/or warm naan.

- 4 tablespoons unsalted butter, cut into 4 pieces and chilled, divided
- 1 onion, chopped fine
- 5 garlic cloves, minced
- 4 teaspoons grated fresh ginger
- 1 serrano chile, stemmed, seeded, and minced
- 1 tablespoon garam masala
- 1 teaspoon ground coriander
- ½ teaspoon ground cumin
- ½ teaspoon pepper
- 1½ cups water
- ½ cup tomato paste
- 1 tablespoon sugar
- 2 teaspoons table salt, divided
- 1 cup heavy cream
- 2 pounds boneless, skinless chicken thighs, trimmed
- ½ cup plain Greek yogurt
- 3 tablespoons chopped fresh cilantro, divided

1. Melt 2 tablespoons butter in large saucepan over medium heat. Add onion, garlic, ginger, and serrano and cook, stirring frequently, until mixture is softened and onion begins to brown, 8 to 10 minutes. Add garam masala, coriander, cumin, and pepper and cook, stirring frequently, until fragrant, about 3 minutes. Add water and tomato paste and whisk until no lumps of tomato paste remain. Add sugar and 1 teaspoon salt and bring to boil. Off heat, stir in cream. Using immersion blender or blender, process until smooth, 30 to 60 seconds. Return sauce to simmer over medium heat and whisk in remaining 2 tablespoons butter. Remove saucepan from heat and cover to keep warm. (Sauce can be refrigerated for up to 4 days; gently reheat sauce before adding hot chicken.)

2. Adjust oven rack 6 inches from broiler element and heat broiler. Combine chicken, yogurt, and remaining 1 teaspoon salt in bowl and toss well to coat. Using tongs, transfer chicken to wire rack set in aluminum foil–lined rimmed baking sheet. Broil until chicken is evenly charred on both sides and registers 175 degrees, 16 to 20 minutes, flipping chicken halfway through broiling.

3. Let chicken rest for 5 minutes. While chicken rests, warm sauce over medium-low heat. Cut chicken into ¾-inch pieces and stir into sauce. Stir in 2 tablespoons cilantro and season with salt to taste. Transfer to serving dish, sprinkle with remaining 1 tablespoon cilantro, and serve.

One-Hour Broiled Chicken and Pan Sauce

Serves 4   Total Time 1¼ hours

Why This Recipe Works Broiling is a great way to get a whole chicken on the table in about an hour. We first butterflied the chicken so that it cooked evenly under the intense direct heat. Piercing the skin at ¾-inch intervals helped to render the fat and prevented the skin from bubbling up and burning. To get the white and dark meat to cook in the same amount of time, we used a preheated skillet to jump-start the cooking of the leg quarters, and we started the skillet under a cold broiler to slow down the cooking of the breast. To account for the greater impact of carryover cooking from the broiler, we pulled the chicken from the oven when the breast meat reached 155 degrees instead of the usual 160. Finally, adding garlic and thyme sprigs to the hot pan drippings created an easy, flavorful sauce. If your broiler has multiple settings, choose the highest one. This recipe requires a broiler-safe skillet. In step 3, if the skin is dark golden brown but the breast has not yet reached 155 degrees, cover the chicken with aluminum foil and continue to broil. Monitor the temperature of the chicken carefully during the final 10 minutes of cooking, because it can quickly overcook. Do not attempt this recipe with a drawer broiler.

1 **(4-pound) whole chicken, giblets discarded**
1½ **teaspoons vegetable oil, divided**
¾ **teaspoon table salt, divided**
½ **plus ⅛ teaspoon pepper, divided**
4 **sprigs fresh thyme**
1 **garlic clove, peeled and crushed**
   Lemon wedges

1. Adjust oven rack 12 to 13 inches from broiler element (do not preheat broiler). Place chicken breast side down on cutting board. Using kitchen shears, cut through bones on either side of backbone. Trim off any excess fat and skin and discard backbone. Flip chicken over and press on breastbone to flatten. Using tip of paring knife, poke holes through skin over entire surface of chicken, spacing them approximately ¾ inch apart.

2. Rub ½ teaspoon oil over skin and sprinkle with ½ teaspoon salt and ½ teaspoon pepper. Flip chicken over and sprinkle bone side with remaining ¼ teaspoon salt and remaining ⅛ teaspoon pepper. Tie legs together with kitchen twine and tuck wings under breasts.

3. Heat remaining 1 teaspoon oil in broiler-safe 12-inch skillet over high heat until just smoking. Place chicken in skillet, skin side up, and transfer to oven, positioning skillet as close to center of oven as handle allows (turn handle so it points toward one of oven's front corners.) Turn on broiler and broil chicken for 25 minutes. Rotate skillet by moving handle to opposite front corner of oven and continue to broil until skin is dark golden brown and thickest part of breast registers 155 degrees, 20 to 30 minutes longer.

4. Transfer chicken to carving board and let rest, uncovered, for 15 minutes. While chicken rests, stir thyme sprigs and garlic into juices in pan and let stand for 10 minutes.

5. Using spoon, skim fat from surface of pan juices. Carve chicken and add any accumulated juices to pan. Strain sauce through fine-mesh strainer and season with salt and pepper to taste. Serve chicken, passing pan sauce and lemon wedges.

NOTES FROM THE TEST KITCHEN

PREVENT BLACKENED SKIN
In our early tests, the chicken's skin bubbled up from the meat, which put it closer to the broiler and caused it to burn. Our solution? Pierce the skin at ¾-inch intervals all over the bird, which provided enough vents for steam to escape. The trapped steam caused the skin to blister and burn.

BREADED AND FRIED

Photos (clockwise from top left): Nashville Hot Fried Chicken; Picnic Fried Chicken;
Chicken Schnitzel; Buffalo Wings

Crispy Pan-Fried Chicken Cutlets

Crispy Pan-Fried Chicken Cutlets
Serves 4 to 6   Total Time 30 minutes

Why This Recipe Works Classic breaded chicken cutlets are often plagued by a soggy, greasy, unevenly browned coating. Our first improvement was to replace the often-used home-made bread crumbs with drier, crunchier panko. To streamline the traditional multistep breading process, we ditched the flour and found that we got a more delicate crust. Whisking salt right into the egg meant we could skip seasoning each cutlet separately, and there was no need to pat the chicken dry before starting since there was no flour in the mix. Letting the cutlets rest on a wire rack lined with paper towels after frying ensured that they were not greasy and retained their crunch. If you are working with 8-ounce breasts, the skillet will initially be crowded; the cutlets will shrink slightly as they cook. For more information about making cutlets, see page 8. The first batch of cutlets can be kept warm in a 200-degree oven while you

cook the second batch. In Japan, breaded chicken (called chicken katsu) is often served over rice with an accompanying savory sauce. The cooked cutlets can be sliced into ½-inch-wide strips and served with Tonkatsu Sauce or Garlic-Curry Sauce (page 269). They can also be served simply spritzed with lemon, in a sandwich, or over a green salad.

- 2 cups panko bread crumbs
- 2 large eggs
- 1 teaspoon table salt
- 4 (6- to 8-ounce) boneless, skinless chicken breasts, trimmed
- ½ cup vegetable oil, divided

1. Place panko in large zipper-lock bag and lightly crush with rolling pin. Transfer to shallow dish. Whisk eggs and salt in second shallow dish until well combined.

2. Starting at thick end, cut each chicken breast in half horizontally. Pound cutlets to uniform ¼-inch thickness. Working with 1 cutlet at a time, dredge cutlets in egg mixture, allowing excess to drip off, then coat all sides with panko, pressing gently so crumbs adhere. Transfer cutlets to rimmed baking sheet and let sit for 5 minutes.

3. Set wire rack in second rimmed baking sheet and line rack with paper towels. Heat ¼ cup oil in 12-inch skillet over medium-high heat until shimmering. Place 4 cutlets in skillet and cook until deep golden brown on both sides, 4 to 6 minutes. Drain chicken briefly on paper towels, then transfer cutlets to prepared rack and season with salt to taste. Wipe skillet clean with paper towels. Repeat with remaining ¼ cup oil and remaining 4 cutlets. Serve immediately.

VARIATIONS
Crispy Pan-Fried Chicken Milanese Cutlets
Stir ¼ cup finely grated Parmesan cheese into panko.

Crispy Pan-Fried Chicken Cutlets with Garlic and Oregano
Whisk 3 tablespoons minced fresh oregano and 8 minced garlic cloves into eggs.

Crispy Pan-Fried Deviled Chicken Cutlets
Season each chicken cutlet with generous pinch of cayenne pepper. Whisk 3 tablespoons Dijon mustard, 1 tablespoon Worcestershire, and 2 teaspoons minced fresh thyme into eggs.

Tonkatsu Sauce

Makes about ⅓ cup   **Total Time** 5 minutes
You can substitute yellow mustard for the Dijon, but do not use a grainy mustard.

¼ cup ketchup
2 tablespoons Worcestershire sauce
2 teaspoons soy sauce
1 teaspoon Dijon mustard

Whisk all ingredients together in bowl.

Garlic-Curry Sauce

Makes about ½ cup   **Total Time** 5 minutes
Full-fat and nonfat yogurt will both work well in this recipe.

⅓ cup mayonnaise
¼ cup plain yogurt
2 tablespoons ketchup
2 teaspoons curry powder
1 teaspoon lemon juice
¼ teaspoon minced garlic

Whisk all ingredients together in bowl.

NOTES FROM THE TEST KITCHEN

TEST OIL BEFORE SHALLOW-FRYING
Shimmering can be an indicator that oil is hot enough to start sautéing, but shimmering can be deceptive when the oil is deep enough for shallow frying (it fully coats the pan bottom and can be swirled). The oil in contact with the pan bottom, where the heat is most intense, will shimmer before the oil on top. So how can you know the oil is heated from top to bottom? We add a pinch of panko. Once the crumbs turn brown, it's time to fry.

Crispy Garlic Chicken Cutlets

Serves 3 to 4   **Total Time** 1¼ hours

Why This Recipe Works Using a hefty amount of fresh garlic can be tricky. We wanted crisp cutlets with an intense but not overpowering garlic bite. Using four garlic cloves to marinate the cutlets provided our recipe with good garlic punch. For a crunchy, flavorful coating, we found that garlic powder mixed with bread crumbs held up well and lent a distinct flavor to the cutlets. Finally, we added crushed garlic cloves to the cold cooking oil and heated them together, and then removed the cloves from the now-flavored cooking oil before adding the chicken. For more information about making cutlets, see page 8.

3 (6- to 8-ounce) boneless, skinless chicken breasts, trimmed
3 tablespoons plus 1 cup vegetable oil, divided
10 garlic cloves, peeled (4 minced; 6 smashed, divided)
3 slices hearty white sandwich bread, torn into large pieces
1 cup all-purpose flour
3 large egg whites
¼ cup cornstarch
1 tablespoon garlic powder
¾ teaspoon table salt
½ teaspoon pepper

1. Adjust oven rack to middle position and heat oven to 200 degrees. Starting at thick end, cut each chicken breast in half horizontally. Pound cutlets to uniform ¼-inch thickness. Pat chicken dry with paper towels. Combine 3 tablespoons oil, minced garlic, and cutlets in zipper-lock bag and refrigerate while preparing remaining ingredients. Pulse bread in food processor until coarsely ground. Bake bread crumbs on baking sheet until dry, about 20 minutes.

2. Spread flour in shallow dish. In second shallow dish, whisk egg whites until foamy. Combine bread crumbs, cornstarch, and garlic powder in third shallow dish. Remove cutlets from bag and sprinkle with salt and pepper. Working with 1 cutlet at a time, dredge cutlets lightly with flour, dip in egg whites, and dredge in crumbs, pressing to adhere. Transfer cutlet to rimmed baking sheet, let sit 5 minutes, and repeat with remaining cutlets.

3. Heat ½ cup oil and 3 smashed garlic cloves in large nonstick skillet over medium heat until garlic is lightly browned, about 4 minutes. Discard garlic and fry 3 cutlets until crisp and deep golden, about 2 minutes per side. Drain chicken briefly on paper towels, then transfer to paper towel–lined baking sheet and transfer sheet to oven to keep warm. Discard oil, wipe out skillet, and repeat with remaining oil, garlic cloves, and cutlets. Serve.

Best Chicken Parmesan

Serves 4 **Total Time** 1 hour

Why This Recipe Works Traditional chicken Parmesan is an Italian American classic, and a mainstay of checkered-tablecloth restaurants and home kitchens alike. But this crowd-pleaser can be a minefield of potential problems: dry meat, soggy crust, and a chewy blanket of mozzarella. What good does it do to create a crisp crust if it turns soggy as soon as it's sauced? We wanted a juicy cutlet that kept its crunch. To start, we salted the cutlets for 20 minutes to ensure that the meat would stay moist. For a tender (not rubbery) cheese topping, we mixed the usual shredded mozzarella with creamy fontina. But the key was keeping the exterior crunchy. To accomplish this feat, we took a twofold approach. We replaced more than half of the starchy (and consequently sog-prone) bread crumbs with grated Parmesan cheese, and we placed the cheese mixture directly on the fried cutlets so that it formed a waterproof layer between the crust and the sauce. Tender chicken, crispy exterior, with a cheesy, saucy topping—it's a classic for a reason. Serve with pasta and a simple green salad. For more information about making cutlets, see page 8.

- 2 (6- to 8-ounce) boneless, skinless chicken breasts, trimmed
- 1 teaspoon kosher salt, divided
- 2 ounces whole-milk mozzarella cheese, shredded (½ cup)
- 2 ounces fontina cheese, shredded (½ cup)
- 1 large egg
- 1 tablespoon all-purpose flour
- 1½ ounces Parmesan cheese, grated (¾ cup)
- ½ cup panko bread crumbs
- ½ teaspoon garlic powder
- ¼ teaspoon dried oregano
- ¼ teaspoon pepper
- ⅓ cup vegetable oil
- 1 cup Quick Tomato Sauce (page 271), warmed
- ¼ cup torn fresh basil

1. Starting at thick end, cut each chicken breast in half horizontally. Pound cutlets to uniform ½-inch thickness. Pat chicken dry with paper towels. Sprinkle each side of each cutlet with ⅛ teaspoon salt and let stand at room temperature for 20 minutes. Combine mozzarella and fontina in bowl; set aside.

2. Adjust oven rack 4 inches from broiler element and heat broiler. Whisk egg and flour in shallow dish until smooth. Combine Parmesan, panko, garlic powder, oregano, and pepper in second shallow dish. Pat chicken dry with paper towels.

Best Chicken Parmesan

Working with 1 cutlet at a time, dredge cutlets in egg mixture, allowing excess to drip off. Coat all sides in Parmesan mixture, pressing gently so crumbs adhere. Transfer cutlets to rimmed baking sheet and let sit for 5 minutes.

3. Heat oil in 10-inch nonstick skillet over medium-high heat until shimmering. Cook 2 cutlets until crispy and golden brown on both sides, 3 to 4 minutes. Transfer cutlets to paper towel–lined plate and repeat with remaining cutlets. (Cooked chicken can be frozen for up to 1 month. To reheat, place frozen cutlets on wire rack set in rimmed baking sheet, top with cheese, bake in 400-degree oven on middle rack until crisp and hot throughout, 20 to 30 minutes, and continue with step 5.)

4. Place cutlets on rimmed baking sheet and sprinkle cheese mixture evenly over cutlets, covering as much surface area as possible. Broil until cheese is melted and beginning to brown, 2 to 4 minutes.

5. Transfer chicken to platter and top each cutlet with 2 tablespoons sauce. Sprinkle with basil and serve immediately, passing remaining sauce separately.

Gluten-Free Chicken Parmesan

Serves 4   **Total Time** 1 hour

Why This Recipe Works Having perfected traditional chicken Parmesan, we were up for the challenge of making a satisfying gluten-free version. We found that simply replacing the flour with cornstarch worked well, and as an added bonus, the additional starch helped the coating cling well to the chicken and also contributed to creating and retaining crispness. Store-bought gluten-free bread crumbs vary widely from brand to brand, so we settled on making our own fresh crumbs in the food processor. But because of gluten-free bread's high starch content and lack of structure, the bread crumbs broke down into sticky pieces that clumped together. The solution was to dry them out in the oven and add cornstarch, which helped eliminate clumping. As with our Best Chicken Parmesan recipe (page 270), we added fontina to the usual mozzarella and placed the mixture directly on the fried cutlets; this made for tender cheese and crunchy, juicy cutlets. For more information about making cutlets, see page 8.

- 4 ounces (4 slices) gluten-free multigrain sandwich bread, torn into quarters
- 1 ounce Parmesan cheese, grated (½ cup)
- 1 tablespoon plus ½ cup cornstarch, divided
- ½ teaspoon garlic powder
- ⅛ teaspoon dried oregano
- 1 large egg
- 2 (6- to 8-ounce) boneless, skinless chicken breasts, trimmed
- ½ teaspoon table salt
- ¼ teaspoon pepper
- 6 tablespoons vegetable oil, divided
- 2 ounces whole-milk mozzarella cheese, shredded (½ cup)
- 2 ounces fontina cheese, shredded (½ cup)
- 1 cup Quick Tomato Sauce, warmed
- ¼ cup chopped fresh basil

1. Adjust 1 oven rack to lower-middle position and second rack 4 inches from broiler element. Heat oven to 425 degrees. Process bread in food processor until evenly ground, about 45 seconds. Spread crumbs in even layer on rimmed baking sheet and bake on lower rack, stirring often, until golden brown, about 5 minutes. Transfer crumbs to shallow dish and break up large clumps into fine crumbs. Stir in Parmesan, 1 tablespoon cornstarch, garlic powder, and oregano.

2. Set wire rack in each of 2 rimmed baking sheets and line 1 rack with several layers of paper towels. Beat egg in second shallow dish. Place remaining ½ cup cornstarch in large zipper-lock bag. Starting at thick end, cut each chicken breast in half

horizontally. Pound cutlets to uniform ½-inch thickness. Pat chicken dry with paper towels and sprinkle with salt and pepper. Working with 1 cutlet at a time, add to bag of cornstarch and shake to coat. Remove cutlet from cornstarch and shake off excess, then dip in egg, and finally coat with crumb mixture, pressing gently to adhere. Lay coated cutlets on unlined wire rack and let sit for 5 minutes.

3. Heat broiler element. Heat ¼ cup oil in 12-inch nonstick skillet over medium-high heat until shimmering. Cook 2 cutlets in skillet until crisp and deep golden brown on both sides, 2 to 4 minutes. Transfer to paper towel–lined rack. Add remaining 2 tablespoons oil to skillet and repeat with remaining cutlets, lowering heat if necessary.

4. Remove paper towels underneath chicken. Combine mozzarella and fontina and sprinkle evenly over cutlets to cover completely. Broil on upper rack until cheese is melted and beginning to brown, about 2 minutes. Transfer chicken to platter and top each cutlet with 2 tablespoons sauce. Sprinkle with basil and serve with remaining sauce.

Quick Tomato Sauce

Makes about 2 cups   **Total Time** 30 minutes
This recipe makes enough sauce to top four chicken cutlets as well as four servings of pasta. High-quality canned tomatoes will make a big difference in this sauce.

- 2 tablespoons extra-virgin olive oil, divided
- 2 garlic cloves, minced
- ¾ teaspoon table salt
- ¼ teaspoon dried oregano
    Pinch red pepper flakes
- 1 (28-ounce) can crushed tomatoes
- ¼ teaspoon sugar
- 2 tablespoons chopped fresh basil

Heat 1 tablespoon oil in medium saucepan over medium heat until just shimmering. Add garlic, salt, oregano, and pepper flakes; cook, stirring occasionally, until fragrant, about 30 seconds. Stir in tomatoes and sugar; increase heat to high and bring to simmer. Reduce heat to medium-low and simmer until thickened, about 20 minutes. Off heat, stir in basil and remaining 1 tablespoon oil; season with salt and pepper to taste. (Sauce can be refrigerated for up to 3 days or frozen for up to 1 month. If frozen, thaw completely in refrigerator.)

Apple-Fennel Rémoulade

Serves 6 to 8   **Total Time** 15 minutes

Any variety of apple can be used here, but we recommend a crisp-sweet variety such as Fuji, Gala, or Honeycrisp.

- ¼ cup mayonnaise
- 2 tablespoons whole-grain mustard
- 2 tablespoons lemon juice
- 2 tablespoons capers, rinsed, plus 1 tablespoon brine
- 4 celery ribs, sliced thin on bias
- 1 fennel bulb, 1 tablespoon fronds minced, stalks discarded, bulb halved, cored, and sliced thin crosswise
- 1 apple, cored and cut into 2-inch-long matchsticks

Whisk mayonnaise, mustard, lemon juice, and caper brine together in large bowl. Add celery, fennel bulb, apple, and capers and toss to combine. Season with salt and pepper to taste. Top with fennel fronds and serve.

Cucumber-Dill Salad

Serves 6 to 8   **Total Time** 40 minutes

The fat percentage of the Greek yogurt doesn't matter here; use what you prefer.

- 2 English cucumbers, halved lengthwise and sliced thin
- 2 teaspoons kosher salt
- ⅓ cup plain Greek yogurt
- 4 teaspoons cider vinegar
- 1 tablespoon extra-virgin olive oil
- 2 teaspoons Dijon mustard
- 1 large shallot, halved through root end and sliced thin
- ¼ cup chopped fresh dill

1. Place cucumbers in colander and toss with salt. Set colander in sink and let stand for 30 minutes. Whisk yogurt, vinegar, oil, and mustard together in large bowl and set aside.

2. Gently shake colander to drain excess liquid, then blot cucumbers dry with paper towels. Add cucumbers, shallot, and dill to bowl with dressing and toss gently to combine. Season with salt and pepper to taste, and serve.

Chicken Schnitzel with Apple-Fennel Rémoulade

Chicken Schnitzel

Serves 4 to 6   **Total Time** 50 minutes

Why This Recipe Works Chicken schnitzel is defined by thin, tender, juicy cutlets coated in a fine, wrinkly crust that has puffed away from the meat. Halving and pounding chicken breasts ¼ inch thick ensured that they were tender and delicate. Use fine, unseasoned store-bought bread crumbs for this recipe; substituting panko bread crumbs will produce a crust that lacks the proper texture and appearance. We used Diamond Crystal Kosher Salt in this recipe; if using Morton Kosher Salt, sprinkle each cutlet with only ½ teaspoon. The oil must wash over the cutlets in waves to achieve the desired wrinkles and puff, so the ample space provided by a large Dutch oven is necessary; do not attempt to use a smaller pot. Serve with Apple-Fennel Rémoulade or Cucumber-Dill Salad, if desired. For more information about making cutlets, see page 8.

- ½ cup all-purpose flour
- 2 large eggs
- 1 tablespoon vegetable oil
- 2 cups plain dried bread crumbs

4 (6- to 8-ounce) boneless, skinless chicken breasts, trimmed
2 tablespoons kosher salt, divided
1 teaspoon pepper, divided
2 cups vegetable oil for frying
Lemon wedges

1. Spread flour in shallow dish. Beat eggs and oil in second shallow dish. Place bread crumbs in third shallow dish. Set wire rack in rimmed baking sheet. Line second rimmed baking sheet with double layer of paper towels. Adjust oven rack to middle position and heat oven to 200 degrees.

2. Starting at thick end, cut each chicken breast in half horizontally. Pound cutlets to uniform ¼-inch thickness. Pat chicken dry with paper towels. Sprinkle each cutlet on both sides with ¾ teaspoon salt and ⅛ teaspoon pepper.

3. Working with 1 cutlet at a time, dredge cutlets thoroughly in flour, shaking off excess, then coat with egg mixture, allowing excess to drip back into dish to ensure very thin coating. Coat evenly with bread crumbs, pressing on crumbs to adhere. Place cutlets on prepared wire rack, taking care not to overlap cutlets and let sit for 5 minutes.

4. Add 2 cups oil to large Dutch oven and heat over medium-high heat to 350 degrees. Lay 2 or 3 cutlets (depending on size) in oil, without overlapping them, and cook, shaking pot continuously and gently, until cutlets are wrinkled and light golden brown on both sides, 2 to 3 minutes. Transfer cutlets to paper towel–lined baking sheet, flip to blot excess oil, and transfer sheet to oven to keep warm. Repeat with remaining cutlets. Serve immediately with lemon wedges.

Chicken Fingers
Serves 4   Total Time 45 minutes

Why This Recipe Works Homemade chicken fingers taste much better than any that you can buy. For the best from-scratch chicken fingers, we chose 6-ounce breasts and cut them on the diagonal into ¾-inch strips to yield the most consistently sized pieces. We used a traditional three-step breading process and found that panko crumbs were the best choice, generating a crust with a mild, wheaty flavor and shatteringly crisp texture. Serve with a dipping sauce (page 275), if desired.

1 cup all-purpose flour
2 large eggs
3 cups panko bread crumbs
4 (6-ounce) boneless, skinless chicken breasts, trimmed and cut lengthwise on slight diagonal into ¾-inch-wide strips

½ teaspoon table salt
¼ teaspoon pepper
¾ cup vegetable oil

1. Adjust oven rack to middle position and heat oven to 200 degrees. Spread flour in shallow dish. Beat eggs in second shallow dish. Spread bread crumbs in third shallow dish.

2. Pat chicken dry with paper towels, then sprinkle with salt and pepper. Working with 1 strip of chicken at a time, dredge in flour, then dip into egg, and finally coat with bread crumbs. Press on bread crumbs to make sure they adhere. Transfer breaded chicken to rimmed baking sheet and let sit for 5 minutes.

3. Heat oil in 12-inch nonstick skillet over medium-high heat until just smoking. Add 4 pieces of chicken and cook until light golden brown on both sides, 4 to 6 minutes.

4. Drain fried chicken briefly on paper towels, then transfer to paper towel–lined baking sheet and keep warm in oven. Repeat with remaining breaded chicken. Serve.

CUTTING CHICKEN FINGERS

After trimming each chicken breast, slice it lengthwise on slight diagonal into long, ¾-inch-wide strips.

Gluten-Free Crispy Chicken Fingers
Serves 4   Total Time 1 hour

Why This Recipe Works For gluten-free chicken fingers that cooked up crisp, flavorful, and perfectly browned, we started by processing store-bought gluten-free sandwich bread into crumbs in the food processor; we then toasted them to dry them out for fine, dry crumbs that coated the chicken more evenly. Still, there were some bare spots. Adding cornstarch to the crumbs ensured an evenly browned coating. We used a three-step breading method, dipping in cornstarch, then egg, then the bread crumbs. As for the cooking method, pan-fried won out over oven-baked, delivering chicken fingers with a crispier exterior surrounding perfectly moist, flavorful chicken. The bread may clump together during toasting; make sure to break it apart into fine crumbs before breading.

6 slices (about 6 ounces) gluten-free multigrain sandwich bread, torn into quarters
½ cup cornstarch, divided
½ teaspoon table salt
¼ teaspoon pepper
2 large eggs
1½ pounds boneless, skinless chicken breasts, trimmed
¾ cup vegetable oil

1. Adjust oven rack to lower-middle position and heat oven to 425 degrees. Process bread in food processor until evenly ground, about 45 seconds. Spread crumbs in even layer on rimmed baking sheet and bake, stirring often, until golden brown, 7 to 10 minutes. Reduce oven temperature to 200 degrees.

2. Meanwhile, cut chicken breasts lengthwise on slight diagonal into ¾-inch-wide strips.

3. Transfer crumbs to shallow dish, breaking up any large clumps into fine crumbs. Stir in 1 tablespoon cornstarch, salt, and pepper. Beat eggs in second shallow dish. Place remaining 7 tablespoons cornstarch in large zipper-lock bag.

4. Set wire rack in rimmed baking sheet. Pat chicken dry with paper towels and season with salt and pepper. Working with 1 strip of chicken at a time, place chicken in bag of cornstarch, seal bag, and shake bag to coat chicken. Using tongs, remove chicken pieces from bag, shaking off excess cornstarch, dip in eggs, then coat with bread-crumb mixture, pressing gently to adhere. Place breaded chicken on prepared wire rack and let sit for 5 minutes.

5. Heat oil in 12-inch nonstick skillet over medium-high heat until just smoking. Add half of chicken and cook until golden brown on all sides, 4 to 6 minutes, flipping halfway through cooking. Drain chicken briefly on paper towels, then transfer to paper towel–lined baking sheet and keep warm in oven. Repeat with remaining breaded chicken. Serve.

VARIATION
Gluten-Free Crispy Chicken Cutlets
Omit step 2. Pound chicken breasts to uniform thickness. In step 4, working in 2 batches, cook cutlets until brown on both sides, about 6 minutes.

Chicken Nuggets
Serves 4 to 6   **Total Time** 1¼ hours

Why This Recipe Works Some chicken nugget recipes take the least desirable parts of the chicken and put them through a grinder. Not so, here—we opted for skinless, boneless chicken breasts so we would know exactly which parts of the chicken

Gluten-Free Crispy Chicken Fingers

Chicken Nuggets

we were eating. Brining the chicken prevented it from drying out and seasoning the breast meat combated its inherently simple flavor. We cut the brining time in half by slicing the meat into nuggets beforehand. Crushed panko combined with flour and a bit of baking soda provided a crispy brown exterior for our nuggets. Using whole eggs to adhere the coating made the nuggets too eggy, but the whites alone didn't have as much binding power. We found that resting the nuggets before frying solved the problem. Do not use kosher chicken for this recipe and don't let the chicken soak in the brine for longer than 30 minutes or it will be too salty. To crush the panko, place it in a zipper-lock bag and lightly beat it with a rolling pin. This recipe doubles easily and freezes well. Serve with one (or more) dipping sauce.

- 4 (6- to 8-ounce) boneless, skinless chicken breasts, trimmed
- 2 cups water
- 2 tablespoons Worcestershire sauce for brining
- 1 tablespoon table salt for brining
- 1 cup all-purpose flour
- 1 cup panko bread crumbs, crushed
- 2 teaspoons onion powder
- 1 teaspoon table salt
- ¾ teaspoon pepper
- ½ teaspoon garlic powder
- ½ teaspoon baking soda
- 3 large egg whites
- 1 quart peanut or vegetable oil for frying

1. Cut each chicken breast diagonally into thirds, then cut each third diagonally into ½-inch-thick pieces. Whisk water, Worcestershire, and 1 tablespoon salt in large bowl until salt dissolves. Add chicken pieces and refrigerate, covered, for 30 minutes.

2. Remove chicken from brine, discard brine, and pat chicken dry with paper towels. Combine flour, panko, onion powder, salt, pepper, garlic powder, and baking soda in shallow dish. Whisk egg whites in second shallow dish until foamy. Coat half of chicken with egg whites and dredge in flour-crumb mixture, pressing gently to adhere. Transfer to plate and repeat with remaining chicken (don't discard flour-crumb mixture). Let sit for 10 minutes.

3. Adjust oven rack to middle position and heat oven to 200 degrees. Heat oil in large Dutch oven over medium-high heat to 350 degrees. Return chicken to flour dish and turn to coat, pressing flour-crumb mixture gently to adhere. Fry half of chicken until deep golden brown, about 3 minutes, turning halfway through cooking. Drain chicken on wire rack set inside rimmed baking sheet and place in oven. Return oil to 350 degrees and repeat with remaining chicken. Serve.

DIPPING SAUCES

These easy homemade sauces beat anything out of a bottle and are the perfect dips for our Chicken Fingers (page 273), Chicken Nuggets (page 274), and Air-Fryer Chicken Nuggets (page 405).

BBQ Dipping Sauce
Makes ¾ cup   **Total Time** 5 minutes

- ¾ cup ketchup
- 3 tablespoons molasses
- 1 tablespoon cider vinegar
- 1 teaspoon hot sauce
- ⅛ teaspoon liquid smoke (optional)

Whisk ketchup; molasses; vinegar; hot sauce; and liquid smoke, if using, in medium bowl until smooth. Season with salt and pepper to taste.

Honey-Mustard Dipping Sauce
Makes ¾ cup   **Total Time** 5 minutes

- ½ cup yellow mustard
- ⅓ cup honey

Whisk mustard and honey in medium bowl until smooth. Season with salt and pepper to taste.

Sweet-and-Sour Dipping Sauce
Makes ¾ cup   **Total Time** 5 minutes

- ¾ cup apple jelly, apricot jelly, or hot pepper jelly
- 1 tablespoon white vinegar
- ½ teaspoon soy sauce
- ⅛ teaspoon garlic powder
- Pinch ground ginger
- Pinch cayenne pepper

Whisk all ingredients in medium bowl until smooth. Season with salt and pepper to taste.

Boneless Buffalo Chicken

Serves 4 to 6   **Total Time** 1¼ hours

Why This Recipe Works For buffalo chicken that could compete with the best bar fiery finger food, we created great flavor and texture from the inside out. Taking a tip from our fried chicken recipes, we soaked the chicken in a buttermilk brine to keep the meat juicy and seasoned before dredging it in a mixture of cornstarch, flour, baking soda, and a touch of hot sauce. This coating crisped beautifully, and our buffalo sauce—thickened with cornstarch—clung to the crags nicely, ensuring a dose of heat in every bite. Served with our home-made blue cheese dressing (made with pungent, slightly sweet Stilton), this buffalo chicken was game day–ready. In step 4, the fried chicken pieces can be held in a 200-degree oven for 30 minutes before being tossed with the sauce. A relatively mild cayenne pepper–based hot sauce, like Frank's RedHot Original Cayenne Pepper Sauce, is essential; avoid hotter sauces like Tabasco. The dressing yields about 1½ cups. Do not use kosher chicken for this recipe and don't let the chicken soak in the brine for longer than 2 hours or it will be too salty. Use a Dutch oven that holds 6 quarts or more for this recipe. Serve with celery and carrot sticks.

Boneless Buffalo
Chicken

Dressing

- 3 ounces Stilton cheese, crumbled (¾ cup)
- ¾ cup mayonnaise
- 6 tablespoons sour cream
- 1½ tablespoons cider vinegar
- ¼ teaspoon pepper
- ⅛ teaspoon garlic powder

Chicken

- 1½ pounds boneless, skinless chicken breasts, trimmed and cut into 1½-inch pieces
- ½ cup buttermilk
- 1 teaspoon table salt
- ¾ cup hot sauce
- ¼ cup water
- 1½ cups cornstarch, divided
- 1 tablespoon unsalted butter
- ¼ teaspoon sugar
- 4 large egg whites
- ½ cup all-purpose flour
- ½ teaspoon baking soda
- 1 quart peanut or vegetable oil for frying

1. For the dressing Process all ingredients in food processor until smooth, about 15 seconds, scraping down sides of bowl as needed. Cover and refrigerate while making chicken. (Dressing can be refrigerated for up to 1 week.)

2. For the chicken Combine chicken, buttermilk, and salt in large zipper-lock bag and refrigerate for 30 minutes or up to 2 hours. Combine hot sauce, water, 2 teaspoons cornstarch, butter, and sugar in small saucepan. Whisk over medium heat until thickened, about 5 minutes; set aside.

3. Whisk egg whites in shallow dish until foamy. Stir flour, baking soda, remaining cornstarch, and 6 tablespoons hot sauce mixture in second shallow dish until mixture resembles coarse meal. Remove chicken from marinade and pat dry with paper towels. Coat half of chicken with egg whites, then dredge in cornstarch mixture. Transfer chicken to rimmed baking sheet, let sit 5 minutes, and repeat with remaining chicken.

4. Heat oil in large Dutch oven over medium-high heat until oil registers 350 degrees. Fry half of chicken until golden brown on both sides, about 4 minutes. Transfer chicken to paper towel–lined plate. Return oil to 350 degrees and repeat with remaining chicken.

5. Warm remaining hot sauce mixture over medium-low heat until simmering. Combine chicken and hot sauce mixture in large bowl and toss to coat. Serve with dressing.

Nut-Crusted Chicken Breasts with Lemon and Thyme

4 (6-to 8-ounce) boneless, skinless chicken breasts, trimmed

1¼ teaspoons table salt, divided

1 cup almonds, chopped coarse

4 tablespoons unsalted butter, cut into 4 pieces

1 shallot, minced (about 3 tablespoons)

1 cup panko bread crumbs

2 teaspoons finely grated lemon zest, plus lemon wedges for serving

1 teaspoon minced fresh thyme

⅛ teaspoon cayenne pepper

3 large eggs

2 teaspoons Dijon mustard

¼ teaspoon pepper

1 cup all-purpose flour

1. Adjust oven rack to lower-middle position and heat oven to 350 degrees. Using fork, poke thickest half of each breast 5 or 6 times. Place on wire rack set in rimmed baking sheet and evenly sprinkle each breast with ¼ teaspoon salt. Refrigerate, uncovered, while preparing coating.

2. Pulse nuts in food processor until they resemble coarse meal, about 20 pulses. Heat butter in 12-inch skillet over medium heat; cook, swirling pan constantly, until butter turns golden brown and has nutty aroma, 4 to 5 minutes. Add shallot and remaining ¼ teaspoon salt; cook, stirring constantly, until just beginning to brown, about 2 minutes. Reduce heat to medium-low, add panko and ground nuts; cook, stirring frequently, until golden brown, 10 to 12 minutes. Transfer panko mixture to shallow dish or pie plate and stir in lemon zest, thyme, and cayenne.

3. Lightly beat eggs, mustard, and black pepper together in second shallow dish or pie plate. Place flour in third shallow dish or pie plate. Pat chicken dry with paper towels. Working with 1 piece at a time, dredge chicken breast in flour, shaking off excess, then coat with egg mixture, allowing excess to drip off. Coat all sides of chicken with panko mixture, pressing gently so that crumbs adhere. Transfer breaded chicken to clean wire rack set in rimmed baking sheet.

4. Bake until chicken registers 160 degrees, 20 to 25 minutes. Let rest for 5 minutes before serving with lemon wedges.

VARIATIONS

Nut-Crusted Chicken Breasts with Orange and Oregano

Substitute 1 teaspoon orange zest for lemon zest (cut zested orange into wedges for serving) and 1 teaspoon oregano for thyme.

Nut-Crusted Chicken Breasts with Lemon and Thyme

Serves 4 Total Time 1¼ hours

Why This Recipe Works Incorporating chopped nuts into the coating of a chicken breast not only adds a more robust flavor element, but also boosts the crust's crunch factor. To ensure juicy, flavorful meat we salted the breasts (poking them with a fork first helped the salt penetrate) and rested them briefly before dredging and frying. For the crust, a mixture of half nuts and half panko bread crumbs gave us just the light, crisp texture we wanted, but it wasn't particularly nutty. To increase the nuttiness, we cooked the panko, ground nuts, and a minced shallot in browned butter until fragrant and russet-colored. This recipe is best with almonds but works well with any type of nut. We love serving it with Spiced Apple Chutney (page 278) for a sweet element that pairs beautifully with the savory, nutty chicken. Make sure to grate the zest from the lemon before cutting it into wedges for serving.

Nut-Crusted Chicken Breasts with Lime and Chipotle

This version works particularly well with peanuts. Substitute 1 teaspoon grated lime zest for lemon zest (cut zested lime into wedges for serving). Omit thyme and add 1 teaspoon chipotle chile powder, ½ teaspoon ground cumin, and ½ teaspoon ground coriander to toasted bread crumbs with lime zest.

Pecan-Crusted Chicken Breasts with Bacon

Substitute coarsely chopped pecans for almonds. Cook 2 finely chopped slices bacon in 12-inch skillet over medium heat until crisp, 5 to 7 minutes. Remove bacon from skillet with slotted spoon and transfer to paper towel–lined plate. Pour off all but 2 tablespoons fat left in skillet. Reduce butter to 2 tablespoons and melt in fat left in skillet over medium heat before adding shallot. Increase shallots to 2. Omit lemon zest and lemon wedges and substitute 1 tablespoon minced fresh parsley for thyme. Add crisp bacon to toasted panko along with parsley.

Spiced Apple Chutney

Makes about 2 cups   Total Time 25 minutes (plus 2 hours cooling time)

    1 tablespoon vegetable oil
    3 Granny Smith apples, peeled, cored, and chopped
    1 shallot, minced
    1 tablespoon grated fresh ginger
    ½ teaspoon ground cinnamon
    ¼ teaspoon ground nutmeg
    ½ cup apple jelly
    ⅓ cup white wine vinegar

Heat oil in 12-inch nonstick skillet over medium-high heat until shimmering. Cook apples until lightly browned, about 5 minutes. Stir in shallot, ginger, cinnamon, and nutmeg and cook until fragrant, about 1 minute. Stir in apple jelly and vinegar, bring to simmer, and cook until thickened and measures about 2 cups, about 5 minutes. Transfer to bowl and let cool to room temperature, about 2 hours. (Chutney can be refrigerated for up to 1 week; bring to room temperature before serving.)

Chicken Cordon Bleu

Serves 4 to 6   Total Time 1¼ hours

Why This Recipe Works Chicken cordon bleu (meaning "blue ribbon" in French) certainly lives up to its name. It's cheesy, deeply savory, and decadent—like all the best parts of a grilled ham and cheese sandwich. Although it's usually made by pounding a piece of chicken and then wrapping it around some ham and cheese, we found that cutting a pocket into the breast was a much more efficient method. To get the same swirl effect, we simply rolled the ham slices into cylinders around shredded cheese and tucked the cylinders into each chicken breast. Adding a healthy dose of Dijon mustard to the egg wash boosted the flavor. To help prevent the filling from leaking, use large, 8-ounce chicken breasts and thoroughly chill the stuffed breasts before breading. We like Black Forest ham here.

    25 Ritz crackers (about ¾ sleeve)
     4 slices hearty white sandwich bread, torn into pieces
     6 tablespoons unsalted butter, melted
     8 thin slices deli ham (about 8 ounces)
     8 ounces Swiss cheese, shredded (2 cups)
     4 (8-ounce) boneless, skinless chicken breasts, trimmed
     ½ teaspoon table salt
     ¼ teaspoon pepper
     3 large eggs
     2 tablespoons Dijon mustard
     1 cup all-purpose flour

1. Adjust oven racks to middle and lowest positions and heat oven to 450 degrees. Pulse crackers and bread in food processor until coarsely ground. Drizzle in melted butter; pulse to incorporate. Bake crumbs on rimmed baking sheet on upper rack, stirring occasionally, until light brown, 3 to 5 minutes. Transfer to shallow dish. Leave oven on.

2. Top each ham slice with ¼ cup cheese and roll tightly; set aside. Pat chicken dry with paper towels and sprinkle with salt and pepper. Cut pocket in thickest part of chicken and stuff each breast with 2 ham-and-cheese rolls. Transfer chicken to plate, cover with plastic wrap, and refrigerate for at least 20 minutes.

3. Beat eggs and mustard in second shallow dish. Place flour in third shallow dish. Working with one at a time, coat stuffed chicken lightly with flour, dip into egg mixture, and dredge in crumbs, pressing to adhere. (Breaded chicken can be refrigerated, covered, for 1 day.) Transfer breaded chicken to rimmed baking sheet and let sit for 5 minutes. Bake on lower rack until bottom of chicken is golden brown, about 10 minutes; move baking sheet to upper rack and reduce oven temperature to 400 degrees. Bake until golden brown, chicken is cooked through, and filling registers at least 160 degrees, 20 to 25 minutes. Transfer to cutting board, tent with foil, and let rest for 5 minutes. Serve.

Chicken Kiev

Serves 4   **Total Time** 3¼ hours

Why This Recipe Works Chicken Kiev consists of a crisp fried chicken breast encasing a buttery herb sauce that dramatically oozes out when cut. The biggest challenge is preventing all that butter from leaking out while the chicken is cooking. Our answer was to butterfly the chicken breast—slicing it lengthwise, almost in half, and then opening it up to create a single, flat cutlet. We then placed a slab of herb butter on the cutlet and rolled it up like a burrito. Traditional recipes use butter spiked with nothing more than parsley and chives, but we found that minced shallots were more flavorful than chives and a small amount of minced tarragon added a pleasant hint of sweetness. A squeeze of lemon juice tamed the rich butter with a bit of acidity. For another layer of flavor, we whisked Dijon mustard into the egg wash for coating the chicken. Chilling the rolled cutlets for an hour in the refrigerator further sealed the seams. Unbaked, breaded chicken Kievs can be refrigerated overnight and baked the next day or frozen for up to one month. To cook frozen chicken Kievs, increase the baking time to 50 to 55 minutes (do not thaw chicken).

Herb Butter

- 8 tablespoons unsalted butter, softened
- 1 tablespoon minced fresh parsley
- 1 tablespoon minced shallot
- ½ teaspoon minced fresh tarragon
- 1 tablespoon lemon juice
- ⅜ teaspoon table salt
- ⅛ teaspoon pepper

Chicken

- 4–5 slices white sandwich bread, torn into pieces
- 1⅛ teaspoons table salt, divided
- ¾ teaspoon pepper, divided
- 2 tablespoons vegetable oil
- 4 (6- to 8-ounce) boneless, skinless chicken breasts, trimmed and tenderloins removed
- 1 cup all-purpose flour
- 3 large eggs, beaten
- 1 teaspoon Dijon mustard

1. For the herb butter Mix all ingredients in medium bowl with rubber spatula until thoroughly combined. Form into 3-inch square on plastic wrap; wrap tightly and refrigerate until firm, about 1 hour.

2. For the chicken Adjust oven rack to lower-middle position; heat oven to 300 degrees. Add half of bread to food processor and pulse until coarsely ground, about 16 pulses. Transfer crumbs to large bowl and repeat with remaining bread

Chicken Kiev

Chicken
Cordon Bleu

(you should have about 3½ cups crumbs). Add ⅛ teaspoon salt and ⅛ teaspoon pepper to bread crumbs. Add oil and toss until crumbs are evenly coated. Spread crumbs on rimmed baking sheet and bake until golden brown and dry, about 25 minutes, stirring twice during baking time. Let cool to room temperature (you should have about 2½ cups bread crumbs).

3. Starting on thinnest side, slice 1 breast lengthwise almost in half and open up to create single, flat cutlet. Repeat with remaining breasts. Place cutlets cut side up between sheets of plastic wrap and gently pound to uniform ¼-inch thickness. Pound outer perimeter to ⅛ inch. Pat chicken dry with paper towels and sprinkle both sides with ¼ teaspoon salt and ¼ teaspoon pepper.

4. Unwrap butter and cut into 4 rectangular pieces. Place 1 piece of butter in center of bottom half of 1 breast. Roll bottom edge of chicken over butter, then fold in sides and continue rolling to form neat, tight package, pressing on seam to seal. Repeat with remaining butter and chicken. Refrigerate chicken, uncovered, to allow edges to seal, about 1 hour.

5. Adjust oven rack to middle position and heat oven to 350 degrees. Place flour, eggs, and bread crumbs in separate pie plates or shallow dishes. Season flour with ¼ teaspoon salt and ⅛ teaspoon pepper; season bread crumbs with remaining ½ teaspoon salt and remaining ¼ teaspoon pepper. Add mustard to eggs and whisk to combine. Dredge 1 chicken breast in flour, shaking off excess, then coat with egg mixture, allowing excess to drip off. Coat all sides of chicken breast with bread crumbs, pressing gently so that crumbs adhere. Transfer breaded chicken to clean wire rack set in rimmed baking sheet and repeat with remaining chicken.

6. Bake until chicken is cooked through and filling registers at least 160 degrees, 40 to 45 minutes. Let rest for 5 minutes on wire rack before serving.

ASSEMBLING CHICKEN KIEV

1. Cut herb butter into 4 rectangular pieces. Place 1 butter piece near tapered end of cutlet.

2. Roll up tapered end of chicken over butter, then fold in sides and continue rolling, pressing on seam to seal. Repeat with remaining butter pieces and cutlets. Chicken is now ready to be breaded.

Ultimate Stuffed Chicken Breasts with Ham and Cheddar

Serves 4   **Total Time** 2 hours

Why This Recipe Works Ham and cheese is a classic combination (see Chicken Cordon Bleu on page 278), but we wanted to amp up the creamy luxuriousness, so we added cream cheese to the equation. We mixed together cream cheese, cheddar, herbs, and sautéed onion and garlic, spread it over a pounded chicken breast, and rolled it up. As with our Chicken Kiev (page 279), we refrigerated the rolls to firm up the filling so it wouldn't ooze out during cooking. We coated the chilled breasts with flour, egg, and fresh bread crumbs and browned them in a skillet on the stovetop. The last step in our stuffed chicken breast recipe, finishing them in the oven, allowed the breasts to cook through without burning. The cooked breasts sliced into medallions look lovely on the plate. The chicken breasts can be filled and rolled in advance and refrigerated for up to 24 hours.

 4 (6- to 8-ounce) boneless, skinless chicken breasts, trimmed
 1 tablespoon unsalted butter
 1 onion, chopped fine
 ½ teaspoon table salt, divided
 ¼ teaspoon pepper, divided
 1 garlic clove, minced
 4 ounces cream cheese, softened
 4 ounces cheddar cheese, shredded (1 cup)
 1 teaspoon chopped fresh thyme
 4 thin slices deli ham (4 ounces)
 1 cup all-purpose flour
 4 large eggs
 1 tablespoon vegetable oil
 1 tablespoon water
 1½ cups fresh bread crumbs
 ¾ cup vegetable oil for frying

1. Place chicken breasts between sheets of plastic wrap and gently pound to uniform thickness; each pounded breast should measure roughly 6 inches wide and 8½ inches long. Cover and refrigerate while preparing filling.

2. Melt butter in medium skillet over low heat; add onion, ¼ teaspoon salt, and ⅛ teaspoon pepper; and cook, stirring occasionally, until deep golden brown, 15 to 20 minutes. Stir in garlic and cook until fragrant, about 30 seconds longer; set aside. Using hand mixer, beat cream cheese in medium bowl on medium speed until light and fluffy, about 1 minute. Stir in onion mixture, cheddar, and thyme; set aside.

3. Place breasts skinned side down on work surface; pat chicken dry with paper towels and sprinkle with remaining ¼ teaspoon salt and remaining ⅛ teaspoon pepper. Spread each breast with one-quarter of cheese mixture, then place 1 slice ham on top of cheese on each breast, folding ham as necessary to fit onto surface of breast. Roll each cutlet up from tapered end, folding in edges to form neat cylinders. Refrigerate chicken, uncovered, to allow edges to seal, about 1 hour.

4. Adjust oven rack to lower-middle position; heat oven to 400 degrees. Spread flour in shallow dish. Beat eggs with oil and water in second shallow dish. Spread bread crumbs in third shallow dish. Unwrap chicken breasts and roll in flour; shake off excess. Using tongs, roll breasts in egg mixture; let excess drip off. Transfer to bread crumbs; shake pan to roll breasts in crumbs, then press with your fingers to help crumbs adhere. Place breaded chicken breasts on wire rack set in rimmed baking sheet.

5. Heat ¾ cup oil in medium skillet over medium-high heat until shimmering, but not smoking; add chicken, seam side down, and cook until medium golden brown, about 2 minutes. Turn each roll and cook until medium golden brown on all sides, 2 to 3 minutes longer. Return chicken rolls, seam side down, to wire rack; bake until deep golden brown, chicken is cooked through, and filling registers at least 160 degrees, about 15 minutes. Let stand 5 minutes before slicing each roll crosswise diagonally into 5 medallions; arrange on individual dinner plates and serve.

Spinach and Goat Cheese–Stuffed Chicken Breasts

Spinach and Goat Cheese–Stuffed Chicken Breasts

Serves 4   Total Time 50 minutes

Why This Recipe Works Hearty spinach is the perfect companion to creamy, tangy goat cheese in this supersimple recipe. Because we weren't worried about the rustic filling oozing out, we didn't have to worry about pounding, rolling, and chilling. Instead, we took a cue from our Chicken Cordon Bleu (page 278), and cut a pocket into the chicken before stuffing. To protect the meat and keep it moist, we brushed the breasts with mayonnaise before adding an easy bread-crumb topping.

- 2 slices hearty white sandwich bread, torn into pieces
- 2 tablespoons chopped fresh tarragon, divided
- 10 ounces frozen chopped spinach, thawed and squeezed dry
- 3 ounces goat cheese, crumbled (¾ cup)
- 2 garlic cloves, minced
- ¾ teaspoon table salt, divided
- ½ teaspoon pepper, divided
- 4 (6- to 8-ounce) boneless, skinless chicken breasts, trimmed
- 1½ tablespoons mayonnaise

1. Adjust oven rack to lower-middle position and heat oven to 425 degrees. Pulse bread and 1 tablespoon tarragon in food processor until coarsely ground and set aside. Combine remaining 1 tablespoon tarragon, spinach, cheese, garlic, ¼ teaspoon salt, and ¼ teaspoon pepper in bowl.

2. Pat chicken dry with paper towels and sprinkle with remaining ½ teaspoon salt and remaining ¼ teaspoon pepper. Working with 1 breast at a time, using paring knife, cut deep pocket in thickest part of chicken, extending into most of breast. Spoon one-quarter of spinach mixture into pocket and seal by threading toothpick through chicken about ¼ inch from the edge.

3. Arrange stuffed chicken breasts in baking dish. Brush top of chicken with mayonnaise and top with bread-crumb mixture, pressing gently to adhere. Bake until crumbs are golden brown, chicken is cooked through, and filling registers at least 160 degrees, 20 to 25 minutes. Let rest for 5 minutes and serve.

Chicken Croquettes

Serves 4 to 6 **Total Time** 1¼ hours

Why This Recipe Works The word croquette comes from the French word croquer, meaning "to crunch." To stay true to the name, we developed a chicken croquette with a crunchy exterior to contrast with its soft, rich chicken filling. Taking a nontraditional route, we tried mixing shredded chicken with leftover mashed potatoes before shaping, breading, and frying, but instant mashed potato flakes proved to be just as tasty, more consistent, and much easier. A coating of fresh bread crumbs resulted in the crunchiest exterior, and fresh scallions, garlic, and spicy cayenne pepper added intrigue to the filling. Shallow frying worked just as well as deep frying (and saved a ton of oil). As a serving option, we stirred together a quick lemon-scallion sauce. We like using Perfect Poached Chicken (page 60) here but any cooked chicken would work.

Lemon-Scallion Sauce
- ½ cup mayonnaise
- 1 scallion, minced
- 1 teaspoon grated lemon zest plus 1 tablespoon juice
- 1 tablespoon water

Croquettes
- 3 slices hearty white sandwich bread, torn into 1-inch pieces
- 1 tablespoon all-purpose flour
- 2 large eggs
- 1½ cups finely shredded chicken
- 1¼ cups plain instant mashed potato flakes
- 4 scallions, sliced thin
- 2 garlic cloves, minced
- 1¼ teaspoons table salt
- 1 teaspoon pepper
- ⅛ teaspoon cayenne pepper
- 1½ cups half-and-half
- 2 tablespoons unsalted butter
- 2 cups vegetable oil for frying

1. For the lemon-scallion sauce Combine all ingredients in bowl. Cover with plastic wrap and refrigerate until ready to serve.

2. For the croquettes Process bread and flour in food processor until finely ground, about 30 seconds; transfer to shallow dish. Beat eggs together in second shallow dish. Set aside bread-crumb mixture and eggs.

Chicken Croquettes

3. Combine chicken, potato flakes, scallions, garlic, salt, pepper, and cayenne in large bowl. Combine half-and-half and butter in 2-cup liquid measuring cup and microwave, covered, until butter is melted and mixture is hot, about 3 minutes. Add to chicken mixture and stir to combine (mixture will thicken as it sits).

4. Divide chicken mixture into 20 equal portions (about 2 tablespoons each). Using your moistened hands, shape each portion into 3-inch log with pointed ends. Working with 3 or 4 croquettes at a time, dip in eggs, turning to coat and allowing excess to drip off; then coat with bread-crumb mixture. Transfer to rimmed baking sheet. (Breaded croquettes can be covered with plastic wrap and refrigerated for up to 24 hours.)

5. Line second rimmed baking sheet with triple layer of paper towels. Heat oil in 12-inch nonstick skillet over medium heat to 350 degrees. Add 10 croquettes and cook until deep golden brown on first side, about 2 minutes. Using tongs, carefully flip croquettes and continue to cook until deep golden brown on second side, about 3 minutes longer. Adjust burner, if necessary, to maintain oil temperature between 300 and 350 degrees.

6. Transfer croquettes to paper towel–lined sheet. Return oil to 350 degrees and repeat with remaining croquettes. Serve with lemon-scallion sauce.

Karaage

Serves 4 to 6 **Total Time** 1 hour

Why This Recipe Works Juicy, deeply seasoned thigh meat encased in a supercrispy crust makes Japanese karaage a fried chicken lover's dream. Minimal oil and fast frying make it a cinch to cook. We briefly marinated the meat in a mixture of soy sauce, sake, ginger, and garlic (seasoned with a little salt and sugar), which imbued the chicken with deeply savory, aromatic flavor. We then dredged the chicken in cornstarch and let the dredged pieces rest while the oil heated, which gave the starch time to hydrate. Just before frying, we dabbed dry patches with reserved marinade to prevent dustiness. Lemon wedges are the traditional karaage accompaniment, and for good reason: The acid cuts through the richness of the fried dark meat, and underscores (without overpowering) the bright heat of the ginger in the marinade. We recommend using a rasp-style grater to grate the ginger. Do not substitute chicken breasts for the thighs; they will dry out during frying. Leftover frying oil can be cooled, strained, and saved for later use. Use a Dutch oven that holds 6 quarts or more for this recipe.

Karaage

- 3 tablespoons soy sauce for marinade
- 2 tablespoons sake for marinade
- 1 tablespoon grated fresh ginger for marinade
- 2 garlic cloves, minced for marinade
- ¾ teaspoon sugar for marinade
- ⅛ teaspoon table salt for marinade
- 1½ pounds boneless, skinless chicken thighs, trimmed and cut crosswise into 1- to 1½-inch-wide strips
- 1¼ cups cornstarch
- 1 quart peanut or vegetable oil for frying
  Lemon wedges

1. Combine soy sauce, sake, ginger, garlic, sugar, and salt in medium bowl. Add chicken and toss to combine. Let sit at room temperature for 30 minutes. While chicken is marinating, line rimmed baking sheet with parchment paper. Set wire rack in second rimmed baking sheet and line rack with triple layer of paper towels. Place cornstarch in wide bowl.

2. Lift chicken from marinade, 1 piece at a time, allowing excess marinade to drip back into bowl but leaving any garlic or ginger bits on chicken. Coat chicken with cornstarch, shake off excess, and place on parchment-lined sheet. Reserve marinade.

3. Add oil to large Dutch oven until it measures about ¾ inch deep and heat over medium-high heat to 375 degrees. While oil heats, check chicken pieces for white patches of dry cornstarch. Dip back of spoon in reserved marinade and gently press onto dry spots to lightly moisten.

4. Using tongs, add half of chicken, 1 piece at a time, to oil in single layer. Cook, adjusting burner, if necessary, to maintain oil temperature between 300 and 325 degrees, until chicken is golden brown and crispy, 4 to 5 minutes. Using spider skimmer or slotted spoon, transfer chicken to paper towel–lined rack. Return oil to 325 degrees and repeat with remaining chicken. Serve with lemon wedges.

SLICING THIGHS INTO STRIPS

Arrange each thigh, skinned side up, with long side parallel to edge of counter. Slice crosswise into 1- to 1½-inch-wide strips.

Ultimate Crispy Fried Chicken

7 cups buttermilk for brining

3 garlic heads, cloves separated, peeled, and smashed, for brining

½ cup plus 2 tablespoons table salt for brining

¼ cup sugar for brining

2 tablespoons paprika for brining

3 bay leaves, crumbled, for brining

3½ pounds bone-in chicken pieces (split breasts halved crosswise, drumsticks, and/or thighs), trimmed

1 quart peanut or vegetable oil for frying

4 cups all-purpose flour

1 large egg

1 teaspoon baking powder

½ teaspoon baking soda

1 cup buttermilk

1. Whisk 7 cups buttermilk, garlic, salt, sugar, paprika, and bay leaves together in large container. Add chicken and turn to coat. Cover and refrigerate for 2 to 3 hours.

2. Set wire rack in rimmed baking sheet. Place chicken in single layer on prepared rack, and refrigerate, uncovered, for 2 hours. (At this point, chicken can be covered with plastic wrap and refrigerated for up to 6 hours.)

3. Adjust oven rack to middle position and heat oven to 200 degrees. Line large plate with triple layer of paper towels. Set second wire rack in second rimmed baking sheet. Add oil to large Dutch oven until it measures about ¾ inch deep and heat over medium-high heat to 375 degrees.

4. Meanwhile, spread flour in shallow dish. Lightly beat egg, baking powder, and baking soda together in medium bowl, then whisk in buttermilk (mixture will bubble and foam). Working with 1 piece at a time, dredge chicken in flour, shaking off excess, then dip in buttermilk mixture, letting excess drip off. Dredge chicken in flour again, shaking off excess, and return to rack.

5. Carefully place half of chicken in pot, skin side down. Cover and fry until deep golden brown, 7 to 11 minutes. Adjust burner, if necessary, to maintain oil temperature between 300 and 325 degrees. (After 4 minutes, check chicken for even browning and rearrange if some pieces are browning faster than others.) Turn chicken pieces over and continue to cook, uncovered, until breasts register 160 degrees and drumsticks/thighs register 175 degrees, 6 to 8 minutes. (Remove pieces from pot as they reach correct temperature.) Let chicken drain briefly on prepared plate, then transfer to second prepared rack and place in oven to keep warm.

6. Return oil to 375 degrees and repeat with remaining chicken. Serve.

Ultimate Crispy Fried Chicken

Ultimate Crispy Fried Chicken

Serves 4 to 6   **Total Time** 50 minutes (plus 4 hours brining and chilling time)

Why This Recipe Works The best homemade fried chicken—seasoned, tender meat coated with a crisp mahogany crust—is worth the splatter and mess. But we wanted to avoid that hassle. We started by brining chicken parts in a mixture of buttermilk, salt, and spices and then air-drying the brined chicken to achieve an extra-crisp skin. To finish, we coated the chicken with flour and a mixture of buttermilk, baking powder, and baking soda for a light, shatteringly crisp crust. Shallow frying made this recipe manageable; we chose peanut oil for its high smoke point and ability to produce a crisp crust. Covering the Dutch oven during the first half of frying reduced splatters, maintained the oil temperature impeccably, and cooked the chicken in about 15 minutes. This time-efficient frying method made up for needing to fry the chicken in two batches. Do not use kosher chicken for this recipe and don't let the chicken soak in the brine for longer than 3 hours or it will be too salty. Use a Dutch oven that holds 6 quarts or more. Maintaining an even oil temperature is key here. If the chicken breasts are particularly large (about 1 pound each), cut each crosswise into three pieces.

Extra-Crunchy Fried Chicken

Serves 4   Total Time 1 hour (plus 1 hour brining time)

Why This Recipe Works We love using buttermilk to brine our chicken and create a well-seasoned, crunchy coating, too. For this recipe, we added some buttermilk right to the flour to create a thick slurry that clung tightly to the meat. We took a cue from our Ultimate Crispy Fried Chicken (page 284) and kept the lid on the pot for half the cooking time. This resulted in crunchy fried chicken that was neither too browned nor too greasy. Do not use kosher chicken for this recipe and don't let the chicken soak in the brine for longer than 1 hour or it will be too salty.

- 2   tablespoons table salt for brining
- 2   cups buttermilk for brining
- 3½ pounds bone-in chicken pieces (split breasts halved crosswise, drumsticks, and/or thighs), trimmed
- 1   quart peanut or vegetable oil for frying
- 3   cups all-purpose flour
- 2   teaspoons baking powder
- ¾   teaspoon dried thyme
- ½   teaspoon pepper
- ¼   teaspoon garlic powder
- 6   tablespoons buttermilk

1. Dissolve salt in 2 cups buttermilk in large container. Submerge chicken in brine, cover, and refrigerate for 1 hour.

2. Line platter with triple layer of paper towels. Set wire rack in rimmed baking sheet. Add oil to large Dutch oven until it measures about ¾ inch deep and heat over medium-high heat to 375 degrees.

3. Meanwhile, whisk flour, baking powder, thyme, pepper, and garlic powder together in large bowl. Add buttermilk; with your fingers rub flour and buttermilk together until buttermilk is evenly incorporated into flour and mixture resembles coarse, wet sand. Dredge chicken pieces in flour mixture and turn to coat thoroughly, gently pressing flour mixture onto chicken. Shake excess flour from each piece of chicken and transfer to prepared baking sheet.

4. Place chicken pieces skin side down in oil, cover, and fry until deep golden brown, 8 to 10 minutes. Adjust burner, if necessary, to maintain oil temperature between 300 and 325 degrees. (After 4 minutes, check chicken for even browning and rearrange if some pieces are browning faster than others.) Turn chicken pieces over and continue to fry, uncovered, until chicken pieces are deep golden brown on second side and breasts register 160 degrees and thighs and drumsticks register 175 degrees, 6 to 8 minutes. Using tongs, transfer chicken to prepared platter; let stand for 5 minutes. Serve.

Extra-Crunchy Fried Chicken

VARIATION

Extra-Spicy, Extra-Crunchy Fried Chicken

Add ¼ cup hot sauce to buttermilk mixture in step 1. Substitute 2 tablespoons cayenne pepper and 2 teaspoons chili powder for dried thyme and garlic powder.

NOTES FROM THE TEST KITCHEN

SECRET INGREDIENT: BAKING POWDER
Baking powder is composed of an acid and an alkali and acts like a salt: The salt helps draw moisture to the surface of the poultry skin, where it can evaporate. (Adding table salt to the baking powder enhances this effect.) The acid helps break down proteins within the skin, and the alkali accelerates the browning process, meaning that the skin can crisp more quickly.

Cast Iron Easier Fried Chicken

Serves 4 **Total Time** 1¼ hours

Why This Recipe Works Juicy, crisp bone-in fried chicken is a cast iron classic. While we love a classic fried chicken recipe, we wanted to come up with a faster alternative that still ensured chicken with a moist, perfectly seasoned interior and a super-crunchy crust. To start, we brined the chicken in salted buttermilk, and for a perfectly crunchy coating, we combined flour with a little baking powder and some seasonings, then added more buttermilk to make a thick, craggy coating that became crisp when fried. We briefly shallow-fried the chicken in a cast-iron skillet, and then to finish cooking, we moved the pieces to a hot oven (perched on a wire rack set in a sheet pan to prevent burnt spots and promote air circulation around the meat). This hybrid method gave us perfectly crisp, evenly cooked results. Any combination of chicken pieces will work well here; just be sure the total amount equals 2½ pounds. You will need a 12-inch cast-iron skillet with at least 2-inch sides for this recipe. Do not use kosher chicken for this recipe and don't let the chicken soak in the brine for longer than 1 hour or it will be too salty. Covering the skillet with a splatter screen will reduce the mess that frying inevitably makes.

- 1   cup buttermilk for brining
- 1   tablespoon table salt for brining
- 1   tablespoon pepper, divided
- 1¼ teaspoons garlic powder, divided
- 1¼ teaspoons paprika, divided
- ½   teaspoon cayenne pepper, divided
- 2½ pounds bone-in chicken pieces (split breasts halved crosswise, drumsticks, and/or thighs), trimmed
- 2   cups all-purpose flour
- 2   teaspoons baking powder
- 1   teaspoon table salt
- ¼   cup buttermilk
- 1   quart peanut or vegetable oil

1. Whisk 1 cup buttermilk, 1 tablespoon salt, 1 teaspoon pepper, ¼ teaspoon garlic powder, ¼ teaspoon paprika, and ¼ teaspoon cayenne together in large bowl. Add chicken, cover, and refrigerate for at least 30 minutes or up to 1 hour.

2. Meanwhile, adjust oven rack to middle position and heat oven to 400 degrees. Whisk flour, baking powder, salt, remaining 2 teaspoons pepper, remaining 1 teaspoon garlic powder, remaining 1 teaspoon paprika, and remaining ¼ teaspoon cayenne together in large bowl. Add buttermilk and rub into flour mixture using your hands until evenly incorporated and small clumps form. Working with 1 piece of chicken at a time, dredge in flour mixture, pressing gently to adhere, then transfer to large plate.

3. Set wire rack in rimmed baking sheet. Heat oil in 12-inch cast-iron skillet over medium-high heat to 375 degrees.

4. Carefully place half of chicken skin side down in oil. Fry until deep golden brown, about 6 minutes, turning chicken over halfway through frying. Adjust burner, if necessary, to maintain oil temperature between 350 and 375 degrees. Transfer chicken to prepared rack. Return oil to 375 degrees and repeat with remaining chicken; transfer to prepared rack.

5. Bake chicken until breasts register 160 degrees and drumsticks/thighs register 175 degrees, 12 to 18 minutes. Serve.

Gluten-Free Fried Chicken

Serves 4 **Total Time** 1½ hours (plus 1 hour brining time)

Why This Recipe Works There are many different methods for frying chicken, but recipes usually involve flour; its protein helps the coating cling to the chicken and its starch ensures that the coating will be brown and crisp. For a gluten-free version, we settled on cornstarch and cornmeal as the perfect substitute that still delivered a crackly crust. We started by lightly coating the chicken in cornstarch, then dipping it in a buttermilk-egg mixture bolstered with baking soda and baking powder for lightness and lift, and finally dredging it in a coating of seasoned cornstarch and cornmeal. Letting the dredged chicken sit for 30 minutes before frying evenly hydrated the coating and prevented dry spots. This chicken fried up just as juicy, crisp, and brown as the traditional standby. Skinless chicken pieces are an acceptable substitute, but the meat will come out slightly drier. Do not use kosher chicken for this recipe and don't let the chicken soak in the brine for longer than 1 hour or it will be too salty. Check labels to be sure that your baking powder and cornmeal are gluten-free. Use a Dutch oven that holds 6 quarts or more for this recipe.

- ¼   cup table salt for brining
- ¼   cup sugar for brining
- 3½ pounds bone-in chicken pieces (split breasts halved crosswise, drumsticks, and/or thighs), trimmed
- 1   cup cornstarch, divided
- 1   large egg
- 1   teaspoon baking powder
- ½   teaspoon baking soda
- 1   cup buttermilk
- 1   cup cornmeal
- 1½ teaspoons garlic powder
- 1½ teaspoons paprika
- 1   teaspoon table salt
- ¼   teaspoon cayenne pepper
- 3   quarts peanut or vegetable oil for frying

1. Whisk 1 quart cold water, ¼ cup salt, and sugar in large bowl until sugar and salt dissolve. Add chicken, cover, and refrigerate for 1 hour. Remove chicken from brine and pat dry with paper towels. Set wire rack in rimmed baking sheet.

2. Place ½ cup cornstarch in large zipper-lock bag. Beat egg, baking powder, and baking soda together in medium bowl; stir in buttermilk (mixture will bubble and foam). Whisk remaining ½ cup cornstarch, cornmeal, garlic powder, paprika, salt, and cayenne together in shallow dish.

3. Working with half of chicken at a time, place chicken in bag of cornstarch, seal bag, and shake bag to coat chicken. Using tongs, remove chicken pieces from bag, shaking off excess cornstarch, dip in buttermilk mixture, then coat with cornmeal mixture, pressing gently to adhere. Place dredged chicken on prepared wire rack, skin side up. Cover loosely with plastic wrap and let sit for 30 minutes.

4. Meanwhile, adjust oven rack to middle position and heat oven to 200 degrees. Line large plate with triple layer of paper towels. Set second wire rack in second rimmed baking sheet. Heat oil in large Dutch oven over medium-high heat to 350 degrees.

5. Carefully place half of chicken in pot skin side down. Cover and fry, stirring occasionally to prevent pieces from sticking together, until deep golden brown, 7 to 11 minutes. Adjust burner, if necessary, to maintain oil temperature between 300 and 325 degrees. (After 4 minutes, check chicken pieces for even browning and rearrange if some pieces are browning faster than others.) Turn chicken pieces over and continue to cook until breasts register 160 degrees and drumsticks/thighs register 175 degrees, 6 to 8 minutes. (Remove pieces from pot as they reach correct temperature.) Drain chicken briefly on prepared plate, then transfer to second prepared rack and place in oven to keep warm.

6. Return oil to 350 degrees and repeat with remaining chicken. Serve.

Batter-Fried Chicken

Serves 4 to 6   **Total Time** 1¼ hours

Why This Recipe Works Batter frying chicken is an old-fashioned technique where the chicken is dipped in a mixture similar to pancake batter and shallow-fried in lard. Using equal parts cornstarch and flour in the batter ensured a crisp crust on the chicken, and baking powder added lift and lightness. We flavored our batter with black pepper, paprika, and cayenne. We preferred deep-frying the chicken pieces to ensure that the chicken bobbed in the oil and cooked evenly (and didn't stick to the bottom). The finished chicken was juicy and had a picture-perfect, golden-brown crust. Do not use kosher

Gluten-Free Fried Chicken

Cast Iron Easier Fried Chicken

Buttermilk Coleslaw

Serves 4 to 6   **Total Time** 45 minutes (plus 1 hour salting time)

This crisp and creamy coleslaw makes an excellent side for fried chicken.

½ head red or green cabbage, cored, quartered, and shredded (6 cups)
¼ teaspoon table salt, plus salt for salting cabbage
1 carrot, peeled and shredded
½ cup buttermilk
2 tablespoons mayonnaise
2 tablespoons sour cream
1 small shallot, minced
2 tablespoons minced fresh parsley
½ teaspoon cider vinegar
½ teaspoon sugar
¼ teaspoon Dijon mustard
⅛ teaspoon pepper

1. Toss shredded cabbage and 1 teaspoon salt in colander set over large bowl and let sit until wilted, at least 1 hour or up to 4 hours. Rinse cabbage under cold running water. Press, but do not squeeze, to drain, and blot dry with paper towels.

2. Combine wilted cabbage and carrot in large bowl. In separate bowl, whisk buttermilk, mayonnaise, sour cream, shallot, parsley, vinegar, sugar, mustard, pepper, and salt together. Pour dressing over cabbage and toss to combine. Refrigerate until chilled, about 30 minutes. Serve. (Coleslaw can be refrigerated for up to 3 days.)

VARIATIONS

Buttermilk Coleslaw with Scallions and Cilantro

Omit mustard. Substitute 1 tablespoon minced fresh cilantro for parsley and 1 tablespoon lime juice for cider vinegar. Add 2 thinly sliced scallions to dressing.

Lemony Buttermilk Coleslaw

Substitute 1 teaspoon lemon juice for cider vinegar. Add 1 teaspoon minced fresh thyme and 1 tablespoon minced fresh chives to dressing.

Batter-Fried Chicken

chicken for this recipe and don't let the chicken soak in the brine for longer than 1 hour or it will be too salty. Use a Dutch oven that holds 6 quarts or more for this recipe.

¼ cup table salt for brining
¼ cup sugar for brining
3½ pounds bone-in chicken pieces (split breasts halved crosswise, drumsticks, and/or thighs), trimmed
1 cup all-purpose flour
1 cup cornstarch
5 teaspoons pepper
2 teaspoons baking powder
1 teaspoon table salt
1 teaspoon paprika
½ teaspoon cayenne pepper
3 quarts peanut or vegetable oil for frying

1. Dissolve ¼ cup salt and sugar in 1 quart cold water in large bowl until dissolved. Add chicken and refrigerate for at least 30 minutes or up to 1 hour.

2. Whisk flour, cornstarch, pepper, baking powder, salt, paprika, cayenne, and 1¾ cups cold water in large bowl until smooth. Refrigerate batter while chicken is brining.

3. Meanwhile, adjust oven rack to middle position and heat oven to 200 degrees. Line large plate with triple layer of paper towels. Set wire rack in rimmed baking sheet. Heat oil in large Dutch oven over medium-high heat to 350 degrees.

4. Remove chicken from brine and pat dry with paper towels. Rewhisk batter. Transfer half of chicken to batter. One piece at a time, remove chicken from batter (allowing excess to drip back into bowl) and carefully place in pot. Fry chicken, adjusting burner as necessary to maintain oil temperature between 300 and 325 degrees, until deep golden brown and breasts register 160 degrees and drumsticks/thighs register 175 degrees, 12 to 15 minutes. (Remove pieces from pot as they reach correct temperature.) Let chicken drain briefly on prepared plate, then transfer to prepared rack and place in oven to keep warm.

5. Return oil to 350 degrees and repeat with remaining chicken. Serve.

Honey-Dipped Fried Chicken
Serves 4   **Total Time** 1½ hours

Why This Recipe Works Honey-dipped fried chicken should be juicy and tender, with a crispy, honey-kissed coating—it's a fantastic combination of crunch, heat, and sweet. After a dusting of cornstarch, we dipped our brined chicken in a thin cornstarch-and-water batter, but the key find for a crunchy crust was double frying. We partially fried the chicken and let it rest to allow moisture from the skin to evaporate before frying a second time. A dunk in a mixture of honey and hot sauce gave this chicken an irresistibly sticky coating. Do not use kosher chicken for this recipe and don't let the chicken soak in the brine for longer than 1 hour or it will be too salty. Use a Dutch oven that holds 6 quarts or more for this recipe.

Chicken
- ½ cup table salt for brining
- ½ cup sugar for brining
- 3½ pounds bone-in chicken pieces (split breasts halved crosswise, drumsticks, and/or thighs), trimmed
- 1½ cups cornstarch, divided
- 2 teaspoons pepper
- 1 teaspoon table salt
- 3 quarts peanut or vegetable oil for frying

Honey Glaze
- ¾ cup honey
- 2 tablespoons hot sauce

1. For the chicken Dissolve ½ cup salt and sugar in 2 quarts cold water in large bowl. Add chicken, cover, and refrigerate for 30 minutes or up to 1 hour. Whisk 1 cup cornstarch, ¾ cup cold water, pepper, and salt in bowl until smooth. Refrigerate batter while chicken is brining.

2. Sift remaining ½ cup cornstarch into medium bowl. Remove chicken from brine and dry thoroughly with paper towels. Working with 1 piece at a time, coat chicken thoroughly with cornstarch, shaking to remove excess; transfer to platter.

3. Set wire rack in rimmed baking sheet. Heat oil in large Dutch oven over medium-high heat to 350 degrees.

4. Whisk batter to recombine. Transfer half of chicken to batter and turn to coat. Remove chicken from batter, allowing excess to drip back into bowl, and add chicken to hot oil. Fry chicken, stirring to prevent pieces from sticking together, until slightly golden and just beginning to crisp, 5 to 7 minutes. Adjust burner, if necessary, to maintain oil temperature between 325 and 350 degrees. (Chicken will not be cooked through at this point.) Transfer parcooked chicken to platter. Return oil to 350 degrees and repeat with remaining raw chicken and batter. Let each batch of chicken rest for 5 to 7 minutes.

5. Return oil to 350 degrees. Return first batch of chicken to oil and fry until breasts register 160 degrees and drumsticks/thighs register 175 degrees, 5 to 7 minutes. (Remove pieces from pot as they reach correct temperature.) Transfer to prepared wire rack. Return oil to 350 degrees and repeat with remaining chicken.

6. For the honey glaze Combine honey and hot sauce in large bowl and microwave until hot, about 1½ minutes. Add chicken pieces one at a time to honey mixture and turn to coat; return to wire rack, skin side up, to drain. Serve.

Garlic Fried Chicken
Serves 4   **Total Time** 1¼ hours (plus 1 hour marinating time)

Why This Recipe Works Savory garlic can make fried chicken even more lip-smackingly good. To deeply season the chicken, we marinated it in a mixture of extra-virgin olive oil, fresh minced garlic, and granulated garlic for at least an hour. To ensure that the coating adhered to the chicken, we dipped pieces in egg whites before dredging them in flour seasoned with more granulated garlic, salt, and pepper. For the sauce, we sautéed some minced garlic in just 1 tablespoon of butter and a little water (the water kept the garlic from burning) before combining the mixture with more butter and parsley. Use a Dutch oven that holds 6 quarts or more for this recipe. Mince the garlic with a knife rather than with a garlic press.

Garlic Fried Chicken

Koji Fried Chicken

Chicken

- 3 tablespoons extra-virgin olive oil
- 2 tablespoons granulated garlic, divided
- 5 garlic cloves, minced
- 4 teaspoons pepper, divided
- 2 teaspoons table salt, divided
- 3½ pounds bone-in chicken pieces (split breasts halved crosswise, drumsticks, thighs, and/or wings), trimmed
- 2 cups all-purpose flour
- 4 large egg whites
- 3 quarts peanut or vegetable oil for frying

Garlic Butter

- 8 tablespoons unsalted butter, softened, divided
- 2 tablespoons minced fresh parsley
- ¼ teaspoon pepper
- ⅛ teaspoon table salt
- 8 garlic cloves, minced
- 1 tablespoon water

1. For the chicken Combine olive oil, 1 tablespoon granulated garlic, minced garlic, 2 teaspoons pepper, and 1 teaspoon salt in large bowl. Add chicken and toss to thoroughly coat with garlic mixture. Cover with plastic wrap and refrigerate for at least 1 hour or up to 24 hours.

2. Set wire rack in rimmed baking sheet. Whisk flour, remaining 1 tablespoon granulated garlic, remaining 2 teaspoons pepper, and remaining 1 teaspoon salt together in separate bowl. Lightly beat egg whites together in shallow dish.

3. Remove chicken from marinade and brush away any solidified clumps of oil with paper towels. Working with 1 piece at a time, dip chicken into egg whites to thoroughly coat, letting excess drip back into dish; then dredge in flour mixture, pressing firmly to adhere. Transfer chicken to prepared wire rack and refrigerate, uncovered, for at least 30 minutes or up to 2 hours.

4. Meanwhile, adjust oven rack to middle position and heat oven to 200 degrees. Line large plate with triple layer of paper towels. Set second wire rack in second rimmed baking sheet. Heat peanut oil in large Dutch oven to 325 degrees. Add half of chicken to hot oil and fry until breasts register 160 degrees and drumsticks/thighs register 175 degrees, 13 to 16 minutes. (Remove pieces from pot as they reach correct temperature.) Adjust burner, if necessary, to maintain oil temperature between 300 and 325 degrees. Let chicken drain briefly on prepared plate, then transfer to second prepared rack and place in oven to keep warm. Return oil to 325 degrees and repeat with remaining chicken.

5. For the garlic butter While chicken rests, combine 7 tablespoons butter, parsley, pepper, and salt in bowl; set aside. Melt remaining 1 tablespoon butter in 8-inch nonstick skillet over medium heat. Add garlic and water and cook, stirring frequently, until garlic is softened and fragrant, 1 to 2 minutes. Add hot garlic mixture to butter-parsley mixture and whisk until well combined.

6. Transfer chicken to platter and spoon garlic butter over top. Serve.

Koji Fried Chicken
Serves 4 to 6   **Total Time** 1 hour (plus 9½ hours chilling time and 7 days curing time)

Why This Recipe Works Shio koji is a traditional use of koji, the ancient mold that gives us soy sauce, miso, fermented bean paste, and sake. It is made by adding water and salt to cooked rice that has been inoculated with koji spores and dried and then letting the mixture ferment for about a week, during which time it develops a sweet, fruity, slightly funky aroma. Shio koji is primarily used as a marinade and it can transform many foods. We wanted to take advantage of its amazing tenderizing and flavor-boosting properties to make fried chicken, so we marinated chicken parts in about a half-cup of shio koji for a good long time. We then dunked the chicken in buttermilk and dredged it in a mixture of cornstarch, flour, and dried granular rice koji. We used a fry-and-then-bake method to prevent the sugar-rich rice koji in the coating from burning; the resulting chicken was deeply meaty and juicy, with a golden-brown, crunchtastic crust. This recipe improves with age: The longer you marinate the chicken (up to three days), the better and meatier it gets. And the longer you let the dredge sit on the chicken (up to 24 hours), the better and crispier the crust becomes. There are a few options for buying rice koji. Some well stocked high-end supermarkets carry it, but for the majority of us, online is the best option. Use a Dutch oven that holds 6 quarts or more for this recipe.

3½ pounds bone-in chicken pieces (split breasts halved crosswise, drumsticks, and/or thighs), trimmed

7 tablespoons Shio Koji

1 cup cornstarch

½ cup plus ⅓ cup all-purpose flour

½ cup plus 2 tablespoons firm granular rice koji

1 tablespoon kosher salt, divided, plus extra for seasoning

2 teaspoons pepper, divided

1 teaspoon baking powder

1 cup buttermilk

1½ quarts peanut or vegetable oil for frying

1. Combine chicken and shio koji in 1-gallon zipper-lock bag. Press out excess air, seal, and massage bag to evenly distribute shio koji. Refrigerate chicken for at least 8 hours or up to 3 days.

2. Combine cornstarch, flour, koji, 2 teaspoons salt, 1 teaspoon pepper, and baking powder in blender and process on high speed until finely ground, about 2 minutes. Transfer koji mixture to large shallow dish. Whisk buttermilk, remaining 1 teaspoon salt, and remaining 1 teaspoon pepper in large bowl. Working with 3 pieces at a time, dunk chicken in buttermilk mixture, then dredge in flour mixture, pressing mixture onto chicken to form thick, even coating. Place chicken, skin side up, on wire rack set in rimmed baking sheet. Refrigerate, uncovered, for at least 1½ hours or up to 24 hours.

3. Adjust oven rack to middle position and heat oven to 350 degrees. Set second wire rack in second rimmed baking sheet. Meanwhile, heat oil in large Dutch oven over medium-high heat to 375 degrees. Place half of chicken in oil, reduce heat to medium, and fry until first side is deep golden brown, 2 to 3 minutes. Flip chicken and continue to fry until second side is deep golden brown, 2 to 3 minutes longer. (Adjust heat

---

Shio Koji
Makes about 1 quart   **Total Time** 7 days
We prefer using a plastic food storage container for this recipe, but any medium (1-quart or more) food-safe container will work. There are a few options for buying rice koji. Some well-stocked high-end supermarkets carry it, but for the majority of us, online is the best option. See Koji Turkey (page 245) for another way to use Shio Koji.

1¾ cups water

2¼ cups firm granular rice koji

9 tablespoons kosher salt

In medium saucepan, heat water to 140 degrees. Combine hot water, koji, and salt in lidded container and whisk until salt is dissolved, about 30 seconds. Cover with lid and let ferment at room temperature until mixture is thickened and smells sweet, fruity, and slightly funky, at least 7 days or up to 14 days, stirring once per day. After initial fermentation, store in refrigerator for up to 6 months.

as necessary to maintain oil temperature around 300 degrees.) Transfer chicken to clean wire rack. Return oil to 375 degrees and repeat with remaining chicken.

4. Bake chicken until breasts register 160 degrees and thighs/drumsticks register 170 degrees, 10 to 20 minutes, transferring pieces to platter as they reach correct temperature. Season chicken with salt to taste, and serve.

Nashville Hot Fried Chicken

Serves 4 to 6

Total Time 1¼ hours (plus 30 minutes brining time)

Why This Recipe Works The slow burn of Nashville hot fried chicken is well worth reproducing at home. We found that quartering the chicken instead of cutting it into the typical eight pieces was key—the larger pieces of meat balanced out the heat in this recipe. Speaking of heat, we added a healthy amount of hot sauce to our brine to inject spicy flavor into the chicken from the start, making the flavor more than skin deep. We then created a spicy exterior to the chicken by "blooming" the spices (cooking them in oil for a short period) to create a complex yet still lip-burning spicy flavor. This chicken was pretty darn spicy, but for the brave of palate, we came up with an extra-hot version. Do not use kosher chicken for this recipe and don't let the chicken soak in the brine for longer than 1 hour or it will be too salty. To quarter a chicken, start by removing the leg quarters (see page 12) then remove the backbone (see page 11). Finally, cut through the breastbone to separate the breast and wing sections into halves. Chicken quarters take longer to cook than smaller pieces. To ensure that the exterior doesn't burn before the inside cooks through, keep the oil temperature between 300 and 325 degrees while the chicken is frying. Use a Dutch oven that holds 6 quarts or more for this recipe. Serve on white bread with pickles.

- ½ **cup hot sauce for brining**
- ½ **cup table salt for brining**
- ½ **cup sugar for brining**
- 1 **(3½- to 4-pound) whole chicken, giblets discarded, quartered**
- 3 **tablespoons peanut or vegetable oil**
- 1 **tablespoon cayenne pepper**
- 1 **teaspoon table salt, divided**
- ½ **teaspoon paprika**
- ½ **teaspoon sugar**
- ¼ **teaspoon garlic powder**
- 2 **cups all-purpose flour**
- ½ **teaspoon pepper**
- 3 **quarts peanut or vegetable oil for frying**

Nashville Hot Fried Chicken

1. Whisk 2 quarts cold water, hot sauce, ½ cup salt, and ½ cup sugar in large bowl until salt and sugar dissolve. Add chicken and refrigerate, covered, for 30 minutes or up to 1 hour.

2. Heat 3 tablespoons oil in small saucepan over medium heat until shimmering. Add cayenne, ½ teaspoon salt, paprika, sugar, and garlic powder and cook until fragrant, about 30 seconds. Transfer to small bowl.

3. Remove chicken from brine and dry thoroughly with paper towels. Combine flour, pepper, and remaining ½ teaspoon salt in large bowl. Dredge chicken pieces two at a time in flour mixture. Shake excess flour from chicken and transfer to wire rack. (Do not discard seasoned flour.)

4. Adjust oven rack to middle position and heat oven to 200 degrees. Line large plate with triple layer of paper towels. Set second wire rack in second rimmed baking sheet. Heat 3 quarts oil in large Dutch oven over medium-high heat to 350 degrees. Return chicken pieces to flour mixture and turn to coat. Fry half of chicken, adjusting burner as necessary to maintain oil temperature between 300 and 325 degrees, until deep golden brown and breasts register 160 degrees and legs register 175 degrees, 20 to 25 minutes. (Remove pieces from pot as they reach correct temperature.) Drain chicken on second prepared rack and place in oven to keep warm.

5. Return oil to 350 degrees and repeat with remaining chicken. Stir spicy oil mixture to recombine and brush over both sides of chicken. Serve.

VARIATION
Nashville Extra-Hot Fried Chicken
In step 2, increase oil to ¼ cup, cayenne to 3½ tablespoons, and sugar to ¾ teaspoon and add 1 teaspoon dry mustard.

Picnic Fried Chicken

Serves 4   Total Time 1¼ hours (plus 1 hour brining time)

Why This Recipe Works For fried chicken that's crispy and delicious even when cold, we pulled out a few tricks. A combination of Wondra flour and cornstarch made for a coat that kept its crunch, and dredging the chicken twice with a water dip in between created a thick, craggy crust. Double-frying the chicken allowed extra moisture to evaporate from the skin, and chilling it uncovered further guarded against sogginess. Finally, since cold dulls flavors, we made sure to brine the chicken and to season the flour coating heavily. We like it best the day it's made, but you can refrigerate this fried chicken for up to 24 hours. Do not use kosher chicken for this recipe and don't let the chicken soak in the brine for longer than 1 hour or it will be too salty. Use a Dutch oven that holds 6 quarts or more for this recipe.

- ¼ cup table salt for brining
- 3 pounds bone-in chicken pieces (split breasts halved crosswise, drumsticks, and/or thighs), trimmed
- 1½ cups Wondra flour
- 1½ cups cornstarch
- 1 tablespoon pepper
- 2 teaspoons white pepper
- 1½ teaspoons baking powder
- 1 teaspoon dried thyme
- 1 teaspoon dried sage leaves
- 1 teaspoon garlic powder
- 1 teaspoon table salt
- ¼ teaspoon cayenne pepper
- 3 quarts peanut or vegetable oil for frying

1. Dissolve ¼ cup salt in 1 quart cold water in large bowl. Submerge chicken in brine, cover, and refrigerate for 1 hour.

2. While chicken is brining, whisk flour and cornstarch together in large bowl. Transfer 1 cup flour mixture to shallow dish; set aside. Whisk pepper, white pepper, baking powder, thyme, sage, garlic powder, salt, and cayenne into remaining

flour mixture. Add ¼ cup water to seasoned flour mixture. Rub flour and water together with your fingers until water is evenly incorporated and mixture contains craggy bits of dough. Pour 2 cups cold water into medium bowl.

3. Set wire rack in rimmed baking sheet. Working with 2 pieces of chicken at a time, remove chicken from brine and dip in unseasoned flour mixture, pressing to adhere; dunk quickly in water, letting excess drip off; and dredge in seasoned flour mixture, pressing to adhere. Place chicken on prepared wire rack and refrigerate for at least 30 minutes or up to 2 hours.

4. Heat oil in large Dutch oven over medium-high heat to 350 degrees. Fry half of chicken until slightly golden and just beginning to crisp, 5 to 7 minutes. Adjust burner, if necessary, to maintain oil temperature between 300 and 325 degrees. (Chicken will not be cooked through at this point.) Return parcooked chicken to wire rack. Return oil to 350 degrees and repeat with remaining raw chicken. Let each batch of chicken rest for 5 to 7 minutes.

5. Return oil to 350 degrees. Return first batch of chicken to oil and fry until breasts register 160 degrees and thighs/drumsticks register 175 degrees, 5 to 7 minutes. (Remove pieces from pot as they reach correct temperature.) Adjust burner, if necessary, to maintain oil temperature between 300 and 325 degrees. Transfer chicken to clean wire rack. Return oil to 350 degrees and repeat with remaining chicken. Let chicken cool to room temperature, transfer to paper towel–lined plate, and refrigerate uncovered until ready to eat, up to 24 hours in advance. (Serve cold or let chicken come to room temperature.)

Garlic-Lime Fried Chicken

Serves 4   Total Time 1½ hours (plus 1 hour marinating time)

Why This Recipe Works For a version of fried chicken with zesty flavors, we started with a potent marinade, combining plenty of fresh lime juice and zest with garlic, cumin, paprika, and oregano. We left the garlic coarsely chopped, which made it easier to scrape off the chicken parts before frying (we didn't want any pieces of burnt garlic in our crust). We added spices to a simple flour coating, along with cornstarch and baking powder for an extra-crispy, light crust. Dipping the chicken in egg whites before coating it further enhanced the light texture, and after frying, our chicken was crunchy, juicy, and golden brown. Don't let the chicken marinate any longer than 2 hours or it will toughen from the lime juice. Use a Dutch oven that holds 6 quarts or more for this recipe. Serve with lime wedges.

Marinade

- 2 tablespoons kosher salt for marinade
- 6 garlic cloves, chopped coarse
- 1 tablespoon pepper
- 1 tablespoon ground cumin
- 2 teaspoons smoked paprika
- 2 teaspoons dried oregano
- 2 teaspoons grated lime zest plus ¼ cup juice (2 limes)
- 3½ pounds bone-in chicken pieces (split breasts halved crosswise, drumsticks, thighs, and/or wings), trimmed

Coating

- 1¼ cups all-purpose flour
- ¾ cup cornstarch
- 1 tablespoon pepper
- 1 tablespoon granulated garlic
- 1 teaspoon baking powder
- 1 teaspoon white pepper
- 1 teaspoon kosher salt
- 1 teaspoon ground cumin
- ¼ teaspoon cayenne pepper
- 3 large egg whites, lightly beaten
- 3 quarts peanut or vegetable oil for frying

1. For the marinade Combine salt, garlic, pepper, cumin, paprika, oregano, and lime zest and juice in bowl. Add chicken and turn to coat thoroughly. Cover with plastic wrap and refrigerate for at least 1 hour or up to 2 hours.

2. For the coating Whisk flour, cornstarch, pepper, granulated garlic, baking powder, white pepper, salt, cumin, and cayenne together in bowl. Place egg whites in shallow dish.

3. Set wire rack in rimmed baking sheet. Remove chicken from marinade and scrape off solids. Pat chicken dry with paper towels. Working with 1 piece at a time, dip chicken into egg whites to thoroughly coat, letting excess drip back into dish. Dredge chicken in flour mixture, pressing to adhere. Transfer chicken to prepared wire rack and refrigerate for at least 30 minutes or up to 2 hours.

4. Meanwhile, adjust oven rack to middle position and heat oven to 200 degrees. Line large plate with triple layer of paper towels. Set second wire rack in second rimmed baking sheet. Heat oil in large Dutch oven over medium-high heat to 325 degrees.

5. Add half of chicken to hot oil and fry until breasts register 160 degrees and drumsticks/thighs register 175 degrees, 13 to 16 minutes. (Remove pieces from pot as they reach correct temperature.) Adjust burner, if necessary, to maintain oil temperature between 300 and 325 degrees. Let chicken drain briefly on prepared plate, then transfer to second prepared rack and place in oven to keep warm. Return oil to 325 degrees and repeat with remaining chicken. Serve.

Authentic Maryland Fried Chicken and Gravy

Serves 4 to 6   Total Time 1½ hours

Why This Recipe Works In Maryland, fried chicken is marked by a thin, crisp crust, standout seasoning, and a dribble of peppery cream gravy. To get our version of this chicken on the right track, we injected a kick of spicy flavor with a generous dose of dry mustard, salt, and garlic powder. Dredging in flour and baking powder and then refrigerating the seasoned chicken before frying in peanut oil made for an extra-crisp coating. A sprinkling of Old Bay on the just-fried pieces reinforced the chicken's bold seasoning. For the gravy, we used some of the remaining frying oil in our pot to brown flour and then whisked in chicken broth, heavy cream, and pepper. Use a Dutch oven that holds 6 quarts or more for this recipe.

Fried Chicken

- 4 pounds bone-in chicken pieces (split breasts halved crosswise, drumsticks, and/or thighs), trimmed
- 1 tablespoon dry mustard
- 1 tablespoon garlic powder
- 1 teaspoon table salt
- 2 cups all-purpose flour
- 1 teaspoon baking powder
- 3 cups peanut or vegetable oil for frying
  Old Bay seasoning

Cream Gravy

- ¼ cup all-purpose flour
- 2 cups chicken broth
- 1 cup heavy cream
- 1 teaspoon pepper

1. For the fried chicken Pat chicken dry with paper towels. Combine mustard, garlic powder, and salt in small bowl and sprinkle mixture evenly over chicken. Combine flour and baking powder in shallow dish. Working with 1 piece at a time, dredge chicken in flour mixture until well coated, shaking off excess. Transfer to plate and refrigerate for at least 30 minutes or up to 2 hours.

2. Meanwhile, adjust oven rack to middle position and heat oven to 200 degrees. Set wire rack in rimmed baking sheet. Heat oil in large Dutch oven over medium-high heat to 375 degrees.

3. Place half of chicken skin side down in pot, cover, and fry until well browned, about 10 minutes, turning chicken over halfway through frying. Reduce heat to medium, adjusting burner, if necessary, to maintain oil temperature between 300 and 325 degrees. Cook, uncovered and turning chicken as needed, until breasts register 160 degrees and drumsticks/ thighs register 175 degrees, about 5 minutes. (Remove pieces from pot as they reach correct temperature.) Transfer chicken to prepared wire rack, season with Old Bay, and keep warm in oven. Return oil to 375 degrees and repeat with remaining chicken.

4. For the cream gravy Pour off all but ¼ cup oil from pot. Stir in flour and cook until golden, about 2 minutes. Slowly whisk in broth, cream, and pepper and simmer gravy until thickened, about 5 minutes. Season with salt to taste. Serve chicken with gravy.

Oven-Fried Chicken

Serves 8   Total Time 1 hour (plus 1 hour marinating time)

Why This Recipe Works We wanted to mimic the juicy meat and crunchy exterior of fried chicken but in a more hands-off method for when you don't feel like standing over the stove. First, we soaked chicken pieces in highly seasoned buttermilk flavored with mustard, garlic powder, black pepper, and hot pepper sauce. Soaking the chicken for at least 1 hour or, even better, overnight, allowed the flavors to penetrate deep into the meat. For the coating, a blend of cornflakes and bread crumbs, seasoned heavily with spices and lightly coated with oil, baked up as crisp as a deep-fried crust. We baked the chicken in a hot oven on a wire rack set on a baking sheet. The rack allowed hot air to circulate beneath the chicken, ensuring that all sides of the pieces became crisp. To crush the corn-flakes, place them inside a plastic bag and use a rolling pin to break them into pieces no smaller than ½ inch. To make this recipe ahead, marinate the chicken in the buttermilk mixture and combine the dry ingredients in a zipper-lock bag (all but the oil) the night before. Heat the oven, toss the crumb mixture with oil, coat the chicken, and bake.

- 2 cups buttermilk for marinade
- 2 tablespoons Dijon mustard for marinade
- 2 teaspoons table salt for marinade
- 1½ teaspoons garlic powder, divided
- 1½ teaspoons ground black pepper, divided
- 1 teaspoon hot pepper sauce for marinade
- 8 (10- to 12-ounce) bone-in split chicken breasts, skin removed and ribs trimmed
- 2½ cups crushed cornflakes
- ¾ cup fresh bread crumbs
- ½ teaspoon ground poultry seasoning
- ½ teaspoon paprika

Oven-Fried Chicken

- ¼ teaspoon table salt
- ⅛ teaspoon cayenne pepper
- 2 tablespoons vegetable oil

1. Whisk buttermilk, mustard, 2 teaspoons salt, 1 teaspoon garlic powder, 1 teaspoon black pepper, and hot sauce together in large bowl. Add chicken, turn to coat well, cover, and refrigerate at least 1 hour or overnight.

2. Adjust oven rack to upper-middle position and heat oven to 400 degrees. Line rimmed baking sheet with foil, set wire rack on sheet, and coat rack with nonstick cooking spray.

3. Gently toss cornflakes, bread crumbs, poultry seasoning, paprika, salt, cayenne, remaining ½ teaspoon garlic powder, and remaining ½ teaspoon black pepper in shallow dish until combined. Drizzle oil over crumbs and toss until well coated. Working with 1 piece at a time, remove chicken from marinade and dredge in crumb mixture, firmly pressing crumbs onto all sides of chicken. Place chicken on prepared rack, leaving ½ inch of space between each piece. Bake until chicken is deep golden brown and registers 160 degrees and juices run clear, 35 to 45 minutes. Serve.

Buttermilk Oven-Fried Chicken

Serves 4   **Total Time** 1¼ hours

Why This Recipe Works For our buttermilk oven-fried chicken, we added ranch dressing mix and sour cream to the buttermilk brine to up the tanginess factor and thicken the liquid even more so that the bread-crumb coating stayed put. Adding ranch dressing mix to the bread crumbs further enhanced the buttermilk flavor. Do not use kosher chicken for this recipe and don't let the chicken soak in the brine for longer than 1 hour or it will be too salty. Use any combination of white and dark meat. For even cooking, halve breasts crosswise and separate leg quarters into thighs and drumsticks.

- 2 cups buttermilk for brining
- ¼ cup sour cream for brining
- 1 (1-ounce) envelope ranch seasoning mix, divided
- 1 tablespoon table salt for brining
- 3½ pounds bone-in chicken pieces (split breasts halved crosswise, drumsticks, and/or thighs), skin removed, trimmed
- 5 slices hearty white sandwich bread, torn into pieces
  Vegetable oil spray

1. Adjust oven racks to middle and lowest positions and heat oven to 450 degrees. Whisk buttermilk, sour cream, 2 tablespoons ranch seasoning mix, and salt in large bowl until salt dissolves. Add chicken and toss to coat. Refrigerate, covered, 30 minutes or up to 1 hour.

2. Meanwhile, pulse bread and remaining ranch seasoning mix in food processor until finely ground. Bake bread crumbs on rimmed baking sheet on middle rack, stirring occasionally, until light golden, about 5 minutes. Transfer to shallow dish.

3. Line rimmed baking sheet with foil and spray lightly with oil spray. Remove chicken from bowl (allowing excess brine to drip back into bowl) and dredge in bread crumbs, pressing to adhere. Transfer coated chicken to prepared baking sheet and spray lightly with oil spray.

4. Bake on lower rack until bottom of chicken is golden brown, about 10 minutes. Move baking sheet to upper rack and reduce oven temperature to 400 degrees. Bake until chicken is golden brown and breasts register 160 degrees and drumsticks/thighs register 175 degrees, 20 to 25 minutes. Serve.

Korean Fried Chicken Wings

Korean Fried Chicken Wings

Serves 4 to 6   **Total Time** 1 hour

Why This Recipe Works A thin, crispy exterior and a spicy-sweet-salty sauce are the hallmarks of Korean fried chicken. The biggest challenge is preventing the sauce from destroying the crust. Wings offer a high exterior-to-interior ratio for maximum crunch and also cook quickly, so we went with those. We dunked them in a loose batter of flour, cornstarch, and water, which clung nicely to the chicken and fried up brown and crispy. To help the coating withstand a wet sauce, we double-fried the wings, which removed more water from the skin than a single fry did, making the coating extra-crispy. Gochujang, Korean chili paste, gave our sauce the proper spicy, fermented notes, while sugar tempered the heat and garlic and ginger—cooked briefly with sesame oil—provided depth. A rasp-style grater makes quick work of turning the garlic into a paste. Tailor the heat level of your wings by adjusting the amount of gochujang. If you can't find gochujang, substitute an equal amount of sriracha and add only 2 tablespoons of water to the sauce. Use a Dutch oven that holds 6 quarts or more for this recipe. If you buy chicken wings that are already split, with the tips removed, you will need only 2½ pounds.

1 tablespoon toasted sesame oil
1 garlic clove, minced to paste
1 teaspoon grated fresh ginger
1¾ cups water, divided
3 tablespoons sugar
2-3 tablespoons gochujang
1 tablespoon soy sauce
2 quarts peanut or vegetable oil for frying
1 cup all-purpose flour
3 tablespoons cornstarch
3 pounds chicken wings, cut at joints,
   wingtips discarded

1. Combine sesame oil, garlic, and ginger in large bowl and microwave until mixture is bubbly and garlic and ginger are fragrant but not browned, 40 to 60 seconds. Whisk in ¼ cup water, sugar, gochujang, and soy sauce until smooth; set aside.

2. Heat peanut oil in Dutch oven over medium-high heat to 350 degrees. While oil heats, whisk flour, cornstarch, and remaining 1½ cups water in second large bowl until smooth. Set wire rack in rimmed baking sheet and set aside.

3. Place half of wings in batter and stir to coat. Using tongs, remove wings from batter one at a time, allowing any excess batter to drip back into bowl, and add to hot oil. Increase heat to high and cook, stirring occasionally to prevent wings from sticking, until coating is light golden and beginning to crisp, about 7 minutes. (Oil temperature will drop sharply after adding wings.) Transfer wings to prepared rack. Return oil to 350 degrees and repeat with remaining wings. Reduce heat to medium and let second batch of wings rest for 5 minutes.

4. Heat oil to 375 degrees. Carefully return all wings to oil and cook, stirring occasionally, until deep golden brown and very crispy, about 7 minutes. Return wings to rack and let stand for 2 minutes. Transfer wings to reserved sauce and toss until coated. Return wings to rack and let stand for 2 minutes to allow coating to set. Transfer to platter and serve.

CUTTING UP CHICKEN WINGS

1. Using kitchen shears or sharp chef's knife, cut through joint between drumette and wingette.

2. Cut off and discard wingtip.

Buffalo Wings

Serves 6 to 8   **Total Time** 1 hour

Why This Recipe Works Great buffalo wings boast juicy meat; a crisp coating; and a spicy, slightly sweet, and vinegary sauce. But dry, flabby wings are often the norm and the sauce can be scorchingly hot. We wanted perfectly cooked wings, coated in a well-seasoned sauce—good enough to serve with our homemade creamy blue cheese dressing. We coated the wings with cornstarch for a supercrisp exterior; as a bonus, this makes them naturally gluten-free. We chose to deep-fry the wings (rather than roasting, sautéing, or pan-frying them) for the best texture. Then we deepened the flavor of the traditional hot sauce by adding brown sugar and cider vinegar. For heat, we chose Frank's RedHot Original Cayenne Pepper Sauce, which is traditional, but not very spicy, so we added a little Tabasco for even more kick. The fried, unsauced wings can be kept warm in the oven for up to 1½ hours. Toss them with the sauce just before serving. Use a Dutch oven that holds 6 quarts or more for this recipe. If you buy chicken wings that are already split, with the tips removed, you will need only 2½ pounds. Serve with Creamy Blue Cheese Dressing (page 299) and celery and carrot sticks.

Sauce
4 tablespoons unsalted butter
½ cup hot sauce, preferably Frank's RedHot Original
   Cayenne Pepper Sauce
2 tablespoons Tabasco sauce or other hot sauce,
   plus more to taste
1 tablespoon dark brown sugar
2 teaspoons cider vinegar

Wings
3 quarts peanut or vegetable oil for frying
3 tablespoons cornstarch
1 teaspoon table salt
1 teaspoon pepper
1 teaspoon cayenne pepper
3 pounds chicken wings, cut at joints,
   wingtips discarded

1. For the sauce Melt butter in small saucepan over low heat. Whisk in hot sauces, brown sugar, and vinegar until combined. Add extra hot sauce to taste, if desired. Remove from heat and set aside.

2. For the wings Preheat oven to 200 degrees. Line baking sheet with paper towels. Heat oil in large Dutch oven over medium-high heat to 360 degrees. While oil heats, mix cornstarch, salt, pepper, and cayenne together in small bowl. Dry chicken with paper towels and place pieces in large mixing bowl. Sprinkle spice mixture over wings and toss with rubber spatula until evenly coated. Fry half of chicken wings until golden and crisp, 10 to 15 minutes. Transfer fried chicken wings to prepared sheet and place in oven to keep warm. Return oil to 360 degrees and repeat with remaining wings.

3. Pour sauce mixture into large bowl, add chicken wings, and toss until wings are uniformly coated. Serve immediately.

Oven-Fried Chicken Wings

Serves 4 to 6   **Total Time** 1½ hours

Why This Recipe Works To get crispy chicken wings without frying, we had to find a way to dry out the skin. Our secret weapon was baking powder; it helped break down the proteins within the skin as well as aid in browning. After we tossed the wings with baking powder and salt, we started them in a low oven—on a wire rack for better air circulation—to fully dry the skin and begin rendering the fat. Then we cranked the oven to finish roasting the wings and crisping the skin. All these wings needed was a coating of flavorful sauce and they were ready to be devoured—we came up with three options, all with sweet and savory notes. If you buy chicken wings that are already split, with the tips removed, you will need only 3 ½ pounds.

- 4 pounds chicken wings, cut at joints, wingtips discarded
- 2 tablespoons baking powder
- ¾ teaspoon table salt
- 1 recipe wing sauce

1. Adjust oven racks to upper-middle and lower-middle positions and heat oven to 250 degrees. Set wire rack in aluminum foil–lined rimmed baking sheet. Pat wings dry with paper towels and transfer to 1-gallon zipper-lock bag. Combine baking powder and salt, add to wings, seal bag, and toss to evenly coat.

2. Arrange wings, skin side up, in single layer on prepared wire rack. Bake wings on lower oven rack for 30 minutes. Move wings to upper rack, increase oven temperature to 425 degrees, and roast until wings are golden brown and crispy, 40 to 50 minutes longer, rotating sheet halfway through baking. Remove sheet from oven and let stand for 5 minutes. Transfer wings to bowl with wing sauce of your choice, toss to coat, and serve.

Buffalo Wing Sauce

Makes about ¾ cup   **Total Time** 5 minutes

- ½ cup Frank's RedHot Original Cayenne Pepper Sauce
- 4 tablespoons unsalted butter, melted
- 1 tablespoon molasses

Combine hot sauce, melted butter, and molasses in large bowl.

Smoky Barbecue Wing Sauce

Makes about ¾ cup   **Total Time** 5 minutes

- ¼ cup chicken broth
- ¼ cup ketchup
- 1 tablespoon molasses
- 1 tablespoon cider vinegar
- 1 tablespoon minced canned chipotle chile in adobo sauce
- ¼ teaspoon liquid smoke

Combine all ingredients in large bowl.

Sweet and Spicy Wing Sauce

Makes about ¾ cup   **Total Time** 10 minutes

- ½ cup packed brown sugar
- ¼ cup lime juice (2 limes)
- 1 tablespoon toasted sesame oil
- 1 teaspoon red pepper flakes
- 1 garlic clove, minced
- 2 tablespoons fish sauce

Combine sugar, lime juice, oil, pepper flakes, and garlic in small saucepan; bring to simmer over medium heat. Cook until slightly thickened, about 5 minutes. Off heat, stir in fish sauce. Transfer to large bowl.

Oven-Fried Soy Sauce Chicken Wings

Serves 4 to 6   **Total Time** 1¼ hours (plus 2 hours marinating time)

Why This Recipe Works For tender, soy sauce–flavored oven-fried chicken wings, we marinated split wings in a simple combination of soy sauce, vegetable oil, brown sugar, garlic, and cayenne pepper. Rather than crowd them into a baking dish, we spread the wings out on a foil-lined baking sheet so the hot air could circulate around them. We found that inadequate cooking led to unpleasantly chewy skin, because the fat hadn't been fully rendered. Our solution was to leave the wings in a moderate 350-degree oven for a little more than an hour; this way, we got meltingly tender meat and sticky, savory skin. A sprinkling of scallions added a fresh note. If you buy chicken wings that are already split, with the tips removed, you will need only 2½ pounds.

- ¾ cup soy sauce for marinade
- ¼ cup vegetable oil for marinade
- ¼ cup packed brown sugar for marinade
- 12 garlic cloves, smashed and peeled, for marinade
- ½ teaspoon cayenne pepper for marinade
- 3 pounds chicken wings, cut at joints, wingtips discarded
- 2 scallions, sliced thin on bias

1. Combine soy sauce, oil, sugar, garlic, and cayenne in 1-gallon zipper-lock bag. Add wings to marinade, press out air, seal bag, and turn to distribute marinade. Refrigerate for at least 2 hours or up to 6 hours.

2. Adjust oven rack to middle position and heat oven to 350 degrees. Line rimmed baking sheet with aluminum foil and spray with vegetable oil spray. Remove wings from marinade and arrange in single layer, fatty side up, on prepared sheet; discard marinade. Bake until evenly well browned, about 1 hour 5 minutes. Transfer wings to platter, sprinkle with scallions, and serve.

Oven-Fried Soy Sauce Chicken Wings

Creamy Blue Cheese Dressing

Makes about ¾ cup   **Total Time** 10 minutes

- 2½ ounces blue cheese, crumbled (about ½ cup)
- 3 tablespoons buttermilk
- 3 tablespoons sour cream
- 2 tablespoons mayonnaise
- 2 teaspoons white wine vinegar

Mash blue cheese and buttermilk in small bowl with fork until mixture resembles cottage cheese with small curds. Stir in sour cream, mayonnaise, and vinegar. Season with salt and pepper to taste, cover, and refrigerate until ready to serve. (Dressing can be refrigerated for up to 4 days.)

PASTA AND NOODLES

Photos (clockwise from top left): Saltimbocca Spaghetti; Pasta Roll-Ups with Chicken, Sun-Dried Tomatoes, and Pine Nuts; Campanelle with Roasted Garlic, Chicken Sausage, and Arugula; Sesame Noodles with Shredded Chicken

Penne alla Vodka with Chicken

Serves 4 to 6   **Total Time** 45 minutes

Why This Recipe Works For a heartier yet still luxurious version of the classic penne alla vodka, we added thin, freshly sautéed slices of boneless chicken breast. We knew we had to get just the right balance of vodka, cream, and tomatoes for our sauce. We found we needed more than a splash of vodka to cut through the richness of the creamy sauce and add some zing, but we had to add it to the tomatoes early on to allow the alcohol to mostly (but not completely) cook off and tame its boozy flavor. If possible, use premium vodka; inexpensive brands will taste harsh in this sauce. Pepper-infused vodka can also be used here. Adjust the amount of red pepper flakes as desired to increase or decrease the amount of spice. To make the chicken easier to slice, freeze it for 15 minutes.

  1 pound boneless, skinless chicken breasts, trimmed and sliced thin crosswise
 ¾ teaspoon table salt, divided, plus salt for cooking pasta
 ⅛ teaspoon pepper
  2 tablespoons extra-virgin olive oil, divided
  1 onion, chopped fine
  1 tablespoon tomato paste
  3 garlic cloves, minced
 ⅛–¼ teaspoon red pepper flakes
  1 (28-ounce) can crushed tomatoes
 ⅓ cup vodka
 ⅔ cup heavy cream
  1 pound penne
  3 tablespoons chopped fresh basil
    Grated Parmesan cheese

1. Sprinkle chicken with ¼ teaspoon salt and pepper. Heat 1 tablespoon oil in 12-inch nonstick skillet over medium-high heat until just smoking. Add chicken in single layer and cook, without stirring, until beginning to brown, about 1 minute. Stir chicken and continue to cook until cooked through, about 4 minutes; transfer to bowl and cover to keep warm.

2. Add remaining 1 tablespoon oil, onion, and tomato paste to now-empty skillet and cook over medium heat until onion has softened, about 3 minutes. Stir in garlic and pepper flakes and cook until fragrant, about 30 seconds. Stir in tomatoes and remaining ½ teaspoon salt.

3. Off heat, carefully add vodka. Return pan to medium-high heat and simmer, stirring often, until alcohol flavor has cooked off, 5 to 8 minutes. Stir in cream and chicken with any accumulated juices and cook until warmed through, about 1 minute; remove from heat and cover.

4. Meanwhile, bring 4 quarts water to boil in large pot. Add pasta and 1 tablespoon salt and cook, stirring often, until al dente. Reserve ½ cup cooking water, then drain pasta and return it to pot. Stir in chicken mixture and toss to combine. Adjust consistency with reserved cooking water as needed. Season with salt and pepper to taste. Stir in basil and serve with Parmesan.

Penne with Chicken, Artichokes, Cherry Tomatoes, and Olives

Serves 4   **Total Time** 1 hour

Why This Recipe Works Penne pairs well with brothy sauces because the liquid binds to the tubes, making it perfect for a lightly sauced one-pot pasta with chicken and vegetables. After cooking sliced chicken, we built a flavorful liquid in which to simmer our pasta. We browned aromatics, deglazed with wine, poured in chicken broth and water, and added penne to simmer. Frozen artichokes went in partway through. Once the pasta was nearly cooked and the liquid had reduced to a sauce, we stirred in cherry tomatoes, olives, and Parmesan. Other pasta shapes can be substituted for the penne; however, their cup measurements may vary. To make the chicken easier to slice, freeze it for 15 minutes.

  1 pound boneless, skinless chicken breasts, trimmed and sliced thin crosswise
 ¾ teaspoon table salt, divided
 ⅛ teaspoon pepper
  3 tablespoons extra-virgin olive oil, divided
  1 onion, chopped fine
  6 garlic cloves, minced
  1 teaspoon minced fresh oregano or ¼ teaspoon dried
 ⅛ teaspoon red pepper flakes
 ½ cup dry white wine
  2 cups chicken broth
 1¾ cups water
  8 ounces (2½ cups) penne
  9 ounces frozen artichoke hearts, thawed
 12 ounces cherry tomatoes, quartered
 ½ cup pitted kalamata olives
  2 ounces Parmesan cheese, grated (1 cup), plus extra for serving
  2 tablespoons minced fresh parsley

Penne with Chicken, Artichokes, Cherry Tomatoes, and Olives

1. Pat chicken dry with paper towels and sprinkle with ¼ teaspoon salt and pepper. Heat 2 tablespoons oil in Dutch oven over medium-high heat until just smoking. Add chicken in single layer and cook, without stirring, until beginning to brown, about 1 minute. Stir chicken and continue to cook until cooked through, 2 to 3 minutes; transfer to bowl and cover to keep warm.

2. Add remaining 1 tablespoon oil and onion to pot and cook over medium heat until onion is softened, about 5 minutes. Stir in garlic, oregano, and pepper flakes and cook until fragrant, about 30 seconds. Stir in wine, scraping up any browned bits, and cook until nearly evaporated, 1 minute.

3. Stir in broth, water, pasta, and remaining ½ teaspoon salt, increase heat to high, and bring to boil. Reduce heat to medium and simmer vigorously, stirring often, for 10 minutes. Stir in artichokes and continue to cook until pasta is tender and sauce is thickened, 5 to 8 minutes.

4. Reduce heat to low and stir in chicken and any accumulated juices, tomatoes, olives, and Parmesan. Cook, tossing pasta gently, until well coated, 1 to 2 minutes. Adjust consistency with reserved cooking water as needed. Season with salt and pepper to taste, sprinkle with parsley, and serve with additional Parmesan.

Penne with Chicken, Sun-Dried Tomato Pesto, and Goat Cheese

Serves 4 to 6   **Total Time** 45 minutes

Why This Recipe Works Flavorful pestos can be made from lots of different ingredients, and they taste great tossed with pasta and chicken. We whipped up a quick, make-anytime pesto from handy sun-dried tomatoes along with frequent pesto partners Parmesan cheese, olive oil, and toasted nuts. While waiting for the pasta water to boil, we quickly sautéed thin slices of boneless chicken breast. We finished our simple pasta dish by mixing in peppery arugula and topping it with a sprinkle of goat cheese for tangy richness. We prefer to buy sun-dried tomatoes that are packed in oil, rather than just dried. Not only do they have more flavor, but their texture is softer and more easily incorporated into the pesto. Crisp fried capers make an excellent garnish for this dish. To make the chicken easier to slice, freeze it for 15 minutes.

1½ cups oil-packed sun-dried tomatoes, rinsed, patted dry, and chopped
1½ ounces Parmesan cheese, grated (¾ cup)
10 tablespoons extra-virgin olive oil, divided
⅓ cup walnuts, toasted
1 garlic clove, minced
1 pound boneless, skinless chicken breasts, trimmed and sliced thin crosswise
¼ teaspoon table salt, plus salt for cooking pasta
⅛ teaspoon pepper
1 pound penne
5 ounces (5 cups) baby arugula, chopped coarse
3 ounces goat cheese, crumbled (¾ cup)

1. Process tomatoes, Parmesan, 9 tablespoons oil, walnuts, and garlic in food processor until smooth, 30 to 60 seconds, scraping down bowl as needed. Transfer to bowl and season with salt and pepper to taste.

2. Sprinkle chicken with salt and pepper. Heat remaining 1 tablespoon oil in 12-inch nonstick skillet over medium-high heat until just smoking. Add chicken in single layer and cook, without stirring, until beginning to brown, about 1 minute. Stir chicken and continue to cook until cooked through, about 4 minutes; transfer to bowl and cover to keep warm.

3. Meanwhile, bring 4 quarts water to boil in large pot. Add pasta and 1 tablespoon salt and cook, stirring often, until al dente. Reserve 1½ cups cooking water, then drain pasta and return it to pot.

Chicken Riggies

Garlicky Tuscan Chicken Pasta

4. Stir ¾ cup of reserved cooking water into pesto to loosen, then add to pasta and toss to combine. Stir in arugula until wilted, about 1 minute. Adjust consistency with reserved cooking water as needed. Season with salt and pepper to taste. Sprinkle with goat cheese and serve.

Chicken Riggies
Serves 6   Total Time 1½ hours

Why This Recipe Works In Utica, New York, this spicy dish of chicken and rigatoni with vegetables is so popular it has its own food festival. Starting with the sauce, we developed rustic Italian flavor with crushed tomatoes, onion, garlic, oregano, bell pepper, and mushrooms. To inject riggies' signature spice, we stirred in chopped hot pickled cherry peppers and their brine before balancing out the sauce's acidity with cream. To infuse the meat with a little heat, we brined the chicken in cherry pepper brine and olive oil for just 30 minutes. With this much flavor in place, we could afford to simply poach the chicken in the sauce at the end. The sauce is stirred into al dente rigatoni (where "riggies" get their name) with a generous helping of Pecorino Romano. If you can find only sweet cherry peppers, add ¼ to ½ teaspoon red pepper flakes with the garlic in step 2. Parmesan cheese can be substituted for the Pecorino Romano.

- 1½ pounds boneless, skinless chicken breasts, trimmed and cut into 1-inch pieces
- ¼ cup finely chopped jarred sliced hot cherry peppers, plus 3 tablespoons cherry pepper brine, divided
- 3 tablespoons extra-virgin olive oil, divided
- 1½ teaspoons table salt, divided, plus salt for cooking pasta
- 10 ounces white mushrooms, trimmed and quartered
- 2 red bell peppers, stemmed, seeded, and cut into 1-inch pieces
- 1 onion, cut into 1-inch pieces
- 5 garlic cloves, minced
- 1½ teaspoons dried oregano
- 1 (28-ounce) can crushed tomatoes
- ¾ cup heavy cream
- ½ teaspoon pepper
- ¾ cup pitted kalamata olives, halved lengthwise
- 1 pound rigatoni
- 2½ ounces Pecorino Romano cheese, grated (1¼ cups), plus more for serving

1. Combine chicken, 2 tablespoons cherry pepper brine, 1 tablespoon oil, and 1 teaspoon salt in zipper-lock bag and refrigerate for at least 30 minutes or up to 1 hour.

2. Heat 1 tablespoon oil in Dutch oven over medium-high heat until shimmering. Stir in mushrooms, bell peppers, and remaining ½ teaspoon salt and cook until browned, about 8 minutes. Transfer vegetables to bowl; set aside. Add remaining 1 tablespoon oil and onion to now-empty pot and cook over medium heat until softened, about 5 minutes. Stir in cherry peppers, garlic, and oregano and cook until fragrant, about 30 seconds. Add tomatoes, cream, and pepper and bring to boil. Reduce heat to medium and simmer, stirring occasionally, until sauce is very thick, 10 to 15 minutes. Stir in chicken and reserved vegetables and simmer, covered, until chicken is cooked through, 6 to 8 minutes. Add olives and remaining 1 tablespoon cherry pepper brine. Cover to keep warm.

3. Meanwhile, bring 4 quarts water to boil in large pot. Add rigatoni and 1 tablespoon salt and cook, stirring often, until al dente. Reserve ½ cup cooking water, then drain rigatoni and return it to pot. Add sauce and Pecorino and toss to combine. Adjust consistency with reserved cooking water as needed. Season with salt and pepper to taste, and serve.

Garlicky Tuscan Chicken Pasta

Serves 4 to 6   **Total Time** 1½ hours

Why This Recipe Works Traditionally, Tuscan chicken combines mild, tender chicken with lots of garlic and lemon to create an intensely flavored dish. We added penne to the mix for an easy weeknight supper. We started by coating boneless, skinless chicken breasts with flour and pan-fried them to golden perfection before setting them aside to build the garlic sauce. To infuse the sauce with intense garlic flavor that wasn't harsh, we sliced a full 12 cloves thin and sautéed them over moderate heat for a few minutes. This slow-and-low approach mellowed the garlic's harshness and drew out its sweet, nutty notes. Adding sliced shallots to the mix enhanced its sweetness and provided insulation against burnt garlic. Red pepper flakes, white wine, and chicken broth served as the base of the sauce, and arugula added peppery flavor and color.

3 (6- to 8-ounce) boneless, skinless chicken breasts, trimmed
¼ teaspoon table salt, plus salt for cooking pasta
⅛ teaspoon pepper
½ cup plus 1 tablespoon all-purpose flour, divided
3 tablespoons extra-virgin olive oil, divided
12 garlic cloves, sliced thin
3 shallots, sliced thin
   Pinch red pepper flakes
¾ cup dry white wine
3 cups chicken broth
1 pound penne
5 ounces (5 cups) baby arugula
1½ ounces Parmesan cheese, grated (¾ cup), plus extra for serving
1 tablespoon lemon juice

1. Pat chicken dry with paper towels and sprinkle with salt and pepper. Place ½ cup flour in shallow dish. Working with 1 piece of chicken at a time, dredge in flour, shaking off excess.

2. Heat 2 tablespoons oil in 12-inch skillet over medium-high heat until just smoking. Carefully lay chicken in skillet and cook until well browned on first side, 6 to 8 minutes. Flip chicken over, reduce heat to medium, and continue to cook until chicken registers 160 degrees, 6 to 8 minutes; transfer to plate and tent with aluminum foil.

3. Add remaining 1 tablespoon oil, garlic, and shallots to now-empty skillet and cook over medium-low heat until softened and beginning to brown, about 3 minutes. Stir in pepper flakes and remaining 1 tablespoon flour and cook for 30 seconds. Whisk in wine, then broth, scraping up any browned bits and smoothing out any lumps. Increase heat to medium-high, bring to simmer, and cook until sauce is slightly thickened and measures 2½ cups, about 15 minutes; transfer to liquid measuring cup and cover to keep warm.

4. Meanwhile, bring 4 quarts water to boil in large pot. Add pasta and 1 tablespoon salt and cook, stirring often, until al dente. Reserve ½ cup cooking water, then drain pasta and return it to pot. Add 2 cups sauce, arugula, Parmesan, and lemon juice and toss until arugula is slightly wilted. Adjust consistency with reserved cooking water as needed. Season with salt and pepper to taste.

5. Slice chicken thin on bias. Portion pasta into individual bowls, lay chicken over top, and drizzle remaining ½ cup sauce over chicken. Serve with extra Parmesan.

Saltimbocca Spaghetti

Serves 4 **Total Time** 1 hour

Why This Recipe Works For a deconstructed chicken saltimbocca, we kept the key elements in place—crisp prosciutto, browned chicken, and fried sage—but changed things up a bit. First, saving the fried prosciutto and sage for a garnish, rather than layering them on the chicken, ensured a dish permeated with meaty crunch and woodsy sweetness. Slicing the chicken breasts into strips, instead of leaving them whole, promised more bites of tender chicken throughout; browning the strips in the rendered fat left behind from the prosciutto gave the chicken rich, meaty flavor. Building our sauce in the pan with plenty of chicken broth, water, and wine provided enough volume to cook our pasta. At the end, our saltimbocca spaghetti was flavored through and through with the rich, savory notes of sage, prosciutto, and chicken. Fresh sage is important to the flavor of this dish; do not substitute dried sage. To make the chicken easier to slice, freeze it for 15 minutes.

Saltimbocca
Spaghetti

- 3 tablespoons extra-virgin olive oil, divided
- 4 ounces thinly sliced prosciutto, sliced crosswise ⅓ inch thick
- 8 large fresh sage leaves plus 3 tablespoons minced
- 1 pound boneless, skinless chicken breasts, trimmed and sliced thin crosswise
- ¼ teaspoon table salt
- ⅛ teaspoon pepper
- 1 onion, chopped fine
- 4 garlic cloves, minced
- 2 teaspoons all-purpose flour
- 1 cup dry white wine
- 3 cups chicken broth
- 1½ cups water
- 12 ounces thin spaghetti or spaghettini, broken in half
- 3 tablespoons capers, rinsed
- 2 tablespoons unsalted butter
- ½ teaspoon lemon zest plus 3 tablespoons juice

1. Heat 2 tablespoons oil in 12-inch nonstick skillet over medium high heat until shimmering. Add prosciutto and cook until crisp, about 5 minutes. Add sage leaves and continue to cook until leaves are crisp, about 20 seconds. Using slotted spoon, transfer prosciutto and sage to paper towel–lined plate.

2. Pat chicken dry with paper towels and sprinkle with salt and pepper. Heat remaining 1 tablespoon oil in now-empty skillet over medium-high heat until just smoking. Add chicken in single layer and cook, without stirring, until beginning to brown, about 1 minute. Stir chicken and continue to cook until nearly cooked through, about 2 minutes; transfer to bowl and cover to keep warm.

3. Add onion to fat left in skillet and cook over medium heat until softened and golden, 7 to 10 minutes. Stir in garlic and minced sage and cook until fragrant, about 30 seconds. Stir in flour and cook for 1 minute. Stir in wine, scraping up any browned bits and smoothing out any lumps, and simmer until reduced by half, about 1 minute.

4. Stir in broth, water, and pasta. Increase heat to medium-high and cook at vigorous simmer, stirring often, until pasta is tender and sauce has thickened, 12 to 15 minutes.

5. Stir in chicken along with any accumulated juices, capers, butter, and lemon zest and juice and cook until chicken is warmed through, about 1 minute. Off heat, season with salt and pepper to taste. Sprinkle individual portions with crisped prosciutto and sage and serve.

Chicken Bolognese with Linguine

Serves 4 to 6   **Total Time** 1½ hours

Why This Recipe Works Bolognese, traditionally made with ground beef, pork, and veal, achieves deep flavor from hours of simmering. We wanted a richly flavored Bolognese that relied on ground chicken in place of the three kinds of meat. To get rich flavor from lean ground chicken, we deployed two flavor powerhouses: pancetta and dried porcini mushrooms. The pancetta gave our sauce a hearty backbone, and the meaty mushrooms contributed depth. Sautéing our aromatics in butter imparted further richness, and tomato paste gave the sauce intensity. Simmering the meat in milk—a classic Bolognese method—kept the ground chicken from becoming tough and turning grainy while cooking. We found that sweet white wine tasted better than either a dry white or a dry red wine. Mincing the vegetables is important for the texture of the sauce; if desired, use a food processor and pulse each vegetable separately until finely minced. Also, be sure to break the chicken into small pieces in step 3, or the sauce will be too chunky. Be sure to use ground chicken or turkey, not ground chicken or turkey breast (also labeled 99 percent fat-free), in this recipe.

- 1 (28-ounce) can diced tomatoes
- 1¼ cups sweet white wine, such as Gewürztraminer, Riesling, or white Zinfandel
- 4 tablespoons unsalted butter
- 4 ounces pancetta, cut into ¼-inch pieces
- ½ carrot, peeled and minced
- ½ cup finely chopped onion
- ½ ounce dried porcini mushrooms, rinsed and minced
- ¼ teaspoon table salt, plus salt for cooking pasta
- 1 garlic clove, minced
- 1 teaspoon sugar
- 1¼ pounds ground chicken or turkey
- 1½ cups whole milk
- 2 tablespoons tomato paste
- 1 pound linguine
  Grated Parmesan cheese

1. Pulse tomatoes in food processor until finely chopped, about 8 pulses; set aside. Simmer wine in 10-inch nonstick skillet over medium-low heat until reduced to 2 tablespoons, about 20 minutes; set aside.

Chicken Bolognese with Linguine

2. Cook butter and pancetta in 12-inch skillet over medium heat until pancetta is lightly browned, 3 to 5 minutes. Add carrot, onion, porcini, and salt and cook, stirring often, until vegetables are softened, about 4 minutes. Stir in garlic and sugar and cook until fragrant, about 30 seconds.

3. Add chicken and cook, breaking up meat with wooden spoon, for 1 minute (chicken will still be pink). Stir in milk and simmer gently, breaking meat into small pieces, until most of liquid has evaporated and meat begins to sizzle, about 15 minutes. Stir in tomato paste and cook for 1 minute. Stir in processed tomatoes and simmer until sauce is thickened, 12 to 15 minutes. Stir in reduced wine and simmer until flavors are blended, about 5 minutes.

4. Meanwhile, bring 4 quarts water to boil in large pot. Add pasta and 1 tablespoon salt and cook, stirring often, until al dente. Reserve ½ cup cooking water, then drain pasta and return it to pot. Add sauce and toss to combine. Adjust consistency with reserved cooking water as needed. Season with salt and pepper to taste. Serve with Parmesan.

Pasta with Chicken Sausage,
Swiss Chard, and White Beans

Campanelle with
Roasted Garlic,
Chicken Sausage,
and Arugula

Pasta with Chicken Sausage, Swiss Chard, and White Beans

Serves 4   **Total Time** 45 minutes

Why This Recipe Works The rustic pairing of pasta with hearty greens and beans makes for a quick weeknight meal. We made it even more satisfying by adding cooked chicken sausage. In our supereasy recipe, we cooked Swiss chard in the same pot as the spaghetti. In the time it took to heat the water and cook the pasta, we browned the sausage, added a dose of garlic, and created a brothy sauce using a can of white beans and their liquid. The bean liquid helped to thicken the sauce. For a spicy kick, add a pinch of red pepper flakes with the Pecorino. Chicken sausage is available in a variety of flavors; feel free to substitute any flavor that you think will pair well with this dish.

8 ounces spaghetti
¼ teaspoon table salt, plus salt for cooking pasta
12 ounces Swiss chard, stems chopped fine, leaves sliced into ½-inch-wide strips
1 tablespoon extra-virgin olive oil, plus extra for drizzling
12 ounces cooked chicken sausage, halved lengthwise and sliced ½ inch thick
3 garlic cloves, minced
¼ teaspoon pepper
1 (15-ounce) can cannellini beans
½ cup chicken broth
2 ounces Pecorino Romano cheese, grated (1 cup)
1½ tablespoons lemon juice

1. Bring 4 quarts water to boil in large pot. Add pasta and 1 tablespoon salt and cook, stirring often, until just al dente. Add chard and cook until tender, about 1 minute. Drain pasta and chard and return to pot.

2. Meanwhile, heat oil in 12-inch skillet over medium heat until shimmering. Add sausage and cook, stirring occasionally, until well browned, about 8 minutes. Add garlic, pepper, and salt and cook until fragrant, about 30 seconds. Add beans and their liquid and broth and bring to boil, scraping up any browned bits.

3. Add ½ cup Pecorino, lemon juice, and sausage-bean mixture to pasta and toss to combine. Season with salt and pepper to taste. Serve drizzled with extra oil, and pass remaining ½ cup Pecorino separately.

Campanelle with Roasted Garlic, Chicken Sausage, and Arugula

Serves 4 to 6   **Total Time** 1 hour

Why This Recipe Works Roasted garlic adds sweet, intense flavor to this simple pasta dinner. To speed up the time required to deliver richly flavored, perfectly tender garlic, we had to rethink our method for roasting garlic. First, we found we could roast the garlic more quickly when the cloves were separated, rather than bunched together in a compact head. Removing the skins also made the cloves easier to handle after being roasted. Combining the peeled garlic cloves, oil, and seasonings in a small baking dish made it a snap to both roast and mash them into a paste. We also found we could crank the oven all the way up to 425 degrees and cut the roasting time to just 20 minutes. Covering the dish with aluminum foil was essential; otherwise, the exposed parts of the garlic cloves turned tough and overly brown during roasting. The mashed garlic paste ensured evenly distributed garlic and gave us a head start on the sauce—crumbled goat cheese turned it into a full-fledged thick and creamy coating for our campanelle. Lightly browned chicken sausage and a few handfuls of baby arugula made this flavorful dish filling, too. Chicken sausage is available in a variety of flavors; feel free to substitute any flavor that you think will pair well with this dish.

⅓ cup plus 1 tablespoon extra-virgin olive oil, divided
16 garlic cloves, peeled
½ teaspoon table salt, plus salt for cooking pasta
½ teaspoon pepper
12 ounces cooked chicken sausage, sliced ½ inch thick on bias
1 pound campanelle
5 ounces (5 cups) baby arugula
4 ounces goat cheese, crumbled (1 cup)

1. Adjust oven rack to upper-middle position and heat oven to 425 degrees. Combine ⅓ cup oil, garlic, salt, and pepper in 8-inch square baking dish and cover with aluminum foil. Bake, stirring occasionally, until garlic is caramelized and soft, about 20 minutes. Let cool slightly, then mash garlic and oil into paste with fork.

2. Heat remaining 1 tablespoon oil in 12-inch skillet over medium-high heat until shimmering. Add sausage and cook until lightly browned, about 4 minutes. Off heat, stir in garlic mixture.

3. Meanwhile, bring 4 quarts water to boil in large pot. Add pasta and 1 tablespoon salt and cook, stirring often, until al dente. Reserve 1½ cups cooking water, then drain pasta and return it to pot. Add sausage mixture, arugula, cheese, and ½ cup reserved cooking water and toss to combine. Adjust consistency with reserved cooking water as needed. Season with salt and pepper to taste, and serve.

Italian-Style Turkey Meatballs

Serves 4 to 6   **Total Time** 1½ hours

Why This Recipe Works Our turkey meatballs rival those made from beef or pork, thanks to a few test kitchen tricks. We skipped the 99 percent lean turkey, which didn't have enough fat to create a palatable meatball, and opted for a fattier grind (better still was grinding our own). Next, we added an egg and fresh bread crumbs (instead of a panade, which made the meatballs too wet) to help bind the meat. We also added a small amount of unflavored gelatin, which mitigated graininess by trapping moisture and giving the meatballs a juicy mouthfeel. To boost meaty flavor, we added glutamate-rich Parmesan cheese, anchovies, tomato paste, and dried shiitake mushrooms. Be sure to use ground turkey, not ground turkey breast (also labeled 99 percent fat-free). Buy store-ground turkey if you can, which is coarser than commercial ground. If you have time, we recommend grinding your own turkey thighs for the best results (see page 92). Serve with spaghetti.

1 cup chicken broth
½ ounce dried shiitake mushrooms
2 slices hearty white sandwich bread, torn into 1-inch pieces
1 ounce Parmesan cheese, grated (½ cup), plus extra≈for serving
1 tablespoon chopped fresh parsley
1½ teaspoons unflavored gelatin
1 teaspoon table salt
½ teaspoon pepper, divided
4 anchovy fillets, rinsed, patted dry, and minced
1½ pounds 85 or 93 percent lean ground turkey
1 large egg, lightly beaten
4 garlic cloves, minced, divided
1 (14.5-ounce) can whole peeled tomatoes
½ teaspoon dried oregano
⅛ teaspoon red pepper flakes
3 tablespoons extra-virgin olive oil
2 tablespoons tomato paste
¼ cup chopped fresh basil
Sugar

Italian-Style
Turkey Meatballs

Chicken Noodle
Casserole

1. Microwave broth and mushrooms in covered bowl until steaming, about 1 minute. Let sit until softened, about 5 minutes. Drain mushrooms in fine-mesh strainer and reserve liquid.

2. Pulse bread in food processor until finely ground, 10 to 15 pulses; transfer bread crumbs to large bowl (do not wash processor bowl). Add Parmesan, parsley, gelatin, salt, and ¼ teaspoon pepper to bowl with bread crumbs and mix until thoroughly combined. Pulse mushrooms and half of anchovies in food processor until chopped fine, 10 to 15 pulses. Add mushroom mixture, turkey, egg, and half of garlic to bowl with bread-crumb mixture and mix with your hands until thoroughly combined. Divide mixture into 16 portions (about ¼ cup each). Using your hands, roll each portion into ball; transfer meatballs to plate and refrigerate for 15 minutes.

3. Pulse tomatoes and their juice in food processor to coarse puree, 10 to 15 pulses. Combine oregano, pepper flakes, remaining anchovies, remaining ¼ teaspoon pepper, and remaining garlic in small bowl; set aside.

4. Heat oil in 12-inch nonstick skillet over medium-high heat until shimmering. Add meatballs and cook until well browned all over, 5 to 7 minutes. Transfer meatballs to paper towel–lined plate, leaving fat in skillet.

5. Add reserved anchovy mixture to skillet and cook, stirring constantly, until fragrant, about 30 seconds. Increase heat to high; stir in tomato paste, reserved mushroom liquid, and pureed tomatoes; and bring to simmer. Return meatballs to skillet, reduce heat to medium-low, cover, and cook until meatballs register 160 degrees, 12 to 15 minutes, turning meatballs once. Transfer meatballs to platter, increase heat to high, and simmer sauce until slightly thickened, 3 to 5 minutes. Stir in basil and season with sugar, salt, and pepper to taste. Pour sauce over meatballs and serve, passing extra Parmesan separately.

NOTES FROM THE TEST KITCHEN

CONSIDER GRINDING YOUR OWN TURKEY
If you have the time and inclination, we recommend grinding your own turkey thighs for the very best results: Start with one 2-pound turkey thigh, skinned, boned, trimmed, and cut into ½-inch pieces. Place pieces on large plate in single layer. Freeze until pieces are very firm and hardened around edges, 35 to 45 minutes. Pulse one-third of turkey in food processor until chopped into ⅛-inch pieces, 18 to 22 pulses, stopping and redistributing turkey around bowl as needed to ensure even grinding. Transfer turkey to large bowl and repeat 2 times with remaining turkey. Yields 1½ pounds.

Chicken Noodle Casserole

Serves 8 to 10   Total Time 1¾ hours

Why This Recipe Works Our updated version of the classic comfort-food chicken noodle casserole features a homemade sauce and boneless, skinless chicken breasts. We cooked egg noodles until just al dente and then shocked them in cold water to prevent them from overcooking in the oven. A flour-thickened sauce made up of half-and-half and chicken broth created a rich, savory base, and a combination of cheeses—cheddar for flavor, American for smooth melting—was key. Precooked chicken turned rubbery after being baked into the casserole, so we simmered boneless, skinless chicken breasts in the sauce until they were nearly cooked through before shredding them and tossing them in with the noodles. Crushed buttery Ritz Crackers became a quick, crunchy topping for our casserole. The casserole needed just 15 minutes in the oven before it came out bubbling and golden brown.

12 ounces (6 cups) wide egg noodles
1½ teaspoons table salt, plus salt for cooking pasta
3   tablespoons unsalted butter, divided
1   red bell pepper, stemmed, seeded, and chopped fine
1   onion, chopped fine
3   tablespoons all-purpose flour
2½ cups half-and-half
2½ cups chicken broth
1   pound boneless, skinless chicken breasts, trimmed and halved lengthwise
4   ounces deli American cheese, chopped coarse
4   ounces sharp cheddar cheese, shredded (1 cup)
1½ cups frozen peas
1¼ teaspoons pepper
25 Ritz Crackers, crushed coarse

1. Bring 4 quarts water to boil in Dutch oven. Add noodles and 1 tablespoon salt and cook, stirring often, until just al dente, about 3 minutes. Drain noodles and rinse with cold water until cool, about 2 minutes. Drain again and set aside.

2. Melt 1 tablespoon butter in now-empty pot over medium-high heat. Add bell pepper and onion and cook, stirring occasionally, until softened, about 5 minutes. Transfer to bowl; set aside. Melt remaining 2 tablespoons butter in again-empty pot over medium heat. Add flour and cook, whisking constantly, for 1 minute. Slowly whisk in half-and-half and broth, scraping up any browned bits and smoothing out any lumps, and bring to boil. Reduce heat to medium-low and simmer until slightly thickened, about 5 minutes. Add chicken and cook until no longer pink, 8 to 10 minutes.

3. Adjust oven rack to upper-middle position and heat oven to 425 degrees. Off heat, transfer chicken to plate. Let chicken cool slightly, then shred with 2 forks into bite-size pieces. Whisk cheeses into sauce until smooth. Stir peas, pepper, salt, noodles, bell pepper mixture, and shredded chicken into cheese sauce.

4. Transfer mixture to 13 by 9-inch baking dish (or similar size casserole dish) and top with crackers. Bake until golden brown and bubbling, about 15 minutes. Let casserole cool on wire rack for 10 minutes before serving.

To make ahead Do not add peas or top casserole with crushed crackers. Casserole can be refrigerated for up to 1 day. To serve, cover casserole dish tightly with greased aluminum foil and bake in 400-degree oven until hot throughout, 45 minutes. Uncover, stir in peas and top with crushed crackers; bake until topping is crisp and golden, 10 minutes.

Chicken, Broccoli, and Ziti Casserole

Serves 8   Total Time 1½ hours

Why This Recipe Works Chicken, broccoli, and ziti is such a crowd-pleaser (protein, pasta, and vegetable all in one dish) that we decided to turn the combination into a hearty casserole to feed a crowd. We wanted our recipe to have it all: moist chicken, crisp-tender broccoli, and firm ziti served in a cheesy sauce that stayed creamy even after baking. We made an enhanced béchamel sauce by sautéing onion, lots of garlic, and red pepper flakes before stirring in flour, milk, and savory chicken broth. The strips of boneless, skinless chicken breast needed to be precooked to prevent the other ingredients from overcooking by the time the chicken was done. We found that poaching the chicken in the sauce was the best method—it flavored the meat and kept it moist. Our first disastrous attempt at simmering the broccoli right in the sauce infused the whole dish with an off-flavor and dirty color. Microwaving the broccoli was easy and reliable. To prepare the pasta for the oven, we undercooked it and then rinsed it with cold water to stop any carryover cooking. A final topping of fresh bread crumbs, minced garlic, and Asiago was as flavorful as the casserole itself. If you can't find Asiago, Parmesan is an acceptable substitute.

Chicken, Broccoli, and Ziti Casserole

2. Adjust oven rack to middle position and heat oven to 400 degrees. Bring 4 quarts water to boil in large pot. Add pasta and 1 tablespoon salt and cook until nearly al dente. Drain in colander and rinse under cold water until cool.

3. Melt remaining 3 tablespoons butter in now-empty pot over medium heat. Add onion and cook until softened, about 5 minutes. Add pepper flakes and remaining garlic and cook until fragrant, about 30 seconds. Stir in flour and cook until golden, about 1 minute. Slowly whisk in wine and cook until liquid is almost evaporated, about 1 minute. Slowly whisk in milk and broth, scraping up any browned bits and smoothing out any lumps, and bring to boil. Add chicken and simmer until no longer pink, about 5 minutes. Off heat, stir in remaining 2 cups Asiago until melted.

4. Microwave broccoli, covered, in large bowl until bright green and nearly tender, 2 to 4 minutes. Stir broccoli and pasta into pot and season with salt and pepper to taste. Transfer to 13 by 9-inch baking dish (or similar size casserole dish). (Casserole can be assembled, minus bread crumbs, and refrigerated for up to 24 hours. Bring to room temperature before adding bread crumbs and baking.) Sprinkle with bread-crumb mixture and bake until sauce is bubbling around edges and topping is golden brown, 20 to 25 minutes. Let cool for 5 minutes before serving.

4 slices hearty white sandwich bread, torn into pieces
5 ounces Asiago cheese, grated (2½ cups), divided
2 tablespoons unsalted butter, melted, plus
   3 tablespoons unsalted butter
8 garlic cloves, minced, divided
1 pound ziti
   Table salt for cooking pasta
1 onion, chopped fine
¼ teaspoon red pepper flakes
¼ cup all-purpose flour
½ cup white wine
3 cups whole milk
2 cups chicken broth
4 (6- to 8-ounce) boneless, skinless chicken breasts,
   trimmed and sliced crosswise ¼ inch thick
12 ounces broccoli florets, cut into 1-inch pieces

1. Pulse bread, ½ cup Asiago, melted butter, and one-quarter of garlic in food processor until coarsely ground, about 10 pulses. Set aside.

Creamy Chicken and Spinach Whole-Wheat Pasta Casserole

Serves 4 Total Time 1¼ hours

Why This Recipe Works Hearty, nutty tasting whole-wheat pasta stands up well to a rich, creamy casserole starring tender chicken and spinach. We created a basic sauce with sautéed aromatics, a bit of flour for thickening, milk and Parmesan for creaminess and savory flavor, and lemon juice for bright, clean notes. Sliced chicken, sautéed to golden perfection, amped up the heartiness of our casserole, and frozen spinach was a convenient way to get in our vegetables. To prevent the pasta from becoming mushy and overdone, we undercooked it slightly. This way, the pasta could finish cooking in the sauce as the casserole baked; stirring in some of the pasta cooking water ensured that it stayed moist. Shredded mozzarella, sprinkled over the top, gave our casserole a bubbling golden crown when we pulled it from the oven. Do not use fat-free mozzarella here. Be sure to squeeze the spinach thoroughly so it is as dry as possible.

12 ounces boneless, skinless chicken breasts, trimmed and sliced thin

¼ teaspoon table salt, plus salt for cooking pasta

⅛ teaspoon pepper

1½ tablespoons extra-virgin olive oil, divided

1 onion, chopped fine

3 garlic cloves, minced

⅛ teaspoon red pepper flakes

2 tablespoons all-purpose flour

4 cups whole milk

1 bay leaf

1 ounce Parmesan cheese, grated (½ cup)

2 teaspoons lemon juice

10 ounces frozen spinach, thawed, squeezed dry, and chopped coarse

8 ounces (2⅔ cups) whole-wheat penne

2 ounces mozzarella cheese, shredded (½ cup)

1. Adjust oven rack to middle position and heat oven to 425 degrees. Grease 8-inch square baking dish with vegetable oil spray.

2. Pat chicken dry with paper towels and sprinkle with salt and pepper. Heat 1½ teaspoons oil in 12-inch nonstick skillet over high heat until just smoking. Add chicken in single layer and cook, without stirring, until beginning to brown, about 1 minute. Stir chicken and continue to cook until nearly cooked through, about 2 minutes; transfer to bowl.

3. Add remaining 1 tablespoon oil and onion to now-empty skillet and cook over medium heat until softened, about 5 minutes. Stir in garlic and pepper flakes and cook until fragrant, about 30 seconds. Stir in flour and cook for 1 minute. Slowly whisk in milk, scraping up any browned bits and smoothing out any lumps, add bay leaf, and simmer, stirring occasionally, until slightly thickened, about 10 minutes.

4. Return chicken along with any accumulated juices to skillet and simmer until chicken is cooked through, about 1 minute. Off heat, remove bay leaf and stir in Parmesan and lemon juice. Stir in spinach, breaking up any clumps. Season with salt and pepper to taste.

5. Meanwhile, bring 4 quarts water to boil in large pot. Add pasta and 1 tablespoon salt and cook, stirring often, until nearly al dente. Reserve ¼ cup cooking water, then drain pasta and return it to pot. Stir in chicken-spinach mixture and reserved cooking water and toss to combine. Transfer to prepared baking dish and sprinkle with mozzarella. Bake until sauce is bubbling and cheese is lightly browned, about 15 minutes. Let cool for 10 to 15 minutes before serving.

Baked Penne with Spinach, Artichokes, and Chicken

Baked Penne with Spinach, Artichokes, and Chicken

Serves 4 to 6   **Total Time** 1¼ hours

Why This Recipe Works We took our cue from the flavors of creamy spinach and artichoke dip and created an easy pasta casserole using frozen spinach and frozen artichoke hearts. First, we built a simple cream sauce, then stirred in the star vegetables, which simply needed to be thawed, dried, and cut into smaller pieces. So that our baked pasta dish offered the same cheesy appeal as the appetizer version, we stirred in a hefty amount of mozzarella and Parmesan. Shredded cooked chicken elevated our appetizer to main-dish status, and lemon juice perked up the flavors of the sauce. Penne worked well for the pasta; its short, tubular shape ensured that every forkful held an even mix of pasta, vegetables, and chicken. Do not use fat-free mozzarella here. We like using Perfect Poached Chicken (page 60) here but any cooked chicken would work. Be sure to squeeze the spinach thoroughly so it is as dry as possible.

12 ounces (3¾ cups) penne
¼ teaspoon table salt, plus salt for cooking pasta
3 tablespoons unsalted butter
1 onion, chopped fine
3 garlic cloves, minced
3 tablespoons all-purpose flour
2½ cups chicken broth
1 cup heavy cream
18 ounces frozen artichoke hearts, thawed, patted dry, and quartered
10 ounces frozen spinach, thawed, squeezed dry, and chopped fine
10 ounces mozzarella cheese, shredded (2½ cups), divided
2 ounces Parmesan cheese, grated (1 cup), divided
2 tablespoons lemon juice
4 cups shredded cooked chicken

1. Adjust oven rack to middle position and heat oven to 450 degrees. Bring 4 quarts water to boil in large Dutch oven. Add pasta and 1 tablespoon salt and cook, stirring often, until nearly al dente. Drain pasta and set aside.

2. Dry now-empty pot, add butter, and melt over medium heat. Add onion and salt and cook until softened, about 5 minutes. Stir in garlic and cook until fragrant, about 30 seconds. Stir in flour and cook for 1 minute. Slowly whisk in broth and cream, scraping up any browned bits and smoothing out any lumps, and bring to simmer. Stir in artichokes and spinach and continue to simmer until vegetables are heated through, about 1 minute.

3. Stir in 1½ cups mozzarella and ½ cup Parmesan until melted. Off heat, stir in lemon juice and season with salt and pepper to taste. Fold in cooked pasta and shredded chicken, breaking up any clumps of pasta. Pour into 13 by 9-inch baking dish (or similar size casserole dish) and sprinkle with remaining 1 cup mozzarella and remaining ½ cup Parmesan. (Casserole can be assembled, cooled [add cheese topping when cool], covered with plastic wrap, and refrigerated for up to 2 days. To bake, remove plastic and cover with aluminum foil; bake in 450-degree oven until hot, about 20 minutes, then remove foil and bake until cheese is spotty brown, about 15 minutes.)

4. Bake until bubbling around edges and cheese is spotty brown, 12 to 15 minutes. Let cool for 10 to 15 minutes before serving.

Pasta Roll-Ups with Chicken, Sun-Dried Tomatoes, and Pine Nuts

Serves 6 to 8   **Total Time** 1¾ hours

Why This Recipe Works This baked pasta is inspired by manicotti but more dressed up. We rolled softened lasagna noodles around a cheesy chicken filling before laying on a rich (but not heavy) white sauce. Poaching boneless breasts and thighs gave us a flavorful mix of white and dark meat for our filling, and the poaching liquid doubled as the base for our sauce. Three kinds of cheese, pine nuts, fresh herbs, and savory sun-dried tomatoes added richness and flavor to the chicken filling, which we thinned with some of the sauce. We covered the roll-ups with a white cream sauce and baked them, covered, using a low-heat/high-heat method until the noodles were soft and the filling was hot. A quick run under the broiler browned the top of our casserole to perfection. Note that this recipe requires 16 noodles; some brands of no-boil noodles contain only 12 noodles per package. Do not overbake this dish; be sure to remove the casserole from the oven once the sauce begins to bubble around the edges in step 7.

Chicken and Sauce
1 pound boneless, skinless chicken breasts and/or thighs, trimmed
2½ cups chicken broth
4 tablespoons unsalted butter
1 onion, chopped fine
4 garlic cloves, minced
⅓ cup all-purpose flour
¼ cup dry white wine
1 cup heavy cream
2 bay leaves
½ teaspoon fresh grated nutmeg
1 ounce Parmesan cheese, grated (½ cup)
2 tablespoons chopped fresh basil

Filling and Noodles
10 ounces goat cheese
6 ounces whole-milk mozzarella cheese, shredded (1½ cups)
2 ounces Parmesan cheese, grated (1 cup), divided
1 large egg, lightly beaten
1 teaspoon grated lemon zest plus 1 tablespoon juice

1 garlic clove, minced
½ teaspoon table salt
½ teaspoon pepper
¼ cup pine nuts, toasted
2 teaspoons minced fresh oregano
½ cup plus 2 tablespoons chopped fresh basil, divided
½ cup oil-packed sun-dried tomatoes, rinsed, patted dry, and chopped fine
16 no-boil lasagna noodles

1. For the chicken and sauce Adjust oven rack to middle position and heat oven to 350 degrees. Combine chicken and broth in large saucepan, cover, and bring to simmer over medium heat. Cook until breasts register 160 degrees and thighs register 175 degrees, 8 to 12 minutes. Remove chicken from pot and pour liquid into measuring cup. Let chicken cool slightly, then, using 2 forks, shred into bite-size pieces.

2. Wipe pot dry, add butter, and melt over medium heat. Add onion and cook until softened, 5 to 7 minutes. Stir in garlic and cook until fragrant, about 30 seconds. Stir in flour and cook for 1 minute. Slowly whisk in white wine, bring to simmer, and cook until nearly evaporated, about 30 seconds.

3. Gradually whisk in reserved broth and cream. Stir in bay leaves and nutmeg and bring to simmer, whisking often. Cook until sauce is thickened and measures about 3½ cups, about 10 minutes. Off heat, discard bay leaves. Whisk in Parmesan and basil and season with salt and pepper to taste. Cover sauce to keep warm; set aside.

4. For the filling and noodles In large bowl, combine goat cheese, mozzarella, ½ cup Parmesan, egg, lemon zest and juice, garlic, salt, and pepper until uniform. Gradually stir ½ cup of sauce into cheese mixture, then fold in shredded chicken, pine nuts, oregano, ½ cup basil, and sun-dried tomatoes; set aside.

5. Pour 1 inch of boiling water into 13 by 9-inch broiler-safe baking dish and slip noodles into water, one at a time. Let noodles soak until pliable, about 5 minutes, separating noodles with tip of knife to prevent sticking. Remove noodles from water and place in single layer on clean dish towels; discard water and dry baking dish.

6. Spread 1 cup sauce over bottom of 13 by 9-inch baking dish. Mound ¼ cup of chicken-cheese mixture evenly over bottom of each noodle and roll, into compact, tidy log. Lay noodle roll-ups seam side down in baking dish. Spoon remaining sauce evenly over filled noodles, covering pasta completely. (Casserole can be covered with plastic wrap and refrigerated for up to 1 day. Remove plastic and bake as directed in steps 7 and 8, increasing covered baking time in step 7 to 45 to 55 minutes.)

Pasta Roll-Ups with Chicken, Sun-Dried Tomatoes, and Pine Nuts

7. Cover dish tightly with greased aluminum foil (or use nonstick foil). Bake until edges are just bubbling, 25 to 30 minutes, rotating pan halfway through baking time.

8. Remove baking dish from oven and discard foil. Adjust oven rack 6 inches from broiling element and heat broiler. Sprinkle with remaining ½ cup Parmesan, and broil until top is spotty brown, 4 to 6 minutes. Let casserole cool for 10 minutes, then sprinkle with remaining 2 tablespoons basil and serve.

Chicken Lo Mein with Broccoli and Bean Sprouts

Serves 4 to 6   Total Time 50 minutes

Why This Recipe Works For this classic dish, we used fresh noodles, which turned out pleasantly chewy and absorbed more of the sauce than dried noodles would. To tenderize and season the chicken before stir-frying, we marinated it in soy sauce, Shaoxing wine, cornstarch, and baking soda. We then created a sauce base with more soy sauce and Shaoxing wine, oyster sauce, hoisin, and five-spice powder for aromatic

Chicken Lo Mein with Broccoli and Bean Sprouts

Chicken Pad Kee Mao

sweetness. Stir-frying in batches (chicken, then vegetables) ensured that everything cooked properly. In the empty pan we cooked the sauce and briefly tossed the noodles in it to soak up the flavor without becoming mushy. Then we tossed the noodles, chicken, and vegetables together, and the lo mein was ready to serve. If fresh lo mein noodles are unavailable, 8 ounces dried lo mein noodles or linguine may be substituted. You will need a 12-inch nonstick skillet or a 14-inch flat-bottomed wok, each with a tight-fitting lid, for this recipe. To make the chicken easier to slice, freeze it for 15 minutes.

⅛ teaspoon baking soda
12 ounces boneless, skinless chicken breasts, trimmed, halved lengthwise, and sliced thin crosswise
3 tablespoons soy sauce, divided
2 tablespoons Shaoxing wine or dry sherry, divided
1½ teaspoons cornstarch, divided
10 scallions, white parts minced, green parts cut into 1-inch pieces
2 tablespoons plus 1 teaspoon vegetable oil, divided
2 garlic cloves, minced
2 teaspoons grated fresh ginger
½ cup chicken broth
2 tablespoons oyster sauce
2 tablespoons hoisin sauce
1 tablespoon toasted sesame oil
⅛ teaspoon five-spice powder
12 ounces broccoli florets, cut into 1-inch pieces
4 ounces (2 cups) bean sprouts
12 ounces fresh lo mein noodles

1. Combine 2 teaspoons water and baking soda in medium bowl. Add chicken and toss to coat; let sit for 5 minutes. Add 2 teaspoons soy sauce, 2 teaspoons wine, and ½ teaspoon cornstarch and toss until well combined.

2. Combine scallion whites, 1 tablespoon vegetable oil, garlic, and ginger in small bowl; set aside. Whisk broth, oyster sauce, hoisin, sesame oil, five-spice powder, remaining 7 teaspoons soy sauce, remaining 4 teaspoons wine, and remaining 1 teaspoon cornstarch together in second small bowl; set aside.

3. Heat 2 teaspoons vegetable oil in nonstick skillet or flat-bottomed wok over medium-high heat until just smoking. Add chicken and increase heat to high. Cook, tossing chicken slowly but constantly, until no longer pink, 2 to 6 minutes; transfer to large bowl.

4. Heat remaining 2 teaspoons vegetable oil in now-empty pan over high heat until just smoking. Add broccoli and ¼ cup water (water will sputter), and cover immediately. Cook, without stirring, until broccoli is bright green, about

2 minutes. Uncover and continue to cook, tossing slowly but constantly, until all water has evaporated and broccoli is crisp-tender and spotty-brown, 1 to 3 minutes. Add bean sprouts and scallion greens and cook until softened, about 1 minute; transfer to bowl with chicken.

5. Meanwhile, bring 4 quarts water to boil in large pot. Add noodles and cook, stirring often, until almost tender (center should still be firm, with slightly opaque dot). Drain noodles and rinse under cold running water until chilled. Drain noodles again and set aside.

6. Whisk reserved broth mixture to recombine. Return again-empty pan to medium heat. Add scallion whites mixture and cook, mashing mixture into pan, until fragrant, about 30 seconds. Add broth mixture and noodles and increase heat to high. Cook, tossing slowly but constantly, until noodles are heated through, about 2 minutes. Transfer to bowl with chicken and vegetables and toss to combine. Serve.

STIR-FRYING CHICKEN

High heat is best for stir-frying chicken whether in a flat-bottomed wok or a nonstick skillet.

Chicken Pad Kee Mao

Serves 4 **Total Time** 1 hour

Why This Recipe Works Sometimes called drunken noodles but translated from Thai as "drunkard noodles," pad kee mao contains no alcohol but rather gets its unique flavor from a spicy, potent sauce flavored with lots of basil. Soaking wide rice noodles in very hot water just until pliable meant we could finish cooking the noodles in the aromatic sauce without making them mushy. Meanwhile, we tossed the chicken with soy sauce, cornstarch, and a bit of baking soda before cooking to boost flavor and keep it moist. After we stir-fried the chicken and vegetables, we added the noodles to the pan, along with a mixture of soy sauce, lime juice, brown sugar, fish sauce, and Thai chiles for spicy heat. Waiting to add the basil until the last minute ensured that its flavor and color stayed fresh. Do not substitute other types of noodles for the rice noodles here.

If fresh Thai chiles are unavailable, substitute one serrano or one-half jalapeño (remove the seeds to make the dish milder). To make the chicken easier to slice, freeze it for 15 minutes. You will need a 12-inch nonstick skillet or a 14-inch flat-bottomed wok for this recipe.

8	ounces (⅜-inch-wide) rice noodles
2	tablespoons vegetable oil, divided
⅛	teaspoon baking soda
12	ounces boneless, skinless chicken breasts, trimmed and sliced thin crosswise
¼	cup plus 2 teaspoons soy sauce, divided
½	teaspoon cornstarch
½	cup packed brown sugar
3	tablespoons lime juice (2 limes), plus lime wedges for serving
2	tablespoons fish sauce
3	Thai chiles, stemmed and sliced into thin rings
½	head napa cabbage, cored and cut into 1-inch pieces (6 cups)
1½	cups coarsely chopped fresh Thai or Italian basil

1. Bring 4 quarts water to boil in large pot. Remove from heat, add noodles, and let sit, stirring occasionally, until soft and pliable but not fully tender. Drain noodles and rinse under cold running water until chilled. Drain noodles well again and toss with 2 teaspoons oil; set aside.

2. Combine 2 teaspoons water and baking soda in medium bowl. Add chicken and toss to coat; let sit for 5 minutes. Add 2 teaspoons soy sauce and cornstarch, and toss until well combined. Whisk remaining ¼ cup soy sauce, sugar, lime juice, fish sauce, 2 tablespoons water, and Thai chiles in small bowl until sugar has dissolved; set aside.

3. Heat 2 teaspoons oil in nonstick skillet or flat-bottomed wok over medium-high heat until just smoking. Add chicken and increase heat to high. Cook, tossing chicken slowly but constantly, until no longer pink, 2 to 6 minutes; transfer to clean medium bowl.

4. Heat remaining 2 teaspoons oil in now-empty pan over high heat until just smoking. Add cabbage and cook, tossing slowly but constantly, until crisp-tender, about 3 minutes. Add noodles, sauce, and chicken and cook, tossing slowly but constantly, until thoroughly combined and noodles are well coated and tender, 2 to 4 minutes. Off heat, fold in basil. Serve with lime wedges.

Chicken Pad See Ew

Serves 4 to 6   **Total Time** 1 hour

Why This Recipe Works Pad see ew, a Thai street food now popular around the world, is said to have been born out of the Chinese style of stir-frying but is a distinctly Thai dish, with sweet-spicy-tart flavors and flat rice noodles. We combined the noodles with tender chicken, crisp Chinese broccoli, and moist egg, bound together by a sweet-salty soy sauce–based sauce. Chile vinegar is served separately, allowing diners to make their portion as spicy as they like. If fresh Thai chiles are unavailable, substitute one serrano or one-half jalapeño. You can substitute an equal amount of broccolini, but be sure to trim and peel the stalks before cutting. Do not substitute other types of noodles for the rice noodles here. To make the chicken easier to slice, freeze it for 15 minutes. You will need a 12-inch nonstick skillet or a 14-inch flat-bottomed wok, each with a tight-fitting lid, for this recipe.

Chile Vinegar

⅓ cup distilled white vinegar
3 Thai chiles, stemmed and sliced into thin rings

Stir-Fry

8 ounces (¼-inch-wide) rice noodles
3 tablespoons vegetable oil, divided
⅛ teaspoon baking soda
12 ounces boneless, skinless chicken breasts, trimmed and sliced thin crosswise
1 tablespoon plus 2 teaspoons soy sauce, divided
½ teaspoon cornstarch
¼ cup oyster sauce
2 tablespoons packed dark brown sugar
1 tablespoon distilled white vinegar
1 teaspoon molasses
1 teaspoon fish sauce
3 garlic cloves, sliced thin
3 large eggs
10 ounces Chinese broccoli or broccolini, trimmed, florets cut into 1-inch pieces, stalks cut ½ inch thick on bias

1. For the chile vinegar Combine vinegar and Thai chiles in bowl; set aside for serving. (Chile vinegar can be refrigerated for up to 1 day; bring to room temperature before serving.)

2. For the stir-fry Bring 4 quarts water to boil in large pot. Remove from heat, add noodles, and let sit, stirring occasionally, until soft and pliable but not fully tender. Drain noodles and rinse under cold running water until chilled. Drain noodles well again and toss with 2 teaspoons oil; set aside.

3. Combine 2 teaspoons water and baking soda in medium bowl. Add chicken and toss to coat; let sit for 5 minutes. Add 2 teaspoons soy sauce and cornstarch and toss until well combined. Whisk oyster sauce, sugar, vinegar, molasses, fish sauce, and remaining 1 tablespoon soy sauce in small bowl until sugar dissolves; set aside.

4. Cook 2 teaspoons oil and garlic in nonstick skillet or flat-bottomed wok over medium-low heat until garlic is deep golden brown, 1 to 2 minutes. Add chicken and increase heat to high. Cook, tossing chicken slowly but constantly, until no longer pink, 2 to 6 minutes; transfer to large bowl.

5. Heat 1 tablespoon oil in now-empty pan over high heat until shimmering. Add eggs and scramble quickly using rubber spatula. Continue to cook, scraping slowly but constantly along bottom and sides of pan, until eggs just form cohesive mass, 15 to 30 seconds (eggs will not be completely dry). Transfer to bowl with chicken and break up any large egg curds.

6. Heat remaining 2 teaspoons oil in now-empty pan over high heat until just smoking. Add Chinese broccoli and ¼ cup water (water will sputter) and cover immediately. Cook, without stirring, until broccoli is bright green, about 2 minutes. Uncover and continue to cook, tossing slowly but constantly, until all water has evaporated and broccoli is crisp-tender and spotty-brown, 1 to 3 minutes. Add noodles, oyster sauce mixture, and chicken-egg mixture and cook, tossing slowly but constantly, until thoroughly combined and noodles are well coated and tender, 2 to 4 minutes. Serve, passing chile vinegar separately.

Sesame Noodles with Shredded Chicken

Serves 4   **Total Time** 35 minutes

Why This Recipe Works For easy sesame noodles, we turned to chunky peanut butter and toasted sesame seeds, grinding them together in the food processor along with soy sauce, rice vinegar, hot sauce, and brown sugar. To avoid pasty noodles, we made sure to rinse the cooked noodles with cold water, and to avoid clumping we tossed them with some sesame oil, which also boosted the sesame flavor. Scallions, carrot, and red bell pepper lent the dish fresh flavor, color, and crunch. We prefer the flavor and texture of chunky peanut butter here; however, creamy peanut butter can be used. If you cannot find fresh Chinese egg noodles, substitute 12 ounces dried spaghetti or linguine. Cooking the noodles until completely tender and leaving them slightly wet after rinsing are important for the texture of the finished dish. We like using Seared Chicken Breasts here (page 60) but any cooked chicken would work.

Sauce

- 5 tablespoons soy sauce
- ¼ cup chunky peanut butter
- 3 tablespoons sesame seeds, toasted
- 2 tablespoons rice vinegar
- 2 tablespoons packed light brown sugar
- 1 tablespoon grated fresh ginger
- 2 garlic cloves, minced
- 1 teaspoon hot sauce
- ½ cup hot tap water

Noodles

- 1 pound fresh Chinese egg noodles
  Table salt for cooking noodles
- 2 tablespoons toasted sesame oil
- 4 cups shredded cooked chicken
- 4 scallions, sliced thin on bias
- 1 carrot, peeled and shredded
- 1 red bell pepper, stemmed, seeded, and cut into ½-inch pieces
- 2 tablespoons minced fresh cilantro
- 1 tablespoon sesame seeds, toasted

1. For the sauce Process soy sauce, peanut butter, sesame seeds, vinegar, sugar, ginger, garlic, and hot sauce in blender until smooth, about 30 seconds. With blender running, add hot water, 1 tablespoon at a time, until sauce has consistency of heavy cream (you may not need all of water).

2. For the noodles Bring 4 quarts water to boil in large pot. Add noodles and 1 tablespoon salt and cook, stirring often, until tender. Drain noodles, rinse with cold water, and drain again, leaving noodles slightly wet. Transfer noodles to large bowl and toss with sesame oil.

3. Add sauce, shredded chicken, scallions, carrot, and bell pepper and gently toss to combine. Season with salt and pepper to taste. Sprinkle individual portions with cilantro and sesame seeds before serving.

Chicken
Pad See Ew

Sesame Noodles with
Shredded Chicken

SAVORY PIES AND CASSEROLES

For baked pasta casseroles, see Chapter 11 Pasta and Noodles

Photos (clockwise from top left): Lattice-Topped Dutch Oven Chicken Pot Pie with Spring Vegetables; Chicken Enchiladas Rojas; Chicken Divan; Chicken Chilaquiles

Classic Chicken Pot Pie

Serves 6 to 8   **Total Time** 1½ hours with premade dough

Why This Recipe Works This recipe yields moist meat; bright, fresh vegetables; and a creamy but not excessively rich filling, draped with a flaky pie crust. To simplify the cooking process, we poached boneless, skinless chicken breasts in broth before shredding them into bite-size pieces. For the sauce, we sautéed our aromatics and vegetables before adding flour to make a roux. Whisking in the reserved chicken poaching liquid along with milk built rich flavor. A bit of sherry brightened up the filling. We stirred in the shredded chicken, peas, and parsley just before topping the pie to ensure that these delicate ingredients didn't overcook in the oven. You can use store-bought pie dough in place of homemade in this recipe.

1½ pounds boneless, skinless chicken breasts, trimmed
2 cups chicken broth
4 tablespoons unsalted butter
1 onion, chopped fine
3 carrots, peeled and sliced ¼ inch thick
2 celery ribs, sliced ¼ inch thick
1 teaspoon table salt
2 garlic cloves, minced
2 teaspoons minced fresh thyme or ½ teaspoon dried
½ cup all-purpose flour
1½ cups milk
¼ cup dry sherry
1 cup frozen peas
3 tablespoons minced fresh parsley
1 recipe Foolproof All-Butter Double-Crust Pie Dough (page 323)
1 egg, lightly beaten with 1 teaspoon water

1. Adjust oven rack to lower-middle position and heat oven to 400 degrees. Bring chicken and broth to simmer in Dutch oven over medium heat. Reduce heat to low, cover, and cook until chicken registers 160 degrees, 10 to 15 minutes. Transfer chicken to cutting board and broth to bowl.

2. Melt butter in now-empty pot over medium heat. Add onion, carrots, celery, and salt and cook until softened, about 5 minutes. Stir in garlic and thyme and cook until fragrant, about 30 seconds. Stir in flour and cook for 1 minute. Whisk in reserved broth and milk, scraping up any browned bits and smoothing out any lumps. Bring to simmer and cook until sauce is thickened, about 3 minutes. Season with salt and pepper to taste, then stir in sherry.

3. Once chicken is cool enough to handle, shred with 2 forks into bite-size pieces, then add to sauce, along with any accumulated juices, peas, and parsley. Transfer to 13 by 9-inch baking dish (or similar size casserole dish). (Filling can be frozen

for up to 1 month; to bake, thaw completely in refrigerator, then bring to gentle simmer, covered, stirring often, before transferring to baking dish and continuing with step 4.)

4. Roll each dough disk into 9-inch round on well-floured counter, then overlap by half, brushing with water where dough overlaps. Roll together to seal, then roll into 16 by 12-inch rectangle. Loosely roll dough around rolling pin and gently unroll it over filling in dish, letting excess dough hang over edge. Trim dough to ½ inch beyond lip of dish, then tuck overhang under itself; folded edge should be flush with edge of dish. Crimp dough evenly around edge of dish using your fingers. Cut five 2-inch slits in top of dough. (Assembled pot pie can be refrigerated for up to 24 hours; to bake, continue with step 5, increasing cooking time to 40 to 50 minutes.)

5. Brush surface with egg wash and bake until topping is golden and filling is bubbling, about 30 minutes, rotating dish halfway through cooking. Let cool for 20 minutes before serving.

Chicken, Spinach, and Artichoke Pot Pie

Serves 4   **Total Time** 1 hour

Why This Recipe Works The creamy-vegetal flavors of spinach and artichoke dip inspire this simple but luscious chicken pot pie, which takes advantage of several of our favorite convenience foods. Mixing thawed frozen spinach with jarred artichokes and Boursin cheese gave us an incredible base. To create a velvety sauce, we stirred in broth, cream, and—for thickening without the need for a roux—Wondra flour, a finely ground precooked flour that instantly dissolves in liquids. Placing the chicken atop the vegetables kept the meat from drying out. A buttery sheet of puff pastry made the perfect top to our updated pot pie. While we prefer the flavor and texture of jarred whole baby artichoke hearts, you can substitute 6 ounces frozen artichoke hearts, thawed and patted dry. To thaw frozen puff pastry, let it sit either in the refrigerator for 24 hours or on the counter for 30 minutes to 1 hour. You can substitute an equal amount of all-purpose flour for the Wondra flour, if necessary; however, the sauce will have a pasty, slightly gritty texture.

1¼ pounds frozen spinach, thawed and squeezed dry
1 (5.2-ounce) package Boursin Garlic & Fine Herbs cheese
1 cup jarred whole artichoke hearts packed in water, halved
2 carrots, peeled and shredded
¾ cup chicken broth
½ cup heavy cream

Chicken, Spinach, and Artichoke Pot Pie

¼ cup capers, rinsed

1 tablespoon Wondra flour

12 ounces boneless, skinless chicken breasts, trimmed and sliced thin

1 teaspoon grated lemon zest

⅛ teaspoon table salt

⅛ teaspoon pepper

1 (9½ by 9-inch) sheet puff pastry, thawed

1 large egg, lightly beaten with 2 tablespoons water

1. Adjust oven rack to middle position and heat oven to 425 degrees. Spray 8-inch square baking dish with vegetable oil spray. Stir spinach, Boursin, artichokes, carrots, broth, cream, capers, and flour together in bowl, then transfer to prepared dish.

2. Toss chicken with lemon zest in second bowl, sprinkle with salt and pepper, and spread in even layer over spinach mixture. Cut puff pastry into 8-inch square and place over top of chicken. Cut four 2-inch slits in center of dough, then brush dough with egg wash.

3. Bake until crust is golden brown and filling is bubbling, 30 to 35 minutes, rotating dish halfway through baking. Remove pot pie from oven and let cool for 10 minutes before serving.

Foolproof All-Butter Double-Crust Pie Dough

Makes one 9-inch double crust
Total Time 2½ hours

20 tablespoons (2½ sticks) unsalted butter, chilled, divided

2½ cups (12½ ounces) all-purpose flour, divided

2 tablespoons sugar

1 teaspoon table salt

½ cup (4 ounces) ice water, divided

1. Grate 4 tablespoons butter on large holes of box grater and place in freezer. Cut remaining 16 tablespoons butter into ½-inch cubes.

2. Pulse 1½ cups flour, sugar, and salt in food processor until combined, 2 pulses. Add cubed butter and process until homogeneous paste forms, 40 to 50 seconds. Using your hands, carefully break paste into 2-inch pieces and redistribute evenly around processor blade. Add remaining 1 cup flour and pulse until mixture is broken into pieces no larger than 1 inch (most pieces will be much smaller), 4 to 5 pulses. Transfer mixture to bowl. Add grated butter and toss until butter pieces are separated and coated with flour.

3. Sprinkle ¼ cup ice water over mixture. Toss with rubber spatula until mixture is evenly mois-tened. Sprinkle remaining ¼ cup ice water over mixture and toss to combine. Press dough with spatula until dough sticks together. Using spatula, divide dough into 2 equal portions. Transfer each portion to sheet of plastic wrap. Working with 1 portion at a time, draw edges of plastic over dough and press firmly on sides and top to form compact, fissure-free mass. Wrap in plastic and form into 5-inch disk. Refrigerate dough for at least 2 hours or up to 2 days. Let chilled dough sit on counter to soften slightly, about 10 minutes, before rolling. (Wrapped dough can be frozen for up to 1 month. If frozen, let dough thaw completely on counter before rolling.)

Lattice-Topped Dutch-Oven Chicken
Pot Pie with Spring Vegetables

Biscuit-Topped Dutch Oven
Chicken Pot Pie

Lattice-Topped Dutch Oven Chicken Pot Pie with Spring Vegetables

Serves 6   **Total Time** 1½ hours

Why This Recipe Works In this one-pot approach to chicken pot pie, we completed all of the cooking within (and on top of!) a Dutch oven, starting it on the stovetop before transferring it to the oven to bake. Boneless, skinless chicken thighs were easy and stayed moist through cooking. We stirred them right into the gravy and turned to tomato paste and soy sauce to boost savoriness without being distinguishable in their own right. To give our pot pie fresh spring flavor we swapped in leeks for onions and stirred in fresh asparagus, peas, and tarragon after pulling the pot from the oven. As for the crust, store-bought puff pastry was convenient; we wove it into a simple but stunning lattice. Baking the delicate lattice top separate from the filling ensured it held its shape. We simply turned the lid of the Dutch oven upside down to act as a baking sheet before covering the pot and baked the pastry on top. To thaw frozen puff pastry, let it sit either in the refrigerator for 24 hours or on the counter for 30 minutes to 1 hour. We prefer to place the baked pastry on top of the filling in the pot just before serving for an impressive presentation; however, you can also cut the pastry into wedges and place them over individual portions of the filling.

1 (9½ by 9-inch) sheet puff pastry, thawed
4 tablespoons unsalted butter
1 pound leeks, white and light green parts only, halved lengthwise, cut into ½-inch pieces, and washed thoroughly
4 carrots, peeled and cut into ½-inch pieces
1 teaspoon table salt
4 garlic cloves, minced
2 teaspoons tomato paste
½ cup all-purpose flour
3 cups chicken broth, plus extra as needed
¼ cup heavy cream
1 teaspoon soy sauce
2 bay leaves
2 pounds boneless, skinless chicken thighs, trimmed and cut into 1-inch pieces
1 large egg, lightly beaten
1 pound asparagus, trimmed and cut on bias into 1-inch lengths
1 cup frozen peas
2 tablespoons chopped fresh tarragon or parsley
1 tablespoon grated lemon zest plus 2 teaspoons juice

1. Cut sheet of parchment paper to match outline of Dutch oven lid and place on large plate or overturned rimmed baking sheet. Roll puff pastry sheet into 15 by 11-inch rectangle on lightly floured counter. Using pizza cutter or sharp knife, cut pastry widthwise into ten 1½-inch-wide strips.

2. Space 5 pastry strips parallel and evenly across parchment circle. Fold back first, third, and fifth strips almost completely. Lay additional pastry strip perpendicular to second and fourth strips, keeping it snug to folded edges of pastry, then unfold strips. Repeat laying remaining 4 pastry strips evenly across parchment circle, alternating between folding back second and fourth strips and first, third, and fifth strips to create lattice pattern. Using pizza cutter, trim edges of pastry following outline of parchment circle. Cover loosely with plastic wrap and refrigerate while preparing filling.

MAKING A LATTICE TOP

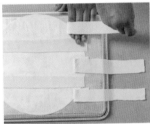

1. Space 5 pastry strips parallel and evenly across parchment circle. Fold back first, third, and fifth strips almost completely.

2. Lay pastry strip perpendicular to second and fourth strips, keeping it snug to folded edges of pastry, then unfold strips.

3. Repeat laying remaining 4 pastry strips evenly across parchment circle, alternating between folding back second and fourth strips and first, third, and fifth strips to create lattice pattern.

4. Using pizza cutter, trim edges of pastry following outline of parchment circle.

3. Adjust oven rack to lower-middle position and heat oven to 400 degrees. Melt butter in Dutch oven over medium heat. Add leeks, carrots, and salt and cook until vegetables are softened, 5 to 7 minutes. Stir in garlic and tomato paste and cook until fragrant, about 1 minute. Stir in flour and cook for 1 minute.

4. Slowly stir in broth, scraping up any browned bits and smoothing out any lumps. Stir in cream, soy sauce, and bay leaves. Bring to simmer and cook until mixture is thickened, about 3 minutes. Stir in chicken and return to simmer.

5. Off heat, cover pot with inverted lid and carefully place parchment with pastry on lid. Brush pastry with egg and sprinkle with salt. Transfer pot to oven and bake until pastry is puffed and golden brown, 25 to 30 minutes, rotating pot halfway through baking.

6. Remove pot from oven. Transfer parchment with pastry to wire rack; discard parchment. Remove lid and discard bay leaves. Stir asparagus into filling and cook over medium heat until crisp-tender, 3 to 5 minutes. Off heat, stir in peas and let sit until heated through, about 5 minutes. Adjust filling consistency with extra hot broth as needed. Stir in tarragon and lemon zest and juice. Season with salt and pepper to taste. Set pastry on top of filling and serve.

Biscuit-Topped Dutch Oven Chicken Pot Pie

Serves 8 **Total Time** 2 hours

Why This Recipe Works For those who prefer their chicken pot pie crowned with flaky biscuits, it pays to bake the biscuits on their own, not directly atop the filling, in order to avoid soggy bottoms. A simple cream biscuit dough eliminated the need to cut butter into flour, and 30 seconds of kneading developed just enough gluten to trap gas during baking, helping the biscuits rise to lofty heights. Rather than bake our biscuits prior to baking our pot pie, we consolidated by flipping the Dutch oven's lid to create a surface area upon which our biscuits could bake while the filling cooked below. Since biscuits benefit from a hot oven (425 degrees) but the filling prefers gentler heat, we placed the biscuit-laden lid on top of room-temperature filling, allowing the oven to bring it to a simmer. Then, once the biscuits were baked, we removed the lid and biscuits, reduced the oven to 300 degrees, and let the filling continue to cook until chicken and vegetables were tender. Finally, we warmed the biscuits by placing them on the cooked filling as it cooled for 10 minutes. Do not substitute boneless, skinless chicken breasts for the thighs in this recipe or the meat will taste very dry.

Biscuits

2 cups (10 ounces) all-purpose flour
2 teaspoons sugar
2 teaspoons baking powder
½ teaspoon table salt
1½ cups heavy cream

Filling

3½ pounds boneless chicken thighs, trimmed and cut into 1-inch pieces
¾ teaspoon table salt
½ teaspoon pepper
3 tablespoons vegetable oil, divided
2 onions, chopped fine
4 garlic cloves, minced
1 teaspoon minced fresh thyme leaves or ¼ teaspoon dried
½ cup all-purpose flour
⅓ cup dry white wine
3½ cups chicken broth
1 pound celery root, peeled and cut into ½-inch pieces
1 pound carrots, peeled and cut into ½-inch pieces
1 cup frozen peas
¾ cup heavy cream
¼ cup minced fresh tarragon
1 tablespoon dry sherry

1. For biscuits Adjust oven rack to lowest position and heat oven to 425 degrees.

2. Whisk flour, sugar, baking powder, and salt together in large bowl. Stir in cream until dough forms, about 30 seconds. Transfer dough to lightly floured counter, gather into ball, and knead until smooth, about 30 seconds. Flatten dough into 7-inch circle and cut into 8 wedges.

3. Place sheet of parchment paper on upside-down lid of large Dutch oven and nestle lid securely inside nest of towels to hold it steady. Arrange biscuits on parchment-lined pot lid; set aside while preparing filling.

4. For filling Pat chicken dry with paper towels and sprinkle with salt and pepper. Heat 1 tablespoon oil in Dutch oven over medium-high heat until just smoking. Brown half of chicken on both sides, 6 to 8 minutes; transfer to bowl. Repeat with 1 tablespoon oil and remaining chicken; transfer to bowl.

5. Add remaining 1 tablespoon oil and onions to pot and cook over medium heat until softened, 5 to 7 minutes. Stir in garlic and thyme and cook until fragrant, about 30 seconds. Stir in flour and cook for 1 minute. Whisk in wine and broth, scraping up any browned bits and smoothing out any lumps.

6. Stir in celery root, carrots, and browned chicken along with any accumulated juices. Off heat, cover pot with inverted, biscuit-topped lid and transfer to oven. Bake until biscuits are dark brown, about 35 minutes, rotating pot halfway through baking.

7. Remove pot from oven and reduce oven to 300 degrees. Transfer parchment and biscuits to cooling rack. Return pot to oven and continue to cook, uncovered, until filling is thickened and vegetables are tender, 20 to 25 minutes, stirring occasionally.

8. Remove pot from oven, stir in the peas, cream, tarragon, and sherry and season with salt and pepper to taste. Arrange biscuits on hot filling and let sit for 10 minutes before serving.

VARIATION

Biscuit-Topped Dutch Oven Chicken Pot Pie with Bell Pepper, Corn, Zucchini, and Basil

Omit celery root, carrots, and peas. Add 1 red bell pepper, stemmed, seeded, and cut into ½-inch pieces, to pot with onions. Add 1 teaspoon chili powder to pot with garlic. After removing biscuits from oven in step 7, stir 2 zucchini, halved lengthwise, seeded, and cut into ½-inch pieces, and 2 cups fresh or frozen corn into filling and continue to cook as directed. Substitute ¼ cup chopped fresh basil leaves for tarragon.

Gluten-Free Chicken Pot Pie

Serves 4 to 6   Total Time 2 hours with premade dough

Why This Recipe Works To create a gluten-free version of this quintessential comfort food, we knew we'd be using our own gluten-free pie dough for the topping. To overcome the structural challenge of using gluten-free flours, which produced too-soft dough, we added a modest amount of xanthan gum, but to our surprise, even with ample amounts of butter and sour cream, the dough was tough. We tried several common tenderizers (baking soda, lemon juice, and vinegar), and found vinegar produced a pie crust that was not only tender but also light and flaky. Moving on, we needed to find a roux replacement that would deliver a velvety, rich sauce. We tested every gluten-free thickener we could think of but sauces were gloppy and unappetizing. Finally, we turned to our own flour blend, the same one used in our crust. Because it contains a combination of flours and starches, it didn't turn the gravy slimy, like starches alone, or gritty, like flour alone. To ensure that our perfected dough baked up nice and flaky, rather than bake it atop the crust, we parbaked the rolled-out dough until golden, then slide it over the filling. All the assembled pie needed was about 10 minutes in the oven to finish cooking through and unify the flaky crust and hearty, comforting filling. If you don't have a rimless baking sheet to use for baking the crust, use an inverted rimmed baking sheet. We prefer to use our ATK All-Purpose Gluten-Free Flour Blend (page 328); however, an equal amount by weight of your favorite store-bought gluten-free flour blend can be substituted.

1 recipe Single-Crust Gluten-Free Pie Dough
4 tablespoons unsalted butter
1 onion, chopped fine
2 carrots, peeled and sliced ¼ inch thick
1 celery rib, sliced ¼ inch thick
¼ teaspoon table salt
¼ teaspoon pepper
1 teaspoon tomato paste
1 teaspoon minced fresh thyme
1½ ounces (⅓ cup) ATK All-Purpose Gluten-Free Flour Blend (page 328)
2 cups chicken broth
1½ pounds boneless, skinless chicken breasts and/or thighs, trimmed
½ cup frozen green peas
¼ cup heavy cream
3 tablespoons minced fresh parsley
1 tablespoon dry sherry

1. Roll pie dough between 2 sheets of parchment paper into 10-inch circle. Remove top parchment sheet. Fold in outer ½-inch rim of dough (creating 9½-inch circle). Using index finger of one hand and thumb and index finger of other hand, crimp folded edge of dough to make attractive fluted rim. Using paring knife, cut 4 oval-shaped vents, each about 2 inches long and ½ inch wide, in center of dough. Transfer dough, still on parchment, to baking sheet and chill in freezer until firm, about 15 minutes.

2. Adjust oven racks to upper-middle and lower-middle positions and heat oven to 400 degrees. Bake shaped dough on upper rack until golden brown and crisp, 18 to 20 minutes. Transfer crust, still on sheet, to wire rack and let cool slightly. (Do not turn off oven.)

3. Meanwhile, melt butter in Dutch oven over medium-high heat. Add onion, carrots, celery, salt, and pepper and cook until tender and lightly browned, about 8 minutes. Stir in tomato paste and thyme and cook until browned, about 2 minutes. Stir in flour blend and cook until golden, about 1 minute.

Single-Crust Gluten-Free Pie Dough

Makes one 9-inch single crust
Total Time 1¾ hours
We prefer to use our ATK All-Purpose Gluten-Free Flour Blend (page 328); however, an equal amount by weight of your favorite store-bought gluten-free flour blend can be substituted.

3 tablespoons ice water
1½ tablespoons sour cream
1½ teaspoons rice vinegar
6½ ounces (¾ cup plus ⅔ cup) ATK All-Purpose Gluten-Free Flour Blend (page 328)
1½ teaspoons sugar
½ teaspoon table salt
¼ teaspoon xanthan gum
8 tablespoons unsalted butter, cut into ¼-inch pieces and frozen for 10 to 15 minutes

1. Combine ice water, sour cream, and vinegar in bowl. Process flour blend, sugar, salt, and xanthan gum in food processor until combined, about 5 seconds. Scatter butter over top and pulse until crumbs look uniform and distinct pieces of butter are no longer visible, 20 to 30 pulses.

2. Pour sour cream mixture over flour mixture and pulse until dough comes together in large pieces around processor blade, about 20 pulses.

3. Transfer dough to sheet of plastic wrap and form into 5-inch disk. Wrap tightly in plastic and refrigerate for at least 1 hour or up to 2 days. Let chilled dough sit on counter to soften slightly, about 30 minutes, before rolling. (Dough cannot be frozen.)

PREPARING GLUTEN-FREE POT PIE CRUST

Bake crust on baking sheet. Carefully slide parbaked pie crust on top of warm filling.

4. Slowly whisk in broth, scraping up any browned bits and smoothing out any lumps. Add chicken, cover, and bring to simmer. Reduce heat to medium-low and continue to simmer, covered, stirring occasionally, until chicken registers 160 degrees for breasts and 175 degrees for thighs, and sauce has thickened, 15 to 18 minutes. Off heat, transfer chicken to large bowl and let cool slightly. Shred with 2 forks into bite-size pieces.

5. Stir peas, heavy cream, parsley, and sherry into thickened sauce, then stir in shredded chicken along with any accumulated juices. Season with salt and pepper to taste. Pour mixture into 9½-inch deep-dish pie plate and place parbaked pie crust on top of filling. Bake on lower rack until crust is deep golden brown and filling is bubbly, about 10 minutes. Let pot pie cool for 5 to 10 minutes before serving.

ATK All-Purpose Gluten-Free Flour Blend

Makes 42 ounces (about 9⅓ cups)
Total Time 10 minutes

No single gluten-free flour or starch behaves like wheat flour—a blend is a must. We found that two flours—white rice and brown rice—provided the right baseline of protein, starch, and flavor. Tapioca and potato starch offered structure and chew. Milk powder contributed proteins that improved structure and aided in browning. Be sure to use potato starch, not potato flour, in this blend. Tapioca starch is also sold as tapioca flour; they are interchangeable. We vastly prefer Bob's Red Mill white and brown rice flours to other brands. You can omit the milk powder, but your baked goods won't brown as well and they will taste less rich. We strongly recommend that you weigh your ingredients, as the ratios of ingredients are integral to successful gluten-free baking. If you measure by volume, spoon each ingredient into the measuring cup (do not pack or tap) and scrape off the excess.

24 ounces (4½ cups plus ⅓ cup) white rice flour
7½ ounces (1⅔ cups) brown rice flour
7 ounces (1⅓ cups) potato starch
3 ounces (¾ cup) tapioca starch
¾ ounce (¼ cup) nonfat dry milk powder

Whisk all ingredients in large bowl until well combined. Transfer to airtight container and refrigerate for up to 3 months. Bring to room temperature before using.

Chicken Shepherd's Pie

Serves 6   **Total Time** 2 hours

Why This Recipe Works Trading beef or lamb for chicken makes for a shepherd's pie that's fresh and full-flavored, while still filling enough for a winter's night. We initially tried ground chicken, but it came out dry and chalky. Bone-in, skin-on thighs proved far better; we seared and braised them, rendering needed fat and building flavorful fond in the pan before discarding the skin and bones and shredding the meat, which would soak up some of the liquid and make a moist, cohesive filling. For the vegetables, we stuck with traditional onion, carrots, and peas, along garlic, thyme, and lemon juice for brightness. As for the topping, we decided to skip the fussy process of preparing mashed potatoes. We simply boiled chunks of peeled russet potatoes, tossed them with butter, and—after spooning them over the filling—brushed on egg before baking, and found that we loved the rustic topping; it was both easy and delicious. You will need a 10-inch ovensafe skillet for this recipe. You can use dry white wine in place of the sherry. Make sure to use russet potatoes here. The skillet will be crowded initially but the cutlets will shrink as they cook.

2 pounds bone-in chicken thighs, trimmed
¾ teaspoon table salt, divided, plus salt for cooking potatoes
¾ teaspoon pepper, divided
6 tablespoons unsalted butter, cut into 6 pieces, divided
1 onion, chopped
3 carrots, peeled, halved lengthwise, and cut crosswise ½ inch thick
2 garlic cloves, minced
1½ teaspoons minced fresh thyme
¼ cup dry sherry
2 cups chicken broth
2 pounds russet potatoes, peeled and cut into 1-inch chunks
¼ cup cornstarch
1 cup frozen peas, thawed
1 tablespoon lemon juice
1 large egg, lightly beaten

1. Adjust oven rack to upper-middle position and heat oven to 375 degrees. Pat chicken dry with paper towels and sprinkle with ½ teaspoon salt and ¼ teaspoon pepper. Melt 1 tablespoon butter in 10-inch ovensafe skillet over medium-high heat. Cook chicken until well browned on both sides, about 10 minutes (skillet will be crowded). Transfer chicken to plate and pour off all but 2 tablespoons fat from skillet.

Chicken
Shepherd's Pie

5. Whisk cornstarch and ¼ cup water together in bowl. Bring broth mixture in skillet to boil and whisk in cornstarch mixture. Return to boil and cook until thickened, about 1 minute. Remove from heat and stir in peas, lemon juice, and shredded chicken. Season with salt and pepper to taste.

6. Spoon potatoes over entire surface of filling. Brush potatoes with egg. Transfer to oven and bake until pie is bubbling, about 15 minutes. Turn oven to broil and cook until potatoes are golden brown, 5 to 7 minutes. Let cool for 15 minutes before serving.

Rustic Farmhouse Chicken Casserole

Serves 6 to 8   **Total Time** 45 minutes

Why This Recipe Works This satisfying casserole combines moist cooked chicken and tender potatoes and carrots in a velvety sauce and gets topped off with a layer of crunchy croutons. Rendering bacon provided a rich, smoky base in which to sauté vegetables before adding some flour for thickening and broth and cream to build our gravy. To avoid boiling potatoes separately, we microwaved them to jump-start their cooking before stirring them into the pan along with cooked, shredded chicken and some fresh parsley. We transferred everything to a casserole dish and fashioned rustic croutons by tearing up a baguette. The uneven pieces offered plenty of craggy edges that became toasted in the oven, a nice contrast to the creamy, potato-y filling. We like using Perfect Poached Chicken (page 60) here but any cooked chicken would work.

2. Return skillet to medium-high heat, add onion and carrots, and cook until golden brown, about 5 minutes. Add garlic and thyme and cook until fragrant, about 30 seconds. Add sherry and cook until pan is nearly dry, scraping up any browned bits, about 1 minute. Stir in broth.

3. Return chicken to skillet, skin side up, along with any accumulated juices, and bring to boil. Cover, reduce heat to medium-low, and simmer until chicken registers 175 degrees, 12 to 14 minutes. Remove skillet from heat and transfer chicken to plate. Let chicken cool slightly, shred chicken with 2 forks into bite-size pieces; discard skin and bones.

4. Meanwhile, place potatoes and 1 tablespoon salt in large saucepan and cover with water by 1 inch. Bring to boil over high heat, reduce heat to medium, and cook at strong simmer until tender, 15 to 18 minutes. Drain potatoes and return to saucepan. Place saucepan over low heat and cook to drive off any remaining moisture from potatoes, about 1 minute. Off heat, gently fold remaining 5 tablespoons butter, remaining ¼ teaspoon salt, and remaining ½ teaspoon pepper into potatoes. Cover and set aside.

4	slices bacon, chopped
1	onion, chopped fine
3	carrots, peeled and sliced ¼ inch thick
1	red bell pepper, stemmed, seeded, and cut into ½-inch pieces
3	tablespoons vegetable oil, divided
¼	cup all-purpose flour
3	garlic cloves, minced
1	teaspoon minced fresh thyme or ¼ teaspoon dried
3½	cups chicken broth
½	cup heavy cream
1	pound Yukon Gold potatoes, peeled and cut into ½-inch pieces
1	(18-inch) baguette, torn into ¾-inch pieces
⅛	teaspoon table salt
	Pinch pepper
3	cups shredded cooked chicken
2	tablespoons minced fresh parsley

1. Adjust oven rack to middle position and heat oven to 475 degrees. Cook bacon in Dutch oven over medium-high heat until crisp, 5 to 7 minutes. Stir in onion, carrots, bell pepper, and 1 tablespoon oil and cook until vegetables are softened, about 5 minutes. Stir in flour, garlic, and thyme and cook until fragrant, about 30 seconds.

2. Gradually whisk in broth and cream, scraping up any browned bits and smoothing out any lumps. Simmer until thickened and vegetables are nearly tender, 3 to 5 minutes.

3. Meanwhile, microwave potatoes in covered bowl, stirring occasionally, until tender, about 10 minutes. In separate bowl, toss bread with remaining 2 tablespoons oil and sprinkle with salt and pepper. Grease 13 by 9-inch broiler-safe baking dish (or similar size casserole dish).

4. Stir shredded chicken, microwaved potatoes, and parsley into sauce and season with salt and pepper to taste. Transfer to prepared baking dish and sprinkle with bread. Bake until bread is deep golden and toasted, about 10 minutes. Let cool slightly and serve.

Maple-Glazed Brussels Sprouts

Serves 6 to 8   **Total Time** 30 minutes
Choose brussels sprouts with small, tight heads no more than 1½ inches in diameter.

  4 tablespoons unsalted butter, divided
  2 pounds brussels sprouts, trimmed and halved
  ½ cup chicken broth
  2 tablespoons maple syrup, divided
  1 teaspoon minced fresh thyme
  ⅛ teaspoon cayenne pepper
  4 teaspoons cider vinegar

1. Melt 2 tablespoons butter in 12-inch skillet over medium-high heat. Add brussels sprouts and cook until browned, 6 to 8 minutes. Stir in broth, 1 tablespoon maple syrup, thyme, and cayenne; reduce heat to medium-low; and cook, covered, until brussels sprouts are nearly tender, 6 to 8 minutes.

2. Uncover and increase heat to medium-high. Continue to cook until liquid is nearly evaporated, about 5 minutes. Off heat, stir in vinegar, remaining 2 tablespoons butter, and remaining 1 tablespoon maple syrup. Season with salt and pepper to taste, and serve.

Chicken Divan

Serves 4   **Total Time** 1 hour

Why This Recipe Works Chicken divan began its life in a fancy New York restaurant, where chefs combined poached chicken and broccoli with both béchamel and hollandaise sauces, fortified with Parmesan cheese and whipped cream. Later versions became considerably more down-market, relying on canned soup, frozen broccoli, sour cream, and mayonnaise. This version dispenses with the multiple sauces and the convenience products. We browned and poached both chicken and broccoli before arranging them on a platter and then completing our creamy, cheesy sauce. Instead of making a separate hollandaise, we incorporated egg yolks and lemon juice right into our pan sauce before pouring it over our chicken and broccoli, adding extra Parmesan, and running the platter under the broiler to create the browned crust that is arguably the best part of a divan.

  3 tablespoons vegetable oil, divided
  1 pound broccoli florets, cut into 1-inch pieces
  2½ cups chicken broth, divided
  ¼ cup all-purpose flour
  4 (6- to 8-ounce) boneless, skinless chicken breasts, trimmed
  ½ teaspoon table salt
  ¼ teaspoon pepper
  2 shallots, minced
  1 cup heavy cream
  ½ cup dry sherry
  2 teaspoons Worcestershire sauce
  3 ounces Parmesan cheese, grated (1½ cups), divided
  3 large egg yolks
  1 tablespoon lemon juice
  3 tablespoons unsalted butter

1. Heat 1 tablespoon oil in 12-inch skillet over medium-high heat until just smoking. Add broccoli and cook until spotty brown, about 1 minute. Add ½ cup broth, cover, and steam until just tender, about 1½ minutes. Remove lid and cook until liquid has evaporated, about 1 minute. Transfer broccoli to paper towel–lined plate; wipe skillet clean.

2. Heat remaining 2 tablespoons oil in now-empty skillet over medium-high heat until smoking. Meanwhile, place flour in shallow dish. Sprinkle chicken with salt and pepper and dredge in flour to coat. Cook chicken until golden brown on both sides, 4 to 6 minutes. Transfer chicken to plate.

3. Add shallots to skillet and cook until just softened, about 1 minute. Add cream and remaining 2 cups broth, scraping up any browned bits and smoothing out any lumps. Return chicken to skillet and simmer over medium-high heat until cooked through, about 10 minutes. Transfer chicken to clean plate and continue to simmer sauce until reduced to 1 cup, about 10 minutes. Add sherry and Worcestershire and simmer until reduced again to 1 cup, about 3 minutes. Stir in 1 cup Parmesan.

4. Adjust oven rack to lower-middle position and heat broiler. Whisk egg yolks and lemon juice in small bowl, then whisk in about ¼ cup sauce. Off heat, whisk egg yolk mixture into sauce in skillet, then whisk in butter.

5. Cut chicken into ½-inch-thick slices and arrange on broiler-safe platter. Scatter broccoli over chicken and pour sauce over broccoli. Sprinkle with remaining ½ cup Parmesan and broil until golden brown, 3 to 5 minutes. Serve.

King Ranch Casserole

Serves 6 to 8   **Total Time** 2 hours

Why This Recipe Works King Ranch just might be the most famous casserole in Texas, packed with tender pieces of chicken, corn tortillas, and spicy tomatoes bound in a rich, cheesy sauce. We wanted to keep its mildly spicy Southwestern flavors intact while avoiding soggy tortillas or relying on canned soup for body. Crisping the tortillas in the oven prevented them from disintegrating into mush. We then built a sauce with sautéed onions, jalapeños, and Ro-Tel tomatoes, the Texas brand of spicy canned tomatoes that are a hallmark of the recipe. Instead of discarding their juice, we reduced the liquid to intensify the tomato flavor. As a nod to this dish's roots, we sprinkled crushed Fritos over the casserole to brown, crowning this Texas classic with crunchy corn flavor. If you can't find Ro-Tel tomatoes, use 2 cups of diced tomatoes combined with 2 finely chopped, stemmed, and seeded jalapeño chiles. Monterey Jack can be substituted for the Colby Jack here.

12 (6-inch) corn tortillas
    Vegetable oil spray
 1 tablespoon unsalted butter
 2 onions, chopped fine
 2 jalapeño chiles, stemmed, seeded, and minced
 2 teaspoons ground cumin
 2 (10-ounce) cans Ro-Tel Diced Tomatoes
    & Green Chilies
 5 tablespoons all-purpose flour
 3 cups chicken broth
 1 cup heavy cream
 4 (6-ounce) boneless, skinless chicken breasts,
    trimmed, halved lengthwise, and cut crosswise
    ½ inch thick
 1 pound Colby Jack cheese, shredded (4 cups)
 2 tablespoons minced fresh cilantro
 6 ounces Fritos corn chips, crushed (2¼ cups)

Chicken Divan

King Ranch
Casserole

1. Adjust oven racks to upper-middle and lower-middle positions and heat oven to 450 degrees. Arrange tortillas on 2 baking sheets and lightly spray both sides of tortillas with oil spray. Bake until slightly crisp and browned, about 12 minutes. Let tortillas cool slightly, then break into bite-size pieces. Adjust upper oven rack to middle position (oven rack will be hot).

2. Heat butter in Dutch oven over medium-high heat. Add onions, jalapeños, and cumin and cook until lightly browned, about 8 minutes. Add tomatoes and their juice and cook until most of liquid has evaporated, about 10 minutes. Stir in flour and cook for 1 minute. Add broth and cream, scraping up any browned bits and smoothing out any lumps, bring to simmer, and cook until thickened, 2 to 3 minutes. Stir in chicken and cook until no longer pink, about 4 minutes. Off heat, add Colby Jack and cilantro and stir until cheese is melted. Season with salt and pepper to taste.

3. Scatter half of tortilla pieces in 13 by 9-inch baking dish (or similar size casserole dish) set in rimmed baking sheet. Spoon half of filling evenly over tortilla pieces. Scatter remaining tortilla pieces over filling, then top with remaining filling. (Unbaked casserole can be wrapped tightly in aluminum foil and refrigerated for up to 24 hours; increase covered baking time to 30 minutes.)

4. Cover dish with foil and bake until filling is bubbling, about 15 minutes. Remove foil, sprinkle with Fritos, and bake until lightly browned, about 10 minutes. Let casserole cool for 10 minutes before serving.

Carolina Chicken Bog

Serves 6 to 8   **Total Time** 1¾ hours

Why This Recipe Works By name it may not sound like much, but chicken bog—a one-pot dish of chicken, smoky sausage, and white rice—is a delicious dish from South Carolina kitchens, packing hearty taste into every last bite. To get in on that flavor, we set our sights on pilaf-like rice cooked in a deeply flavorful broth with generous chunks of chicken and sausage. Rather than risk overcooking white meat, we turned to chicken thighs for juicy meat and maximum flavor. We browned the thighs and set them aside, using the skin's rendered fat to infuse chicken flavor into the onion and kielbasa. Next, we created an aromatic broth, blooming minced garlic before stirring in chicken broth. The thighs cooked in this superflavorful liquid at a low simmer before we added the rice. As the rice cooked to a tender, slightly sticky consistency, we shredded the chicken and folded it into the sausage-studded rice. We now had all of the meaty, seasoned flavors of a Loris Bog-Off Festival contender, but in the comfort of our own kitchen.

Carolina
Chicken Bog

6 (5- to 7-ounce) bone-in chicken thighs, trimmed
1½ teaspoons table salt, divided
1¼ teaspoons, divided
1 tablespoon vegetable oil
8 ounces smoked kielbasa sausage,
    cut into ½-inch-thick rounds
1 onion, chopped fine
3 garlic cloves, minced
4 cups chicken broth
2 cups long-grain white rice

1. Pat chicken dry with paper towels and sprinkle with ½ teaspoon salt and ¼ teaspoon pepper. Heat oil in Dutch oven over medium heat until just smoking. Cook chicken skin side down until browned, 5 to 8 minutes. Transfer chicken to plate; discard skin.

2. Pour off all but 1 tablespoon fat from pot and return to medium heat. Add sausage and onion and cook until onion is translucent and sausage begins to brown, 3 to 5 minutes. Add garlic and cook until fragrant, about 30 seconds. Add broth, chicken, remaining 1 teaspoon salt, and remaining 1 teaspoon pepper and bring to boil. Reduce heat to low, cover, and simmer until chicken is tender, about 30 minutes.

3. Remove chicken from pot and set aside. Stir rice into pot, cover, and continue to cook over low heat until rice is tender, about 20 minutes.

4. Shred chicken with 2 forks into bite-size pieces; discard bones. Gently fold shredded chicken into rice mixture. Remove from heat and let sit, covered, for 10 minutes. Serve.

Chicken and Rice Casserole with Peas, Carrots, and Cheddar

Serves 8 **Total Time** 2¼ hours

Why This Recipe Works This hearty chicken and rice casserole is a weeknight workhorse sure to appeal to kids and adults alike. A two-step cooking method, poaching the chicken breasts in the sauce first and then removing them and stirring in the rice, worked like a charm: Both elements cooked evenly and each absorbed the sauce's flavor while lending their own key attributes to the mix. Chicken cooked this way tasted juicier and maintained its texture better, even when held overnight. Shredded cheddar cheese added a pleasant bite. Fresh bread crumbs added great crunch and held up nicely in the fridge or freezer. After adding the rice, be sure to stir the sauce often for the first few minutes, using a heatproof rubber spatula; this is when the rice is most likely to clump and stick to the bottom of the pot. Serve with lemon wedges, if desired.

  4 slices hearty white sandwich bread, torn into quarters
  2 tablespoons unsalted butter, melted, plus 4 tablespoons unsalted butter
  5 tablespoons minced fresh parsley, divided
  1 onion, chopped fine
  1 teaspoon table salt
  3 garlic cloves, minced
  ⅛ teaspoon cayenne pepper
  ¼ cup all-purpose flour
  6 cups chicken broth
  1 cup heavy cream
  2 pounds boneless, skinless chicken breasts, trimmed
  1½ cups long-grain white rice
  1 pound frozen peas and carrots
  8 ounces sharp cheddar cheese, shredded (2 cups)
  2 tablespoons lemon juice

1. Adjust oven rack to middle position and heat oven to 300 degrees. Pulse bread and 2 tablespoons melted butter in food processor to coarse crumbs, about 6 pulses. Spread crumbs evenly over rimmed baking sheet and bake, stirring occasionally, until light golden and dry, 20 to 30 minutes. Let crumbs cool completely, about 20 minutes, then toss with 2 tablespoons parsley and season with salt and pepper to taste; set aside.

2. Increase oven temperature to 400 degrees. Melt remaining 4 tablespoons butter in Dutch oven over medium heat. Add onion and salt and cook until softened and lightly browned, 5 to 7 minutes. Stir in garlic and cayenne and cook until fragrant, about 30 seconds. Stir in flour and cook, stirring constantly, until golden, about 1 minute. Slowly whisk in broth and cream, scraping up any browned bits and smoothing out any lumps.

3. Add chicken and bring to simmer. Reduce heat to low, cover, and cook until chicken registers 160 degrees, 10 to 15 minutes. Transfer chicken to cutting board. Let chicken cool slightly, then shred with 2 forks into bite-size pieces.

4. Stir rice into liquid in pot, cover, and cook over low heat, stirring often, until rice has absorbed much of liquid and is just tender, 15 to 20 minutes.

5. Off heat, stir in shredded chicken along with any accumulated juices, peas and carrots, cheddar, and lemon juice and season with salt and pepper to taste. Pour mixture into 13 by 9-inch baking dish (or similar size casserole dish) and sprinkle evenly with crumb topping. (Casserole can be refrigerated for up to 2 days. To bake, cover with greased aluminum foil and bake in 400-degree oven until hot throughout, 40 to 50 minutes; remove foil and continue to bake until crumbs are crisp, 10 to 20 minutes, before garnishing as directed.)

6. Bake until sauce is bubbling and hot throughout, 10 to 15 minutes. Sprinkle with remaining 3 tablespoons parsley before serving.

Chicken and Rice with Caramelized Onions, Cardamom, and Raisins

Serves 6 **Total Time** 2 hours

Why This Recipe Works The warming, complex spices used in traditional biryani inspire the chicken and rice here. After browning bone-in chicken thighs, we created a darkly sweet base by caramelizing sliced onions with brown sugar. To that we added fresh ginger, cardamom, cumin, and saffron—and bloomed their flavors before adding our cooking liquid: chicken broth. We simmered the browned chicken in this richly flavored liquid before adding the rice and moving the whole production to the oven to finish cooking in its gentle, even heat. After about 20 minutes and a few periodic stirs, the grains had taken on a golden hue and tender texture. We shredded the chicken for easier eating, removing the skin and bones, and stirred in some raisins and minced cilantro for bursts of sweetness and freshness. To keep the dish from becoming greasy, remove excess fat from the chicken thighs and trim most of the skin. Be sure to stir the rice gently when cooking in step 3; aggressive stirring will make it gluey. You can substitute long-grain white, jasmine, or Texmati rice for the basmati.

2½ pounds bone-in chicken thighs, trimmed
  1 teaspoon table salt, divided
  ¼ teaspoon pepper
  1 tablespoon extra-virgin olive oil
  3 onions, sliced thin
  1 teaspoon packed brown sugar
  4 garlic cloves, minced
  2 teaspoons grated fresh ginger
  1 teaspoon minced fresh thyme or ¼ teaspoon dried
  ½ teaspoon ground cardamom
  ½ teaspoon ground cumin
  ⅛ teaspoon saffron threads, crumbled
2½ cups chicken broth
  2 cups basmati rice, rinsed
  ⅓ cup raisins
  3 tablespoons minced fresh cilantro
  ½ teaspoon grated lemon zest plus 4 teaspoons juice

1. Adjust oven rack to middle position and heat oven to 350 degrees. Pat chicken dry with paper towels and sprinkle with ½ teaspoon salt and pepper. Heat oil in Dutch oven over medium-high heat until just smoking. Brown half of chicken, skin side down, 6 to 8 minutes; transfer to large plate. Repeat with remaining chicken.

2. Pour off all but 2 tablespoons fat left in pot. Add onions, sugar, and remaining ½ teaspoon salt and cook over medium heat, stirring often, until onions are deep golden brown, 25 to 35 minutes. Stir in garlic, ginger, thyme, cardamom, cumin, and saffron and cook until fragrant, about 30 seconds. Stir in broth, scraping up any browned bits. Add chicken, browned side up, along with any accumulated juices and bring to simmer. Cover and simmer gently for 20 minutes.

3. Stir in rice. Cover, transfer pot to oven, and cook, stirring occasionally, until chicken registers 175 degrees, rice is tender, and liquid has been absorbed, 20 to 30 minutes.

4. Remove pot from oven and transfer chicken to cutting board; cover pot and set aside. Let chicken cool slightly, then shred chicken with 2 forks into bite-size pieces; discard skin and bones. Gently stir shredded chicken, raisins, cilantro, and lemon zest and juice into rice, and season with salt and pepper to taste. Cover and let stand until chicken is warmed through, about 5 minutes. Serve.

Arroz con Pollo
Serves 6   Total Time 2 hours

Why This Recipe Works For arroz con pollo full of classic flavors, we briefly marinated bone-in chicken thighs in a mixture of vinegar, salt, pepper, and oregano. Next we stewed the meat with tomato sauce, olives, capers, and rice until it became fall-off-the-bone tender while the rice cooked evenly. We started the chicken skin-on to maximize the flavorful renderings but then removed it after cooking. Using spoons rather than forks to pull the cooked meat apart gave us appealing chunks instead of shreds. To keep the dish from becoming greasy, it is important to remove excess fat and most of the skin from the chicken thighs, leaving just enough skin to protect the meat. Long-grain rice can be substituted for the medium-grain rice; however, you will need to increase the amount of water to ¾ cup.

  6 garlic cloves, minced
  5 teaspoons distilled white vinegar, divided
1½ teaspoons minced fresh oregano or
      ½ teaspoon dried
1¾ teaspoons table salt, divided
  ½ teaspoon pepper
  4 pounds bone-in chicken thighs, trimmed
  2 tablespoons extra-virgin olive oil, divided
  1 onion, chopped fine
  1 small green bell pepper, stemmed, seeded, and chopped fine
  ¼ teaspoon red pepper flakes
  ¼ cup minced fresh cilantro, divided
1¾ cups chicken broth
  1 (8-ounce) can tomato sauce
  ¼ cup water, plus extra as needed
  3 cups medium-grain white rice
  ½ cup pitted green Manzanilla olives, halved
  1 tablespoon capers, rinsed
  ½ cup jarred whole pimentos, cut into
      2 by ¼-inch strips
      Lemon wedges

1. Adjust oven rack to middle position and heat oven to 350 degrees. Combine garlic, 1 tablespoon vinegar, oregano, 1 teaspoon salt, and pepper in large bowl. Add chicken, toss to coat, and cover; let sit at room temperature for 15 minutes.

2. While chicken marinates, heat 1 tablespoon oil in Dutch oven over medium heat until shimmering. Add onion and bell pepper and cook until softened, 5 to 7 minutes. Stir in pepper flakes and cook until fragrant, about 30 seconds. Stir in 2 tablespoons cilantro.

3. Push vegetables to side of pot and increase heat to medium-high. Add chicken, skin side down, to cleared area of pot and brown lightly, 2 to 4 minutes per side, reducing heat if chicken begins to burn. Stir in broth, tomato sauce, and water and bring to simmer. Cover, reduce heat to medium-low, and simmer for 20 minutes.

4. Stir in rice, olives, capers, and remaining ¾ teaspoon salt and bring to simmer. Cover, transfer pot to oven, and cook, stirring often, until chicken registers 175 degrees, rice is tender, and liquid has been absorbed, about 30 minutes. (If pot appears dry and begins to scorch after 20 minutes, stir in additional ¼ cup water.)

5. Remove pot from oven and transfer chicken to cutting board; cover pot and set aside. Let chicken cool slightly, then shred chicken into large chunks using 2 soupspoons; discard skin and bones. Toss chicken chunks, pimentos, remaining 2 teaspoons vinegar, remaining 1 tablespoon oil, and remaining 2 tablespoons cilantro in clean bowl and season with salt and pepper to taste.

6. Place chicken on top of rice, cover, and let stand until warmed through, about 5 minutes. Serve with lemon wedges.

Chicken Enchiladas Rojas
Serves 4 to 6   **Total Time** 1¾ hours

Why This Recipe Works Enchiladas with red sauce are a great dish to assemble the day before; we found it best to store the enchiladas separately from the sauce so that we could bake the enchiladas partway through before adding the sauce, giving the top a chance to crisp and brown. We first created a simple red chile sauce; blooming a full 3 tablespoons of chili powder in oil along with cumin and coriander gave it deep flavor. We poached the chicken directly in the sauce, which both enhanced the flavor of the sauce and ensured moist, flavorful meat. Sharp cheddar cheese complemented the filling nicely, while jarred jalapeños and fresh cilantro provided tang and brightness. Brushing the tortillas with oil and microwaving them not only made them easier to roll and fill, but also sealed the surface of the tortillas, preventing them from becoming soggy during baking. If you prefer, Monterey Jack cheese can be used instead of cheddar, or, for a mellower flavor and creamier texture, try substituting an equal amount of queso fresco. Serve with sour cream, diced avocado, shredded romaine lettuce, and/or lime wedges.

Arroz con Pollo

Chicken Enchiladas Rojas

¼ cup vegetable oil, divided
1 onion, chopped fine
3 tablespoons chili powder
3 garlic cloves, minced
2 teaspoons ground coriander
2 teaspoons ground cumin
2 teaspoons sugar
½ teaspoon table salt
1 pound boneless, skinless chicken thighs, trimmed and cut into ¼-inch-wide strips
2 (8-ounce) cans tomato sauce
⅓ cup water
½ cup minced fresh cilantro
⅓ cup jarred jalapeños, rinsed, patted dry, and chopped
10 ounces sharp cheddar cheese, shredded (2½ cups), divided
12 (6-inch) corn tortillas
Vegetable oil spray

1. Adjust oven rack to middle position and heat oven to 400 degrees. Heat 2 tablespoons oil in large saucepan over medium heat until shimmering. Add onion and cook until softened and lightly browned, 5 to 7 minutes. Stir in chili powder, garlic, coriander, cumin, sugar, and salt and cook until fragrant, about 30 seconds. Stir in chicken, tomato sauce, and water and bring to gentle simmer. Cook, stirring occasionally, until chicken is tender and flavors meld, 8 to 10 minutes.

2. Pour mixture through fine-mesh strainer into bowl, pressing on strained chicken mixture to extract as much sauce as possible; set sauce aside. Transfer chicken mixture to bowl, refrigerate for 20 minutes to chill, then stir in cilantro, jalapeños, and 2 cups cheddar.

3. Brush both sides of tortillas with remaining 2 tablespoons oil. Stack tortillas, wrap in damp dish towel, and place on plate; microwave until warm and pliable, about 1 minute. Working with 1 warm tortilla at a time, spread ⅓ cup chicken filling across center of tortilla, roll tortilla tightly around filling, and place seam side down in greased 13 by 9-inch baking dish (or similar size casserole dish); arrange enchiladas in 2 columns

across width of dish. (Enchiladas, wrapped tightly in plastic wrap and covered with aluminum foil, and sauce can be refrigerated separately for up to 24 hours or frozen for up to 1 month; if frozen, thaw completely in the refrigerator.)

4. Spray top of enchiladas with oil spray and bake uncovered until lightly toasted on top, 10 to 15 minutes. Pour sauce over enchiladas, covering tortillas completely, then sprinkle remaining ½ cup cheddar across center of enchiladas. Cover dish tightly with greased aluminum foil and bake until enchiladas are hot throughout, bubbling around edges, and cheese is melted, 20 to 25 minutes. Serve immediately.

Chicken Enchiladas Verdes
Serves 4 to 6   **Total Time** 1¾ hours

Why This Recipe Works In enchiladas verdes, the bright, citrusy flavors of green chiles and tomatillos offer fresh contrast to the richness of chicken wrapped in soft corn tortillas and topped with melted cheese. To give the sauce its characteristic char, the chiles and fresh tomatillos are often roasted on a comal. Instead we ran them under the broiler before pulsing them in a food processor and thinning our sauce with a bit of the poaching liquid, giving us a well-seasoned, chunky sauce. To enrich the filling, we liked pepper Jack cheese—and sprinkled more on top of the dish. The enchiladas required just a brief stint in the oven to heat through and melt the cheese. To increase spiciness, reserve some of the chiles' ribs and seeds and add them to the food processor in step 4. To avoid soggy enchiladas, be sure to cool the chicken filling before filling the tortillas.

3 tablespoons vegetable oil, divided
1 onion, chopped
½ teaspoon ground cumin
3 garlic cloves, minced, divided
1½ cups chicken broth
1 pound boneless, skinless chicken breasts, trimmed
1½ pounds tomatillos, husks and stems removed, rinsed well, dried, and halved
3 poblano chiles, stemmed, halved, and seeded
1-2½ teaspoons sugar
1 teaspoon table salt
8 ounces pepper Jack or Monterey Jack cheese, shredded (2 cups), divided
½ cup chopped fresh cilantro
12 (6-inch) corn tortillas
2 scallions, sliced thin
Thinly sliced radishes
Sour cream

ARRANGING ENCHILADAS

In order to fit 12 enchiladas in a 13 by 9-inch casserole dish, you need to arrange them widthwise in the pan, in two rows of six enchiladas.

Chicken
Enchiladas
Verdes

4. Transfer vegetables, along with any accumulated juices, to food processor. Add 1 teaspoon sugar, salt, remaining garlic, and reserved cooking liquid to food processor and pulse until sauce is somewhat chunky, about 8 pulses. Season with salt and pepper to taste, and adjust tartness by stirring in remaining sugar, ½ teaspoon at a time; set aside.

5. When chicken is cool, shred with 2 forks into bite-size pieces. Combine chicken with 1½ cups pepper Jack and cilantro; season with salt to taste.

6. Grease 13 by 9-inch baking dish (or similar size casserole dish). Brush both sides of tortillas with remaining 2 tablespoons oil. Stack tortillas, wrap in damp dish towel, and place on plate. Microwave until warm and pliable, about 1 minute. Working with 1 warm tortilla at a time, spread ⅓ cup chicken filling across center. Roll tortilla tightly around filling and place seam side down in dish, arranging enchiladas in 2 columns across width of dish. Cover completely with remaining sauce. Sprinkle with remaining ½ cup pepper Jack.

7. Cover dish tightly with greased aluminum foil and bake until enchiladas are heated through, 15 to 20 minutes. Let enchiladas cool for 10 minutes. Sprinkle with scallions, and serve, passing radishes and sour cream separately.

Chicken Chilaquiles
Serves 4   **Total Time** 1¼ hours

Why This Recipe Works Chilaquiles is a comforting Mexican dish made from fried tortilla wedges that are tossed in a deeply flavored red or green chile sauce. The crisp chips soften slightly in the sauce, giving the dish a unique crunchy-chewy texture. The finished dish is topped with a variety of fresh garnishes along with a fried egg and served for breakfast or lunch. We decided to swap the fried egg for shredded chicken to make the dish into an even heartier meal. We quickly discovered that store-bought chips led to disappointing results; they either turned mushy or never softened properly so we switched to making our own from corn tortillas. Although most recipes call for frying tortillas, we opted to bake them, which was not only more hands-off but made for a lighter finished dish. We made a simple sauce by pureeing both dried and fresh chiles, vegetables, and aromatics in a blender and then simmering the mixture in a Dutch oven. Poaching the chicken directly in the sauce infused both with more depth of flavor. An assortment of fresh garnishes made the perfect counterpoint to the rich sauce, chips, and chicken. For the best texture, we prefer to use 100 percent corn tortillas in this recipe. Serve with crema and lime wedges.

1. Adjust 1 oven rack to middle position and second rack 6 inches from broiler element; heat broiler. Heat 2 teaspoons oil in medium saucepan over medium heat until shimmering. Add onion and cook until softened and lightly browned, 5 to 7 minutes. Stir in cumin and two-thirds of garlic and cook until fragrant, about 30 seconds. Stir in broth and bring to simmer.

2. Add chicken and reduce heat to medium-low. Cover and simmer until chicken registers 160 degrees, 15 to 20 minutes, flipping chicken halfway through cooking. Transfer chicken to cutting board and let cool slightly.

3. While chicken cools, measure out ½ cup cooking liquid and set aside; discard remaining liquid. Toss tomatillos and poblanos with 1 teaspoon oil. Arrange tomatillos cut side down and poblanos skin side up on aluminum foil–lined rimmed baking sheet. Broil on upper rack until vegetables blacken and start to soften, 5 to 10 minutes, rotating sheet halfway through broiling. Let tomatillos and poblanos cool slightly, then remove skins from poblanos (leave tomatillo skins intact). Heat oven to 450 degrees.

Chicken Chilaquiles

Pastel Azteca

16 (6-inch) corn tortillas, cut into 8 wedges
¼ cup extra-virgin olive oil, divided
1 teaspoon table salt, divided
5 dried guajillo chiles, stemmed, seeded, and torn into ½-inch pieces (⅔ cup)
1 (28-ounce) can whole peeled tomatoes
1 cup finely chopped onion, divided
1 poblano chile, stemmed, seeded, and chopped
1 jalapeño chile, stemmed, seeded, and chopped
3 garlic cloves, peeled and chopped
8 sprigs fresh cilantro plus 2 tablespoons minced, divided
1½ cups chicken broth
1½ pounds boneless, skinless chicken breasts, trimmed
4 ounces queso fresco, crumbled (1 cup)
1 avocado, halved, pitted, and cut into ½-inch pieces
2 radishes, trimmed and sliced thin

1. Adjust oven racks to upper-middle and lower-middle positions and heat oven to 425 degrees. Spread tortillas evenly over 2 rimmed baking sheets. Drizzle each sheet with 2 tablespoons oil and ¼ teaspoon salt and toss until evenly coated. Bake, stirring occasionally, until tortillas are golden brown and crisp, 15 to 20 minutes, switching sheets halfway through baking.

2. Toast guajillos in Dutch oven over medium heat, stirring frequently, until fragrant, 2 to 6 minutes. Transfer toasted guajillos to blender and process until finely ground, 60 to 90 seconds. Add tomatoes and their juice, ¾ cup onion, poblano, jalapeño, garlic, cilantro sprigs, and remaining ¾ teaspoon salt to blender and process until very smooth, 60 to 90 seconds.

3. Combine guajillo-tomato mixture and broth in now-empty Dutch oven and bring to boil over medium-high heat. Nestle chicken into sauce. Cover, reduce heat to medium-low, and cook until chicken registers 160 degrees, 10 to 15 minutes, flipping halfway through cooking.

4. Transfer chicken to plate, let cool slightly, then shred with 2 forks into bite-size pieces. Meanwhile, increase heat to medium and simmer sauce until thickened and measures 4½ cups, about 5 minutes.

5. Stir in shredded chicken and cook until warmed through, about 2 minutes. Off heat, stir in tortillas, cover, and let sit until tortillas have softened slightly, 2 to 5 minutes. Transfer tortilla mixture to serving dish and sprinkle with queso fresco, avocado, radishes, remaining ¼ cup onion, and minced cilantro. Serve immediately.

Pastel Azteca

Serves 6 to 8   **Total Time** 1¾ hours

Why This Recipe Works Traditional Mexican pastel Azteca (literally meaning "Aztec cake") features corn tortillas layered with chicken, cheese, and a simple enchilada-style sauce. We added a bit of flour to our sauce, which allowed it to cling to the tortillas nicely. Toasting the tortillas in a dry skillet was preferable to using untoasted tortillas, which disintegrated, and it was less messy and oily than frying them, as some pastel Azteca recipes do. A combination of melty Monterey Jack and tangy queso fresco provided contrasting flavors and textures that helped bring the dish to life, and we topped the casserole with cilantro, scallions, and chopped tomatoes for a pop of bright freshness.

 2 dried ancho chiles, stemmed, seeded, and torn into ½-inch pieces (½ cup)
 1 tablespoon vegetable oil
 1 onion, chopped
 1 tablespoon tomato paste
 3 garlic cloves, minced
 2 teaspoons dried oregano
 1 teaspoon ground cumin
 1 teaspoon ground coriander
 1 teaspoon table salt
 ½ teaspoon pepper
 3 tablespoons all-purpose flour
 3 cups chicken broth
 2½ pounds boneless, skinless chicken breasts, trimmed
 5 scallions, sliced thin, divided
 ⅓ cup chopped fresh cilantro, divided
 1 tablespoon lime juice
 18 (6-inch) corn tortillas
 8 ounces Monterey Jack cheese, shredded (2 cups)
 8 ounces queso fresco, crumbled (2 cups)
 2 tomatoes, cored and chopped

1. Adjust oven rack to middle position and heat oven to 425 degrees. Toast anchos in 12-inch skillet over medium heat, stirring frequently, until fragrant, 2 to 6 minutes; transfer to blender.

2. Heat oil in Dutch oven over medium-high heat until shimmering. Add onion and cook until softened, about 5 minutes. Stir in tomato paste, garlic, oregano, cumin, coriander, salt, and pepper and cook until fragrant, about 1 minute. Stir in flour and cook until slightly deepened in color, about 1 minute. Slowly whisk in broth, scraping up any browned bits and smoothing out any lumps, and bring to simmer. Reduce heat to medium-low and cook, whisking often, until sauce is slightly thickened, about 3 minutes.

3. Add sauce to blender and process until smooth, about 30 seconds; return to now-empty pot. Nestle chicken into sauce, cover, and cook over medium-low heat until chicken registers 160 degrees, about 15 minutes. Transfer chicken to cutting board, let cool slightly, then shred with 2 forks into bite-size pieces; transfer to bowl. Add 1½ cups sauce, two-thirds of scallions, ¼ cup cilantro, and lime juice and toss to combine.

4. Meanwhile, toast tortillas, one at a time, in 8-inch skillet over medium-high heat until lightly browned, about 20 seconds per side; transfer to plate and cover with dish towel. Combine Monterey Jack and queso fresco in bowl.

5. Spread ½ cup remaining sauce over bottom of 13 by 9-inch baking dish (or similar size casserole dish). Lay 6 tortillas into dish, overlapping them slightly. Spread ½ cup sauce over tortillas and top with half of chicken mixture and one-third of cheese mixture. Repeat with 6 more tortillas, ½ cup sauce, remaining chicken mixture, and half of remaining cheese mixture. Top with remaining 6 tortillas, remaining sauce, and remaining cheese.

6. Cover dish with aluminum foil and bake until sauce is bubbling and cheese is melted, 15 to 20 minutes. Let casserole cool for 10 minutes. Sprinkle with tomatoes, remaining scallions, and remaining cilantro. Serve.

Phyllo Pie with Chicken

Serves 6 to 8   **Total Time** 1½ hours

Why This Recipe Works Inspired by Greek phyllo-topped meat pies, we created a flaky, savory phyllo pie encasing a filling of ground chicken, feta, and scallions brightened with lemon and mint. We found that 16 sheets of phyllo (eight on top, eight on the bottom) made crusts that were substantial but still tender. Adding a middle layer of four sheets of phyllo helped the pie keep its shape after it was sliced. Almost every recipe utilizing phyllo calls for brushing each layer with some sort of fat, usually oil or clarified butter, to encourage flakiness. We found that lightly spraying our phyllo with olive oil spray enabled us to coat the sheets with a thinner (but still adequate) layer of fat, and it simplified the process. To prevent the top phyllo layers from curling and separating in the hot oven, we dusted grated Parmesan across each of the top sheets, which yielded a cohesive, crisp crust, with a nice boost in flavor. Phyllo dough is also available in 18 by 14-inch sheets; if using those, cut them to make 14 by 9-inch sheets. Do not thaw the phyllo in the microwave; let it sit in the refrigerator overnight or on the counter for 4 to 5 hours. While working with the phyllo, cover the sheets with plastic wrap, then a damp dish towel to prevent drying. Be sure to use ground chicken and not ground chicken breast (also labeled 99 percent fat-free) in this recipe.

1 tablespoon extra-virgin olive oil
2 pounds ground chicken
8 ounces feta cheese, crumbled into fine
  pieces (2 cups)
3 large eggs, lightly beaten
1 bunch scallions, sliced thin
½ cup pitted kalamata olives, chopped coarse
⅓ cup minced fresh mint leaves
3 tablespoons lemon juice
2 garlic cloves, minced
1 teaspoon table salt
¼ teaspoon black pepper
¼ teaspoon cayenne pepper
  Olive oil spray
20 (14 by 9-inch) sheets phyllo
  (about 8 ounces), thawed
1 ounce Parmesan cheese, grated (½ cup)

1. Adjust oven rack to middle position and heat oven to 400 degrees. Heat oil in 12-inch skillet over medium heat until shimmering. Add chicken and cook, breaking meat into small pieces with wooden spoon, until no longer pink, about 5 minutes. Transfer meat to strainer and let drain, about 5 minutes.

2. Mix feta, eggs, scallions, olives, mint, lemon juice, garlic, salt, pepper, and cayenne together in large bowl, then stir in drained chicken.

3. Spray 13 by 9-inch baking dish (or similar size casserole dish) liberally with olive oil spray. Lay 1 phyllo sheet in bottom of prepared dish and coat thoroughly with olive oil spray. Repeat with 7 more phyllo sheets, spraying each with oil. Spread half of chicken mixture evenly into dish. Cover with 4 more phyllo sheets, spraying each with oil.

4. Spread remaining chicken mixture evenly into dish. Cover with 7 more phyllo sheets, spraying each with oil and sprinkling each with generous tablespoon of Parmesan. Lay final sheet of phyllo over top and coat thoroughly with oil (do not sprinkle final layer with Parmesan).

5. Working from center outward, use palms of your hands to compress layers and press out any air pockets. Using sharp knife, lightly score pie into serving squares but do not cut through more than top 3 sheets of phyllo. (Casserole can be assembled and covered with plastic wrap and refrigerated up to 1 day. Remove plastic wrap and bake as directed in step 6, increasing the cooking time to 35 to 40 minutes.)

6. Bake until phyllo is golden and crisp, 30 to 35 minutes. Let casserole cool for at least 10 minutes or up to 2 hours before serving.

Chicken B'stilla
Serves 10 to 12   **Total time** 2½ hours

Why This Recipe Works B'stilla is an impressive Moroccan tart whose savory filling is customarily made with pigeon and richly flavored with almonds and cinnamon sugar. The most cherished qualities of this dish are its many contrasts: crisp yet juicy, sweet yet savory, succulent yet wholesome. We started by swapping the pigeon for chicken thighs, which we cooked gently in a spiced broth to ensure that they were moist and flavorful. We used the rich cooking liquid as the base of the traditional custard-like component of the pie. Although b'stilla is usually made with layers of a paper-thin dough called warqa, we found that phyllo worked perfectly. We decided to assemble the pie in the same skillet we had used to cook the chicken, which created a wide, thin pie that was easy to serve. We lined the pan with phyllo, poured in the chicken-egg mixture, and topped it with more phyllo as well as a traditional mixture of slivered almonds tossed with cinnamon and sugar. The pie tasted great, but the nut topping was dry and loose. Instead, we encased the almond mixture in phyllo to make the base of the pie; that way, it could soak up the rich juices from the chicken above it. A customary sprinkling of cinnamon sugar on the baked pie drove home the sweet-savory contrasts. Phyllo dough is also available in larger 18 by 14-inch sheets; if using, cut them in half to make 14 by 9-inch sheets. Do not thaw the phyllo in the microwave; let it sit in the refrigerator overnight or on the counter for 4 to 5 hours. While working with the phyllo, cover the sheets with plastic wrap, then a damp dish towel to prevent drying.

½ cup extra-virgin olive oil, divided
1 onion, chopped fine
¾ teaspoon table salt
1 tablespoon grated fresh ginger
½ teaspoon pepper
½ teaspoon ground turmeric
½ teaspoon paprika
1½ cups water
2 pounds boneless, skinless chicken thighs, trimmed
6 large eggs
½ cup minced fresh cilantro
1 pound (14 by 9-inch) phyllo, thawed
1½ cups slivered almonds, toasted and chopped
¼ cup confectioners' sugar, divided
1 tablespoon ground cinnamon, divided

1. Heat 1 tablespoon oil in 12-inch nonstick skillet over medium heat until shimmering. Add onion and salt and cook until softened, about 5 minutes. Stir in ginger, pepper, turmeric, and paprika and cook until fragrant, about 30 seconds. Add water and chicken and bring to simmer. Reduce heat

Chicken B'stilla

1. Brush 1 phyllo sheet with oil and arrange in bottom of skillet with short side against side of pan. Continue layering 11 more phyllo sheets in skillet in pinwheel pattern.

2. Sprinkle almond mixture over phyllo in skillet, then lay 2 phyllo sheets across top and brush with oil. Rotate skillet 90 degrees and lay 2 more phyllo sheets across top.

3. Spoon chicken mixture into skillet and spread into even layer. Stack 5 phyllo sheets and brush with oil. Fold in half, brush top with oil, and lay on chicken mixture.

4. Fold overhanging phyllo over filling and phyllo stack, pleating phyllo every 2 to 3 inches, and press to seal. Brush top with oil before baking.

to low, cover, and cook until chicken registers 175 degrees, 15 to 20 minutes. Transfer chicken to cutting board, let cool slightly, then shred into bite-size pieces using 2 forks; transfer to large bowl.

2. Whisk eggs together in small bowl. Bring cooking liquid to boil over high heat and cook until reduced to about 1 cup, about 10 minutes. Reduce heat to low. Whisking constantly, slowly pour eggs into broth and cook until mixture resembles loose scrambled eggs, 6 to 8 minutes; transfer to bowl with chicken. Stir in cilantro until combined. Wipe skillet clean with paper towels and let cool completely.

3. Adjust oven rack to middle position and heat oven to 375 degrees. Brush 1 phyllo sheet with oil and arrange in bottom of cooled skillet with short side against side of pan. Some phyllo will overhang edge of skillet; leave in place. Turn skillet 30 degrees. Brush second phyllo sheet with oil and arrange in skillet, leaving any overhanging phyllo in place. Repeat turning and layering with 10 more phyllo sheets in pinwheel pattern, brushing each with oil, to cover entire circumference of skillet (you should have total of 12 layers of phyllo).

4. Combine almonds, 3 tablespoons sugar, and 2 teaspoons cinnamon and sprinkle over phyllo in skillet. Lay 2 phyllo sheets evenly across top of almond mixture and brush top with oil.

Rotate skillet 90 degrees and lay 2 more phyllo sheets evenly across top; do not brush with oil. Spoon chicken mixture into skillet and spread into even layer.

5. Stack 5 phyllo sheets on counter and brush top with oil. Fold phyllo in half crosswise and brush top with oil. Lay phyllo stack on center of chicken mixture.

6. Fold overhanging phyllo over filling and phyllo stack, pleating phyllo every 2 to 3 inches, and press to seal. Brush top with oil and bake until phyllo is crisp and golden, 35 to 40 minutes.

7. Combine remaining 1 tablespoon sugar and remaining 1 teaspoon cinnamon in small bowl. Let b'stilla cool in skillet for 15 minutes. Using rubber spatula, carefully slide b'stilla out onto cutting board. Dust top with cinnamon sugar, slice, and serve.

ON THE GRILL

Photos (clockwise from top left): Grilled Jerk Chicken; Grilled Tequila Chicken with Orange, Avocado, and Pepita Salad; Best Grilled Chicken Thighs; Grilled Glazed Boneless Chicken Breasts

USING A CHARCOAL GRILL

Chicken is a summertime grilling staple, and with careful cooking you can make grilled chicken memorable for all the right reasons. Each recipe in this chapter contains specific instructions for cooking on either a charcoal or a gas grill. Follow the fire setup instructions to ensure success.

Use a Chimney Starter We strongly recommend using a chimney starter for charcoal fires. (Lighter fluid imparts an off-flavor to grilled foods.) This simple device gets all of the charcoal ready at once. Fill the bottom of the chimney starter with crumpled newspaper, set it on the charcoal grate, and fill the top with charcoal as directed. A large starter holds about 6 quarts of charcoal.

Get the Coals Hot Allow the charcoal to burn until the briquettes on top are partially covered with a thin layer of gray ash. The ash is a sign that the coals are fully lit and hot and are ready to be turned out into the grill. Don't pour out the coals prematurely; you will be left with unlit coals at the bottom of the pile that may never ignite, as well as a cooler fire.

Arrange the Coals Carefully Once the coals are covered with gray ash, empty them evenly onto the charcoal grate or as instructed in the recipe. A single-level fire is a common fire setup that delivers a uniform level of heat across the entire cooking surface.

Using a Disposable Pan Some fire setups call for using a disposable aluminum pan. Piling coals on either side of the pan creates a cool area over the pan for foods such as bone-in chicken. Alternatively, corralling the coals in the pan concentrates the heat to create an intense fire ideal for quicker-cooking foods such as burgers and scallops.

Half-Grill Charcoal Fire A half-grill fire has two cooking zones for foods that require longer cooking: You can brown the food on the hotter side and finish it on the cooler side's indirect heat. To set up this fire, distribute ash-covered coals over half of the grill, piling them in an even layer. Leave the other half free of coals.

Clean and Oil the Cooking Grate Properly heating and cleaning your grill are important steps to successful grilling. To ensure that food will release with ease, heat the grate before scraping it clean with a grill brush. For further insurance against sticking, dip a wad of paper towels into vegetable oil and run it over the cleaned grate several times.

Grilled Chicken Kebabs with Garlic and Herb Marinade

Serves 4 Total Time 1 hour (plus 3 hours marinating time)

Why This Recipe Works Grilled chicken kebabs are a great way to take boneless, skinless chicken breasts up a notch, but the lean meat requires some help to keep from becoming dried out over a hot grill. To counter this, we started with a simple olive oil marinade. Brining meat helps it retain moisture, but we worried that a true brine would make the small pieces of chicken too salty. Instead, we simply added a teaspoon of salt to the marinade, along with a mix of herbs and garlic—you can tweak the herbs based on what you like best, or try one of our spiced-up variations. Because there is no acid in the marinade and thus no danger of breaking down the texture of the meat, the chicken can be soaked for up to 24 hours before cooking. If you have thin pieces of chicken, cut them larger than 1 inch and roll or fold them into approximate 1-inch cubes. You will need four 12-inch metal skewers for this recipe.

½ cup extra-virgin olive oil
6 small garlic cloves, minced
¼ cup chopped fresh chives, minced fresh basil, parsley, tarragon, oregano, cilantro, or mint; or 2 tablespoons minced fresh thyme or rosemary
1 teaspoon table salt
Pinch pepper
1½ pounds boneless, skinless chicken breasts, trimmed and cut into 1-inch pieces
2 red bell peppers, stemmed, seeded, and cut into 1-inch pieces
1 large red onion, cut into 1-inch pieces, 3 layers thick

1. Whisk oil, garlic, herbs, salt, and pepper in small bowl.

2. Mix marinade and chicken in 1-gallon zipper-lock plastic bag; seal bag and refrigerate, turning once or twice, at least 3 hours or up to 24 hours.

3. Remove chicken from marinade, letting excess drip off. Thread each of four 12-inch skewers with 2 pieces bell pepper, 1 section onion, 2 pieces chicken, and 1 section onion. Repeat twice more, ending with 2 additional pieces bell pepper.

4A. For a charcoal grill Open bottom vent completely. Light large chimney starter filled with charcoal briquettes (6 quarts). When top coals are partially covered with ash, pour evenly over grill. Set cooking grate in place, cover, and open lid vent completely. Heat grill until hot, about 5 minutes.

4B. For a gas grill Turn all burners to high, cover, and heat grill until hot, about 15 minutes. Leave all burners on high.

5. Clean and oil cooking grate. Place kebabs on grill. Cook (covered if using gas), turning as needed, until vegetables and chicken are charred around edges and chicken is cooked through, about 12 minutes. Transfer kebabs to platter and serve.

VARIATIONS

Grilled Chicken Kebabs with Cilantro and Curry Powder

Substitute ¼ cup minced fresh cilantro or mint for herbs and add 1 teaspoon curry powder to marinade.

Grilled Chicken Kebabs with Cumin and Chili Powder

Substitute ¼ cup minced fresh parsley for herbs and add 1 teaspoon ground cumin, 1 teaspoon chili powder, ½ teaspoon ground allspice, ½ teaspoon pepper, and ¼ teaspoon ground cinnamon to marinade.

Grilled Chicken Kebabs with Cinnamon and Allspice

Substitute ¼ cup minced fresh mint or parsley (alone or in combination) for herbs and add ½ teaspoon ground cinnamon, ½ teaspoon ground allspice, and ¼ teaspoon cayenne pepper to marinade.

Grilled Chicken Kebabs with Jalapeño

Substitute ¼ cup minced fresh cilantro for herbs. Decrease salt to ½ teaspoon and add 1 teaspoon ground cumin, 1 teaspoon chili powder, 1 teaspoon turmeric, and 1 jalapeño, seeded and minced.

Grilled Chicken Kebabs with Yogurt Marinade

Substitute following mixture for herb marinade: Combine ½ cup plain whole-milk yogurt, ¼ cup extra-virgin olive oil, 3 minced garlic cloves, 2 teaspoons dried thyme, 2 teaspoons dried oregano, 1 teaspoon table salt, 1 teaspoon pepper, and ¼ teaspoon cayenne pepper. In step 2, marinate chicken for 3 to 6 hours. Whisk ¼ cup extra-virgin olive oil, 3 tablespoons lemon juice, 2 tablespoons chopped fresh basil, and 1 minced garlic clove together in bowl; set aside. Skewer chicken and grill as directed. Brush cooked kebabs with lemon dressing before serving.

Barbecued Chicken Kebabs

Serves 6   Total Time 1¼ hours (plus 1 hour marinating time)

Barbecued Chicken Kebabs

Why This Recipe Works In theory, barbecued chicken kebabs sound pretty great: char-streaked chunks of juicy meat lacquered with sweet and tangy barbecue sauce. Brining is one common way to safeguard against dry meat, but the brine made the meat so slick that the barbecue sauce refused to stick. A salt rub worked much better; the rub crisped up on the chicken's exterior, forming a craggy surface that the sauce could cling to. For depth of flavor, we turned to an unusual technique: grinding bacon to a paste and applying it to the salted meat. Combined with both sweet and smoked paprika and turbinado sugar for excellent browning, our bacon-y rub created juicy, full-flavored chicken. Use the large holes of a box grater to grate the onion. We prefer dark thigh meat for these kebabs, but white meat can be used. Don't mix white and dark meat on the same skewer, since they cook at different rates. If you have thin pieces of chicken, cut them larger than 1 inch and roll or fold them into approximate 1-inch cubes. Turbinado sugar is commonly sold as Sugar in the Raw. Demerara sugar can be substituted. You will need four 12-inch metal skewers for this recipe.

Sauce

- ½ cup ketchup
- ¼ cup molasses
- 2 tablespoons grated onion
- 2 tablespoons Worcestershire sauce
- 2 tablespoons Dijon mustard
- 2 tablespoons cider vinegar
- 1 tablespoon packed light brown sugar

Chicken

- 2 tablespoons paprika
- 4 teaspoons turbinado sugar
- 2 teaspoons kosher salt
- 2 teaspoons smoked paprika
- 2 slices bacon, cut into ½-inch pieces
- 2 pounds boneless, skinless chicken thighs or breasts, trimmed and cut into 1-inch pieces

1. For the sauce Bring all ingredients to simmer in small saucepan over medium heat and cook, stirring occasionally, until reduced to about 1 cup, 5 to 7 minutes. Transfer ½ cup sauce to small bowl and set remaining sauce aside for serving.

2. For the chicken Combine paprika, sugar, salt, and smoked paprika in large bowl. Process bacon in food processor until smooth paste forms, 30 to 45 seconds, scraping down sides of bowl as needed. Add bacon paste and chicken to spice mixture and mix with your hands or rubber spatula until ingredients are thoroughly blended and chicken is completely coated. Cover with plastic wrap and refrigerate for 1 hour. Thread chicken tightly onto four 12-inch metal skewers.

3A. For a charcoal grill Open bottom vent completely. Light large chimney starter three-quarters filled with charcoal briquettes (4½ quarts). When top coals are partially covered with ash, pour evenly over half of grill. Set cooking grate in place, cover, and open lid vent completely. Heat grill until hot, about 5 minutes.

3B. For a gas grill Turn all burners to high, cover, and heat grill until hot, about 15 minutes. Turn all burners to medium-high.

4. Clean and oil cooking grate. Place skewers on hotter part of grill (if using charcoal), and cook (covered if using gas), turning kebabs every 2 to 2½ minutes, until well browned and slightly charred, 8 to 10 minutes. Brush top surface of skewers with ¼ cup sauce, flip, and cook until sauce is sizzling and browning in spots, about 1 minute. Brush second side with remaining ¼ cup sauce, flip, and continue to cook until sizzling and browning in spots, about 1 minute.

5. Transfer skewers to serving platter, tent with aluminum foil, and let rest for 5 to 10 minutes. Serve, passing reserved sauce separately.

Grilled Boneless, Skinless Chicken Breasts

Serves 4   **Total Time** 1 hour

Why This Recipe Works The perfect grilled boneless, skinless chicken breasts are juicy, savory, and well browned and can be served as is or added to salads or sandwiches. We started by pounding them to an even thickness so that they cooked through evenly. Soaking the chicken for 30 minutes in a potent "brinerade" seasoned it and added moisture that helped keep it juicy during cooking; we spiked the salt water with just enough umami-rich fish sauce to add savory depth without any trace of fishiness, as well as honey that encouraged browning and balanced the salt. Coating the chicken in a little oil before grilling kept it from sticking to the grate, and cooking it over a hot fire ensured that it browned deeply. Serve this chicken with Red Pepper–Almond Sauce or Poblano-Pepita Sauce (page 386), pair it with Grilled Asparagus (page 353), use it in sandwiches or tacos, or slice it and add it to a salad. This recipe can easily be doubled.

- 4 (6- to 8-ounce) boneless, skinless chicken breasts, trimmed
- 3 tablespoons fish sauce for brining
- 2 tablespoons honey for brining
- 1 teaspoon table salt for brining
- ⅛ teaspoon pepper for brining
- 1 tablespoon vegetable oil

1. Pound chicken breasts to uniform thickness. Whisk ⅓ cup water, fish sauce, honey, salt, and pepper together in bowl. Transfer mixture to 1-gallon zipper-lock bag. Add chicken, press out air, seal bag, and turn bag so contents are evenly distributed. Refrigerate for 30 minutes.

2A. For a charcoal grill Open bottom vent completely. Light large chimney starter filled with charcoal briquettes (6 quarts). When top coals are partially covered with ash, pour evenly over grill. Set cooking grate in place, cover, and open lid vent completely. Heat grill until hot, about 5 minutes.

2B. For a gas grill Turn all burners to high, cover, and heat grill until hot, about 15 minutes. Leave all burners on high.

3. Remove chicken from brine, letting excess drip off, then toss with oil in second bowl until evenly coated. Clean and oil cooking grate. Place chicken, skinned side down, on grill and cook (covered if using gas) until chicken develops dark grill marks, 3 to 5 minutes. Gently release chicken from cooking grate, flip, and continue to cook until chicken registers 160 degrees, 3 to 5 minutes. Transfer chicken to cutting board and tent with aluminum foil. Let rest for 5 minutes before serving.

CREATING A SINGLE-LEVEL OR OTHER GAS FIRE

To create a single-level fire on a gas grill, turn all burners to the heat setting specified in the recipe after preheating. To create other fires, adjust the primary burner as directed and turn off or adjust other burner(s).

Grilled Lemon-Parsley Chicken Breasts

Serves 4   **Total Time** 1¼ hours

Why This Recipe Works This easy upgrade for grilled boneless, skinless chicken breasts flavors the chicken inside and out, first infusing it with a lemon marinade and then topping it with an herbal sauce. We started by soaking the chicken in a marinade of olive oil, lemon juice, garlic, salt, and pepper, along with some sugar to cut the acidity and help with browning. Adding 2 tablespoons of water diluted the marinade's concentration of salt and flavor molecules enough for an exchange of dissolved molecules to flow in and out of the chicken. Thirty minutes of marinating did the trick. While the chicken marinated, we set up the grill with a hot side and a cooler side (called a half-grill fire). We started the breasts on the cooler side, cooking them covered until they were nearly done, and then gave them a quick sear over direct heat to cook them through without drying them out. A quick sauce, made from the same ingredients we used in the marinade—plus a little chopped parsley for color and some Dijon mustard for extra flavor and emulsification—added even more moisture to the chicken as well as another layer of flavor. The chicken should be marinated for at least 30 minutes and no more than 1 hour. Serve with a vegetable or use in a sandwich or salad.

- 6 tablespoons extra-virgin olive oil, divided
- 2 tablespoons lemon juice, divided
- 1 tablespoon minced fresh parsley
- 1¼ teaspoons sugar, divided
- 1 teaspoon Dijon mustard
- 1¾ teaspoons table salt, divided
- ¾ teaspoon pepper, divided
- 3 garlic cloves, minced
- 4 (6- to 8-ounce) boneless, skinless chicken breasts, trimmed
- 1 (13 by 9-inch) disposable aluminum roasting pan

1. Whisk 3 tablespoons oil, 1 tablespoon lemon juice, parsley, ¼ teaspoon sugar, mustard, ¼ teaspoon salt, and ¼ teaspoon pepper together in bowl and set aside.

2. Whisk 2 tablespoons water, garlic, remaining 3 tablespoons oil, remaining 1 tablespoon lemon juice, remaining 1 teaspoon sugar, remaining 1½ teaspoons salt, and remaining ½ teaspoon pepper together in bowl. Transfer marinade to 1-gallon zipper-lock bag, add chicken, and toss to coat; press out as much air as possible and seal bag. Refrigerate for at least 30 minutes or up to 1 hour, flipping bag every 15 minutes.

3A. For a charcoal grill Open bottom vent completely. Light large chimney starter filled with charcoal briquettes (6 quarts). When top coals are partially covered with ash, pour evenly over half of grill. Set cooking grate in place, cover, and open lid vent completely. Heat grill until hot, about 5 minutes.

3B. For a gas grill Turn all burners to high, cover, and heat grill until hot, about 15 minutes. Leave primary burner on high and turn off other burner(s).

4. Clean and oil cooking grate. Remove chicken from marinade, allowing excess to drip off. Place chicken skinned side down on cooler side of grill with thicker side facing coals. Place disposable pan over chicken, cover grill, and cook until bottom begins to develop light grill marks and is no longer translucent, 6 to 9 minutes.

5. Flip chicken and rotate so that thinner side faces coals. Place disposable pan over chicken, cover grill, and continue to cook until chicken is opaque and registers 140 degrees, 6 to 9 minutes.

6. Slide chicken to hotter side of grill and cook, uncovered, until dark grill marks develop on both sides and chicken registers 160 degrees, 2 to 6 minutes.

7. Transfer chicken to cutting board, tent with aluminum foil, and let rest for 5 minutes. Slice chicken on bias ¼ inch thick and transfer to individual plates. Drizzle with reserved sauce and serve.

Grilled Glazed Boneless Chicken Breasts

Serves 4   Total Time 1 hour

Why This Recipe Works Painting on a glaze seems like a quick fix to add extra flavor to simple grilled chicken. But if you apply the glaze after the meat is browned, the chicken ends up dry. And if you apply the glaze too soon, the chicken won't brown, and the glaze burns before the meat cooks through. Our solution was to brown the chicken faster with the help of an unusual ingredient: dry milk powder. Just ½ teaspoon per

breast browned the chicken twice as fast; it also created a tacky surface that was perfect for holding on to the glaze. We created a variety of glazes featuring ingredients with balanced acidity and spice and just the right consistency. Applying the glaze immediately after the chicken was flipped meant less glaze stuck to the grill; it also meant that the glaze applied to the top of the chicken had time to dry out and cling. If using kosher chicken, do not brine. Use one of the following glazes: Spicy Hoisin Glaze, Honey-Mustard Glaze, Coconut-Curry Glaze, or Miso-Sesame Glaze (see pages 387–388).

¼ cup sugar for brining
¼ cup table salt for brining
4 (6- to 8-ounce) boneless, skinless chicken breasts, trimmed
2 teaspoons nonfat dry milk powder
¼ teaspoon pepper
   Vegetable oil spray
1 recipe glaze (pages 387–388)

1. Dissolve sugar and salt in 1½ quarts cold water in large container. Pound chicken to uniform thickness, then submerge in brine, cover, and refrigerate for at least 30 minutes or up to 1 hour.

2A. For a charcoal grill Open bottom vent completely. Light large chimney starter mounded with charcoal briquettes (7 quarts). When top coals are partially covered with ash, pour two-thirds evenly over half of grill, then pour remaining coals over other half of grill. Set cooking grate in place, cover, and open lid vent completely. Heat grill until hot, about 5 minutes.

2B. For a gas grill Turn all burners to high, cover, and heat grill until hot, about 15 minutes. Leave primary burner on high and turn other burner(s) to medium-high.

3. Remove chicken from brine and pat dry with paper towels. Combine milk powder and pepper in bowl. Sprinkle half of milk powder mixture over 1 side of chicken breasts. Lightly spray coated side of breasts with oil spray until milk powder is moistened. Flip chicken and sprinkle remaining milk powder mixture over second side. Lightly spray with oil spray.

4. Clean and oil cooking grate. Place chicken skinned side down on hotter part of grill and cook until browned on first side, 2 to 2½ minutes. Flip chicken, brush with 2 tablespoons glaze, and cook until browned on second side, 2 to 2½ minutes. Flip chicken, move to cooler side of grill, brush with 2 tablespoons glaze, and cook for 2 minutes. Repeat flipping and brushing 2 more times, cooking for 2 minutes on each side. Flip chicken, brush with remaining glaze, and cook until chicken registers 160 degrees, 1 to 3 minutes. Transfer chicken to plate and let rest for 5 minutes before serving.

Grilled Monterey Chicken

Serves 4 **Total Time** 1½ hours

Why This Recipe Works As invented by the Bonanza Steakhouse chain, Chicken Monterey consisted of a boneless chicken breast in the restaurant's "exclusive Monterey marinade," flame-broiled and then topped with bacon strips and melted Monterey Jack cheese. Our challenge was to create a version for home grillers. Recipes that we tried out tended to be bland and dry. To improve on these disappointing results, we started by butterflying boneless, skinless chicken breasts to provide more surface area for tasty char. For our marinade we developed a simple mixture of honey, Dijon mustard, salt, and pepper that could also double as a basting sauce on the grill. While the chicken cooked on the hotter side of a half-grill fire, we let red onion slices—basted with the reserved fat from cooking the bacon—soften on the cooler side of the grill. To finish, we slid the chicken away from the fire and topped it with the smoky onions and a mixture of cooked diced bacon and spicy shredded pepper Jack cheese. The onion slices are skewered with toothpicks to keep them from falling apart on the grill; you will need four sturdy uncolored toothpicks for this recipe. You won't need an entire red onion for this recipe; you can use the remainder to make Pico de Gallo to serve on top.

½ cup Dijon mustard
¼ cup honey
1 teaspoon table salt
½ teaspoon pepper
4 (6- to 8-ounce) boneless, skinless chicken breasts, trimmed
4 slices bacon, cut into ½-inch pieces
6 ounces pepper Jack cheese, shredded (1½ cups)
4 (½-inch-thick) slices red onion
Lime wedges

1. Whisk mustard, honey, salt, and pepper together in bowl. Reserve ¼ cup honey-mustard mixture for basting chicken. Transfer remaining honey-mustard mixture to 1-gallon zipper-lock bag.

2. Working with 1 breast at a time, starting on thick side, cut chicken in half horizontally, stopping ½ inch from edge so halves remain attached. Open up breast like book, creating single flat piece. Place chicken in bag with honey-mustard mixture, toss to coat, and refrigerate for 30 minutes to 1 hour.

3. Meanwhile, cook bacon in 10-inch skillet over medium heat until crisp, 5 to 7 minutes. Using slotted spoon, transfer bacon to paper towel–lined plate. Reserve bacon fat. Once cool, toss bacon with pepper Jack.

Grilled Monterey Chicken

Pico de Gallo

Makes about 1½ cups **Total Time** 40 minutes

To make this sauce spicier, include the jalapeño ribs and seeds.

3 tomatoes, cored and chopped
¼ teaspoon table salt
¼ cup finely chopped red onion
¼ cup chopped fresh cilantro
1 jalapeño chile, stemmed, seeded, and minced
1 tablespoon lime juice
1 garlic clove, minced

Toss tomatoes with salt in bowl. Transfer to colander and let drain for 30 minutes. Combine drained tomatoes, onion, cilantro, jalapeño, lime juice, and garlic in bowl. Season with salt and pepper to taste.

4A. For a charcoal grill Open bottom vent completely. Light large chimney starter filled with charcoal briquettes (6 quarts). When top coals are partially covered with ash, pour two-thirds evenly over half of grill, then pour remaining coals over other half of grill. Set cooking grate in place, cover, and open lid vent completely. Heat grill until hot, about 5 minutes.

4B. For a gas grill Turn all burners to high, cover, and heat grill until hot, about 15 minutes. Leave primary burner on high and turn other burner(s) to medium.

5. Push toothpick horizontally through each onion slice to keep rings intact while grilling and brush onion slices lightly with reserved bacon fat. Clean and oil cooking grate. Remove chicken from marinade, letting excess drip off. Place chicken on hotter side of grill and onion slices on cooler side of grill. Cover and cook until chicken is lightly charred, about 5 minutes. Flip onion slices and chicken. Brush chicken with reserved honey-mustard mixture, cover, and cook until lightly charred on second side, about 5 minutes.

6. Remove onion slices from grill and move chicken to cooler side of grill. Quickly remove toothpicks and separate onion rings. Divide onion rings evenly among chicken breasts. Divide bacon–pepper Jack mixture evenly over onion rings. Cover and cook until pepper Jack is melted and chicken registers 160 degrees, about 2 minutes. Transfer chicken to platter, tent with aluminum foil, and let rest for 5 to 10 minutes. Serve with lime wedges.

Grilled Tequila Chicken with Orange, Avocado, and Pepita Salad

Serves 4 Total Time 1¼ hours

Why This Recipe Works Tequila is for far more than margaritas. Here, a complexly flavored tequila-lime mixture boosts grilled chicken's flavor both in a quick marinade before cooking and, when cooked down with fresh orange juice, as a sauce drizzled over the cooked chicken. Grilled avocados gave smoky depth to a salad topped with oranges, pepitas, and a vinaigrette of lime juice, olive oil, cayenne, and honey. We cooked the chicken over the hotter part of a half-grill fire to get a good char while cooking the avocados on the cooler side. Ripe but firm avocados are critical for successful grilling. If your avocados are overripe, skip seasoning and grilling; peel and slice the avocados before assembling the salad.

- ½ cup tequila
- ½ cup water
- 6 tablespoons lime juice (3 limes), divided
- 4 garlic cloves, minced
- 2½ teaspoons table salt, divided
- 4 (6- to 8-ounce) boneless, skinless chicken breasts, trimmed and pounded to even thickness
- 3 oranges, peeled and cut into ½-inch pieces
- 5 tablespoons extra-virgin olive oil, divided
- 1 tablespoon honey
- ¼ teaspoon cayenne pepper
- ¼ teaspoon plus ⅛ teaspoon pepper, divided
- 2 ripe but firm avocados, halved and pitted
- 6 ounces (6 cups) watercress, chopped
- ⅓ cup pepitas, toasted
- 1 shallot, sliced thin

1. Whisk tequila, water, 3 tablespoons lime juice, garlic, and 2 teaspoons salt in bowl until salt is dissolved. Transfer ½ cup marinade to small saucepan. Pour remaining marinade into 1-gallon zipper-lock bag, add chicken, and toss to coat. Press out as much air as possible, seal bag, and refrigerate for 30 minutes to 1 hour, flipping bag occasionally.

2. Let oranges drain in colander set over large bowl, reserving juice. In second large bowl, whisk ¼ cup oil, honey, cayenne, ¼ teaspoon salt, ¼ teaspoon pepper, and remaining 3 tablespoons lime juice together; set aside for salad.

3A. For a charcoal grill Open bottom vent completely. Light large chimney starter filled with charcoal briquettes (6 quarts). When top coals are partially covered with ash, pour two-thirds evenly over half of grill, then pour remaining coals over other half of grill. Set cooking grate in place, cover, and open lid vent completely. Heat grill until hot, about 5 minutes.

3B. For a gas grill Turn all burners to high, cover, and heat grill until hot, about 15 minutes. Leave primary burner on high and turn other burner(s) to medium.

4. Brush avocado halves with remaining 1 tablespoon oil and sprinkle with remaining ¼ teaspoon salt and remaining ⅛ teaspoon pepper. Clean and oil cooking grate. Remove chicken from marinade, letting excess marinade drip off. Place chicken on hotter side of grill. Cook (covered if using gas), turning as needed, until chicken is nicely charred and registers 160 degrees, 8 to 12 minutes. Meanwhile, place avocados cut side down on cooler side of grill and cook until lightly charred, 3 to 5 minutes. Transfer chicken and avocados to cutting board and tent with aluminum foil.

5. Add drained orange juice to reserved marinade in saucepan, bring to simmer over medium-high heat, and cook until reduced to ¼ cup, 3 to 5 minutes. Whisk dressing to recombine, then add watercress, pepitas, shallot, and drained oranges and toss gently to coat; transfer to platter. Peel grilled avocado, slice thin, and lay on top of salad. Slice chicken on bias ½ inch thick, lay on top of salad, and drizzle with reduced marinade. Serve.

Seattle Grilled Chicken Teriyaki

Serves 6 to 8   **Total Time** 1 hour (plus 1 hour marinating time)

Why This Recipe Works Teriyaki, which translates roughly as "shiny grilled" in Japanese, describes both the sauce and the cooking style in which it's used. Inspired by the teriyaki served at Toshi's Teriyaki Grill in Mill Creek, Washington, we made a traditional sauce of soy sauce, sugar, and mirin. We pureed a portion of the sauce with garlic and ginger to use as a marinade for boneless, skinless chicken thighs. After marinating, we grilled the thighs until they were slightly charred and caramelized, and then we sliced them and served them with white rice and the reserved teriyaki sauce, just as they do at Toshi's. Serve with white rice.

    1 cup soy sauce for marinade
    ½ cup sugar for marinade
    2 tablespoons mirin for marinade
    1 (2-inch) piece ginger, peeled and sliced thin,
       for marinade
    5 garlic cloves, peeled, for marinade
    3 pounds boneless, skinless chicken thighs, trimmed

1. Bring soy sauce, sugar, and mirin to boil in small saucepan over medium-high heat, stirring to dissolve sugar. Remove from heat and let teriyaki sauce cool completely.

2. Combine ¾ cup teriyaki sauce, ginger, and garlic in blender and process until smooth, about 20 seconds. Set aside remaining teriyaki sauce for serving (you should have about ½ cup).

3. Place chicken in 1-gallon zipper-lock bag and add teriyaki sauce–ginger mixture. Press out air, seal bag, and turn to coat chicken with marinade. Refrigerate for at least 1 hour or up to 24 hours.

4A. For a charcoal grill Open bottom vent completely. Light large chimney starter filled with charcoal briquettes (6 quarts). When top coals are partially covered with ash, pour evenly over grill. Set cooking grate in place, cover, and open lid vent completely. Heat grill until hot, about 5 minutes.

4B. For a gas grill Turn all burners to high, cover, and heat grill until hot, about 15 minutes. Turn all burners to medium-high.

5. Clean and oil cooking grate. Remove chicken from marinade, letting excess marinade drip off. Place chicken on grill and cook (covered if using gas) until chicken is lightly charred and registers at least 175 degrees, 6 to 8 minutes per side, rearranging as needed to ensure even browning. Transfer to cutting board, tent with aluminum foil, and let rest for 5 minutes. Slice crosswise ½ inch thick and serve with reserved teriyaki sauce.

Grilled Tequila Chicken with Orange, Avocado, and Pepita Salad

Seattle Grilled Chicken Teriyaki

Easy Grilled Stuffed Chicken Breasts

Serves 4   Total Time 1¼ hours

Why This Recipe Works Two promising ways to add big flavor to chicken breasts are with smoke and char from grilling and with a savory stuffing. We started with a simple stuffing technique, in which we cut a pocket in the chicken breast, packed it with stuffing, and sealed it with a toothpick. Herb purees (made with garlic and olive oil) packed the most flavor and came together quickly, but oozed out of the chicken as it cooked. Creamy fontina cheese and a small amount of bread crumbs helped keep the herbs in place. With the added bulk from the stuffing, these chicken breasts had to spend extra time on the grill, so we cooked them gently over indirect heat and incorporated an olive oil–based marinade both before and after cooking to help protect against drying out and add even more flavor. Our variation plays with the flavors in both the stuffing and the marinade. You will need four sturdy, uncolored toothpicks for this recipe. We prefer the taste and texture of homemade bread crumbs (simply tear one slice of hearty white sandwich bread into pieces, grind in a food processor, and toast in a dry skillet until golden), but store-bought bread crumbs are acceptable here.

Easy Grilled Stuffed Chicken Breasts

- 6 tablespoons extra-virgin olive oil
- ½ teaspoon grated lemon zest plus 1 tablespoon juice
- 3 garlic cloves, minced
- 1 teaspoon sugar
- ¾ teaspoon table salt
- ½ teaspoon pepper
- 1 cup chopped fresh basil
- 2 ounces fontina cheese, shredded (½ cup)
- 3 tablespoons toasted bread crumbs
- 4 (6- to 8-ounce) boneless, skinless chicken breasts, trimmed

1. Whisk oil, zest and juice, garlic, sugar, salt, and pepper in small bowl. Pulse 2 tablespoons oil mixture, basil, cheese, and bread crumbs in food processor until coarsely ground, about 10 pulses.

2. Cut pocket in thick part of each chicken breast, spoon in filling, and secure with toothpick. Transfer stuffed chicken to large plate or baking dish and toss with ¼ cup oil mixture. Cover with plastic wrap and refrigerate for 30 minutes to 1 hour.

3A. For a charcoal grill Open bottom vent completely. Light large chimney starter filled with charcoal briquettes (6 quarts). When top coals are partially covered with ash, pour evenly over half of grill. Set cooking grate in place, cover, and open lid vent completely. Heat grill until hot, about 5 minutes.

3B. For a gas grill Turn all burners to high, close lid, and heat grill until very hot, about 15 minutes. Leave primary burner on high and turn off other burner(s).

4. Clean and oil cooking grate. Arrange chicken, skinned side down, on cooler side of grill with thicker side facing hotter side of grill. Cook (covered if using gas) until chicken is beginning to brown and meat registers 140 degrees, 16 to 20 minutes, flipping and rotating breasts halfway through cooking time. Move chicken to hotter side of grill and cook covered, flipping every few minutes, until chicken registers 160 degrees, 4 to 8 minutes. Transfer chicken to platter and brush with remaining oil mixture. Tent with aluminum foil and let rest for 5 minutes. Remove toothpicks. Serve.

VARIATION

Grilled Stuffed Chicken Breasts with Parsley, Oregano, and Feta

Substitute ¾ cup chopped fresh parsley and ¼ cup chopped fresh oregano for basil. Substitute ⅓ cup crumbled feta for fontina.

Grilled Pesto Chicken

Serves 4   **Total Time** 1¼ hours (plus 1 hour marinating time)

Why This Recipe Works Basil pesto isn't just for pasta. We found a way to imbue chicken with basil and garlic that would hold up on the grill. How did we get enough flavor into the chicken? We used homemade pesto, which tastes stronger and fresher than store-bought. We added the pesto base to separate mixtures for marinating, stuffing, and saucing the bone-in chicken breasts. To stuff the chicken breasts, we cut pockets in them to fill with pesto and then marinated the stuffed breasts in more pesto. We added a third dose of pesto in a sauce to serve with the chicken after it was grilled.

- 4 cups fresh basil leaves
- ¾ cup extra-virgin olive oil, divided
- 5 garlic cloves, peeled
- 1½ tablespoons lemon juice
- 1¼ teaspoons table salt, divided
- 2 ounces Parmesan cheese, grated (1 cup)
- 4 (10- to 12-ounce) bone-in split chicken breasts, trimmed
- ¼ teaspoon pepper

1. Process basil, ½ cup oil, garlic, lemon juice, and ¾ teaspoon salt in food processor until smooth, about 1 minute, scraping down bowl as needed. Transfer ¼ cup pesto to large bowl and set aside for marinating. Add Parmesan to pesto left in processor and pulse to incorporate, about 3 pulses; transfer ¼ cup pesto to small bowl and set aside for stuffing. Add remaining ¼ cup oil to pesto left in processor and pulse to incorporate, about 3 pulses; set aside for serving.

2. Starting on thick side of breast, closest to breastbone, cut horizontal pocket in each breast, stopping ½ inch from edge so halves remain attached. Sprinkle chicken, inside and out, with remaining ½ teaspoon salt and pepper. Place 1 tablespoon pesto reserved for stuffing in each pocket. Tie each chicken breast with 2 pieces kitchen twine to secure. In large bowl, rub chicken with pesto reserved for marinating, cover, and refrigerate for 1 hour.

3A. For a charcoal grill Open bottom vent completely. Light large chimney starter filled with charcoal briquettes (6 quarts). When top coals are partially covered with ash, pour evenly over half of grill. Set cooking grate in place, cover, and open lid vent completely. Heat grill until hot, about 5 minutes.

3B. For a gas grill Turn all burners to high, cover, and heat grill until hot, about 15 minutes. Turn all burners to medium-low. (Adjust primary burner [or, if using 3-burner grill, primary burner and second burner] as needed to maintain grill temperature around 350 degrees.)

4. Clean and oil cooking grate. Place chicken skin side up on grill (cooler side if using charcoal). Cover and cook until chicken registers 155 degrees, 25 to 35 minutes.

5. Slide chicken to hotter side of grill (if using charcoal) or turn all burners to high (if using gas), and flip skin side down. Cover and cook until well browned and chicken registers 160 degrees, 5 to 10 minutes.

6. Transfer chicken to carving board, tent with aluminum foil, and let rest for 5 to 10 minutes. Remove twine, carve chicken, and serve with remaining sauce.

Grilled Asparagus

Serves 4 to 6   **Total Time** 40 minutes
Use asparagus spears that are at least ½ inch thick at the base. Grill the asparagus while the chicken is resting. If using a different fire setup, grill over the highest heat.

- 1½ pounds thick asparagus, trimmed
- 3 tablespoons unsalted butter, melted

1A. For a charcoal grill Open bottom vent completely. Light large chimney starter three-quarters filled with charcoal briquettes (4½ quarts). When top coals are partially covered with ash, pour evenly over grill. Set cooking grate in place, cover, and open lid vent completely. Heat grill until hot, about 5 minutes.

1B. For a gas grill Turn all burners to high, cover, and heat grill until hot, about 15 minutes. Turn all burners to medium-high.

2. Brush asparagus with melted butter and season with salt and pepper.

3. Clean and oil cooking grate. Place asparagus in even layer on grill and cook until just tender and browned, 4 to 10 minutes, turning halfway through cooking. Transfer asparagus to platter and serve.

VARIATIONS
Grilled Asparagus with Garlic Butter
Add 3 minced small garlic cloves to melted butter.

Grilled Asparagus with Chili-Lime Butter
Add 1 teaspoon grated lime zest, ½ teaspoon chili powder, ¼ teaspoon cayenne pepper, and ⅛ teaspoon red pepper flakes to melted butter.

Best Grilled Chicken Thighs

Serves 4 to 6   Total Time 1½ hours

Why This Recipe Works For juicy, meaty chicken thighs with crispy seasoned skin, the best grilling method is also the easiest. Cooking the chicken over indirect heat until it registered 185 to 190 degrees, which took about an hour, allowed collagen in the meat to break down into gelatin, which kept it moist and silky. Grilling the thighs skin side down enabled fat under the skin's surface to thoroughly render, turning it paper-thin, and collagen in the skin to break down and soften—both of which allowed the skin to get nicely crisp once we seared it over direct heat for the last few minutes of cooking. We coated the thighs with a bold-flavored paste, applying most of it to the flesh side so as not to introduce too much extra moisture to the skin that would interfere with crisping. Briefly searing the flesh side before serving took the raw edge off the paste on that side. To keep the dish from becoming greasy, remove excess fat from the chicken thighs and trim the skin.

8   (5- to 7-ounce) bone-in chicken thighs, trimmed
½   teaspoon kosher salt
1   recipe seasoned paste

1. Place chicken, skin side up, on large plate. Sprinkle skin side with salt and spread evenly with one-third of spice paste. Flip chicken and spread remaining two-thirds of paste evenly over flesh side. Refrigerate while preparing grill. (Chicken can be refrigerated for up to 2 hours before grilling.)

2A. For a charcoal grill Open bottom vent halfway. Light large chimney starter mounded with charcoal briquettes (7 quarts). When top coals are partially covered with ash, pour evenly over half of grill. Set cooking grate in place, cover, and open lid vent halfway. Heat grill until hot, about 5 minutes.

2B. For a gas grill Turn all burners to high, cover, and heat grill until hot, about 15 minutes. Leave primary burner on high and turn off other burner(s). (Adjust primary burner [or, if using 3-burner grill, primary burner and second burner] as needed to maintain grill temperature around 350 degrees.)

3. Clean and oil cooking grate. Place chicken, skin side down, on cooler side of grill. Cover and cook for 20 minutes. Rearrange chicken, keeping skin side down, so that pieces that were positioned closest to edge of grill are now closer to heat source and vice versa. Cover and continue to cook until chicken registers 185 to 190 degrees, 15 to 20 minutes.

4. Move all chicken, skin side down, to hotter side of grill and cook until skin is lightly charred, about 5 minutes. Flip chicken and cook until flesh side is lightly browned, 1 to 2 minutes. Transfer to platter, tent with aluminum foil, and let rest for 10 minutes. Serve.

SEASONED PASTES

These pastes can be refrigerated for up to 2 days.

Garam Masala Paste

Makes about ⅓ cup   **Total Time** 10 minutes
Adjust the amount of cayenne to suit your taste. When using this paste, we like to serve the chicken with lime wedges.

3   tablespoons vegetable oil
1½   tablespoons garam masala
2   garlic cloves, minced
2   teaspoons grated fresh ginger
2   teaspoons finely grated lime zest
1¼   teaspoons kosher salt
⅛–¼   teaspoon cayenne pepper

Combine all ingredients in bowl.

Gochujang Paste

Makes about ⅓ cup   **Total Time** 10 minutes

3   tablespoons gochujang
1   tablespoon soy sauce
2   garlic cloves, minced
2   teaspoons sugar
1   teaspoon kosher salt

Combine all ingredients in bowl.

Mustard-Tarragon Paste

Makes about ⅓ cup   **Total Time** 10 minutes
Rosemary or thyme can be substituted for the tarragon, if desired. When using this paste, we like to serve the chicken with lemon wedges.

3   tablespoons Dijon mustard
5   garlic cloves, minced
1   tablespoon finely grated lemon zest
2   teaspoons minced fresh tarragon
1½   teaspoons kosher salt
1   teaspoon water
½   teaspoon pepper

Combine all ingredients in bowl.

Grilled Spice-Rubbed Chicken Drumsticks

Serves 6   **Total Time** 2 hours

Why This Recipe Works If you know how to do them justice, economical chicken drumsticks can be a delicious choice for the grill. We started by soaking the drumsticks in a brine to season them and help them retain their juices, and then we coated them with a flavorful spice rub. We cooked them to between 185 and 190 degrees over indirect heat, allowing their connective tissue to soften and the skin to render its fat gently. We finished by cooking briefly over the coals to capture some char and crispiness. Before applying the spice rub, smooth the skin over the drumsticks so it is covering as much surface area as possible. This will help the skin render evenly and prevent the meat from drying out. You can use any of the spice rubs on page 389.

½ cup table salt for brining
5 pounds chicken drumsticks
1 recipe spice rub (page 389)

1. Dissolve salt in 2 quarts cold water in large container. Submerge drumsticks in brine, cover, and refrigerate for 30 minutes to 1 hour.

2. Place spice rub on plate. Remove drumsticks from brine and pat dry with paper towels. Holding 1 drumstick by bone end, press lightly into rub on all sides. Pat gently to remove excess rub. Repeat with remaining drumsticks.

3A. For a charcoal grill Open bottom vent halfway. Light large chimney starter filled with charcoal briquettes (6 quarts). When top coals are partially covered with ash, pour evenly over half of grill. Set cooking grate in place, cover, and open lid vent halfway. Heat grill until hot, about 5 minutes.

3B. For a gas grill Turn all burners to high, cover, and heat grill until hot, about 15 minutes. Leave primary burner on high and turn off other burner(s). (Adjust primary burner [or, if using three-burner grill, primary burner and second burner] as needed to maintain grill temperature between 325 and 350 degrees.)

4. Clean and oil cooking grate. Place drumsticks, skin side down, on cooler side of grill. Cover and cook for 25 minutes. Rearrange pieces so that drumsticks that were closest to edge are now closer to heat source and vice versa. Cover and cook until drumsticks register 185 to 190 degrees, 20 to 30 minutes.

5. Move all drumsticks to hotter side of grill and cook, turning occasionally, until skin is nicely charred, about 5 minutes. Transfer to platter, tent with aluminum foil, and let rest for 10 minutes. Serve.

Best Grilled
Chicken Thighs

Grilled Spice-Rubbed
Chicken Drumsticks

Grilled Chicken Leg Quarters with Lime Dressing

Serves 4   Total Time 1¼ hours (plus 1 hour chilling time)

Why This Recipe Works Chicken leg quarters, which have plenty of skin to crisp, are a perfect cut for grilling. We flavored them with garlic, lime zest, fresh cilantro and oregano, and spices, which we mixed with just enough oil to create a paste. To help the unevenly shaped leg quarters cook evenly, we made a few deep slashes in each piece and rubbed the paste all over the legs and into the slashes, reserving some paste. A two-level fire (two-thirds of the coals on one side of the grill and one-third on the other side) worked best; we started the quarters on the cooler side to render some of the fat and then moved them to the hotter side to finish cooking without the risk of flare-ups. We mixed the extra paste with lime juice, oil, and fresh herbs to make a bright dressing. A garlic press makes quick work of mincing the six cloves. You can use 1 teaspoon of dried oregano in place of the fresh called for in the dressing, but make sure to use fresh cilantro. Some leg quarters are sold with the backbone attached; removing it before cooking makes the chicken easier to serve (see page 11).

6 garlic cloves, minced
4 teaspoons kosher salt
1 tablespoon sugar
2 teaspoons grated lime zest plus 2 tablespoons juice
2 teaspoons plus ¼ cup extra-virgin olive oil, divided
1½ teaspoons ground cumin
1 teaspoon pepper
½ teaspoon cayenne pepper
4 (10- to 12-ounce) chicken leg quarters, trimmed
2 tablespoons chopped fresh cilantro
2 teaspoons chopped fresh oregano

1. Combine garlic, salt, sugar, lime zest, 2 teaspoons oil, cumin, pepper, and cayenne in bowl and mix to form paste. Reserve 2 teaspoons garlic paste for dressing.

2. Position chicken skin side up on cutting board and pat dry with paper towels. Leaving drumsticks and thighs attached, make 4 parallel diagonal slashes in chicken: 1 across drumsticks, 1 across leg joints, and 2 across thighs (each slash should reach bone). Flip chicken over and make 1 more diagonal slash across back of drumsticks. Rub remaining garlic paste all over chicken and into slashes. Refrigerate chicken for at least 1 hour or up to 24 hours.

3A. For a charcoal grill Open bottom vent completely. Light large chimney starter filled with charcoal briquettes (6 quarts). When top coals are partially covered with ash, pour two-thirds evenly over half of grill, then pour remaining coals

over other half of grill. Set cooking grate in place, cover, and open lid vent completely. Heat grill until hot, about 5 minutes.

3B. For a gas grill Turn all burners to high, cover, and heat grill until hot, about 15 minutes. Turn primary burner to medium and turn other burner(s) to low. (Adjust primary burner [or, if using 3-burner grill, primary burner and second burner] as needed to maintain grill temperature between 400 and 425 degrees.)

4. Clean and oil cooking grate. Place chicken on cooler side of grill, skin side up. Cover and cook until underside of chicken is lightly browned, 9 to 12 minutes. Flip chicken, cover, and cook until chicken registers 165 degrees, 7 to 10 minutes.

5. Transfer chicken to hotter side of grill, skin side down, and cook (covered if using gas) until skin is well browned, 3 to 5 minutes. Flip chicken and continue to cook until chicken registers 175 degrees, about 3 minutes. Transfer to platter, tent with aluminum foil, and let rest for 5 to 10 minutes.

6. Meanwhile, whisk cilantro, oregano, reserved garlic paste, lime juice, and remaining ¼ cup oil together in bowl. Spoon half of dressing over chicken and serve, passing remaining dressing separately.

Grilled Mojo Chicken

Serves 4 to 6   Total Time 1½ hours (plus 1 hour marinating time)

Why This Recipe Works Mojo sauce is a cornerstone of Cuban cookery, and its tart, sweet, and garlicky flavors make for great grilled chicken. To mimic the juice of sour oranges common in mojo marinades, we used a combination of orange and lime juices as well as their zests. Toasting the garlic took off its raw edge. Pineapple juice added sweetness while oregano, black pepper, and cumin provided a spicy backbone. Our bone-in chicken leg quarters stayed juicy on the grill and soaked up marinade well, especially when we slashed them to allow the marinade access to the meat. Basting the meat with the marinade multiple times as it grilled gave the chicken an extra dose of mojo flavor. Canned and bottled pineapple juices are great in this recipe, but when it comes to the citrus, we recommend using freshly squeezed juice. A garlic press makes quick work of mincing the six cloves. Some leg quarters are sold with the backbone attached; removing it before cooking makes the chicken easier to serve (see page 11).

⅓ cup extra-virgin olive oil
6 garlic cloves, minced
⅓ cup pineapple juice
1 tablespoon yellow mustard
2 teaspoons grated orange zest plus ⅓ cup juice

Grilled Mojo
Chicken

2 teaspoons lime zest plus ⅓ cup juice (3 limes)
1¼ teaspoons ground cumin
1 teaspoon pepper, divided
¾ teaspoon dried oregano
2 tablespoons coarsely chopped fresh cilantro
1 tablespoon minced jalapeño chile
1 teaspoon table salt
1 tablespoon table salt for marinade
6 (10- to 12-ounce) chicken leg quarters, trimmed

1. Heat oil and garlic in small saucepan over low heat, stirring often, until tiny bubbles appear and garlic is fragrant and straw-colored, 3 to 5 minutes. Let cool for at least 5 minutes.

2. Whisk pineapple juice, mustard, orange zest and juice, lime zest and juice, cumin, ¾ teaspoon pepper, and oregano together in medium bowl. Slowly whisk in cooled garlic oil until emulsified.

3. Transfer half of mojo mixture to small bowl and stir in cilantro, jalapeño, salt, and remaining ¼ teaspoon pepper; set aside mojo sauce.

4. Whisk 1 tablespoon salt into remaining mojo mixture until dissolved. Transfer mojo marinade to 1-gallon zipper-lock bag.

5. Place chicken, skin side up, on cutting board and pat dry with paper towels. Leaving drumsticks and thighs attached, make 4 parallel diagonal slashes in each piece of chicken: 1 across drumstick, 1 across leg-thigh joint, and 2 across thigh (slashes should reach bone). Flip chicken and make 1 more diagonal slash across back of each drumstick. Transfer chicken to bag with mojo marinade. Seal bag, turn to coat chicken, and refrigerate for at least 1 hour or up to 24 hours.

6A. For a charcoal grill Open bottom vent completely. Light large chimney starter filled with charcoal briquettes (6 quarts). When top coals are partially covered with ash, pour two-thirds evenly over half of grill, then pour remaining coals over other half of grill. Set cooking grate in place, cover, and open lid vent completely. Heat grill until hot, about 5 minutes.

6B. For a gas grill Turn all burners to high, cover, and heat grill until hot, about 15 minutes. Turn primary burner to medium and turn other burner(s) to low. (Adjust primary burner [or, if using 3-burner grill, primary burner and second burner] as needed to maintain grill temperature between 400 and 425 degrees.)

7. Clean and oil cooking grate. Divide reserved mojo sauce equally between 2 bowls. Remove chicken from marinade, letting excess marinade drip off. Place on cooler side of grill, skin side up, cover, and cook until underside of chicken is lightly browned, about 15 minutes. Using first bowl of mojo, baste chicken, then flip chicken and baste second side (use all of first bowl). Cover and continue to cook until chicken registers 165 degrees, about 15 minutes.

8. Slide chicken to hotter side of grill, keeping skin side down, and cook (covered if using gas) until skin is well browned, 3 to 5 minutes. Flip chicken and continue to cook until chicken registers 175 degrees, about 3 minutes. Transfer chicken to platter and spoon remaining mojo sauce from second bowl over top. Tent with aluminum foil and let rest for 5 minutes. Serve.

Barbecued Pulled Chicken

Serves 6 to 8   Total Time 2¼ hours

Why This Recipe Works Meltingly tender shredded chicken coated in a sweet, tangy barbecue sauce makes for a delicious (if messy) sandwich. For an excellent barbecued pulled chicken recipe that wouldn't take all day, we chose whole chicken legs, which combine great flavor, low cost, and resistance to overcooking. The legs cooked gently but thoroughly over indirect heat, absorbing plenty of smoke flavor along the way. Once the chicken finished cooking, we hand-shredded half and machine-processed the other half to produce the perfect texture. The chicken then just had to be combined with a quick barbecue sauce for a truly sandwich-worthy pulled chicken recipe. Some

Barbecued Pulled Chicken

Grilled Chicken Wings

leg quarters are sold with the backbone attached; removing it before cooking makes the chicken easier to serve; see page 11. If you'd like to use wood chunks instead of wood chips when using a charcoal grill, substitute two medium wood chunks, soaked in water for 1 hour, for the wood chip packets. Serve the pulled chicken on hamburger buns or sandwich bread, with pickles and coleslaw.

Chicken

  2 cups wood chips, soaked in water for 15 minutes and drained
  1 (16 by 12-inch) disposable aluminum roasting pan (if using charcoal)
  8 (10- to 12-ounce) chicken leg quarters, trimmed
  1 teaspoon table salt
  ½ teaspoon pepper

Sauce

  1 large onion, peeled and quartered
  ¼ cup water
  1½ cups ketchup
  1½ cups apple cider
  ¼ cup molasses
  ¼ cup cider vinegar, divided
  3 tablespoons Worcestershire sauce
  3 tablespoons Dijon mustard
  ½ teaspoon pepper
  1 tablespoon vegetable oil
  1½ tablespoons chili powder
  2 garlic cloves, minced
  ½ teaspoon cayenne pepper
    Hot sauce

1. For the chicken Using large piece of heavy-duty aluminum foil, wrap soaked chips in 8 by 4½-inch foil packet. (Make sure chips do not poke holes in sides or bottom of packet.) Cut 2 evenly spaced 2-inch slits in top of packet.

2A. For a charcoal grill Open bottom vent halfway and place disposable pan in center of grill. Light large chimney starter three-quarters filled with charcoal briquettes (4½ quarts). When top coals are partially covered with ash, pour into 2 even piles on either side of disposable pan. Place wood chip packet on 1 pile of coals. Set cooking grate in place, cover, and open lid vent halfway. Heat grill until hot and wood chips are smoking, about 5 minutes.

2B. For a gas grill Remove cooking grate and place wood chip packet directly on primary burner. Set cooking grate in place, turn all burners to high, cover, and heat grill until hot and wood chips are smoking, about 15 minutes. Turn all burners to medium. (Adjust primary burner [or, if using 3-burner grill, primary burner and second burner] as needed to maintain grill temperature between 250 and 350 degrees.)

3. Clean and oil cooking grate. Pat chicken dry with paper towels and sprinkle with salt and pepper. Place chicken skin side up on grill (over disposable pan if using charcoal). Cover (position lid vent over meat if using charcoal) and cook until chicken registers 185 degrees, 1 to 1½ hours, rotating chicken pieces halfway through cooking. Transfer chicken to carving board, tent with aluminum foil, and let rest until cool enough to handle.

4. For the sauce Meanwhile, process onion and water in food processor until mixture resembles slush, about 30 seconds. Strain through fine-mesh strainer set over liquid measuring cup, pressing on solids with rubber spatula (you should have ¾ cup strained onion juice). Discard solids.

5. Whisk onion juice, ketchup, cider, molasses, 3 tablespoons vinegar, Worcestershire, mustard, and pepper together in bowl. Heat oil in large saucepan over medium heat until shimmering. Stir in chili powder, garlic, and cayenne and cook until fragrant, about 30 seconds. Stir in ketchup mixture, bring to simmer, and cook over medium-low heat until slightly thickened, about 15 minutes (you should have about 4 cups of sauce). Transfer 2 cups sauce to serving bowl; leave remaining sauce in saucepan.

6. Remove and discard skin from chicken legs. Using your fingers, pull meat off bones, separating larger pieces (which should fall off bones easily) from smaller, drier pieces into 2 equal piles.

7. Pulse smaller chicken pieces in food processor until just coarsely chopped, 3 or 4 pulses, stirring chicken with rubber spatula after each pulse. Add chopped chicken to sauce in saucepan. Using your fingers or 2 forks, pull larger chicken pieces into long shreds and add to saucepan. Stir in remaining 1 tablespoon vinegar, cover, and heat chicken over medium-low heat, stirring occasionally, until heated through, about 10 minutes. Add hot sauce to taste, and serve, passing remaining sauce separately.

VARIATION

Barbecued Pulled Chicken for a Crowd

This technique works well on a charcoal grill but not so well on a gas grill. If your gas grill is large and can accommodate more than eight legs, follow the master recipe, adding as many legs as will comfortably fit in a single layer. Increase charcoal briquettes to 6 quarts. Use 12 chicken legs and slot into V-shaped roasting rack set on top of cooking grate over disposable aluminum pan. Increase cooking time in step 3 to 1½ to 1¾ hours. In step 5, remove only 1 cup sauce from saucepan. In step 7, pulse chicken in food processor in 2 batches.

Grilled Chicken Wings

Serves 4   Total Time 1½ hours

Why This Recipe Works To take this barroom classic from the fryer to the grill we had to figure out how to handle the fat and connective tissue from the wings, which creates a problem as it drips into the fire. To get crisp, well-rendered chicken wings with lightly charred skin; succulent, smoky meat; and minimal flare-ups, we quick-brined the wings and tossed them in cornstarch and pepper. These steps helped the meat retain moisture and kept the wings from sticking to the grill. We then cooked them right over a gentle medium-low fire. The moderate temperature minimized flare-ups and the direct heat accelerated the cooking process. Also, though we normally cook white chicken meat to 160 degrees, wings are chock-full of collagen, which begins to break down upwards of 170 degrees. Cooking the wings to 180 degrees produced meltingly tender wings. These few minor adjustments gave us crispy, juicy chicken that made a great alternative to fried wings. We also developed several easy spice rubs if you're looking for new flavor options (see page 389). We prefer to buy whole chicken wings and butcher them ourselves because they tend to be larger than wings that come presplit. If you can find only presplit wings, opt for larger ones, if possible. If you buy whole wings, cut them into two pieces before brining (see page 10). Don't brine the wings for more than 30 minutes or they'll be too salty.

½ cup table salt for brining
2 pounds chicken wings, cut at joints, wingtips discarded
1½ teaspoons cornstarch
1 teaspoon pepper

1. Dissolve salt in 2 quarts cold water in large container. Prick chicken wings all over with fork. Submerge chicken in brine, cover, and refrigerate for 30 minutes. Combine cornstarch and pepper in bowl and set aside.

2A. For a charcoal grill Open bottom vent completely. Light large chimney starter half filled with charcoal briquettes (3 quarts). When top coals are partially covered with ash, pour evenly over grill. Set cooking grate in place, cover, and open lid vent completely. Heat grill until hot, about 5 minutes.

2B. For a gas grill Turn all burners to high, cover, and heat grill until hot, about 15 minutes. Turn all burners to medium-low.

3. Remove chicken from brine and pat dry with paper towels. Transfer wings to large bowl and sprinkle with cornstarch mixture, tossing until evenly coated. Clean and oil cooking grate. Place wings on grill and cook (covered if using gas), thicker skin side up, until browned on bottom, 12 to 15 minutes. Flip chicken and grill until skin is crisp and lightly charred and meat registers 180 degrees, about 10 minutes. Transfer chicken to platter, tent with aluminum foil, and let rest for 5 to 10 minutes. Serve.

VARIATIONS

Grilled BBQ Chicken Wings

Reduce pepper to ½ teaspoon. Add 1 teaspoon chili powder, 1 teaspoon paprika, ½ teaspoon garlic powder, ½ teaspoon dried oregano, and ½ teaspoon sugar to cornstarch mixture in step 1.

Grilled Chicken Wings with Creole Seasonings

Add ¾ teaspoon dried oregano, ½ teaspoon garlic powder, ½ teaspoon onion powder, ½ teaspoon white pepper, and ¼ teaspoon cayenne pepper to cornstarch mixture in step 1.

Grilled Chicken Wings with Tandoori Seasonings

Reduce pepper to ½ teaspoon. Add 1 teaspoon garam masala, ½ teaspoon ground cumin, ¼ teaspoon garlic powder, ¼ teaspoon ground ginger, and ⅛ teaspoon cayenne pepper to cornstarch mixture in step 1.

PREPPING GRILLED CHICKEN WINGS

1. Puncturing each wing with fork lets brine easily penetrate meat and helps fat render away.

2. Quick saltwater brine seasons wings and keeps them juicy.

3. Dusting wings with cornstarch and black pepper prevents sticking and encourages crisping.

Grill-Fried Chicken Wings

Serves 4 to 6   **Total Time** 2¼ hours (plus 1 hour brining time)

Why This Recipe Works Grill-fried chicken sounds like an oxymoron, but it's actually possible to make great fried chicken without deep frying. To make it happen on the grill, we separated whole chicken wings at the joints into drumettes and flats. Then we brined the chicken to ensure that it stayed moist. We coated the chicken with flour that we seasoned heavily with black pepper, granulated garlic, paprika, and cayenne pepper and then built a hot fire with the coals banked on one side of the grill. We put the chicken opposite the coals, on the cooler side of the grill, to cook until the coating was dry and set, about 30 minutes. Then, to get the fried texture we were looking for, we brushed the wings with a mere 3 tablespoons of oil and let them continue to cook until they were golden brown, which took another 30 minutes. We prefer to buy whole chicken wings and butcher them ourselves because they tend to be larger than wings that come presplit. If you can find only presplit wings, opt for larger ones, if possible. If you buy whole wings, cut them into two pieces before brining. Do not brine the chicken for longer than 3 hours in step 1 or it will be too salty.

¼ cup table salt for brining
¼ cup sugar for brining
3 pounds chicken wings, cut at joints, wingtips discarded
2 cups all-purpose flour
1 tablespoon granulated garlic
1 tablespoon pepper
2 teaspoons paprika
1 teaspoon table salt
½ teaspoon cayenne pepper
3 tablespoons vegetable oil

1. Dissolve ¼ cup salt and sugar in 2 quarts cold water in large container. Add chicken and refrigerate, covered, for at least 1 hour or up to 3 hours.

2. Set wire rack in rimmed baking sheet. Whisk flour, granulated garlic, pepper, paprika, salt, and cayenne together in large bowl. Remove chicken from brine, letting excess drip off. Working in batches of four, dredge chicken pieces in flour mixture, pressing to adhere. Place chicken on prepared rack. Refrigerate chicken, uncovered, for at least 30 minutes or up to 2 hours.

Grill-Fried Chicken Wings

3A. For a charcoal grill Open bottom vent completely. Light large chimney starter mounded with charcoal briquettes (7 quarts). When top coals are partially covered with ash, pour into steeply banked pile against side of grill. Set cooking grate in place, cover, and open lid vent completely. Heat grill until hot, about 5 minutes.

3B. For a gas grill Turn all burners to high, cover, and heat grill until hot, about 15 minutes. Turn primary burner to high and turn off other burner(s). (Adjust primary burner [or, if using three-burner grill, primary burner and second burner] as needed to maintain grill temperature of around 425 degrees.)

4. Clean and oil cooking grate. Place chicken, fatty side up, on cooler side of grill, arranging drumettes closest to coals. Cook chicken, covered, until lightly browned and coating is set, about 30 minutes for charcoal or about 45 minutes for gas.

5. Brush chicken with oil until no traces of flour remain (use all of oil). Cover and continue to cook until coating is golden brown and chicken registers between 180 and 200 degrees, about 30 minutes for charcoal or about 45 minutes for gas. Transfer chicken to clean wire rack and let cool for 10 minutes. Serve.

Grilled Bone-In Chicken
Serves 4 to 6   **Total Time** 1 hour

Why This Recipe Works Flare-ups can turn chicken into a charred mess if you're not paying attention. The method we developed for bone-in chicken avoids this pitfall by starting the chicken over a relatively cool area of the grill. This allows the fat in the chicken skin to render slowly, thereby avoiding flare-ups and encouraging ultracrisp skin. Finishing it over the hotter side yields browned parts. In addition to the quality of the finished product, we like this approach because it is effectively hands-off: You don't have to constantly move and monitor the chicken pieces. This recipe works with breasts, legs, thighs, or a combination of parts. For extra flavor, rub the chicken with a spice rub (page 389) before cooking.

4 pounds bone-in chicken pieces (split breasts halved crosswise, drumsticks, and/or thighs), trimmed
¾ teaspoon table salt
½ teaspoon pepper
1 (13 by 9-inch) disposable aluminum roasting pan (if using charcoal)

1. Pat chicken dry with paper towels and sprinkle with salt and pepper.

2A. For a charcoal grill Open bottom vent completely and place disposable pan in center of grill. Light large chimney starter filled with charcoal briquettes (6 quarts). When top coals are partially covered with ash, pour into 2 even piles on either side of disposable pan. Set cooking grate in place, cover, and open lid vent completely. Heat grill until hot, about 5 minutes.

2B. For a gas grill Turn all burners to high, cover, and heat grill until hot, about 15 minutes. Turn all burners to medium-low.

3. Clean and oil cooking grate. Place chicken, skin side down, on grill (over disposable pan if using charcoal). Cover and cook until skin is crisp and golden, about 20 minutes.

4. Slide chicken to hotter sides of grill if using charcoal, or turn all burners to medium-high if using gas. Cook (covered if using gas), turning as needed, until well browned on both sides and breasts register 160 degrees and drumsticks/thighs register 175 degrees, 5 to 15 minutes.

5. Transfer chicken to platter, tent with aluminum foil, and let rest for 5 to 10 minutes before serving.

Classic Barbecued Chicken

Sweet and Tangy Barbecued Chicken

Classic Barbecued Chicken

Serves 4 to 6   Total Time 1¼ hours

Why This Recipe Works Classic barbecued chicken is one of America's favorite summer meals. But despite its popularity, barbecued chicken recipes cause backyard grillers plenty of headaches. We set out to develop a recipe for barbecued chicken with perfect, evenly cooked meat; golden-brown skin; and intense, multidimensional barbecue flavor. Most recipes call for searing chicken quickly over high heat, but we found that starting barbecued chicken over low heat slowly rendered the fat without the danger of flare-ups and gave us evenly cooked meat all the way through. Our homemade sauce has the perfect balance of sweetness and smokiness from brewed coffee, vinegar, and molasses. We created a complex layer of barbecue flavor by applying the sauce in coats and turning the chicken as it cooked over moderate heat. The sauce turned out thick and caramelized, and it perfectly glazed the chicken. Using homemade barbecue sauce makes a big difference, but you can substitute 3 cups of store-bought sauce. Don't try to grill more than 10 pieces of chicken at a time; you won't be able to line them up as directed in step 4. You can use a mix of chicken breasts, thighs, and drumsticks, making sure they add up to about 10 pieces.

- 1 teaspoon table salt
- 1 teaspoon pepper
- ¼ teaspoon cayenne pepper
- 3 pounds bone-in chicken pieces (split breasts halved crosswise, drumsticks, and/or thighs), trimmed
- 1 recipe Kansas City Barbecue Sauce (page 387)
- 1 (13 by 9-inch) disposable aluminum roasting pan (if using charcoal)

1. Combine salt, pepper, and cayenne in bowl. Pat chicken dry with paper towels and rub with spices. Reserve 2 cups barbecue sauce for cooking; set aside 1 cup sauce for serving.

2A. For a charcoal grill Open bottom vent completely and place disposable pan on 1 side of grill. Light large chimney starter filled with charcoal briquettes (6 quarts). When top coals are partially covered with ash, pour evenly over other side of grill. Set cooking grate in place, cover, and open lid vent completely. Heat grill until hot, about 5 minutes.

2B. For a gas grill Turn all burners to high, cover, and heat grill until hot, about 15 minutes. Leave primary burner on high and turn off other burner(s). (Adjust primary burner [or, if using 3-burner grill, primary burner and second burner] as needed to maintain grill temperature around 350 degrees.)

3. Clean and oil cooking grate. Place chicken, skin side down, on cooler side of grill. Cover and cook until chicken begins to brown, 30 to 35 minutes.

4. Slide chicken into single line between hotter and cooler sides of grill. Cook uncovered, flipping chicken and brushing every 5 minutes with some of sauce reserved for cooking, until sticky, about 20 minutes.

5. Slide chicken to hotter side of grill and cook, uncovered, flipping and brushing with remaining sauce for cooking, until well glazed, breasts register 160 degrees, and drumsticks/thighs register 175 degrees, about 5 minutes. Transfer chicken to platter, tent with aluminum foil, and let rest for 5 to 10 minutes. Serve with remaining sauce.

Sweet and Tangy Barbecued Chicken

Serves 6 to 8   **Total Time** 1¾ hours (plus 6 hours chilling time)

Why This Recipe Works Barbecued chicken can stand up to boldly flavored sauces, so we wanted to take our classic barbecued chicken technique and create a sweet-and-spicy version. For chicken that was well seasoned all the way to the bone, we applied a rub and let the chicken chill: Salt, onion and garlic powders, paprika, a touch of cayenne, and some brown sugar maintained a bold presence even after grilling. Placing a disposable aluminum pan opposite the coals in our grill setup and filling the pan partially with water lowered the temperature inside the grill, which ensured that all the chicken pieces cooked at a slow, steady rate. We waited to apply the sauce until after searing the chicken, which prevented the sauce from burning and gave the chicken skin a chance to develop color first. Applying the sauce in stages, rather than all at once, ensured that its bright tanginess wasn't lost. When browning the chicken over the hotter side of the grill, move it away from any flare-ups. Use the large holes of a box grater to grate the onion for the sauce.

    2 tablespoons packed dark brown sugar
    1½ tablespoons kosher salt
    1½ teaspoons onion powder
    1½ teaspoons garlic powder
    1½ teaspoons paprika
    ¼ teaspoon cayenne pepper
    6 pounds bone-in chicken pieces (split breasts and/or leg quarters), trimmed
    1 recipe Sweet and Tangy Barbecue Sauce (page 387)
    1 (13 by 9-inch) disposable aluminum roasting pan (if using charcoal) or 2 (9-inch) disposable aluminum pie plates (if using gas)

1. Combine sugar, salt, onion powder, garlic powder, paprika, and cayenne in bowl. Arrange chicken on rimmed baking sheet and sprinkle both sides evenly with spice rub. Cover with plastic wrap and refrigerate for at least 6 hours or up to 24 hours. Measure out ⅔ cup sauce and set aside to baste chicken; set aside remaining sauce for serving.

2A. For a charcoal grill Open bottom vent halfway. Place disposable pan on 1 side of grill and add 3 cups water to pan. Light large chimney starter filled with charcoal briquettes (6 quarts). When top coals are partially covered with ash, pour evenly over other side of grill. Set cooking grate in place, cover, and open lid vent halfway. Heat grill until hot, about 5 minutes.

2B. For a gas grill Remove cooking grate, place 2 disposable pie plates directly on 1 burner (opposite primary burner), and add 1½ cups water to each. Set grate in place, turn all burners to high, cover, and heat grill until hot, about 15 minutes. Turn primary burner to medium-high and turn off other burner(s). (Adjust primary burner [or, if using 3-burner grill, primary burner and second burner] as needed to maintain grill temperature between 325 and 350 degrees.)

3. Clean and oil cooking grate. Place chicken, skin side down, over hotter part of grill and cook until browned and blistered in spots, 2 to 5 minutes. Flip chicken and cook until second side is browned, 4 to 6 minutes. Move chicken to cooler side and brush both sides with ⅓ cup basting sauce. Arrange chicken, skin side up, with leg quarters closest to fire and breasts farthest away. Cover (positioning lid vent over chicken if using charcoal) and cook for 25 minutes.

4. Brush both sides of chicken with remaining ⅓ cup basting sauce and continue to cook, covered, until breasts register 160 degrees and leg quarters register 175 degrees, 25 to 35 minutes.

5. Transfer chicken to serving platter, tent with aluminum foil, and let rest for 10 minutes. Serve, passing reserved sauce separately.

Citrus-and-Spice Grilled Chicken

Serves 4 to 6   **Total Time** 1¼ hours (plus 1 hour marinating time)

Why This Recipe Works Grilled citrus- and spice-marinated chicken is a popular Latin dish that appears on just about every Mexican restaurant menu, but the recipes vary dramatically, often turning out dry, bland results. Some recipes call for marinating chicken in a blend of orange and lime juices (to substitute for the more authentic sour oranges), along with spices and herbs, but this combination didn't deliver the bold flavors we were after. Instead, we started with just lime juice and gave it a boost with orange zest and lime zest. Mixed with onion, garlic, and olive oil to make a paste, this gave our chicken great citrus flavor. We created a split fire, with a central cooler zone and coals on either side, using a disposable roasting pan in the center of the grill. Then, we cooked the chicken over indirect heat with a brief sear over the fire at the end; this gave us succulent meat and crisp, flavorful skin.

1 onion, chopped coarse
6 garlic cloves, peeled
2 tablespoons extra-virgin olive oil
1 tablespoon grated orange zest
2 teaspoons dried oregano
1½ teaspoons table salt
1 teaspoon grated lime zest plus ¼ cup juice (2 limes)
½ teaspoon pepper
½ teaspoon ground cinnamon
½ teaspoon ground cumin
⅛ teaspoon ground cloves
3 pounds bone-in chicken pieces (split breasts halved crosswise, drumsticks, and/or thighs), trimmed
1 (13 by 9-inch) disposable aluminum roasting pan (if using charcoal)

1. Process onion, garlic, oil, orange zest, oregano, salt, lime zest and juice, pepper, cinnamon, cumin, and cloves in food processor until smooth, about 30 seconds; transfer to 1-gallon zipper-lock bag. Add chicken to bag with marinade and toss to coat; press out as much air as possible and seal bag. Refrigerate for at least 1 hour or up to 24 hours, turning bag occasionally.

2A. For a charcoal grill Open bottom vent completely and place disposable pan in center of grill. Light large chimney starter filled with charcoal briquettes (6 quarts). When top coals are partially covered with ash, pour into 2 even piles on either side of disposable pan. Set cooking grate in place, cover, and open lid vent completely. Heat grill until hot, about 5 minutes.

2B. For a gas grill Turn all burners to high, cover, and heat grill until hot, about 15 minutes. Turn all burners to medium-low. (Adjust primary burner [or, if using 3-burner grill, primary burner and second burner] as needed to maintain grill temperature around 350 degrees.)

3. Clean and oil cooking grate. Remove chicken from marinade, letting excess drip off. Place chicken skin side up on grill (over disposable pan if using charcoal). Cover and cook until bottom is browned and chicken registers 155 degrees, about 25 minutes.

4. Flip chicken skin side down. Slide chicken over coals if using charcoal, or turn all burners to high if using gas. Cook until well browned and breasts register 160 degrees and drumsticks/thighs register 175 degrees, 5 to 10 minutes. Transfer chicken to large platter, tent with aluminum foil, and let rest for 5 to 10 minutes before serving.

Grilled Chicken Diavolo

Serves 4 **Total Time** 1¼ hours (plus 1 hour marinating time)

Why This Recipe Works Chicken diavolo is one of those dishes that has no universally accepted recipe. The one constant (other than the chicken) is plenty of peppery heat. To make a truly fiery chicken diavolo we took it to the grill and used a mixture of herbs, spices, lemon, oil, sugar, and both black and red pepper. We built a two-level fire, starting the chicken on the cooler side and then searing it over the hotter side to char and crisp the skin. For extra smoky flavor, we added a foil-wrapped packet of soaked wood chips. We cooked the reserved marinade mixture to mellow the garlic bite, added a shot of lemon juice, and spooned our supercharged vinaigrette over the grilled chicken. If you'd like to use wood chunks instead of wood chips when using a charcoal grill, substitute one medium wood chunk, soaked in water for 1 hour, for the wood chip packet.

3 pounds bone-in chicken pieces (split breasts halved crosswise, drumsticks, and/or thighs), trimmed
½ cup extra-virgin olive oil
4 garlic cloves, minced
1 tablespoon chopped fresh rosemary
2 teaspoons grated lemon zest plus 4 teaspoons juice
2 teaspoons red pepper flakes
1 teaspoon sugar
1 teaspoon pepper
½ teaspoon paprika
2½ teaspoons table salt, divided
1 cup wood chips

1. Pat chicken dry with paper towels. Whisk oil, garlic, rosemary, lemon zest, pepper flakes, sugar, pepper, and paprika in bowl until combined. Reserve ¼ cup oil mixture for sauce. (Oil mixture can be covered and refrigerated for up to 24 hours.) Whisk 2¼ teaspoons salt into oil mixture remaining in bowl and transfer to 1-gallon zipper-lock bag. Add chicken, turn to coat, and refrigerate for at least 1 hour or up to 24 hours.

2. Just before grilling, soak wood chips in water for 15 minutes, then drain. Using large piece of heavy-duty aluminum foil, wrap soaked chips in 8 by 4½-inch foil packet. (Make sure chips do not poke holes in sides or bottom of packet.) Cut 2 evenly spaced 2-inch slits in top of packet.

3A. For a charcoal grill Open bottom vent halfway. Light large chimney starter filled with charcoal briquettes (6 quarts). When top coals are partially covered with ash, pour two-thirds evenly over half of grill, then pour remaining coals over other half of grill. Place wood chip packet on larger pile of coals. Set cooking grate in place, cover, and open lid vent halfway. Heat grill until hot and wood chips are smoking, about 5 minutes.

3B. For a gas grill Place wood chip packet over primary burner. Turn all burners to high, cover, and heat grill until hot and wood chips are smoking, about 15 minutes. Turn primary burner to medium and turn other burner(s) to low. (Adjust primary burner [or, if using 3-burner grill, primary burner and second burner] as needed to maintain grill temperature between 400 and 425 degrees.)

4. Remove chicken from marinade and pat dry with paper towels. Clean and oil cooking grate. Place chicken on cooler side of grill, skin side up. Cover and cook until underside of chicken is lightly browned, 8 to 12 minutes. Flip chicken, cover, and cook until white meat registers 155 degrees and dark meat registers 170 degrees, 7 to 10 minutes.

5. Transfer chicken to hotter side of grill, skin side down, and cook (covered if using gas) until skin is well browned, about 3 minutes. Flip and continue to cook (covered if using gas) until white meat registers 160 degrees and dark meat registers 175 degrees, 1 to 3 minutes. Transfer chicken to platter, tent with foil, and let rest for 5 to 10 minutes.

6. Meanwhile, heat reserved oil mixture in small saucepan over low heat until fragrant and garlic begins to brown, 3 to 5 minutes. Off heat, whisk in lemon juice and remaining ¼ teaspoon salt. Spoon sauce over chicken. Serve.

Grilled Chicken Diavolo

MAKING A FOIL PACKET FOR WOOD CHIPS

1. Soak wood chips in water for 15 minutes; spread drained chips in center of 15 by 12-inch piece of heavy-duty aluminum foil. Fold to seal edges, then cut 2 evenly spaced 2-inch slits in top of packet to allow smoke to escape.

2. Place aluminum foil packet of chips on lit coals of charcoal grill or over primary burner on gas grill.

Grilled Jerk Chicken

Serves 4   **Total Time** 1¼ hours (plus 1 hour marinating time)

Why This Recipe Works Our bold, spicy-but-nuanced grilled jerk chicken starts with the jerk paste. We blended fiery habaneros (more readily available and less intense than the traditionally used Scotch bonnet peppers), scallions, and garlic with 10 whole thyme sprigs for a big herby punch. Soy sauce added depth, cider vinegar contributed brightness, and warm spices (allspice, cinnamon, and ginger) provided the characteristic jerk flavor, while brown sugar rounded out the spicy edge. After marinating bone-in chicken pieces in the paste, we first cooked the chicken on the cooler side of the grill, covered, which helped the marinade to stick to the chicken and not slide off over direct heat and burn. Once the chicken was cooked through, we brushed it with a little reserved marinade for a fresh burst of jerk flavor and seared it on the hotter side of the grill. Tasters preferred the chicken charred over the hotter side of the grill, not smoked per tradition. It picked up plenty of grill flavor and tasted cleaner, without any acrid or harsh smokiness. Use more or fewer habaneros depending on your desired

Grilled Jerk Chicken

Peri Peri Grilled Chicken

level of spiciness. You can also remove the seeds and ribs from the habaneros or substitute jalapeños for less heat. We recommend wearing rubber gloves or plastic bags on your hands when handling the chiles. Use thyme sprigs with a generous amount of leaves; there's no need to separate the leaves from the stems. Keep a close eye on the chicken in step 5 since it can char quickly. When browning the chicken over the hotter side of the grill, move it away from any flare-ups.

4	scallions
¼	cup vegetable oil
¼	cup soy sauce
2	tablespoons cider vinegar
2	tablespoons packed brown sugar
1–2	habanero chiles, stemmed
10	sprigs fresh thyme
5	garlic cloves, peeled
2½	teaspoons ground allspice
1½	teaspoons table salt
½	teaspoon ground cinnamon
½	teaspoon ground ginger
3	pounds bone-in chicken pieces (split breasts halved crosswise, drumsticks, and/or thighs), trimmed
	Lime wedges

1. Process scallions, oil, soy sauce, vinegar, sugar, habanero(s), thyme sprigs, garlic, allspice, salt, cinnamon, and ginger in blender until smooth, about 30 seconds, scraping down sides of blender jar as needed. Measure out ¼ cup marinade and refrigerate until ready to use.

2. Place chicken and remaining marinade in 1-gallon zipper-lock bag. Press out air, seal bag, and turn to coat chicken in marinade. Refrigerate for at least 1 hour or up to 24 hours, turning occasionally.

3A. For a charcoal grill Open bottom vent completely. Light large chimney starter mounded with charcoal briquettes (7 quarts). When top coals are partially covered with ash, pour evenly over half of grill. Set cooking grate in place, cover, and open lid vent completely. Heat grill until hot, about 5 minutes.

3B. For a gas grill Turn all burners to high, cover, and heat grill until hot, about 15 minutes. Leave primary burner on high and turn off other burner(s). (Adjust primary burner [or, if using 3-burner grill, primary burner and second burner] as needed to maintain grill temperature between 450 and 500 degrees.)

4. Clean and oil cooking grate. Place chicken skin side up on cooler side of grill, with breast pieces farthest away from heat. Cover and cook until breasts register 160 degrees and drumsticks/thighs register 175 degrees, 22 to 30 minutes, transferring pieces to plate, skin side up, as they come to temperature. (Re-cover grill after checking pieces for doneness.)

5. Brush skin side of chicken with half of reserved marinade. Place chicken skin side down on hotter side of grill. (Turn all burners to high if using gas.) Brush with remaining reserved marinade and cook until lightly charred, 1 to 3 minutes per side. Check browning often and move pieces as needed to avoid flare-ups.

6. Transfer chicken to platter, tent with aluminum foil, and let rest for 5 to 10 minutes. Serve with lime wedges.

Peri Peri Grilled Chicken

Serves 6 to 8   **Total Time** 2¼ hours (plus 6 hours marinating time)

Why This Recipe Works The spicy grilled dish known as peri peri chicken has African roots; at its most basic, it is chicken marinated in a paste of garlic, herbs, spices, lemon juice, and fiery African peppers called peri peri and then grilled over a hot fire. We wanted to develop a version that kept the flavor profile while presenting an alternative to the hard-to-come-by peri peri chiles. We used a half-grill fire plus an aluminum pan filled with water to eliminate hot spots. For the spice paste, we combined olive oil, garlic, shallot, lemon, bay leaves, paprika, black pepper, and five-spice powder. To mimic the fruity, complex heat of the peri peri peppers we turned to dried arbol chiles and cayenne. Tomato paste and chopped peanuts gave the dish a balanced richness and hint of sweetness. When browning the chicken over the hotter side of the grill, move it away from any flare-ups. Serve with white rice.

- 2 tablespoons table salt
- 3 tablespoons extra-virgin olive oil
- 8 garlic cloves, peeled
- 2 tablespoons tomato paste
- 1 shallot, chopped
- 1 tablespoon sugar
- 1 tablespoon paprika
- 1 tablespoon five-spice powder
- 1 teaspoon pepper
- ½ teaspoon cayenne pepper
- 3 bay leaves, crushed
- 2 teaspoons grated lemon zest plus ¼ cup juice (2 lemons), plus lemon wedges for serving
- 4–10 arbol chiles, stems removed
- 6 pounds bone-in chicken pieces (split breasts, thighs, and/or drumsticks), trimmed
- ½ cup dry-roasted peanuts, chopped fine
- 1 (13 by 9-inch) disposable roasting pan (if using charcoal) or 2 (9-inch) disposable pie plates (if using gas)

1. Process salt, oil, garlic, tomato paste, shallot, sugar, paprika, five-spice powder, pepper, cayenne, bay leaves, lemon zest and juice, and 4 arbol chiles in blender until smooth paste forms, 10 to 20 seconds. Taste paste and add up to 6 additional arbol chiles, depending on desired level of heat (spice paste should be slightly hotter than desired heat level of cooked chicken); process until smooth. Using metal skewer, poke skin side of chicken pieces 8 to 10 times. Place chicken parts, peanuts, and spice paste in large bowl or container and toss until chicken is evenly coated with spice paste. Cover and refrigerate for at least 6 hours or up to 24 hours.

2A. For a charcoal grill Open bottom vent halfway. Place disposable pan on 1 side of grill and add 3 cups water to pan. Light large chimney starter filled with charcoal briquettes (6 quarts). When top coals are partially covered with ash, pour evenly over other side of grill. Set cooking grate in place, cover, and open lid vent halfway. Heat grill until hot, about 5 minutes.

2B. For a gas grill Remove cooking grate, place 2 disposable pie plates directly on 1 burner (opposite primary burner), and add 1½ cups water to each. Set grate in place, turn all burners to high, cover, and heat grill until hot, about 15 minutes. Turn primary burner to medium-high and turn off other burner(s). (Adjust primary burner [or, if using 3-burner grill, primary burner and second burner] as needed to maintain grill temperature between 325 and 350 degrees.)

3. Clean and oil cooking grate. Place chicken, skin side down, on hotter side of grill and cook until browned and blistered in spots, 2 to 5 minutes. Flip chicken and cook until second side is browned, 4 to 6 minutes. Move chicken to cooler side and arrange, skin side up, with drumsticks/thighs closest to fire and breasts farthest away. Cover (positioning lid vent over chicken if using charcoal) and cook until breasts register 160 degrees and drumsticks/thighs register 175 degrees, 50 minutes to 1 hour.

4. Transfer chicken to serving platter, tent with aluminum foil, and let rest for 10 minutes before serving with lemon wedges.

Smoked Chicken

Serves 6 to 8   **Total Time** 2½ hours

Why This Recipe Works Smoking is a gentle process in which a low fire burns slowly to keep pieces of wood smoldering, allowing chicken to cook gradually. We wanted a foolproof grill version, but getting the heat just right is a challenge, and the smoke flavor can be fickle. We needed a fire setup and specific window of smoking time that would produce tender, juicy meat with clean, full-bodied smoke flavor. We started by brining the chicken for additional moisture, which kept it from drying out. We used chicken parts rather than a whole bird so we could arrange the white meat as far from the heat as possible. Covering a small pile of unlit coals with a batch of lit coals in our grill allowed the heat from the lit briquettes to trickle down and light the cold coals—a technique that extended the life of the fire. A pan of water under the chicken on the cooler side of the grill provided humidity, which helped stabilize the temperature of the grill and prevented the delicate breast meat from drying out. Adding wood chips just once at the beginning of cooking—and not refueling them once they had burned out—gave us fresh, clean-tasting smoke flavor. If using kosher chicken, do not brine in step 1. If you'd like to use wood chunks instead of wood chips when using a charcoal grill, substitute two medium wood chunks, soaked in water for 1 hour, for the wood chip packets.

- 1 cup table salt for brining
- 1 cup sugar for brining
- 6 pounds bone-in chicken pieces (split breasts, drumsticks and/or thighs), trimmed
- 3 tablespoons vegetable oil
- ½ teaspoon pepper
- 3 cups wood chips (1½ cups soaked in water for 15 minutes and drained, 1½ cups unsoaked)
- 1 (16 by 12-inch) disposable aluminum roasting pan (if using charcoal) or 1 (9-inch) disposable aluminum pie plate (if using gas)

1. Dissolve salt and sugar in 4 quarts cold water in large container. Submerge chicken pieces in brine, cover, and refrigerate for 30 minutes to 1 hour.

2. Using large piece of heavy-duty aluminum foil, wrap soaked chips in 8 by 4½-inch foil packet. (Make sure chips do not poke holes in sides or bottom of packet.) Cut 2 evenly spaced 2-inch slits in top of packet. Repeat with another sheet of foil and unsoaked wood chips.

3A. For a charcoal grill Open bottom vent halfway. Place disposable pan on 1 side of grill and add 2 cups water to pan. Arrange 2 quarts unlit charcoal banked against other side of grill. Light large chimney starter half filled with charcoal briquettes (3 quarts). When top coals are partially covered with ash, pour on top of unlit charcoal, to cover one-third of grill with coals steeply banked against side of grill. Place wood chip packets on top of coals. Set cooking grate in place, cover, and open lid vent halfway. Heat grill until hot and wood chips begin to smoke, about 5 minutes.

3B. For a gas grill Remove cooking grate and place wood chip packets directly on primary burner. Place disposable pie plate on other burner(s) and add 2 cups water to plate. Set cooking grate in place, turn all burners to high, cover, and heat grill until hot and wood chips begin to smoke, about 15 minutes.

Turn primary burner to medium-high and turn off other burner(s). (Adjust primary burner [or, if using 3-burner grill, primary burner and second burner] as needed to maintain grill temperature around 325 degrees.)

4. Remove chicken from brine and pat dry with paper towels. Brush chicken evenly with oil and sprinkle with ½ teaspoon pepper. Clean and oil cooking grate. Place chicken on cooler side of grill, skin side up, as far away from heat as possible with thighs closest to heat and breasts farthest away. Cover (positioning lid vent over chicken if using charcoal) and cook until breasts register 160 degrees and thighs and drumsticks register 175 degrees, 1¼ to 1½ hours.

5. Transfer chicken to serving platter, tent with foil, and let rest for 5 to 10 minutes. Serve.

Easy Grill-Roasted Whole Chicken
Serves 4 **Total Time** 2 hours

Why This Recipe Works Our dead-simple grill roasting method delivers juicy, subtly smoky meat with bronzed skin. Grilling a whole chicken over indirect heat for the majority of the cooking time allowed it to cook gently and evenly throughout. To ensure that it picked up distinct grill flavor, we moved the chicken over direct heat for the last few minutes of cooking and added a wood chip packet to the fire, which subtly infused the meat with smoke. Draining the bird's cavity midway through cooking prevented the fatty juices from dripping onto the fire and causing flare-ups. With no salt treatments or knife work, the chicken was ready for the grill in no time. If you're using a two-burner gas grill, use the side with the wood chips as the primary burner and the other side as the secondary burner. Adjust the primary burner to maintain a grill temperature between 375 and 400 degrees. Place the chicken 6 inches from the primary burner and rotate it after 25 minutes of cooking in step 4 so that it cooks evenly. If you'd like to use wood chunks instead of wood chips when using a charcoal grill, substitute one medium wood chunk, soaked in water for 1 hour, for the wood chip packet.

- 1 tablespoon kosher salt
- ½ teaspoon pepper
- 1 (3½- to 4-pound) whole chicken, giblets discarded
- 1 tablespoon vegetable oil
- ¼–½ cup wood chips

1. Combine salt and pepper in bowl. Pat chicken dry with paper towels, then rub entire surface of chicken with oil. Sprinkle salt mixture all over chicken and rub in mixture

Easy Grill-Roasted Whole Chicken

4. Clean and oil cooking grate. Place chicken, breast side up with cavity facing toward you, in center of grill, making sure chicken is centered between hotter sides of grill. Cover (position lid vent over chicken if using charcoal) and cook until breast registers 130 degrees, 45 to 55 minutes.

5. Using long grill tongs, reach into cavity and carefully lift chicken by breast. Holding chicken over bowl or container, tilt chicken toward you to allow fat and juices to drain from cavity. Transfer chicken, breast side up, to hotter side of grill (without wood chip packet) and cook, covered, until back is deep golden brown, about 5 minutes. Using tongs, flip chicken breast side down; cover and continue to cook over hotter side of grill until breast is deep golden brown, about 5 minutes. Using tongs, flip chicken breast side up and return it to center of grill; take internal temperature of breast. If breast registers 155 degrees, transfer chicken to carving board. If breast registers less than 155 degrees, cover and continue to cook in center of grill, checking temperature every 2 minutes, until it registers 155 degrees, 2 to 10 minutes. Let chicken rest, uncovered, for 20 minutes. Carve chicken and serve.

Chicken Under a Brick

Serves 4   **Total Time** 2 hours (plus 1 hour marinating time)

Why This Recipe Works In Tuscany, whole chicken is often spatchcocked (that is, the backbone is removed and the bird is opened and flattened) and then grilled al mattone, or "under a brick." Weighing down the spatchcocked bird accomplishes a few goals: It ensures even cooking of all the parts, it speeds up the cooking process, and it maximizes contact with the cooking grate for perfectly crisp skin. We started by salting the bird so it would retain its juices, even while being pressed and cooked over a hot flame. We gave the chicken a couple of flips on the grill to further ensure evenly cooked meat, and we loosened the chicken's skin from the meat to guarantee that an ultra-crisp sheath developed. Preheated foil-wrapped bricks provided a scorching start by delivering heat from above, and using two of them distributed the weight evenly. Rosemary, garlic, and lemon are typical flavorings for this dish; we tried adding them to a wet marinade, but it foiled our efforts for crispy skin. Instead, we utilized a homemade garlic-and-herb-infused oil; we strained the solids from the oil, rubbed them like a paste on the chicken's flesh, and whisked the flavorful oil with lemon juice to make a sauce for serving. This recipe calls for two standard-size bricks. (A cast-iron skillet or other heavy pan can be used in place of the bricks.) Use a pot holder or dish towel to safely grip and maneuver the hot bricks onto the chicken. The hot bricks ensure that the chicken's skin will be evenly browned and well rendered.

with your hands to evenly coat. Tie legs together with kitchen twine and tuck wingtips behind back.

2. Using large piece of heavy-duty aluminum foil, wrap chips (¼ cup if using charcoal; ½ cup if using gas) in 8 by 4½-inch foil packet. (Make sure chips do not poke holes in sides or bottom of packet.) Cut 2 evenly spaced 2-inch slits in top of packet.

3A. For a charcoal grill Open bottom vent halfway. Light large chimney starter mounded with charcoal briquettes (7 quarts). When top coals are partially covered with ash, pour into 2 banked piles on either side of grill. Place wood chip packet on 1 pile of coals. Set cooking grate in place, cover, and open lid vent halfway. Heat grill until hot and wood chips are smoking, about 5 minutes. (Grill temperature will reach about 400 degrees and will fall to about 350 degrees by end of cooking.)

3B. For a gas grill Remove cooking grate and place wood chip packet directly on 1 primary burner. Set grate in place, turn all burners to high, cover, and heat grill until hot and wood chips are smoking, about 15 minutes. Turn primary burner (with wood chips) to medium-high and turn off other burner (or, if using 3-burner grill, turn 2 outside burners to medium-high and turn off center burner).

⅓ cup extra-virgin olive oil
8 garlic cloves, minced
1 teaspoon grated lemon zest plus 2 tablespoons juice
Pinch red pepper flakes
4 teaspoons minced fresh thyme, divided
1 tablespoon minced fresh rosemary, divided
1 (3½- to 4-pound) whole chicken, giblets discarded
1½ teaspoons table salt
1 teaspoon pepper

1. Heat oil, garlic, lemon zest, and pepper flakes in small saucepan over medium-low heat until sizzling, about 3 minutes. Stir in 1 tablespoon thyme and 2 teaspoons rosemary and continue to cook for 30 seconds. Strain mixture through fine-mesh strainer set over small bowl, pushing on solids to extract oil. Transfer garlic-herb mixture to second bowl and let cool; set aside oil and garlic-herb mixture.

2. With chicken breast side down, use kitchen shears to cut along both sides of backbone. Discard backbone and trim any excess fat or skin at neck. Flip chicken over and use heel of your hand to flatten breastbone. Tuck wingtips behind back. Using your fingers, gently loosen skin covering breast and thighs and remove any excess fat.

3. Combine salt and pepper in bowl. Mix 2 teaspoons salt mixture into cooled garlic-herb mixture. Spread garlic-herb mixture evenly under skin of breast and thighs. Flip chicken and spread remaining ½ teaspoon salt mixture on bone side. Place chicken, skin side up, on wire rack set in rimmed baking sheet and refrigerate for 1 to 2 hours.

4A. For a charcoal grill Open bottom vent halfway. Light large chimney starter three-quarters filled with charcoal briquettes (4½ quarts). When top coals are partially covered with ash, pour evenly over half of grill. Set cooking grate in place, wrap 2 bricks tightly in aluminum foil, and place bricks on cooking grate. Cover and open lid vent halfway. Heat grill until hot, about 5 minutes.

4B. For a gas grill Wrap 2 bricks tightly in aluminum foil and place on cooking grate. Turn all burners to high, cover, and heat grill until hot, about 15 minutes. Leave primary burner on high and turn off other burner(s). (Adjust primary burner [or, if using 3-burner grill, primary burner and second burner] as needed to maintain grill temperature around 350 degrees.)

5. Clean and oil cooking grate. Place chicken on cooler side of grill, skin side down, with legs facing coals. Place 1 hot brick lengthwise over each breast half, cover, and cook until skin is lightly browned and faint grill marks appear, 22 to 25 minutes. Remove bricks. Using tongs, grip legs and flip chicken (chicken should release freely from grill; use thin metal spatula to loosen if stuck), then transfer, skin side up, to hotter side of grill. Place bricks over breast, cover, and cook until chicken is well browned, 12 to 15 minutes.

6. Remove bricks, flip chicken, skin side down, and continue to cook until skin is well browned and breast registers 160 degrees and thighs register 175 degrees, 5 to 10 minutes. Transfer chicken to carving board, tent with foil, and let rest for 15 minutes.

7. Whisk lemon juice, remaining 1 teaspoon thyme, and remaining 1 teaspoon rosemary into reserved oil and season with salt and pepper to taste. Carve chicken and serve, passing sauce separately.

Grilled Wine-and-Herb Marinated Chicken

Serves 4 **Total Time** 2¼ hours (plus 2 hours marinating time)

Why This Recipe Works Wine is a natural fit with chicken. The bold acidity and fruity, complex flavors of both red and white wines pair beautifully with the mild meat. We wanted to develop a recipe for winey, herby grilled chicken. First off, we used a dry white wine, which imparted a more distinct flavor to the meat. Whizzing our marinade in a blender broke down the herbs for optimal flavor and distribution, and poking holes in the chicken with a skewer helped the flavors of the marinade penetrate the bird. Butterflying increased the meat's exposure to heat, allowing it to cook more quickly and evenly. We started the chicken over the cooler part of the grill with the skin side down until the meat was almost done before flipping it and finishing directly above the fire, which ensured evenly cooked meat with a crisp skin. We also included a thin basting sauce, or mop, to add complexity and freshness to the grilled meat by reserving a small amount of marinade to brush on the chicken near the end of cooking. Use a dry white wine, such as Sauvignon Blanc, for this recipe. An inexpensive wine will work just fine, but pick one that's good enough to drink.

2 cups dry white wine
3 tablespoons lemon juice
3 tablespoons extra-virgin olive oil
2 tablespoons chopped fresh parsley
2 tablespoons chopped fresh thyme
2 tablespoons packed light brown sugar
4 garlic cloves, minced
1 teaspoon pepper
2 tablespoons table salt for marinade
1 (3½- to 4-pound) whole chicken, giblets discarded

Grilled Wine-and-Herb Marinated Chicken

1. Process wine, lemon juice, oil, parsley, thyme, sugar, garlic, and pepper in blender until emulsified, about 40 seconds. Measure out ¼ cup marinade and set aside. Add salt to remaining marinade in blender and process to dissolve, about 20 seconds.

2. With chicken breast side down, use kitchen shears to cut along both sides of backbone. Discard backbone and trim any excess fat or skin at neck. Flip chicken over and use heel of your hand to flatten breastbone. Tuck wingtips behind back.

3. Poke holes all over chicken with skewer. Place chicken in 1-gallon zipper-lock bag, pour in salted marinade, seal bag, and turn to coat. Set bag in baking dish, breast side down, and refrigerate for 2 to 3 hours.

4A. For a charcoal grill Open bottom vent completely. Light large chimney starter filled with charcoal briquettes (6 quarts). When top coals are partially covered with ash, pour evenly over half of grill. Set cooking grate in place, cover, and open lid vent completely. Heat grill until hot, about 5 minutes.

4B. For a gas grill Turn all burners to high, cover, and heat grill until hot, about 15 minutes. Turn primary burner to medium and other burner(s) to low. (Adjust primary burner [or, if using 3-burner grill, primary burner and second burner] as needed to maintain grill temperature between 350 and 375 degrees.)

5. Remove chicken from marinade and pat dry with paper towels. Clean and oil cooking grate. Place chicken skin side down on cooler side of grill, with legs closest to hotter side of grill. Cover and cook until chicken is well browned and thighs register 160 degrees, 50 minutes to 1 hour 5 minutes. Brush chicken with half of reserved marinade. Flip chicken skin side up, move it to hotter side of grill, and brush with remaining reserved marinade. Cook, covered, until breasts register 160 degrees and thighs register 175 degrees, 10 to 15 minutes.

6. Transfer chicken to carving board, tent with aluminum foil, and let rest for 15 minutes. Carve and serve.

Grill-Roasted Beer Can Chicken

Serves 4   Total Time 2¼ hours (plus 1 hour brining time)

Why This Recipe Works Beer can chicken has a number of things going for it: The beer in the open can simmers and turns to steam as the chicken roasts, which makes the meat remarkably juicy and rich-textured, similar to braised chicken. And the dry heat of the grill crisps the skin and renders the fat away. After brining the chicken, we rubbed it inside and out with a simple but flavorful blend of pantry staples including garlic powder, thyme, celery seeds, and cayenne. To cook the bird, we simply propped it up on an open can of beer on the grill in the center of the coals, using the drumsticks to form a tripod, and put the lid on the grill. It took about 4 quarts of coals (two-thirds of a chimney starter) to maintain the grill at the proper temperature for the duration. A few hardwood chunks atop the smoldering coals added just the right amount of smoky flavor. Roughly an hour and a half later we had a perfectly cooked chicken with moist meat and crispy skin. We like both mesquite wood and hickory wood in this recipe. Don't use a chicken weighing less than 3½ pounds here; its cavity will be too small to hold a beer can. You can substitute lemonade for the beer, if desired; fill an empty 12-ounce soda or beer can with 10 ounces (1¼ cups) of lemonade and proceed with the recipe as directed. If you'd like to use wood chunks instead of wood chips when using a charcoal grill, substitute four medium wood chunks, soaked in water for 1 hour (while the chicken brines), for the wood chip packet. Do not use a kosher chicken for this recipe.

½ cup table salt for brining
1 (3½- to 4-pound) whole chicken, giblets discarded
2 cups wood chips
3 tablespoons Basic Spice Rub (page 389)
1 (13 by 9-inch) disposable aluminum roasting pan (if using gas)
1 (12-ounce) can beer

1. Dissolve salt in 2 quarts cold water in large container. Submerge chicken in brine, cover, and refrigerate for 1 hour.

2. Remove chicken from brine and pat dry with paper towels. Rub chicken evenly, inside and out, with spice rub, gently loosening skin covering breast and rubbing spice rub directly onto meat. Just before grilling, soak wood chips in water for 15 minutes, then drain. Using large piece of heavy-duty aluminum foil, wrap soaked chips in 8 by 4½-inch foil packet. (Make sure chips do not poke holes in sides or bottom of packet.) Cut 2 evenly spaced 2-inch slits in top of packet.

3A. For a charcoal grill Open bottom vent halfway. Light large chimney starter two-thirds filled with charcoal briquettes (4 quarts). When top coals are partially covered with ash, pour into 2 even piles on either side of grill; use grill tongs to move any stray coals into piles. Place wood chip packet on 1 pile of coals. Set cooking grate in place, cover, and open lid vent halfway. Heat grill until hot and wood chunks are smoking, about 5 minutes.

3B. For a gas grill Remove cooking grate. Place soaked wood chips in disposable pan and place pan over primary burner. Set grate in place, turn all burners to high, cover, and heat grill until hot and wood chips are smoking, about 15 minutes. Turn primary burner to medium and turn other burner(s) off. (Adjust primary burner [or, if using 3-burner grill, primary burner and second burner] as needed to maintain grill temperature between 325 and 350 degrees.)

4. Open beer can and pour out (or drink) ¼ cup. Using church key, punch several large holes in top of can. Slide chicken over can so that drumsticks are level with bottom of can and chicken stands upright.

5. Clean and oil cooking grate. Place chicken with can in center of grill (if using charcoal), or on cooler side of grill with wing side facing primary burner (if using gas), using drumsticks to help steady chicken. Cover (position lid vent over chicken if using charcoal) and cook, rotating chicken and can 180 degrees halfway through cooking, until breast registers 160 degrees and thighs register 175 degrees, 1 hour 10 minutes to 1½ hours.

6. Using large wad of paper towels, carefully transfer chicken (with can) to tray, making sure to keep can upright. Tent with foil and let rest for 15 minutes. Using wads of paper towels, carefully lift chicken off can and transfer to carving board. Discard remaining beer and can. Carve chicken and serve.

Two Glazed Grill-Roasted Chickens
Serves 6 to 8 **Total Time** 2¼ hours

Why This Recipe Works We wanted a recipe for smoky grill-roasted chicken finished with a sweet, sticky glaze. To get direct heat on the chicken without burning it, we used a V-rack to elevate the two birds above the flame. We pricked the chicken skin all over with a skewer to allow the fat an escape route. To evenly brown and render the skin before glazing, we grilled the chickens on each side, rotating the V-rack 180 degrees halfway through. To help this recipe fulfill its potential as a summer grilling staple, we came up with a variety of glazes. To ensure that the glaze would adhere when brushed on the skin, we pre-cooked it, which thickened the mixture to a viscous consistency and concentrated its flavor. Glazing the chickens too soon slowed their cooking to a crawl. We found it best to wait until the chickens had reached an internal temperature of 155 degrees before beginning to glaze them. For a substantial coating, we brushed the chickens with the glaze and turned the birds at least three times during their final minutes on the grill. To prevent flare-ups, be sure that your grill is clean. Use any of the glazes on pages 387–388.

2 (3½- to 4-pound) whole chickens, giblets discarded
1 tablespoon sugar
1 tablespoon table salt
1 teaspoon pepper
1 recipe glaze (pages 387–388)

SETTING UP BEER CAN CHICKEN

With legs pointing down, slide chicken over open beer can. Two legs and beer can form tripod that steadies chicken on grill.

1. Spray V-rack with vegetable oil spray. Pat chickens dry with paper towels and prick skin all over with skewer or paring knife. Combine sugar, salt, and pepper in small bowl, then rub seasoning mixture all over chickens. Tuck wings behind back and tie legs together with kitchen twine. Arrange chickens, breast side up, head to tail on prepared V-rack.

2A. For a charcoal grill Open bottom vent completely. Light large chimney starter filled with charcoal briquettes (6 quarts). When top coals are partially covered with ash, pour evenly over grill. Set cooking grate in place, cover, and open lid vent completely. Heat grill until hot, about 5 minutes.

2B. For a gas grill Turn all burners to high, cover, and heat grill until hot, about 15 minutes. Turn all burners to low. (Adjust primary burner [or, if using 3-burner grill, primary burner and second burner] as needed to maintain grill temperature around 325 degrees.)

3. Arrange V-rack on cooking grate and grill, covered, until back of each chicken is well browned, about 30 minutes, carefully rotating V-rack 180 degrees after 15 minutes. Flip chickens and repeat until breasts are well browned and thighs register 155 degrees, 30 to 40 minutes. Brush chickens with glaze and continue grilling with lid on, flipping and glazing chicken every 5 minutes, until lightly charred in spots and breasts register 160 degrees and thighs register 175 degrees, 15 to 25 minutes.

4. Transfer chickens to carving board, tent with aluminum foil, and let rest for 10 minutes. Carve and drizzle chicken with remaining glaze. Serve.

Two Kentucky Bourbon–Brined Grilled Chickens

Serves 4 to 6 **Total Time** 2½ hours (plus 1 hour marinating time)

Why This Recipe Works A bourbon-spiked barbecue sauce slathered on whole grilled chicken is a perfect combination, but infusing smoke and bourbon flavors while keeping the meat from drying out is a challenge. We started by using two split chickens so we could cook each half skin side up for crispier skin. For good bourbon flavor, we made a marinade that paired the bourbon with brown sugar, shallot, garlic, and soy sauce. We also slashed the surface of the chickens to help them absorb the marinade. Our science editor suggested heating the marinade, which would help activate the aroma compounds, so we boiled the mixture before adding it to the chickens.

Two Glazed Grill-Roasted Chickens

Two Kentucky Bourbon–Brined Grilled Chickens

Now the meat had smokiness, bold bourbon flavor, and deep, well-rounded seasoning. Use a bourbon you'd be happy drinking. Use all the basting liquid in step 5. Do not use kosher chickens in this recipe. If you'd like to use wood chunks instead of wood chips when using a charcoal grill, substitute one medium wood chunk, soaked in water for 1 hour, for the wood chip packet.

1¼ cups bourbon
1¼ cups soy sauce
½ cup packed brown sugar
1 shallot, minced
4 garlic cloves, minced
2 teaspoons pepper
2 (3½- to 4-pound) whole chickens, giblets discarded
1 cup wood chips
4 (12-inch) wooden skewers

1. Bring bourbon, soy sauce, sugar, shallot, garlic, and pepper to boil in medium saucepan over medium-high heat and cook for 1 minute. Remove from heat and let cool completely. Set aside ¾ cup bourbon mixture for basting chicken. (Bourbon mixture can be refrigerated for up to 3 days.)

2. With 1 chicken breast side down, use kitchen shears to cut along both sides of backbone. Discard backbone and trim any excess fat or skin at neck. Flip chicken over and, using chef's knife, cut through breastbone to separate chicken into halves. Cut ½-inch-deep slits across breast, thigh, and leg of each half, about ½ inch apart. Tuck wingtips behind backs. Repeat with second chicken. Divide chicken halves between two 1-gallon zipper-lock bags and divide remaining bourbon mixture between bags. Seal bags, turn to distribute marinade, and refrigerate for at least 1 hour or up to 24 hours, flipping occasionally.

3. Just before grilling, soak wood chips in water for 15 minutes, then drain. Using large piece of heavy-duty aluminum foil, wrap soaked chips in 8 by 4½-inch foil packet. (Make sure chips do not poke holes in sides or bottom of packet.) Cut 2 evenly spaced 2-inch slits in top of packet. Remove chicken halves from marinade and pat dry with paper towels. Insert 1 skewer lengthwise through thickest part of breast down through thigh of each chicken half.

4A. For a charcoal grill Open bottom vent halfway. Light large chimney starter filled with charcoal briquettes (6 quarts). When top coals are partially covered with ash, pour into steeply banked pile against side of grill. Place wood chip packet on coals. Set cooking grate in place, cover, and open lid vent halfway. Heat grill until hot and wood chips are smoking, about 5 minutes.

4B. For a gas grill Remove cooking grate and place wood chip packet directly on primary burner. Set grate in place, turn all burners to high, cover, and heat grill until hot and wood chips are smoking, about 15 minutes. Leave primary burner on high and turn off other burners. (Adjust primary burner [or, if using 3-burner grill, primary burner and second burner] as needed to maintain grill temperature between 350 and 375 degrees.)

5. Clean and oil cooking grate. Place chicken halves skin side up on cooler side of grill with legs pointing toward fire. Cover and cook, basting every 15 minutes with reserved bourbon mixture, until breasts register 160 degrees and thighs register 175 degrees, 1¼ to 1½ hours, switching placement of chicken halves after 45 minutes. (All of bourbon mixture should be used.) Transfer chicken to carving board, tent with foil, and let rest for 20 minutes. Carve and serve.

Two Sinaloa-Style Grill-Roasted Chickens

Serves 4 to 6 **Total Time** 2½ hours (plus 2 hours marinating time)

Why This Recipe Works In Mexico's Sinaloa region, chicken is marinated with orange, garlic, and herbs and roasted over embers. Fresh orange juice gave lackluster flavor, so we made our marinade with orange juice concentrate, which packed a citrusy punch. We used two chickens and scored them before marinating so the flavor would penetrate. Butterflying, halving, and skewering the chickens made them easier to handle. We reserved some marinade and added oregano, thyme, and chipotle chile in adobo to baste the chicken while grilling. A wood chip packet on the grill infused the chickens with smoky flavor. You will need four 12-inch metal skewers for this recipe. If you'd like to use wood chunks instead of wood chips when using a charcoal grill, substitute two medium wood chunks, soaked in water for 1 hour, for the wood chip packets.

2 (3½- to 4-pound) whole chickens, giblets discarded
2 onions, chopped
1 (12-ounce) can frozen orange juice concentrate, thawed
¼ cup extra-virgin olive oil
2 garlic heads, cloves separated and peeled (20 cloves)
2 tablespoons table salt
1 tablespoon chopped fresh oregano
1 tablespoon minced fresh thyme
2 teaspoons minced canned chipotle chile in adobo sauce
1½ cups wood chips
Lime wedges

Two Sinaloa-Style Grill-Roasted Chickens

4A. For a charcoal grill Open bottom vent halfway. Light large chimney starter filled with charcoal briquettes (6 quarts). When top coals are partially covered with ash, pour into steeply banked pile against side of grill. Place wood chip packet on coals. Set cooking grate in place, cover, and open lid vent halfway. Heat grill until hot and wood chips are smoking, about 5 minutes.

4B. For a gas grill Remove cooking grate and place wood chip packet directly on primary burner. Set cooking grate in place, turn all burners to high, cover, and heat grill until hot and wood chips are smoking, about 15 minutes. Leave primary burner on high and turn off other burner(s). (Adjust primary burner [or, if using 3-burner grill, primary burner and second burner] as needed to maintain grill temperature between 350 and 375 degrees.)

5. Clean and oil cooking grate. Place chicken halves skin side up on cooler side of grill with legs pointing toward fire. Cover and cook for 45 minutes, basting every 15 minutes with reserved marinade.

6. Switch placement of chickens, with legs pointing toward fire, and continue to cook, covered, until breasts register 160 degrees and thighs register 175 degrees, 30 to 45 minutes. Transfer to carving board, tent with foil, and let rest for 20 minutes. Carve and serve with lime wedges.

Two Huli Huli Grilled Chickens

Serves 4 to 6   **Total Time** 2 hours (plus 1 hour brining time)

Why This Recipe Works Hawaiian huli huli chicken is typically something home cooks buy instead of make. The birds are continually basted with a sticky-sweet glaze and "huli"-ed, which means "turned" in Hawaiian. To adapt this recipe for an achievable homemade option, we had to change both the sauce and the technique. For the teriyaki-like glaze, we developed a version with soy sauce, rice vinegar, ginger, garlic, chili sauce, ketchup, brown sugar, and lots and lots of pineapple juice. We reduced the sauce until it was thick, glossy, and sweet to get the same effect as constantly basting without having to babysit the chicken on the grill. To mimic a Hawaiian rotisserie, we spread the coals in a single layer. The direct heat rendered the fat and crisped the skin, but the chicken was far enough from the coals to avoid burning. If you'd like to use wood chunks instead of wood chips when using a charcoal grill, substitute two medium wood chunks, soaked in water for 1 hour, for the wood chip packets. Do not brine the chicken for longer than 8 hours or it will become too salty. Do not use kosher chickens in this recipe.

1. With 1 chicken breast side down, use kitchen shears to cut along both sides of backbone. Discard backbone and trim any excess fat or skin at neck. Flip chicken over and split in half length-wise through breastbone using chef's knife. Cut ½-inch-deep slits across breast, thighs, and legs, about ½ inch apart. Tuck wingtips behind back. Repeat with second chicken.

2. Process onions, orange juice concentrate, oil, garlic, and salt in blender until smooth, about 1 minute. Transfer ¾ cup mixture to bowl and stir in oregano, thyme, and chipotle; set aside for grilling. Divide remaining marinade between two 1-gallon zipper-lock bags. Add chickens to bags and toss to coat. Press out as much air as possible, seal bags, and refrigerate for at least 2 hours or up to 24 hours, flipping occasionally.

3. Just before grilling, soak wood chips in water for 15 minutes, then drain. Using large piece of heavy-duty aluminum foil, wrap soaked chips in 8 by 4½-inch foil packet. (Make sure chips do not poke holes in sides or bottom of packet.) Cut 2 evenly spaced 2-inch slits in top of packet. Remove chickens from marinade and pat dry with paper towels. Insert 1 skewer lengthwise through thickest part of breast down through thigh of each chicken half.

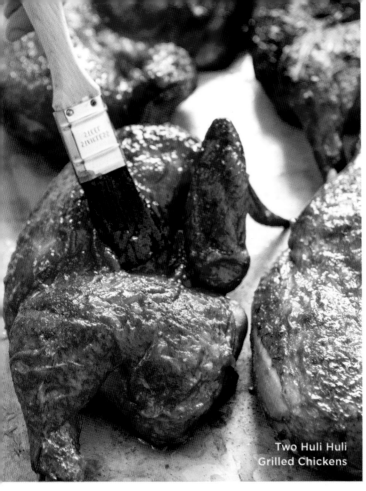

Two Huli Huli Grilled Chickens

Two Cornell Chickens

Chicken

- 2 (3½- to 4-pound) whole chickens, giblets discarded
- 2 cups soy sauce for brining
- 1 tablespoon vegetable oil
- 6 garlic cloves, minced
- 1 tablespoon grated fresh ginger

Glaze

- 3 (6-ounce) cans pineapple juice
- ¼ cup packed light brown sugar
- ¼ cup soy sauce
- ¼ cup ketchup
- ¼ cup rice vinegar
- 2 tablespoons grated fresh ginger
- 4 garlic cloves, minced
- 2 teaspoons Asian chili-garlic sauce

- 2 cups wood chips

1. For the chicken With 1 chicken breast side down, use kitchen shears to cut along both sides of backbone. Discard backbone and trim any excess fat or skin at neck. Flip chicken over and, using chef's knife, cut through breastbone to separate chicken into halves. Tuck wingtips behind back. Repeat with second chicken. Combine soy sauce and 2 quarts cold water in large container. Heat oil in large saucepan over medium-high heat until shimmering. Add garlic and ginger and cook until fragrant, about 30 seconds. Stir into soy sauce mixture. Add chicken, cover, and refrigerate for at least 1 hour or up to 8 hours.

2. For the glaze Meanwhile, combine all glaze ingredients in empty saucepan and bring to boil. Reduce heat to medium and simmer until thick and syrupy (you should have about 1 cup), 20 to 25 minutes. (Glaze can be refrigerated for up to 3 days.)

3. Just before grilling, soak wood chips in water for 15 minutes, then drain. Using large piece of heavy-duty aluminum foil, wrap soaked chips in 8 by 4½-inch foil packet. (Make sure chips do not poke holes in sides or bottom of packet.) Cut 2 evenly spaced 2-inch slits in top of packet.

4A. For a charcoal grill Open bottom vent halfway. Light large chimney starter three-quarters filled with charcoal briquettes (4½ quarts). When top coals are partially covered with ash, pour evenly over grill. Place foil packet on coals. Set cooking grate in place, cover, and open lid vent halfway. Heat grill until hot and wood chips are smoking, about 5 minutes.

4B. For a gas grill Remove cooking grate and place wood chip packet directly on primary burner. Set grate in place, turn all burners to high, cover, and heat grill until hot and wood chips are smoking, about 15 minutes. Turn all burners to medium-low. (Adjust primary burner [or, if using 3-burner grill, primary burner and second burner] as needed to maintain grill temperature around 350 degrees.)

5. Remove chicken from brine and pat dry with paper towels. Clean and oil cooking grate. Place chicken skin side up on grill (do not place chicken directly above foil packet). Cover and cook chicken until well browned on bottom and thighs register 120 degrees, 25 to 30 minutes. Flip chicken skin side down and continue to cook, covered, until skin is well browned and crisp, breasts register 160 degrees, and thighs register 175 degrees, 20 to 25 minutes. Transfer chicken to platter, brush with half of glaze, and let rest for 5 minutes. Serve, passing remaining glaze at table.

Two Cornell Chickens

Serves 4 to 6   **Total Time** 2 hours (plus 1 hour brining time)

Why This Recipe Works Invented in the 1940s by Robert Baker, a Cornell University professor, this grilled chicken has been a star attraction at the New York State Fair ever since, thanks to a vinegary sauce and a gentle cooking method that make the chicken tangy and crisp-skinned but still juicy. Grilling two split chickens over gentle heat gave us the requisite tender meat. To crisp the skin without burning it, we started the chicken skin side up to render the fat slowly, then flipped the chicken skin side down to brown until crisp. Poultry seasoning worked great as a rub but tasted dusty in the sauce, so we replaced it with fresh rosemary and sage. Dijon mustard contributed even more flavor to the sauce and thickened it perfectly. If using kosher chicken, do not brine. Do not brine the chicken longer than 2 hours or the vinegar will turn the meat mushy. Poultry seasoning is a mix of herbs and spices that can be found in the supermarket spice aisle.

Chicken
2   (3½- to 4-pound) whole chickens, giblets discarded
¼   cup table salt for brining
3½   cups cider vinegar

Seasoning and Sauce
1   tablespoon ground poultry seasoning
2½   teaspoons table salt, divided
2½   teaspoons pepper, divided

½   cup cider vinegar
3   tablespoons Dijon mustard
1   tablespoon chopped fresh sage leaves
1   tablespoon chopped fresh rosemary
½   cup extra-virgin olive oil

1. For the chicken With 1 chicken breast side down, use kitchen shears to cut along both sides of backbone. Discard backbone and trim any excess fat or skin at neck. Flip chicken over and, using chef's knife, cut through breastbone to separate chicken into halves. Tuck wingtips behind back. Repeat with second chicken. In large container, dissolve salt in vinegar and 2 quarts cold water. Submerge chickens in brine, cover, and refrigerate for 1 to 2 hours.

2. For the seasoning and sauce Combine poultry seasoning, 2 teaspoons salt, and 2 teaspoons pepper in small bowl; set aside. Process vinegar, mustard, sage, rosemary, remaining ½ teaspoon salt, and remaining ½ teaspoon pepper in blender until smooth, about 1 minute. With blender running, slowly add oil until incorporated. Measure out ¾ cup vinegar sauce and set aside to baste chicken; set aside remaining sauce for serving.

3A. For a charcoal grill Open bottom vent completely. Light large chimney starter three-quarters filled with charcoal briquettes (4½ quarts). When top coals are partially covered with ash, pour evenly over grill. Set cooking grate in place, cover, and open lid vent halfway. Heat grill until hot, about 5 minutes.

3B. For a gas grill Turn all burners to high, cover, and heat grill until hot, about 15 minutes. Turn all burners to medium-low. (Adjust primary burner [or, if using 3-burner grill, primary burner and second burner] as needed to maintain grill temperature around 350 degrees.)

4. Remove chickens from brine, pat dry with paper towels, and rub evenly with poultry seasoning mixture. Clean and oil cooking grate. Place chicken skin side up on grill and brush with 6 tablespoons vinegar sauce for basting. Cover and cook chicken until well browned on bottom and thighs register 120 degrees, 25 to 30 minutes, brushing with more sauce for basting halfway through grilling.

5. Flip chicken skin side down and brush with remaining sauce for basting. Cover and continue to cook chicken until skin is golden brown and crisp and breasts register 160 degrees and thighs register 175 degrees, 20 to 25 minutes.

6. Transfer chicken to carving board and let rest for 10 minutes. Carve chicken and serve with reserved sauce.

Two Alabama Barbecued Chickens

Two Alabama Barbecued Chickens

Serves 4 to 6   **Total Time** 2¼ hours (plus 1 hour chilling time)

Why This Recipe Works Alabama chicken with white barbecue sauce can be traced to a single place: the Big Bob Gibson Bar-B-Q restaurant in Decatur. The mayonnaise-based sauce is the perfect complement to grilled chicken: creamy and tart, with a hint of sweetness and decent heat. To replicate Big Bob's sauce, we added sweet-tart cider vinegar to mayonnaise to achieve a loose consistency not unlike that of salad dressing. A little granulated sugar reinforced the subtle sweetness and a touch of black pepper and cayenne, along with some prepared horseradish, amped up the heat without making it overpowering. Cutting two chickens in half made for quicker and more even grilling, and brushing them with the sauce twice (once when they came off the grill and again 10 minutes later) gave us a thorough coating that clung nicely. If you'd like to use wood chunks instead of wood chips when using a charcoal grill, substitute two medium wood chunks, soaked in water for 1 hour, for the wood chip packet.

Sauce
- ¾ cup mayonnaise
- 2 tablespoons cider vinegar
- 2 teaspoons sugar
- ½ teaspoon prepared horseradish
- ½ teaspoon table salt
- ½ teaspoon pepper
- ¼ teaspoon cayenne pepper

Chicken
- 1 teaspoon table salt
- 1 teaspoon pepper
- ½ teaspoon cayenne pepper
- 2 (3½- to 4-pound) whole chickens, giblets discarded
- 2 cups wood chips, soaked in water for 15 minutes and drained
- 1 (13 by 9-inch) disposable aluminum roasting pan (if using charcoal)

1. For the sauce Process all ingredients in blender until smooth, about 1 minute. Refrigerate sauce for at least 1 hour or up to 2 days.

2. For the chicken Combine salt, pepper, and cayenne in small bowl. With 1 chicken breast side down, use kitchen shears to cut along both sides of backbone. Discard backbone and trim any excess fat or skin at neck. Flip chicken over and, using chef's knife, cut through breastbone to separate chicken into halves. Tuck wingtips behind back. Repeat with remaining chicken. Pat chicken dry with paper towels and rub evenly with spice mixture. Using large piece of heavy-duty aluminum foil, wrap soaked chips in 8 by 4½-inch foil packet. (Make sure chips do not poke holes in sides or bottom of packet.) Cut 2 evenly spaced 2-inch slits in top of packet.

3A. For a charcoal grill Open bottom vent halfway and place disposable pan in center of grill. Light large chimney starter filled with charcoal briquettes (6 quarts). When top coals are partially covered with ash, pour into 2 even piles on either side of disposable pan. Place wood chip packet on 1 pile of coals. Set cooking grate in place, cover, and open lid vent halfway. Heat grill until hot and wood chips are smoking, about 5 minutes.

3B. For a gas grill Remove cooking grate and place wood chip packet directly on primary burner. Set grate in place, turn all burners to high, cover, and heat grill until hot and wood chips are smoking, about 15 minutes. Turn all burners to medium-low. (Adjust primary burner [or, if using 3-burner grill, primary burner and second burner] as needed to maintain grill temperature around 350 degrees.)

4. Clean and oil cooking grate. Place chicken skin side down on grill (in center of grill over disposable pan if using charcoal). Cover (position lid vent opposite wood chips if using charcoal) and cook until skin is browned and thighs register 120 degrees, 35 to 45 minutes.

5. Flip chicken skin side up. Cover and continue to cook until skin is deep golden brown and crispy and breasts register 160 degrees and thighs register 175 degrees, 15 to 20 minutes.

6. Transfer chicken to carving board and brush each half with 2 tablespoons sauce. Tent chicken with foil and let rest for 10 minutes. Brush chicken with remaining sauce, carve, and serve.

Thai Grilled Cornish Hens

Serves 4   **Total Time** 2 hours (plus 6 hours marinating time)

Why This Recipe Works Gai yang, a popular Thai street food, features small whole chickens with juicy meat, bronzed skin, and smoky char—made extraordinary by a flavor-packed marinade. For our take, we started with Cornish hens, which are similar in size to the hens traditionally used by chicken vendors in Thailand. Butterflying and flattening the hens helped them cook more quickly and evenly on the grill. For the marinade we used cilantro leaves and stems (a substitute for hard-to-find cilantro root), lots of garlic, white pepper, ground coriander, brown sugar, and fish sauce; thanks to its pesto-like consistency, it clung to the hens instead of sliding off. We set up a half-grill fire and started cooking the hens skin side up over the cooler side of the grill so the skin had time to slowly render while the meat cooked; we finished them over the hotter side to crisp the skin. This dish is traditionally served with sweet-tangy-spicy dipping sauce. We made our own with equal parts white vinegar and sugar and simmered the mixture until it was slightly thickened. Minced garlic and Thai chiles balanced the sauce with savory, fruity heat. The hens need to marinate for at least 6 hours before cooking (a longer marinating time is preferable). If your hens weigh 1½ to 2 pounds, grill three hens instead of four and extend the initial cooking time in step 6 by 5 minutes. If you can't find Thai chiles, substitute Fresno or red jalapeño chiles. Serve with white rice.

Hens
- 4 (1¼- to 1½-pound) whole Cornish game hens, giblets discarded
- 1 cup fresh cilantro leaves and stems, chopped coarse
- 12 garlic cloves, peeled
- ¼ cup packed light brown sugar
- 2 teaspoons ground white pepper
- 2 teaspoons ground coriander
- 2 teaspoons table salt
- ¼ cup fish sauce

Dipping Sauce
- ½ cup distilled white vinegar
- ½ cup granulated sugar
- 1 tablespoon minced Thai chiles
- 3 garlic cloves, minced
- ¼ teaspoon table salt

1. For the hens With 1 hen breast side down, use kitchen shears to cut along both sides of backbone. Discard backbone. Flip hen and press on breastbone to flatten. Trim any excess fat and skin. Repeat with remaining hens.

2. Pulse cilantro leaves and stems, garlic, sugar, pepper, coriander, and salt in food processor until finely chopped, 10 to 15 pulses; transfer to small bowl. Add fish sauce and stir until marinade has consistency of loose paste.

3. Rub hens all over with marinade. Transfer hens and any excess marinade to 1-gallon zipper-lock bag and refrigerate for at least 6 hours or up to 24 hours, flipping bag halfway through marinating.

4. For the dipping sauce Meanwhile, bring vinegar to boil in small saucepan. Add sugar and stir to dissolve. Reduce heat to medium-low and simmer until vinegar mixture is slightly thickened, 5 minutes. Remove from heat and let vinegar mixture cool completely. Add chiles, garlic, and salt and stir until combined. Transfer sauce to airtight container and refrigerate

Thai Grilled Cornish Hens

until ready to use. (Sauce can be refrigerated for up to 2 weeks. Bring to room temperature before serving.)

5A. For a charcoal grill Open bottom vent completely. Light large chimney starter filled with charcoal briquettes (6 quarts). When top coals are partially covered with ash, pour evenly over half of grill. Set cooking grate in place, cover, and open lid vent completely. Heat grill until hot, about 5 minutes.

5B. For a gas grill Turn all burners to high, cover, and heat grill until hot, about 15 minutes. Leave primary burner on high and turn off other burner(s). (Adjust primary burner [or, if using 3-burner grill, primary burner and second burner] as needed to maintain grill temperature between 400 and 450 degrees.)

6. Clean and oil cooking grate. Remove hens from bag, leaving any marinade that sticks to hens in place. Tuck wingtips behind backs and turn legs so drumsticks face inward toward breasts. Place hens, skin side up, on cooler side of grill (if using charcoal, arrange hens so that legs and thighs are facing coals). Cover and cook until skin is browned and breasts register 145 to 150 degrees, 30 to 35 minutes, rotating hens halfway through cooking.

7. Using tongs, carefully flip hens skin side down and move to hotter side of grill. Cover and cook until skin is crisp, deeply browned, and charred in spots and breasts register 160 degrees, 3 to 5 minutes, being careful to avoid burning.

8. Transfer hens, skin side up, to cutting board; tent with aluminum foil and let rest for 10 minutes. Slice each hen in half or into 4 pieces and serve, passing dipping sauce separately.

Grill-Roasted Boneless Turkey Breast

Serves 6 to 8   **Total Time** 2 hours (plus 1 hour salting time)

Why This Recipe Works Turkey breast easily dries out on the grill, but we wanted a recipe that would deliver a grill-roasted breast with crisp skin and rich, juicy meat. We started with a bone-in whole breast, removed the skin and bones, and then salted the meat to add flavor and moisture. Next we stacked the breast halves on top of one another, draped them with the skin, and tied the "roast" together. Removing the breast halves from the bone and arranging them so that the thick end of one was pressed against the tapered end of the other created an even thickness. The skin protected the meat from the fire and the stacked breasts ensured that the meat cooked more slowly. We started the turkey on the cooler side of the grill, then finished with a quick sear on the hotter side to crisp the skin. We prefer either a natural (unbrined) or kosher turkey breast for this recipe. If using a kosher turkey breast (rubbed with salt and rinsed during processing) or self-basting turkey breast

(injected with salt and water), do not salt it in step 1. If the breast has a pop-up timer, remove it before cooking. If you'd like to use wood chunks instead of wood chips when using a charcoal grill, substitute one small wood chunk, soaked in water for 1 hour, for the wood chip packet. For more information on cutting the bones from a turkey breast, see page 13.

> 1 (5- to 7-pound) bone-in whole turkey breast, trimmed
> 2 teaspoons table salt
> ½ cup wood chips (optional)
> 1 teaspoon vegetable oil
> 1 teaspoon pepper

1. Remove skin from breast meat and then cut along rib cage to remove breast halves (discard bones or save for stock). Pat turkey breast halves dry with paper towels and sprinkle with salt. Stack breast halves on top of one another with cut sides facing each other, and alternating thick and tapered ends. Stretch skin over exposed meat and tuck in ends. Tie kitchen twine lengthwise around roast. Then tie 5 to 7 pieces of twine at 1-inch intervals crosswise along roast. Transfer roast to wire rack set in rimmed baking sheet and refrigerate for 1 hour.

2. If using wood chips Just before grilling, soak wood chips in water for 15 minutes, then drain. Using large piece of heavy-duty aluminum foil, wrap soaked chips in 8 by 4½-inch foil packet. (Make sure chips do not poke holes in sides or bottom of packet.) Cut 2 evenly spaced 2-inch slits in top of packet.

3A. For a charcoal grill Open bottom vent halfway. Light large chimney starter filled with charcoal briquettes (6 quarts). When top coals are partially covered with ash, pour evenly over half of grill. Place wood chip packet, if using, on coals. Set cooking grate in place, cover, and open lid vent halfway. Heat grill until hot and wood chips are smoking, about 5 minutes.

3B. For a gas grill Place wood chip packet, if using, directly on primary burner. Turn all burners to high, cover, and heat grill until hot and wood chips are smoking, about 15 minutes. Turn all burners to medium-low. (Adjust primary burner [or, if using 3-burner grill, primary burner and second burner] as needed to maintain grill temperature around 350 degrees.)

4. Clean and oil cooking grate. Rub surface of roast with oil and sprinkle with pepper. Place roast on grill (on cooler side if using charcoal). Cover (position lid vent over meat if using charcoal) and cook until roast registers 150 degrees, 40 minutes to 1 hour, turning roast 180 degrees halfway through grilling.

5. Slide roast to hotter side of grill (if using charcoal) or turn all burners to medium-high (if using gas). Cook until roast is browned and skin is crisp on all sides, 8 to 10 minutes, rotating every 2 minutes.

6. Transfer roast to carving board, tent with foil, and let rest for 15 minutes. Cut into ½-inch-thick slices, removing twine as you cut. Serve.

Smoked Turkey Breast

Serves 6 to 8   **Total Time** 2¾ hours (plus 8 hours salting time)

Why This Recipe Works For smoked turkey with plump, juicy meat lightly perfumed with smoke, we chose a turkey breast, which cooked relatively quickly on the grill. Rubbing salt and brown sugar under and over the skin and resting the turkey breast in the refrigerator overnight allowed the seasonings to penetrate the meat. Before grilling, we dried the skin and applied a second round of rub, replacing the salt with pepper for kick. Piercing the skin before grilling allowed some of the fat to drain away, which helped crisp the skin. A half-cup of wood chips added enough smokiness without overwhelming the mild meat. After grilling the bird for an hour and a half, we had smoky, well-seasoned, juicy meat with golden, crisp skin. We prefer either a natural (unbrined) or kosher turkey breast for this recipe. If using a kosher turkey breast (rubbed with salt and rinsed during processing) or self-basting turkey breast (injected with salt and water), do not salt it in step 1, but do sugar. If the breast has a pop-up timer, remove it before cooking. If you'd like to use wood chunks instead of wood chips when using a charcoal grill, substitute two medium wood chunks, soaked in water for 1 hour, for the wood chip packet.

> 3 tablespoons packed brown sugar, divided
> 1 tablespoon table salt
> 1 (5-to 7-pound) bone-in whole turkey breast, trimmed
> ½ cup wood chips
> 2 teaspoons pepper
> 1 (13 by 9-inch) disposable aluminum roasting pan (if using charcoal)

1. Combine 2 tablespoons sugar and salt in bowl. Pat turkey dry with paper towels. Using your fingers, gently loosen skin covering each side of breast and rub sugar-salt mixture evenly over and under skin. Tightly wrap turkey with plastic wrap and refrigerate for 8 to 24 hours.

2. Just before grilling, soak wood chips in water for 15 minutes, then drain. Using large piece of heavy-duty aluminum foil, wrap soaked chips in 8 by 4½-inch foil packet. (Make sure chips do not poke holes in sides or bottom of packet.) Cut 2 evenly spaced 2-inch slits in top of packet. Combine remaining 1 tablespoon sugar and pepper in bowl. Unwrap turkey, pat dry with paper towels, and rub sugar-pepper mixture under and over skin. Poke skin all over with skewer.

3A. For a charcoal grill Open bottom vent halfway and place disposable pan in center of grill. Light large chimney starter filled with charcoal briquettes (6 quarts). When top coals are partially covered with ash, pour into 2 even piles on either side of disposable pan. Place wood chip packet on 1 pile

Grill-Roasted Boneless Turkey Breast

Smoked Turkey Breast

of coals. Set cooking grate in place, cover, and open lid vent halfway. Heat grill until hot and wood chips are smoking, about 5 minutes.

3B. For a gas grill Remove cooking grate and place wood chip packet directly on primary burner. Set cooking grate in place, turn all burners to high, cover, and heat grill until hot and wood chips are smoking, about 15 minutes. Turn all burners to medium-low. (Adjust primary burner [or, if using 3-burner grill, primary burner and second burner] as needed to maintain grill temperature around 350 degrees.)

4. Clean and oil cooking grate. Place turkey breast, skin side up, in center of grill (over disposable pan if using charcoal). Cover (position lid vent over turkey if using charcoal) and cook until skin is well browned and breast registers 160 degrees, about 1½ hours.

5. Transfer turkey to carving board, tent with foil, and let rest for 15 to 20 minutes. Carve turkey and serve.

Classic Grill-Roasted Turkey

Serves 10 to 12   **Total Time** 3½ hours (plus 6 hours brining time)

Why This Recipe Works This turkey isn't your average Thanksgiving dinner, but cooking a whole turkey on the grill produces unbeatable intense, smoky flavor. Grill-roasting a whole turkey can be hard to manage, but it can also produce the best-tasting, best-looking turkey ever, with crispy skin and moist meat perfumed with smoke. We wanted to take the guesswork out of preparing the holiday bird on the grill. Because the skin on larger birds will burn before the meat cooks, we chose a small turkey (less than 14 pounds). To season the meat and help prevent it from drying out, we brined the turkey. Brushing the brined bird with melted butter guaranteed the best browning. To protect the skin and promote slow cooking, we placed the turkey on the opposite side of the glowing coals or lit gas burner. Using a V-rack, sprayed with vegetable oil spray to prevent sticking, improved air circulation and we turned the turkey three times so all four sides received equal exposure to the hot side of the grill for evenly bronzed skin. If using a self-basting turkey (such as a frozen Butterball) or a kosher turkey, do not brine in step 1. If you'd like to use wood chunks instead of wood chips when using a charcoal grill, substitute six medium wood chunks, soaked in water for 1 hour, for the wood chip packets. If you plan to make the Gravy for Classic Grill-Roasted Turkey (page 383), reserve the turkey neck and giblets.

Classic Grill-Roasted Turkey

1 cup table salt for brining
1 (12- to 14-pound) turkey, neck and giblets removed, wingtips tucked behind back
2 tablespoons unsalted butter, melted
6 cups wood chips

1. Dissolve salt in 2 gallons cold water in large container. Submerge turkey in brine, cover, and refrigerate or store in very cool spot (40 degrees or less) for 6 to 12 hours.

2. Lightly spray V-rack with vegetable oil spray. Remove turkey from brine and pat dry, inside and out, with paper towels. Brush both sides of turkey with melted butter and place breast side down in prepared V-rack.

3. Just before grilling, soak wood chips in water for 15 minutes, then drain. Using large piece of heavy-duty aluminum foil, wrap 2 cups soaked chips in 8 by 4½-inch foil packet. (Make sure chips do not poke holes in sides or bottom of packet.) Cut 2 evenly spaced 2-inch slits in top of packet. Repeat twice with remaining 4 cups chips for total of 3 packets. Cut 2 evenly spaced 2-inch slits in top of each packet.

Gravy for Classic Grill-Roasted Turkey

Makes 6 cups   Total Time 2¾ hours

- 1 tablespoon vegetable oil
  Reserved turkey neck, cut into 1-inch pieces, and giblets
- 1 pound onions, chopped coarse, divided
- 4 cups chicken broth
- 4 cups beef broth
- 2 small carrots, peeled and chopped coarse
- 2 small celery ribs, chopped coarse
- 6 tablespoons unsalted butter
- ½ cup all-purpose flour
- 2 bay leaves
- ½ teaspoon dried thyme
- 10 whole black peppercorns

1. Heat oil in Dutch oven over medium-high heat until shimmering. Add turkey neck and giblets; cook, stirring occasionally, until browned, about 5 minutes. Add half of onions and cook, stirring occasionally, until softened, about 3 minutes. Reduce heat to low; cover and cook, stirring occasionally, until turkey parts and onions release their juices, about 20 minutes.

2. Add chicken and beef broths; increase heat to high and bring to boil. Reduce heat to low and simmer, covered, skimming any foam that rises to surface, until broth is rich and flavorful, about 30 minutes. Strain broth into large bowl (you should have about 8 cups), reserving giblets, if desired; discard neck. Reserve broth. If using giblets, when cool enough to handle, remove gristle from giblets, dice, and set aside. (Broth and giblets can be refrigerated for up to 2 days.)

3. Pulse carrots in food processor until broken into rough ¼-inch pieces, about 5 pulses. Add celery and remaining onions; pulse until all vegetables are broken into ⅛-inch pieces, about 5 pulses.

4. Melt butter in now-empty Dutch oven over medium-high heat. Add vegetables and cook, stirring frequently, until softened and well browned, about 10 minutes. Reduce heat to medium; stir in flour and cook, stirring constantly, until thoroughly browned and fragrant, 5 to 7 minutes. Whisking constantly, gradually add reserved broth; bring to boil, skimming off any foam that forms on surface. Reduce heat to medium-low and add bay leaves, thyme, and peppercorns; simmer, stirring occasionally, until thickened and reduced to 6 cups, 30 to 35 minutes.

5. Strain gravy through fine-mesh strainer into clean saucepan, pressing on solids to extract as much liquid as possible; discard solids. Stir in diced giblets, if using. Season with salt and pepper to taste, and serve.

4A. For a charcoal grill Open bottom vent halfway. Light large chimney starter mounded with charcoal briquettes (7 quarts). When top coals are partially covered with ash, pour into steeply banked pile against side of grill. Place 2 wood chip packets on pile of coals. Set cooking grate in place, cover, and open lid vent halfway. Heat grill until hot and wood chips are smoking, about 5 minutes.

4B. For a gas grill Remove cooking grate and place 1 wood chip packet directly on primary burner. Set cooking grate in place, turn all burners to high, cover, and heat grill until hot and wood chips are smoking, about 15 minutes. Turn primary burner to medium-high and turn off other burner(s). (Adjust primary burner [or, if using 3-burner grill, primary burner and second burner] as needed to maintain grill temperature around 325 degrees.)

5. Clean and oil cooking grate. Place V-rack with turkey on cooler side of grill with leg and wing facing coals, cover (position lid vent over turkey if using charcoal), and cook for 1 hour.

6. Using pot holders, transfer V-rack with turkey to rimmed baking sheet or roasting pan. If using charcoal, remove cooking grate and add 12 new briquettes and third wood chip packet to pile of coals; set cooking grate in place. If using gas, place remaining wood chip packets directly on primary burner. With wad of paper towels in each hand, flip turkey breast side up in rack and return V-rack with turkey to cooler side of grill, with other leg and wing facing coals. Cover (position lid vent over turkey if using charcoal) and cook for 45 minutes.

7. Using pot holders, carefully rotate V-rack with turkey (breast remains up) 180 degrees. Cover and continue to cook until breast registers 160 degrees and thighs register 175 degrees, 15 to 45 minutes. Transfer turkey to carving board, tent with foil, and let rest for 20 to 30 minutes. Carve and serve.

Grilled Corn with Basil-Lemon Butter

Serves 4 to 6   **Total Time** 40 minutes

We recommend using a disposable aluminum pan that measures at least 2¾ inches deep. Grill the corn while the chicken or turkey is resting. If using a different fire setup, grill over the highest heat.

    6 tablespoons unsalted butter, softened
    2 tablespoons chopped fresh basil
    1 tablespoon minced fresh parsley
    1 tablespoon finely grated lemon zest
    ½ teaspoon table salt
    ¼ teaspoon pepper
    1 (13 by 9-inch) disposable aluminum
       roasting pan
    8 ears corn, husks and silk removed
    2 tablespoons vegetable oil

1. Combine butter, basil, parsley, lemon zest, salt, and pepper in small bowl.

2. Place flavored butter in disposable pan. Brush corn evenly with oil and season with salt and pepper.

3A. For a charcoal grill Open bottom vent completely. Light large chimney starter three-quarters filled with charcoal briquettes (4½ quarts). When top coals are partially covered with ash, pour evenly over grill. Set cooking grate in place, cover, and open lid vent completely. Heat grill until hot, about 5 minutes.

3B. For a gas grill Turn all burners to high, cover, and heat grill until hot, about 15 minutes. Turn all burners to medium-high.

4. Clean and oil cooking grate. Place corn on grill and cook, turning occasionally, until lightly charred on all sides, 5 to 9 minutes. Transfer corn to disposable pan and cover tightly with aluminum foil.

5. Place disposable pan on grill and cook, shaking pan frequently, until butter is sizzling, about 3 minutes. Remove pan from grill and carefully remove foil, allowing steam to escape away from you. Serve corn, spooning any butter in pan over individual ears.

VARIATION

Grilled Corn with Honey Butter

Omit basil, parsley, lemon zest, and pepper. Add 2 tablespoons honey and ¼ teaspoon red pepper flakes to butter in step 1.

Spice-Rubbed Grill-Roasted Turkey

Serves 10 to 12   **Total Time** 3¾ hours (plus 6 hours brining time)

Why This Recipe Works Mild turkey is a perfect candidate for amping up with a bold spice rub and grilled char. For a rub that was balanced with salty, sweet, and spicy flavors, we used an intense combination of five-spice powder, salt, cumin, pepper, garlic, cayenne, and cardamom. To thoroughly season the bird inside and out, we used the flavorful rub both on and under the skin of the turkey. Moderate, indirect heat was key for this recipe. Too hot and the skin (including the spice rub on it) would burn before the inside of the bird cooked. A pan of water placed on the grill helped cook our spice-rubbed turkey gently and kept the meat moist. Setting up the grill with a pile of unlit charcoal under lit briquettes created a long-burning fire that stayed hot long enough to cook the whole bird. A double dose of wood chips imbued the turkey with deeply smoky flavor. More spice mixture was brushed on the turkey with melted butter during cooking for perfectly burnished skin. If using a self-basting turkey (such as a frozen Butterball) or a kosher turkey, do not brine in step 1. Make sure you have plenty of fuel if you're using a gas grill. If you'd like to use wood chunks instead of wood chips when using a charcoal grill, substitute two medium wood chunks, soaked in water for 1 hour, for the wood chip packets.

    1 cup table salt for brining
    2 teaspoons five-spice powder
    2 teaspoons table salt
 1½ teaspoons ground cumin
    1 teaspoon pepper
    1 teaspoon granulated garlic
    ¼ teaspoon cayenne pepper
    ¼ teaspoon ground cardamom
    2 tablespoons unsalted butter, softened, plus
       4 tablespoons unsalted butter, divided
    1 tablespoon packed brown sugar
    2 tablespoons vegetable oil
    1 (12- to 14-pound) turkey,
       neck and giblets discarded
    2 cups wood chips, soaked in water for
       15 minutes and drained
    1 (13 by 9-inch) disposable aluminum roasting
       pan (if using charcoal) or 2 (9-inch) disposable
       aluminum pie plates (if using gas)

Spice-Rubbed Grill-Roasted Turkey

1. Dissolve 1 cup salt in 2 gallons cold water in large container. Submerge the turkey in the brine, cover, and refrigerate or store in a very cool spot (40 degrees or less) for 6 to 12 hours.

2. Combine five-spice powder, salt, cumin, pepper, granulated garlic, cayenne, and cardamom in bowl. Combine 1 tablespoon spice mixture with 2 tablespoons softened butter and sugar in second bowl. Combine 1 tablespoon spice mixture with oil in third bowl.

3. Pat turkey dry, inside and out, with paper towels. With turkey breast side up, use your fingers to gently loosen skin covering each side of breast. Rub spiced butter evenly under skin of breast. Tuck wingtips behind back and tie legs together with kitchen twine. Rub spiced oil evenly over entire surface of turkey. Using large piece of heavy-duty aluminum foil, wrap soaked chips in 8 by 4½-inch foil packet. (Make sure chips do not poke holes in sides or bottom of packet.) Cut 2 evenly spaced 2-inch slits in top of packet.

4A. For a charcoal grill Open bottom vent completely. Place disposable pan on 1 side of grill and add 3 cups water to pan. Arrange 3 quarts unlit charcoal briquettes evenly on

other side of grill. Light large chimney starter three-quarters filled with charcoal briquettes (4½ quarts). When top coals are partially covered with ash, pour evenly over unlit coals. Place wood chip packet on coals. Set cooking grate in place, cover, and open lid vent completely. Heat grill until hot and wood chips are smoking, about 5 minutes.

4B. For a gas grill Remove cooking grate and place wood chip packet directly on primary burner. Place disposable pie plates directly on secondary burner(s) and add 2 cups water to each. Set cooking grate in place, turn all burners to high, cover, and heat grill until hot and wood chips are smoking, about 15 minutes. Leave primary burner on high and turn off other burner(s). (Adjust primary burner [or, if using 3-burner grill, primary burner and second burner] as needed to maintain grill temperature around 325 degrees.)

5. Clean and oil cooking grate. Place turkey, breast side up, on cooler side of grill with legs pointing toward hotter side of grill. Cover (position lid vent over turkey if using charcoal) and cook for 1 hour.

6. Meanwhile, melt remaining 4 tablespoons butter in small saucepan over medium heat. Add remaining 2 teaspoons spice mixture and cook until fragrant, about 1 minute. Remove from heat. After turkey has been on grill for 1 hour, brush all over with spiced butter, rotating turkey if using gas grill (if turkey looks too dark, cover breast lightly with foil). Cover and continue to cook until breast registers 160 degrees and thighs/drumsticks register 175 degrees, 1 to 2 hours.

7. Transfer turkey to carving board and let rest, uncovered, for 45 minutes. Carve turkey and serve.

NOTES FROM THE TEST KITCHEN

MODERATING THE HEAT
One of the keys to our Spice-Rubbed Grill-Roasted Turkey is moderating the heat—the fire needs to be hot enough to cook the turkey, but not so hot that the turkey cooks unevenly or burns. For both gas and charcoal, we place disposable aluminum pans filled with water on the bottom of the grill (next to the briquettes for charcoal, directly on the secondary burners for gas). The water absorbs heat and helps keep the temperature consistently low. For a charcoal grill, use a 13 by 9-inch disposable aluminum roasting pan. For a gas grill, use 9-inch aluminum disposable pie plates.

SAUCES, GLAZES, AND SPICE RUBS

These simple sauces, spice rubs, and glazes add a wide variety of flavor and richness to all kinds of grilled chicken.

Red Pepper–Almond Sauce

Serves 4   **Total Time** 25 minutes

We like the complexity that toasted sesame oil gives to this sauce, but extra-virgin olive oil can be substituted.

  5 teaspoons sherry vinegar
  1 garlic clove, minced
  ¾ teaspoon table salt
  2 red bell peppers, stemmed, seeded, and quartered
  1 tablespoon vegetable oil
  ¼ cup whole almonds, toasted
  2 teaspoons toasted sesame oil
  ½ teaspoon smoked paprika
    Pinch cayenne pepper

1. Combine vinegar, garlic, and salt in small bowl and set aside.

2. Toss bell peppers with vegetable oil in bowl until evenly coated. Grill bell peppers, skin side down, over hot fire (covered if using gas), until most of surface is well charred, 5 to 7 minutes. Flip and cook until lightly charred on second side, about 2 minutes. Transfer bell peppers to bowl and cover tightly with aluminum foil.

3. Pulse almonds in food processor until finely chopped, 10 to 12 pulses. Add sesame oil, paprika, cayenne, vinegar mixture, and bell peppers (do not remove skins) and process until smooth, about 45 seconds, scraping down sides of bowl as needed. Loosen with water as needed and season with salt to taste.

Poblano-Pepita Sauce

Serves 4   **Total Time** 25 minutes

Parsley can be substituted for the cilantro in the sauce, if desired.

  2 small poblano chiles, stemmed, seeded, and quartered
  1 small jalapeño chile
  1½ teaspoons vegetable oil
  1 tablespoon raw pepitas, toasted
  3 tablespoons water
  2 tablespoons fresh cilantro leaves
  1 tablespoon white wine vinegar
  1½ teaspoons extra-virgin olive oil
  ¼ teaspoon table salt

1. Toss poblanos and jalapeño with vegetable oil in bowl until evenly coated.

2. Grill poblanos (skin side down) and jalapeño over hot fire (covered if using gas) until most of surface is well charred, 5 to 7 minutes for poblanos and 7 to 10 minutes for jalapeño, rotating chiles every 2 to 3 minutes. Flip poblanos and cook until lightly charred on second side, about 2 minutes. Transfer poblanos and jalapeño to bowl and cover tightly with aluminum foil.

3. Stem and seed jalapeño. Pulse pepitas in food processor until finely chopped, 10 to 12 pulses. Add water, cilantro, vinegar, olive oil, salt, poblanos, and jalapeño (do not remove skins from poblanos or jalapeño) and process until smooth, about 45 seconds, scraping down sides of bowl as needed. Loosen with water as needed and season with salt to taste.

Basic Barbecue Sauce

Makes about 2 cups   **Total Time** 1¼ hours

For a thinner, smoother texture, strain the sauce after it has finished cooking. This recipe can be doubled or tripled.

  1 tablespoon vegetable oil
  1 onion, chopped fine
    Pinch table salt
  1 garlic clove, minced
  1 teaspoon chili powder
  ¼ teaspoon cayenne pepper
  1¼ cups ketchup
  6 tablespoons molasses
  3 tablespoons cider vinegar
  2 tablespoons Worcestershire sauce
  2 tablespoons Dijon mustard
  1 teaspoon hot sauce

1. Heat oil in medium saucepan over medium heat until shimmering. Add onion and salt and cook until softened, 5 to 7 minutes. Stir in garlic, chili powder, and cayenne and cook until fragrant, about 30 seconds.

2. Whisk in ketchup, molasses, vinegar, Worcestershire, mustard, and hot sauce. Bring sauce to simmer and cook, stirring occasionally, until thickened and measures 2 cups, about 25 minutes.

3. Let sauce cool to room temperature. Season with salt and pepper to taste.

Kansas City Barbecue Sauce

Makes about 4 cups   **Total Time** 2 hours

For a thinner, smoother texture, strain the sauce after it has finished cooking.

- 1 tablespoon vegetable oil
- 1 onion, chopped fine
- Pinch table salt
- 4 cups chicken broth
- 1 cup brewed coffee
- 1¼ cups cider vinegar
- ¾ cup molasses
- ½ cup tomato paste
- ½ cup ketchup
- 2 tablespoons brown mustard
- 1 tablespoon hot sauce
- ½ teaspoon garlic powder
- ¼ teaspoon liquid smoke

1. Heat oil in large saucepan over medium heat until shimmering. Add onion and salt and cook until softened, 5 to 7 minutes. Whisk in broth, coffee, vinegar, molasses, tomato paste, ketchup, mustard, hot sauce, and garlic powder.

2. Bring sauce to simmer and cook, stirring occasionally, until thickened and measures 4 cups, about 1 hour.

3. Off heat, stir in liquid smoke. Let sauce cool to room temperature. Season with salt and pepper to taste.

Sweet and Tangy Barbecue Sauce

Makes about 1 cup   **Total Time** 30 minutes

For a thinner, smoother texture, strain the sauce after it has finished cooking.

- 1 cup ketchup
- 5 tablespoons molasses
- 3 tablespoons cider vinegar
- 2 tablespoons Worcestershire sauce
- 2 tablespoons Dijon mustard
- ¼ teaspoon pepper
- 2 tablespoons vegetable oil
- ⅓ cup grated onion
- 1 garlic clove, minced
- 1 teaspoon chili powder
- ¼ teaspoon cayenne pepper

Whisk ketchup, molasses, vinegar, Worcestershire, mustard, and pepper together in bowl. Heat oil in medium saucepan over medium heat until shimmering. Add onion and garlic; cook until onion is softened, 2 to 4 minutes. Add chili powder and cayenne and cook until fragrant, about 30 seconds. Whisk in ketchup mixture and bring to boil. Reduce heat to medium-low and simmer gently for 5 minutes. (Sauce can be refrigerated for up to 1 week.)

Grilled Boneless, Skinless Chicken Breasts with Poblano-Pepita Sauce

Spicy Hoisin Glaze

Makes about ⅔ cup   **Total Time** 15 minutes

For a spicier glaze, use the larger amount of sriracha.

- 2 tablespoons rice vinegar
- 1 teaspoon cornstarch
- ⅓ cup hoisin sauce
- 2 tablespoons corn syrup
- 1–2 tablespoons sriracha
- 1 teaspoon grated fresh ginger
- ¼ teaspoon five-spice powder

Whisk vinegar and cornstarch in small saucepan until cornstarch has dissolved. Whisk in hoisin, corn syrup, sriracha, ginger, and five-spice powder. Bring mixture to boil over high heat. Cook, stirring constantly, until thickened, about 1 minute. Transfer glaze to bowl. (Glaze can be refrigerated for up to 3 days. Gently warm glaze in small saucepan or microwave before using.)

Honey-Mustard Glaze

Makes about ⅔ cup   **Total Time** 15 minutes

- 2 tablespoons cider vinegar
- 1 teaspoon cornstarch
- 3 tablespoons Dijon mustard
- 3 tablespoons honey
- 2 tablespoons corn syrup
- 1 garlic clove, minced
- ¼ teaspoon ground fennel seeds

Whisk vinegar and cornstarch in small saucepan until cornstarch has dissolved. Whisk in mustard, honey, corn syrup, garlic, and fennel seeds. Bring mixture to boil over high heat. Cook, stirring constantly, until thickened, about 1 minute. Transfer glaze to bowl. (Glaze can be refrigerated for up to 3 days. Gently warm glaze in small saucepan or microwave before using.)

Coconut-Curry Glaze

Makes about ⅔ cup   **Total Time** 15 minutes

- 2 tablespoons lime juice
- 1½ teaspoons cornstarch
- ⅓ cup canned coconut milk
- 3 tablespoons corn syrup
- 1 tablespoon fish sauce
- 1 tablespoon Thai red curry paste
- 1 teaspoon grated fresh ginger
- ¼ teaspoon ground coriander

Whisk lime juice and cornstarch in small saucepan until cornstarch has dissolved. Whisk in coconut milk, corn syrup, fish sauce, curry paste, ginger, and coriander. Bring mixture to boil over high heat. Cook, stirring constantly, until thickened, about 1 minute. Transfer glaze to bowl. (Glaze can be refrigerated for up to 3 days. Gently warm glaze in small saucepan or microwave before using.)

Miso-Sesame Glaze

Makes about ⅔ cup   **Total Time** 15 minutes

- 3 tablespoons rice vinegar
- 1 teaspoon cornstarch
- 3 tablespoons white miso
- 2 tablespoons corn syrup
- 1 tablespoon toasted sesame oil
- 2 teaspoons grated fresh ginger
- ¼ teaspoon ground coriander

Two Glazed Grill-Roasted Chickens
with Honey-Mustard Glaze

Whisk vinegar and cornstarch in small saucepan until cornstarch has dissolved. Whisk in miso, corn syrup, oil, ginger, and coriander. Bring mixture to boil over high heat. Cook, stirring constantly, until thickened, about 1 minute. Transfer glaze to bowl. (Glaze can be refrigerated for up to 3 days. Gently warm glaze in small saucepan or microwave before using.)

Orange-Chipotle Glaze

Makes about ¾ cup   **Total Time** 20 minutes
For a spicier glaze, use the greater amount of chipotle chile. Reserve half of glaze for serving and use remaining glaze to brush on chicken.

- 1–2 tablespoons minced canned chipotle chile in adobo sauce
- 1 small shallot, minced
- 2 teaspoons minced fresh thyme
- 1 teaspoon grated orange zest plus ⅔ cup juice (2 oranges)
- 1 tablespoon molasses
- ¾ teaspoon cornstarch

Combine chipotle, shallot, thyme, and orange zest and juice in small saucepan. Whisk in molasses and cornstarch, bring to simmer, and cook over medium heat until thickened, about 5 minutes. Season with salt to taste. (Glaze can be refrigerated for up to 3 days. Gently warm glaze in small saucepan or microwave before using.)

Basic Spice Rub
Makes 1 cup   **Total Time** 10 minutes

½ cup paprika
2 tablespoons kosher salt
2 tablespoons garlic powder
1 tablespoon dried thyme
2 teaspoons ground celery seeds
2 teaspoons pepper
2 teaspoons cayenne pepper

Combine all ingredients in bowl. (Store leftover spice rub for up to 3 months.)

Cajun Spice Rub
Makes about 1 cup   **Total Time** 10 minutes
Omit the salt from the spice rub if brining the chicken.

½ cup paprika
2 tablespoons kosher salt
2 tablespoons garlic powder
1 tablespoon dried thyme
2 teaspoons ground celery seeds
2 teaspoons pepper
2 teaspoons cayenne pepper

Combine all ingredients in bowl. (Store leftover spice rub for up to 3 months.)

Jamaican Spice Rub
Makes about 1 cup   **Total Time** 10 minutes
Omit the salt from the spice rub if brining the chicken.

¼ cup packed brown sugar
3 tablespoons kosher salt
3 tablespoons ground coriander
2 tablespoons ground ginger
2 tablespoons garlic powder
1 tablespoon ground allspice

1 tablespoon pepper
2 teaspoons cayenne pepper
2 teaspoons ground nutmeg
1½ teaspoons ground cinnamon

Combine all ingredients in bowl. (Store leftover spice rub for up to 3 months.)

Tex-Mex Spice Rub
Makes about 1 cup   **Total Time** 10 minutes
Omit the salt from the spice rub if brining the chicken.

¼ cup ground cumin
2 tablespoons chili powder
2 tablespoons ground coriander
2 tablespoons dried oregano
2 tablespoons garlic powder
4 teaspoons kosher salt
2 teaspoons unsweetened cocoa powder
1 teaspoon cayenne pepper

Combine all ingredients in bowl. (Store leftover spice rub for up to 3 months.)

Ras el Hanout Spice Rub
Makes about ½ cup   **Total Time** 10 minutes
Though not strictly authentic, smoked paprika may be substituted for half the sweet paprika to produce an even more complex flavor.

2 tablespoons paprika
4 teaspoons ground coriander
4 teaspoons ground cumin
1 tablespoon packed brown sugar
1 teaspoon ground cardamom
1 teaspoon ground cinnamon
¾ teaspoon table salt
½ teaspoon ground cloves
½ teaspoon ground nutmeg
½ teaspoon cayenne pepper

Combine all ingredients in bowl. (Store leftover spice rub for up to 3 months.)

INSTANT POT, AIR FRYER, AND SOUS VIDE

*All Instant Pot recipes work in a 6- to 8-quart Instant Pot or other electric pressure cooker.

Photos (clockwise from top left): Pressure-Cooker Spiced Chicken in a Pot with Pear, Cherry, and Walnut Chutney; Air-Fryer Chicken Lettuce Wraps with Herbs and Mango; Air-Fryer Chicken Nuggets; Sous Vide Easy Boneless Turkey Breast

Pressure-Cooker Classic Chicken Noodle Soup

Serves 6 to 8   **Total Time** 1 hour

Why This Recipe Works With its velvety broth and deep, comforting flavor, old-fashioned chicken noodle soup is a perfect candidate for the pressure cooker: You can't beat the sheer convenience, and the closed environment is ideal for extracting tons of flavor and body-building gelatin from the meat, skin, and bones of a whole chicken. We started by using our Instant Pot's sauté function to brown aromatics; tomato paste and soy sauce boosted the savory flavor of our soup. We found we didn't need to spend time cutting up the chicken—we could put the whole chicken right in the pot. We made sure to place it breast side up: The pressure cooker heats from the bottom, so positioning the chicken this way exposed the dark meat thighs to more direct heat and protected the delicate breast meat from overcooking. Once cooked, the tender meat practically fell off the bones, making it easy to shred and stir back in. Rather than using a second pot to cook the noodles, we simply used the sauté function to simmer them right in the broth. We prefer to use wide egg noodles in this soup, but thin egg noodles can be substituted; thin egg noodles will have a shorter cooking time in step 4. Cook the noodles just before serving to keep them from overcooking and turning mushy.

Pressure-Cooker Classic
Chicken Noodle Soup

1   tablespoon vegetable oil
1   onion, chopped fine
1¼ teaspoons table salt, divided
1   tablespoon tomato paste
3   garlic cloves, minced
2   teaspoons minced fresh thyme or ½ teaspoon dried
8   cups water, divided
4   carrots, peeled, halved lengthwise, and sliced
     ½ inch thick
2   celery ribs, sliced ½ inch thick
2   tablespoons soy sauce
1   (4-pound) whole chicken, giblets discarded
½   teaspoon pepper
4   ounces (2 cups) wide egg noodles
¼   cup minced fresh parsley

1. Using highest sauté or browning function, heat oil in electric pressure cooker until shimmering. Add onion and ½ teaspoon salt and cook until onion is softened, 3 to 5 minutes. Stir in tomato paste, garlic, and thyme and cook until fragrant, about 30 seconds. Stir in 6 cups water, carrots, celery, and soy sauce, scraping up any browned bits. Sprinkle chicken with remaining ¾ teaspoon salt and pepper and place breast side up in pot.

2. Lock lid in place and close pressure release valve. Select high pressure cook function and cook for 20 minutes. Turn off pressure cooker and quick-release pressure. Carefully remove lid, allowing steam to escape away from you.

3. Transfer chicken to cutting board, let cool slightly, then shred into bite-size pieces using 2 forks; discard skin and bones.

4. Meanwhile, stir remaining 2 cups water into soup. If necessary, cook using highest sauté or browning function until vegetables are just tender, 5 to 10 minutes. Stir in noodles and cook until tender, about 8 minutes. Turn off pressure cooker. Stir in chicken and let sit until heated through, about 2 minutes. Stir in parsley and season with salt and pepper to taste. Serve.

VARIATIONS

Pressure-Cooker Classic Chicken Noodle Soup with Orzo, Green Beans, and Peas

Substitute 1 leek, white and light green parts only, quartered lengthwise, sliced thin, and washed thoroughly, for onion; ¾ cup orzo for egg noodles; and 2 tablespoons minced fresh tarragon for parsley. Stir 8 ounces green beans, trimmed and cut into 1-inch lengths, into soup with orzo. Stir ½ cup thawed frozen peas into soup with shredded chicken.

Pressure-Cooker Classic Chicken Noodle Soup with Shells, Tomatoes, and Zucchini
Substitute 1 cup small pasta shells for egg noodles and chopped fresh basil for parsley. Stir 1 chopped tomato and 1 zucchini, cut into ½-inch pieces, into soup with pasta.

Pressure-Cooker Spicy Moroccan Chicken and Lentil Soup

Serves 8   Total Time 55 minutes

Why This Recipe Works This soup takes inspiration from harira, an intensely flavored Moroccan lentil soup full of warm spices and fresh herbs that's often bulked up with meat and garnished with harissa, the spicy, smoky chile paste. Like many regional soups, harira's exact ingredients vary from region to region. To give ours balanced complexity, we used a mix of spices that brought varied flavor notes (cumin and cinnamon for warmth, paprika and saffron for depth, fresh ginger for brightness, cayenne for heat). We bloomed them in the rendered fat left after browning bone-in chicken breasts, adding some flour to help thicken the soup. We returned our chicken to the pot along with lentils and chicken broth and cooked everything at pressure for just 8 minutes. The chicken came out perfectly tender, ready to be shredded and stirred back into the soup. Plum tomatoes, cut into large pieces, added traditional bright flavor. Harissa, a spicy paste of chiles, spices, garlic, and olive oil, was a delicious finishing touch. Large green or brown lentils work well in this recipe; do not use French green lentils (lentilles du Puy). We prefer to use our homemade Harissa (page 125) but you can substitute store-bought harissa, though the spiciness varies greatly by brand.

Pressure-Cooker Spicy Moroccan Chicken and Lentil Soup

1½ pounds bone-in split chicken breasts, trimmed
¼ teaspoon table salt
⅛ teaspoon plus ¼ teaspoon pepper, divided
1 tablespoon extra-virgin olive oil
1 tablespoon all-purpose flour
1 teaspoon grated fresh ginger
1 teaspoon ground cumin
½ teaspoon paprika
¼ teaspoon ground cinnamon
¼ teaspoon cayenne pepper
  Pinch saffron threads, crumbled
10 cups chicken broth
1 cup brown or green lentils, picked over and rinsed
4 plum tomatoes, cored and cut into ¾-inch pieces
⅓ cup minced fresh cilantro
¼ cup harissa, plus extra for serving

1. Pat chicken dry with paper towels and sprinkle with salt and ⅛ teaspoon pepper. Using highest sauté or browning function, heat oil in electric pressure cooker for 5 minutes (or until just smoking). Cook chicken until browned on both sides, 6 to 10 minutes; transfer to plate.

2. Add flour, ginger, cumin, paprika, cinnamon, cayenne, saffron, and remaining ¼ teaspoon pepper to fat left in pot and cook until fragrant, about 1 minute. Slowly whisk in broth, scraping up any browned bits and smoothing out any lumps. Stir in lentils, then nestle chicken, skin side up, in pot, along with any accumulated juices.

3. Lock lid in place and close pressure release valve. Select high pressure cook function and cook for 8 minutes. Turn off pressure cooker and quick-release pressure. Carefully remove lid, allowing steam to escape away from you.

4. Transfer chicken to cutting board, let cool slightly, then shred into bite-size pieces using 2 forks; discard skin and bones.

5. If lentils are still firm, continue to cook lentils using highest sauté or browning function until lentils are just tender, about 5 minutes. Turn off pressure cooker. Stir in chicken and tomatoes and let sit until heated through, about 2 minutes. Stir in cilantro and harissa and season with salt and pepper to taste. Serve, passing extra harissa separately.

Pressure-Cooker Turkey Meatball Soup with Kale

Pressure-Cooker Chicken in a Pot with Lemon-Herb Sauce

Pressure-Cooker Turkey Meatball Soup with Kale

Serves 6 to 8   **Total Time** 1 hour

Why This Recipe Works This Spanish-inspired meatball soup has a vibrantly flavored and colored broth and lean turkey meatballs kept moist and tender thanks to a panade (a paste made from bread and milk) and Manchego cheese. For our broth, we started with a sofrito, a traditional Spanish base of onion, bell pepper, and garlic, then added smoked paprika. After deglazing the pot with white wine, we poured in chicken broth, then carefully dropped in the meatballs and some chopped fresh kale. The soup required a mere 3 minutes under pressure, after which we brightened it with a sprinkling of minced parsley and a touch of extra Manchego. Be sure to use ground turkey, not ground turkey breast (also labeled 99 percent fat-free), in this recipe.

1 slice hearty white sandwich bread, torn into quarters

¼ cup whole milk

1 ounce Manchego cheese, grated (½ cup), plus extra for serving

5 tablespoons minced fresh parsley, divided

½ teaspoon table salt

1 pound ground turkey

1 tablespoon extra-virgin olive oil

1 onion, chopped

1 red bell pepper, stemmed, seeded, and cut into ¾-inch pieces

4 garlic cloves, minced

2 teaspoons smoked paprika

½ cup dry white wine

8 cups chicken broth

8 ounces kale, stemmed and chopped

1. Using fork, mash bread and milk together into paste in large bowl. Stir in Manchego, 3 tablespoons parsley, and salt until combined. Add turkey and knead mixture with your hands until well combined. Pinch off and roll 2-teaspoon-size pieces of mixture into balls and arrange on large plate (you should have about 35 meatballs); set aside.

2. Using highest sauté or browning function, heat oil in electric pressure cooker until shimmering. Add onion and bell pepper and cook until softened and lightly browned, 5 to 7 minutes. Stir in garlic and paprika and cook until fragrant, about 30 seconds. Stir in wine, scraping up any browned bits, and cook until almost completely evaporated, about 5 minutes. Stir in broth and kale, then gently submerge meatballs.

3. Lock lid in place and close pressure release valve. Select high pressure cook function and cook for 3 minutes. Turn off pressure cooker and quick-release pressure. Carefully remove lid, allowing steam to escape away from you.

4. Stir in remaining 2 tablespoons parsley and season with salt and pepper to taste. Serve, passing extra Manchego separately.

NOTES FROM THE TEST KITCHEN

DEALING WITH UNDERCOOKED FOOD WHEN PRESSURE COOKING
Since it's impossible to test the doneness of food as it cooks under pressure, sometimes food might be slightly underdone. Simply finish cooking by switching to the highest sauté or browning function, adding extra liquid as needed.

Pressure-Cooker Chicken in a Pot with Lemon-Herb Sauce

Serves 4 **Total Time** 1 hour

Why This Recipe Works Cooking a whole chicken in a moist covered environment isn't a new concept. In fact, the classic French method of cooking en cocotte relies on this principle to create unbelievably tender, moist meat and a savory sauce enhanced with the chicken's own concentrated juices. We knew this would be a perfect use for the pressure cooker, and started with a 4-pound chicken, which fit nicely into the narrow pot. Since we wanted to focus on achieving succulent meat and not on getting crisp skin, we didn't bother with browning the chicken. Sautéing some onion and garlic in the pot gave the chicken and the jus layers of deep flavor. The controlled environment of the pressure cooker gave us chicken with perfectly cooked light and dark meat. A couple of tablespoons of flour, added at the start, ensured that our jus was transformed into a velvety smooth sauce after cooking. Butter, lemon juice, and fresh herbs gave our sauce a final boost of rich, bright flavor.

1 tablespoon vegetable oil
1 onion, chopped fine
2 tablespoons all-purpose flour
3 garlic cloves, minced
2 teaspoons minced fresh rosemary

½ cup dry white wine
1 cup chicken broth
1 (4-pound) whole chicken, giblets discarded
¼ teaspoon table salt
⅛ teaspoon pepper
¼ cup minced fresh chives, parsley, or tarragon
2 tablespoons unsalted butter, cut into 2 pieces and chilled
2 tablespoons lemon juice

1. Using highest sauté or browning function, heat oil in electric pressure cooker until shimmering. Add onion and cook until softened, 3 to 5 minutes. Stir in flour, garlic, and rosemary and cook until fragrant, about 1 minute. Slowly whisk in wine, scraping up any browned bits and smoothing out any lumps, then stir in broth. Sprinkle chicken with salt and pepper and place breast side up in pot.

2. Lock lid in place and close pressure release valve. Select high pressure cook function and cook for 30 minutes. Turn off pressure cooker and quick-release pressure. Carefully remove lid, allowing steam to escape away from you.

3. Transfer chicken to carving board, tent with aluminum foil, and let rest for 5 to 10 minutes. Let cooking liquid settle, then skim excess fat from surface using wide, shallow spoon. Whisk in chives, butter, and lemon juice. Carve chicken, discarding skin if desired. Serve with sauce.

Pressure-Cooker Spiced Chicken in a Pot with Pear, Cherry, and Walnut Chutney

Serves 4 **Total Time** 1¾ hours

Why This Recipe Works This recipe gives you a company-worthy entrée of warm-spiced chicken and a sweet-savory chutney—all made in your pressure cooker. Rubbing a whole chicken with spices is always a great way to infuse it with flavor; the pressure cooker's concentrated heat brought out the spices' nuanced flavors, and the tight-fitting lid ensured that no flavor escaped during cooking. To create more depth of flavor, we browned the chicken before locking on the lid. A simple pear, cherry, and walnut chutney made for an elegant accompaniment. Since chutneys taste best when their flavors have time to meld, we used the pressure cooker's sauté function to cook the chutney before turning our attention to the chicken; we lightly browned the pears, then added shallot, ginger, and cherry preserves to give the chutney a thick, jammy texture.

A healthy dose of white wine vinegar balanced the sweetness of the pears and cherry preserves. To maintain the textural contrast of the crunchy toasted walnuts, we waited to add them until after cooking the chutney.

3 tablespoons vegetable oil, divided
1½ pounds ripe but firm Bosc or Bartlett pears, peeled, halved, cored, and cut into ½-inch pieces
1 shallot, minced
1 tablespoon grated fresh ginger
2¼ teaspoons table salt, divided
½ cup cherry preserves
2 tablespoons plus 1 cup water, divided
⅓ cup white wine vinegar
¼ cup walnuts, toasted and chopped
2 teaspoons five-spice powder
1½ teaspoons ground cumin
1 teaspoon pepper
1 teaspoon garlic powder
¼ teaspoon cayenne pepper
¼ teaspoon ground cardamom
1 (4-pound) whole chicken, giblets discarded

1. Using highest sauté or browning function, heat 1 table-spoon oil in electric pressure cooker until shimmering. Cook pears until softened and lightly browned, 8 to 10 minutes. Stir in shallot, ginger, and ¼ teaspoon salt and cook until fragrant, about 1 minute. Stir in cherry preserves, 2 tablespoons water, and vinegar and cook until thickened and mixture measures about 1½ cups, 6 to 8 minutes. Turn off pressure cooker. Transfer chutney to bowl and stir in walnuts; set aside for serving. (Chutney can be refrigerated for up to 1 week; bring to room temperature before serving.) Wipe pressure cooker clean with paper towels.

2. Combine five-spice powder, cumin, pepper, garlic powder, cayenne, cardamom, 1 tablespoon oil, and remaining 2 teaspoons salt in small bowl. Pat chicken dry with paper towels and, using your fingers, gently loosen skin covering breast and thighs. Rub spice paste evenly over and under skin.

3. Using highest sauté or browning function, heat remaining 1 tablespoon oil in pressure cooker for 5 minutes (or until just smoking). Place chicken, breast side down, in pot and cook until well browned, 6 to 8 minutes. Using tongs, gently flip chicken and cook until well browned on second side, 6 to 8 minutes. Add remaining 1 cup water to pot.

4. Lock lid in place and close pressure release valve. Select high pressure cook function and cook for 27 minutes. Turn off pressure cooker and quick-release pressure. Carefully remove lid, allowing steam to escape away from you.

5. Transfer chicken to carving board, tent with aluminum foil, and let rest for 5 to 10 minutes. Carve chicken, discarding skin if desired. Serve with chutney.

Pressure-Cooker Braised Chicken Breasts with Tomatoes and Capers
Serves 4 Total Time 1 hour

Why This Recipe Works Bone-in, skin-on chicken breasts are a great candidate for pressure cooking: The appliance sidesteps many of the usual problems that plague white meat chicken— namely bland, dry meat—by providing a moist cooking environment that requires very little monitoring, and the bones and skin help to insulate the delicate white meat and give it better flavor, even after high-heat pressure cooking. To turn our simple chicken breasts into an appealing weeknight dinner, we paired them with a vibrant caper-spiked tomato sauce. Browning the chicken in batches rendered some fat (which we used to sauté our shallot) and created flavorful fond. From there, we threw together a simple pantry-ready sauce. The pressure cooker concentrated our easy tomato sauce into something with the complexity of a much more labor-intensive sauce. While the chicken rested, we simmered the sauce briefly to thicken it to just the right consistency. Serve over orzo or rice.

4 (12-ounce) bone-in split chicken breasts, trimmed
1 teaspoon table salt, divided
¼ teaspoon pepper
1 tablespoon extra-virgin olive oil
1 shallot, minced
1 tablespoon tomato paste
⅛ teaspoon red pepper flakes
½ cup dry white wine
1 (28-ounce) can diced tomatoes, drained
2 tablespoons capers, rinsed
¼ cup chopped fresh basil

1. Pat chicken dry with paper towels and sprinkle with ½ teaspoon salt and pepper. Using highest sauté or browning function, heat oil in electric pressure cooker for 5 minutes (or until just smoking). Place half of chicken, skin side down, in pot and cook until browned, 5 to 7 minutes; transfer to plate. Repeat with remaining chicken; transfer to plate.

2. Add shallot to fat left in pot and cook until softened, about 1 minute. Stir in tomato paste, pepper flakes, and remaining ½ teaspoon salt and cook until fragrant, about 1 minute.

Stir in wine, scraping up any browned bits, then stir in tomatoes. Nestle chicken, skin side up, into pot, along with any accumulated juices.

3. Lock lid in place and close pressure release valve. Select high pressure cook function and cook for 9 minutes. Turn off pressure cooker and quick-release pressure. Carefully remove lid, allowing steam to escape away from you.

4. Transfer chicken to serving dish and discard skin, if desired. Tent with aluminum foil and let rest while finishing sauce.

5. Stir capers into sauce. Using highest sauté or browning function, cook sauce, stirring occasionally, until thickened slightly and reduced to about 2 cups, 8 to 10 minutes. Season with salt and pepper to taste. Spoon sauce over chicken and sprinkle with basil. Serve.

Pressure-Cooker Chicken and Couscous with Chorizo and Saffron

Serves 4   **Total Time** 1 hour

Why This Recipe Works A Spanish-inspired combination of saffron, smoked chorizo, red bell pepper, and garlic gives deep flavor to a simple dish of chicken and couscous. When developing this recipe, we started with rice but found that it was not cooking at the same rate as the chicken in the pressure cooker—we ended up with either stubbornly crunchy rice or egregiously overcooked chicken. So we traded rice for couscous. Since couscous needs only soaking, we could add it to the pot after pressure and allow it to absorb the ultraflavorful cooking liquid, and it proved an ideal base for the other flavors.

   4 (12-ounce) bone-in split chicken breasts, trimmed
   ¾ teaspoon table salt, divided
   ¼ teaspoon pepper
   1 tablespoon extra-virgin olive oil
   1 red bell pepper, stemmed, seeded, and chopped fine
   4 ounces Spanish-style chorizo sausage, cut into ¼-inch pieces
   4 garlic cloves, minced
   ⅛ teaspoon saffron threads, crumbled
   ½ cup chicken broth
1½ cups couscous
   1 cup frozen peas, thawed
   2 teaspoons lemon juice
   3 tablespoons minced fresh parsley

Pressure-Cooker Braised Chicken Breasts with Tomatoes and Capers

Pressure-Cooker Chicken and Couscous with Chorizo and Saffron

1. Pat chicken dry with paper towels and sprinkle with ½ teaspoon salt and pepper. Using highest sauté or browning function, heat oil in electric pressure cooker for 5 minutes (or until just smoking.) Place half of chicken, skin side down, in pot and cook until browned, 5 to 7 minutes; transfer to plate. Repeat with remaining chicken; transfer to plate.

2. Add bell pepper, chorizo, and remaining ¼ teaspoon salt to fat left in pot and cook until bell pepper is softened, 3 to 5 minutes. Stir in garlic and saffron and cook until fragrant, about 30 seconds. Stir in broth, scraping up any browned bits. Nestle chicken, skin side up, into pot, along with any accumulated juices.

3. Lock lid in place and close pressure release valve. Select high pressure cook function and cook for 9 minutes. Turn off pressure cooker and quick-release pressure. Carefully remove lid, allowing steam to escape away from you.

4. Transfer chicken to serving dish and discard skin, if desired. Tent with aluminum foil and let rest while preparing couscous.

5. Stir couscous, peas, and lemon juice into liquid in pot, cover, and let sit until couscous is tender, about 5 minutes. Add parsley and fluff couscous gently with fork to combine. Season with salt and pepper to taste. Serve with chicken.

Pressure-Cooker Chicken Tagine

Pressure-Cooker Chicken Tagine
Serves 4   Total time 1 hour

Why This Recipe Works Heady with spices, salty with olives, and bright with lemon, a chicken tagine is a balancing act of flavors ready-made for the pressure cooker, as the enclosed environment ensures none of that flavor escapes. For the chicken, we used bone-in thighs instead of breasts for deeper flavor; the bones would enrich and give body to the braising liquid. But, since we weren't rendering fat or building fond, we didn't need the skin, which would end up flabby, so we discarded it before cooking. Fresh fennel and convenient canned chickpeas (some of them mashed into a paste to thicken the tagine) gave our meal heft. Next we tackled the defining spices: Paprika, cumin, and ground ginger lent depth and a little sweetness; cayenne added subtle heat; and aromatic turmeric colored the broth a deep, attractive yellow. Raisins lent a pleasant floral flavor, as did a few wide strips of lemon zest. Brine-cured olives provided a salty counterpart to the sweet and complex broth. Do not core the fennel before cutting it into wedges; the core helps hold the wedges together during cooking. Serve with Simple Couscous (page 189).

2 (15-ounce) cans chickpeas, rinsed, divided
1 tablespoon extra-virgin olive oil
5 garlic cloves, minced
1½ teaspoons paprika
½ teaspoon ground turmeric
½ teaspoon ground cumin
¼ teaspoon ground ginger
¼ teaspoon cayenne pepper
1 fennel bulb, 1 tablespoon fronds minced, stalks discarded, bulb halved and cut lengthwise into ½-inch-thick wedges
1 cup chicken broth
3 (2-inch) strips lemon zest, plus lemon wedges for serving
4 (5- to 7-ounce) bone-in chicken thighs, skin removed, trimmed
½ teaspoon table salt
½ cup pitted large brine-cured green or black olives, halved
⅓ cup raisins
2 tablespoons chopped fresh parsley

1. Using potato masher, mash ½ cup chickpeas in bowl to paste. Using highest sauté or browning function, cook oil, garlic, paprika, turmeric, cumin, ginger, and cayenne in electric pressure cooker until fragrant, about 1 minute. Turn off pressure cooker, then stir in remaining whole chickpeas, mashed chickpeas, fennel wedges, broth, and zest.

2. Sprinkle chicken with salt. Nestle chicken skinned side up into pot and spoon some of cooking liquid over top. Lock lid in place and close pressure release valve. Select high pressure cook function and cook for 10 minutes.

3. Turn off pressure cooker and quick-release pressure. Carefully remove lid, allowing steam to escape away from you. Discard lemon zest. Stir in olives, raisins, parsley, and fennel fronds. Season with salt and pepper to taste. Serve with lemon wedges.

Pressure-Cooker Lemony Chicken with Fingerling Potatoes and Olives

Serves 4 **Total Time** 1 hour

Why This Recipe Works In this simple dish, tender, juicy chicken thighs and delicate fingerling potatoes absorb the bright aromas of a classic Provençal combination: garlic, lemon, and olives. We started by browning the chicken thighs in olive oil in our pressure cooker. We then set the chicken aside so we could toast garlic cloves and add chicken broth and a whole sliced lemon to create a vibrant cooking liquid. We returned the chicken to the pot, added potatoes, and cooked it all under pressure; the small fingerlings cooked through in the same time as the chicken. We especially loved the brightness and supple texture of the braised lemon slices. Olives, fresh parsley, and a drizzle of olive oil were the perfect finish. Use potatoes that are approximately 1 inch in diameter. Slice the lemon as thin as possible; this allows the slices to melt into the sauce.

    4 (5- to 7-ounce) bone-in chicken thighs, trimmed
    ½ teaspoon table salt
    ¼ teaspoon pepper
    2 teaspoons extra-virgin olive oil, plus extra
       for drizzling
    4 garlic cloves, peeled and smashed
    ½ cup chicken broth
    1 small lemon, sliced thin
 1½ pounds fingerling potatoes, unpeeled
    ¼ cup pitted brine-cured green or black olives, halved
    2 tablespoons coarsely chopped fresh parsley

Pressure-Cooker Lemony Chicken with Fingerling Potatoes and Olives

1. Pat chicken dry with paper towels and sprinkle with salt and pepper. Using highest sauté function, heat oil in electric pressure cooker for 5 minutes (or until just smoking). Place chicken skin side down in pot and cook until well browned on first side, about 5 minutes; transfer to plate.

2. Add garlic to fat left in pot and cook, using highest sauté function, until golden and fragrant, about 2 minutes. Stir in broth and lemon, scraping up any browned bits. Return chicken skin side up to pot and add any accumulated juices. Arrange potatoes on top. Lock lid in place and close pressure release valve. Select high pressure cook function and cook for 9 minutes.

3. Turn off pot and quick-release pressure. Carefully remove lid, allowing steam to escape away from you. Transfer chicken to serving dish and discard skin, if desired. Stir olives and parsley into potatoes and season with salt and pepper to taste. Serve chicken with potatoes.

Pressure-Cooker Braised Chicken Thighs with White Beans, Pancetta, and Rosemary

Serves 4   Total Time 50 minutes

Why This Recipe Works For a Tuscan-inspired one-pot chicken dinner, we combined rich chicken thighs with bold, salty pancetta; woodsy rosemary; and creamy, mild cannellini beans. We started by browning the chicken thighs to render the fat and give the dish extra richness and savory depth, then used the fat to crisp the pancetta and brown the garlic. Canned beans worked perfectly, softening just enough in the pressure cooker and absorbing lots of flavor. A couple of sprigs of rosemary, added to the pot with the beans, brought subtle floral notes. This recipe was an ideal fit for the pressure cooker, producing tender, juicy meat and creamy, savory beans infused with aromatic flavor. Don't be shy with the olive oil drizzle at the end; add at least a tablespoon to each serving to boost the creaminess of the bean mixture considerably.

- 8 (5- to 7-ounce) bone-in chicken thighs, trimmed
- ½ teaspoon table salt
- ½ teaspoon pepper, divided
- 1 tablespoon extra-virgin olive oil, plus extra for drizzling
- 2 ounces pancetta, chopped fine
- 5 garlic cloves, peeled and smashed
- 2 (15-ounce) cans cannellini beans, rinsed
- ½ cup water
- 2 sprigs fresh rosemary
- 1 tablespoon chopped fresh parsley

1. Pat chicken dry with paper towels and sprinkle with salt and ¼ teaspoon pepper. Using highest sauté or browning function, heat oil in electric pressure cooker for 5 minutes (or until just smoking.) Place half of chicken, skin side down, in pot and cook until browned, 5 to 7 minutes; transfer to plate. Repeat with remaining chicken; transfer to plate.

2. Add pancetta, garlic, and remaining ¼ teaspoon pepper to fat left in pot and cook until garlic is golden and pancetta is crisp and browned, about 3 minutes. Stir in beans, water, and rosemary sprigs. Nestle chicken, skin side up, in pot, along with any accumulated juices.

3. Lock lid in place and close pressure release valve. Select high pressure cook function and cook for 9 minutes. Turn off pressure cooker and quick-release pressure. Carefully remove lid, allowing steam to escape away from you.

4. Transfer chicken to serving dish and discard skin, if desired. Tent with aluminum foil and let rest while finishing beans.

5. Cook beans using highest sauté or browning function until liquid is thickened slightly, about 3 minutes. Discard rosemary sprigs. Stir in parsley and season with pepper to taste. Drizzle individual portions of beans with extra oil before serving with chicken.

Pressure-Cooker Buffalo Chicken Wings

Serves 6   Total Time 1 hour

Why This Recipe Works Given that good Buffalo wings depend upon a crisp coating, you might not think of making them in your pressure cooker, but this appliance turned out to be the perfect all-in-one vessel for this bar snack. Pressure cooking rendered excess fat from the wings and produced fall-off-the-bone meat. Using hot sauce as our cooking liquid infused the wings with great flavor. To achieve the hallmark crisp exteriors of truly great wings, frying is usually necessary, and successful frying depends on monitoring the temperature of the oil. It occurred to us that the electric pressure cooker has a temperature regulator built right in: The heating element is designed to reach a specific temperature on each setting. It reaches this temperature quickly and then self-regulates to maintain the heat—which means there's no need to babysit a thermometer or fuss with stovetop burners. The highest sauté or browning function reaches a temperature that's perfect for frying (between 325 and 350 degrees), so we used it to heat just enough oil to submerge the wings in batches. Once the oil came up to temperature, we fried the wings and were happy to find that the high sides of the pot also prevented the oil from splattering and making a mess. Finally, we tossed our crisp, golden-brown wings with a classic Buffalo sauce that we quickly stirred together using a combination of Frank's RedHot sauce and Tabasco for extra kick. Brown sugar and cider vinegar deepened the sauce's flavor. Serve with celery and carrot sticks.

Creamy Blue Cheese Dressing

2½ ounces blue cheese, crumbled (½ cup)
3 tablespoons buttermilk
3 tablespoons sour cream
2 tablespoons mayonnaise
2 teaspoons white wine vinegar

Wings

3 pounds chicken wings, cut at joints, wingtips discarded
1 cup hot sauce, preferably Frank's RedHot Original Cayenne Pepper Sauce, divided
4 cups vegetable oil, for frying
4 tablespoons unsalted butter, melted
2 tablespoons Tabasco sauce or other hot sauce
1 tablespoon packed dark brown sugar
2 teaspoons cider vinegar

1. For the creamy blue cheese dressing Mash blue cheese and buttermilk in small bowl with fork until mixture resembles cottage cheese with small curds. Stir in sour cream, mayonnaise, and vinegar and season with salt and pepper to taste. Cover and refrigerate until ready to serve. (Dressing can be refrigerated for up to 4 days.)

2. For the wings Combine chicken wings and ½ cup hot sauce in electric pressure cooker.

3. Lock lid in place and close pressure release valve. Select high pressure cook function and cook for 5 minutes. Turn off pressure cooker and quick-release pressure. Carefully remove lid, allowing steam to escape away from you.

4. Adjust oven rack to middle position and heat oven to 200 degrees. Set wire rack in rimmed baking sheet. Using slotted spoon, transfer wings to paper towel–lined plate and pat dry with paper towels. Discard cooking liquid and wipe pressure cooker clean with additional paper towels.

5. Using highest sauté or browning function, heat oil in now-empty pot until it registers between 325 and 350 degrees. Carefully place one-third of wings in oil and cook until golden and crisp, about 15 minutes, turning halfway through cooking. Using slotted spoon or wire skimmer, place wings on prepared sheet and keep warm in oven. Return oil to 325 to 350 degrees and repeat with remaining wings in 2 batches.

6. Whisk melted butter, Tabasco, sugar, vinegar, and remaining ½ cup hot sauce together in large bowl. Add wings and toss to coat. Serve immediately.

Pressure-Cooker Braised Chicken Thighs with White Beans, Pancetta, and Rosemary

Pressure-Cooker Buffalo Chicken Wings

Air-Fryer Apricot-Thyme Glazed Chicken Breasts

Serves 2   **Total Time** 40 minutes

Why This Recipe Works To make glazed boneless chicken breasts especially hands-off, with no need to turn on the oven, we placed two breasts, rubbed with oil, in the air fryer and let the hot air work its magic. Brushing on the glaze after flipping the chicken prevented it from sticking to the basket. When it comes to glaze for chicken, many recipes invest too much time creating a mixture that just slides off and ends up in the bottom of the pan. For a slightly sweet, no-fuss glaze that stayed put, we reached for apricot preserves. The chunkier preserves offered a more pleasant texture than jam or jelly; their thick, sticky consistency helped them adhere; and the chunky bits browned up nicely. Just a few seconds in the microwave made the preserves much easier to spread, and a little fresh thyme added a slight woodsy flavor that balanced the apricot's sweet tartness. For a simple variation, we combined the sweetness of pineapple preserves and the warm, spicy bite of fresh ginger.

- 2 tablespoons apricot preserves
- ½ teaspoon minced fresh thyme or ⅛ teaspoon dried
- 2 (8-ounce) boneless, skinless chicken breasts, trimmed and pounded to uniform thickness
- 1 teaspoon vegetable oil
- ¼ teaspoon table salt
- ⅛ teaspoon pepper

1. Microwave apricot preserves and thyme in bowl until fluid, about 30 seconds; set aside. Pat chicken dry with paper towels, rub with oil, and sprinkle with salt and pepper.

2. Arrange breasts skinned side down in air-fryer basket, spaced evenly apart, alternating ends. Place basket in air fryer, set temperature to 400 degrees, and cook chicken for 4 minutes. Flip and rotate chicken, then brush skinned side with apricot-thyme mixture. Return basket to air fryer and cook until chicken registers 160 degrees, 8 to 12 minutes.

3. Transfer chicken to serving platter, tent with aluminum foil, and let rest for 5 minutes. Serve.

VARIATION
Air-Fryer Pineapple-Ginger Glazed Chicken Breasts
Substitute pineapple preserves for apricot preserves and grated fresh ginger for thyme.

Air-Fryer Roasted Bone-In Chicken Breasts with Lemon-Basil Salsa Verde

Air-Fryer Roasted Bone-In Chicken Breasts

Serves 2   **Total Time** 30 minutes

Why This Recipe Works Bone-in chicken cooks beautifully in the air fryer, and the circulated hot air does nearly all the work. We rubbed two bone-in breasts with just a teaspoon of oil to ensure crispy skin and flipped and rotated them halfway through cooking, starting them skin side down to help the fat in the skin to render, then flipping them so the skin could brown. A moderate 350 degrees minimized moisture loss and resulted in perfectly juicy meat. For a sauce to drizzle over our roasted breasts, we created two bright, fresh options, either of which can be prepared while the chicken cooks (neither requires a pan). With our chicken roasted, all that remained was to toss a simple salad, perhaps open a bottle of wine, and voilà—a fancy dinner for two, ready in 30 minutes.

- 2 (12-ounce) bone-in split chicken breasts, trimmed
- 1 teaspoon extra-virgin olive oil
- ¼ teaspoon table salt
- ⅛ teaspoon pepper

Pat chicken dry with paper towels, rub with oil, and sprinkle with salt and pepper. Arrange breasts skin side down in air-fryer basket, spaced evenly apart, alternating ends. Place basket in air fryer and set temperature to 350 degrees. Cook until chicken registers 160 degrees, 20 to 25 minutes, flipping and rotating breasts halfway through cooking. Transfer chicken to serving platter, tent with aluminum foil, and let rest for 5 minutes. Serve.

Peach-Ginger Chutney
Makes about 2 cups   **Total Time** 20 minutes

- 1 teaspoon extra-virgin olive oil
- 1 small shallot, minced
- 1 garlic clove, minced
- 1 teaspoon grated fresh ginger
- ⅛ teaspoon table salt
- Pinch red pepper flakes
- 1½ cups frozen peaches, thawed and cut into ½-inch pieces
- 2 tablespoons packed light brown sugar
- 1½ tablespoons cider vinegar
- 1 tablespoon chopped crystallized ginger

Microwave oil, shallot, garlic, fresh ginger, salt, and pepper flakes in medium bowl until shallot has softened, about 1 minute. Stir in peaches, sugar, and vinegar. Microwave until peaches have softened and liquid is thick and syrupy, 6 to 8 minutes, stirring occasionally. Stir in crystallized ginger.

Lemon-Basil Salsa Verde
Makes about 1 cup   **Total Time** 10 minutes

- ¼ cup minced fresh parsley
- ¼ cup chopped fresh basil
- 3 tablespoons extra-virgin olive oil
- 1 tablespoon capers, rinsed and minced
- 1 tablespoon water
- 2 garlic cloves, minced
- 1 anchovy fillet, rinsed and minced
- ½ teaspoon grated lemon zest, plus 2 teaspoons juice
- ⅛ teaspoon table salt

Whisk all ingredients together in bowl.

Air-Fryer Roasted Bone-In Chicken Breasts and Potatoes with Sun-Dried Tomato Relish
Serves 2   Total Time 40 minutes

Why This Recipe Works One of our favorite ways to roast chicken is on a pile of potatoes, which become flavored by the chicken's savory drippings as they roast. Moving the process to the air fryer gave us crispier, less greasy results, as the circulated hot air cooked the potatoes from all sides, while the wire basket allowed excess fat to drip below. We filled the basket with quick-cooking fingerling potatoes tossed with garlic, oil, and herbs. Then we placed two bone-in chicken breasts—rubbed with more oil and herbs—on the potatoes. We started the chicken skin side down to render drippings, which seasoned the potatoes, then flipped it to allow the skin to crisp. Afterward, we collected a small spoonful of drippings from the bottom of the air fryer and used it to flavor a sun-dried tomato relish, which brought savory depth to our meal. Look for fingerling potatoes about 3 inches in length.

- 1 pound fingerling potatoes, unpeeled
- 2 teaspoons extra-virgin olive oil, divided, plus extra as needed
- 2 teaspoons minced fresh thyme or ¾ teaspoon dried, divided
- 2 teaspoons minced fresh oregano or ¾ teaspoon dried, divided
- 1 garlic clove, minced
- ½ teaspoon plus ⅛ teaspoon table salt, divided
- ½ teaspoon pepper, divided
- 2 (12-ounce) bone-in split chicken breasts, trimmed
- ¼ cup oil-packed sun-dried tomatoes, patted dry and chopped fine
- 1 small shallot, minced
- 1½ tablespoons red wine vinegar
- 1 tablespoon capers, rinsed and minced

1. Toss potatoes with 1 teaspoon oil, 1 teaspoon thyme, 1 teaspoon oregano, garlic, ¼ teaspoon salt, and ¼ teaspoon pepper in bowl to coat; transfer to air-fryer basket.

2. Pat chicken dry with paper towels. Rub with remaining 1 teaspoon oil and sprinkle with ¼ teaspoon salt, ⅛ teaspoon pepper, remaining 1 teaspoon thyme, and remaining 1 teaspoon oregano. Arrange breasts skin side down on top of potatoes, spaced evenly apart, alternating ends. Place basket in air fryer and set temperature to 350 degrees. Cook until potatoes are tender and chicken registers 160 degrees, 20 to 25 minutes, flipping and rotating breasts halfway through cooking.

3. Transfer chicken and potatoes to serving platter, tent with aluminum foil, and let rest for 5 minutes. Pour off and reserve 1½ tablespoons juices from air-fryer drawer (add extra oil as needed to equal 1½ tablespoons). Combine tomatoes, shallot, vinegar, capers, remaining ⅛ teaspoon salt, remaining ⅛ teaspoon pepper, and reserved chicken juices in bowl. Serve chicken and potatoes with tomato relish.

Air-Fryer Tandoori Chicken Thighs
Serves 2   Total Time 55 minutes

Why This Recipe Works Tandoori chicken depends on intense, dry heat (traditionally supplied by a superhot clay oven) to lightly char chicken pieces that have been marinated in yogurt and spices. While our bake-then-broil approach (see page 261) produces terrific results, we were impressed at how the air fryer produced good tandoori with fewer steps, ideal for a simple dinner for two. Bone-in chicken thighs gave us moist, rich meat. We mixed yogurt with garlic, ginger, garam marsala, cumin, and chili powder for a spicy marinade. Blooming the seasonings in the microwave released their flavors and softened the garlic's raw edge. Poking holes in the chicken skin allowed the marinade to penetrate more deeply and helped render fat, and keeping the thighs skin side up throughout cooking encouraged better charring. To complement the chicken, we whisked together a cooling yogurt and lime sauce. We prefer this dish with whole-milk yogurt, but low-fat yogurt can be substituted.

    3 garlic cloves, minced
    1 tablespoon grated fresh ginger
 1½ teaspoons garam masala
    1 teaspoon ground cumin
    1 teaspoon chili powder
    1 teaspoon vegetable oil
  ¼ teaspoon table salt
  ¼ teaspoon pepper
  ½ cup plain whole-milk yogurt, divided
    4 teaspoons lime juice, divided
    4 (5-ounce) bone-in chicken thighs, trimmed

1. Combine garlic, ginger, garam masala, cumin, chili powder, oil, salt, and pepper in large bowl and microwave until fragrant, about 30 seconds. Set aside to cool slightly, then stir in ¼ cup yogurt and 1 tablespoon lime juice.

2. Pat chicken dry with paper towels. Using metal skewer, poke skin side of chicken 10 to 15 times. Add to bowl with yogurt-spice mixture and toss to coat; set aside to marinate

Air-Fryer Tandoori Chicken Thighs

Air-Fryer Fried Chicken

for 10 minutes. Meanwhile, combine remaining ¼ cup yogurt and remaining 1 teaspoon lime juice in clean bowl; season with salt and pepper to taste, and set aside.

3. Remove chicken from marinade, letting excess drip off, and arrange skin side up in air-fryer basket, spaced evenly apart. Place basket in air fryer and set temperature to 400 degrees. Cook until chicken is well browned and crisp and registers 195 degrees, 20 to 30 minutes, rotating chicken halfway through cooking (do not flip).

4. Transfer chicken to serving platter, tent with aluminum foil, and let rest for 5 minutes. Serve with yogurt-lime sauce.

Air-Fryer Fried Chicken

Serves 2 **Total Time** 50 minutes

Why This Recipe Works Our air-fried chicken comes out golden and crispy on the outside and moist and juicy on the inside, and needs only a light spray of vegetable oil to become crisp. The secret was removing the skin and finding a coating that would become crunchy without needing to be fried in a pan of hot oil. In a side-by-side taste test, crushed cornflakes won out over bread crumbs and Melba toast, offering the best color and crispness, but the results tasted a bit like breakfast cereal. Spicing up the cornflakes with poultry seasoning, paprika, and cayenne pepper gave the coating the savory element it needed. Dredging the floured chicken pieces in buttermilk added tang. To crush the cornflakes, place them inside a zipper-lock bag and use a rolling pin or the bottom of a large skillet to break them into fine crumbs. To help remove the skin from the chicken, use a paper towel to grasp the skin. If you prefer, you can use two 5-ounce thighs and two 5-ounce drumsticks instead of the chicken breasts; if using drumsticks and thighs, cook them until they register 175 degrees, 20 to 25 minutes.

  Vegetable oil spray
 2 (12-ounce) bone-in split chicken breasts, skin removed, trimmed, and halved crosswise
 1 teaspoon table salt, divided
 ⅛ teaspoon plus ¼ teaspoon pepper, divided
 ⅓ cup buttermilk
 ½ teaspoon dry mustard
 ½ teaspoon garlic powder
 ¼ cup all-purpose flour
 2 cups (2 ounces) cornflakes, finely crushed
 1½ teaspoons poultry seasoning
 ½ teaspoon paprika
 ⅛ teaspoon cayenne pepper

1. Lightly spray base of air-fryer basket with oil spray. Pat chicken dry with paper towels and sprinkle with ¼ teaspoon salt and ⅛ teaspoon pepper. Whisk buttermilk, mustard, garlic powder, ½ teaspoon salt, and remaining ¼ teaspoon pepper together in medium bowl. Spread flour in shallow dish. Combine cornflakes, poultry seasoning, paprika, cayenne, and remaining ¼ teaspoon salt in second shallow dish.

2. Working with 1 piece of chicken at a time, dredge in flour, dip in buttermilk mixture, letting excess drip off, then coat with cornflake mixture, pressing gently to adhere; transfer to large plate. Lightly spray chicken with oil spray.

3. Arrange chicken pieces in prepared basket, spaced evenly apart. Place basket in air fryer and set temperature to 400 degrees. Cook until chicken is crisp and registers 160 degrees, 16 to 24 minutes, flipping and rotating pieces halfway through cooking. Serve.

Air-Fryer Chicken Nuggets

Serves 4 (Makes 36 nuggets) **Total Time** 1 hour (plus 4 hours freezing time)

Why This Recipe Works These homemade nuggets are tender and juicy, not gristly and spongy, and achieve a crispy coating without the need to deep-fry in a pot of oil. Since a big plus of the air fryer is its ability to crisp up frozen food at the last minute, we decided to develop a recipe for chicken nuggets that could be made ahead and frozen, ready to be popped in the air fryer. A 15-minute brine seasoned the white meat and guarded against dryness, even after freezing. The air fryer cooks up to 18 nuggets at once; this recipe makes double that, so you'll have plenty on hand. The nuggets can be cooked from fresh without freezing; reduce the cooking time to 10 to 12 minutes, tossing halfway through cooking. Respray the basket before cooking additional batches. For a variety of dipping sauces, see page 275.

 4 (8-ounce) boneless, skinless chicken breasts, trimmed and pounded to uniform thickness
 3 tablespoons table salt for brining
 3 tablespoons sugar for brining
 3 cups panko bread crumbs
 ¼ cup extra-virgin olive oil
 3 large eggs
 3 tablespoons all-purpose flour
 1 tablespoon onion powder
 1 teaspoon table salt
 ¾ teaspoon garlic powder
 ¼ teaspoon pepper

1. Cut each breast diagonally into thirds, then cut each piece into thirds. Dissolve 3 tablespoons salt and sugar in 2 quarts cold water in large container. Add chicken, cover, and let sit for 15 minutes.

2. Meanwhile, toss panko with oil in bowl until evenly coated. Microwave, stirring frequently, until light golden brown, about 5 minutes. Transfer to shallow dish and let cool slightly. Whisk eggs, flour, onion powder, salt, garlic powder, and pepper together in second shallow dish.

3. Set wire rack in rimmed baking sheet. Remove chicken from brine and pat dry with paper towels. Working with several chicken pieces at a time, dredge in egg mixture, letting excess drip off, then coat with panko mixture, pressing gently to adhere; transfer to prepared rack. Freeze until firm, about 4 hours. (Frozen nuggets can be transferred to zipper-lock bag and stored in freezer for up to 1 month.)

4. Lightly spray base of air-fryer basket with vegetable oil spray. Place up to 18 nuggets in prepared basket. Place basket in air fryer, set temperature to 400 degrees, and cook for 6 minutes. Transfer nuggets to clean bowl and gently toss to redistribute. Return nuggets to air fryer and cook until chicken is crisp and registers 160 degrees, 6 to 10 minutes. Serve.

Air-Fryer Chicken Parmesan

Air-Fryer Chicken Parmesan

Serves 2   Total Time 45 minutes

Why This Recipe Works Crisp and gooey when done right, but too often oily and soggy, chicken Parmesan is the ideal candidate for the air fryer. We aimed to eliminate pan frying and simplify this multistep dish. But we soon learned that, without a pan of hot oil, the coating of crunchy panko bread crumbs refused to brown. This was easily fixed: Pretoasting the panko in the microwave with a bit of olive oil turned it richly golden. To streamline the breading process, we whisked the flour and egg together, adding garlic powder and dried oregano for flavor. We dipped our chicken in this mixture and then pressed it in the toasted panko that we'd combined with grated Parmesan for an extra hit of cheesiness and an even crunchier texture. A short stint in the air fryer gave us chicken that was perfectly juicy inside and crunchy outside. We sprinkled on shredded mozzarella and cooked the cutlets just long enough to melt the cheese. A little warmed pasta sauce poured over the top kept our recipe simple and avoided soggy cutlets, and a sprinkle of chopped basil added a fresh finish. Serve with pasta, if desired.

¾ **cup panko bread crumbs**
2 **tablespoons extra-virgin olive oil**
¼ **cup grated Parmesan cheese**

1 **large egg**
1 **tablespoon all-purpose flour**
¾ **teaspoon garlic powder**
½ **teaspoon dried oregano**
⅛ **teaspoon plus ¼ teaspoon table salt, divided**
¼ **teaspoon pepper, divided**
2 **(8-ounce) boneless, skinless chicken breasts, trimmed**
2 **ounces whole-milk mozzarella cheese, shredded (½ cup)**
¼ **cup jarred marinara sauce, warmed**
2 **tablespoons chopped fresh basil**

1. Toss panko with oil in bowl until evenly coated. Microwave, stirring frequently, until light golden brown, 1 to 3 minutes. Transfer to shallow dish, let cool slightly, then stir in Parmesan. Whisk egg, flour, garlic powder, oregano, ⅛ teaspoon salt, and ⅛ teaspoon pepper together in second shallow dish.

2. Pound chicken breasts to even thickness. Pat dry with paper towels and sprinkle with remaining ¼ teaspoon salt and remaining ⅛ teaspoon pepper. Working with 1 breast at a time, dredge in egg mixture, letting excess drip off, then coat with panko mixture, pressing gently to adhere.

3. Lightly spray base of air-fryer basket with vegetable oil spray. Arrange breasts in prepared basket, spaced evenly apart, alternating ends. Place basket in air fryer and set temperature to 400 degrees. Cook until chicken is crisp and registers 160 degrees, 12 to 16 minutes, flipping and rotating breasts halfway through cooking.

4. Sprinkle chicken with mozzarella. Return basket to air fryer and cook until cheese is melted, about 1 minute. Transfer chicken to individual serving plates. Top each breast with 2 tablespoons warm marinara sauce and sprinkle with basil. Serve.

Air-Fryer Shredded Chicken Tacos

Serves 2 to 4   **Total Time** 40 minutes

Why This Recipe Works The perfect weeknight chicken tacos should be the kind of no-brainer meal you can turn to again and again. But often this means wet, oversimmered chicken and tired ingredients. The air fryer gave us something better: crispier, more deeply seasoned chicken, and downtime to prepare lively toppings. Our first step was to skip the expected boneless chicken breasts in favor of boneless thighs, which are equally convenient but richer and more deeply flavored. Rubbed with just a teaspoon of oil and sprinkled with chili powder, cumin, garlic powder, salt, pepper, and cayenne, they went into the air fryer to cook while we prepared a pico de gallo from chopped tomato, red onion, jalapeño, and lime juice. Letting the cooked chicken rest for a few minutes before shredding ensured that the juices remained in the meat and didn't wind up all over the cutting board. Crisp iceberg lettuce and shredded cheddar gave that familiar taco bar feel.

> 1 teaspoon chili powder
> ½ teaspoon ground cumin
> ½ teaspoon garlic powder
> ½ teaspoon table salt
> ¼ teaspoon pepper
>   Pinch cayenne pepper
> 1 pound boneless, skinless chicken thighs, trimmed
> 1 teaspoon vegetable oil
> 1 tomato, cored and chopped
> 2 tablespoons finely chopped red onion
> 2 teaspoons minced jalapeño chile
> 1½ teaspoons lime juice
> 6–12 (6-inch) corn tortillas, warmed
> 1 cup shredded iceberg lettuce
> 3 ounces cheddar cheese, shredded (¾ cup)

1. Combine chili powder, cumin, garlic powder, salt, pepper, and cayenne in bowl. Pat chicken dry with paper towels, rub with oil, and sprinkle evenly with spice mixture. Place chicken in air-fryer basket. Place basket in air fryer and set temperature to 400 degrees. Cook until chicken registers 175 degrees, 12 to 16 minutes, flipping and rotating chicken halfway through cooking.

2. Meanwhile, combine tomato, onion, jalapeño, and lime juice in bowl; season with salt and pepper to taste, and set aside until ready to serve.

3. Transfer chicken to cutting board, let cool slightly, then shred into bite-size pieces using 2 forks. Serve chicken on warm tortillas, topped with salsa, lettuce, and cheddar.

Air-Fryer Chicken Lettuce Wraps with Herbs and Mango

Serves 2 to 4   **Total Time** 40 minutes

Why This Recipe Works Inspired by Thai larb, a category of minced meat salads, this chicken salad served in lettuce leaves offers balanced sweet, sour, salty, and hot flavors. But even the most flavorful salad can't make up for dry chicken. Using boneless thighs ensured that the meat would stay moist in the air fryer, which quickly cooked the meat while we mixed an aromatic dressing from lime juice, fish sauce, brown sugar, shallot, garlic, and pepper flakes. Shredding the chicken enabled it to soak up plenty of dressing. Fresh herbs (mint, cilantro, and Thai basil), mango, and Thai chiles brightened our salad, which we spooned into Bibb lettuce cups and sprinkled with chopped peanuts for crunch. If you can't find Thai basil, you can substitute regular basil. If you can't find Thai chiles, you can substitute two Fresno or red jalapeño chiles.

> 1 pound boneless, skinless chicken thighs, trimmed
> 1 teaspoon vegetable oil
> 2 tablespoons lime juice
> 1 shallot, minced
> 1 tablespoon fish sauce, plus extra for serving
> 2 teaspoons packed brown sugar
> 1 garlic clove, minced
> ⅛ teaspoon red pepper flakes
> 1 mango, peeled, pitted, and cut into ¼-inch pieces
> ⅓ cup chopped fresh mint
> ⅓ cup chopped fresh cilantro
> ⅓ cup chopped fresh Thai basil
> 1 head Bibb lettuce (8 ounces), leaves separated
> ¼ cup dry-roasted peanuts, chopped
> 2 Thai chiles, stemmed and sliced thin

1. Pat chicken dry with paper towels and rub with oil. Place chicken in air-fryer basket. Place basket in air fryer and set temperature to 400 degrees. Cook until chicken registers 175 degrees, 12 to 16 minutes, flipping and rotating chicken halfway through cooking.

2. Meanwhile, whisk lime juice, shallot, fish sauce, sugar, garlic, and pepper flakes together in large bowl; set aside.

3. Transfer chicken to cutting board, let cool slightly, then shred into bite-size pieces using 2 forks. Add shredded chicken, mango, mint, cilantro, and basil to bowl with dressing and toss to coat. Serve chicken in lettuce leaves, passing peanuts, Thai chiles, and extra fish sauce separately.

Air-Fryer Buffalo Chicken Drumsticks

Serves 2   Total Time 45 minutes

Why This Recipe Works An air fryer produces great buffalo chicken with the crunch that typically comes from deep frying. The catch is that, for well-crisped pieces, you must cook wings in batches—even for two servings—which didn't thrill us. To avoid this, we opted for more substantial drumsticks, turning the snack into a main dish, and found we liked the meatier pieces (still with plenty of crispy skin) prepared buffalo style. We poked holes in the skin to render the fat efficiently and rubbed them with a touch of oil to ensure crispness. To build flavor, we coated the drumsticks with a blend of paprika, cayenne, salt, and pepper before cooking. For the namesake sauce, we microwaved equal parts melted butter and hot sauce but found the coating to be greasy. Using less butter fixed that problem but did not keep the sauce from sliding off the chicken. Adding just ¼ teaspoon of cornstarch yielded a thicker, glazy sauce that coated the drumsticks perfectly, and a bit of molasses deepened its flavor and brought a hint of sweetness. Instead of preparing a blue cheese sauce, we simply crumbled blue cheese over the drumsticks, which balanced the buffalo sauce's addictive heat. Classic buffalo sauce is made with Frank's RedHot Original Cayenne Pepper Sauce.

1½ teaspoons paprika
½ teaspoon cayenne pepper
¼ teaspoon table salt
¼ teaspoon pepper
4 (5-ounce) chicken drumsticks, trimmed
1 teaspoon vegetable oil

Air-Fryer Buffalo Chicken Drumsticks

3 tablespoons hot sauce
2 tablespoons unsalted butter
2 teaspoons molasses
¼ teaspoon cornstarch
2 tablespoons crumbled blue cheese

1. Combine paprika, cayenne, salt, and pepper in bowl. Pat drumsticks dry with paper towels. Using metal skewer, poke 10 to 15 holes in skin of each drumstick. Rub with oil and sprinkle evenly with spice mixture.

2. Arrange drumsticks in air-fryer basket, spaced evenly apart, alternating ends. Place basket in air fryer and set temperature to 400 degrees. Cook until chicken is crisp and registers 195 degrees, 22 to 25 minutes, flipping and rotating chicken halfway through cooking. Transfer chicken to large plate, tent with aluminum foil, and let rest for 5 minutes.

3. Meanwhile, microwave hot sauce, butter, molasses, and cornstarch in large bowl, stirring occasionally, until hot, about 1 minute. Add chicken and toss to coat. Transfer to serving platter and sprinkle with blue cheese. Serve.

Air-Fryer Spicy Fried-Chicken Sandwich

Serves 4 **Total Time** 40 minutes

Why This Recipe Works Crunchy, juicy, and slicked with mayo, a spicy fried-chicken sandwich is a lunchtime favorite, and using the air fryer means you don't need to heat up a skillet of oil whenever the craving strikes. For our sandwich to live up to its name, we added heat in three stages. First, we whisked hot sauce into the egg-flour dredging mixture to ensure that the heat would directly coat the chicken rather than get lost in the breading. Combining more hot sauce with mayonnaise for a creamy spread upped the heat level further. An unwritten rule of fried sandwiches states that a pickled element is a must; this was our opportunity to add even more heat with fiery sweet pickled jalapeños in lieu of pickle chips. Shredded lettuce provided a crisp, fresh component that tempered the heat a bit. You can use your air fryer to toast the buns; see page 410.

Air-Fryer Spicy Fried-Chicken Sandwich

1 cup panko bread crumbs
2 tablespoons extra-virgin olive oil
1 large egg
3 tablespoons hot sauce, divided
1 tablespoon all-purpose flour
½ teaspoon garlic powder
¼ teaspoon table salt, divided
⅛ teaspoon plus pinch pepper, divided
2 (8-ounce) boneless, skinless chicken breasts, trimmed
¼ cup mayonnaise
4 hamburger buns, toasted if desired
2 cups shredded iceberg lettuce
¼ cup jarred sliced jalapeños

1. Toss panko with oil in bowl until evenly coated. Microwave, stirring frequently, until light golden brown, 1 to 3 minutes. Transfer to shallow dish and set aside to cool slightly. Whisk egg, 2 tablespoons hot sauce, flour, garlic powder, ⅛ teaspoon salt, and ⅛ teaspoon pepper together in second shallow dish.

2. Pound chicken breasts to uniform thickness. Halve each breast crosswise, pat dry with paper towels, and sprinkle with remaining ⅛ teaspoon salt and remaining pinch pepper. Working with 1 piece of chicken at a time, dredge in egg mixture, letting excess drip off, then coat with panko mixture, pressing gently to adhere.

3. Lightly spray base of air-fryer basket with vegetable oil spray. Arrange chicken pieces in prepared basket, spaced evenly apart. Place basket in air fryer and set temperature to 400 degrees.

Cook until chicken is crisp and registers 160 degrees, 12 to 16 minutes, flipping and rotating chicken pieces halfway through cooking.

4. Combine mayonnaise and remaining 1 tablespoon hot sauce in small bowl. Spread mayonnaise mixture evenly over bun bottoms, then top each with 1 piece chicken, lettuce, jalapeños, and bun top. Serve.

Air-Fryer Turkey Burgers

Serves 2 **Total Time** 35 minutes

Why This Recipe Works The air fryer offers a convenient way to prepare turkey burgers for two, but it's not quite as simple as forming two patties and tossing them in the basket. On its own, ground turkey cooks up dry and dense—the extra-lean meat can't hold on to its own moisture during cooking. Mixing in a bit of Monterey Jack cheese went a long way in keeping the burgers moist, and the cheese crisped around the burger's edges, creating a crust. We also added a mixture of sandwich bread and yogurt known as a panade. Acting like a

Air-Fryer Turkey Burgers

Air-Fryer Mini Glazed Turkey Meatloaves

sponge, this helped the burgers retain moisture and kept them from becoming too dense. Pressing a slight dimple in the raw patties prevented them from puffing up too much when they cooked. Be sure to use ground turkey, not ground turkey breast (also labeled 99 percent fat-free) in this recipe. See below for how to use your air fryer to toast the buns. Serve with your favorite burger toppings.

- ½ slice hearty white sandwich bread, crust removed, torn into ½-inch pieces
- 2 tablespoons plain yogurt
- ¼ teaspoon plus ⅛ teaspoon table salt, divided
- ¼ teaspoon plus pinch pepper, divided
- 8 ounces ground turkey or chicken
- 1 ounce Monterey Jack cheese, shredded (¼ cup)
- 2 hamburger buns, toasted if desired
- ½ tomato, sliced thin
- 1 cup baby arugula

1. Mash bread, yogurt, ¼ teaspoon salt, and ¼ teaspoon pepper to paste in medium bowl using fork. Break up ground turkey into small pieces over bread mixture in bowl, add Monterey Jack, and lightly knead with your hands until mixture forms cohesive mass.

2. Divide turkey mixture into 2 lightly packed balls, then gently flatten each into 1-inch-thick patty. Press center of each patty with your fingertips to create ¼-inch-deep depression. Sprinkle with remaining ⅛ teaspoon salt and remaining pinch pepper.

3. Arrange patties in air-fryer basket, spaced evenly apart. Place basket in air fryer and set temperature to 350 degrees. Cook until burgers are browned and register 160 degrees, 12 to 16 minutes, flipping and rotating burgers halfway through cooking.

4. Transfer burgers to large plate, tent with aluminum foil, and let rest for 5 minutes. Serve burgers on buns, topped with tomato and arugula.

NOTES FROM THE TEST KITCHEN

TOASTING BURGER OR SANDWICH BUNS IN THE AIR FRYER

Wipe out the air-fryer basket with paper towels after cooking burgers or other food and arrange two split buns cut side down in the basket. Place the basket in the air fryer and set the temperature to 400 degrees. Cook until lightly golden, 2 to 3 minutes.

VARIATION
Air-Fryer Turkey Burgers with Sun-Dried Tomatoes and Basil

Add ¼ cup sun-dried tomatoes, rinsed, patted dry, and chopped coarse, and 2 tablespoons chopped fresh basil to turkey mixture in step 1.

Air-Fryer Mini Glazed Turkey Meatloaves

Serves 2 **Total Time** 1 hour

Why This Recipe Works For a lighter version of meatloaf, we started with ground turkey, perking up its mild flavor with garlic, shallot, and thyme. Worcestershire sauce provided savory meatiness, while cayenne added subtle heat. To hold the loaf together, we mixed in an egg and a panade made from white sandwich bread and milk, which also helped the meatloaf stay moist. Shaping two free-form mini loaves, rather than one big loaf, enabled the dish to cook in just 25 minutes and provided more surface area for a flavorful glaze. To ensure that the glaze stuck, we applied it in two coats. Once the first coat of glaze was tacky, we added the second coat of glaze, which stuck to this base coat in an even layer. Since the loaves were delicate, we placed them on an aluminum foil sling, which allowed us to rotate and remove them easily. Be sure to use ground turkey, not ground turkey breast (also labeled 99 percent fat-free), in this recipe.

- 1 shallot, minced
- 1 tablespoon vegetable oil
- 1 garlic clove, minced
- ½ teaspoon minced fresh thyme or ⅛ teaspoon dried
  Pinch cayenne pepper
- 1 slice hearty white sandwich bread, crust removed, torn into ½-inch pieces
- 1 large egg, lightly beaten
- 1 tablespoon whole milk
- 1 tablespoon Worcestershire sauce
- ¼ teaspoon table salt
- ¼ teaspoon pepper
- 1 pound ground turkey
- ¼ cup ketchup
- 1 tablespoon cider vinegar
- 1 tablespoon packed brown sugar
- ½ teaspoon hot sauce

1. Make foil sling for air-fryer basket by folding 1 long sheet of aluminum foil so it is 4 inches wide. Lay sheet of foil widthwise across basket, pressing foil into and up sides of basket. Fold excess foil as needed so that edges of foil are flush with top of basket. Lightly spray foil and basket with vegetable oil spray.

2. Microwave shallot, oil, garlic, thyme, and cayenne in large bowl until fragrant, about 1 minute. Add bread, egg, milk, Worcestershire, salt, and pepper and mash mixture to paste using fork. Break up ground turkey into small pieces over bread mixture and knead with hands until well combined. Shape turkey mixture into two 5 by 3-inch loaves. Arrange loaves on sling in prepared basket, spaced evenly apart.

3. Combine ketchup, vinegar, sugar, and hot sauce in small bowl, then brush loaves with half of ketchup mixture. Place basket in air fryer and set temperature to 350 degrees. Cook until meatloaves register 160 degrees, 25 to 30 minutes, brushing with remaining ketchup mixture and rotating meatloaves using sling halfway through cooking.

4. Using foil sling, carefully remove meatloaves from basket. Tent with foil and let rest for 5 minutes. Serve.

MAKING A FOIL SLING

Fold long sheet of foil so it is 4 inches wide. Lay sheet widthwise across basket, pressing up and into sides of basket. Fold excess as needed so that edges are flush with top of basket.

Sous Vide Foolproof Poached Chicken

Serves 4 **Cook Time** 1 to 3 hours

Why This Recipe Works Poached chicken gets a bad rap for being tough and dry, and that's probably because poaching can be a relatively imprecise cooking method: If your poaching water's too hot, the meat overcooks. If you leave the meat in water too long, it overcooks. If you use too little water, the meat—you guessed it—undercooks. Our Perfect Poached Chicken (page 60) employs a few tricks to work around these issues for a juicy result. But with sous vide, no tricks are needed. Sous vide allows us to cook chicken breasts at a consistent moderate temperature, which results in a juicy, tender texture that's just firm enough that it doesn't fall apart.

Sous Vide Foolproof
Poached Chicken

Sous Vide Crispy-Skinned Bone-In Chicken
Breasts with Leek and White Wine Pan Sauce

While this recipe is finished in an hour, you can hold the chicken in the bath for up to 3 hours before the texture starts to change—giving you some flexibility. This perfectly poached chicken is great on its own, or used in Creamy Chicken Salad with Fresh Herbs (page 54) or the other salads on pages 54–66. This method is a great starting point for experimentation and variation, so feel free to add spices, herbs, or boldly flavored marinades to the bag (just don't add fresh garlic; it is particularly susceptible to botulism).

  4 8-ounce boneless, skinless chicken breasts, trimmed
  ½ teaspoon table salt
  ¼ teaspoon pepper
  ¼ cup vegetable oil

  1. Using sous vide circulator, bring water to 150 degrees in 7-quart container.
  2. Sprinkle chicken with salt and pepper. Place chicken and oil in 1-gallon zipper-lock freezer bag and toss to coat. Seal bag, pressing out as much air as possible. Gently lower bag into prepared water bath until chicken is fully submerged, and then clip top corner of bag to side of water bath container, allowing remaining air bubbles to rise to top of bag. Reopen 1 corner of zipper, release remaining air bubbles, and reseal bag. Cover and cook for at least 1 hour or up to 3 hours. (Chicken can be rapidly chilled in ice bath [see page 413] and then refrigerated in zipper-lock bag after step 2 for up to 5 days. To reheat, return sealed bag to water bath set to 150 degrees for 20 minutes and then proceed with step 3.)
  3. Transfer chicken to paper towel–lined plate and let rest for 5 to 10 minutes. Serve.

VARIATIONS
Sous Vide Foolproof Lemon-Thyme Poached Chicken
Combine 1 teaspoon salt, ½ teaspoon pepper, ½ teaspoon garlic powder, ½ teaspoon minced fresh thyme, and 1 teaspoon grated lemon zest in bowl. Sprinkle chicken with salt mixture in step 2.

Sous Vide Foolproof Soy-Ginger Poached Chicken
Omit salt and pepper. Whisk ¼ cup soy sauce, ¼ cup sugar, 1 teaspoon grated fresh ginger, 1 teaspoon toasted sesame oil, and ½ teaspoon white pepper together in bowl. Substitute soy sauce mixture for oil.

PREPARING FOOD FOR SOUS VIDE

1. Place ingredients in zipper-lock freezer bag, press out as much air as possible, and gently lower bag into prepared bath.

2. Clip corner of bag to side of container with binder clip. Open 1 corner of zipper and release any remaining air, and then reseal bag. To prevent cold spots, make sure bag isn't touching circulator or container.

Sous Vide Crispy-Skinned Bone-In Chicken Breasts

Serves 4 **Cook Time** 1½ to 3 hours

Why This Recipe Works Cooking a perfect skin-on chicken breast is a tall order: You want a juicy, firm interior and a crackling crisp skin. In a hot oven, by the time skin crisps up, the meat within has turned dry. One solution is to gently cook the chicken until tender and juicy (usually in a low oven) and finish with a quick sear in a hot skillet to crisp the skin, a two-step process known as reverse searing. For more control over the process (and less moisture loss), we used sous vide for the first step. We let the chicken rest for 5 to 10 minutes before searing to retain juiciness. To get a really good sear, we aggressively patted the exterior of the chicken dry with paper towels. Serve the chicken as is, or use the fond left in the skillet after searing to make a pan sauce (page 414).

4   12-ounce bone-in split chicken breasts, trimmed
½   teaspoon table salt
¼   teaspoon pepper
6   tablespoons vegetable oil, divided

  1. Using sous vide circulator, bring water to 150 degrees in 7-quart container.

  2. Sprinkle chicken with salt and pepper. Place chicken and ¼ cup oil in 1-gallon zipper-lock freezer bag and toss to coat. Seal bag, pressing out as much air as possible. Gently lower bag into prepared water bath until chicken

NOTES FROM THE TEST KITCHEN

SOUS VIDE COOKING TIPS
Picking a Container
These recipes call for either a 7-quart or 12-quart container; use a Dutch oven or stockpot, or a large plastic container like a Cambro. Fill it with water to 1 inch above the immersion circulator's minimum water level line. Since the food will raise the water level, avoid filling to the maximum water line.

Choosing a Bag
While vacuum-sealing food cooked sous vide is common, especially in restaurants, the home sous-vider can be content with using zipper-lock bags. It's safe. The zipper-lock bags we use are made from polyethylene or polypropylene, which are considered among the safest plastics, resistant to the sub-boiling temperatures involved in sous vide cooking.

Chilling in an Ice Bath
If you're not serving the food right away, it's important to rapidly chill the food before storage. Why? Food safety. Plunge the still-sealed bags into a large ice bath to stop the cooking, let sit until chilled, and then refrigerate it for later.

Doneness Temperatures for Chicken and Turkey Cooked Sous Vide
While we traditionally cook poultry to 160 degrees or higher, our favorite temperature for cooking chicken breasts using sous vide is 150 degrees (and 145 degrees for turkey). Why? Cooking meat to lower temperatures reduces moisture loss, ensuring that our chicken and turkey emerge from the bag incredibly juicy and tender. Is it safe? Yes—because killing harmful bacteria is a function of both time and temperature. With enough time, most pathogens are killed at 130 degrees according to the U.S. Food and Drug Administration. The sous vide process of holding food at a constant temperature for an hour or sometimes much longer means that there is ample time to render poultry safe at 150 or 145 degrees.

Leek and White Wine Pan Sauce

Makes about ¾ cup   **Total Time** 30 minutes
Note that this recipe is meant to be started after you have seared the chicken breasts.

    Vegetable oil, if needed
1 leek, white and light green parts only, halved lengthwise, sliced ¼ inch thick, and washed thoroughly
1 teaspoon all-purpose flour
¾ cup chicken broth
½ cup dry white wine or dry vermouth
1 tablespoon unsalted butter, chilled
2 teaspoons chopped fresh tarragon
1 teaspoon whole-grain mustard

1. Pour off all but 2 tablespoons fat from skillet used to sear chicken. (If necessary, add oil to equal 2 tablespoons.) Add leek and cook over medium heat until softened and lightly browned, about 5 minutes. Stir in flour and cook for 1 minute. Slowly whisk in broth and wine, scraping up any browned bits and smoothing out any lumps. Bring to simmer and cook until thickened and reduced to ¾ cup, 3 to 5 minutes.

2. Off heat, whisk in butter until melted, and then whisk in tarragon, mustard, and any accumulated meat juices. Season with salt and pepper to taste.

Hoisin-Sesame Pan Sauce

Makes about ¾ cup   **Total Time** 20 minutes
Note that this recipe is meant to be started after you have seared the chicken breasts.

    Vegetable oil, if needed
2 teaspoons grated fresh ginger
¼ cup hoisin sauce
½ cup orange juice
½ cup chicken broth
2 scallions sliced thin on bias
1 teaspoon toasted sesame oil

1. Pour off all but 1 tablespoon fat from skillet used to sear chicken. (If necessary, add oil to equal 1 tablespoon.) Add ginger and cook over medium heat until fragrant, about 15 seconds. Stir in hoisin, orange juice, and broth, scraping up any browned bits. Bring to simmer and cook until liquid is reduced to ¾ cup, about 4 minutes.

2. Off heat, stir in scallions, sesame oil, and any accumulated meat juices. Season with pepper to taste.

is fully submerged, and then clip top corner of bag to side of water bath container, allowing remaining air bubbles to rise to top of bag. Reopen 1 corner of zipper, release remaining air bubbles, and reseal bag. Cover and cook for at least 1½ hours or up to 3 hours.

3. Transfer chicken to paper towel–lined plate and let rest for 5 to 10 minutes. Pat chicken thoroughly dry with paper towels. Heat remaining 2 tablespoons oil in 12-inch skillet over medium-high heat until just smoking. Place chicken skin side down in skillet and cook until skin is well browned and crisp, 4 to 6 minutes. Serve. (Chicken can be rapidly chilled in ice bath [see page 413] and then refrigerated in zipper-lock bag after step 2 for up to 5 days. To reheat, return sealed bag to water bath set to 150 degrees for 20 minutes and then proceed with step 3.)

Sous Vide Peri Peri Chicken

Serves 4   **Cook Time** 1½ to 3 hours (plus 6 hours chilling time)

Why This Recipe Works A grilled dish with roots in Africa and the West Indies, peri peri chicken gets its name from the paste of fiery peri peri chiles used to marinate the chicken. Our indoor version employed sous vide followed by a stint under the broiler. We tossed bone-in chicken breasts with a paste made from arbol chiles, garlic powder, tomato paste, five-spice powder, and salt in a plastic bag and let the chicken marinate for up to a day so the seasoning penetrated the meat. During cooking, the sealed bag retained all of the chicken's juices that would have dripped away on the grill, so they could combine with the paste. We reduced these juices to intensify their flavors, and then brushed the mixture over the chicken before a final broil to brown the skin. If you can find peri peri chiles, use them instead of arbols. For a spicier dish, use the greater amount of chiles.

2–5 arbol chiles, stemmed
1 shallot, chopped
2 tablespoons extra-virgin olive oil
1 tablespoon table salt
1 tablespoon tomato paste
2 teaspoons sugar
1½ teaspoons paprika
1½ teaspoons five-spice powder
1 teaspoon garlic powder
1 teaspoon grated lemon zest plus 2 tablespoons juice, plus lemon wedges for serving
½ teaspoon pepper
¼ teaspoon cayenne pepper
2 bay leaves, crumbled
4 (12-ounce) bone-in split chicken breasts, trimmed

Sous Vide Peri Peri Chicken

4. Pour accumulated juices into 8-inch skillet, bring to simmer over medium heat, and cook until reduced by two-thirds, 3 to 5 minutes. Brush chicken with sauce and broil until skin is crisp and lightly charred, 6 to 8 minutes. Serve with lemon wedges

Sous Vide Easy Boneless Turkey Breast

Serves 6 to 8   **Cook Time** 3½ to 5 hours

Why This Recipe Works Cooking a turkey breast sous vide guarantees turkey that is moist and succulent with crispy skin. We first took the meat off of the breastbone for easy handling and better crisping of the skin. A long bath in our immersion circulator delivered tender, juicy meat with a uniform texture. Resting the turkey before searing to crisp the skin helped retain juiciness. You can make any number of turkey breasts ahead of time and sear them off as needed. If using a self-basting or kosher turkey breast, do not salt the breast halves in step 2. Serve with Red Bell Pepper Chutney (page 416) or All-Purpose Gravy (page 242).

1 (7-pound) bone-in turkey breast
1½ teaspoons table salt
¾ teaspoon pepper
½ cup plus 2 tablespoons vegetable oil, divided

1. Process arbols, shallot, oil, salt, tomato paste, sugar, paprika, five-spice powder, garlic powder, lemon zest and juice, pepper, cayenne, and bay leaves in blender until smooth, scraping down sides of blender jar as needed, about 1 minute. Place chicken and chile paste in 1-gallon zipper-lock freezer bag and toss to coat. Seal bag, pressing out as much air as possible. Refrigerate chicken for at least 6 hours or up to 24 hours.

2. Using sous vide circulator, bring water to 150 degrees in 7-quart container. Gently lower bag into prepared water bath until chicken is fully submerged, and then clip top corner of bag to side of water bath container, allowing remaining air bubbles to rise to top of bag. Reopen 1 corner of zipper, release remaining air bubbles, and reseal bag. Cover and cook chicken for at least 1½ hours or up to 3 hours. (Chicken and accumulated juices can be rapidly chilled in ice bath [see page 413] and then refrigerated in zipper-lock bag after step 2 for up to 5 days. To reheat, return sealed bag to water bath set to 150 degrees for 20 minutes. Proceed with step 3.)

3. Adjust oven rack 6 inches from broiler element and heat broiler. Set wire rack in aluminum foil–lined rimmed baking sheet and spray with vegetable oil spray. Transfer chicken skin side up to prepared rack and let rest while preparing sauce.

1. Using sous vide circulator, bring water to 145 degrees in 7-quart container.

2. Using sharp knife, cut along rib cage of breast to remove breast halves; discard bones. Trim excess skin from turkey and sprinkle with salt and pepper. Place 1 breast half and ¼ cup oil in 1-gallon zipper-lock freezer bag. Repeat with second breast half. Seal bags, pressing out as much air as possible. Gently lower bags into prepared water bath until turkey is fully submerged, and then clip top corner of each bag to side of water bath container, allowing remaining air bubbles to rise to top of bags. Reopen 1 corner of each zipper, release remaining air bubbles, and reseal bags. Cover and cook for at least 3½ hours or up to 5 hours. (Turkey can be rapidly chilled in ice bath [see page 413] and then refrigerated in zipper-lock bag after step 2 for up to 5 days. To reheat, return sealed bag to water bath set to 145 degrees for 30 minutes. Proceed with step 3.)

3. Transfer turkey to paper towel–lined plate and let rest for 5 to 10 minutes. Pat turkey dry with paper towels. Heat remaining 2 tablespoons oil in 12-inch skillet over medium-high heat until just smoking. Place turkey skin side down in skillet and cook, adjusting position with tongs as needed, until well-browned and crisp, 4 to 6 minutes. Transfer turkey to carving board and slice into ½-inch-thick slices. Serve.

Red Bell Pepper Chutney

Makes about 2 cups   **Total Time** 3 hours
Avoid adding the parsley to the chutney before it is fully cooled, or the parsley will wilt. This recipe is best served at room temperature.

    1 tablespoon extra-virgin olive oil
    1 red onion, chopped fine
    4 red bell peppers, stemmed, seeded,
       and cut into ½-inch pieces
    1 cup white wine vinegar
    ½ cup plus 2 tablespoons sugar
    2 garlic cloves, peeled and smashed
    1 1-inch piece ginger, peeled, sliced into
       thin coins, and smashed
    1 teaspoon yellow mustard seeds
    1 teaspoon table salt
    ½ teaspoon red pepper flakes
    ¼ cup minced fresh parsley

Heat oil in large saucepan over medium heat until shimmering. Add onion and cook until softened, about 5 minutes. Stir in bell peppers, vinegar, sugar, garlic, ginger, mustard seeds, salt, and pepper flakes. Bring to simmer and cook until thickened and measures about 2 cups, about 40 minutes. Transfer to bowl and let cool to room temperature, about 2 hours. Discard garlic and ginger and stir in parsley. (Chutney can be refrigerated for up to 1 week; bring to room temperature before serving.)

Sous Vide Turkey Thigh Confit with Citrus-Mustard Sauce

Serves 6 to 8   **Cook Time** 17¾ hours to 21¾ hours (plus 4 days salting time)

Why This Recipe Works The process of confit, or salt-curing and slow-poaching in fat, is a near miracle for turkey, producing unbelievably compact, succulent, silky meat and concentrated savory flavor. This recipe takes at least five days to make, mostly to allow time for the turkey thighs to cure, but almost all the time is hands-off. And making confit using sous vide, rather than in the oven, offers a huge benefit: You only need 1 cup of fat or oil instead of the 6 cups traditionally required. We first coated bone-in turkey thighs in a paste of pureed onion, salt, pepper, sugar, and thyme for at least four days, which allowed time for the turkey to become seasoned down to the bone. We rinsed away the cure and cooked the thighs sous vide with duck fat or oil until fully tender. To ensure proper seasoning, make sure the total weight of the turkey is within 2 ounces of the 4-pound target weight (you should have four thighs in all); do not use enhanced or kosher turkey thighs. Though duck fat is traditional, we found that any chicken fat or even vegetable oil will work. Reserve remaining chicken or duck fat for further use; used oil should be discarded. We double-bag the turkey thighs to protect against seam failure, so you will need four 1-gallon zipper-lock freezer bags for this recipe. If preferred, you may bag the turkey using a vacuum sealer, and skip the double-bagging. The thighs can be refrigerated for up to a week or immediately browned and served with our bright and tangy citrus-mustard sauce.

    3 large onions, chopped coarse (4¾ cups)
   12 thyme sprigs
   2½ tablespoons table salt, for curing
   4½ teaspoons sugar
   1½ teaspoons pepper
    4 pounds bone-in turkey thighs
    1 cup duck fat, chicken fat, or vegetable oil,
       for cooking, divided
    ½ teaspoon granulated garlic, divided
    2 bay leaves, divided
    ½ cup orange marmalade
    2 tablespoons whole-grain mustard
    ¾ teaspoon lime zest plus 2 tablespoons juice
    ¼ teaspoon table salt
    ⅛ teaspoon cayenne pepper

1. 5 to 12 days before serving Process onions, thyme sprigs, 2½ tablespoons salt, sugar, and pepper in food processor until finely chopped, about 20 seconds, scraping down sides of bowl as needed. Spread ⅓ of mixture evenly in bottom of 13 by 9-inch baking dish. Arrange turkey thighs, skin side up, in single layer in dish. Spread remaining onion mixture evenly over thighs. Wrap dish tightly with plastic wrap, and refrigerate for 4 to 6 days (whichever is most convenient).

2. Using sous vide circulator, bring 4 inches (about 6 quarts) water to 158 degrees in 12-quart stockpot or similar-size heatproof container. Remove thighs from onion mixture and rinse well (if you don't have a garbage disposal, do not allow onion pieces to go down drain). Pat thighs dry with paper towels. Fold back top of 1-gallon zipper-lock freezer bag. Place 2 thighs skin side up in single layer in bag. Add ½ cup fat, ¼ teaspoon granulated garlic, and 1 bay leaf. Seal bag, pressing out as much air as possible. Gently lower bag into prepared water bath until thighs are fully submerged, allowing air bubbles to rise to top of bag. Open 1 corner of zipper, release air bubbles, and reseal bag. Repeat bagging and resealing with second zipper-lock bag and remaining thighs, ½ cup fat, ¼ teaspoon granulated garlic, and bay leaf.

3. Seal each bag inside separate 1-gallon zipper-lock freezer bag. Gently lower 1 bag into prepared water bath until thighs are fully submerged, then clip top corner of bag to side of container, allowing remaining air bubbles to rise to top of bag. Open 1 corner of zipper of outer bag, release air bubbles, and reseal bag. Repeat with second bag. Cover container with plastic and cook for at least 16 hours or up to 20 hours. Remove bags from water bath and let cool completely, about 1 hour. Refrigerate, still double-bagged, for up to 6 days.

4. To serve Using sous vide circulator, bring 4 inches (about 6 quarts) water to 140 degrees in 12-quart stockpot or similar-size heatproof container. Fully submerge each bag in water bath, cover container with plastic, and cook for at least 1½ hours.

5. Adjust oven rack to lower-middle position and heat oven to 500 degrees. While oven heats, crumple 20-inch length of aluminum foil into loose ball. Uncrumple foil, place in rimmed baking sheet, and top with wire rack. Using tongs, gently transfer thighs, skin side up, to prepared rack, being careful not to tear delicate skin. Set aside. Strain fat through fine-mesh strainer set into large bowl. Working in batches, pour liquid into fat separator, letting liquid settle for 5 minutes before separating fat from turkey stock. (Alternatively, use bulb baster to extract turkey stock from beneath fat.) Transfer 4 teaspoons turkey stock to small bowl; add marmalade; and microwave until mixture is fluid, about 30 seconds. Stir in mustard, lime zest and juice, salt, and cayenne. Transfer to serving bowl.

6. Transfer thighs to oven and roast until well-browned, 12 to 15 minutes. Transfer thighs to cutting board, skin side up, and let rest until just cool enough to handle, about 15 minutes.

7. Flip 1 thigh skin side down. Using tip of paring knife, cut along sides of thighbone, exposing bone. Carefully remove bone and any stray bits of cartilage. Flip thigh skin side up. Using sharp chef's knife, slice thigh crosswise ¾ inch thick. Transfer to serving platter, skin side up. Repeat with remaining thighs. Serve, passing sauce separately.

Sous Vide Turkey Thigh Confit with Citrus-Mustard Sauce

CARVING TURKEY THIGHS

1. Place thigh skin side down. Using tip of paring knife, cut along sides of thighbone, exposing bone.

2. Carefully remove bone and any stray bits of cartilage. Flip thigh skin side up.

3. Using sharp chef's knife, slice thigh crosswise ¾ inch thick.

SLOW COOKER

Photos (clockwise from top left): Slow-Cooker Chicken with Mushrooms and Tarragon Cream Sauce; Slow-Cooker Lemon Chicken Thighs; Slow-Cooker Chicken and Corn Chowder; Slow-Cooker Sweet and Tangy Pulled Chicken

Slow-Cooker Old-Fashioned Chicken Noodle Soup

Serves 6 to 8   **Cook Time** 3 to 4 hours on low

Why This Recipe Works Making a deeply flavored chicken noodle soup in the slow cooker is surprisingly easy, but it requires getting out a skillet to start things off right. We found that searing skin-on chicken breasts and using the flavorful fat to sweat our vegetables and aromatics gave us unbelievable depth of flavor. We then removed the chicken skin to prevent too much fat from getting into our soup. Using chicken broth instead of water also provided a backbone of flavor. We tried many iterations of cooking our noodles in the soup but found that the heat of the slow cooker was not sufficient to cook the noodles (or pasta or couscous, depending on the recipe) properly, so we cooked them on the side and added them at the end. You can substitute bone-in chicken thighs for the bone-in breasts, if desired; increase the cooking time to 4 to 5 hours.

Slow-Cooker Old-Fashioned Chicken Noodle Soup

1½ pounds bone-in split chicken breasts, trimmed
 1 teaspoon table salt, divided, plus salt for cooking pasta
 ⅛ teaspoon pepper
 4 teaspoons vegetable oil, divided
 3 carrots, peeled and cut into ½-inch pieces
 2 celery ribs, cut into ½-inch pieces
 1 onion, chopped fine
 1 teaspoon tomato paste
 1 teaspoon minced fresh thyme
10 cups chicken broth, divided
 2 ounces wide egg noodles
 2 tablespoons minced fresh parsley

1. Pat chicken dry with paper towels; sprinkle with ¼ teaspoon salt and pepper. Heat 1 tablespoon oil in 12-inch skillet over medium-high heat until just smoking. Brown chicken on both sides, 6 to 8 minutes; transfer to plate and discard skin.

2. Add carrots, celery, onion, and remaining ¾ teaspoon salt to fat left in skillet; cook over medium heat until softened, about 8 minutes. Stir in tomato paste and thyme; cook until fragrant, about 30 seconds. Stir in 1 cup broth, scraping up any browned bits; transfer to slow cooker.

3. Stir in remaining 9 cups broth. Nestle chicken into slow cooker, cover, and cook until chicken is tender, 3 to 4 hours on low.

4. Bring 2 quarts water to boil in large saucepan. Add noodles and 1½ teaspoons salt; cook until al dente. Drain noodles, rinse with cold water, then toss with remaining 1 teaspoon oil.

5. Transfer chicken to cutting board, let cool slightly, then shred into bite-size pieces using 2 forks; discard bones. Stir noodles and chicken into soup; let sit for 5 minutes. Stir in parsley; season with salt and pepper to taste. Serve.

VARIATIONS
Slow-Cooker Spring Vegetable Chicken Soup
Serves 6 to 8   **Cook Time** 3 to 4 hours on low

1½ pounds bone-in split chicken breasts, trimmed
 1 teaspoon table salt, divided, plus salt for cooking noodles
 ⅛ teaspoon pepper
 4 teaspoons vegetable oil, divided
 1 onion, chopped fine
 1 teaspoon tomato paste
 1 teaspoon minced fresh thyme
10 cups chicken broth, divided
 2 ounces medium shells
 2 cups frozen lima beans, thawed
 1 zucchini, quartered lengthwise and sliced ¼ inch thick
 1 ounce Parmesan cheese, grated fine (½ cup)
 2 tablespoons minced fresh basil

1. Pat chicken dry with paper towels; sprinkle with ¼ teaspoon salt and pepper. Heat 1 tablespoon oil in 12-inch skillet over medium-high heat until just smoking. Brown chicken on both sides, 6 to 8 minutes; transfer to plate and discard skin.

2. Add onion and remaining ¾ teaspoon salt to fat left in skillet; cook over medium heat until softened, about 5 minutes. Stir in tomato paste and thyme; cook until fragrant, about 30 seconds. Stir in 1 cup broth, scraping up any browned bits; transfer to slow cooker.

3. Stir in remaining 9 cups broth. Nestle chicken into slow cooker, cover, and cook until chicken is tender, 3 to 4 hours on low.

4. Bring 2 quarts water to boil in large saucepan. Add pasta and 1½ teaspoons salt; cook until al dente. Drain pasta, rinse with cold water, then toss with remaining 1 teaspoon oil.

5. Transfer chicken to cutting board, let cool slightly, then shred into bite-size pieces using 2 forks; discard bones. Stir lima beans and zucchini into soup, cover, and cook on high until tender, about 30 minutes. Stir in noodles and chicken; let sit for 5 minutes. Stir in Parmesan and basil; season with salt and pepper to taste. Serve.

Slow-Cooker Spicy Chipotle Chicken Noodle Soup

Serves 6 to 8   Cook Time 3 to 4 hours on low

1½ pounds bone-in split chicken breasts, trimmed
1 teaspoon table salt, divided, plus salt for cooking pasta
⅛ teaspoon pepper
4 teaspoons vegetable oil, divided
4 teaspoons minced canned chipotle chile in adobo sauce
3 garlic cloves, minced
1 tablespoon tomato paste
1 teaspoon minced fresh oregano
1 teaspoon ground cumin
10 cups chicken broth, divided
1 (28-ounce) can diced tomatoes, drained
2 ounces wide egg noodles
2 cups frozen corn, thawed
2 tablespoons minced fresh cilantro

1. Pat chicken dry with paper towels; sprinkle with ¼ teaspoon salt and pepper. Heat 1 tablespoon oil in 12-inch skillet over medium-high heat until just smoking. Brown chicken on both sides, 6 to 8 minutes; transfer to plate and discard skin.

2. Add chipotle, garlic, tomato paste, oregano, cumin, and remaining ¾ teaspoon salt to fat left in skillet; cook until fragrant, about 30 seconds. Stir in 1 cup broth, scraping up any browned bits; transfer to slow cooker.

3. Stir in remaining 9 cups broth and tomatoes. Nestle chicken into slow cooker, cover, and cook until chicken is tender, 3 to 4 hours on low.

4. Bring 2 quarts water to boil in large saucepan. Add noodles and 1½ teaspoons salt; cook until al dente. Drain noodles, rinse, then toss with remaining 1 teaspoon oil.

5. Transfer chicken to cutting board, let cool slightly, then shred into bite-size pieces using 2 forks; discard bones. Stir noodles, chicken, and corn into soup; let sit for 5 minutes. Stir in cilantro; season with salt and pepper to taste. Serve.

Slow-Cooker Curried Chicken and Couscous Soup

Serves 6 to 8   Cook Time 3 to 4 hours on low

1½ pounds bone-in split chicken breasts, trimmed
1 teaspoon table salt, divided, plus salt for cooking pasta
⅛ teaspoon pepper
4 teaspoons vegetable oil, divided
12 ounces Swiss chard, stems and leaves separated and chopped
3 carrots, peeled and cut into ½-inch pieces
2 tablespoons grated fresh ginger
2 teaspoons curry powder
1 teaspoon tomato paste
10 cups chicken broth, divided
⅓ cup pearl couscous
2 tablespoons minced fresh mint

1. Pat chicken dry with paper towels; sprinkle with ¼ teaspoon salt and pepper. Heat 1 tablespoon oil in 12-inch skillet over medium-high heat until just smoking. Brown chicken on both sides, 6 to 8 minutes; transfer to plate and discard skin.

2. Add chard stems, carrots, and remaining ¾ teaspoon salt to fat left in skillet; cook over medium heat until softened, about 8 minutes. Stir in ginger, curry powder, and tomato paste and cook until fragrant, about 30 seconds. Stir in 1 cup broth, scraping up any browned bits; transfer to slow cooker.

3. Stir in remaining 9 cups broth. Nestle chicken into slow cooker, cover, and cook until chicken is tender, 3 to 4 hours on low.

4. Bring 2 quarts water to boil in large saucepan. Add couscous and 1½ teaspoons salt; cook until al dente. Drain couscous, rinse with cold water, then toss with remaining 1 teaspoon oil.

5. Transfer chicken to cutting board, let cool slightly, then shred into bite-size pieces using 2 forks; discard bones. Stir chard leaves into soup, cover, and cook on high until tender, about 30 minutes. Stir in couscous and chicken; let sit for 5 minutes. Stir in mint and season with salt and pepper to taste. Serve.

Slow-Cooker Chicken Tortilla Soup

Slow-Cooker Turkey
and Rice Soup

Slow-Cooker Chicken Tortilla Soup

Serves 6 to 8 **Cook Time** 4 to 5 hours on low

Why This Recipe Works A good chicken tortilla soup has deep, smoky, roasted notes (achieved by charring vegetables) and toasty corn flavor from steeping tortillas in the soup. To create this in our slow cooker and avoid watered-down flavor, we browned some of the vegetables in a skillet first. Including chipotle chiles in adobo sauce added smokiness along with a spicy kick. For deep corn flavor, we added torn-up tortillas to simmer for hours in the broth, and shallow-fried fresh tortillas in just 5 minutes for a garnish along with plentiful toppings. For even more heat, include the jalapeño seeds. Do not omit the garnishes; the flavor of the soup depends heavily on them.

 1 tablespoon plus 1 cup vegetable oil, divided
 2 tomatoes, cored and chopped
 1 onion, chopped fine
 2 jalapeño chiles, stemmed, seeded, and minced, divided
 6 garlic cloves, minced
 1 tablespoon minced canned chipotle chile in adobo sauce, divided
 1 tablespoon tomato paste
 6 cups chicken broth, divided
10 (6-inch) corn tortillas (4 torn into ½-inch pieces, 6 halved and cut crosswise into ½-inch strips)
1½ pounds boneless, skinless chicken thighs, trimmed
 ¼ teaspoon table salt
 ⅛ teaspoon pepper
 8 ounces Cotija cheese, crumbled (2 cups)
 1 avocado, halved, pitted, and cut into ½-inch pieces
 ½ cup sour cream
 ½ cup minced fresh cilantro
   Lime wedges

1. Heat 1 tablespoon oil in 12-inch nonstick skillet over medium-high heat until shimmering. Add tomatoes, onion, half of jalapeños, garlic, 2 teaspoons chipotle, and tomato paste and cook until onion is softened and beginning to brown, 8 to 10 minutes. Stir in 1 cup broth, scraping up any browned bits; transfer to slow cooker.

2. Stir remaining 5 cups broth and tortilla pieces into slow cooker. Sprinkle chicken with salt and pepper and nestle into slow cooker. Cover and cook until chicken is tender, 4 to 5 hours on low.

3. Meanwhile, wipe skillet clean with paper towels. Heat remaining 1 cup oil in skillet over medium-high heat until shimmering. Add tortilla strips and cook, stirring occasionally, until golden brown, 4 to 6 minutes. Using slotted spoon, transfer tortilla strips to paper towel–lined plate; discard remaining oil. Season tortilla strips with salt to taste and let cool slightly to crisp.

4. Transfer chicken to cutting board, let cool slightly, then shred into bite-size pieces using 2 forks. Whisk soup vigorously for 30 seconds to break down tortilla pieces. Stir in chicken, remaining jalapeños, and remaining 1 teaspoon chipotle and let sit until heated through, about 5 minutes. Season with salt and pepper to taste. Serve, passing tortilla strips, Cotija, avocado, sour cream, cilantro, and lime wedges separately.

Slow-Cooker Turkey and Rice Soup

Serves 6 to 8   Cook Time 6 to 7 hours on low

Why This Recipe Works Turkey soup is a dish perfectly suited for a slow cooker. The hearty flavor of turkey translates easily into a full-flavored soup without requiring any tricks, and turkey thighs (which we prefer for soup) seem to have been designed for the slow cooker's low and steady cooking environment. Turkey thighs, which are made up entirely of dark meat, are quite big and thick, which means they are nearly impossible to overcook, and they have lots of flavor to spare. (As a bonus, they're also inexpensive.) Be sure to use instant rice (sometimes labeled minute rice); traditional rice takes much longer to cook and won't work here. You can substitute an equal amount of bone-in chicken thighs for the turkey, if desired; reduce the cooking time to 4 to 5 hours.

- 2 onions, chopped fine
- 4 garlic cloves, minced
- 1 tablespoon vegetable oil
- 1 tablespoon tomato paste
- 2 teaspoons minced fresh thyme or ½ teaspoon dried
- 1 teaspoon table salt, divided
- 8 cups chicken broth
- 3 carrots, peeled and sliced ¼ inch thick
- 2 celery ribs, sliced ¼ inch thick
- 2 bay leaves
- 2 pounds bone-in turkey thighs, skin removed, trimmed
- ⅛ teaspoon pepper
- 2 cups instant brown rice
- 2 tablespoons minced fresh parsley

1. Microwave onions, garlic, oil, tomato paste, thyme, and ¾ teaspoon salt in bowl, stirring occasionally, until onions are softened, about 5 minutes; transfer to slow cooker. Stir in broth, carrots, celery, and bay leaves. Sprinkle turkey with remaining ¼ teaspoon salt and pepper and nestle into slow cooker. Cover and cook until turkey is tender, 6 to 7 hours on low.

2. Transfer turkey to cutting board, let cool slightly, then shred into bite-size pieces using 2 forks; discard bones. Discard bay leaves.

3. Stir rice into soup, cover, and cook on high until tender, 30 to 40 minutes. Stir in turkey and let sit until heated through, about 5 minutes. Stir in parsley and season with salt and pepper to taste. Serve.

Slow-Cooker Hearty Turkey and Vegetable Soup

Serves 6 to 8   Cook Time 6 to 7 hours on low

Why This Recipe Works In this recipe, turkey delivers a full-flavored soup without requiring a lot of extra steps. To complement the meaty turkey thighs, we microwaved leeks and colorful chard stems to bring out their sweetness, which added valuable depth to the broth. Chopped chard leaves were added during the last 20 minutes of cooking for an earthy, colorful contrast. Orzo was the perfect addition to this soup, adding substance. You can substitute an equal amount of bone-in chicken thighs for the turkey, if desired; reduce the cooking time to 4 to 5 hours.

- 1½ pounds leeks, white and light green parts only, halved lengthwise, sliced ¼ inch thick, and washed thoroughly
- 8 ounces Swiss chard, stems chopped, leaves cut into 1-inch pieces, divided
- 4 teaspoons vegetable oil, divided
- 1 teaspoon tomato paste
- 1 teaspoon minced fresh thyme or ¼ teaspoon dried
- 1 teaspoon table salt, divided, plus salt for cooking orzo
- 8 cups chicken broth
- 2 carrots, peeled and cut into ½-inch pieces
- 2 bay leaves
- 2 pounds bone-in turkey thighs, trimmed
- ⅛ teaspoon pepper
- ¼ cup orzo

1. Microwave leeks, chard stems, 1 tablespoon oil, tomato paste, thyme, and ¾ teaspoon salt in bowl, stirring occasionally, until vegetables are softened, about 5 minutes; transfer to slow cooker. Stir in broth, carrots, and bay leaves. Sprinkle turkey with remaining ¼ teaspoon salt and pepper and nestle into slow cooker. Cover and cook until turkey is tender, 6 to 7 hours on low.

2. Meanwhile, bring 2 quarts water to boil in large saucepan. Add orzo and 1½ teaspoons salt and cook, stirring often, until al dente. Drain orzo, rinse with cold water, then toss with remaining 1 teaspoon oil in bowl; set aside.

3. Transfer turkey to cutting board, let cool slightly, then shred into bite-size pieces using 2 forks; discard bones. Discard bay leaves.

4. Stir chard leaves into soup, cover, and cook on high until tender, 20 to 30 minutes. Stir in orzo and turkey and let sit until heated through, about 5 minutes. Season with salt and pepper to taste. Serve.

Slow-Cooker Chicken and Corn Chowder

Serves 6 to 8   **Cook Time** 7 to 8 hours on low or 4 to 5 hours on high

Why This Recipe Works For this ultracomforting hands-off chowder, we decided to use corn and chicken instead of clams. Carefully layering a mixture of potatoes, celery, shallot, and salt pork on the bottom of the slow cooker and adding bone-less, skinless chicken thighs on top ensured that the potatoes cooked evenly. We then added corn and chicken broth to prevent the chicken from drying out. After shredding the chicken, we pureed some of the soup for a silky texture. We finished the chowder with cream for richness and chopped chives for a fresh garnish. It's important to layer the ingredients in the order listed to ensure that the potatoes fully cook and the chicken doesn't dry out. If you can't find salt pork, you can use two slices of bacon. You can substitute fresh corn kernels for the frozen corn, if desired.

1½ pounds boneless, skinless chicken thighs, trimmed
½ teaspoon table salt
1½ pounds Yukon Gold potatoes, peeled and cut into ½-inch pieces
4 ounces salt pork, cut into 4 pieces
¼ cup minced celery
1 shallot, minced
3 garlic cloves, minced
1 teaspoon sugar
½ teaspoon pepper
1 bay leaf
3 cups frozen corn
3 cups chicken broth
¾ cup heavy cream
3 tablespoons chopped fresh chives

1. Pat chicken dry with paper towels and sprinkle with salt. Toss potatoes, salt pork, celery, shallot, garlic, sugar, pepper, and bay leaf together in slow cooker; spread into even layer. Layer chicken over top of potato mixture to cover. Scatter corn over chicken. Add chicken broth; do not stir contents of slow cooker. Cover and cook until chicken is tender, 7 to 8 hours on low or 4 to 5 hours on high.

2. Discard bay leaf and salt pork. Transfer chicken to cutting board and shred into bite-size pieces with 2 forks; set aside.

3. Transfer 2 cups chowder to blender and process until smooth, 1 to 2 minutes. Return blended chowder to slow cooker.

4. Stir cream and chicken into chowder. Season with salt and pepper to taste. Serve, sprinkled with chives.

Slow-Cooker Chicken and Sausage Gumbo

Serves 6 to 8   **Cook Time** 4 to 5 hours on low

Why This Recipe Works The key to a remarkable gumbo is a dark roux: flour toasted in oil until it's the color of peanut butter. Since a slow cooker doesn't get hot enough to make the roux, we started it on the stovetop. Heating the oil and flour in a 12-inch nonstick skillet offered enough surface area to create a nice brown roux in 10 minutes. In a few more minutes we softened our trinity of vegetables (onion, celery, and bell pepper) before transferring everything to the slow cooker along with chicken, andouille sausage, okra, and broth to cook in the gentle heat. Trimming the fat from the raw chicken thighs reduces the amount of fat you'll need to skim off the finished gumbo.

½ cup vegetable oil
¾ cup all-purpose flour
2 onions, chopped
1 green bell pepper, stemmed, seeded, and chopped
1 celery rib, chopped fine
4 garlic cloves, minced
1 tablespoon Creole seasoning
4 cups chicken broth, divided
1½ pounds boneless, skinless chicken thighs, trimmed
   Salt and pepper
12 ounces andouille sausage, sliced ½ inch thick
10 ounces frozen cut okra
2 bay leaves
4 scallions, white and green parts separated and sliced thin
4 cups cooked white rice
   Hot sauce

1. Heat oil in 12-inch nonstick skillet over medium-high heat until just smoking. Using rubber spatula, stir in flour and cook until mixture is color of peanut butter, about 3 minutes, stirring constantly. Reduce heat to medium and continue to cook, stirring constantly, until roux is slightly darker and color of ground cinnamon, 5 to 10 minutes longer.

2. Stir in onions, bell pepper, celery, garlic, and Creole seasoning and cook until vegetables are softened, 7 to 10 minutes. Stir in 2 cups broth and bring to simmer over high heat; transfer to slow cooker.

3. Season chicken with salt and pepper and transfer to slow cooker. Stir in andouille, okra, bay leaves, and remaining 2 cups broth. Cook on low until chicken is tender, 4 to 5 hours.

4. Transfer chicken to plate. Using 2 forks, shred chicken into bite-size pieces. Skim any excess fat from surface of gumbo and discard bay leaves. Stir in scallion whites and chicken. Serve over rice, sprinkled with scallion greens, passing hot sauce separately.

Slow-Cooker Homey Chicken Stew

Serves 6 to 8   Cook Time 4 to 5 hours on low

Why This Recipe Works To make a chicken stew in which the simple, pure flavor of a rich broth married with tender chicken and vegetables would shine through, we had to start by browning boneless, skinless thighs, which both gave them extra flavor and rendered some of their fat and juice (which later made their way into the slow cooker). We also sautéed aromatics with a little tomato paste, which added richness without a noticeable tomatoey presence. In early tests we discovered that our chunky potatoes as well as the sliced carrots were just not tender by the time the chicken had finished

---

NOTES FROM THE TEST KITCHEN

FOR BETTER SLOW COOKING, GET OUT A SKILLET (SOMETIMES)

Slow cookers promise hands-off cooking, and we partly agree, but we think it's often better to start with a skillet. Just 5 or 10 minutes of sautéing or browning can make all the difference between a meal that's simply expedient and one that is great. Browning a flavorful fond, rendering fat, even making a roux all build richness and depth up front before the slow cooker's low, gentle cooking finishes the work. And we turn to skillets (or the microwave) to soften aromatics and vegetables to ensure that they come out perfectly tender.

Slow-Cooker Chicken and Corn Chowder

Slow-Cooker Chicken and Sausage Gumbo

Slow-Cooker Homey Chicken Stew

Slow-Cooker Chicken Mulligatawny Soup

cooking. So we gave them a head start by briefly simmering them in the skillet with the aromatics, which ensured that we could have tender vegetables in our finished stew.

 3 pounds boneless, skinless chicken thighs, trimmed, divided
 ½ teaspoon table salt
 ¼ teaspoon pepper
 3 tablespoons vegetable oil, divided
 2 onions, chopped fine
 ⅓ cup all-purpose flour
 6 garlic cloves, minced
 1 tablespoon tomato paste
 2 teaspoons minced fresh thyme or ½ teaspoon dried
 4 cups chicken broth, divided, plus extra as needed
 ½ cup dry white wine
12 ounces red potatoes, unpeeled, cut into ½-inch pieces
 4 carrots, peeled and sliced ¼-inch thick
 2 bay leaves
 1 cup frozen peas
 2 tablespoons minced fresh parsley

1. Pat chicken dry with paper towels and sprinkle with salt and pepper. Heat 1 tablespoon oil in 12-inch skillet over medium-high heat until just smoking. Cook half of chicken until browned on both sides, about 8 minutes; transfer to slow cooker. Repeat with 1 tablespoon oil and remaining chicken; transfer to slow cooker.

2. Heat remaining 1 tablespoon oil in now-empty skillet over medium heat until shimmering. Add onions and cook until softened and lightly browned, 8 to 10 minutes. Stir in flour, garlic, tomato paste, and thyme and cook until fragrant, about 1 minute. Slowly whisk in 2 cups broth and wine, scraping up any browned bits and smoothing out any lumps. Stir in potatoes and carrots and bring to simmer. Cover, reduce heat to medium-low, and simmer until vegetables just begin to soften, about 10 minutes; transfer to slow cooker.

3. Stir remaining 2 cups broth and bay leaves into slow cooker, cover, and cook until chicken is tender, 4 to 5 hours on low.

4. Transfer chicken to cutting board, let cool slightly, then pull apart into large chunks using 2 forks. Discard bay leaves.

5. Stir chicken and peas into stew and let sit until heated through, about 5 minutes. Adjust consistency with extra hot broth as needed. Stir in parsley and season with salt and pepper to taste. Serve.

Slow-Cooker Chicken Mulligatawny Soup

Serves 8   **Cook Time** 4 to 5 hours on low

Why This Recipe Works This classic Anglo-Indian soup features a spiced and pureed base enriched with lentils and tender shredded chicken. To make it in the slow cooker, we started by sautéing aromatics (which would never soften in the cooker) on the stovetop. Since the slow cooker doesn't allow for evaporation and reduction, using a higher ratio of flour to liquid gave our soup the right consistency. Shredded coconut turned stringy in our soup, but we found that swapping out some of the liquid for canned coconut milk gave just the right sweet creaminess to balance the bold spices—a heady mix of ginger, curry powder, garam masala, and cayenne. Cut the carrots into ½-inch pieces or they won't cook through. If the carrots are more than ½ inch in diameter, halve or quarter them lengthwise.

  3 tablespoons unsalted butter
  2 onions, chopped
  4 carrots, peeled and cut into ½-inch pieces
  1 celery rib, minced
1½ tablespoons grated fresh ginger
  4 garlic cloves, minced
  1 tablespoon tomato paste
  1 tablespoon curry powder
  2 teaspoons garam masala
  1 teaspoon table salt
  ¼ teaspoon cayenne pepper
  ⅓ cup all-purpose flour
  5 cups chicken broth
1½ pounds boneless, skinless chicken thighs, trimmed and cut into 1½-inch pieces
  1 (14-ounce) can coconut milk
  ½ cup brown lentils, picked over and rinsed
    Plain yogurt
    Chopped fresh cilantro leaves
    Lime wedges

1. Melt butter in large saucepan over medium heat. Add onions, carrots, and celery and cook until onions are softened and just beginning to brown, 10 to 14 minutes. Add ginger, garlic, tomato paste, curry powder, garam masala, salt, and cayenne and cook until fragrant, about 30 seconds. Stir in flour and cook for 1 minute. Slowly whisk in broth, scraping up any browned bits. Bring to boil, reduce heat to medium-low, and simmer until thickened, about 5 minutes. Transfer to slow cooker. Stir in chicken, coconut milk, and lentils.

2. Cover and cook until chicken and lentils are tender, 4 to 5 hours on low. Let sit, uncovered, for 5 minutes. Using large spoon, skim fat from surface of soup. Season soup with salt and pepper to taste. Ladle into serving bowls. Garnish with yogurt and cilantro. Serve with lime wedges.

Slow-Cooker Chicken and Dumplings

Serves 8   **Cook Time** 4 to 5 hours on low

Why This Recipe Works Chicken and dumplings on the stovetop is a classic winter meal, but move it to a slow cooker and you get a slew of problems—chewy chicken, lackluster flavor, and gummy dumplings, to name a few. Since dark meat is flavorful and can stand up to long cooking without drying out, we started with boneless, skinless chicken thighs. We browned the meat, vegetables, and aromatics on the stovetop to build a base of flavor, and added tomato paste, dried herbs, and bay leaves—hardy ingredients that could stand up to the slow cooker. After the chicken and vegetables cooked for 4 to 5 hours, we arranged the dumplings around the perimeter of the slow-cooker insert (where heating elements are) to ensure that they cooked through. You will need an oval slow cooker for this recipe.

Filling
  3 pounds boneless, skinless chicken thighs, trimmed
  ½ teaspoon table salt
  ¼ teaspoon pepper
  3 tablespoons vegetable oil, divided
  2 onions, chopped fine
  2 celery ribs, sliced ¼ inch thick
  2 carrots, peeled and cut into ¼-inch pieces
  ¼ cup all-purpose flour
  4 garlic cloves, minced
  1 tablespoon tomato paste
  1 tablespoon minced fresh thyme or 1 teaspoon dried
  4 cups chicken broth, divided, plus extra as needed
  ½ cup dry white wine
  2 bay leaves
  1 cup frozen peas, thawed

Dumplings
1¾ cups (8¾ ounces) all-purpose flour
  1 tablespoon baking powder
  1 teaspoon table salt
  1 cup whole milk
  4 tablespoons unsalted butter, melted

1. For the filling Pat chicken dry with paper towels and sprinkle with salt and pepper. Heat 1 tablespoon oil in 12-inch skillet over medium-high heat until just smoking. Cook half of chicken until browned on both sides, about 8 minutes; transfer to slow cooker. Repeat with 1 tablespoon oil and remaining chicken; transfer to slow cooker.

2. Heat remaining 1 tablespoon oil in now-empty skillet over medium heat until shimmering. Add onions, celery, and carrots and cook until softened and lightly browned, 8 to 10 minutes. Stir in flour, garlic, tomato paste, and thyme and cook until fragrant, about 1 minute. Slowly stir in 1 cup broth and wine, scraping up any browned bits and smoothing out any lumps; transfer to slow cooker.

3. Stir remaining 3 cups broth and bay leaves into slow cooker. Cover and cook until chicken is tender, 4 to 5 hours on low.

4. Discard bay leaves. Transfer chicken to cutting board, let cool slightly, then pull apart into large chunks using 2 forks. Stir chicken and peas into filling. Adjust consistency with extra hot broth as needed.

5. For the dumplings Whisk flour, baking powder, and salt together in large bowl. Stir in milk and melted butter until just incorporated. Using greased ¼-cup measure, drop 8 dumplings around perimeter of filling. Cover and cook on high until dumplings have doubled in size, 30 to 40 minutes. Serve.

ARRANGING DUMPLINGS IN THE SLOW COOKER

Using ¼-cup measure, drop dumplings around perimeter of slow cooker.

Slow-Cooker Spicy Chipotle Chicken Chili

Serves 2   **Total Time** 2 to 3 hours on low

Why This Recipe Works This hearty chili features a spicy broth with bites of tender shredded chicken and chickpeas. We microwaved aromatics, chili powder and canned chipotles to soften them and release their flavor, creating a smoky base for the chili. We then stirred this mixture into the slow cooker, adding our chicken and broth, and let everything gently cook. Creamy canned chickpeas were an easy addition to bulk up

the chili, and we mashed a portion of the beans after cooking to thicken it. Frozen corn, another easy addition, lent a pop of color and a nice textural contrast when stirred in at the end to just heat through. Bright, herbaceous cilantro, stirred in just before serving, added freshness and balance to our spicy, healthy chili. Serve with your favorite chili garnishes.

 1 onion, chopped fine
 1 teaspoon canola oil
 1 teaspoon minced canned chipotle chile in
    adobo sauce
 1 garlic clove, minced
 1 teaspoon tomato paste
 ½ teaspoon chili powder
1½ cups chicken broth
 1 (15-ounce) can chickpeas, rinsed
 ¼ teaspoon table salt
 1 (12-ounce) bone-in split chicken breast,
    skin removed, trimmed of all visible fat
 1 cup frozen corn, thawed
 2 tablespoons minced fresh cilantro

1. Lightly spray inside of slow cooker with vegetable oil spray. Microwave onion, oil, chipotle, garlic, tomato paste, and chili powder in bowl, stirring occasionally, until onion is softened, about 5 minutes; transfer to slow cooker. Stir in broth, chickpeas, and salt. Nestle chicken into slow cooker, cover, and cook until chicken is tender, 2 to 3 hours on low.

2. Transfer chicken to carving board, let cool slightly, then shred into bite-size pieces using 2 forks; discard bones.

3. Transfer 1 cup cooked chickpeas to bowl and mash with potato masher until mostly smooth. Stir shredded chicken, mashed chickpeas, and corn into chili and let sit until heated through, about 5 minutes. Stir in cilantro and season with salt and pepper to taste. Serve.

Slow-Cooker Turkey Chili

Serves 8 to 10   **Cook Time** 4 to 5 hours on low

Why This Recipe Works Turkey chili is a great alternative to classic beef chili, providing a leaner but no less flavorful meal for the dinner table. To help protect our ground turkey from drying out, we enlisted the help of a panade—typically a paste of bread and milk—to provide added moisture. Here, however, in place of milk we used soy sauce, which helped reinforce the meatiness of the lean meat. Here, be sure to use ground turkey, not ground turkey breast (also labeled 99 percent fat-free), in this recipe. Serve with your favorite chili garnishes.

- 2 slices hearty white sandwich bread, torn into 1-inch pieces
- ¼ cup soy sauce
- 2 pounds ground turkey
- 3 tablespoons vegetable oil
- 3 onions, chopped fine
- 1 red bell pepper, stemmed, seeded, and chopped
- ¼ cup chili powder
- ¼ cup tomato paste
- 6 garlic cloves, minced
- 1 tablespoon ground cumin
- ¾ teaspoon dried oregano
- 1¼ cups chicken broth, plus extra as needed
- 2 (15-ounce) cans kidney beans, rinsed
- 1 (28-ounce) can diced tomatoes, drained
- 1 (15-ounce) can tomato sauce
- 1 tablespoon packed brown sugar
- 2 teaspoons minced canned chipotle chile in adobo sauce

1. Mash bread and soy sauce into paste in large bowl using fork. Add ground turkey and knead with your hands until well combined.

2. Heat oil in 12-inch skillet over medium heat until shimmering. Add onions and bell pepper and cook until softened and lightly browned, 8 to 10 minutes. Stir in chili powder, tomato paste, garlic, cumin, and oregano and cook until fragrant, about 1 minute.

3. Add half of turkey mixture and cook, breaking up turkey with wooden spoon, until no longer pink, about 5 minutes. Repeat with remaining turkey mixture. Stir in broth, scraping up any browned bits; transfer to slow cooker.

4. Stir beans, tomatoes, tomato sauce, sugar, and chipotle into slow cooker. Cover and cook until turkey is tender, 4 to 5 hours on low. Break up any remaining large pieces of turkey with spoon. Adjust consistency with extra hot broth as needed. Season with salt and pepper to taste. Serve.

MAKING A PANADE

Using fork, mash bread and milk (or other liquid) into paste.

Slow-Cooker Spicy Chipotle Chicken Chili

Slow-Cooker Chicken with "Roasted" Garlic Sauce

Serves 4   Cook Time 2 to 3 hours on low

Why This Recipe Works It's often the simplest meals that are the hardest to re-create in the slow cooker; tender, perfectly cooked bone-in chicken with a garlicky gravy is no exception. For a richly flavored and satisfying gravy, we turned to 15 whole cloves of garlic plus a shallot to lend a roasted flavor and body to our sauce. To end up with aromatics soft enough to puree into a smooth gravy, we found it necessary to jump-start their cooking by sautéing them on the stovetop until lightly browned. Giving the shallots and garlic time to brown also added to the subtle roasted taste and deepened their overall flavor, which became sweeter and mellower after hours in the slow cooker. With the aromatics already in the skillet, adding a small amount of flour was a quick and easy way to thicken the sauce, and deglazing with wine and broth ensured that the flavorful browned bits in the bottom of the pan ended up in the slow cooker. The addition of soy sauce helped to round out the overall flavor of the sauce. Rosemary

Slow-Cooker Chicken with "Roasted" Garlic Sauce

and chives enlivened the gravy with fresh flavors. You will need an oval slow cooker for this recipe. Check the chicken's temperature after 2 hours of cooking and continue to monitor until it registers 160 degrees.

4 (12-ounce) bone-in split chicken breasts, trimmed
¼ teaspoon table salt
⅛ teaspoon pepper
1 tablespoon vegetable oil
15 garlic cloves, peeled
1 shallot, peeled and quartered
3 tablespoons all-purpose flour
½ teaspoon minced fresh rosemary or ⅛ teaspoon dried
⅔ cup dry white wine
½ cup chicken broth
1 tablespoon soy sauce
1 tablespoon minced fresh chives

1. Pat chicken dry with paper towels and sprinkle with salt and pepper. Heat oil in 12-inch skillet over medium-high heat until just smoking. Cook chicken until browned on both sides, 6 to 8 minutes; transfer to plate and discard skin.

2. Add garlic and shallot to fat left in skillet and cook over medium-low heat until lightly browned and fragrant, 8 to 10 minutes. Stir in flour and rosemary and cook for 1 minute. Slowly whisk in wine, broth, and soy sauce, scraping up any browned bits and smoothing out any lumps; transfer to slow cooker.

3. Arrange chicken, skinned side up, in even layer in slow cooker, adding any accumulated juices. Cover and cook until chicken registers 160 degrees, 2 to 3 hours on low.

4. Transfer chicken to serving dish. Process cooking liquid in blender until smooth, about 30 seconds. Stir in chives and season with salt and pepper to taste. Serve chicken with sauce.

Slow-Cooker Chicken with Mushrooms and Tarragon Cream Sauce

Serves 4   Cook Time 2 to 3 hours on low

Why This Recipe Works To get the richest and deepest chicken flavor for this creamy, company-worthy braised chicken, we opted to get out a skillet and brown bone-in chicken breasts. Since we had our skillet out, we also browned the mushrooms and aromatics and deglazed the pan with white wine, seriously

Slow-Cooker Chicken with Mushrooms and Tarragon Cream Sauce

elevating the overall flavor. We further boosted the flavor with an unusual ingredient, soy sauce, which brought an extra level of meatiness without taking over. We added cream at the end of the cooking time, along with a hefty dose of fresh tarragon for bright flavor. You will need an oval slow cooker for this recipe. Check the chicken's temperature after 2 hours of cooking and continue to monitor until it registers 160 degrees.

4 (12-ounce) bone-in split chicken breasts, trimmed
½ teaspoon table salt, divided
⅛ teaspoon pepper
2 tablespoons vegetable oil, divided
1¼ pounds cremini mushrooms, trimmed and halved if small or quartered if large
2 onions, chopped fine
¼ cup all-purpose flour
4 garlic cloves, minced
2 teaspoons minced fresh thyme or ½ teaspoon dried
¾ cup dry white wine
2 tablespoons soy sauce
2 bay leaves
¼ cup heavy cream
2 tablespoons minced fresh tarragon

1. Pat chicken dry with paper towels and sprinkle with ¼ teaspoon salt and pepper. Heat 1 tablespoon oil in 12-inch skillet over medium-high heat until just smoking. Cook chicken until browned on both sides, 6 to 8 minutes; transfer to plate and discard skin.

2. Heat remaining 1 tablespoon oil in now-empty skillet over medium heat until shimmering. Add mushrooms, onions, and remaining ¼ teaspoon salt, cover, and cook until vegetables are softened and mushrooms have released their liquid, about 5 minutes. Uncover and continue to cook until vegetables are dry and lightly browned, 5 to 7 minutes. Stir in flour, garlic, and thyme and cook until fragrant, about 1 minute. Slowly stir in wine, scraping up any browned bits and smoothing out any lumps; transfer to slow cooker.

3. Stir soy sauce and bay leaves into slow cooker. Arrange chicken, skinned side up, in even layer in slow cooker, adding any accumulated juices. Cover and cook until chicken registers 160 degrees, 2 to 3 hours on low.

4. Transfer chicken to serving dish. Discard bay leaves. Stir cream and tarragon into cooking liquid. Adjust consistency with hot water as needed. Season with salt and pepper to taste. Spoon vegetables and sauce over chicken and serve.

Slow-Cooker Chicken with Tomatoes, Olives, and Cilantro

Serves 4   **Cook Time** 2 to 3 hours on low

Why This Recipe Works The bright flavors of cilantro and lime juice enliven this simple dish of chicken in a chunky tomato sauce, while green olives offer briny contrast. Most slow-cooker tomato-based recipes result in a dull, waterlogged tomato sauce, so we looked to give our dish a richer texture with a bright and assertive tomato flavor. Our testing revealed that canned diced tomatoes with their juice had the fresh tomato taste we wanted but created too much liquid during cooking. Compounded with the juices from the chicken, they created a thin, dull sauce. Draining the diced tomatoes, plus adding tomato paste and a small amount of tapioca, created the thickened sauce we were after. Oregano and cumin added depth to balance the brighter elements. Adding the green olives, cilantro, and lime juice at the last minute kept their flavors fresh. You will need an oval slow cooker for this recipe. Check the chicken's temperature after 2 hours of cooking and continue to monitor until it registers 160 degrees.

1 onion, halved and sliced thin
4 garlic cloves, sliced thin
1 tablespoon vegetable oil
1 tablespoon tomato paste
2 teaspoons minced fresh oregano or ½ teaspoon dried
¼ teaspoon ground cumin
1 (14.5-ounce) can diced tomatoes, drained
1 teaspoon instant tapioca
4 (12-ounce) bone-in split chicken breasts, skin removed, trimmed
½ teaspoon table salt
¼ teaspoon pepper
⅓ cup pitted large brine-cured green olives, chopped coarse
2 tablespoons minced fresh cilantro
1 tablespoon lime juice

1. Microwave onion, garlic, oil, tomato paste, oregano, and cumin in bowl, stirring occasionally, until onion is softened, about 5 minutes; transfer to slow cooker. Stir in tomatoes and tapioca. Sprinkle chicken with salt and pepper and arrange, skinned side up, in even layer in slow cooker. Cover and cook until chicken registers 160 degrees, 2 to 3 hours on low.

2. Transfer chicken to serving dish. Stir olives, cilantro, and lime juice into sauce and season with salt and pepper to taste. Spoon sauce over chicken and serve.

Slow-Cooker Chicken with Fennel and Tomato Couscous

Serves 4   **Total Time** 2 to 3 hours on low

Why This Recipe Works For a simple braised chicken dinner with fresh Italian flavors, we combined bone-in chicken breasts with fennel and bright cherry tomatoes. Chicken broth flavored with garlic, salt, and pepper made a simple cooking liquid that seasoned the chicken as it simmered and helped it to cook gently and evenly. Once the chicken was cooked, we used the flavorful cooking liquid, enriched with the chicken's juices, to cook couscous for a quick and easy side dish. A quick basil vinaigrette brought freshness and acidity when drizzled over both the chicken and the couscous. Be sure to use regular (or fine-grain) couscous; large-grain couscous, often labeled "Israeli-style" or pearl, takes much longer to cook and won't work in this recipe. You will need an oval slow cooker for this recipe. Check the chicken's temperature after 2 hours of cooking and continue to monitor until it registers 160 degrees.

- 1 fennel bulb, stalks discarded, bulb halved, cored, and sliced thin
- 5 tablespoons extra-virgin olive oil, divided
- 3 garlic cloves, minced, divided
- ¾ teaspoon table salt, divided
- ½ teaspoon plus ⅛ teaspoon pepper, divided
- ½ cup chicken broth
- 4 (12-ounce) bone-in split chicken breasts, skin removed, trimmed
- 8 ounces cherry tomatoes, halved
- 1 cup couscous
- ¼ cup chopped fresh basil
- 2 tablespoon white wine vinegar
- 2 teaspoons honey
- ½ teaspoon Dijon mustard

1. Microwave fennel, 1 tablespoon oil, two-thirds of garlic, ½ teaspoon salt, and ½ teaspoon pepper in bowl, stirring occasionally, until fennel is tender, about 5 minutes; transfer to slow cooker. Stir in broth. Sprinkle chicken with remaining ¼ teaspoon salt and remaining ⅛ teaspoon pepper and arrange, skinned side up, in even layer in slow cooker. Sprinkle tomatoes over chicken, cover, and cook until chicken registers 160 degrees, 2 to 3 hours on low.

2. Transfer chicken to serving dish and tent with aluminum foil. Strain cooking liquid into fat separator, reserving vegetables. Return vegetables and 1 cup defatted liquid to now-empty slow cooker; discard remaining liquid. Stir in couscous, cover, and cook on high until tender, about 15 minutes.

3. Whisk basil, vinegar, honey, mustard, remaining ¼ cup oil, and remaining garlic together in bowl. Season with salt and pepper to taste. Add 3 tablespoons dressing to cooked couscous and fluff with fork to combine. Drizzle chicken with remaining dressing and serve with couscous.

Slow-Cooker Sesame-Ginger Chicken and Sweet Potatoes

Serves 4   **Cook Time** 2 to 3 hours on low

Why This Recipe Works Sesame and ginger make a classic flavoring for chicken and pair well with earthy sweet potatoes. To ensure deep seasoning, we used both flavors at multiple stages. We first bloomed a ginger-garlic oil in the microwave and rubbed that directly onto bone-in chicken breasts (skin removed) for a flavor boost. Microwaving the sweet potatoes before placing them in the bottom of the slow cooker softened them enough to ensure they would be fully tender when the chicken finished cooking. Once our chicken and potatoes were done, we whisked together a dressing with more ginger plus sesame oil, which we balanced with honey, spicy chili-garlic sauce, and rice vinegar. A sprinkle of toasted sesame seeds and sliced scallions adding a nutty, aromatic finish. You will need an oval slow cooker for this recipe. Check the chicken's temperature after 2 hours of cooking and continue to monitor until it registers 160 degrees.

- 3 tablespoons vegetable oil, divided
- 4 teaspoons grated fresh ginger, divided
- 3 garlic cloves, minced
- 1 teaspoon table salt, divided
- ¾ teaspoon pepper, divided
- 1½ pounds sweet potatoes, peeled, cut into 1-inch pieces
- 1 red bell pepper, stemmed, seeded, and cut into ¼-inch-wide strips
- 4 (12-ounce) bone-in split chicken breasts, skin removed, trimmed
- 2 tablespoons toasted sesame oil
- 1 tablespoon water
- 1 tablespoon rice vinegar
- 1 teaspoon honey
- 1 teaspoon Asian chili-garlic sauce
- 2 teaspoons sesame seeds, toasted
- 2 scallions, sliced thin on bias

1. Microwave 2 tablespoons vegetable oil, 1 tablespoon ginger, garlic, ½ teaspoon salt, and ½ teaspoon pepper in bowl until fragrant, about 30 seconds; let cool slightly.

2. Toss potatoes with remaining 1 tablespoon vegetable oil, remaining ½ teaspoon salt, and remaining ¼ teaspoon pepper in large bowl. Cover potatoes and microwave, stirring occasionally, until almost tender, 8 to 10 minutes; transfer to slow cooker with bell pepper. Rub chicken with ginger-oil mixture; arrange skinned side up in even layer in slow cooker. Cover and cook until chicken registers 160 degrees, 2 to 3 hours on low.

3. Whisk sesame oil, water, vinegar, honey, chili-garlic sauce, and remaining 1 teaspoon ginger in bowl until combined. Season with salt and pepper to taste. Transfer chicken to serving dish. Using slotted spoon, transfer vegetables to dish with chicken; drizzle with half of dressing. Sprinkle with sesame seeds and scallions. Serve, passing remaining dressing separately.

Slow-Cooker Lemon Chicken Thighs

Serves 6   **Cook Time** 4 to 6 hours on low

Why This Recipe Works We wanted braised lemon chicken with an appealing, vibrant, balanced lemon flavor that held true through hours of slow cooking. We chose bone-in chicken thighs for their ability to stay juicy for a long time, trimming them carefully and removing the skin to keep the finished dish from becoming too greasy. We tossed the trimmed chicken with olive oil and a pantry-friendly mix of black pepper, paprika, dried oregano, and granulated garlic. To give the dish a bright punch of lemon, we added lemon juice to the seasoned chicken before cooking and whisked finely grated lemon zest into the finished sauce. Serve with white rice.

- 8 (5- to 7-ounce) bone-in chicken thighs, skin removed, trimmed
- ¼ cup extra-virgin olive oil
- 2 teaspoons table salt
- 1 teaspoon pepper
- 1 teaspoon paprika
- 1 teaspoon dried oregano
- ¾ teaspoon granulated garlic
- 10 sprigs fresh thyme
- 1 teaspoon finely grated lemon zest plus ¼ cup juice (2 lemons)
- 2 tablespoons coarsely chopped fresh parsley

Slow-Cooker Chicken with Fennel and Tomato Couscous

Slow-Cooker Lemon Chicken Thighs

1. Add chicken, oil, salt, pepper, paprika, oregano, and granulated garlic to slow cooker and toss until chicken is well coated with spices. Nestle thyme sprigs into chicken mixture. Add lemon juice, taking care not to wash spices from top of chicken. Cover and cook until chicken is tender, 4 to 6 hours on low.

2. Discard thyme sprigs. Transfer chicken to shallow serving dish. Stir parsley and lemon zest into sauce in slow cooker, then spoon sauce over chicken. Serve.

Slow-Cooker Chicken Thighs with Black-Eyed Pea Ragout

Serves 4   **Cook Time** 4 to 5 hours on low

Why This Recipe Works Juicy chicken, tender black-eyed peas, and earthy kale are a great combination for a healthy and comforting supper. Sturdy kale is a perfect match for the slow cooker; after a quick spin in the microwave (along with onion, garlic, and oil) it could be added to the slow cooker to fully soften and cook through. To complement the bitter kale we wanted rich, slightly spicy black-eyed peas. We found that a combination of dry mustard and hot sauce was the key to getting the right balance between heat and spice. Dry mustard added to the slow cooker at the beginning of cooking infused the chicken with a subtle flavor, and finishing the peas with hot sauce punched up the heat and acidity of the dish. Pureeing a portion of the peas also helped to thicken the juices released from the chicken during cooking.

- 1 pound kale, stemmed and chopped coarse
- 1 onion, chopped fine
- 4 garlic cloves, minced
- 1 tablespoon vegetable oil
- 1 teaspoon dry mustard
- 2 teaspoons minced fresh thyme or ½ teaspoon dried
- ½ cup chicken broth
- 2 (15-ounce) cans black-eyed peas, rinsed, divided
- 8 (5- to 7-ounce) bone-in chicken thighs, skin removed, trimmed
- ¼ teaspoon table salt
- ⅛ teaspoon pepper
- 2 teaspoons hot sauce

1. Microwave kale, onion, garlic, oil, mustard, and thyme in covered bowl, stirring occasionally, until vegetables are softened, 5 to 7 minutes; transfer to slow cooker.

2. Process broth and one-third of peas in food processor until smooth, about 30 seconds; transfer to slow cooker.

Stir in remaining peas. Sprinkle chicken with salt and pepper and nestle into slow cooker. Cover and cook until chicken is tender, 4 to 5 hours on low.

3. Transfer chicken to serving dish. Stir hot sauce into ragout and season with salt and pepper to taste. Serve chicken with ragout.

Slow-Cooker Curried Chicken Thighs with Acorn Squash

Serves 4   **Cook Time** 4 to 5 hours on low

Why This Recipe Works Meaty chicken thighs are a perfect match for the slow cooker, as they become meltingly tender in its moist heat environment. Here we opted to pair them with wedges of acorn squash, which are hearty enough to withstand a few hours in the slow cooker and still hold their shape. To give this dish a distinct flavor profile we rubbed the chicken with curry powder that we had bloomed in the microwave with a little bit of oil. To finish, we microwaved a mixture of honey and cayenne, to which we added lime juice, and then drizzled the mixture over the chicken and squash. This simple step tied together the flavors of this easy one-dish meal. You will need an oval slow cooker for this recipe.

- 2 small acorn squashes (1 pound each), quartered pole to pole and seeded
- 1 tablespoon vegetable oil
- 2 teaspoons curry powder
- ½ teaspoon table salt
- ¼ teaspoon pepper
- 8 (5- to 7-ounce) bone-in chicken thighs, skin removed, trimmed
- 3 tablespoons honey
- ⅛ teaspoon cayenne pepper
- 1 tablespoon lime juice
- ¼ cup fresh cilantro leaves

1. Shingle squash wedges, cut side down, into slow cooker, then add ½ cup water. Microwave oil, curry powder, salt, and pepper in bowl until fragrant, about 30 seconds; let cool slightly. Rub chicken with curry mixture and arrange in single layer on top of squash. Cover and cook until chicken is tender, 4 to 5 hours on low.

2. Transfer chicken and squash to serving dish; discard cooking liquid. Microwave honey and cayenne in bowl until heated through, about 30 seconds. Stir in lime juice. Drizzle chicken and squash with honey mixture and sprinkle with cilantro. Serve.

Slow-Cooker Kimchi-Braised Chicken Thighs

Serves 4 **Cook Time** 4 to 5 hours on low

Why This Recipe Works In this Korean-inspired dish, spicy kimchi pairs well with rich bone-in chicken thighs, which are fattier and meatier than breasts. We reinforced the flavors by flavoring our braising liquid with scallions, garlic, soy sauce, sugar, sesame oil, and fresh ginger. To get the most flavor from the kimchi and prevent it from tasting washed out, we added it toward the end of cooking.

1 cup chicken broth
4 scallions, white and green parts separated and sliced thin
6 garlic cloves, minced
2 tablespoons instant tapioca
1 tablespoon soy sauce
1 tablespoon sugar
1 tablespoon toasted sesame oil
1 teaspoon grated fresh ginger
8 (5- to 7-ounce) bone-in chicken thighs, skin removed, trimmed
⅛ teaspoon pepper
2 cups cabbage kimchi, drained and chopped coarse

1. Combine broth, scallion whites, garlic, tapioca, soy sauce, sugar, oil, and ginger in slow cooker. Sprinkle chicken with pepper and nestle into slow cooker. Cover and cook until chicken is tender, 4 to 5 hours on low.

2. Stir in kimchi, cover, and cook on high until tender, 20 to 30 minutes. Transfer chicken and kimchi to serving dish. Spoon 1 cup sauce over chicken and sprinkle with scallion greens. Serve, passing remaining sauce separately.

Slow-Cooker Chicken Tikka Masala

Serves 4 **Cook Time** 2 to 3 hours on low

Why This Recipe Works We wanted to create a flavorful take on chicken tikka masala that had tender, moist pieces of chicken napped with a robustly spiced creamy tomato sauce. While traditionally this dish calls for marinating the chicken overnight to infuse flavor and then cooking the sauce separately, we turned to our slow cooker for a hands-off version that would infuse big flavor into the chicken without marinating while cooking the dish to perfection. First we needed the

Slow-Cooker Curried Chicken Thighs with Acorn Squash

Slow-Cooker Chicken Tikka Masala

perfect sauce. Fresh tomatoes and canned tomato sauce both released too much liquid during cooking, which created a thin sauce made worse by the juices released by the chicken. Switching to drained canned diced tomatoes along with flavor-packed tomato paste proved to be the answer; and when we added garlic, ginger, a serrano chile for heat, plus garam masala, our sauce had the bold, zesty flavor that is the hallmark of this dish. After cooking, to finish the dish, we added some yogurt, tempering it first with a bit of braising liquid to ensure a velvety sauce. For a spicier dish, do not remove the ribs and seeds from the chile.

1 onion, chopped fine
3 tablespoons vegetable oil
1 serrano chile, stemmed, seeded, and minced
2 tablespoons tomato paste
4 teaspoons garam masala
3 garlic cloves, minced
1 tablespoon grated fresh ginger
2 teaspoons sugar
1 teaspoon table salt, divided
1 (14.5-ounce) can diced tomatoes, drained
2 pounds boneless, skinless chicken breasts, trimmed and cut into 1½-inch pieces
¼ teaspoon pepper
¾ cup plain whole-milk yogurt
¼ cup minced fresh cilantro

1. Microwave onion, oil, serrano, tomato paste, garam masala, garlic, ginger, sugar, and ½ teaspoon salt in bowl, stirring occasionally, until onion is softened, about 5 minutes; transfer to slow cooker. Stir in tomatoes. Sprinkle chicken with pepper and remaining ½ teaspoon salt and stir into slow cooker. Cover and cook until chicken is tender, 2 to 3 hours on low.

2. Whisk ½ cup sauce and yogurt together in bowl (to temper), then stir mixture back into slow cooker and let sit until heated through, about 5 minutes. Stir in cilantro and season with salt and pepper to taste. Serve.

Slow-Cooker Southern Smothered Chicken

Serves 4   Cook Time 4 to 5 hours on low

Why This Recipe Works The traditional Southern style of "smothered" chicken involves cooking the chicken low-and-slow in a rich gravy. Too often, though, versions of smothered chicken taste like whatever else is in the dish, rather than the chicken itself. But smothered chicken is designed to coax

out as much flavor as possible from the chicken, and the slow cooker is the perfect tool for the job. To start, we tossed chicken thighs in flour and browned them in batches in a skillet to render some fat and build a base of flavor. Once the chicken was browned, we moved it to the slow cooker and used some of the residual fat to sauté the aromatic ingredients for the sauce. A simple mix of onion, celery, garlic, and sage gave a clean, savory base that enhanced the rich chicken flavor. Achieving the right consistency for the sauce took some tinkering. In the end, we found that just 1 cup of chicken broth with 2 tablespoons of flour made for a velvety rich sauce, and was plenty to smother the chicken for serving. Once the sauce was added to the slow cooker, we cooked everything until the chicken was tender and our sauce was deeply flavorful. This simple braise may not be flashy, but its robust chicken flavor, brought to life in the slow cooker, is deeply satisfying.

8 (5- to 7-ounce) bone-in chicken thighs, trimmed
1¼ teaspoons table salt, divided
⅛ teaspoon plus ½ teaspoon pepper, divided
½ cup plus 2 tablespoons all-purpose flour, divided
¼ cup vegetable oil
2 onions, chopped fine
2 celery ribs, chopped fine
3 garlic cloves, minced
1 tablespoon minced fresh sage or 1 teaspoon dried
1 cup chicken broth
1 tablespoon cider vinegar
1 tablespoon minced fresh parsley

1. Pat chicken dry with paper towels and sprinkle with ¼ teaspoon salt and ⅛ teaspoon pepper. Spread ½ cup flour in shallow dish. Working with 1 piece at a time, dredge chicken in flour, shaking off excess, and transfer to plate.

2. Heat oil in 12-inch skillet over medium-high heat until just smoking. Cook half of chicken until deep golden brown on both sides, 8 to 12 minutes. Transfer chicken, skin side up, to slow cooker; repeat with remaining chicken, adjusting heat as needed if flour begins to burn.

3. Pour off all but 2 tablespoons fat from skillet. Add onions, celery, remaining 1 teaspoon salt, and remaining ½ teaspoon pepper and cook over medium heat until vegetables are softened, about 8 minutes. Stir in garlic, sage, and remaining 2 tablespoons flour and cook until fragrant, about 1 minute. Slowly whisk in broth, scraping up any browned bits and smoothing any lumps; transfer to slow cooker. Cover and cook until chicken is tender, 4 to 5 hours on low.

4. Transfer chicken to serving dish. Using large spoon, skim excess fat from surface of sauce. Stir in vinegar and parsley, and season with salt and pepper to taste. Spoon 1 cup sauce over chicken. Serve, passing remaining sauce separately.

Slow-Cooker Jerk Chicken

8 scallions, chopped

¼ cup vegetable oil

2 habanero chiles, stemmed and seeded

1 (1-inch) piece ginger, peeled and sliced into ¼-inch-thick rounds

2 tablespoons molasses

3 garlic cloves, peeled

1 tablespoon dried thyme

2 teaspoons ground allspice

1 teaspoon table salt

4 pounds bone-in chicken pieces (thighs and/or drumsticks), trimmed

Lime wedges

1. Process scallions, oil, habaneros, ginger, molasses, garlic, thyme, allspice, and salt in food processor until smooth, about 30 seconds.

2. Lightly coat slow cooker with vegetable oil spray. Transfer ½ cup mixture to prepared slow cooker; reserve remaining mixture separately. Add chicken to slow cooker and turn to coat evenly with scallion mixture. Cover and cook until chicken is tender, 4 to 5 hours on low.

3. Adjust oven rack 6 inches from broiler element and heat broiler. Set wire rack in aluminum foil–lined rimmed baking sheet and coat with vegetable oil spray. Transfer chicken to prepared rack; discard cooking liquid. Broil chicken until browned, about 10 minutes, flipping chicken halfway through broiling.

4. Brush chicken with half of reserved scallion mixture and continue to broil until lightly charred, about 5 minutes, flipping and brushing chicken with remaining scallion mixture halfway through broiling. Serve with lime wedges.

Slow-Cooker Jerk Chicken

Serves 4 to 6   **Cook Time** 4 to 5 hours on low

Why This Recipe Works We wanted to use a slow cooker to create a satisfying jerk chicken, with fiery chiles, warm spices, and fragrant herbs—and we wanted it to taste just as good as its more common grilled counterpart. First, we used a food processor to make a smooth paste of the aromatic ingredients—scallions, garlic, habanero chiles (in place of traditionally used Scotch bonnets), and ginger—along with sticky molasses, dried thyme, allspice, salt, and oil to bind everything together. We coated the chicken with some of this paste before cooking and saved the rest for basting later on. Following a slow braise in the slow cooker, after which the chicken was tender but still intact, we finished it under the broiler, brushing it with more of the paste until it was lightly charred and crisp. If you can't find habanero chiles, substitute two to four jalapeño chiles. For even more heat, include the chile seeds.

WORKING WITH HABANERO PEPPERS

Wear gloves when working with very hot peppers like habaneros to avoid direct contact with oils that supply heat. Wash your hands, knife, and cutting board well after prepping chiles.

Slow-Cooker Barbecue Pulled Chicken

Slow-Cooker Barbecue Pulled Chicken

Serves 10 **Cook Time** 5 hours on low

Why This Recipe Works To produce a big batch of tender barbecued chicken in the slow cooker that tastes likes it's straight off the grill, we ditched the bottled sauce and made our own. We found that microwaving the onion both softened and caramelized it, and including tomato paste, chili powder, garlic, and cayenne deepened the flavors. We supplemented our sauce with liquid smoke (a natural product) to replicate the smoky grill flavor. For chicken, two cuts were better than one: Bone-in breasts shredded nicely and boneless thighs added meaty flavor. Use a relatively mild hot sauce, like Frank's, or the sauce will be too hot.

- 5 (10- to 12-ounce) bone-in split chicken breasts, trimmed
- 7 (3-ounce) boneless, skinless chicken thighs, trimmed
- ½ teaspoon table salt
- ¼ teaspoon pepper
- 1 onion, chopped fine
- ½ cup tomato paste
- 2 tablespoons vegetable oil
- 5 teaspoons chili powder
- 3 garlic cloves, minced
- ¼ teaspoon cayenne pepper
- 1 cup ketchup
- ⅓ cup molasses
- 2 tablespoons brown mustard
- 4 teaspoons cider vinegar
- 4 teaspoons hot sauce
- ¾ teaspoon liquid smoke
- 10 sandwich rolls

1. Pat chicken dry with paper towels and sprinkle with salt and pepper. Combine onion, tomato paste, oil, chili powder, garlic, and cayenne in bowl and microwave until onion softens slightly, about 3 minutes, stirring halfway through microwaving. Transfer mixture to slow cooker and whisk in ketchup, molasses, mustard, and vinegar. Add chicken to slow cooker and toss to combine with sauce. Cover and cook on low until chicken shreds easily with fork, about 5 hours.

2. Transfer cooked chicken to carving board, tent with aluminum foil, and let rest for 15 minutes. Using large spoon, remove any fat from surface of sauce. Whisk hot sauce and liquid smoke into sauce and cover to keep warm. Remove and discard chicken skin and bones. Roughly chop thigh meat into ½-inch pieces. Shred breast meat into thin strands using 2 forks. Return meat to slow cooker and toss to coat with sauce. Season with salt and pepper to taste. Serve on sandwich rolls.

Slow-Cooker Sweet and Tangy Pulled Chicken

Slow-Cooker Sweet and Tangy Pulled Chicken

Serves 4   **Cook Time** 2 to 3 hours on low

Why This Recipe Works A simple spice mixture and a quick homemade barbecue sauce made it easy to turn slow-cooked bone-in chicken breasts into tangy, silky, shredded chicken—perfect for piling onto buns. Microwaving the aromatics with chili powder, paprika, and cayenne softened the onions and infused them with flavor while at the same time blooming the spices. We found that simply seasoning the chicken with salt and pepper before nestling the breasts into our sauce mixture of ketchup, molasses, and spiced aromatic was enough to infuse the chicken with the rich essence of the sauce. Stirring in vinegar at the beginning of cooking made the sauce too thin and dulled its acidity, but adding 2 tablespoons of vinegar at the end of cooking, along with a small amount of mustard, ensured that the sauce retained its bright flavors. Check the chicken's temperature after 2 hours of cooking and continue to monitor until it registers 160 degrees. Serve with pickle chips and Sweet and Tangy Coleslaw.

- 1 onion, chopped fine
- ¼ cup tomato paste
- 1 tablespoon chili powder
- 1 tablespoon vegetable oil
- 1 teaspoon paprika
- ½ teaspoon table salt
- ¼ teaspoon pepper
- ⅛ teaspoon cayenne pepper
- ¼ cup ketchup
- 2 tablespoons molasses
- 2 (12-ounce) bone-in split chicken breasts, skin removed, trimmed
- 2 tablespoons cider vinegar
- 2 teaspoons Dijon mustard
- 4 hamburger buns

1. Lightly coat slow cooker with vegetable oil spray. Microwave onion, tomato paste, chili powder, oil, paprika, salt, pepper, and cayenne in bowl, stirring occasionally, until onion is softened, about 5 minutes; transfer to prepared slow cooker. Stir in ketchup and molasses. Add chicken to slow cooker and coat evenly with sauce mixture. Cover and cook until chicken registers 160 degrees, 2 to 3 hours on low.

2. Transfer chicken to cutting board, let cool slightly, then shred into bite-size pieces using 2 forks; discard bones. Stir vinegar and mustard into sauce. Adjust consistency with hot water as needed. Stir in chicken and season with salt and pepper to taste. Serve on hamburger buns.

Sweet and Tangy Coleslaw

Serves 4

If you don't have a salad spinner, use a colander to drain the cabbage, pressing out the excess moisture with a rubber spatula. This recipe can be easily doubled.

- ¼ cup cider vinegar, plus extra for seasoning
- 2 tablespoons vegetable oil
- ¼ teaspoon celery seeds
- ¼ teaspoon pepper
- ½ head green or red cabbage, cored and shredded (6 cups)
- ¼ cup sugar, plus extra for seasoning
- 1 teaspoon table salt
- 1 large carrot, peeled and shredded
- 2 tablespoons chopped fresh parsley

1. Whisk vinegar, oil, celery seeds, and pepper together in medium bowl. Place bowl in freezer and chill until dressing is cold, at least 15 minutes or up to 30 minutes.

2. Meanwhile, in large bowl, toss cabbage with sugar and salt. Cover and microwave until cabbage is just beginning to wilt, about 1 minute. Stir briefly, cover, and continue to microwave until cabbage is partially wilted and has reduced in volume by one-third, 30 to 60 seconds.

3. Transfer cabbage mixture to salad spinner and spin until excess water is removed, 10 to 20 seconds. Remove bowl from freezer, add cabbage mixture, carrot, and parsley to cold dressing, and toss to coat. Season with salt, pepper, vinegar, and sugar to taste. Refrigerate until chilled, about 15 minutes. Toss coleslaw again before serving.

Slow-Cooker Tomatillo Chicken Soft Tacos

1 cup jarred tomatillo or tomato salsa
2 poblano chiles, stemmed, seeded, and chopped
¼ teaspoon table salt
¼ teaspoon pepper
1 teaspoon minced fresh oregano or ¼ teaspoon dried
3 pounds boneless, skinless chicken thighs, trimmed
¼ cup minced fresh cilantro
2 tablespoons lime juice
18 (6-inch) flour tortillas, warmed

1. Combine salsa, poblanos, salt, pepper, and oregano in slow cooker. Nestle chicken into slow cooker, cover, and cook until tender, 4 to 6 hours on low.

2. Using tongs, break chicken into bite-size pieces. Stir in cilantro and lime juice and season with salt and pepper to taste. Serve with tortillas.

Slow-Cooker Buffalo Chicken Wings

Serves 4 to 6   **Cook Time** 4 to 5 hours on low

Why This Recipe Works Great wings should have juicy, tender meat and a crisp coating. You might not consider making them in your slow cooker. True, the gentle heat of the slow cooker is great for achieving meltingly tender wings, but it is terrible at producing a good crisp coating. However, with a little re-imagining, great wings are possible in the slow cooker. To add serious flavor, we first tossed the wings with a hefty blend of spices and aromatics. We then cooked the wings on low for 4 to 5 hours, which turned them moist and incredibly tender. For a crisp exterior, a few minutes under the broiler was all it took. We found that basting the wings with sauce while they broiled kept the skin from fully crisping. Instead, we broiled the wings sans sauce and gently tossed them with it after broiling. These recipes can easily be doubled in a 7-quart slow cooker; you will need to broil the wings in two batches. Serve with Creamy Blue Cheese Dressing (page 299) and celery and carrot sticks.

4 pounds chicken wings, cut at joints and trimmed, wingtips discarded
1 tablespoon paprika
1 teaspoon cayenne pepper
1 teaspoon table salt
½ teaspoon pepper
½ cup Frank's RedHot Original Cayenne Pepper Sauce
6 tablespoons unsalted butter, melted
2 tablespoons molasses

Slow-Cooker Tomatillo Chicken Soft Tacos

Serves 6   **Cook Time** 4 to 6 hours on low

Why This Recipe Works The slow cooker offers a hands-off method for these simple chicken tacos. Cooking the chicken for our taco filling in store-bought tomatillo salsa flavored it in a big way without the time-consuming prep necessary for fresh tomatillos. Fresh poblano chiles lent a little heat to the sauce and created a more complex flavor profile than salsa alone, and a small amount of oregano enhanced and deepened the flavors even further. We found that boneless chicken thighs worked best here; they required little prep and after 4 to 6 hours in the slow cooker they were meltingly tender and easily shredded. Finishing with a little lime juice and cilantro added fresh flavor. Jarred tomatillo salsa is also called salsa verde. We don't discard any of the cooking liquid, as it helps season the chicken and keep the filling moist; a slotted spoon works best for serving the filling. Serve with lime wedges, diced avocado, queso fresco, and/or sour cream. For more information on warming tortillas, see page 97.

1. Lightly coat slow cooker with vegetable oil spray. Toss chicken with paprika, cayenne, salt, and pepper in slow cooker. Cover and cook until chicken is tender, 4 to 5 hours on low.

2. Adjust oven rack 6 inches from broiler element; heat broiler. Set wire rack in aluminum foil–lined rimmed baking sheet; coat with vegetable oil spray. Transfer chicken to pre-pared rack. Broil chicken until lightly charred and crisp, 15 to 20 minutes, flipping chicken halfway through broiling.

3. Whisk hot sauce, melted butter, and molasses in large bowl until combined. Gently toss chicken with sauce to coat. Serve.

VARIATIONS
Slow-Cooker Sticky Wings

Serves 4 to 6   **Cook Time** 4 to 5 hours on low

- ¾ cup packed dark brown sugar, divided
- ¼ cup soy sauce, divided
- 1 (3-inch) piece fresh ginger, peeled and chopped
- 4 garlic cloves, peeled
- ½ teaspoon cayenne pepper, divided
- 4 pounds chicken wings, cut at joints and trimmed, wingtips discarded
- ¼ cup water
- ¼ cup tomato paste

1. Pulse ¼ cup sugar, 1 tablespoon soy sauce, ginger, garlic, and ¼ teaspoon cayenne in food processor until finely ground. Add mixture to slow cooker. Add chicken and toss until combined.

2. Cover and cook until chicken is tender, 4 to 5 hours on low. Using slotted spoon, remove wings from slow cooker and transfer to clean large bowl (discard liquid in slow cooker). Let wings cool for 20 minutes (or cool briefly and refrigerate for up to 24 hours).

3. Adjust oven rack 6 inches from broiler element; heat broiler. Set wire rack in aluminum foil–lined rimmed baking sheet; coat with vegetable oil spray. Whisk water, tomato paste, remaining ½ cup sugar, remaining 3 tablespoons soy sauce, and remaining ¼ teaspoon cayenne in bowl. Add half of sauce to bowl with cooled wings and toss gently to coat. Arrange wings, skin side up, on prepared rack. Broil until wings are lightly charred and crisp around edges, about 15 minutes. Flip wings, brush with remaining sauce, and continue to broil until well caramelized, 3 to 5 minutes. Serve.

Slow-Cooker Mango-Curry Wings

Serves 4 to 6   **Cook Time** 4 to 5 hours on low

- 4 pounds chicken wings, cut at joints and trimmed, wingtips discarded
- 1 tablespoon paprika

Slow-Cooker Sticky Wings

- 1 tablespoon curry powder
- 2 teaspoons ground cumin
- 1 teaspoon table salt
- ½ teaspoon pepper
- ¾ cup mango chutney
- 1 shallot, minced
- 3 tablespoons water
- 1 tablespoon minced fresh cilantro
- 1 teaspoon grated lime zest

1. Lightly coat slow cooker with vegetable oil spray. Toss chicken with paprika, curry powder, cumin, salt, and pepper in slow cooker. Cover and cook until chicken is tender, 4 to 5 hours on low.

2. Adjust oven rack 6 inches from broiler element; heat broiler. Set wire rack in aluminum foil–lined rimmed baking sheet; coat with vegetable oil spray. Transfer chicken to pre-pared rack. Broil chicken until lightly charred and crisp, 15 to 20 minutes, flipping chicken halfway through broiling.

3. Whisk chutney, shallot, water, cilantro, and lime zest together in bowl. Gently toss chicken with sauce to coat. Serve.

Slow-Cooker Harissa-Spiced Chicken in a Pot

Serves 4   Cook Time 4 to 5 hours on low

Why This Recipe Works There's lots to like about slow-cooking a whole chicken: There's no need to monitor the oven or truss or rotate the bird. But getting good results does require a few tricks. We discovered that when we placed a whole chicken breast side down, a moister bird resulted because the dark meat rendered its fat and juices down over and through the breast and kept it from overcooking as the dark meat reached the proper temperature. As the juices pooled in the bottom of the cooker, they submerged the breast, enabling it to retain more moisture. Without the flavor contributed from browning, we needed to rely on potent seasonings. Here, we prepared a harissa spice mix in the microwave and rubbed a portion under the skin to give it direct contact with the meat while it cooked, rubbing the remainder onto the skin, coating the entire bird. Check the chicken's temperature after 4 hours of cooking and continue to monitor until the breast registers 160 degrees and the thighs register 175 degrees. You will need an oval slow cooker for this recipe.

    3 tablespoons extra-virgin olive oil
    4 garlic cloves, minced
    4 teaspoons paprika
    2 teaspoons ground coriander
 1½ teaspoons table salt
    ¾ teaspoon red pepper flakes
    ½ teaspoon pepper
    ½ teaspoon ground cumin
    ½ teaspoon caraway seeds
    1 (4-pound) whole chicken, giblets discarded
    1 tablespoon chopped fresh mint

1. Microwave oil, garlic, paprika, coriander, salt, pepper flakes, pepper, cumin, and caraway in bowl until fragrant, about 30 seconds; let cool slightly.

2. Using your fingers, gently loosen skin covering breast and thighs of chicken. Place half of oil mixture under skin, directly on meat in center of each side of breast and on thighs. Gently press on skin to distribute oil mixture over meat. Rub entire exterior surface of chicken with remaining oil mixture. Place chicken, breast side down, in slow cooker. Cover and cook until breast registers 160 degrees and thighs register 175 degrees, 4 to 5 hours on low.

3. Transfer chicken to carving board, tent with aluminum foil, and let rest for 20 minutes. Carve chicken, discarding skin if desired. Sprinkle with mint and serve.

APPLYING A SPICE RUB

1. Gently separate skin from breast and thighs using your fingers.

2. Apply half of rub under skin; press on skin to distribute. Apply remaining rub on exterior of chicken.

Slow-Cooker Herbed Chicken with Warm Spring Vegetable Salad

Serves 4   Cook Time 4 to 5 hours on low

Why This Recipe Works This flavorful recipe features a juicy whole chicken and crunchy, vibrant spring vegetables, but comes in handy year-round. A simple aromatic mixture of oil, shallot, garlic, and thyme gave the chicken layers of flavor. We rubbed the mixture under the skin to give it direct contact with the meat. We placed the chicken breast side down in the slow cooker to keep the breast meat moist during cooking, and scattered seasoned radish halves around the chicken. While the chicken rested before carving, we stirred fresh sugar snap peas into the braised radishes in the slow cooker and cooked on high until the snap peas were crisp-tender yet still vibrant. A creamy dill dressing was the perfect flavorful accompaniment to our spring vegetable salad. Check the chicken's temperature after 4 hours of cooking and continue to monitor until the breast registers 160 degrees and the thighs register 175 degrees. You will need a 5- to 7-quart oval slow cooker for this recipe.

    ¼ cup extra-virgin olive oil, divided
    1 shallot, minced
    4 garlic cloves, minced, divided
    2 teaspoons minced fresh thyme or
      ½ teaspoon dried
    ¾ teaspoon plus ⅛ teaspoon table salt, divided
    ½ teaspoon pepper, divided
    1 (4-pound) whole chicken, giblets discarded
    1 pound radishes, trimmed and halved
    1 pound sugar snap peas, strings removed
    ¼ cup plain whole-milk yogurt
    ¼ cup mayonnaise

2 tablespoons minced fresh dill
1 tablespoon red wine vinegar
1 teaspoon sugar
  Lemon wedges

1. Microwave 3 tablespoons oil, shallot, three-quarters of garlic, thyme, ½ teaspoon salt, and ¼ teaspoon pepper in bowl until fragrant, about 30 seconds; let cool slightly.

2. Using your fingers, gently loosen skin covering breast and thighs of chicken. Place half of oil mixture under skin, directly on meat in center of each side of breast and on thighs. Gently press skin to distribute oil mixture over meat. Rub entire exterior surface of chicken with remaining oil mixture. Place chicken, breast side down, into slow cooker.

3. Toss radishes with remaining 1 tablespoon oil, ¼ teaspoon salt, and remaining ¼ teaspoon pepper in clean bowl, then arrange around chicken. Cover and cook until breast registers 160 degrees and thighs register 175 degrees, 4 to 5 hours on low.

4. Transfer chicken to carving board, tent with aluminum foil, and let rest while finishing vegetables. Stir snap peas into slow cooker, cover, and cook on high until crisp-tender, about 20 minutes.

5. Whisk yogurt, mayonnaise, dill, vinegar, sugar, remaining ⅛ teaspoon salt, and remaining garlic together in large bowl. Using slotted spoon, transfer vegetables to bowl with dressing and toss to coat; discard cooking liquid. Season salad with salt and pepper to taste. Carve chicken, discarding skin if desired. Serve with radish salad and lemon wedges.

Slow-Cooker Herbed Chicken with Warm Spring Vegetable Salad

Slow-Cooker Spice-Rubbed Chicken with Black Bean Salad

Serves 4   Cook Time 4 to 5 hours on low

Why This Recipe Works For this flavorful chicken recipe, we started with a Southwestern-inspired spice rub. We rubbed the mix under the skin to give it direct contact with the meat while it cooked. A simple black bean salad seemed like the perfect accompaniment to our chicken. Combining the beans with some chipotle chile and cooking them along with the chicken allowed the beans to absorb some of the chicken's juices and become even more flavorful and tender. While the chicken rested, we drained the beans and tossed them with bell pepper, corn, sliced scallions, lime juice, and olive oil to finish the salad. Check the chicken's temperature after 4 hours of cooking and continue to monitor until the breast registers 160 degrees and the thighs register 175 degrees. You will need an oval slow cooker for this recipe.

Slow-Cooker Spice-Rubbed Chicken with Black Bean Salad

5 teaspoons extra-virgin olive oil, divided
1 teaspoon ground cumin
1 teaspoon paprika
2 teaspoons grated lime zest plus ¼ cup juice (2 limes)
1½ teaspoons packed brown sugar
¼ teaspoon table salt
¼ teaspoon pepper
1 (4-pound) whole chicken, giblets discarded
1 (15-ounce) can black beans, rinsed
1 teaspoon minced canned chipotle chile in adobo sauce
1 red bell pepper, stemmed, seeded, and chopped fine
1 cup frozen corn, thawed
2 scallions, sliced thin

1. Microwave 2 teaspoons oil, cumin, and paprika in bowl until fragrant, about 30 seconds. Let spice mixture cool slightly, then stir in lime zest, sugar, salt, and pepper.

2. Using your fingers, gently loosen skin covering breast and thighs of chicken. Place half of spice mixture under skin, directly on meat in center of each side of breast and on thighs. Gently press skin to distribute spice mixture over meat. Rub entire exterior surface of chicken with remaining spice mixture.

3. Combine beans and chipotle in slow cooker. Place chicken, breast side down, on top of beans. Cover and cook until breast registers 160 degrees and thighs register 175 degrees, 4 to 5 hours on low.

4. Transfer chicken to carving board, tent with aluminum foil, and let rest for 20 minutes.

5. Drain beans and transfer to large bowl. Stir in bell pepper, corn, scallions, lime juice, and remaining 1 tablespoon oil. Season with salt and pepper to taste. Carve chicken, discarding skin if desired. Serve with bean salad.

Slow-Cooker Braised Chicken Sausages with White Bean Ragout

Serves 4   Cook Time 3 to 4 hours on low

Why This Recipe Works For this hearty winter braise, a simple combination of sausage, beans, and rosemary is transformed into a rich, warming bean ragout by the gentle simmer of the slow cooker. For the main components of the dish, we chose delicately flavored cannellini beans and Italian chicken sausage, which was full of spices like fennel and caraway that would flavor the dish. We combined broth, wine, minced garlic, and rosemary for a flavorful cooking liquid that would season the beans as they cooked. Cherry tomatoes

added a pop of bright color and fresh flavor. Once the sausage was cooked and the beans were tender, we mashed a portion of the beans and tomatoes together to help thicken the ragout. Stirring in some baby spinach right before serving brightened up this comforting dish. Italian turkey sausage can be substituted for the chicken sausage.

2 (15-ounce) cans cannellini beans, rinsed
¼ cup chicken broth
¼ cup dry white wine
2 garlic cloves, minced
1 sprig fresh rosemary
½ teaspoon table salt
½ teaspoon pepper
1½ pounds hot or sweet Italian chicken sausage
8 ounces cherry tomatoes
4 ounces (4 cups) baby spinach
2 tablespoons extra-virgin olive oil

1. Combine beans, broth, wine, garlic, rosemary sprig, salt, and pepper in slow cooker. Nestle sausage into slow cooker and top with tomatoes. Cover and cook until sausage is tender, 3 to 4 hours on low.

2. Transfer sausage to serving dish and tent with aluminum foil. Discard rosemary sprig. Transfer 1 cup bean-tomato mixture to bowl and mash with potato masher until mostly smooth.

3. Stir spinach, 1 handful at a time, and mashed bean mixture into slow cooker and let sit until spinach is wilted, about 5 minutes. Stir in oil and season with salt and pepper to taste. Serve sausages with ragout.

Slow-Cooker Italian Braised Chicken Sausages with Potatoes and Peppers

Serves 4   Cook Time 3 to 4 hours on low

Why This Recipe Works The gentle, moist heat of the slow cooker perfectly cooks sausage and a trio of vegetables to create this satisfying meal. We started with chicken sausages and chose to pair them with creamy red potatoes, bell peppers, and onion. We microwaved the vegetables with tomato paste, garlic, oregano, and red pepper flakes, which served two purposes: This step infused the potatoes, peppers, and onion with plenty of flavor and also gave them a head start so that they would finish cooking at the same time as the sausages. Fresh basil stirred in right before serving brightened up this dish. Chicken sausage is available in a variety of flavors; feel free to use any flavor that you think will work well in this dish. Turkey sausage can be substituted for the chicken sausage. You will need a 5- to 7-quart oval slow cooker for this recipe.

- 12 ounces red potatoes, unpeeled, quartered and sliced ¼ inch thick
- 3 red or green bell peppers, stemmed, seeded, and cut into ¼-inch-wide strips
- 1 onion, halved and sliced ½ inch thick
- ¼ cup tomato paste
- 2 tablespoons water
- 3 garlic cloves, minced
- 2 teaspoons minced fresh oregano or ½ teaspoon dried
- ¼ teaspoon red pepper flakes
- ¼ cup chicken broth
- 1½ pounds raw chicken sausage
- 2 tablespoons chopped fresh basil

1. Microwave potatoes, bell peppers, onion, tomato paste, water, garlic, oregano, and pepper flakes in covered bowl, stirring occasionally, until vegetables are almost tender, about 15 minutes; transfer to slow cooker. Stir in broth. Nestle sausage into slow cooker, cover, and cook until sausage and vegetables are tender, 3 to 4 hours on low.

2. Transfer sausage to serving platter. Stir basil into vegetable mixture and season with salt and pepper to taste. Transfer vegetable mixture to platter with sausage. Serve.

Slow-Cooker Sun-Dried Tomato and Basil Turkey Meatballs

Makes 24 meatballs and about 10 cups sauce; enough for 2 pounds pasta   **Cook Time** 4 to 5 hours on low

Why This Recipe Works Turkey meatballs often turn out bland and dry, so we set out to develop a recipe that rivaled those made from beef or pork in terms of tenderness and flavor. To start, we wanted to pack them with a bright savoriness, and decided to try adding a hefty dose of chopped basil, sun-dried tomatoes, and Parmesan along with the usual aromatics. We microwaved a large amount of aromatics first, thinking we'd split it between the sauce and the meatballs. This worked perfectly, infusing their flavors throughout the whole dish. The addition of a panade (milk and bread mixed to a paste) and egg yolks helped bind the turkey mixture while keeping it moist and tender. But if we tried to place our meatballs directly in the slow cooker, they were apt to fall apart during

Slow-Cooker Braised Chicken Sausages with White Bean Ragout

Slow-Cooker Sun-Dried Tomato and Basil Turkey Meatballs

the long cooking time. An extra step solved the problem: just 10 minutes in the oven browned them and firmed them up just enough to withstand the simmering time in the slow cooker, where they imparted flavor to the sauce. The sauce was super-simple to make—we combined crushed tomatoes, tomato puree, and wine, along with half the onion mix. Sugar stirred in at the end balanced out any sharpness in the sauce, and chopped basil gave the meatballs a fresh finishing touch. Be sure to use ground turkey, not ground turkey breast (also labeled 99 percent fat-free), in this recipe.

2 onions, chopped fine
6 garlic cloves, minced
2 tablespoons tomato paste
½ cup oil-packed sun-dried tomatoes, chopped fine, plus 2 tablespoons packing oil
2 tablespoons minced fresh oregano or 2 teaspoons dried
½ teaspoon red pepper flakes
1 teaspoon table salt, divided
2 (28-ounce) cans crushed tomatoes
1 (28-ounce) can tomato puree
½ cup dry red wine
2 slices hearty white sandwich bread, torn into 1-inch pieces
⅓ cup whole milk
1 ounce Parmesan cheese, grated (½ cup)
¼ cup chopped fresh basil, plus extra for serving
2 large egg yolks
½ teaspoon pepper
2 pounds ground turkey
2 teaspoons sugar, plus extra for seasoning

1. Adjust oven rack to middle position and heat oven to 475 degrees. Set wire rack in aluminum foil–lined rimmed baking sheet and coat with vegetable oil spray.

2. Microwave onions, garlic, tomato paste, tomato packing oil, oregano, pepper flakes, and ½ teaspoon salt in bowl, stirring occasionally, until onions are softened, about 5 minutes. Transfer half of onion mixture to slow cooker. Stir in tomatoes, tomato puree, and wine.

3. Mash bread, milk, and remaining ½ teaspoon salt to paste in large bowl using fork. Stir in sun-dried tomatoes, remaining onion mixture, Parmesan, basil, egg yolks, and pepper. Add ground turkey and knead with your hands until well combined. Pinch off and roll mixture into 1½-inch meatballs (about 24 meatballs) and arrange on prepared rack. Bake until firm and no longer pink, about 10 minutes.

4. Gently nestle meatballs into slow cooker, cover, and cook until meatballs are tender, 4 to 5 hours on low. Stir in sugar and season with salt, pepper, and extra sugar to taste. Before serving, stir in 2 tablespoons basil for every 5 cups sauce.

Slow-Cooker Turkey Breast with Cherry-Orange Sauce

Serves 8 to 10   **Cook Time** 5 to 6 hours on low

Why This Recipe Works We often think of turkey as being reserved for big holiday dinners, but some hands-off cooking in the slow cooker makes turkey breast a weeknight-friendly dinner. The bone-in turkey breast is prep-free, and the gentle heat of the slow cooker produces juicy and tender meat every time. For a fresh accompaniment to our "roast" turkey, a cherry-orange sauce seemed like the perfect choice. To keep it simple, we started with frozen cherries, which we chopped; we then added orange zest and a little thyme for aroma. By the time the turkey was fully cooked, the cherries were tender and the juices of the turkey had melded with the aromatics to create a flavorful sauce. To give it a thicker consistency, we added a small amount of instant tapioca. Many supermarkets sell "hotel-cut" turkey breasts, which still have the wings and rib cage attached. If this is the only type of breast you can find, you will need to remove the wings and cut away the rib cage with kitchen shears before proceeding with the recipe. Check the turkey's temperature after 5 hours of cooking and continue to monitor until the breast registers 160 degrees. You will need an oval slow cooker for this recipe.

12 ounces frozen sweet cherries, thawed and chopped
2 (2-inch) strips orange zest
1 teaspoon instant tapioca
½ teaspoon minced fresh thyme or ⅛ teaspoon dried
¾ teaspoon table salt, divided
½ teaspoon pepper
1 (6- to 7-pound) bone-in whole turkey breast, trimmed
½ cup apple butter
2 tablespoons unsalted butter
2 tablespoons lemon juice

1. Combine cherries, orange zest, tapioca, thyme, and ¼ teaspoon salt in slow cooker. Sprinkle turkey with pepper and remaining ½ teaspoon salt and place skin side up into slow cooker. Cover and cook until breast registers 160 degrees, 5 to 6 hours on low.

2. Transfer turkey to carving board, tent with aluminum foil, and let rest for 20 minutes.

3. Discard orange zest. Whisk apple butter, butter, and lemon juice into cherry mixture until combined. Season with salt and pepper to taste. Carve turkey and discard skin. Serve with sauce.

Slow-Cooker Turkey Breast with Gravy

Serves 8 to 10   **Total Time** 5 to 6 hours on low

Why This Recipe Works No one will ever guess that this dinner-table classic was turned out of a slow cooker as you serve up moist slices of turkey drizzled with a rich brown gravy. But it takes a little advance work (and a skillet) to get it right. We found that it was possible to skip the cumbersome step of browning the turkey breast, but to get a real gravy, we still needed the skillet to build a proper flavor base and make a roux. First we browned the onion, carrot, celery, and garlic. Then we added flour and cooked it until golden brown, deglazing the pan with water. Added to the slow cooker with the turkey and chicken broth and white wine, this base mingled with the juices released as the turkey cooked, resulting in a hearty gravy. Many supermarkets sell "hotel-cut" turkey breasts, which still have the wings and rib cage attached. If this is the only type of breast you can find, you will need to remove the wings and cut away the rib cage with kitchen shears before proceeding with the recipe. Check the turkey's temperature after 5 hours of cooking and continue to monitor until the breast registers 160 degrees. You will need an oval slow cooker for this recipe.

3 tablespoons unsalted butter
1 onion, chopped
1 carrot, peeled and chopped
1 celery rib, chopped
6 garlic cloves, peeled and smashed
⅓ cup all-purpose flour
1 cup water
2 cups chicken broth
½ cup dry white wine
2 sprigs fresh thyme
2 bay leaves
1 (6- to 7-pound) bone-in whole turkey breast, trimmed
½ teaspoon table salt
½ teaspoon pepper

Slow-Cooker Turkey Breast with Gravy

1. Melt butter in 12-inch skillet over medium heat. Add onion, carrot, celery, and garlic and cook until softened and lightly browned, 8 to 10 minutes. Stir in flour and cook until golden brown, about 2 minutes. Stir in water, scraping up any browned bits and smoothing out any lumps; transfer to slow cooker.

2. Stir broth, wine, thyme sprigs, and bay leaves into slow cooker. Sprinkle turkey with salt and pepper and place skin side up into slow cooker. Cover and cook until breast registers 160 degrees, 5 to 6 hours on low.

3. Transfer turkey to carving board, tent with aluminum foil, and let rest for 20 minutes.

4. Strain cooking liquid into saucepan; discard solids. Bring to simmer over medium heat and cook until thickened, about 15 minutes. Season with salt and pepper to taste. Carve turkey and discard skin. Serve with gravy.

COOKING FOR TWO

Photos (clockwise from top left): Chicken Lettuce Wraps with Hoisin for Two; Chicken Scarpariello for Two; Barbecued Dry-Rubbed Chicken for Two; Thai Red Curry with Chicken for Two

Pantry Garlicky
Chicken and Rice
Soup for Two

Chicken and
Coconut
Soup for Two

Pantry Garlicky Chicken and Rice Soup for Two

Serves 2   **Total Time** 40 minutes

Why This Recipe Works Whether you're under the weather or just in need of something warming and filling, few things nourish like a well-rounded chicken and rice soup enriched with a hefty dose of sinus-clearing garlic. But while Grandma's big-batch recipe may have you sautéing and simmering for hours, we wanted a simplified and small-batch version that would still be loaded with flavor and complexity. (Plus, if you're really not feeling well, the last thing you want to do is embark on a project.) For our scaled-down recipe, one shallot replaced the traditional onion, and a garlic press made quick work of mincing the whopping five cloves of garlic. Some herbes de Provence gave floral brightness (dried thyme is fine, too), and a touch of anchovy paste brought meaty depth without the need to make homemade stock. We added broth, boneless chicken thighs, a single carrot, and rice and simmered it all until everything was perfectly cooked. Convenient frozen peas and a squeeze of lemon juice brought garden freshness—just what the doctor ordered.

2 teaspoons vegetable oil
1 shallot, minced
5 garlic cloves, minced
½ teaspoon herbes de Provence or dried thyme
½ teaspoon anchovy paste
3 cups chicken broth
6 ounces boneless, skinless chicken thighs, trimmed and cut into ½-inch pieces
¼ cup long-grain white rice, rinsed
1 carrot, peeled, halved lengthwise, and sliced ¼ inch thick
⅛ teaspoon table salt
¼ cup frozen peas
   Lemon wedges

   1. Heat oil, shallot, and garlic in medium saucepan over medium-low heat, stirring occasionally, until shallot and garlic are softened and beginning to brown, 3 to 5 minutes. Stir in herbes de Provence and anchovy paste and cook until fragrant, about 30 seconds.

   2. Stir in broth, chicken, rice, carrot, and salt, scraping up any browned bits. Bring to simmer and cook until rice is tender, about 12 minutes.

   3. Off heat, stir in peas and let sit until warmed through, about 2 minutes. Season with salt and pepper to taste. Serve with lemon wedges. (Soup can be refrigerated for up to 3 days.)

Hearty Chicken Soup with Leeks, Fennel, and Orzo for Two

Serves 2   **Total Time** 1¼ hours

Why This Recipe Works We wanted to streamline chicken noodle soup and make it quick enough to prepare for two any night of the week—without losing any of its soul-satisfying flavor. While homemade stock was out, we found that we could get great results from store-bought chicken broth with just a couple of extra steps. Adding sautéed aromatics lent our broth a welcome depth and complexity, while creating a simple roux contributed a nutty flavor and also thickened the broth slightly, giving our soup a long-simmered consistency. A bone-in chicken breast gave our broth more flavor than a boneless one did, and quick-cooking orzo turned our soup into a hearty one-dish meal. Be careful not to overcook the chicken in step 3 or it will taste dry.

- 1 (12-ounce) bone-in split chicken breast, trimmed
  Pinch table salt
  Pinch pepper
- 2 teaspoons vegetable oil
- ½ leek, white and light green parts only, halved and sliced ¼ inch thick
- ½ fennel bulb, cored and chopped
- 1 carrot, peeled and cut into ½-inch pieces
- 1 teaspoon minced fresh thyme or ¼ teaspoon dried
- 1 tablespoon all-purpose flour
- 3 cups chicken broth
- 1 bay leaf
- ¼ cup orzo
- 1 tablespoon minced fresh parsley

1. Pat chicken dry with paper towels and sprinkle with salt and pepper. Heat oil in medium saucepan over medium-high heat until just smoking. Brown chicken, skin side down, until golden, about 6 minutes; transfer to plate. Pour off all but 1 tablespoon fat from saucepan.

2. Add leek, fennel, and carrot to fat left in saucepan and cook over medium heat until softened, about 5 minutes. Stir in thyme and cook until fragrant, about 30 seconds. Stir in flour and cook for 1 minute. Slowly whisk in broth, scraping up any browned bits.

3. Add browned chicken with any accumulated juices and bay leaf. Bring to simmer and cook until chicken registers 160 degrees, 20 to 22 minutes, flipping chicken halfway through cooking. Transfer chicken to cutting board, let cool slightly, then shred into bite-size pieces using 2 forks, discarding skin and bones.

4. Discard bay leaf. Return soup to simmer, stir in orzo, and cook until vegetables and orzo are tender, about 8 minutes. Off heat, stir in shredded chicken and let sit until heated through, about 2 minutes. Stir in parsley and season with salt and pepper to taste. Serve.

VARIATION

Hearty Chicken Soup with Tomato, Zucchini, and Shells for Two

Omit carrot. Substitute ½ cup medium shells for orzo and simmer for 5 minutes. Stir in 1 zucchini, cut into ½-inch pieces, and 1 tomato, cored and chopped, and continue to simmer until pasta and zucchini are tender, about 5 minutes. Stir in shredded chicken and proceed with recipe.

Chicken and Coconut Soup for Two

Serves 2   **Total Time** 50 minutes

Why This Recipe Works Thai red curry paste combines a number of aromatics—including lemongrass, coriander root, and makrut lime leaves—in one jar. It added flavor and depth to this soup in record time. Browning a boneless chicken breast and then simmering it briefly in coconut milk and chicken broth kept the meat moist and infused it with flavor, while fish sauce, sugar, and lime juice added salty, sweet, and sour notes. Mushrooms and snow peas rounded out the soup. Although we prefer the deeper, richer flavor of regular coconut milk, light coconut milk can be substituted. Be careful not to overcook the chicken in step 3 or it will taste dry.

- 1 (8-ounce) boneless, skinless chicken breast, trimmed
  Pinch table salt
  Pinch pepper
- 1 tablespoon vegetable oil
- 1 shallot, minced
- 2 cups chicken broth
- 1 cup canned coconut milk
- 1 tablespoon fish sauce, divided
- 1 teaspoon sugar
- 3 ounces white or cremini mushrooms, trimmed and sliced thin
- 3 ounces snow peas, strings removed, cut in half on bias
- 1 tablespoon lime juice
- 1 teaspoon Thai red curry paste
- ¼ cup minced fresh cilantro

1. Pat chicken dry with paper towels and sprinkle with salt and pepper. Heat oil in medium saucepan over medium-high heat until just smoking. Cook chicken until browned lightly on both sides, 4 to 6 minutes; transfer to plate.

2. Add shallot to fat left in saucepan and cook over medium heat until softened, about 3 minutes. Stir in broth, coconut milk, 1 teaspoon fish sauce, and sugar, scraping up any browned bits.

3. Add browned chicken and any accumulated juices, bring to simmer, and cook until it registers 160 degrees, about 10 minutes, flipping chicken halfway through cooking. Transfer chicken to cutting board, let cool slightly, then shred into bite-size pieces using 2 forks.

4. Return soup to simmer, stir in mushrooms and snow peas, and cook until just tender, about 3 minutes. Whisk lime juice, curry paste, and remaining 2 teaspoons fish sauce together in bowl. Off heat, stir in lime juice mixture and shredded chicken into soup and let sit until heated through, about 2 minutes. Season with salt and pepper to taste. Sprinkle individual portions with cilantro before serving.

Escarole, Chicken Sausage, and Orzo Soup for Two

Serves 2 **Total Time** 50 minutes

Why This Recipe Works For a quick yet satisfying weeknight meal, we combined tender bites of sausage, delicate pasta, and hearty greens in a warming Italian-inspired soup. We browned the sausage to create a flavorful fond on the bottom of the pot and then added onion and garlic. Red pepper flakes infused our soup with a subtle heat. Cooking orzo pasta right in the broth streamlined our dish, and the starch from the pasta gave the broth body and substance. Chopped escarole brought a pleasant, mildly bitter flavor to the soup. Chicken sausage is available in a wide variety of flavors; feel free to choose one that you think will pair well with the other flavors in this dish.

 1 tablespoon olive oil, divided
 6 ounces cooked chicken sausage, sliced ½ inch thick
 1 small onion, chopped fine
 1 garlic clove, minced
 ⅛ teaspoon red pepper flakes
 3 cups chicken broth
 2 ounces escarole, trimmed and chopped coarse (2 cups)
 ¼ cup orzo
 ¼ cup grated Parmesan cheese
 1 tablespoon minced fresh parsley

1. Heat 2 teaspoons oil in medium saucepan over medium-high heat until shimmering. Add sausage and cook until browned, about 5 minutes; transfer to bowl.

2. Heat remaining 1 teaspoon oil in now-empty saucepan over medium heat until shimmering. Add onion and cook until softened and lightly browned, 5 to 7 minutes. Stir in garlic and pepper flakes and cook until fragrant, about 30 seconds.

3. Stir in broth, scraping up any browned bits. Stir in browned sausage, escarole, and orzo. Bring to simmer and cook until orzo is tender, 10 to 12 minutes. Off heat, stir in Parmesan and parsley and season with salt and pepper to taste. Serve.

White Chicken Chili for Two

Serves 2 **Total Time** 50 minutes

Why This Recipe Works To achieve the right consistency for our white chicken chili, we utilized two thickeners: flour and pureed hominy. Cooking the flour briefly with the aromatics and spices—poblano chiles, onion, garlic, cumin, and coriander—allowed it to not only thicken the chili, but also build depth of flavor. And pureeing a portion of the hominy with some chicken broth created a luxuriously thick texture. Adding store-bought tomatillo salsa was an easy way to boost the flavor of our chili at the end. Both white hominy and yellow hominy will work in this chili; however, we prefer the deeper flavor of white hominy here. To make this dish spicier, add the chile seeds. Be careful not to overcook the chicken in step 3 or it will taste dry. Serve with your favorite chili garnishes.

 1 (15-ounce) can white or yellow hominy, rinsed, divided
 2 cups chicken broth, divided
 1 tablespoon vegetable oil
 2 poblano chiles, stemmed, seeded, and chopped
 1 small onion, chopped fine
 2 garlic cloves, minced
 1 teaspoon ground cumin
 1 teaspoon ground coriander
 1 tablespoon all-purpose flour
12 ounces boneless, skinless chicken breasts, trimmed
 ⅛ teaspoon table salt
 ⅛ teaspoon pepper
 ½ cup jarred tomatillo salsa (salsa verde)
 2 tablespoons minced fresh cilantro

1. Process 1 cup hominy and ½ cup broth in blender until smooth, about 10 seconds.

2. Heat oil in medium saucepan over medium heat until shimmering. Add poblanos, onion, garlic, cumin, and coriander.

Cook, stirring often, until vegetables are softened and spices are fragrant, about 5 minutes. Stir in flour and cook for 1 minute.

3. Slowly whisk in remaining 1½ cups broth, scraping up any browned bits and smoothing out any lumps. Stir in pureed hominy mixture and remaining hominy. Sprinkle chicken with salt and pepper, add to chili mixture, and bring to simmer. Cover, reduce heat to medium-low, and simmer until chicken registers 160 degrees, 10 to 15 minutes, flipping chicken halfway through cooking. Transfer chicken to cutting board, let cool slightly, then shred into bite-size pieces using 2 forks.

4. Return chili to simmer, stir in shredded chicken and tomatillo salsa, and cook until heated through, about 2 minutes. Stir in cilantro and season with salt and pepper to taste. Serve.

NOTES FROM THE TEST KITCHEN

NO-PREP AROMATICS
To save time on prep, we've found easy alternatives to onion and garlic. An equal amount of store-bought frozen chopped onion can replace fresh chopped onion in any recipe. You can also chop extra onion and freeze it to have on hand. And if you don't have fresh garlic, swap ¾ teaspoon granulated garlic for 1 teaspoon fresh minced garlic.

White Chicken
Chili for Two

French-Style White Bean Stew for Two

Serves 2   **Total Time** 1½ hours

Why This Recipe Works Cassoulet, the revered stew from France, is typically composed of garlicky white beans and various meats, including garlic sausage, duck confit, pork shoulder or loin, and sometimes game. For this recipe, we looked to cassoulet as our inspiration for a stew that was both quick to make and perfectly sized for two. We kept the garlic sausage but substituted rich, meaty chicken thighs for the duck confit. Starting with canned cannellini beans eliminated an overnight soak. We sautéed drained tomatoes with onions to concentrate their flavor and used a healthy splash of dry vermouth to enhance the beans and sauce. The dish came together easily on the stovetop before being topped with toasted bread crumbs. Canned navy or great Northern beans can be substituted for the cannellini beans. Traditional cassoulet uses Toulouse sausage, a garlicky sausage from France; use it if you can find it.

French-Style
White Bean
Stew for Two

2½ tablespoons olive oil, divided
2 slices hearty white sandwich bread, torn into
  ½-inch pieces
½ plus ⅛ teaspoon table salt, divided
2 (5- to 7-ounce) bone-in chicken thighs, trimmed
⅛ teaspoon pepper
8 ounces bratwurst or garlic sausage
1 onion, chopped fine
½ cup canned diced tomatoes, drained
3 garlic cloves, minced
1 tablespoon minced fresh thyme
1 cup chicken broth
½ cup dry vermouth or dry white wine
1 (15-ounce) can cannellini beans, rinsed
2 tablespoons minced fresh parsley

1. Heat 1½ tablespoons oil in 10-inch skillet over medium heat until shimmering. Add bread and ¼ teaspoon salt and toast, stirring frequently, until golden and crispy, 5 to 7 minutes. Transfer to bowl and set aside.

2. Pat chicken dry with paper towels and sprinkle with ⅛ teaspoon salt and pepper. Heat remaining 1 tablespoon oil in now-empty skillet over medium-high heat until just smoking. Add chicken, skin side down, and sausage and cook, rotating sausage occasionally but leaving chicken undisturbed, until well browned, about 5 minutes. Transfer to plate.

3. Add onion, tomatoes, and remaining ¼ teaspoon salt to now-empty skillet and cook, stirring occasionally, until softened and beginning to brown, 5 to 7 minutes. Stir in garlic and thyme and cook until fragrant, about 30 seconds. Stir in broth and vermouth, scraping up any browned bits. Add beans and stir to combine.

4. Add chicken, skin side up; sausage; and accumulated juices to bean mixture and bring to boil over high heat. Reduce heat to low, cover, and simmer until chicken registers 175 degrees, 10 to 15 minutes.

5. Remove lid, increase heat to medium-low, and continue to simmer until sauce is slightly thickened and liquid falls just below surface of beans, about 10 minutes longer. (Mixture will still be very loose but will continue to thicken as it sits.) Off heat, top stew with toasted bread and sprinkle with parsley. Let rest for 10 minutes before serving.

Braised Chicken Thighs with Potatoes, Fennel, and Tarragon for Two

Serves 2   Total Time 1¾ hours

Why This Recipe Works Braised chicken thighs are the ultimate comfort food, with juicy meat surrounded by a rich pan sauce and tender vegetables. Most recipes make enough for a crowd, but we wanted a version for two that could be made in a skillet. We chose bone-in thighs, which would retain plenty of flavor and moisture over the extended cooking time. We browned them first to develop a flavorful fond in the pan and then removed the skin to prevent the final dish from being greasy. A combination of chicken broth and wine lent the dish acidity and depth of flavor. To make this dish a hearty meal, we added red potatoes, carrots, and an onion, and some sliced fennel, and we included tarragon for a fresh finish.

4 (5- to 7-ounce) bone-in chicken thighs, trimmed
½ teaspoon table salt, divided
¼ teaspoon pepper
2 teaspoons vegetable oil
8 ounces red potatoes, unpeeled, cut into
  ½-inch pieces
3 carrots, peeled and sliced ½ inch thick
1 small onion, chopped fine
1 garlic clove, minced
½ teaspoon minced fresh thyme or ⅛ teaspoon dried
1¼ cups chicken broth
¼ cup dry white wine
½ fennel bulb, stalks discarded, bulb cored
  and sliced thin
2 tablespoons minced fresh tarragon
1 teaspoon lemon juice

1. Pat chicken dry with paper towels and sprinkle with ¼ teaspoon salt and pepper. Heat oil in 10-inch skillet over medium-high heat until just smoking. Cook chicken until brown on both sides, 8 to 10 minutes; transfer to plate. Let chicken cool slightly, then remove skin.

2. Pour off all but 1 tablespoon fat from skillet. Add potatoes, carrots, onion, and remaining ¼ teaspoon salt and cook over medium heat until onion is softened, about 5 minutes. Stir in garlic and thyme and cook until fragrant, about 30 seconds. Stir in broth and wine, scraping up any browned bits.

3. Nestle browned chicken into vegetables, add any accumulated juices, and bring to simmer. Reduce heat to medium-low, cover, and simmer until chicken is very tender and almost falling off bone, about 1 hour, flipping chicken halfway through cooking. Transfer chicken to serving dish and tent with aluminum foil.

4. Increase heat to medium, stir in fennel, and continue to simmer, uncovered, until vegetables are tender and sauce is slightly thickened, about 8 minutes. Stir in any accumulated chicken juices and simmer for 30 seconds. Off heat, stir in tarragon and lemon juice and season with salt and pepper to taste. Spoon vegetables and sauce over chicken and serve.

Chicken Tagine for Two

Serves 2   Total Time 40 minutes

Why This Recipe Works Tagines are warmly spiced, assertively flavored stews that typically include meats, vegetables, fruits, and numerous spices and are cooked for hours, traditionally in conical earthenware vessels (also called tagines). They're exceedingly delicious and we wanted to make a version with chicken that served just two people. We relied on ras el hanout, a Moroccan spice blend, to deliver big flavor. Quick-cooking chicken thighs were our protein of choice. Dried apricots and chickpeas contributed to the tagine's sweet-savory balance, and just one sweet potato was plenty to amp up the sweetness of the braise. Coarsely mashing the tagine at the end of cooking helped achieve a creamy texture reminiscent of long-cooked stews. Serve over couscous, rice, or other grains.

> 1 tablespoon extra-virgin olive oil
> 1 shallot, chopped fine
> 2 garlic cloves, minced
> 1½ teaspoons ras el hanout
> 1 (15-ounce) can chickpeas, rinsed
> 1½ cups chicken or vegetable broth
> 8 ounces boneless, skinless chicken thighs, trimmed and cut into 1-inch pieces
> 1 small sweet potato (8 ounces), peeled and cut into 1-inch pieces
> ¼ cup dried apricots, quartered
> 2 tablespoons chopped fresh cilantro
> ¼ cup pomegranate seeds

1. Heat oil in medium saucepan over medium-low heat until shimmering. Add shallot, garlic, and ras el hanout and cook, stirring often, until shallot and garlic are softened and spices are fragrant, about 3 minutes.

2. Stir in chickpeas, broth, chicken, sweet potato, and apricots, scraping up any browned bits. Bring to simmer and cook until chicken and sweet potato are tender, about 15 minutes. Using potato masher or back of large spoon, coarsely mash

Chicken Tagine for Two

stew to desired consistency. Off heat, stir in cilantro, season with salt and pepper to taste, and sprinkle with pomegranate seeds. Serve. (Tagine can be refrigerated for up to 3 days.)

Thai Red Curry with Chicken for Two

Serves 2   Total Time 30 minutes

Why This Recipe Works Thai curries are complexly flavored, boasting the perfect balance of aromatic, funky, tangy, and sweet flavors. Red curry paste is an ingredient we go back to again and again, and for good reason—it's fast, and it packs an aromatic punch. For this scaled-down version of chicken, we whisked it into broth to develop a superflavorful base in a snap. Chicken thighs and one potato gave our dish heft; crunchy bell pepper and snap peas brought texture; sugar, fish sauce, and lime juice provided the balance of flavors we were after; and coconut milk added creamy, slightly sweet richness. Serve on its own or over rice.

1½ cups chicken broth
2 tablespoons Thai red curry paste
2 teaspoons sugar
8 ounces boneless, skinless chicken thighs, trimmed and cut into 1-inch pieces
1 Yukon Gold potato (8 ounces), peeled and cut into 1-inch pieces
1 small red bell pepper, stemmed, seeded, and chopped
4 ounces sugar snap peas, strings removed, cut on bias into ½-inch pieces
½ cup canned coconut milk
2 tablespoons chopped fresh basil
1 tablespoon fish sauce
1 tablespoon lime juice

1. Bring broth to simmer in medium saucepan over medium-low heat then whisk in curry paste and sugar until dissolved. Add chicken and potato, bring to simmer, and cook until tender, 8 to 10 minutes. Stir in bell pepper and snap peas and cook until just tender, 3 to 5 minutes.

2. Off heat, stir in coconut milk, basil, fish sauce, and lime juice and season with salt and pepper to taste. Serve. (Curry can be refrigerated for up to 3 days.)

Thai Red Curry with Chicken for Two

Chicken Curry with Cauliflower and Peas for Two

Serves 2   Total Time 1 hour

Why This Recipe Works For a scaled-down version of chicken curry that we could make in an hour, we focused first on the cornerstone of the flavor—the spices. We found that a mix of store-bought curry powder and garam masala provided wonderful flavor and complexity. Blooming the two spice blends in oil released their full flavors. Onion, along with equal amounts of ginger and garlic, provided the aromatic base, while a little tomato paste offered sweet depth. Boneless chicken breasts cooked quickly, and cauliflower and peas—a classic pairing in curries—added heartiness and a burst of color to our curry. Coconut milk contributed a creamy, savory richness. Be careful not to overcook the chicken in step 2 or it will taste dry. Serve with rice.

1 tablespoon vegetable oil
1 small onion, chopped fine
1 tablespoon curry powder
2 teaspoons grated fresh ginger
2 teaspoons tomato paste
2 garlic cloves, minced
½ teaspoon garam masala
¼ teaspoon table salt
1 tablespoon all-purpose flour
1½ cups chicken broth
1½ cups cauliflower florets, cut into 1-inch pieces
12 ounces boneless, skinless chicken breasts, trimmed
½ cup canned coconut milk
¼ cup frozen peas
2 tablespoons minced fresh cilantro

1. Heat oil in medium saucepan over medium heat until shimmering. Add onion, curry powder, ginger, tomato paste, garlic, garam masala, and salt. Cook, stirring often, until onion is softened and spices are fragrant, about 5 minutes. Stir in flour and cook for 1 minute.

2. Slowly whisk in broth, scraping up any browned bits and smoothing out any lumps. Stir in cauliflower. Sprinkle chicken with salt and pepper, add to curry mixture, and bring to simmer. Reduce heat to medium-low, cover, and simmer until chicken registers 160 degrees, 10 to 15 minutes, flipping chicken halfway through cooking. Transfer chicken to cutting board, let cool slightly, then shred into bite-size pieces using 2 forks.

3. Return stew to simmer, stir in shredded chicken, coconut milk, and peas and cook until heated through, about 2 minutes. Stir in cilantro and season with salt and pepper to taste. Serve.

Chicken Marsala for Two

1 small onion, chopped coarse
1 garlic clove, minced
½ cup sweet Marsala
¼ cup chicken broth
1 tablespoon minced fresh parsley

1. Pound chicken breasts to uniform thickness. Pat chicken dry with paper towels and sprinkle with salt and pepper. Spread ¼ cup flour in shallow dish. Working with 1 breast at a time, dredge breasts in flour.

2. Heat oil in 10-inch skillet over medium-high heat until just smoking. Cook chicken until well browned on first side, 6 to 8 minutes. Flip chicken, reduce heat to medium, and continue to cook until chicken registers 160 degrees, 6 to 8 minutes; transfer to plate and tent with aluminum foil.

3. Melt 1 tablespoon butter in now-empty skillet over medium heat. Add mushrooms and onion and cook until mushrooms have released their liquid and vegetables are softened and lightly browned, 5 to 7 minutes. Stir in garlic and cook until fragrant, about 30 seconds; transfer mixture to bowl.

4. Add remaining ½ teaspoon flour to again-empty skillet and cook over medium heat for 1 minute. Whisk in Marsala and broth, scraping up any browned bits. Bring to simmer and cook until sauce is slightly thickened, about 5 minutes. Return chicken and any accumulated juices to skillet and simmer until heated through, about 1 minute; transfer chicken to serving platter. Off heat, whisk mushroom mixture, remaining 2 tablespoons butter, and parsley into sauce and season with salt and pepper to taste. Pour sauce over chicken and serve.

Chicken Marsala for Two

Serves 2 **Total Time** 50 minutes

Why This Recipe Works Boasting juicy meat napped with a rich mushroom-wine sauce, chicken Marsala may taste luxurious but is quite simple to prepare at home for a fancy dinner for two. We first dredged the chicken in flour, which not only protected the meat from overcooking but also ensured that more sauce would cling to the meat. For the sauce, we sautéed onion along with mushrooms before adding chicken broth and a full ½ cup of sweet Marsala (rather than dry) for its depth of flavor. We finished our sauce with butter for silky richness and added a sprinkle of fresh parsley.

2 (6- to 8-ounce) boneless, skinless chicken breasts, trimmed
¼ teaspoon table salt
¼ teaspoon pepper
¼ cup plus ½ teaspoon all-purpose flour, divided
1 tablespoon vegetable oil
3 tablespoons unsalted butter, chilled, divided
4 ounces white mushrooms, trimmed and sliced thin

Chicken Parmesan for Two

Serves 2 **Total Time** 1 hour

Why This Recipe Works Chicken Parmesan is a perennial favorite and we wanted to make this dish feasible for two. We made a quick but flavorful tomato sauce by whirring together canned tomatoes in a food processor. Garlic sautéed in olive oil provided a rich backbone, and basil, sugar, and salt rounded out the flavor. For the chicken, we coated boneless, skinless breasts in flour, dipped them in an egg wash, and then rolled them in a crumb coating of ultracrisp panko bread crumbs and freshly grated Parmesan cheese. Pan frying the chicken produced an evenly browned crust that stayed crisp even when topped with a mix of mozzarella and fontina and broiled until the cheese turned gooey. Spooning the sauce over the cheese, not the chicken, also ensured a crisp crust. We saved the remaining sauce for tossing with a side of hot spaghetti.

Chicken Parmesan for Two

Chicken Scarpariello for Two

Sauce
- 1 (28-ounce) can whole peeled tomatoes, drained
- 2 tablespoons extra-virgin olive oil
- 2 garlic cloves, minced
- 2 tablespoons chopped fresh basil
- ¼ teaspoon sugar, plus extra as needed

Chicken and Spaghetti
- ¼ cup all-purpose flour
- 1 large egg
- ¾ cup panko bread crumbs
- ¼ cup grated Parmesan cheese
- 2 (6- to 8-ounce) boneless, skinless chicken breasts, trimmed
- ¼ teaspoon table salt, plus salt for cooking pasta
- ¼ teaspoon pepper
- 6 tablespoons vegetable oil
- 1 ounce whole-milk mozzarella cheese, shredded (¼ cup)
- 1 ounce fontina cheese, shredded (¼ cup)
- 1 tablespoon chopped fresh basil
- 4 ounces spaghetti

1. For the sauce Pulse tomatoes in food processor until coarsely ground, 6 to 8 pulses. Cook oil and garlic in medium saucepan over medium heat, stirring often, until garlic is fragrant but not browned, about 2 minutes. Stir in pulsed tomatoes, bring to simmer, and cook until sauce is slightly thickened, 10 to 15 minutes. Off heat, stir in basil and sugar and season with salt and extra sugar to taste; cover to keep warm.

2. For the chicken and spaghetti Adjust oven rack 4 inches from broiler element and heat broiler. Spread flour in shallow dish. Beat egg in second shallow dish. Combine panko and Parmesan in third shallow dish. Pound chicken breasts to uniform thickness. Pat chicken dry with paper towels and sprinkle with salt and pepper. Working with 1 breast at a time, dredge breasts in flour, dip in egg, then coat with bread-crumb mixture, pressing gently to adhere.

3. Line large plate with triple layer of paper towels. Heat oil in 10-inch nonstick skillet over medium-high heat until shimmering. Cook chicken until browned on both sides and registers 160 degrees, 8 to 12 minutes. Drain chicken briefly on paper towel–lined plate, then transfer to rimmed baking sheet.

4. Combine mozzarella and fontina in bowl. Sprinkle cheese mixture evenly over chicken, covering as much surface area as possible. Broil until cheese is melted and beginning to brown, 2 to 4 minutes. Transfer chicken to serving platter, top each breast with 2 tablespoons tomato sauce, and sprinkle with basil.

5. Meanwhile, bring 4 quarts water to boil in large pot. Add pasta and 1 tablespoon salt and cook, stirring often, until al dente. Reserve ½ cup cooking water, then drain pasta and return it to pot. Add remaining sauce to pasta and toss to combine. Season with salt and pepper to taste, and add reserved cooking water as needed to adjust consistency. Serve chicken with pasta.

Chicken Scarpariello for Two

Serves 2 **Total Time** 1¼ hours

Why This Recipe Works If you (and whoever is joining you) like strong flavors, try this dish of chicken and sausage bathed in a garlicky sauce full of onions, bell peppers, and pickled hot cherry peppers. Two chicken leg quarters offered a generous portion per person and were forgiving to cook. We browned the chicken and sausage and then cooked the bell pepper and onion in the rendered fat until softened and charred in spots. Just 1 tablespoon of chopped hot pickled cherry peppers, plus a splash of their spicy brine, delivered the dish's signature shot of bright heat, while flour cooked with the vegetables ensured that the sauce would have enough body to tie it to the other elements and make a cohesive dish. Crusty bread provided the perfect accompaniment to mop up any leftover sauce.

- 2 (10-ounce) chicken leg quarters, trimmed
- ¼ teaspoon table salt
- ¼ teaspoon pepper
- 2 teaspoons extra-virgin olive oil
- 6 ounces sweet Italian sausage, casings removed
- 1 cup thinly sliced red bell pepper
- 1 cup thinly sliced onion
- 1 tablespoon chopped hot pickled cherry peppers, plus 1 tablespoon brine
- 2 garlic cloves, minced
- 1 teaspoon all-purpose flour
- ½ teaspoon dried oregano
- ¾ cup chicken broth
- 1 tablespoon chopped fresh parsley

1. Pat chicken dry with paper towels and sprinkle with salt and pepper. Heat oil in 10-inch nonstick skillet over medium-high heat until just smoking. Add chicken skin side down and cook, without moving it, until well browned, about 5 minutes. Flip chicken and continue to cook until browned on second side, about 4 minutes longer. Transfer chicken to plate.

2. Add sausage to fat left in skillet and cook until browned, breaking up meat with wooden spoon, about 2 minutes. Using slotted spoon, transfer sausage to paper towel–lined plate.

3. Heat leftover fat in skillet over medium-high heat until shimmering. Add bell pepper and onion and cook until vegetables are softened and charred in spots, stirring occasionally,

about 7 minutes. Add cherry peppers, garlic, flour, and oregano and cook until fragrant, about 1 minute. Stir in broth, sausage, and cherry pepper brine and bring to simmer, scraping up any browned bits.

4. Nestle chicken, skin side up, into sauce and pour in any accumulated juices. Reduce heat to medium-low; cover; and simmer until chicken registers 200 degrees, about 20 minutes.

5. Off heat, let chicken rest in skillet, uncovered, for 10 minutes. Sprinkle with parsley and serve.

Chicken Imperial for Two

Serves 2 **Total Time** 1¼ hours

Why This Recipe Works A retro classic, chicken imperial blankets boneless chicken breasts with buttery fresh bread crumbs and surrounds them in a cream-and-wine sauce. We wanted to cut this winning recipe down to size. We started by replacing the fresh bread crumbs with panko, which have good flavor and hold up well in the oven. For the chicken, we found that a sprinkle of salt followed by a 30-minute rest imparted deep seasoning. Our original recipe, which serves four people, calls for reducing the sauce on the stovetop after baking the chicken, but we wondered if we could save ourselves a step and just reduce the sauce in the oven. We switched to a 13 by 9-inch baking dish to increase the surface area for better evaporation (and reduction); after baking the chicken and transferring it to a serving platter, we slid the dish with the cream sauce back into the hot oven. Just a few minutes later we had a smooth, velvety sauce. With these easy revisions, we were able to keep the signature richness of chicken imperial while trimming the amount of work. Use chicken breasts of equal size so they cook at the same rate.

- 2 (6- to 8-ounce) boneless, skinless chicken breasts, trimmed
- ½ teaspoon table salt
- ½ cup panko bread crumbs
- 2 tablespoons grated Parmesan cheese
- 1½ tablespoons unsalted butter, softened, plus 1 tablespoon melted
- 1 tablespoon minced fresh parsley, divided
- 1 teaspoon minced fresh thyme
- 1 garlic clove, minced
- ¼ teaspoon pepper
- ½ cup heavy cream
- ⅓ cup chicken broth
- ¼ cup dry white wine
- 1 small shallot, minced
- 1 teaspoon Dijon mustard

Chicken Imperial for Two

1. Sprinkle chicken breasts with salt. Cover with plastic wrap and refrigerate for 30 minutes. Adjust oven rack to middle position and heat oven to 425 degrees.

2. Meanwhile, combine panko, Parmesan, softened butter, 1½ teaspoons parsley, thyme, garlic, and pepper in bowl with fork until butter is fully incorporated into crumbs.

3. Pat chicken dry with paper towels and season with pepper. Arrange chicken, skinned side up, in 13 by 9-inch baking dish, side by side with narrow ends of breasts opposite each other. Brush tops of breasts with melted butter. Top each breast with equal amount panko mixture, pressing firmly to adhere.

4. Whisk cream, broth, wine, shallot, and mustard together in 2-cup liquid measuring cup. Carefully pour cream mixture around chicken breasts, taking care not to wet crumbs. Transfer dish to oven and bake until chicken registers 160 degrees, 17 to 20 minutes.

5. Using spatula, transfer chicken to platter. Return dish to oven and continue to cook until sauce is thickened slightly, 1 to 3 minutes. Season with salt and pepper to taste. Spoon sauce around chicken, sprinkle with remaining 1½ teaspoons parsley, and serve.

Chicken Mole for Two

Serves 2 **Total Time** 1½ hours

Why This Recipe Works "Mole" describes a variety of Mexican sauces, but the most famous is mole poblano, a rich blend of chiles, nuts, dried fruits, spices, and chocolate. Taking inspiration from mole poblano, we obtained depth of flavor from a combination chili powder, chipotles in adobo, warm spices, raisins, sesame seeds, peanut butter, and a little bittersweet chocolate. Downsizing this small recipe to a 10-inch skillet prevented the sauce from burning. For a velvety texture, we processed the sauce in a blender, then poured it over chicken breasts and baked them until tender and flavorful. Take care not to burn the spice and chocolate mixture in step 2; add a small splash of water or broth if it begins to scorch. If using kosher chicken, do not brine. If brining the chicken, do not season with salt in step 3. For more information on brining, see page 15.

1 tablespoon vegetable oil
1 small onion, chopped fine
½ ounce bittersweet, semisweet, or Mexican chocolate, chopped coarse
1 tablespoon chili powder
1 teaspoon minced canned chipotle chile in adobo sauce
¼ teaspoon ground cinnamon
Pinch ground cloves
1 garlic clove, minced
1¼ cups chicken broth
1 tomato, cored, seeded, and chopped
2 tablespoons raisins
1 tablespoon peanut butter
1 tablespoon sesame seeds, toasted, plus extra for serving
Sugar
2 (12-ounce) bone-in split chicken breasts, skin removed, trimmed, and brined if desired
¼ teaspoon table salt
¼ teaspoon pepper

1. Adjust oven rack to middle position and heat oven to 400 degrees. Heat oil in 10-inch skillet over medium heat until shimmering. Add onion and cook until softened, about 5 minutes.

2. Reduce heat to medium-low, stir in chocolate, chili powder, chipotle, cinnamon, and cloves; cook, stirring frequently, until spices are fragrant and chocolate is melted and bubbly, about 1 minute. Stir in garlic and cook until fragrant, about 30 seconds. Stir in broth, tomato, raisins, peanut butter, and sesame seeds. Bring to simmer and cook,

Chicken
Mole for Two

stirring occasionally, until sauce is slightly thickened and reduced to about 1¾ cups, 10 to 15 minutes. Transfer sauce to blender and process until smooth, about 30 seconds. Season with salt, pepper, and sugar to taste.

3. Pat chicken dry with paper towels and sprinkle with salt and pepper. Place chicken, skinned side down, in 8-inch square baking dish and pour pureed sauce over top, turning chicken to coat evenly. Bake chicken for 20 minutes. Flip chicken skinned side up and continue to bake until chicken registers 160 degrees, 15 to 25 minutes. Let chicken rest in sauce for 5 minutes. Sprinkle with extra sesame seeds and serve.

Teriyaki Chicken for Two

Serves 2   **Total Time** 40 minutes

Why This Recipe Works Teriyaki chicken is often prepared on the grill, but since we were cooking just four chicken thighs, we reached for a skillet. To obtain juicy meat and crisp skin covered with a sweet-salty glaze, we needed to ensure that the maximum amount of skin came in contact with that skillet.

Setting a weight on top of the chicken (a saucepan and a couple of cans) helped to brown more surface area and pressed out most of the fat, for thin, ultracrisp skin. Simmering soy sauce, mirin, ginger, garlic, and sugar until thick and glossy made a bright, balanced teriyaki sauce that far surpassed any we could buy in a bottle. In step 1, weight the saucepan with a 28-ounce can or two 15-ounce cans. Serve with rice.

- 4 (5- to 7-ounce) bone-in chicken thighs, trimmed
- ¼ teaspoon pepper
- 1 teaspoon vegetable oil
- ½ cup sugar
- 2 tablespoons soy sauce
- 1 tablespoon mirin, sweet sherry, or dry white wine
- 1 teaspoon grated fresh ginger
- 1 garlic clove, minced
- ½ teaspoon cornstarch
     Pinch red pepper flakes

1. Wrap bottom of large saucepan with aluminum foil, then place 1 large can or 2 smaller cans inside. Pat chicken dry with paper towels and sprinkle with pepper. Heat oil in 10-inch nonstick skillet over medium-high heat until just smoking. Lay chicken skin side down in skillet and weigh down with prepared saucepan. Cook chicken until skin is well browned and crisp, 10 to 15 minutes.

2. Remove saucepan and flip chicken skin side up. Reduce heat to medium and continue to cook, without weight, until chicken registers 175 degrees, about 10 minutes; transfer to plate. Pour off fat from skillet.

3. Meanwhile, whisk sugar, soy sauce, mirin, ginger, garlic, cornstarch, and pepper flakes together in bowl. Add soy sauce mixture to now-empty skillet and bring to simmer. Return chicken, skin side up, and any accumulated juices to skillet and simmer until sauce is thick and glossy, 2 to 3 minutes. Turn chicken to coat evenly with sauce. Serve.

CRISPING CHICKEN SKIN

For chicken skin that stays crisp even when glazed, set weighted saucepan (wrapped in aluminum foil for easy cleanup) on chicken as it browns in pan.

Murgh Makhani for Two

Serves 2   Total Time 1 hour

Why This Recipe Works Murgh makhani, or Indian butter chicken, tastes rich, creamy, vibrant, and complex. We started our version for two by softening onion, garlic, ginger, and chile in butter followed by garam masala, coriander, cumin, and black pepper. Instead of canned tomatoes, we opted for a mix of tomato paste and water, which lent acidity and punch plus deep color without making the sauce liquid-y. Cream gave the sauce lush, velvety body, and we whisked in another tablespoon of butter for extra richness. To imitate the charring produced by a tandoor, we broiled chicken thighs coated in yogurt (its milk proteins and lactose brown quickly and deeply) before cutting them and stirring them into the sauce. Traditionally, butter chicken is mildly spiced. If you prefer a spicier dish, mince and add the ribs and seeds from the chile. Serve with basmati rice and/or warm naan.

- 2 tablespoons unsalted butter, cut into 2 pieces and chilled
- ½ onion, chopped fine
- 3 garlic cloves, minced
- 2 teaspoons grated fresh ginger
- 2 teaspoons minced serrano chile
- 1½ teaspoons garam masala
- ½ teaspoon ground coriander
- ¼ teaspoon ground cumin
- ¼ teaspoon pepper
- ¾ cup water
- ¼ cup tomato paste
- 1½ teaspoons sugar
- 1 teaspoon table salt, divided
- ½ cup heavy cream
- 1 pound boneless, skinless chicken thighs, trimmed
- ¼ cup plain Greek yogurt
- 1½ tablespoons chopped fresh cilantro, divided

1. Melt 1 tablespoon butter in medium saucepan over medium heat. Add onion, garlic, ginger, and serrano and cook, stirring frequently, until mixture is softened and onion begins to brown, 6 to 8 minutes. Add garam masala, coriander, cumin, and pepper and cook, stirring frequently, until very fragrant, about 3 minutes. Add water and tomato paste and whisk until no lumps of tomato paste remain. Add sugar and ½ teaspoon salt and bring to boil. Off heat, stir in cream. Using immersion blender or blender, process until smooth, 30 to 60 seconds. Return sauce to simmer over medium heat

and whisk in remaining 1 tablespoon butter. Remove saucepan from heat and cover to keep warm. (Sauce can be refrigerated for up to 4 days; gently reheat sauce before adding hot chicken.)

2. Adjust oven rack 6 inches from broiler element and heat broiler. Combine chicken, yogurt, and remaining ½ teaspoon salt in bowl and toss well to coat. Using tongs, transfer chicken to wire rack set in aluminum foil–lined rimmed baking sheet. Broil until chicken is evenly charred on both sides and registers 175 degrees, 16 to 20 minutes, flipping chicken halfway through broiling.

3. Let chicken rest for 5 minutes. While chicken rests, warm sauce over medium-low heat. Cut chicken into ¾-inch chunks and stir into sauce. Stir in 1 tablespoon cilantro and season with salt to taste. Transfer to serving dish, sprinkle with remaining 1½ teaspoons cilantro, and serve.

Thai Chicken with Basil for Two

Serves 2   Total Time 35 minutes

Why This Recipe Works A Thai street food often served for lunch, stir-fried ground chicken with basil is cooked at a low heat so that aromatics can be added at the start of cooking without scorching, enabling them to infuse the dish with flavor. Rather than buying preground chicken, we ground our own in a food processor, which gave us coarse-textured meat that retained moisture during cooking. A mix of fish sauce, oyster sauce, and white vinegar added rich but bright flavor. Stirring in more basil at the end provided a fresh finish and bold basil flavor. For a mild version of the dish, remove the seeds from the chiles. If fresh Thai chiles are unavailable, substitute two serranos or one medium jalapeño. Serve with rice.

- 1 cup fresh basil leaves, divided
- 2 green or red Thai chiles, stemmed
- 1 garlic clove, peeled
- 2½ teaspoons fish sauce, divided, plus extra for serving
- 1½ teaspoons oyster sauce
- ½ teaspoon sugar, plus extra for serving
- ½ teaspoon distilled white vinegar, plus extra for serving
- 1 (8-ounce) boneless, skinless chicken breast, trimmed and cut into 2-inch pieces
- 1 shallot, sliced thin
- 1 tablespoon vegetable oil
  Red pepper flakes

Thai Chicken with Basil for Two

1. Pulse ½ cup basil, Thai chiles, and garlic in food processor until finely chopped, 10 to 12 pulses, scraping down sides of bowl as needed. Transfer 1½ teaspoons of basil mixture to small bowl and stir in 1½ teaspoons fish sauce, oyster sauce, sugar, and vinegar. Transfer remaining basil mixture to 10-inch nonstick skillet.

2. Without washing food processor bowl, pulse chicken and remaining 1 teaspoon fish sauce in food processor until meat is coarsely chopped, 6 to 8 pulses; transfer to medium bowl and refrigerate for 15 minutes.

3. Stir shallot and oil into basil mixture in skillet. Cook over medium-low heat, stirring constantly, until garlic and shallot are golden brown, 5 to 8 minutes. (Mixture should start to sizzle after about 1½ minutes; if it doesn't, adjust heat accordingly.)

4. Stir in chopped chicken and cook over medium heat, breaking up chicken with wooden spoon, until only traces of pink remain, 2 to 4 minutes. Add reserved basil–fish sauce mixture and cook, stirring constantly, until chicken is no longer pink, about 1 minute. Stir in remaining ½ cup basil leaves and cook, stirring constantly, until basil is wilted, 30 to 60 seconds. Serve immediately, passing pepper flakes and extra fish sauce, sugar, and vinegar separately.

Simple White Rice for Two

Serves 2   **Total Time** 45 minutes

For really great long-grain rice with distinct, separate grains that didn't clump together, we rinsed the rice of excess starch first. After simmering the rice until all of the liquid was absorbed, we placed a dish towel between the lid and pot to absorb excess moisture and ensure dry, fluffy grains. You will need a small saucepan with a tight-fitting lid for this recipe. A nonstick saucepan will help prevent the rice from sticking.

   1 teaspoon vegetable oil
   ¾ cup long-grain white, basmati,
      or jasmine rice, rinsed
   1¼ cups water
   ¼ teaspoon table salt

1. Heat oil in small saucepan over medium heat until shimmering. Stir in rice and cook until edges of grains begin to turn translucent, about 2 minutes. Stir in water and salt and bring to boil. Reduce heat to low, cover, and simmer until all liquid is absorbed, 18 to 22 minutes.

2. Remove saucepan from heat. Remove lid, place folded clean dish towel over saucepan, then replace lid. Let rice sit for 10 minutes, then gently fluff with fork. Serve.

Chicken Lettuce Wraps with Hoisin for Two

Serves 2   **Total Time** 40 minutes

Why This Recipe Works Here, we made a dead-simple dish out of buttery, crunchy Bibb lettuce leaves encasing chicken thighs that we poached in sweet, tangy, umami-rich hoisin thinned with a little water. That's it. As a bonus, we only needed a skillet. While keeping it simple, we enhanced the dish with a few additions: Scallions, toasted sesame seeds, and lime wedges added depth, crunch, and tanginess, while sriracha provided an extra hit of spice. You will need a 10-inch skillet with a tight-fitting lid for this recipe—any larger and there will be too much evaporation.

2 teaspoons extra-virgin olive oil
2 scallions, white parts minced, green parts
sliced thin
6 tablespoons hoisin sauce
2 tablespoons water
4 (3- to 4-ounce) boneless, skinless chicken
thighs, trimmed
2 teaspoons toasted sesame seeds
8 Bibb, Boston, iceberg, or green leaf lettuce leaves
Lime wedges
Sriracha

1. Heat oil in 10-inch skillet over medium-low heat until shimmering. Add scallion whites and cook, stirring occasionally, until softened, about 2 minutes. Stir in hoisin and water, scraping up any browned bits. Nestle chicken into sauce, cover, and simmer for 5 minutes. Flip chicken and continue to simmer, covered, until chicken registers 175 degrees, 5 to 7 minutes.

2. Transfer chicken to plate and let cool slightly; remove skillet with sauce from heat. Using 2 forks, shred chicken into bite-size pieces. Return shredded chicken to skillet and stir to coat with sauce.

3. Cook chicken and sauce over medium heat until sauce is thickened slightly, 2 to 4 minutes. Sprinkle with sesame seeds and scallion greens. Serve filling in lettuce leaves with lime wedges and sriracha. (Filling can be refrigerated in airtight container for up to 2 days.)

Weeknight Baked
Chicken with Lemon
and Thyme for Two

Weeknight Baked Chicken with Lemon and Thyme for Two

Serves 2   Total Time 1 hour

Why This Recipe Works Recipes for baked chicken parts often produce bland, dry meat and flabby skin. Attempts to cover up such disappointments with potent ingredients only make matters worse for this simple dish. We found that a few simple tricks (and a few ingredients) gave us superb baked chicken. We started with flavorful bone-in, skin-on chicken pieces to help insulate the meat and keep it juicy in the oven. We infused the chicken with flavor by spreading butter, flavored with lemon and thyme, under the skin of each piece before cooking. Then we brushed the chicken pieces with melted butter and baked them in a hot 450-degree oven to encourage crisp skin. Elevating the chicken on a broiler pan allowed the fat to render from the chicken quickly.

2 tablespoons unsalted butter, softened, plus
1 tablespoon melted
2 teaspoons minced fresh thyme
½ teaspoon grated lemon zest
⅛ plus ¼ teaspoon table salt, divided
⅛ plus ¼ teaspoon pepper, divided
1½ pounds bone-in chicken pieces (split breasts,
drumsticks, and/or thighs), trimmed

1. Adjust oven rack to upper-middle position and heat oven to 450 degrees. Line broiler-pan bottom with aluminum foil and top with slotted broiler pan top. Mix softened butter, thyme, lemon zest, ⅛ teaspoon salt, and ⅛ teaspoon pepper together in bowl.

2. Pat chicken dry with paper towels. Use your fingers to gently loosen center portion of skin covering each chicken piece; place softened herb butter evenly under skin, directly on meat in center of each piece. Arrange chicken, skin side up, on prepared broiler pan. Brush chicken with melted butter and season with remaining ¼ teaspoon salt and remaining ¼ teaspoon pepper.

3. Roast chicken until breasts register 160 degrees and drumsticks/thighs register 175 degrees, 30 to 50 minutes. Transfer chicken to cutting board and let rest for 5 minutes before serving.

Weeknight Baked Chicken with Ginger for Two

Substitute 2 teaspoons grated fresh ginger for thyme and ½ teaspoon five-spice powder for lemon zest.

Weeknight Baked Jerk Chicken for Two

Substitute ½ teaspoon grated lime zest for lemon zest and ½ teaspoon Jamaican jerk seasoning for thyme, salt, and pepper. Add 1 minced garlic clove to softened butter mixture.

Cauliflower Gratin for Two

Serves 2 **Total Time** 35 minutes

You will need an 8½ by 5½-inch baking dish for this recipe. Serve it with Weeknight Baked Chicken with Lemon and Thyme for Two (page 464); it bakes at the same temperature.

½ cup panko bread crumbs
1½ teaspoons olive oil
10 ounces cauliflower florets, cut into 1-inch pieces
1 tablespoon water
½ (5.2-ounce) package Boursin Garlic and Fine Herbs cheese
¼ cup heavy cream
¼ teaspoon table salt
⅛ teaspoon pepper

1. Adjust oven rack to middle position and heat oven to 450 degrees. Combine panko and oil in 8-inch nonstick skillet. Toast panko over medium-high heat, stirring often, until golden, about 3 minutes.

2. Meanwhile, microwave cauliflower and water together in covered bowl until tender, about 3 minutes; drain cauliflower.

3. Wipe bowl dry with paper towels. Microwave Boursin, cream, salt, and pepper in cleaned bowl until cheese is melted, about 1 minute. Whisk Boursin mixture until smooth, then add drained cauliflower and toss to coat.

4. Transfer cauliflower mixture to 8½ by 5½-inch baking dish and sprinkle with toasted panko. Bake until hot and lightly bubbling around edges, about 7 minutes. Transfer gratin to wire rack and let cool for 5 to 10 minutes before serving.

Barbecued Dry-Rubbed Chicken for Two

Barbecued Dry-Rubbed Chicken for Two

Serves 2 **Total Time** 1½ hours

Why This Recipe Works Simply brushing grilled chicken with barbecue sauce only flavors the surface of the meat, and worse, it turns the skin flabby. We wanted classic barbecued chicken that was flavored through and through. Our solution was to swap the barbecue sauce for a dry spice rub. Spread over and under the skin before cooking, it flavored the chicken down to the bone, and it didn't prevent the skin from crisping on the grill. To keep the chicken juicy, we let it rest while the salt in the rub penetrated the meat. We also added a generous amount of sugar to the rub; as it melted in the heat, it gave our chicken the glazed sweetness of a sauce. A second coating of the rub partway through cooking thickened the glaze even more. To keep the sugar from burning, we cooked the chicken over indirect heat. Apply the second coating of spices with a light hand or it won't melt into a glaze.

1 tablespoon packed dark brown sugar
1 teaspoon paprika
¾ teaspoon chili powder
¾ teaspoon pepper
½ teaspoon dry mustard
½ teaspoon onion powder
¼ teaspoon table salt
   Pinch cayenne pepper
2 (12-ounce) bone-in split chicken breasts, trimmed

1. Combine sugar, paprika, chili powder, pepper, mustard, onion powder, salt, and cayenne in bowl. Transfer 1½ tablespoons spice mixture to shallow dish; set aside. Pat chicken dry with paper towels. Use your fingers to gently loosen center portion of skin covering each breast, then rub remaining spice mixture over and underneath skin. Transfer chicken to large plate, cover with plastic wrap, and refrigerate for at least 30 minutes or up to 1 hour.

2A. For a charcoal grill Open bottom vent completely. Light large chimney starter three-quarters filled with charcoal briquettes (4½ quarts). When top coals are partially covered with ash, pour evenly over half of grill. Set cooking grate in place, cover, and open lid vent completely. Heat grill until hot, about 5 minutes.

2B. For a gas grill Turn all burners to high, cover, and heat grill until hot, about 15 minutes. Turn primary burner to medium-high and turn off other burner(s). (Adjust primary burner as needed to maintain grill temperature around 350 degrees.)

3. Clean and oil cooking grate. Place chicken, skin side down, on cooler side of grill with thicker ends of breasts facing hotter side of grill. Tent chicken with aluminum foil, cover grill, and cook until chicken is browned and registers 140 degrees, 20 to 25 minutes.

4. Discard foil. Using tongs, lightly dredge skin side of breasts in reserved spice rub. Return chicken, skin side up, to cooler side of grill with thicker ends of breasts facing hotter side of grill. Cover grill and cook until rub has melted into glaze and chicken registers 160 degrees, about 15 minutes. Transfer chicken to serving platter and let rest for 5 to 10 minutes. Serve.

Chicken and Rice for Two

Serves 2   Total Time 1½ hours

Why This Recipe Works Chicken and rice are classic but it can be hard to properly cook them together, especially when using smaller quantities. To get perfectly al dente rice, we parcooked it in the microwave. We chose bone-in, skin-on chicken thighs for rich flavor and seared them in a saucepan to get nicely browned skin. After sautéing onion, garlic, and a little

fresh thyme in the flavorful fat left from the chicken, we added the parcooked rice to the pot, set the chicken on top, and transferred the pot to the oven to cook gently. You will need a medium ovensafe saucepan for this recipe.

1¼ cups chicken broth, divided
½ cup long-grain white rice
¾ teaspoon table salt, divided
4 (5- to 7-ounce) bone-in chicken thighs, trimmed
¼ teaspoon pepper
1 teaspoon vegetable oil
1 small onion, chopped fine
2 garlic cloves, minced
¾ teaspoon minced fresh thyme or ⅛ teaspoon dried
¼ cup dry white wine
2 tablespoons chopped fresh parsley

1. Adjust oven rack to lower-middle position and heat oven to 350 degrees. Combine ¾ cup broth, rice, and ¼ teaspoon salt in bowl. Cover and microwave until rice is softened and most of liquid is absorbed, 6 to 8 minutes.

2. Meanwhile, pat chicken dry with paper towels and sprinkle with pepper and ¼ teaspoon salt. Heat oil in medium saucepan over medium-high heat until just smoking. Cook chicken skin side down until browned, 5 to 8 minutes. Flip chicken and brown on second side, about 5 minutes; transfer to plate.

3. Pour off all but 1 teaspoon fat from saucepan. Add onion and remaining ¼ teaspoon salt and cook over medium-low heat until softened and lightly browned, 5 to 7 minutes. Stir in garlic and thyme and cook until fragrant, about 30 seconds. Stir in wine and remaining ½ cup broth, scraping up any browned bits. Stir in parcooked rice, breaking up any large clumps, and bring to simmer. Place browned chicken skin side up on rice, cover, and bake until rice is cooked through and chicken registers 175 degrees, about 25 minutes.

4. Using pot holders (saucepan handle will be hot), remove saucepan from oven. Transfer chicken to serving platter and tent chicken with aluminum foil. Fluff rice with fork, cover, and let sit for 10 minutes. Stir in parsley and season with salt and pepper to taste. Serve chicken with rice.

VARIATIONS
Chicken and Rice with Five-Spice and Scallions for Two
Substitute ¼ teaspoon five-spice powder for thyme and 2 thinly sliced scallions for parsley.

Chicken and Rice with Smoked Paprika and Cilantro for Two
Substitute ¼ teaspoon smoked paprika for thyme and 2 tablespoons chopped fresh cilantro for parsley.

Arroz con Pollo for Two

Arroz con Pollo for Two

Serves 2 **Total Time** 1¾ hours

Why This Recipe Works For an arroz con pollo full of classic flavors, we briefly marinated bone-in chicken thighs in garlic, vinegar, salt, pepper, and oregano and then stewed them with tomato paste, olives, and rice until fall-off-the-bone tender. We started the chicken skin-on to capture the flavorful fat but removed the skin after cooking. Using spoons to pull apart the meat gave us appealing chunks instead of shreds. To prevent greasiness, be sure to remove excess fat and most of the skin from the thighs, leaving just enough to protect the meat. Long-grain rice can be substituted for the medium-grain rice; however, you will need to increase the amount of broth to 1¼ cups.

 2 garlic cloves, minced
 2 teaspoons distilled white vinegar, divided
 1 teaspoon minced fresh oregano or ¼ teaspoon dried
 ½ teaspoon table salt, divided
 ¼ teaspoon pepper
 1 pound bone-in chicken thighs, trimmed
 4 teaspoons extra-virgin olive oil, divided
 1 small onion, chopped fine

 1 tablespoon tomato paste
   Pinch pepper flakes
 2 tablespoons minced fresh cilantro, divided
 1 cup chicken broth, plus extra as needed
 1 cup medium-grain white rice
 ¼ cup pitted brine-cured green olives, halved
 ¼ cup jarred whole pimentos, cut into
   2 by ¼-inch strips
   Lemon wedges

1. Adjust oven rack to middle position and heat oven to 350 degrees. Combine garlic, 1 teaspoon vinegar, oregano, ¼ teaspoon salt, and pepper in large bowl. Add chicken and toss to coat. Cover and let sit at room temperature for 15 minutes.

2. Meanwhile, heat 1 tablespoon oil in Dutch oven over medium heat until shimmering. Add onion and cook until softened, about 5 minutes. Stir in tomato paste and pepper flakes and cook until fragrant, about 1 minute. Stir in 1 tablespoon cilantro.

3. Push vegetables to sides of pot and increase heat to medium-high. Add chicken skin side down to center of pot and cook on both sides, 2 to 4 minutes per side, reducing heat if chicken begins to brown. Stir in broth and bring to simmer. Cover, reduce heat to medium-low, and cook for 15 minutes.

4. Stir in rice, olives, and remaining ¼ teaspoon salt and bring to simmer. Cover, transfer pot to oven, and cook, stirring often, until chicken registers 175 degrees, rice is tender, and liquid has been absorbed, about 30 minutes. (If pot appears dry and begins to scorch after 20 minutes, stir in 2 tablespoons extra water.)

5. Remove pot from oven and transfer chicken to cutting board; cover pot and set aside. Let chicken cool slightly, then pull into large chunks using 2 spoons; discard skin and bones. Toss chicken, pimentos, remaining 1 teaspoon vinegar, remaining 1 teaspoon oil, and remaining 1 tablespoon cilantro together in clean bowl and season with salt and pepper to taste.

6. Place chicken mixture on top of rice, cover, and let sit until heated through, about 5 minutes. Serve with lemon wedges.

Chicken and Chorizo Paella for Two

Serves 2 **Total Time** 50 minutes

Why This Recipe Works Paella is often loaded with meat, seafood, and vegetables—an abundance of ingredients that makes it a challenge to scale this recipe down and keep the flavor and feel of the original. Luckily, we found that a combination of chorizo sausage and chicken breasts was hearty enough that we could forgo the seafood altogether. To ensure that the rice was evenly cooked, we started it in the microwave and finished it in the pan with our other ingredients. A rich sofrito of onion, garlic, and tomato gave our dish a deep flavor, and bright peas and briny olives added color and dimension. We like to use short-grain Valencia rice for this dish, but you can substitute Arborio rice. Do not substitute long-grain rice. Look for large pitted green olives at the olive bar in the supermarket. Pimento-stuffed olives can be substituted in a pinch. To make the chicken easier to slice, freeze it for 15 minutes.

1½ cups water, divided
½ cup Valencia or Arborio rice
⅛ plus ¼ teaspoon table salt, divided
4 teaspoons vegetable oil, divided
4 ounces chorizo sausage, halved lengthwise and sliced ¼ inch thick
1 (8-ounce) boneless, skinless chicken breast, trimmed and sliced ¼ inch thick
¼ teaspoon pepper
1 small onion, chopped fine
¾ cup canned diced tomatoes, drained with juice reserved
2 garlic cloves, minced
⅛ teaspoon saffron threads, crumbled
¼ cup large pitted green olives, quartered
¼ cup frozen peas

1. Combine 1 cup water, rice, and ⅛ teaspoon salt in bowl. Cover and microwave until rice is softened and most of liquid is absorbed, 6 to 8 minutes

2. Meanwhile, heat 2 teaspoons oil in 10-inch nonstick skillet over medium-high heat until just smoking. Add chorizo and cook until lightly browned, about 2 minutes. Using slotted spoon, transfer chorizo to plate. Pat chicken dry with paper towels and sprinkle with pepper and remaining ¼ teaspoon salt. Add chicken to fat left in skillet, break up any clumps, and cook until lightly browned on all sides, about 4 minutes; transfer to plate with chorizo.

3. Heat remaining 2 teaspoons oil in now-empty skillet over medium heat until shimmering. Add onion and cook until softened, about 5 minutes. Stir in tomatoes and cook until beginning to soften and darken, 3 to 5 minutes. Stir in garlic and saffron and cook until fragrant, about 30 seconds. Stir in remaining ½ cup water and reserved tomato juice, scraping up any browned bits. Stir in parcooked rice, breaking up any large clumps, and bring to simmer. Reduce heat to medium-low, cover, and simmer until rice is tender and liquid is absorbed, 8 to 12 minutes.

4. Stir in browned chorizo and chicken and any accumulated juices, olives, and peas and increase heat to medium-high. Cook, uncovered, until bottom layer of rice is golden and crisp, about 5 minutes, rotating skillet halfway through cooking to ensure even browning. Season with salt and pepper to taste, and serve.

Chicken and Couscous with Dried Fruit and Smoked Almonds for Two

Serves 2 Total Time 45 minutes

Why This Recipe Works This easy yet elegant dish relies on just one skillet to cook the chicken, sauté the aromatics, and simmer the couscous. Cooking the chicken first meant we were able to capitalize on the flavorful browned bits, or fond, left behind to infuse the couscous with deep, savory flavor. And since couscous cooks so quickly, it came together in a flash while the chicken rested. For some crunch and more savory depth, we stirred in a handful of chopped smoked almonds. The smoky flavor contrasted nicely with the sweetness of the dried apricots and added an unexpected twist to this simple dinner.

2 (6- to 8-ounce) boneless, skinless chicken breasts, trimmed
½ teaspoon table salt, divided
¼ teaspoon pepper
¼ cup all-purpose flour
2 tablespoons extra-virgin olive oil, divided
1 shallot, minced
½ cup couscous
½ teaspoon garam masala
¾ cup chicken broth
¼ cup dried apricots, chopped coarse
2 tablespoons coarsely chopped smoked almonds
1 tablespoon minced fresh parsley

1. Pound chicken breasts to uniform thickness. Pat chicken dry with paper towels and sprinkle with ¼ teaspoon salt and pepper. Spread flour in shallow dish. Working with 1 breast at a time, dredge breasts in flour.

2. Heat 1 tablespoon oil in 10-inch skillet over medium-high heat until just smoking. Cook chicken until well browned on first side, 6 to 8 minutes. Flip chicken, reduce heat to medium, and continue to cook until chicken registers 160 degrees, 6 to 8 minutes; transfer to serving platter and tent with aluminum foil.

3. Heat remaining 1 tablespoon oil in now-empty skillet over medium heat until shimmering. Add shallot and remaining ¼ teaspoon salt and cook until softened, about 2 minutes. Stir in couscous and garam masala and cook until fragrant, about 30 seconds. Stir in broth and apricots, scraping up any browned bits. Bring to brief simmer, then remove from heat, cover, and let sit until liquid is absorbed and grains are tender, about 3 minutes.

4. Uncover and fluff grains with fork. Stir in almonds and parsley and season with salt and pepper to taste. Serve chicken with couscous.

Skillet-Roasted Chicken Leg Quarters and Potatoes for Two

Serves 2   Total Time 1 hour

Why This Recipe Works This recipe hits all the right notes of a roast chicken and potato dinner—and in just one skillet. A bit of batch cooking helped develop savory browning on both the chicken leg quarters and the potatoes while adding chicken flavor to the vegetables. Lining the skillet with ½-inch slices of potato and giving them a quick jump start on the stove helped ensure that they browned in the oven. Next, placing the chicken directly on top of the potatoes allowed for chicken drippings to season the potatoes beneath, bumping up their creamy texture and their flavor. Some leg quarters are sold with the backbone attached; removing it before cooking makes the chicken easier to serve (see page 11). You can substitute two 10- to 12-ounce bone-in split chicken breasts for the leg quarters, if desired. Be sure to cook the breasts to 160 degrees in step 4, about 35 minutes.

- 2 (10- to 12-ounce) chicken leg quarters, trimmed
- 1 teaspoon minced fresh thyme
- ¾ teaspoon plus pinch table salt, divided
- ½ teaspoon pepper, divided
- 1 pound Yukon Gold potatoes, peeled and sliced into ½-inch-thick rounds
- 2 shallots, halved through root end
- 2 tablespoons extra-virgin olive oil, divided
- 1 tablespoon chopped fresh parsley
- ½ teaspoon grated lemon zest, plus lemon wedges for serving
- ½ teaspoon minced garlic

1. Adjust oven rack to middle position and heat oven to 400 degrees. Pat chicken dry with paper towels and sprinkle with thyme, ½ teaspoon salt, and ¼ teaspoon pepper.

Chicken and Couscous with Dried Fruit and Smoked Almonds for Two

Skillet-Roasted Chicken Leg Quarters and Potatoes for Two

Toss potatoes, shallots, 1 tablespoon oil, ¼ teaspoon salt, and remaining ¼ teaspoon pepper together in bowl. Combine parsley, lemon zest, garlic, and remaining pinch salt in small bowl; set aside.

2. Heat remaining 1 tablespoon oil in 12-inch ovensafe nonstick skillet over medium heat until shimmering. Cook chicken skin side down until well browned, about 5 minutes. Transfer chicken to plate, skin side up.

3. Place potatoes and shallots in single layer in now-empty skillet. Cook over medium heat, without moving vegetables, until bottoms of potatoes are golden brown, about 5 minutes.

4. Place chicken, skin side up, on top of vegetables and transfer skillet to oven. Roast until chicken registers 175 degrees and potatoes are tender, about 30 minutes. Sprinkle with parsley mixture. Serve, passing lemon wedges separately.

Skillet-Roasted Chicken Breasts with Garlicky Green Beans for Two

Serves 2   Total Time 1¼ hours

Why This Recipe Works This recipe is a twofer from one skillet. First, we seasoned bone-in chicken breasts under the skin with salt. Starting them in a cold skillet helped the skin to slowly render and brown without overcooking the delicate flesh. Once the skin was well browned, we flipped the breasts and finished them gently in a 325-degree oven. While they rested, we reduced the juices with garlic and red pepper flakes before adding green beans along with a little water to help them cook through in a covered the pan. With the skillet uncovered, the savory liquid thickened to coat the green beans. Be sure to remove excess skin from the breasts when trimming.

- 2 (10- to 12-ounce) bone-in split chicken breasts, trimmed
- ¾ teaspoon table salt, divided
  Vegetable oil spray
- 2 garlic cloves, sliced thin
  Pinch red pepper flakes
- 10 ounces green beans, trimmed
- ¼ cup water
- ¼ cup shredded Parmesan cheese

1. Adjust oven rack to lower-middle position and heat oven to 325 degrees. Working with 1 breast at a time, use your fingers to carefully separate skin from meat. Peel back skin, leaving skin attached at top and bottom of breast and at ribs. Sprinkle

Skillet-Roasted Chicken Breasts with Garlicky Green Beans for Two

½ teaspoon salt evenly over chicken. Lay skin back in place. Using metal skewer or tip of paring knife, poke 6 to 8 holes in fat deposits in skin of each breast. Spray skin with oil spray.

2. Place chicken, skin side down, in 10-inch ovensafe skillet and set over medium-high heat. Cook, moving chicken as infrequently as possible, until skin is well browned, 7 to 9 minutes.

3. Carefully flip chicken and transfer skillet to oven. Roast until chicken registers 160 degrees, 25 to 30 minutes.

4. Transfer chicken to plate; do not discard liquid in skillet. Add garlic, pepper flakes, and remaining ¼ teaspoon salt to skillet and cook over medium-high heat, stirring occasionally and scraping up any browned bits, until moisture has evaporated and mixture begins to sizzle, 1 to 3 minutes. Add green beans and water and bring to simmer. Cover skillet, reduce heat to medium, and cook until green beans are tender, 8 to 10 minutes, stirring halfway through cooking. Uncover and continue to cook, stirring frequently, until sauce begins to coat green beans, 2 to 4 minutes longer. Add any accumulated chicken juices to skillet and toss to combine. Season with salt to taste. Transfer green beans to serving platter and sprinkle with Parmesan. Top with chicken and serve.

Skillet-Roasted Chicken Breasts with Garlic-Ginger Broccoli for Two

Omit pepper flakes and add 1 teaspoon grated fresh ginger, 1 teaspoon toasted sesame oil, and ⅛ teaspoon sugar to skillet with garlic and salt in step 4. Substitute 12 ounces broccoli, florets cut into ¾-inch pieces, stalks trimmed, peeled, and sliced on bias ¼ inch thick, for green beans and cook until broccoli is crisp-tender, about 5 minutes, stirring halfway through cooking. Uncover and cook as directed, omitting Parmesan.

Baked Chicken with Fennel, Tomatoes, and Olives for Two

Serves 2   Total Time 1¼ hours (plus 1 hour marinating time)

Why This Recipe Works To turn simple baked chicken breasts into an inspiring main course, we started by flavoring the chicken with a garlic, shallot, and herb marinade. We chose a mix of easy-prep Mediterranean vegetables: whole cherry tomatoes, thinly sliced fennel, and kalamata olives. We tossed the vegetables with some reserved marinade; as they cooked, the tomatoes released juice that combined with the marinade to make a tasty sauce. Some fresh basil and lemon juice at the end completed the dish. You can substitute boneless, skinless breasts here if desired; marinate the boneless chicken as directed, but reduce the baking time by 10 to 15 minutes. The marinade takes the place of a brine in this recipe, so there's no need to brine the chicken.

Chicken
- ⅓ cup extra-virgin olive oil
- 1 shallot, minced
- 2 tablespoons water
- 2 tablespoons chopped fresh basil
- 4 garlic cloves, minced
- ½ teaspoon table salt
- ⅛ teaspoon pepper
- 2 (12-ounce) bone-in split chicken breasts, trimmed

Vegetables
- 1 fennel bulb, stalks discarded, bulb halved, cored, and sliced thin
- 6 ounces cherry tomatoes
- ¼ cup pitted kalamata olives
- ¼ teaspoon table salt
- ⅛ teaspoon pepper
- 1 tablespoon lemon juice
- 2 tablespoons chopped fresh basil

1. For the chicken Whisk oil, shallot, water, basil, garlic, salt, and pepper in bowl until well combined. Measure out ¼ cup marinade and set aside. Pour remaining marinade into 1-gallon zipper-lock bag, add chicken, seal bag tightly, and toss to coat. Marinate chicken in refrigerator for at least 1 hour or up to 24 hours. (If marinating chicken for more than 1 hour, refrigerate ¼ cup reserved marinade as well; return it to room temperature before using.)

2. For the vegetables Adjust oven rack to middle position and heat oven to 450 degrees. In large bowl, combine 1 tablespoon reserved marinade with fennel, tomatoes, olives, salt, and pepper and toss to coat. Transfer vegetables to 8-inch square baking dish.

3. Remove chicken from marinade and lay skin side up on top of vegetables; discard any marinade left in bag. Bake until chicken registers 160 degrees, 35 to 45 minutes. Meanwhile, stir lemon juice into remaining 3 tablespoons reserved marinade.

4. Transfer chicken and vegetables to serving platter along with juices from baking dish. Pour lemon-marinade mixture over chicken and let rest for 5 minutes. Sprinkle with basil and serve.

A Single Pan-Seared Boneless Chicken Breast

Serves 1   Total Time 20 minutes

When cooking a single chicken breast, we found it best to use a smaller skillet to avoid a smoking pan. After letting it brown on one side, we flipped it, added a splash of water, covered the skillet, and reduced the heat to finish cooking it gently. You will need an 8- or 10-inch skillet with a tight-fitting lid.

- 1 (6- to 8-ounce) boneless, skinless chicken breast, trimmed
- ⅛ teaspoon table salt
- ⅛ teaspoon pepper
- 1 teaspoon oil

1. Pound chicken breast to even thickness. Pat chicken dry with paper towels and sprinkle with salt and pepper.

2. Heat oil in 8- or 10-inch skillet over medium heat until just smoking. Add chicken and cook until well browned on first side, about 3 minutes. Flip chicken, add 2 tablespoons water, and cover skillet. Reduce heat to low and continue to cook until chicken registers 160 degrees, about 3 minutes.

3. Transfer chicken to plate, tent with aluminum foil, and let rest for 5 minutes. Serve.

Parmesan and
Basil-Stuffed Chicken
with Roasted Carrots for Two

Chicken and
Dumplings for Two

Parmesan and Basil-Stuffed Chicken with Roasted Carrots for Two

Serves 2 **Total Time** 1 hour

Why This Recipe Works Stuffed chicken breasts may sound like a dish best reserved for entertaining, but they actually make an easy meal for two. The key? A supersimple stuffing. We used a no-fuss cream cheese filling featuring basil, garlic, and Parmesan. Rather than turn to a fussy preparation for stuffing the breasts, we simply spooned the filling under the skin of bone-in chicken breasts; the skin held the filling in place, and the meat emerged from the oven moist and juicy. Brushing the skin with melted butter and baking the breasts in a hot 450-degree oven ensured crisp, golden brown skin. For a simple side, we tossed carrots with melted butter and a little brown sugar and roasted them alongside the chicken until perfectly softened and caramelized. It is important to buy chicken breasts with the skin still attached and intact; otherwise, the stuffing will leak out. Be sure to spread the carrots in an even layer halfway through baking to ensure that they cook through and brown properly. If using kosher chicken, do not brine. If brining the chicken, do not season with salt in step 2. For more information on brining, see page 15.

1 ounce Parmesan cheese, grated (½ cup)
1 ounce cream cheese, softened
2 tablespoons chopped fresh basil
1 tablespoon extra-virgin olive oil
1 small garlic clove, minced
    Pinch plus ¼ teaspoon table salt, divided
    Pinch plus ¼ teaspoon pepper, divided
2 (12-ounce) bone-in split chicken breasts, trimmed and brined if desired
1 tablespoon unsalted butter, melted, divided
6 small carrots, peeled and sliced ½ inch thick on bias
1½ teaspoons packed dark brown sugar

1. Adjust oven rack to middle position and heat oven to 450 degrees. Line rimmed baking sheet with aluminum foil. Mix Parmesan, cream cheese, basil, oil, garlic, pinch salt, and pinch pepper together in bowl.

2. Pat chicken dry with paper towels and season with remaining ¼ teaspoon salt and remaining ¼ teaspoon pepper. Use your fingers to gently loosen center portion of skin covering each breast. Using spoon, place half of cheese mixture underneath skin over center of each breast. Gently press on skin to spread out cheese mixture.

3. Arrange chicken skin side up on 1 side of baking sheet. Brush chicken with half of melted butter. Toss carrots with sugar and remaining melted butter and season with salt and pepper. Mound carrots in pile on baking sheet, opposite chicken.

4. Bake until chicken registers 160 degrees and carrots are browned and tender, 30 to 35 minutes, rotating sheet and spreading out carrots into even layer halfway through baking. Let chicken and carrots rest on sheet for 5 minutes before serving.

VARIATION

Goat Cheese and Olive-Stuffed Chicken with Roasted Carrots for Two

Omit Parmesan, basil, and olive oil. Add 1½ ounces softened goat cheese, 2 tablespoons finely chopped pitted kalamata olives, and 1 teaspoon minced fresh oregano to cream cheese mixture.

STUFFING BONE-IN CHICKEN BREASTS

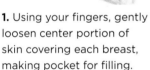

1. Using your fingers, gently loosen center portion of skin covering each breast, making pocket for filling.

2. Using spoon, place filling underneath loosened skin, over center of each breast. Gently press on skin to spread out filling.

Chicken and Dumplings for Two

Serves 2   Total Time 1¼ hours

Why This Recipe Works Chicken and dumplings is a perfect warm-you-up winter stew. Most recipes for chicken and dumplings feed six or so, but if you don't eat the dish right away, any leftover dumplings get soggy and start to disintegrate. To downsize this comfort-food classic, we started by swapping out a whole chicken for boneless, skinless thighs. They're quick-cooking but less apt to dry out than white-meat breasts. Added with the hardier carrots and onion, frozen peas turned mushy and drab, so we sprinkled them over the dish during the last 5 minutes of cooking. As for the dumplings,

when we scaled down the recipe, we found that they used so little cream that it seemed like a nuisance. We wondered if we needed cream at all. Luckily, we found that we could use chicken broth (which we were already using in the filling) in place of the cream, along with a bit of butter to add back richness. The dumplings were more tender and savory than ever. Make the dumplings just before adding them to the stew.

Stew
- 2 tablespoons unsalted butter
- 2 carrots, peeled and sliced ¼ inch thick
- 1 small onion, chopped fine
- 1 garlic clove, minced
- ½ teaspoon minced fresh thyme
- ½ teaspoon table salt
- ½ teaspoon pepper
- 1 tablespoon all-purpose flour
- ¼ cup dry sherry
- 2 cups chicken broth
- 1 pound boneless, skinless chicken thighs, trimmed and cut into 1-inch pieces
- ⅓ cup frozen peas

Dumplings
- ½ cup (2½ ounces) all-purpose flour
- 1 teaspoon baking powder
- ¼ teaspoon salt
- ¼ cup chicken broth
- 1 tablespoon unsalted butter, melted

1. For the stew Melt butter in medium saucepan over medium-high heat. Add carrots and onion and cook until lightly browned, 5 to 8 minutes. Add garlic, thyme, salt, and pepper and cook until fragrant, about 30 seconds. Add flour and cook, stirring, for 1 minute. Stir in sherry, scraping up any browned bits, and cook until nearly dry, about 1 minute. Slowly stir in broth and bring to boil. Add chicken, reduce heat to medium-low, cover, and simmer until chicken is cooked through and tender, about 15 minutes.

2. For the dumplings Meanwhile, combine flour, baking powder, and salt in bowl. Stir in broth and melted butter until just incorporated.

3. Season stew with salt and pepper to taste. Increase heat to medium. Using 2 spoons, drop eight 1-inch dumplings into stew about 1 inch apart. Cover and simmer for 5 minutes. Sprinkle peas around dumplings, cover, and cook 5 minutes longer. Remove from heat and let cool slightly, uncovered, about 10 minutes. Serve.

Chicken Pot Pie for Two

Serves 2   Total Time 1½ hours

Why This Recipe Works To simplify making chicken pot pie for two, we opted to make two individual pies in ramekins. A single boneless, skinless chicken breast was supereasy to work with and substantial enough for two pies when combined with the rest of the ingredients. Cooking the chicken right in the sauce imparted layers of flavor and also saved time on cleanup. A little soy sauce added complex flavor that would normally require hours of simmering to achieve. For the crust, we turned to a store-bought option, which we parcooked on a baking sheet to ensure that it wouldn't collapse into the filling. We use two 12-ounce ovensafe ramekins or bowls to make this dish. If you don't own any, you can use 14-ounce disposable mini loaf pans, cutting the crust to fit.

- 1 Pillsbury Refrigerated Pie Crust
- 2 tablespoons unsalted butter
- 2 carrots, peeled and sliced ¼ inch thick
- 1 small onion, chopped fine
- 1 small celery rib, sliced ¼ inch thick
- ½ teaspoon table salt
- 2 garlic cloves, minced
- 1 teaspoon minced fresh thyme
- 3 tablespoons all-purpose flour
- 1¾ cups chicken broth
- ⅓ cup heavy cream
- ½ teaspoon soy sauce
- 1 (8-ounce) boneless, skinless chicken breast, trimmed
- ¼ cup frozen peas
- 2 teaspoons minced fresh parsley
- ¼ teaspoon lemon juice

1. Adjust oven rack to middle position and heat oven to 450 degrees. Line rimmed baking sheet with parchment paper. Unroll dough on baking sheet. Use 12-ounce ovensafe ramekin as guide to cut out 2 rounds of dough about ½ inch larger than mouth of ramekin. Fold under and crimp outer ½ inch of dough, then cut 3 vents in center of each crust. Bake until crusts just begin to brown and no longer look raw, about 7 minutes; set aside.

2. Meanwhile, melt butter in medium saucepan over medium heat. Add carrots, onion, celery, and salt and cook until vegetables are softened and browned, 8 to 10 minutes. Stir in garlic and thyme, and cook until fragrant, about 30 seconds. Stir in flour and cook for 1 minute.

3. Slowly whisk in broth, cream, and soy sauce, scraping up any browned bits. Nestle chicken into sauce and bring to simmer. Cover, reduce heat to medium-low, and cook until

Chicken Pot Pie for Two

chicken registers 160 degrees, 10 to 15 minutes. Transfer chicken to plate; let cool slightly. Using 2 forks, shred chicken into bite-size pieces.

4. While chicken is cooling, return pan with sauce to medium heat and simmer until thickened and sauce measures 2 cups, about 5 minutes. Off heat, return shredded chicken and accumulated juice to pan. Stir in peas, parsley, and lemon juice and season with salt and pepper to taste.

5. Divide filling between ramekins and place parbaked crusts on top of filling. Place pot pies on baking sheet and bake until crusts are deep golden brown and filling is bubbling, 10 to 15 minutes. Let pot pies cool for 10 minutes before serving.

Chicken Sausage Hash for Two

Serves 2   Total Time 40 minutes

Why This Recipe Works While making hash for a crowd might mean endless chopping, all it takes is two small potatoes to get this scaled-down version going. To drastically cut down the cooking time, we microwaved the cut-up potatoes to give them a head start. Store-bought chicken sausage is filled with flavors and spices, so we didn't have to add many seasonings. For the classic flavor combination of potatoes and cabbage, we used tiny brussels sprouts to stand in for their larger counterpart; it was easy to buy just the amount we needed. To ensure that everything was evenly cooked, we sautéed the components in stages, then added everything back to steam briefly, and then uncovered the pan and cooked until the edges were crispy. This not only gave the hash a savory depth, but also made the mixture more cohesive. Then we cleared a small well in the center of the skillet and cracked an egg in the middle for a poached/fried hybrid that delivered a luxuriously oozy yolk (if desired). You will need a 12-inch nonstick skillet with a tight-fitting lid for this recipe. Sprinkle with fresh herbs, crumbled cheese, and/or a drizzle of your favorite hot sauce or herb sauce.

 2 small Yukon Gold potatoes, peeled and cut into
    ½-inch pieces
 2 tablespoons oil, divided
 ¼ teaspoon table salt, divided
 ¼ teaspoon pepper, divided
 8 ounces chicken sausage, casing removed
 4 ounces brussels sprouts, trimmed and quartered
 2 tablespoons water
 2 large eggs

1. Toss potatoes, 2 teaspoons oil, ⅛ teaspoon salt, and ⅛ teaspoon pepper together in bowl. Cover and microwave until tender, about 5 minutes, stirring once halfway through microwaving; set aside. Heat 2 teaspoons oil in 12-inch nonstick skillet over medium heat until shimmering. Add sausage and cook, breaking up meat with wooden spoon, until sausage is lightly browned, about 5 minutes; add sausage to bowl with potatoes.

2. Heat remaining 2 teaspoons oil in now-empty skillet over medium heat until shimmering. Add brussels sprouts and cook, stirring occasionally, until browned, about 5 minutes. Stir in water and sausage-potato mixture. Reduce heat to medium-low, cover, and cook until brussels sprouts are tender, 3 to 4 minutes, stirring once halfway through. Flip hash, 1 scoop at a time, then lightly repack hash into pan. Repeat flipping and repacking hash every minute until potatoes are well browned, about 4 minutes.

3. Off heat, make 2 shallow wells in hash with back of spoon. Break 1 egg into each well in hash, sprinkle eggs with remaining ⅛ teaspoon salt and remaining ⅛ teaspoon pepper, then cover skillet and place over medium-low heat. Cook to desired doneness: 4 to 5 minutes for runny yolks or 6 to 7 minutes for set yolks. Season with salt and pepper to taste, and serve.

Chicken Noodle Casserole for Two
Serves 2 **Total Time** 50 minutes

Why This Recipe Works For a homemade version of this classic casserole that's commonly made with canned cream of mushroom soup, we first made a copycat soup base. We browned mushrooms and shallots and then added a bit of flour to thicken the half-and-half and chicken broth that followed. We chose chicken thighs because they stayed juicy, and we cut them into small pieces so that they cooked quickly in the sauce. Instead of boiling the egg noodles separately, we streamlined the dish and added them straight to the skillet with the sauce and chicken. Covering the skillet meant that the noodles would cook through while the sauce thickened and the chicken finished cooking. We then stirred in shredded cheddar cheese for more creaminess and frozen peas for wholesome pops of sweetness. For satisfying textural contrast, we topped it all off with a cheesy, crunchy combo of panko bread crumbs and Parmesan.

 3 tablespoons extra-virgin olive oil, divided
 ½ cup panko bread crumbs
 ½ teaspoon table salt, divided
 ½ teaspoon pepper, divided
 3 tablespoons grated Parmesan cheese
 4 ounces white mushrooms, trimmed and sliced thin
 2 shallots, chopped
 8 ounces boneless, skinless chicken thighs,
    trimmed and cut into 1-inch pieces
 4 teaspoons all-purpose flour
 1 cup half-and-half
 1 cup chicken broth
 3 ounces (1½ cups) wide egg noodles
 2 ounces sharp cheddar cheese, shredded (½ cup)
 ½ cup frozen peas

1. Combine 1 tablespoon oil, panko, ⅛ teaspoon salt, and ⅛ teaspoon pepper in 10-inch nonstick skillet. Cook over medium heat, stirring frequently, until evenly browned, 3 to 5 minutes. Off heat, sprinkle Parmesan evenly over panko mixture and stir to combine, breaking up any clumps. Transfer panko mixture to bowl; set aside.

2. Heat remaining 2 tablespoons oil in now-empty skillet over medium heat until shimmering. Add mushrooms, shallots, ¼ teaspoon salt, and ¼ teaspoon pepper and cook until moisture has evaporated and mushrooms are golden brown, about 8 minutes.

3. Add chicken and flour and stir until no dry flour remains. Cook for 1 minute. Stir in half-and-half and broth and bring to simmer. Stir in noodles, submerging them as much as possible, and cook, uncovered, stirring often, until noodles are tender and sauce is thickened (rubber spatula will leave trail that takes about 3 seconds to fill in), about 8 minutes.

4. Stir in cheddar, peas, remaining $\frac{1}{8}$ teaspoon salt, and remaining $\frac{1}{8}$ teaspoon pepper until cheese is completely melted and peas are warmed through, about 2 minutes. Off heat, sprinkle evenly with reserved panko mixture. Serve.

Pasta with Chicken, Broccoli, and Sun-Dried Tomatoes for Two

Serves 2   **Total Time** 1 hour

Why This Recipe Works For our take on this popular pasta, we sought a fresh, not rich sauce that would highlight the crisp broccoli and tender chicken. We kept the chicken tender and added flavor by letting it finish cooking in the sauce, and we kept the broccoli crisp by blanching it in the pasta water. But our real breakthrough was to replace the typical cream sauce with a broth-based sauce, which we rounded out with a little butter, Asiago cheese, and sun-dried tomatoes. Other pasta shapes can be substituted; however, their cup measurements may vary. Parmesan cheese can be substituted for the Asiago. To make the chicken easier to slice, freeze it for 15 minutes.

- 1 (8-ounce) boneless, skinless chicken breast, trimmed and sliced $\frac{1}{4}$ inch thick
- $\frac{1}{4}$ plus $\frac{1}{8}$ teaspoon table salt, divided, plus salt for cooking broccoli and pasta
- $\frac{1}{4}$ teaspoon pepper
- 3 tablespoons unsalted butter, divided
- 1 small onion, chopped fine
- 3 garlic cloves, minced
- 1 teaspoon minced fresh thyme or $\frac{1}{4}$ teaspoon dried
- 1 teaspoon all-purpose flour
- $\frac{1}{8}$ teaspoon red pepper flakes
- 1 cup chicken broth
- $\frac{1}{2}$ cup dry white wine
- 12 ounces broccoli, florets cut into 1-inch pieces, stalks peeled and sliced $\frac{1}{4}$ inch thick
- 6 ounces (2 cups) ziti
- 1 ounce Asiago cheese, grated ($\frac{1}{2}$ cup), plus extra for serving
- $\frac{1}{2}$ cup oil-packed sun-dried tomatoes, patted dry and cut into $\frac{1}{4}$-inch strips
- 1 tablespoon chopped fresh parsley

1. Pat chicken dry with paper towels and sprinkle with $\frac{1}{4}$ teaspoon salt and pepper. Melt 1 tablespoon butter in 10-inch nonstick skillet over high heat until beginning to brown. Add chicken, break up any clumps, and cook, without stirring, until beginning to brown, about 1 minute. Stir chicken and continue to cook until nearly cooked through, about 2 minutes; transfer to bowl.

2. Melt 1 tablespoon butter in now-empty skillet over medium heat. Add onion and remaining $\frac{1}{8}$ teaspoon salt and cook until softened and lightly browned, 5 to 7 minutes. Stir in garlic, thyme, flour, and pepper flakes and cook until fragrant, about 30 seconds. Whisk in broth and wine, bring to simmer, and cook until sauce is slightly thickened and measures about $\frac{2}{3}$ cup, about 10 minutes. Remove from heat and cover to keep warm.

3. Meanwhile, bring 4 quarts water to boil in large pot. Add broccoli florets and stalks and 1 tablespoon salt and cook, stirring often, until florets are crisp-tender, about 2 minutes. Using slotted spoon, transfer broccoli to paper towel–lined plate.

4. Return pot of water to boil. Add pasta and cook, stirring often, until al dente. Reserve $\frac{1}{2}$ cup cooking water, then drain pasta and return it to pot. Stir Asiago, tomatoes, chicken and any accumulated juices, and remaining 1 tablespoon butter into sauce, bring to simmer, and cook until chicken is cooked through, about 1 minute. Add chicken mixture, broccoli, and parsley to pasta and toss to combine. Season with salt and pepper to taste, and adjust consistency with reserved cooking water as needed. Serve with extra Asiago.

Sesame Noodles with Shredded Chicken for Two

Serves 2   **Total Time** 1 hour

Why This Recipe Works For sesame noodles we could make at home whenever the craving struck, we started with the noodles themselves. Fresh Chinese noodles have a chewier texture than dried versions; rinsing them under cold water and tossing them with a little oil prevented clumping. The addition of one chicken breast turned our noodles into a meal, and broiling ensured that it cooked through quickly without drying out. Asian sesame paste is what gives this dish its distinct flavor; we found that peanut butter and freshly ground toasted sesame seeds made a fine substitute. Garlic, ginger, soy sauce, rice vinegar, hot sauce, and brown sugar rounded out our sauce, and thinly sliced red bell pepper, cucumber, and shredded carrot added color and fresh crunch to the dish.

Conventional chunky peanut butter works best in this recipe because it tends to be sweeter than natural or old-fashioned versions; however, creamy peanut butter can be substituted.

Sauce

2½ tablespoons soy sauce
  2 tablespoons chunky peanut butter
1½ tablespoons sesame seeds, toasted
  1 tablespoon rice vinegar
  1 tablespoon packed light brown sugar
1½ teaspoons grated fresh ginger
  1 garlic clove, minced
  ½ teaspoon hot sauce
  3 tablespoons hot tap water

Chicken and Noodles

  1 (8-ounce) boneless, skinless chicken breast, trimmed
  8 ounces fresh Chinese noodles or 6 ounces dried spaghetti or linguine
  1 tablespoon table salt, for cooking noodles
  1 tablespoon toasted sesame oil
  ½ red bell pepper, cut into ¼-inch-wide strips
  ½ cucumber, peeled, halved lengthwise, seeded, and sliced ¼ inch thick
  1 carrot, peeled and shredded
  2 scallions, sliced thin on bias
  1 tablespoon chopped fresh cilantro (optional)
  1 tablespoon sesame seeds, toasted

1. For the sauce Process soy sauce, peanut butter, sesame seeds, vinegar, sugar, ginger, garlic, and hot sauce in blender until smooth, about 30 seconds. With blender running, slowly add hot water, 1 tablespoon at a time, until sauce has consistency of heavy cream (you may not need all of water).

2. For the chicken and noodles Adjust oven rack 6 inches from broiler element and heat broiler. Spray broiler pan top with vegetable oil spray. Pound chicken breast to even thickness. Pat chicken dry with paper towels and lay on prepared pan. Broil until lightly golden on both sides and chicken registers 160 degrees, 10 to 12 minutes, flipping chicken halfway through cooking. Transfer chicken to cutting board, let cool slightly, then shred into bite-size pieces using 2 forks.

3. Meanwhile, bring 4 quarts water to boil in large pot. Add noodles and salt and cook, stirring often, until tender. Drain noodles, rinse with cold water, then drain again, leaving noodles slightly wet. Transfer noodles to large bowl and toss with oil. Add sauce; shredded chicken; bell pepper; cucumber; carrot; scallions; and cilantro, if using, and toss to combine. Sprinkle individual portions with sesame seeds and serve.

Pasta with Chicken, Broccoli, and Sun-Dried Tomatoes for Two

Sesame Noodles with Shredded Chicken for Two

NUTRITIONAL INFORMATION FOR OUR RECIPES

We calculate the nutritional values of our recipes per serving; if there is a range in the serving size, we used the highest number of servings to calculate the nutritional values. We entered all the ingredients, using weights for important ingredients such as most vegetables. We also used our preferred brands in these analyses. We did not include additional salt or pepper for food that's "seasoned to taste."

	Calories	Total Fat (g)	Sat Fat (g)	Chol (mg)	Sodium (mg)	Total Carb (g)	Dietary Fiber (g)	Total Sugars (g)	Protein (g)
EASY DINNERS									
Pan-Seared Chicken Breasts with Artichokes and Spinach	526	22	10	236	846	13	6	2	67
Un-Stuffed Chicken Breasts with Ham and Gruyère and Roasted Broccoli	540	24	8	165	1130	20	0	4	56
Chicken Leg Quarters with Cauliflower and Shallots	690	48	11	192	1357	28	8	11	40
Stir-Fried Chicken Lettuce Wraps	307	17	2	107	794	13	3	3	25
Chicken Sausage with Braised Red Cabbage and Potatoes	490	25	6	75	990	40	4	11	26
Chicken Breasts with Kale and Butternut Squash	263	14	3	38	509	22	4	9	15
Crispy Parmesan Chicken with Warm Fennel, Radicchio, and Arugula Salad	451	24	5	157	807	26	5	5	33
Mustard-Roasted Chicken with Warm Green Bean and Potato Salad	830	51	12	230	1180	32	5	4	57
Teriyaki Chicken Thighs with Sesame Vegetables	490	19	3	160	1920	35	4	21	39
Skillet-Roasted Chicken Breasts with Root Vegetables	680	29	8	175	830	41	6	9	62
Chicken Bonne Femme	726	48	14	238	1039	24	3	3	44
Roasted Chicken Parts with Potatoes, Carrots, and Brussels Sprouts	1080	71	20	355	940	34	4	5	65
Lemon-Thyme Roasted Chicken with Ratatouille	540	32	8	145	920	13	4	7	50
Chicken Kebabs with Potatoes and Broccoli	709	30	5	209	1428	38	4	5	74
Chicken Baked in Foil with Zucchini and Tomatoes	418	14	3	199	995	6	2	2	63
Apricot-Glazed Chicken with Chickpeas, Chorizo, and Spinach	882	46	13	197	1339	44	9	15	72
Honey Mustard–Glazed Chicken with Roasted Sweet Potato Salad	607	20	3	145	1219	59	6	34	50

	Calories	Total Fat (g)	Sat Fat (g)	Chol (mg)	Sodium (mg)	Total Carb (g)	Dietary Fiber (g)	Total Sugars (g)	Protein (g)
EASY DINNERS (cont.)									
Garlic-Lime Roasted Chicken Leg Quarters with Swiss Chard and Sweet Potatoes	890	44	11	365	2620	51	11	16	75
Chicken and Rice with Peas and Scallions	716	19	6	129	1441	84	3	4	50
Turkey Meatballs with Lemony Rice	703	24	6	155	1119	76	2	5	44
Chicken and Shrimp Jambalaya	390	24	7	210	950	8	2	4	34
Chicken and Couscous with Fennel and Orange	858	35	6	199	1301	61	6	9	71
Honey-and-Garlic Roasted Chicken with Pearl Couscous Salad	810	35	9	160	920	68	2	11	51
Roasted Chicken with Harissa and Warm Bulgur Salad	850	49	15	170	1360	51	8	7	53
Pomegranate-Glazed Bone-In Chicken Breasts with Farro Salad	830	34	8	145	810	76	2	17	58
Turkey Cutlets with Barley and Swiss Chard	598	26	7	110	1024	43	10	4	48
Skillet Chicken Cacciatore with Polenta Topping	400	10	2.5	65	420	42	5	3	31
Herbes de Provence (1 tablespoon)	10	0	0	0	0	2	1	0	1
Chicken and Orzo with Tomatoes and Parmesan	620	15	3	130	1020	65	2	6	53
Poached Chicken with Quinoa and Warm Tomato-Ginger Vinaigrette	560	19	3	125	670	46	6	5	48
Penne with Chicken and Broccoli	607	22	5	92	1369	54	4	4	43
Penne with Chicken Sausage and Spinach	592	26	6	95	987	52	4	2	40
Chicken Chow Mein	528	16	2	117	1473	60	5	5	33
SALADS AND BOWLS									
Chicken Salad with Whole-Grain Mustard Vinaigrette	300	17	2.5	125	710	13	2	9	41
Creamy Chicken Salad with Fresh Herbs	383	26	4	120	438	1	0	0	34
Grilled Chicken Salad	603	40	10	169	788	7	2	3	53
California Chicken Salad with Creamy Avocado Dressing	430	19	3	125	1010	21	7	11	43
Chicken Caesar Salad	484	30	6	115	941	17	5	3	38
Kale Caesar Salad with Chicken	510	32	6	75	930	25	2	2	29
Chicken BLT Salad	1010	79	20	175	1400	26	2	9	45
Green Goodness Chicken Salad	480	24	4.5	135	810	17	7	5	49
Spinach Salad with Chicken, Almonds, and Apricots	430	28	4	60	220	22	4	14	23
Classic Cobb Salad	527	39	9	169	893	11	6	3	34
Chicken and Arugula Salad with Figs and Warm Spices	290	13	2	66	459	19	5	9	25
Sichuan-Style Chicken Salad	311	16	2	97	614	9	3	3	33
Chinese Chicken Salad	520	28	4	110	780	25	6	16	44
Chicken Salad with Thai Basil and Mango	225	4	1	97	610	16	2	12	32
Chicken Salad with Spicy Peanut Dressing	837	65	14	184	187	12	2	6	51

	Calories	Total Fat (g)	Sat Fat (g)	Chol (mg)	Sodium (mg)	Total Carb (g)	Dietary Fiber (g)	Total Sugars (g)	Protein (g)
SALADS AND BOWLS (cont.)									
Chicken Salad with Apricots, Almonds, and Chickpeas	620	38	5	80	320	35	7	22	36
Turkey Taco Salad	870	68	16	75	1030	31	8	8	41
Chopped Salad with Apples, Bacon, and Smoked Turkey	600	47	16	95	1460	20	2	14	25
Buffalo Chicken Bowl	380	13	6	150	1460	16	4	9	47
Turkey Meatball and Barley Bowl	620	23	7	50	560	67	10	10	38
Chimichurri Couscous Chicken Bowl	710	31	4	0	520	83	3	4	26
Peanut Soba Noodle Chicken Bowl	660	18	3	125	1670	67	2	9	57
Chicken Zoodle Bowl with Ginger and Garam Masala	350	15	3	90	390	23	3	18	31
Perfect Poached Chicken	286	5	1	145	1841	9	0	6	48
Seared Chicken Breasts	230	7	1	125	370	0	0	0	38
Easy-Peel Hard-Cooked Eggs	72	4	1	186	71	0	0	0	6
Lemon-Dill Vinaigrette (2 tablespoons)	100	11	1.5	0	90	0	0	0	0
Green Goddess Dressing (2 tablespoons)	223	24	4	17	197	1	0	0	1
Blue Cheese Dressing (2 tablespoons)	30	2	1.5	5	170	1	0	1	2
Creamy Avocado Dressing (2 tablespoons)	70	7	1	0	220	3	2	0	1
Quick Toasted Nuts (2 tablespoons)	110	10	1	0	150	4	2	1	4
Spiced Pepitas (1 tablespoon)	60	5	1	0	75	1	1	0	2
Croutons	70	4	0	0	100	7	0	1	1
Quick Pickled Grapes (2 tablespoons)	15	0	0	0	30	4	0	4	0
SANDWICHES, BURGERS, TACOS, AND MORE									
Crispy Chicken Salad Wraps	1025	74	24	241	1083	27	2	2	61
Smoked Turkey Club Panini	839	59	21	139	905	35	3	7	42
Spicy Chicken Subs	650	30	9	95	2370	56	1	10	38
Chicken Parmesan Subs	744	39	10	226	896	57	4	4	40
Barbecue Chicken Sandwiches with Quick Buttermilk Coleslaw	1009	51	13	238	1434	63	4	36	68
Texas-Size Barbecue Chicken and Cheddar Sandwiches	867	35	14	261	1747	53	2	27	80
Indoor Pulled Chicken with Sweet and Tangy Barbecue Sauce	251	5	1	107	654	28	0	24	24
Sloppy Janes	415	18	3	78	695	38	3	14	28
Fried Chicken Sandwiches	670	35	4	65	1020	56	1	4	30
Chicken Souvlaki	564	27	5	131	893	35	5	6	48
Chicken Spiedies	597	31	5	135	624	31	1	1	47
Classic Turkey Burgers	558	32	13	161	593	22	1	3	44
Turkey Burgers with Sun-Dried Tomatoes, Goat Cheese, and Balsamic Glaze	575	34	12	128	396	30	2	9	35
Buffalo Turkey Burgers	569	33	14	187	565	30	2	9	832
Crispy California Turkey Burgers	832	58	12	108	830	46	6	11	33

	Calories	Total Fat (g)	Sat Fat (g)	Chol (mg)	Sodium (mg)	Total Carb (g)	Dietary Fiber (g)	Total Sugars (g)	Protein (g)
SANDWICHES, BURGERS, TACOS, AND MORE (cont.)									
Spiced Turkey Burgers with Mango Chutney	516	24	8	135	687	35	2	13	39
Brie-Stuffed Turkey Burgers with Red Pepper Relish	539	31	13	161	606	22	1	3	44
Turkey-Veggie Burgers with Lemon-Basil Sauce	455	26	6	91	550	25	2	5	30
Grilled Turkey Burgers with Spinach and Feta	420	21	9	126	513	23	1	3	35
Turkey Sliders with Peanut Sauce and Cucumber Salad	513	22	6	88	873	50	3	17	31
Grind-Your-Own Turkey Burgers	348	21	4	121	556	2	0	1	37
Classic Burger Sauce	114	11	2	6	162	4	0	3	0
Jerk Spice–Rubbed Turkey Burgers with Fried Green Tomatoes	532	29	5	59	519	58	4	14	11
Mediterranean Turkey Burgers with Shaved Zucchini Salad and Ricotta	296	18	4	14	464	27	2	6	9
Easy Chipotle Chicken Tacos	500	16	6	145	160	46	0	8	43
Grilled Chicken Tacos with Salsa Verde	670	30	3	125	1450	58	6	12	46
Grilled Chicken Fajitas	640	29	2.5	125	180	54	2	11	44
Chicken Tinga	470	20	4	150	660	38	4	7	37
Chicken Quesadillas with Roasted Corn and Jack Cheese	600	38	13	140	1690	23	2	5	41
California Chicken Burritos	914	48	20	126	1718	77	11	5	44
Chicken Burritos Mojados	810	35	13	130	2610	79	8	11	48
Chicken Chimichangas	770	41	9	115	1040	58	6	3	43
Quick Tomato Salsa	20	0	0	0	330	5	0	2	1
Spicy Chicken Flautas	740	41	7	120	1210	54	6	6	43
Chicken and Avocado Arepas	260	11	1	15	370	30	2	0	9
Red Chile Chicken Tamales	530	29	10	100	850	48	6	3	21
SOUPS									
Old-Fashioned Chicken Noodle Soup	437	17	4	82	1163	33	2	7	35
Matzo Ball Soup	591	36	10	248	1367	32	4	9	33
Hearty Chicken and Cabbage Soup	430	20	8	60	1010	37	7	12	21
Hearty Chicken and Vegetable Soup	210	6	0.5	30	640	23	4	7	15
Lemony Chicken and Rice Soup	290	11	2	180	750	25	3	5	22
Chicken and Rice Soup with Ginger and Scallions	771	42	10	159	2022	44	2	10	51
Garlic Chicken and Wild Rice Soup	188	7	1	21	664	19	2	2	13
Hearty Chicken Soup with Orzo and Spring Vegetables	315	19	5	86	975	11	2	2	23
Easy Alphabet Soup with Chicken	190	5	0.5	55	740	15	1	3	20
Chicken and Spinach Tortellini Soup	500	20	6	105	1480	51	1	5	28

	Calories	Total Fat (g)	Sat Fat (g)	Chol (mg)	Sodium (mg)	Total Carb (g)	Dietary Fiber (g)	Total Sugars (g)	Protein (g)
SOUPS (cont.)									
Italian Chicken Soup with Parmesan Dumplings	333	18	5	81	1311	17	3	5	25
Pennsylvania Dutch Chicken, Corn, and Rivel Soup	501	21	7	147	1354	48	3	11	31
Mulligatawny with Chicken	329	13	7	111	150	17	3	5	37
New Orleans Chicken and Sausage Soup	350	16	4	81	430	24	1	2	28
Avgolemono	397	9	2	154	1135	38	2	5	38
Cock-a-Leekie	170	5	2	35	680	18	2	8	13
Turkey Meatball Soup with Saffron	250	13	3	47	326	12	1	3	18
Harira	280	10	1.5	50	970	22	6	4	27
Harissa (1 tablespoon)	110	11	1.5	0	150	2	1	0	1
Tortilla Soup	481	29	10	75	1261	29	6	4	30
Mexican-Style Chicken and Chickpea Soup	240	11	2.5	55	810	14	3	4	22
Chicken Pho	350	4.5	1	80	1040	51	0	5	26
Crispy Shallots (1 tablespoon)	15	1	0	0	0	1	0	0	0
Tom Kha Gai	340	24	19	42	619	16	2	5	20
Hearty Cream of Chicken Soup	530	24	11	105	1499	46	5	11	31
Farmhouse Chicken Chowder	952	61	21	224	1918	40	4	7	60
Simple Turkey Stock	690	27	350	550	1	0	0	0	105
Turkey Barley Soup	181	3	1	36	309	25	5	2	14
Creamy Turkey and Wild Rice Soup	667	35	15	188	1262	29	3	5	45
Italian Wedding Soup with Kale and Farro	250	8	2	32	969	28	5	5	18
Classic Chicken Broth	240	16	4.5	135	700	1	0	1	22
Simple Chicken Broth with Shredded Breast Meat	450	32	9	150	730	1	0	1	37
Pressure-Cooker Chicken Broth	70	4.5	35	2350	1	0	0	0	5
Slow-Cooker Chicken Broth	120	8	2	70	160	1	0	0	11
Sous Vide Chicken Broth	6	0	0	3	12	0	0	0	1
STEWS, CHILIS, AND CURRIES									
Classic Chicken Stew	409	13	3	160	1138	30	5	6	40
Easiest-Ever Drop Biscuits	347	20	12	71	224	36	1	3	5
Quick Provençal-Style Chicken Stew with Mushrooms and Olives	340	13	1.5	85	1050	24	3	9	31
Chicken and Dumplings	964	63	19	301	747	41	3	6	56
Gluten-Free Chicken and Dumplings	541	22	6	162	1087	47	7	8	39
Southern-Style Stewed Chicken and Rice	527	26	9	130	705	45	0	3	25
Chicken Maque Choux	540	30	8	210	1280	27	4	9	48
Chicken Pepper Pot	260	8	1	80	680	28	7	8	21
Brunswick Stew	464	19	5	169	1322	35	4	11	40
Kentucky Burgoo	960	47	15	295	1690	51	5	8	78

	Calories	Total Fat (g)	Sat Fat (g)	Chol (mg)	Sodium (mg)	Total Carb (g)	Dietary Fiber (g)	Total Sugars (g)	Protein (g)
STEWS, CHILIS, AND CURRIES (cont.)									
Gumbo	650	32	5	355	1860	26	3	5	62
Chicken Posole Verde	520	35	9	190	1050	16	3	4	34
Chicken Stew with Sweet Potato, Pineapple, and Plantains	500	18	3	160	1130	44	8	16	41
White Chicken Chili	360	15	4	85	760	20	6	5	35
Quick Green Chicken Chili	410	11	2.5	95	1680	31	9	7	44
Mole Chicken Chili	570	41	11	190	660	15	4	7	36
Southern-Style Cornbread	412	25	11	90	314	40	2	6	6
Classic Turkey Chili	310	7	2.5	45	1110	30	10	11	36
Pumpkin Turkey Chili	200	10	2	42	761	18	7	6	14
Chicken Curry	157	13	6	10	357	10	3	3	2
Vindaloo-Style Chicken	432	18	3	215	1031	18	4	6	49
Thai Green Curry with Chicken, Bell Peppers, and Mushrooms	560	41	26	85	700	19	3	8	31
Massaman Curry with Potatoes and Peanuts	448	26	14	73	696	34	5	9	24
CLASSIC BRAISES									
Chicken with 40 Cloves of Garlic	733	53	18	274	1081	16	1	2	43
Braised Chicken with Mustard and Herbs	563	36	9	208	726	5	1	1	50
Lemon-Braised Chicken Thighs with Chickpeas and Fennel	1059	46	10	176	1713	103	20	20	56
Braised Chicken with Leeks and Saffron	751	51	13	227	1003	9	1	2	58
Braised Lemon Chicken Breasts	567	27	7	119	168	41	6	19	44
Southern-Style Smothered Chicken	993	67	16	259	1354	25	2	5	69
Braised Chicken Thighs with Chard with Mustard	678	45	12	237	1452	18	3	4	45
Quick Chicken Fricassee	301	12	4	146	788	9	1	3	38
Chicken California	751	50	12	172	880	21	3	5	46
Classic Mashed Potatoes	300	19	12	55	30	29	2	3	4
Country Captain	794	49	13	227	1289	29	7	17	59
Chicken Marbella	539	32	8	140	709	15	2	8	45
Chicken Marengo	562	30	11	134	1354	17	6	9	42
Chicken Canzanese	597	41	12	211	790	7	1	1	37
Spicy Braised Chicken Abruzzo	300	12	2	125	630	6	1	3	39
Chicken Scarpariello	615	40	11	182	928	11	2	4	51
Chicken Arrabbiata	976	71	18	330	1391	20	5	11	64
Chicken Pomodoro	522	25	8	226	1028	9	3	5	63
Chicken Cacciatore with Portobellos and Sage	840	54	15	298	1403	17	4	6	56
Chicken Provençal	592	41	10	196	487	16	2	3	36
Chicken in Adobo	904	60	16	258	1192	20	4	10	68

	Calories	Total Fat (g)	Sat Fat (g)	Chol (mg)	Sodium (mg)	Total Carb (g)	Dietary Fiber (g)	Total Sugars (g)	Protein (g)
CLASSIC BRAISES (cont.)									
Coq au Vin	1430	91	29	385	1440	20	1	8	93
Coq au Riesling	709	41	12	185	1507	20	4	5	49
Chicken Bouillabaisse	1109	70	12	176	1563	54	6	11	59
Rouille (per tablespoon)	140	14	1.5	10	40	3	0	0	1
Garlic Toasts	150	6	0.5	0	240	19	1	1	3
Pollo en Pepitoria	885	63	15	373	1277	17	5	6	57
Chicken with Pumpkin Seed Sauce	360	16	1.5	125	930	8	3	4	42
Pollo Encacahuatado	670	41	5	125	900	24	9	7	53
Chicken Paprikash	632	46	12	204	1033	16	3	6	38
Filipino Chicken Adobo	883	60	32	292	1425	9	1	0	54
Red-Cooked Chicken	860	65	16	396	1452	9	1	5	56
Chicken Tagine with Olives and Lemon	645	44	11	173	1074	17	4	8	47
Chicken Tagine with Fennel, Chickpeas, and Apricots	764	39	10	257	448	44	9	13	59
Simple Couscous	260	5	0.5	0	390	45	3	0	7
SIMPLE SAUTÉS AND STIR-FRIES									
Sautéed Chicken Breasts with Vermouth and Tarragon Sauce	470	23	7	145	810	14	0	3	40
Chicken Piccata	381	19	5	113	565	18	2	2	33
Chicken Marsala	560	23	6	110	1510	30	2	15	35
Scampi-Style Chicken	726	47	12	146	782	41	3	3	28
Chicken Scallopini with Mushrooms and Pepper	570	35	8	134	971	18	2	5	39
Chicken Saltimbocca	977	59	19	264	1127	16	2	1	79
Chicken Florentine	484	28	13	196	952	7	2	2	50
Chicken and Artichokes with Honey and Herbes de Provence	503	31	12	142	697	17	4	9	39
Chicken Véronique	404	18	9	167	776	12	1	7	40
Chicken Francese	544	26	13	286	862	20	1	2	50
Circassian Chicken	449	27	4	110	771	12	3	2	40
Blackened Chicken with Pineapple-Cucumber Salsa	472	15	2	199	989	21	3	13	63
Stir-Fried Sesame Chicken with Broccoli and Red Pepper	299	17	2	62	91	14	4	3	24
Stir-Fried Chicken with Bok Choy and Crispy Noodle Cake	706	36	5	136	858	56	3	4	37
Gingery Stir-Fried Chicken and Bok Choy	568	44	7	83	1283	11	1	3	29
Stir-Fried Chicken and Chestnuts	402	15	2	160	950	31	1	9	36
Sticky Rice	230	0	0	0	200	50	2	0	4
Spicy Stir-Fried Sesame Chicken with Green Beans and Shiitake Mushrooms	840	67	11	83	1688	26	6	10	33
Sweet and Savory Chicken with Pineapple and Broccoli	196	5	1	74	515	13	1	6	25

	Calories	Total Fat (g)	Sat Fat (g)	Chol (mg)	Sodium (mg)	Total Carb (g)	Dietary Fiber (g)	Total Sugars (g)	Protein (g)
SIMPLE SAUTÉS AND STIR-FRIES (cont.)									
Cashew Chicken	596	32	5	125	1548	29	3	9	48
Gai Pad Krapow	349	12	1	124	919	19	3	11	42
Three Cup Chicken	403	21	3	160	1338	14	1	4	37
Spicy Orange Chicken	390	18	2	125	500	14	1	9	40
Kung Pao Chicken	339	18	3	107	716	17	3	8	29
ROASTED									
Pan-Roasted Chicken Breasts with Sage-Vermouth Sauce	289	18	8	79	455	6	1	2	20
Roasted Bone-In Chicken Breasts	460	27	7	160	733	0	0	0	52
Roasted Bone-In Chicken Thighs	650	49	13	285	960	1	0	0	48
Roasted Chicken Thighs with Pistachio and Currant Sauce	370	29	7	120	320	6	1	4	21
Mahogany Chicken Thighs	500	31	9	185	2610	12	0	9	37
Skillet-Roasted Chicken Leg Quarters and Potatoes	740	36	8	165	1620	41	1	0	57
Cast Iron Roast Chicken Parts	794	57	18	270	824	3	1	0	64
Spice-Rubbed Roast Chicken Parts	920	70	17	255	888	6	3	0	65
Pan-Roasted Chicken Parts with Vinegar-Tarragon Sauce	838	57	17	265	1069	10	1	5	66
Skillet-Roasted Chicken in Lemon Sauce	841	59	19	272	1012	8	1	3	66
Slow-Roasted Chicken Parts with Shallot-Garlic Pan Sauce	720	50	16	230	926	10	1	3	56
Weeknight Roast Chicken	602	44	14	188	749	5	1	1	45
Classic Roast Chicken	706	53	17	232	1017	1	0	0	54
Two Roast Chickens	899	58	19	250	826	34	0	33	57
Herbed Roast Chicken	716	56	21	218	840	6	1	1	46
Roast Lemon Chicken	602	44	16	195	1005	5	1	1	46
Garlic-Rosemary Roast Chicken with Jus	596	40	11	173	947	10	2	0	46
Glazed Roast Chicken	539	27	9	125	712	39	1	32	29
Two Honey Roast Chickens	596	38	12	180	761	19	0	18	44
Spice-Roasted Chicken with Chili and Oregano	571	42	11	173	638	4	2	0	43
Chile-Rubbed Roast Chicken	1060	76	18	300	1130	15	6	2	77
Peruvian Roast Chicken with Garlic and Lime	620	45	11	173	603	8	2	3	44
Spicy Mayonnaise	520	57	4.5	45	190	1	0	0	2
Za'atar-Rubbed Butterflied Chicken	610	43	10	165	530	0	0	0	52
Za'atar (1 tablespoon)	20	1.5	0	0	5	2	1	0	1
Crisp-Skin High-Roast Butterflied Chicken with Potatoes	1220	75	23	320	1160	52	4	3	80
Mustard-Garlic Butter with Thyme	72	8	5	20	56	1	0	0	0
Chipotle Butter with Lime and Honey	80	7	4.5	20	0	2	0	2	0

	Calories	Total Fat (g)	Sat Fat (g)	Chol (mg)	Sodium (mg)	Total Carb (g)	Dietary Fiber (g)	Total Sugars (g)	Protein (g)
ROASTED (cont.)									
Roast Chicken with Warm Bread Salad	690	47	11	150	1050	23	2	4	42
Skillet-Roasted Chicken and Stuffing	1003	66	25	277	1481	36	5	3	64
Chicken en Cocotte with Thyme and Lemon	780	56	15	255	530	2	0	0	64
Turkey Breast en Cocotte with Pan Gravy	525	24	6	184	1026	8	1	1	65
Lemon-Thyme Boneless Turkey Breast with Gravy	460	23	8	170	660	4	1	1	54
Easy Roast Turkey Breast	396	21	7	159	310	0	0	0	50
All-Purpose Gravy	90	6	0	0	290	6	0	1	1
Spice-Rubbed Turkey Breast with Sour Orange Sauce	292	14	3	100	564	6	0	3	35
Maple Roast Turkey Breast	81	6	4	16	50	7	0	6	1
Stuffed Roast Turkey Breast	320	11	3.5	110	620	7	1	4	45
Mushroom Marsala Stuffing	106	7	4	17	199	4	1	2	7
Lemon, Spinach, and Fontina Stuffing	173	14	7	38	287	3	1	1	10
Koji Turkey	1748	66	18	731	3575	53	5	32	225
Perfect Roast Turkey and Gravy	510	21	5	230	1520	5	0	2	70
BAKED AND BROILED									
Simple Baked Chicken Parts	1030	74	23	355	460	0	0	0	84
Baked Chicken Imperial	764	41	23	309	1086	22	2	5	71
Chicken Mole Poblano	846	57	14	201	1129	28	5	16	56
Chicken Baked in Foil with Potatoes and Carrots	451	22	3	124	780	22	4	3	41
Un-Stuffed Chicken Breasts with Prosciutto, Sage, and Porcini	796	45	22	313	994	14	2	3	76
Simple Stuffed Bone-In Chicken Breasts with Boursin	660	45	21	235	550	1	0	0	62
Baked Ricotta Chicken	607	34	10	183	912	16	2	6	57
Chicken Vesuvio	541	31	8	156	962	25	3	2	29
Greek Chicken	874	65	17	255	887	6	3	1	64
Turkey Meatloaf with Ketchup–Brown Sugar Glaze	424	22	8	192	696	26	1	19	33
Simple Broiled Bone-In Chicken Parts	740	51	15	255	820	1	0	1	63
Broiled Paprika Chicken	360	22	8	127	432	2	1	0	37
Chipotle Chicken Kebabs with Creamy Cilantro Dipping Sauce	430	16	4.5	180	1030	17	0	15	52
Chicken Tandoori	872	66	17	341	976	8	1	3	59
Raita	40	2	1.5	10	30	3	0	3	2
Chicken Tikka Masala	462	27	9	152	911	18	3	11	39
Garam Masala (1 tablespoon)	6	0	0	0	1	1	1	0	0
Murgh Makhani	453	30	17	220	783	12	2	8	34
One-Hour Broiled Chicken and Pan Sauce	687	48	13	231	1075	2	1	0	58

	Calories	Total Fat (g)	Sat Fat (g)	Chol (mg)	Sodium (mg)	Total Carb (g)	Dietary Fiber (g)	Total Sugars (g)	Protein (g)
BREADED AND FRIED									
Crispy Pan-Fried Chicken Cutlets	418	24	2	159	436	14	1	1	34
Tonkatsu Sauce (1 tablespoon)	25	0	0	0	330	5	0	4	0
Garlic-Curry Sauce (1 tablespoon)	70	6	1	5	100	2	0	1	0
Crispy Garlic Chicken Cutlets	1268	92	12	167	977	45	2	2	63
Best Chicken Parmesan	607	41	10	155	906	24	4	10	39
Gluten-Free Chicken Parmesan	623	40	10	131	816	33	2	4	31
Quick Tomato Sauce	102	6	3	10	345	11	3	6	2
Chicken Schnitzel	1104	85	7	194	751	34	2	2	49
Apple-Fennel Rémoulade	78	6	1	3	165	6	2	4	1
Cucumber-Dill Salad	45	2	1	2	239	5	1	2	2
Chicken Fingers	740	28	3.5	215	500	66	0	2	50
Gluten-Free Crispy Chicken Fingers	590	31	4.5	215	610	31	0	2	44
Chicken Nuggets	1666	155	11	132	1080	25	1	1	46
BBQ Dipping Sauce	70	0	0	0	340	18	0	15	0
Honey-Mustard Dipping Sauce	90	0	0	0	720	17	0	16	0
Sweet-and-Sour Dipping Sauce	150	0	0	0	50	39	0	36	0
Boneless Buffalo Chicken	1738	156	12	138	1062	39	1	2	45
Nut-Crusted Chicken Breasts with Lemon and Thyme	869	41	11	369	990	45	7	4	79
Spiced Apple Chutney	100	2	0	0	0	22	0	19	0
Chicken Cordon Bleu	723	34	17	300	779	38	2	3	62
Chicken Kiev	854	42	18	399	973	42	3	2	73
Ultimate Stuffed Chicken Breasts with Ham and Cheddar	620	38	12	265	780	26	0	3	42
Spinach and Goat Cheese-Stuffed Chicken Breasts	516	19	7	216	931	11	3	1	71
Chicken Croquettes	440	34	11	128	510	20	2	4	13
Karaage	462	28	3	107	550	26	0	1	23
Ultimate Crispy Fried Chicken	850	57	14	215	1670	22	0	16	61
Extra-Crunchy Fried Chicken	2927	267	68	177	1581	78	3	6	57
Cast Iron Easier Fried Chicken	680	43	9	145	1080	31	1	1	40
Gluten-Free Fried Chicken	1000	53	12	250	1100	57	2	4	72
Batter-Fried Chicken	850	54	12	200	1110	35	1	1	52
Buttermilk Coleslaw	80	4.5	1	5	380	8	2	5	2
Honey-Dipped Fried Chicken	1420	81	19	300	1630	95	0	49	74
Garlic Fried Chicken	1400	98	29	335	1490	51	1	0	71
Koji Fried Chicken	1291	96	15	200	953	51	1	2	54
Nashville Hot Fried Chicken	840	54	12	200	1260	30	0	1	53
Picnic Fried Chicken	1698	119	19	255	1186	84	3	0	69

	Calories	Total Fat (g)	Sat Fat (g)	Chol (mg)	Sodium (mg)	Total Carb (g)	Dietary Fiber (g)	Total Sugars (g)	Protein (g)
BREADED AND FRIED (cont.)									
Garlic-Lime Fried Chicken	1190	73	16	255	3010	56	3	1	72
Authentic Maryland Fried Chicken and Gravy	1535	122	33	281	1254	44	2	2	65
Oven-Fried Chicken	432	21	5	114	612	19	1	4	41
Buttermilk Oven-Fried Chicken	927	57	18	268	1210	29	2	9	72
Korean Fried Chicken Wings	730	50	10	250	460	24	0	8	42
Buffalo Wings	1904	197	41	215	981	7	1	3	33
Oven-Fried Chicken Wings	660	48	17	356	1116	4	0	3	53
Buffalo Wing Sauce	80	8	5	20	499	3	0	3	0
Smoky Barbecue Wing Sauce	24	0	0	0	134	6	0	5	0
Sweet and Spicy Wing Sauce	100	2.5	0	0	240	20	0	18	1
Oven-Fried Soy Sauce Chicken Wings	578	39	10	252	1946	13	1	9	43
Creamy Blue Cheese Dressing (2 tablespoons)	142	15	4	15	183	0	0	0	2
PASTA AND NOODLES									
Penne alla Vodka with Chicken	220	15	7	35	570	13	3	8	4
Penne with Chicken, Artichokes, Cherry Tomatoes, and Olives	739	27	9	112	1572	66	8	8	53
Penne with Chicken, Sun-Dried Tomato Pesto, and Goat Cheese	740	40	8	65	400	63	5	2	35
Chicken Riggies	868	33	14	202	1369	77	8	13	65
Garlicky Tuscan Chicken Pasta	708	25	6	145	774	61	3	3	58
Saltimbocca Spaghetti	730	24	7	120	1540	71	4	4	46
Chicken Bolognese with Linguine	660	24	10	100	900	70	6	10	33
Pasta with Chicken Sausage, Swiss Chard, and White Beans	640	23	7	97	1080	74	9	4	35
Campanelle with Roasted Garlic, Chicken Sausage, and Arugula	550	25	6	50	610	59	3	2	24
Italian-Style Turkey Meatballs	330	19	5	116	515	12	1	5	29
Chicken Noodle Casserole	463	22	12	112	658	41	3	6	25
Chicken, Broccoli, and Ziti Casserole	732	25	12	152	1125	65	3	8	59
Creamy Chicken and Spinach Whole-Wheat Pasta Casserole	610	22	9	100	640	56	1	15	43
Baked Penne with Spinach, Artichokes, and Chicken	810	38	22	180	1070	59	9	6	56
Pasta Roll-Ups with Chicken, Sun-Dried Tomatoes, and Pine Nuts	714	40	22	163	782	50	3	3	39
Chicken Lo Mein with Broccoli and Bean Sprouts	270	11	1	60	960	25	2	18	19
Chicken Pad Kee Mao	340	7	0.5	40	1450	52	1	20	12
Chicken Pad See Ew	561	20	3	202	1366	62	3	10	30
Sesame Noodles with Shredded Chicken	600	19	4	146	833	65	4	8	41

	Calories	Total Fat (g)	Sat Fat (g)	Chol (mg)	Sodium (mg)	Total Carb (g)	Dietary Fiber (g)	Total Sugars (g)	Protein (g)
SAVORY PIES AND CASSEROLES									
Classic Chicken Pot Pie	660	38	23	180	821	50	5	8	29
Foolproof All-Butter Double-Crust Pie Dough	410	28	18	75	290	35	0	3	5
Chicken, Spinach, and Artichoke Pot Pie	508	31	16	188	1063	23	8	4	39
Lattice-Topped Dutch Oven Chicken Pot Pie with Spring Vegetables	507	22	10	211	1244	37	6	10	40
Biscuit-Topped Dutch Oven Chicken Pot Pie	760	38	18	265	1030	51	4	9	49
Gluten-Free Chicken Pot Pie	272	15	6	71	434	14	2	3	19
Single-Crust Gluten-Free Pie Dough	190	12	7	30	160	19	1	1	1
ATK All-Purpose Gluten-Free Flour Blend	366	2	1	2	9	81	2	1	5
Chicken Shepherd's Pie	667	39	15	212	1147	45	5	6	33
Rustic Farmhouse Chicken Casserole	370	19	6	70	490	26	1	4	23
Maple-Glazed Brussels Sprouts	117	6	4	15	334	14	4	6	4
Chicken Divan	945	62	29	396	1593	31	6	8	66
King Ranch Casserole	586	36	20	164	950	29	5	5	39
Carolina Chicken Bog	523	25	7	111	800	46	1	3	26
Chicken and Rice Casserole with Peas, Carrots, and Cheddar	670	33	19	170	1080	52	2	4	41
Chicken and Rice with Caramelized Onions, Cardamom, and Raisins	756	35	9	188	936	68	1	9	39
Arroz con Pollo	842	48	11	177	1004	63	2	4	37
Chicken Enchiladas Rojas	705	44	18	146	1899	48	12	12	37
Chicken Enchiladas Verdes	500	25	8	90	840	40	8	11	32
Chicken Chilaquiles	528	24	6	98	1111	43	9	7	37
Pastel Azteca	570	24	10	150	1010	40	2	6	49
Phyllo Pie with Chicken	440	23	9	175	970	28	0	2	30
Chicken B'stilla	420	24	4	165	440	27	3	4	24
ON THE GRILL									
Grilled Chicken Kebabs with Garlic and Herb Marinade	551	41	7	160	749	10	3	5	35
Barbecued Chicken Kebabs	319	11	3	149	514	24	1	20	32
Grilled Boneless, Skinless Chicken Breasts	280	8	1	125	1180	11	0	8	40
Grilled Lemon-Parsley Chicken Breasts	556	32	5	199	739	3	0	2	62
Grilled Glazed Boneless Chicken Breasts	413	10	1	45	615	36	1	34	45
Grilled Monterey Chicken	669	32	13	207	1048	33	4	23	61
Pico de Gallo	25	0	0	0	180	5	1	3	1
Grilled Tequila Chicken with Orange, Avocado, and Pepita Salad	730	42	7	125	1560	30	10	15	46
Seattle Grilled Chicken Teriyaki	285	7	2	160	1914	16	0	13	36
Easy Grilled Stuffed Chicken Breasts	470	30	7	140	640	4	0	2	43
Grilled Pesto Chicken	897	70	15	184	998	4	1	0	63

	Calories	Total Fat (g)	Sat Fat (g)	Chol (mg)	Sodium (mg)	Total Carb (g)	Dietary Fiber (g)	Total Sugars (g)	Protein (g)
ON THE GRILL (cont.)									
Grilled Asparagus	100	8	5	25	0	5	2	2	3
Best Grilled Chicken Thighs	360	27	7	155	220	0	0	0	27
Garam Masala Paste	419	34	8	156	553	2	0	0	26
Gochujang Paste	376	27	7	156	596	5	1	2	28
Mustard-Tarragon Paste	362	27	7	156	557	2	1	0	27
Grilled Spice-Rubbed Chicken Drumsticks	646	35	9	348	904	9	1	7	69
Grilled Chicken Leg Quarters with Lime Dressing	489	36	9	192	693	6	1	3	34
Grilled Mojo Chicken	568	45	11	192	745	5	1	2	34
Barbecued Pulled Chicken	878	57	15	320	873	32	2	24	58
Grilled Chicken Wings	192	7	2	56	174	25	0	25	9
Grill-Fried Chicken Wings	689	37	10	252	668	42	2	9	45
Grilled Bone-In Chicken	650	46	13	225	500	0	0	0	56
Classic Barbecued Chicken	848	35	10	170	1903	87	2	73	44
Sweet and Tangy Barbecued Chicken	858	55	15	255	959	24	1	20	64
Citrus-and-Spice Grilled Chicken	544	39	10	170	599	4	1	1	43
Grilled Chicken Diavolo	986	79	18	255	872	4	1	1	64
Grilled Jerk Chicken	921	66	16	255	1122	15	2	8	66
Peri Peri Grilled Chicken	870	61	16	255	961	11	3	5	67
Smoked Chicken	380	12	2	200	410	1	0	1	61
Easy Grill-Roasted Whole Chicken	526	38	10	173	544	0	0	0	43
Chicken Under a Brick	1040	79	20	300	1150	3	1	0	74
Grilled Wine-and-Herb Marinated Chicken	885	57	15	231	1403	13	1	8	58
Grill-Roasted Beer Can Chicken	960	62	17	300	2560	15	6	0	77
Two Glazed Grill-Roasted Chickens	900	60	17	300	1360	11	0	9	74
Two Kentucky Bourbon–Brined Grilled Chickens	1360	80	23	395	3440	20	0	18	105
Two Sinaloa-Style Grill-Roasted Chickens	1340	89	24	395	2700	26	1	19	101
Two Huli Huli Grilled Chickens	1492	95	27	460	5791	30	1	20	123
Two Cornell Chickens	869	65	16	230	1888	5	2	1	58
Two Alabama Barbecued Chickens	682	55	13	181	607	1	0	1	43
Thai Grilled Cornish Hens	858	47	13	339	1627	45	1	39	60
Grill-Roasted Boneless Turkey Breast	260	4	0.5	130	830	1	0	0	53
Smoked Turkey Breast	280	3.5	0.5	130	1130	6	0	5	53
Classic Grill-Roasted Turkey	480	20	6	235	940	0	0	0	70
Gravy for Classic Grill-Roasted Turkey	50	3.5	2	10	180	4	1	1	1
Spice-Rubbed Grill-Roasted Turkey	540	26	8	245	1330	2	0	1	70
Grilled Corn with Basil-Lemon Butter	250	17	8	30	210	23	3	4	4
Red Pepper–Almond Sauce	120	11	1	0	440	6	2	3	3
Poblano-Pepita Sauce	50	4.5	0.5	0	180	2	1	1	1

	Calories	Total Fat (g)	Sat Fat (g)	Chol (mg)	Sodium (mg)	Total Carb (g)	Dietary Fiber (g)	Total Sugars (g)	Protein (g)
ON THE GRILL (cont.)									
Basic Barbecue Sauce	120	2	0	0	590	26	0	22	0
Kansas City Barbecue Sauce	80	1	0	0	340	16	0	15	1
Sweet and Tangy Barbecue Sauce	145	5	0	0	493	26	1	22	1
Spicy Hoisin Glaze	35	0	0	0	170	7	0	4	0
Honey-Mustard Glaze	151	1	0	0	1129	37	1	35	2
Coconut-Curry Glaze	40	1.5	1.5	0	130	6	0	2	0
Miso-Sesame Glaze	35	1.5	0	0	140	5	0	2	0
Orange-Chipotle Glaze	15	0	0	0	0	3	0	3	0
Basic Spice Rub (1 tablespooon)	20	0	0	0	420	3	1	0	1
Cajun Spice Rub (1 tablespoon)	15	0.5	0	420	3	2	0	0	1
Jamaican Spice Rub (1 tablespoon)	30	0	0	0	630	6	1	3	0
Tex-Mex Spice Rub (1 tablespoon)	15	0.5	0	0	310	3	1	0	1
Ras el Hanout Spice Rub (1 tablespoon)	20	0.5	0	0	220	4	2	2	1
INSTANT POT, AIR FRYER, AND SOUS VIDE									
Pressure-Cooker Classic Chicken Noodle Soup	440	25	7	125	1000	22	2	7	33
Pressure-Cooker Spicy Moroccan Chicken and Lentil Soup	240	9	2	45	890	18	4	3	21
Pressure-Cooker Turkey Meatball Soup with Kale	170	5	2.5	25	810	10	2	4	18
Pressure-Cooker Chicken in a Pot with Lemon-Herb Sauce	1110	78	23	355	610	8	1	2	86
Pressure-Cooker Spiced Chicken in a Pot with Pear, Cherry, and Walnut Chutney	1320	83	21	340	1630	57	6	41	87
Pressure-Cooker Braised Chicken Breasts with Tomatoes and Capers	700	35	10	220	1390	13	4	6	73
Pressure-Cooker Chicken and Couscous with Chorizo and Saffron	1030	46	14	245	1080	59	6	3	89
Pressure-Cooker Chicken Tagine	560	31	7	140	1040	37	9	12	32
Pressure-Cooker Lemony Chicken with Fingerling Potatoes and Olives	280	7	1.5	80	580	33	4	1	20
Pressure-Cooker Braised Chicken Thighs with White Beans, Pancetta, and Rosemary	830	55	15	290	1170	24	7	2	59
Pressure-Cooker Buffalo Chicken Wings	450	38	9	150	1790	3	0	3	24
Air-Fryer Apricot-Thyme Glazed Chicken Breasts	343	8	1	166	582	13	0	9	51
Air-Fryer Roasted Bone-in Chicken Breasts	491	27	8	174	799	1	0	0	57
Peach-Ginger Chutney	140	2.5	0	0	150	30	2	27	1
Lemon-Basil Salsa Verde	383	37	5	2	271	7	1	1	3
Air-Fryer Roasted Bone-in Chicken Breasts and Potatoes with Sun-Dried Tomato Relish	740	32	8	174	1455	49	8	3	63
Air-Fryer Tandoori Chicken Thighs	522	38	11	22	860	9	1	3	36

	Calories	Total Fat (g)	Sat Fat (g)	Chol (mg)	Sodium (mg)	Total Carb (g)	Dietary Fiber (g)	Total Sugars (g)	Protein (g)
INSTANT POT, AIR FRYER, AND SOUS VIDE (cont.)									
Air-Fryer Fried Chicken	670	28	8	175	1330	39	2	5	62
Air-Fryer Chicken Nuggets	671	25	4	305	794	48	2	11	61
Air-Fryer Chicken Parmesan	690	34	11	294	866	24	2	3	69
Air-Fryer Shredded Chicken Tacos	369	15	6	128	578	28	5	2	31
Air-Fryer Chicken Lettuce Wraps with Herbs and Mango	292	11	2	107	473	24	4	17	27
Air-Fryer Buffalo Chicken Drumsticks	363	28	13	131	843	8	1	6	21
Air-Fryer Spicy Fried-Chicken Sandwich	501	24	4	135	667	36	2	4	33
Air-Fryer Turkey Burgers	374	15	6	93	525	27	2	5	32
Air-Fryer Mini Glazed Turkey Meatloaves	567	28	6	250	853	30	2	18	51
Sous Vide Foolproof Poached Chicken	292	21	4	77	374	0	0	0	25
Sous Vide Crispy-Skinned Bone-In Chicken Breasts	516	46	8	146	397	1	0	0	25
Leek and White Wine Pan Sauce	20	1	0.5	5	45	0	0	0	0
Hoisin-Sesame Pan Sauce	20	0.5	0	0	110	4	0	2	0
Sous Vide Peri Peri Chicken	406	23	6	111	569	11	2	6	38
Sous Vide Easy Boneless Turkey Breast	510	22	2	180	790	1	0	0	74
Red Bell Pepper Chutney	151	3	0	0	394	30	2	25	1
Sous Vide Turkey Thigh Confit with Citrus-Mustard Sauce	664	41	13	187	941	28	3	19	46
SLOW COOKER									
Slow-Cooker Old-Fashioned Chicken Noodle Soup	330	14	4	69	1057	22	2	7	27
Slow-Cooker Chicken Tortilla Soup	620	48	9	110	950	24	2	5	27
Slow-Cooker Turkey and Rice Soup	469	14	4	88	1100	52	4	7	33
Slow-Cooker Hearty Turkey and Vegetable Soup	160	4	1	45	1070	13	2	4	19
Slow-Cooker Chicken and Corn Chowder	439	25	11	125	754	32	3	5	24
Slow-Cooker Chicken and Sausage Gumbo	608	32	7	108	1078	50	3	4	30
Slow-Cooker Homey Chicken Stew	360	13	2.5	160	640	21	3	5	37
Slow Cooker Chicken Mulligatawny Stew	389	20	13	96	893	27	4	6	26
Slow-Cooker Chicken and Dumplings	509	20	7	178	1066	36	3	5	42
Slow-Cooker Spicy Chipotle Chicken Chili	550	22	5	110	1260	42	8	6	46
Slow-Cooker Turkey Chili		13	3	63	1078	31	9	10	27
Slow-Cooker Chicken with "Roasted" Garlic Sauce	339	29	8	175	1045	14	1	2	60
Slow-Cooker Chicken with Mushrooms and Tarragon Cream Sauce	718	38	11	195	1467	23	3	6	63
Slow-Cooker Chicken with Tomatoes, Olives, and Cilantro	397	22	5	111	788	12	5	5	38
Slow-Cooker Chicken with Fennel and Tomato Couscous	839	43	10	175	1308	46	5	7	65

	Calories	Total Fat (g)	Sat Fat (g)	Chol (mg)	Sodium (mg)	Total Carb (g)	Dietary Fiber (g)	Total Sugars (g)	Protein (g)
SLOW COOKER (cont.)									
Slow-Cooker Sesame-Ginger Chicken and Sweet Potatoes	803	43	9	174	1354	41	7	10	60
Slow-Cooker Lemon Chicken Thighs	527	42	10	195	501	3	1	0	33
Slow-Cooker Chicken Thighs with Black-Eyed Pea Ragout	715	45	11	234	1720	29	9	9	50
Slow Cooker Curried Chicken Thighs with Acorn Squash	657	41	11	233	1224	32	3	13	41
Slow-Cooker Kimchi-Braised Chicken Thighs	300	11	2.5	160	960	13	2	5	36
Slow-Cooker Chicken Tikka Masala	450	19	3	172	1016	16	4	9	55
Slow-Cooker Southern Smothered Chicken	786	55	12	235	1225	27	3	4	44
Slow-Cooker Jerk Chicken	778	55	14	227	609	11	1	6	57
Slow-Cooker Barbecue Pulled Chicken	467	15	3	89	847	50	3	17	32
Slow-Cooker Sweet and Tangy Pulled Chicken	337	15	4	87	601	20	2	14	30
Sweet and Tangy Coleslaw	123	7	0	0	137	15	1	14	0
Slow-Cooker Tomatillo Chicken Soft Tacos	662	19	4	213	1432	66	4	6	56
Slow-Cooker Buffalo Chicken Wings	712	52	20	366	674	8	1	5	53
Slow-Cooker Harissa-Spiced Chicken in a Pot	773	57	15	231	1099	4	2	0	58
Slow-Cooker Herbed Chicken with Warm Spring Vegetable Salad	950	70	17	230	870	17	5	9	61
Slow-Cooker Spice-Rubbed Chicken with Black Bean Salad	867	53	14	231	1497	31	10	4	66
Slow-Cooker Braised Chicken Sausages with White Bean Ragout	1188	37	8	164	1368	139	35	7	78
Slow-Cooker Italian Braised Chicken Sausages with Potatoes and Peppers	381	14	4	128	1181	27	5	7	36
Slow-Cooker Sun-Dried Tomato and Basil Turkey Meatballs	125	4	1	43	387	12	3	6	11
Slow-Cooker Turkey Breast with Cherry-Orange Sauce	489	21	7	179	815	13	1	10	58
Slow-Cooker Turkey Breast with Gravy	504	23	7	183	960	9	1	2	60
COOKING FOR TWO									
Pantry Garlicky Chicken and Rice Soup for Two	290	9	1.5	80	1200	30	2	5	22
Hearty Chicken Soup with Leeks, Fennel, and Orzo for Two	490	22	5	110	1100	31	3	7	42
Chicken and Coconut Soup for Two	500	35	23	85	1160	16	2	7	32
Escarole, Chicken Sausage, and Orzo Soup for Two	370	19	5	75	1590	23	1	4	26
White Chicken Chili for Two	433	15	2	131	1334	26	4	10	48
French-Style White Bean Stew for Two	1255	73	20	204	1996	81	15	9	59
Braised Chicken Thighs with Potatoes, Fennel, and Tarragon for Two	860	53	13	280	1300	39	7	11	52

	Calories	Total Fat (g)	Sat Fat (g)	Chol (mg)	Sodium (mg)	Total Carb (g)	Dietary Fiber (g)	Total Sugars (g)	Protein (g)
COOKING FOR TWO (cont.)									
Chicken Tagine for Two	540	12	1.5	85	1840	71	11	41	39
Thai Red Curry with Chicken for Two	430	17	12	105	1250	38	2	11	30
Chicken Curry with Cauliflower and Peas for Two	470	25	12	125	870	18	5	5	44
Chicken Marsala for Two	590	28	12	170	450	24	1	7	42
Chicken Parmesan for Two	1256	71	13	252	1792	90	11	21	69
Chicken Scarpariello for Two	994	68	19	348	1201	18	3	7	74
Chicken Imperial for Two	688	41	23	260	915	20	2	5	54
Chicken Mole for Two	846	57	14	201	1129	28	5	16	56
Teriyaki Chicken for Two	788	50	14	292	1993	29	1	25	52
Murgh Makhani for Two	681	45	25	330	1177	19	3	12	51
Thai Chicken with Basil for Two	251	10	1	83	771	12	2	6	28
Simple White Rice for Two	300	7	0.5	0	300	54	0	0	6
Chicken Lettuce Wraps with Hoisin for Two	190	7	1.5	80	470	12	1	7	18
Weeknight Baked Chicken with Lemon and Thyme for Two	880	68	25	300	670	1	0	0	63
Cauliflower Gratin for Two	390	31	19	80	600	24	3	4	8
Barbecued Dry-Rubbed Chicken for Two	630	32	9	220	540	9	1	7	72
Chicken and Rice for Two	255	15	4	83	357	12	0	1	16
Arroz con Pollo for Two	930	44	10	190	1300	89	3	5	42
Chicken and Chorizo Paella for Two	727	37	10	133	1322	52	5	5	45
Chicken and Couscous with Dried Fruit and Smoked Almonds for Two	700	23	3	125	930	71	7	21	49
Skillet-Roasted Leg Quarters Chicken and Potatoes for Two	786	47	11	192	1368	52	8	6	40
Skillet-Roasted Chicken Breasts with Garlicky Green Beans for Two	593	34	9	169	1179	11	4	5	60
Baked Chicken with Fennel, Tomatoes, and Olives for Two	1010	70	14	220	1210	17	5	8	74
A Single Pan-Seared Boneless Chicken Breast	250	9	1.5	125	370	0	0	0	38
Parmesan and Basil-Stuffed Chicken with Roasted Carrots for Two	764	47	17	215	1259	20	5	11	64
Chicken and Dumplings for Two	752	31	14	267	1616	56	5	10	58
Chicken Pot Pie for Two	1026	60	29	168	1488	85	6	7	38
Chicken Sausage Hash for Two	500	28	6	280	1460	34	2	5	30
Chicken Noodle Casserole for Two	1004	56	21	229	1362	72	6	16	54
Pasta with Chicken, Broccoli, and Sun-Dried Tomatoes for Two	1260	39	16	400	1240	87	10	7	128
Sesame Noodles with Shredded Chicken for Two	810	25	3	85	5050	98	5	15	47

CONVERSIONS AND EQUIVALENTS

Some say cooking is a science and an art. We would say that geography has a hand in it, too. Flours and sugars manufactured in the United Kingdom and elsewhere will feel and taste different from those manufactured in the United States. So we cannot promise that the loaf of bread you bake in Canada or England will taste the same as a loaf baked in the States, but we can offer guidelines for converting weights and measures. We also recommend that you rely on your instincts when making our recipes. Refer to the visual cues provided. If the dough hasn't "come together in a ball" as described, you may need to add more flour—even if the recipe doesn't tell you to. You be the judge.

The recipes in this book were developed using standard U.S. measures following U.S. government guidelines. The charts below offer equivalents for U.S. and metric measures. All conversions are approximate and have been rounded up or down to the nearest whole number.

EXAMPLE

1 teaspoon = 4.9292 milliliters, rounded up to 5 milliliters
1 ounce = 28.3495 grams, rounded down to 28 grams

VOLUME CONVERSIONS

U.S.	METRIC
1 teaspoon	5 milliliters
2 teaspoons	10 milliliters
1 tablespoon	15 milliliters
2 tablespoons	30 milliliters
¼ cup	59 milliliters
⅓ cup	79 milliliters
½ cup	118 milliliters
¾ cup	177 milliliters
1 cup	237 milliliters
1¼ cups	296 milliliters
1½ cups	355 milliliters
2 cups (1 pint)	473 milliliters
2½ cups	591 milliliters
3 cups	710 milliliters
4 cups (1 quart)	0.946 liter
1.06 quarts	1 liter
4 quarts (1 gallon)	3.8 liters

WEIGHT CONVERSIONS

OUNCES	GRAMS
½	14
¾	21
1	28
1½	43
2	57
2½	71
3	85
3½	99
4	113
4½	128
5	142
6	170
7	198
8	227
9	255
10	283
12	340
16 (1 pound)	454

CONVERSIONS FOR COMMON BAKING INGREDIENTS

Baking is an exacting science. Because measuring by weight is far more accurate than measuring by volume, and thus more likely to produce reliable results, in our recipes we provide ounce measures in addition to cup measures for many ingredients. Refer to the chart below to convert these measures into grams.

INGREDIENT	OUNCES	GRAMS
Flour		
1 cup all-purpose flour*	5	142
1 cup cake flour	4	113
1 cup whole-wheat flour	5½	156
Sugar		
1 cup granulated (white) sugar	7	198
1 cup packed brown sugar (light or dark)	7	198
1 cup confectioners' sugar	4	113
Cocoa Powder		
1 cup cocoa powder	3	85
Butter†		
4 tablespoons (½ stick or ¼ cup)	2	57
8 tablespoons (1 stick or ½ cup)	4	113
16 tablespoons (2 sticks or 1 cup)	8	227

* U.S. all-purpose flour, the most frequently used flour in this book, does not contain leaveners, as some European flours do. These leavened flours are called self-rising or self-raising. If you are using self-rising flour, take this into consideration before adding leaveners to a recipe.

† In the United States, butter is sold both salted and unsalted. We generally recommend unsalted butter. If you are using salted butter, take this into consideration before adding salt to a recipe.

OVEN TEMPERATURES

FAHRENHEIT	CELSIUS	GAS MARK
225	105	¼
250	120	½
275	135	1
300	150	2
325	165	3
350	180	4
375	190	5
400	200	6
425	220	7
450	230	8
475	245	9

CONVERTING TEMPERATURES FROM AN INSTANT-READ THERMOMETER

We include doneness temperatures in many of the recipes in this book. We recommend an instant-read thermometer for the job. Refer to the table above to convert Fahrenheit degrees to Celsius. Or, for temperatures not represented in the chart, use this simple formula:

Subtract 32 degrees from the Fahrenheit reading, then divide the result by 1.8 to find the Celsius reading.

EXAMPLE
"Roast chicken until thighs register 175 degrees."

To convert:
175°F – 32 = 143°
143° ÷ 1.8 = 79.44°C, rounded down to 79°C

INDEX

Note: Page references in *italics* indicate photographs.